SOCIAL MOVEMENTS IN INDIA

AF656596

Social Movements in India

Studies in Peasant, Backward Classes, Sectarian, Tribal and Women's Movements

Edited by

M.S.A. RAO

MANOHAR

2025

First published in hard cover 1979
New Edition in one volume in papaerback 1984
Reprinted 2000, 2002, 2004, 2006, 2008, 2012, 2016, 2020, 2023, 2025

© M.A. Saroja Rao, 1984, 2000

All rights reserved. No part of this publication may be reproduced or transmitted, in any form or by any means, without prior permission of the publisher.

ISBN 978-81-7304-335-2

Published by
Ajay Kumar Jain *for*
Manohar Publishers & Distributors
4753/23 Ansari Road, Daryaganj
New Delhi 110 002

Printed and bound in India

Preface to the Second Edition

The two Volumes on *Social Movements in India* published separately in 1978-79, went out of print within two years of their publication. The enthusiasm with which the two Volumes were received by the readers prompted the publishers to bring out a paperback reprint edition. This edition puts together the earlier two Volumes into one. Only such organizational changes that are necessary to combine the two Volumes have been made leaving all the essays, the Introduction and the bibliography intact.

The publication of *Social Movements in India* was acclaimed by the critics as a turning point in the development of sociology in India, in so far as it marked a shift from the conventionalist structure-functional approach to the study of dynamic processes and movements highlighting conflict and contradiction as the basis of protest, reform, transformation and revolution. It was also pointed out that the study of social movements which was the preserve of the historians, came to be established as an area of specialization in sociology. Some critics (Bhatia 1979) welcomed the sociological perspective in the understanding of historical processes. However, two developments have taken place since the publication of the two Volumes. First, the theoretical formulations of the editor of the Volumes generated wide ranging controversies. Secondly, many seminars and conferences have been organized centring round the theme of social movements, and many more books have been published. In this preface I wish to capture the excitement in the study of social movements as reflected in seminars and publications, and clarify some of my own ideas regarding the conceptual issues.

It is necessary to stress that there had been studies of social movements before the publication of the two Volumes. For instance, Fuchs (1965) brought out a collection of different types of Messianic movements in Indian Religions. Singh (1966) wrote on the Birsa Munda movement. Alvi (1965) analysed the peasants and revolution. Kathleen Gough (1968) studied peasant resistance and revolts in South India. While Sen (1972) analysed the agrarian struggles in Bengal, Dhanagare (1974) made a study of the Telangana movement. All these studies of peasant movements used the Marxian frame of analysis. However, Oommen (1972) in his study of the Bhoodan movement (a movement among the peasants) used Weberian ideas of charisma and routinization.

The first major all India inter-disciplinary conference, to my knowledge, on Dissent, Protest and Reform Movements was organised by S.C. Dube and Mallik in 1974 at the Indian Institute of Advanced Study, Simla. The proceedings of the conference, published in 1978, included diverse kinds of movements such as Bhakti movement, Versasaiva movement, Bhagat movement, Arya Samaj movement, and Backward Classes movements. Sociologists, historians, literary experts, political scientists—all participated in the conference.

However, the seminar that was organized in the Department of Sociology, University of Delhi in 1976 which resulted in the publication of the two Volumes was mainly focused on sociological analysis of different kinds of social movements. Hence there was pointed discussion on the sociological approach to the study of social movements. The sociological view point on social movements was further expanded at a special panel on social movements at the XII All-India Sociological Conference in December 1976, and at a national seminar on Tribal Movements in India, organized by the Anthropological Survey of India in 1976. International seminar on "Anthropology of Social and Cultural Movements" at the Xth International Congress of Anthropological and Ethnological Sciences, December 1978 further generated discussion on the conceptual issues. Other conferences and seminars with social movements as a component followed: "Agrarian Situation in India" organized by the Anthropological Survey of India, 1982; "Harijans and Mass Religious Conversions" organized by the Department of Sociology, University of Madras in 1982; "Social

Movements of the Under Privileged" organized by the Department of Sociology, SNDT University in 1983; a Summer School on "Social and Political Movements" organized by the Department of Political Science, Marathwada University in 1983.

The discussions on different types of movements at these seminars and summer schools in which I participated, reflected great enthusiasm among scholars belonging to different social science disciplines and keenness on their part to come to grips with the conceptual problems. Before I discuss the latter, let me give a brief account of some major publications on Movements since the publication of the two Volumes in 1978.

A major theme that has attracted the attention of many social scientists has been that of peasant movements. A.R. Desai (1978) published his book on peasant struggles, and his another book is in the press. Siddiqi (1978) wrote on agrarian unrest in north India. Dhanagare's study of seven different peasant movements which occurred during 1920-1950 was published in 1983. Sunil Sen (1979) analysed the agrarian relations in India during 1793-1947 in the political economy framework. Ranjit Guha (1983) has recently published a book on peasant insurgency. It is important to note that almost all the studies of peasant movements use the Marxist frame of reference of class struggle. However some of them stretch the argument too far as to ignore other important forces behind the peasant movements especially during the period of British rule before 1945. A few of them were organized on the basis of the ideology of national struggle for Independence and not of class struggle The peasant movements led by Mahatma Gandhi were not intended to pitch one class of peasants against another, but to incorporate different sections of peasantry including the Harijans (landless agricultural labourers) in the Independence movement against the British through different channels of mobilization. Similarly the chipko and appiko movement, and the Sarvodaya movement cannot be wholly explained in terms of class struggle ideology.

Another main theme of social movements has been the backward classes and tribal movements. The Dalit and Neo-Buddhist movement has come in for special studies. Similarly there are studies of Kurmi movement in Bihar. K.S. Singh has edited (1982, 1983) two volumes on Tribal Movements in India. Sons of the soil movements have attracted the attention of some sociologists and political scientists (Weiner 1978; Gupta 1982; Katzenstein 1979). The Assam and the Akali movements are waiting to be studied by sociologists. Studies of women's movements have gathered some momentum and one might expect shortly major publications in this area. Student, trade union, linguistic, sectarian and other ethnic movements have yet to attract the attention of sociologists. However, studies of political movements have received special attention from historians, political sociologists and party men (Panikar 1980).

This is the state of development of studies of social movements in India in the context of which the present second edition has to be placed. Now let me briefly indicate the theoretical advancements made in the study of social movements.

There is a greater concensus today that social movements constitute an area of sociological analysis in their own right. They are located in the domain of social process and change. The processual changes are no doubt related to the pre-existing structural conditions. In studying social movements, as some critics would fear, the structural context is not neglected but is studied in detail so as to locate the areas of conflict and contradiction which provide the necessary conditions for the emergence of social movements. It is also realized that the awareness and consciousness of the conditions of existence on the part of the concerned section in an effort (collective mobilization) to change them, provide the sufficient conditions in the emergence of movements. While all critics agree that ideology is an important aspect of social movement, some (Dhanagare 1979; Imtiaz Ahmad 1980) hold that the ideology need not be present initially. I am grateful to them for providing this useful clarification. Ideology may emerge later along with collective mobilization. It is necessary to stress further the steering role that ideology plays in the communication process and how crucial it is in developing an *emic* point of view of social movements (Rao 1984).

No doubt the Marxian framework provides important leads in conceptualizing social movements. However, I argue that it is helpful in understanding only certain types of movements such as the peasant movements and trade union and workers' movements where class conflict and struggle are of primary importance. It however, cannot explain every type of movement—sectarian, different caste and ethnic movements—although they are related to social conditions of existence. It is necessary therefore to look for concepts which are more inclusive. In this context the concept of relative deprivation in different areas of social life has proved more useful in understanding those social movements which have emerged among the deprived sections. It incorporates the virtues of the Marxian analysis without necessarily accepting the class struggle ideology. It enables one to take account of the structural conditions of existence (relations of production and class structure) and the elements of conflict and contradiction, the nature of ideological formulations and the nature of social changes envisaged by the leaders of the movement. In my paper on conceptual problems although I have not explicitly mentioned the Marxian perspective, it was implicit in developing the concept of relative deprivation. I do realize that it needed a fully fledged discussion.

Similarly, although I have used Max Weber's notions of church-sect, prophecy, charisma, legitimacy, routinization, they needed an elaborate discussion. I (1981) have elsewhere developed these ideas but suffice it to say here that it will be artificial to impose a conceptual framework on the data, rather the data themselves should lead to particular ways of conceptualization. For instance, it is hard to analyse the sons of the soil (Shivsena) movement in Bombay wholly in the Marxian perspective, as Gupta (1972) has done, because it is ethnicity cutting across classes and not class cutting across natives and aliens that is at the root of the conflict.

There are two other points which need consideration: one regarding the process of routinization and the second concerning the characterization of social change consequent upon social movements. If social movements belong to the logical area of process, over a period of time they, *in that form*, are likely to get routinized and develop into establishments. Their character might change into political movements, or the internal contradictions might become the bases of new movements. This is what I meant when I said that 'when a movement with an ideology becomes a well established political party it ceases to be a movement'. Routinization and deroutinization are dialectically related in the process of change (in response to Dhanagare 1979 and Aurora 1981).

As regards characterizing the nature of change that many social movements bring about, I have found greater confirmation in the notions of reform, transformation and revolution. I agree that all revolutions need not be violent, but they imply a total change in the mode of production, quality of social relations and the nature of dominance, power and the state. Whereas transformation is useful to describe the changes in the superordination and subordination relationships, dominance and the power relations without any basic change in the mode of production. Reform describes changes in the value system and status hierarchy without necessarily changing the existing power relations. Transformatory changes in most cases include reformatory changes. All the three signify different levels of structural changes. Instead of having only a binary distinction between structural and organizational changes, it is useful and realistic to distinguish different levels of structural changes.

Delhi
March 1984

M.S.A. Rao

REFERENCES

Ahmad, Imtiaz (1980) "Social Movements in India" (Review), *Sunday Standard*, 16th March 1980, p. 6.

Alvi, Hamza (1965) "Peasants and Revolution", *The Socialist Register*, ed. by Ralph Miliband *et al.*

Aurora, G.S. (1981) "Social Movements in India, A Review Article".

Bhatia, B.M. (1979) "Radio Talk on Social Movements in India, Vol. I", AIR, 26 Feb. 1979.

Dhanagare, D.N (1974) "Social Origins of the Peasant Insurrection in Telangana, 1946-51", *Contributions to Indian Sociology* NS, Vol. VIII, Dec.

——— (1979) "Analyses of Peasant Movements" (A Review of Social Movements in India, Vol. I ed. by M.S.A. Rao). *The Book Review*, Vol. IV, No. 1, July-August, pp. 3-9.

——— (1983) *Peasant Movements in India*, 1920-1950, Delhi: Oxford University Press.

Desai, A.R. (1978) *Peasant Struggles in India*, Bombay: Oxford University Press.

Fuchs, Stephen (1965) *Rebellious Prophets: A Study of Messianic Movements in Indian Religions*, Bombay: Asia Publishing House.

Gough, Kathleen (1968) "Peasant Resistance and Revolt in South India", *Pacific* Affairs, Vol. 16, No. 4.

Guha, R. (1983) *Elementary Aspects of Peasant Insurgency in India*, Delhi: Oxford University Press.

Gupta, D. (1982) *Nativism in a Metropolis: The Shiv Sena in Bombay*, New Delhi: Manohar.

Katzenstein, Mary F. (1979) *Ethnicity and Equality: The Shiv Sena Party and Preferential Policies in Bombay*, Ithaca: Cornell University Press.

Malik, S.C. (ed.) (1978) *Indian Movements: Some Aspects of Dissent, Protest and Reform*, Simla: Indian Institute of Advanced Study.

Oommen, T.K. (1972) *Charisma, Stability and Change: An Analysis of Bhoodan-Gramdan Movement in India*, New Delhi: Thomson Press.

Panikar K.N. (ed.) (1980) *National and Left Movements in India*, New Delhi: Vikas Publishing House.

Rao, M.S.A. (1981) "Prophecy and Heritage in Social and Cultural Movements", *Social Action*, 31(2) April-June, pp. 174-81.

——— (1984) "Some Subjective Orientations in Understanding Indian Social Reality" in Ravinder Kumar (ed.), *Philosophical Theory and Social Reality*, New Delhi: Allied.

Sen, Sunil K. (1972) *Agrarian Struggles in Bengal, 1946-47*, New Delhi: People's Publishing House.

——— (1979) *Agrarian Relations in India*, 1793-1947, New Delhi: People's Publishing House

Siddiqi, M.H. (1978) *Agrarian Unrest in North India: The United Provinces (1918-22)*, Delhi: Vikas.

Singh, Suresh K. (1966) *Dust Storms and Hanging Mist: Story of Birsa Munda and His Movement*, Calcutta: Forma K.L. Mukhopadhyay.

——— (ed.) (1982, 1983) *Tribal Movements in India*, Vols. I and II, Delhi: Manohar.

Weiner, Myron (1978) *Sons of the Soil: Migration and Ethnic Conflict in India*, New Jersey: Princeton University Press.

The Contributors

M.S.A. RAO is Professor of Sociology, University of Delhi. Currently he is the UGC National Fellow.

PARTHA N. MUKHERJI is Associated Professor of Sociology in the Centre for the Study of Social Systems, Jawaharlal Nehru University. He is currently Senior Fellow, ICSSR, New Delhi.

RAJENDRA SINGH is Lecturer in Sociology, Delhi School of Social Work, University of Delhi.

K. RANGA RAO is Professor of Sociology, Andhra University.

CHANDRASHEKHAR BHAT is Lecturer in Social Anthropology, University of Mysore.

KENNETH W. JONES is Professor of History at Kansas State University, Manhattan (USA).

ARUN P. BALI is Assistant Director, Indian Council of Social Science Research.

KOLLEEN and GAR KELLOM are Graduate Students under the Berkeley Professional Studies Programme—1975-76.

I.S. MARWAH is a Lecturer in Social Anthropology, Department of Anthropology, University of Delhi.

B.K. ROY BURMAN is Professor of Rural Studies in the Vishwabharati, Sriniketan.

JOSEPH TROISI is assistant director of the Department of Research and Publications at the Indian Social Institute, New Delhi.

GERALDINE H. FORBES is Associate Professor of History, State University of New York, College of Arts and Science at Oswego, (USA).

ANJALI ARUN BALI is Research Analyst in the National Institute of Urban Affairs, New Delhi,

Contents

M S A Rao

Introduction

IN RECENT YEARS Indian sociologists and social anthropologists have shown increasing interest in the study of social movements—a field that has long been considered to be the province of historians. No doubt the study of any social movement involves a long or short time span, occurrence of events, and a body of written documents, the analysis of which demands the skills of a historian. However, the theoretical framework of interpretation and explanation that a sociologist uses will be sociological. Hence, there is a case for a sociology of social movements.

Although there is a considerable body of theoretical literature on the sociology of social movements, this area of specialization is still in the formative stages. A body of concepts have, however, been developed which enables a scholar to interpret the genesis of movements, the formation of ideology, the sources of identity, organization and leadership, the event structure, the internal dynamics, and the social consequences. But, the logical boundary of the phenomena needs to be sharpened and more appropriate concepts and techniques need to be developed to handle problems of processual analysis, as social movements logically belong to the area of processes having connections with structure and change.

For long, sociologists and social anthropologists have been preoccupied with the concept of social structure at various levels of abstraction—from empirical relations to the relationship of relationships. There is often an excessive concern either for what goes on in the minds of people or what their actual behaviour is. Social movements deal with a class of social phenomena which are connected with the two in the realm of process. If we consider a social movement to be an organized effort on the part of a section of the population, involving collective mobilization based on an ideology, to bring about changes (either partial or total) in the social system, then we have to see the social process as consisting of interrelated social activities, interactions and events as related to ideology (or structure at a higher level of abstraction) on the one hand, and as connected with social and cultural changes on the other.

The character of a social movement as an instrument of social change is quite different from an imitative or emulative process of mobility and change. While the latter centres around acquiescence, the former is focused on protest of one kind or the other. Following from this, the latter emphasizes the functional unity of the social system, whereas the former places emphasis on contradiction and conflict. The social mobility and change that are brought about by social movements are based on challenge, protest, confrontation, aggression and revolt, as opposed to acquiescence, request, obedience and loyalty. The latter type of process of mobility and change only perpetuates the established order, whereas social mobility and change brought about by social movements lead to social transformation thereby changing the traditional balance of power. Thus, social movements based on protest bring about qualitative changes in the traditional structure of social relationships. Protest and acquiescence are logically opposed to each other and the nature of changes that are brought about by protest is qualitatively different. An approach to the study of change through social movements centred around contradiction and conflict offers a corrective to the simplistic explanation of emulative process of mobility and change.

Many of the papers included in this volume were presented at a workshop on social movements held in March 1976, at the Department of Sociology, University of Delhi. All except one are being published for the first time. The twelve papers included here constitute Part 1 with six sections: conceptual problems, peasant movements, religious and sectarian movements, tribal movements and women's movements.

Part 2 of the Volume includes a select bibliography compiled by Arun P. Bali and Anjali Arun Bali covering the six sections. In addition, select bibliographies on student, trade union and national movements are included for the benefit of the readers interested in these types of social movements which are not included in the book.

Conceptual Problems

Any emerging field of specialization is beset with problems of conceptualization, and the sociology of social movements is no exception. The first section of this volume consists of an essay on 'Conceptual Problems in the Study of Social Movements'. Rao outlines the conceptual problems in terms of definition and classification, genesis, ideology and identity, organization and leadership, internal dynamics and routinization and social consequences. He considers social movements as being characterized by three important features: collective mobilization, ideology and orientation to change. Examining three theories explaining the genesis of social movements—namely, relative deprivation, the strain theory and revitalization—he shows that the latter two do not adequately explain the ideological underpinnings of a social movement and the consequent social changes. He suggests that the theory of relative deprivation, with suitable modifications, has a greater explanatory power as it places the perception of contradiction, conflict and protest at the centre of social movements. He also suggests the notion of opposition reference groups in discussing the formulation of ideology, establishment of identity and the mechanics of confrontation.

Ideology is considered to be a crucial aspect of any social movement. Rao points out the variations in the themes of protest ideologies in terms of reinterpretation and rejection of religious sources of identity, class conflict and millenarian themes.

As regards the problem of the organization of a social movement, Rao discusses the aspects of recruitment, commitment and leadership. He suggests that when a movement develops a high degree of formal organization with sanctions of rewards and punishment, it ceases to be a movement.

Discussing the nature of social changes brought about by social movements, Rao distinguishes three levels of structural change: reform, transformation and revolution. While reform aims at modifying the belief system and life-styles of the members of a group, revolutionary changes aim to bring about sudden and total changes in all the aspects of society. Transformative changes refer to changes in the traditional balance of power relations, altering the economic and political superordination-subordination relationships.

As regards the methodological question, Rao points out that a study of social movements involves acquisition of the skills of a historian and adoption of diverse field techniques such as participant observation, survey, interviews, content analysis and working out social networks. For a sociological analysis, intensive fieldwork is a necessary complement to the analysis of documentary data.

PEASANT MOVEMENTS

Peasant movements, like workers movements belong to a distinct category of social movements with the ideology of class conflict as their basis. While Marx considered the peasantry to be passive, Lenin, Mao and Fanon placed the peasants at the centre of the revolution. In the Indian context two ideologies are associated with peasant movements—the bhoodan and sarvodaya of Vinoba Bhave and Jai Prakash Narain, and the communist. However, significant peasant movements—such as Tebhaga, Telangana, Naxalite and land-grab—have emerged on the basis of communist ideology.

The section on Peasant Movement consists of three papers: Naxalbari Movement in North Bengal, Peasant Movements in Uttar Pradesh and Peasant Movement in Telangana. Partha Nath Mukherji's study on Naxalbari Movement and the Peasant Revolt in North Bengal is based on extensive fieldwork carried out under most difficult circumstances. He handles his rich empirical data in a neat analytical farmework yielding valuable insights. Since the ideological question is central to the Naxalite peasant movement, he examines the evolution of the communist movement in India in the Marxist-Leninist-Maoist ideological framework. He shows that after the split in the CPI, ideological pressures for radicalisation of CPI (M) politics was exerted by the Darjeeling District Committee. But right from the very inception there were two lines of thinking amongst the radicals. One favoured participation in the elections for furthering the revolutionary cause, whilst the other proposed to shun the elections altogether and socialise the masses against it. The former held to the primacy of the land problem and recommended mass struggles to solve it, whereas the latter ridiculed narrow economism and prescribed seizure of political power by guerilla squads.

The Naxalbari peasant revolt owes its origin to the dying waves of *tebhaga* movement in Bengal in the forties. In an agrarian system, which had evolved from a *feudal jotedari system* to a *semi-feudal jotedari-adhiari system* in the context of money market forces, a small group of communist cadres inspired by the *tebhaga* struggle, began systematically unweiling the contradictions between labour and capital that was increasing the burden of exploitation on the poor and marginal peasants. Over a period of time numerous struggles against such exploitation led to the emergence of a strong *Krishak Sabha* with increasing membership. Interestingly enough, it is the peasant leadership that initiated the unionisation of the plantation labour, which constitutes nearly 30 per cent of the population in that area. The unionisation of plantation labour was considered necessary not merely for the plantation labour but also for the peasant struggles. There developed, since the mid-fifties an alliance between the peasants and the workers which is remarkable in as much as it was unique.

Mukherji considers the question of means as important as the goals in a movement. Thus he argues that the Naxalbari struggle like the *tebhaga* is yet another instance of the use of non-institutionalised means for securing intra-systemic changes. However, neither the objective conditions nor the subjective preparations warranted such a strategy. Hence Mukherji points out that it is not sufficient that objective conditions for social transformation exist, it is more important that the actors in the system internalise the contradictions through experience before subjectively preparing for the struggle.

Mukherji evolves a classification of movements on the basis of quality of change it intends to bring about or the kind of change that has already been accomplished. Thus, if social mobilisation has been demanding changes *within* the system, the changes that are likely to occur will be *accumulative*. However, if the social mobilisation is directed towards creating new structures which by their existence would qualitatively affect the entire system, then the change, in the event that it is accomplished, will be *atlernative*. Finally, if a social mobilisation is determined to replace one structure and substitute it by another, the change should it materialise, would be *transformative*. Mobilisations of the first variety are quasi-movements, whilst those of the second and third variety, are *social movements*. Hence all mobilizations in a conflict dimension need not be social movements. In this framework, Naxalbari movement is a transformative movement. Mukherji concludes by pointing out that the search for a radical transformation is on, both among Naxalites and those who subscribe to a radically different methodology of militant struggle, and the movement is kept alive.

Rajendra Singh, in his paper on 'Peasant Movements in Uttar Pradesh' discusses two movements in Basti district: The Nijai-Bol ('declare ownership of land' movement of 1946) and the land-grab movement of 1970. While the former was fostered under the influence of National Congress, the latter was spearheaded by the communists. Rajendra Singh discusses these movements utilizing a body of rich data. He first describes the structural conditions responsible for the emergence of the 'declare ownership of land' movement in terms of the land-tenurial system, British land and revenue policies, the caste system, relations of production and property relations. The tenants suffered from the worst kind of exploitation at the hands of the zamindars. Until the twenties of the present century, the tenants accepted their miserable life as no alternatives seemed available nor was there sufficient awakening among them. Rajendra Singh explains this situation with the aid of the notion of the culture of inequality. However, under the influence of the Indian National Congress during the thirties the peasantry gradually arose from their torpor and became politically aware. There was also the simultaneous growth of an English educated middle class, and the political and military elite. The peasants soon perceived the possibility of changing their conditions of relative deprivation through an organised movement. Thus, in 1946 the Nijai Bol (declare ownership of land) movement emerged among the peasants, who started appropriating ownership of the land they were tilling.

Rajendra Singh shows that the Nijai Bol movement was preceded by about thirty sporadic but frequent violent rebellions of peasants against landlords, in which the latter were killed in open encounters. There were also incidents in which the landlords killed the peasants. He shows that these open confrontations and the emerging class conflict helped to mobilize the peasants who rallied together on the basis of common interest in claiming possession of the land they tilled. The movement attempted to correct the contradiction between the property relations and production relations. It appears that the peasants, although heterogenous in terms of caste and religious composition, were conscious of their interests by this time.

As a consequence of this movement, the land record operation was started by the state administration in 1946. The litigation between the zamindars and peasants increased, and there were also cases of agrarian tension and violence. While many zamindars were dispossessed of their land and other privileges, many peasants became owners of land. The latter built up pressure on the government for the abolition of zamindari.

Rajendra Singh contrasts the 'declare ownership of land' movement of 1946 with the land-grab movement of 1970. The latter was led by communists with a sharply defined ideology and an organized leadership and on an all-India basis. However, the Hindu-Muslim communal conflict emerged in the course of the land-grab movement and led to its eventual failure. The communal element blurred the lines of the class antagonism basic to the movement by bringing the Hindu peasants and zamindars together. Indeed ex-zamindars who had become almost paupers, joined hands with the peasants who had become the new owners of the land. Rajendra Singh shows that while the land-grab movement did not have much of an impact, the Nijai Bol movement did bring about structural changes in the traditional distribution of power and in the system of superordination and subordination relationships.

Ranga Rao's study of Peasant Movement in Telangàna is based on both secondary sources and fieldwork. He makes good use of the Telugu source materials. He places the communist-led peasant movement in the wider context of other social movements which sprang up in Telangana in the beginning of the twentieth century. The Telugu literary movement introduced ideas of renaissance and set the tone of protest against Nizam administration. Further, under the influence of the Indian National Congress the Telangana elite gave a new direction to the activities of the Andhra Mahasabha in the 1930s. They mobilized the public including the peasants for the abolition of forced labour, untouchability and other social evils, and demanded equal educational and economic opportunities and political representation. All these activities of the Andhra Mahasabha became the forerunner of the peasant movement led by the communists in the late 1940s.

Ranga Rao describes the peasant movement with reference to revolutionary ideology of class struggle, collective mobilization and the strategies adopted by the leaders. He portrays the movement in three phases and considers the question of consequences. He concludes that although the movement did not succeed in bringing about social revolution, it brought about significant changes in the traditional distribution of power in the agrarian relations.

Backward Classes Movements

Many social movements among the Scheduled Castes and Other Backward Classes emerged in the nineteenth and early twentieth centuries. They utilized both religious and secular themes of ideology oriented towards reform, emancipation and transformation of the established order of social relationships and values. The section on these movements consists of two essays: 'Reform Movement among the Waddars of Karnatak' by Chandrashekhar Bhat and 'Social Movements among the Backward Classes and the Blacks: Homology in the Sources of Identity' by MSA Rao.

Chandrashekhar Bhat discusses the reform movement among the Waddars of Karnatak. The Waddars were and are a nomadic caste engaged mainly in earthwork and stonework. They were listed as Scheduled Castes in the erstwhile Mysore State, as one of the Waddar sub-castes are scavengers by occupation.

Bhat considers the emergence of the reform movement among the Waddars in the contexts of the sedentarization process in this community and the wider backward classes movements in Mysore. Certain sections of the Waddars started settling down in towns and villages and attempted to attain a more fixed place in the ritual hierarchy of the caste system. Those who settled in the urban areas had access to modern education and pursued occupations other than their traditional ones. Following their sedentarization, the emergence of higher aspirations and a certain degree of educational and occupational achievements, a few educated leaders started organizing their community in the 1930s. They claimed the Kshatriya *varna* status through an appropriate myth and this claim provided the basic ideology for their movement. They established caste associations in different parts of old Mysore, and these associations undertook various welfare activities. In the fifties and sixties, the Waddars became politically active and agitated, under the auspices of the All Karnatak Waddars Association, for the inclusion of Waddars all over Karnatak under the category of Scheduled Castes.

However, in the old Mysore State, where they had already gained Scheduled Caste status, the Waddars contested the Assembly elections in the reserved constituencies and won a few seats defeating some of the prominent Harijan leaders. This brought them into open confrontation with the Harijans who opposed the Waddar claim for Scheduled Caste status. Nevertheless, access to political power has meant greater opportunities for upward social mobility for the Waddars.

Bhat concludes that the reform movement among the Waddars has led to greater ethnic identity and upward social mobility through an ideology of higher *varna* status, political mobilization and conflict with the Harijans.

Rao's paper on 'Social Movements among the Backward Classes and the Blacks: Homology in the Sources of Identity', takes the readers beyond the Indian sub-continent to the United States of America. The comparison is about the homology (at a higher level of abstraction) in the sources of identity of the deprived classes in India and the USA. Both the backward classes and the blacks were faced with a common problem of establishing a new identity in order to gain self-respect and honour. The answers that they have sought to provide have been different but homologous.

The problem of identity is intimately related to ideology which is a symbolic system. Broadly, two alternatives were open to the backward classes and the blacks. One was to adopt an acquiescent posture and the other was to formulate a protest ideology asserting their rights of equality. Many movements chose the latter to gain self-respect. The Protest ideology was logically opposed to the acquiescent approach as it had its own sources of legitimacy, and the efforts towards social mobility and change were not sponsored. The leaders of the protest movements adopted two main themes: religious-cultural and secular. In the former, while the leaders of some movements—like the Sri Narayana Dharma Paripalana movement among the Izhavas of Kerala and the Marcus Garvey and black theology movements among the blacks—made use of the principle of reinterpretation of Hinduism and Christianity respectively, the leaders of other movements—such as the Buddhist movement among the Mahars and the black Muslim movement among the blacks—adopted the principle of rejection of Hinduism and Christianity respectively.

The leaders of some other movements among the blacks and backward classes made use of two secular ideologies: the civil rights and the class conflict. While DuBois and Martin Luther King and the leaders of the SNDP and Mahar movements made use of the civil rights ideology, the Black Panthers and Dalit Panthers made use of the Marxian class-conflict ideology along with an ethnic element.

Religious and Sectarian Movements

Of all types of movements, religious and sectarian movements have, by and large, predominated from very early times in India, as can be seen by the fact that the largest number of entries in the bibliography are for this section. Religious ideas have for long been the language of protest, innovation and expression of individuality and separate identity. They provide vast scope for reinterpretation in order to legitimize the aspiration of various sections of the population and to justify changes in the existing order of social relationships. This section consists of four essays: 'Social Change and Religious Movements in Nineteenth Century Punjab' by Kenneth W Jones; 'Organization of the Virasaiva Movement: An Analysis in the Sect-Church Framework' by Arun P Bali; 'A Guru-centred Movement in the Making' by Kolleen and Gar Kellom; and 'The Tabligh Movement among the Meos of Mewat' by IS Marwah.

Kenneth W Jones examines the interplay of forces which created and sustained competition and conflict between religious movements in nineteenth century Punjab. Jones isolates three sets of forces—the traditional social situation in pre-annexation Punjab, the forces of modernization, and the policies and actions of the British colonial administration—and shows how they interacted with one another to produce conflict and competition among diverse religious movements.

He points out that, in pre-conquest Punjab, there was one evolutionary religion, Hinduism, and two prophetic faiths—Islam and Sikhism. The British added another prophetic faith, Christianity.

Religious movements—such as, the Arya Samaj, Sanathan, Ahmadiya and Singh Sabha—reacted against the orthodox leaders of their faith, but in the conflicting relations between Islam, Hinduism and Christianity. Although British policy oscillated between deliberate attempts at divide and rule and a general desire to limit religious controversy, it contributed to religious competition both deliberately and inadvertently. Thus, Jones provides a framework of interacting forces for an understanding of the conflict and competition among the religious movements in nineteenth century Punjab. His essay demonstrates the fact that a religious movement cannot be understood without reference to other relevant religious and sectarian movements and the wider political context.

Arun P Bali concentrates on analysing the organization of the Virasaiva movement in the sect-church framework. The Virasaiva movement was organized by Basaveswara in the twelfth century AD in Karnatak. He protested against brahmanical Hinduism and the caste system. He particularly attacked the notions of purity and pollution and the corrupt practices of the Brahmins. Basaveswara proclaimed an egalitarian ideology based on the path of devotion and on equal access to spiritual goods. He emphasized the use of the vernacular language (Kannada), rather than Sanskrit, in establishing communication with god, decried the excess of rituals and accorded equal rights of worship to men and women. He abolished all notions of pollution and emphasized work as the means of liberation. Thus, the movement in the early phases was small, spontaneous and anti-establishment (brahmanical) in its orientation.

Gradually, the movement lost its innovative character as it began to achieve significant success and attracted a large number of recruits. At a later stage the leaders of the movement created an elaborate organizational framework parallel to that of the Brahmins, with its own sources of legitimacy, sanctions and codes of conduct, and punishments for the deviants. *Mathas* (monastery) were established with their own internal bureaucracy, an official clergy, ritual specialists to propagate Virasaivism, an elaborate literature both in Sanskrit and Kannada, and agencies of social control with powers to reward and punish. They created a network of educational institutions which provided religious instruction. Thus, the Virasaiva movement became highly routinized. It assumed the form of a caste or church with.

established rules of endogamy, demanded observance of 'caste norms and was armed with powers of excommunication.

Bali argues that it is misleading to borrow the sect-church framework in its entirety, as it has been developed in the Western social context, to analyse the Virasaiva movement, as it obscures to some degree the nexus between meanings and the functional problems of social organization. It is not a mere question of organizational survival through compromise. He also contests the view that when a sect becomes a 'church' or caste within an established order, it does not bring about any change in society. He points out that the Virasaiva movement led to transformations which changed the character of caste society by introducing a new social ethic and by upsetting the traditional power relations between groups.

Kolleen and Går Kellom's account of a sect (Akhand Maha Yoga) in the making is based on direct observation in the real sense of the term as they actually became recruits. Thus, they provide a first-hand account of the process of sect-making. They show that the founder, Sita Ram Pandey's approach to problems of spiritual and mundane life is different from that of other gurus, and that the ideology of the sect appeals to householders as it does not affect their interpersonal relationships within the family nor does it alienate them from economic pursuits. It reinforces brotherhood instead of trying to enforce ascetic other-worldly discipline. At the same time, it does not neglect spiritual attainments. The Kelloms demonstrate the process by which this belief system is built up step by step and the manner in which it is legitimized. They also discuss the process of collective mobilization through initiation and the events leading to the founding of the Akhand Maha Yoga Sangh in Banaras.

The formation of a guru-centred sect, unlike other movements, is the result of the personal interaction between a guru and his disciples and the way individuals come to seek solutions to their personal problems. Hence the Kelloms pay particular attention to the biographic details of the disciples and the communication processes by which individuals were drawn towards the guru.

Another aspect of the process of sect formation is event analysis. The Kelloms build up the event structure of the movement and highlight the event which triggered off the movement and determined its nature. They also show that the social composition of the movement is more masculine and middle-class oriented, and outline the possible future development of the movement.

There are only a few studies of social movements among Indian Muslims. Indian Muslims have shown diverse responses to the changing conditions of cultural and political life in the subcontinent, through the medium of organized movements. Marwah looks at the Tabligh movement among the Meos in the wider context of other movements among the Muslims. Broadly, while some of them—such as the Shah Wali Ullah movement—emphasized orthodoxy and purity of Islamic practices others—like Sir Sayyad Ahmed's movement—emphasized modernization through the adoption of Western education. The Tabligh movement belongs to the former category.

The Tabligh (meaning religious instruction) movement was started by Maulana Ilyas in the late 1920s who laid down six precepts which formed the basis of a new ideology. Discussing the organizational framework of the movement, Marwah points out the crucial part played by the *jammatis* (groups of propagators) who moved from village to village progagating the six precepts of Maulana Ilyas. What have been the consequences of the Tabligh movement especially after Independence? Marwah shows that Islamization has increased, transforming the Hindu social customs and practices which the converts retained. This has heightened their Islamic identity, weakening the traditional ties between the Meos and their Hindu neighbours. Thus, Marwah places the ideology of the Tabligh movement and the establishment of a separate identity in the wider context of dynamic Hindu-Muslim relations, and the two systems of beliefs.

Tribal Movements

Tribal movements in India are as old as other types of movements. They were considered to be rebellious and 'civilized' rulers quelled them as they had superior arms. The tribals were in a position of confrontation both with the Hindu overlords and the British colonists as the latter seriously encroached on their rights and territories. There are two papers comprising the section on tribal movements, namely, 'Challenges and Responses in Tribal India' by BK Roy Burman and 'Social Movements among the Santals by Joseph Troisi.

Roy Burman identifies eight kinds of responses of the tribals to he different challenges that they faced: response to threats to the rivacy of habitat; response to threats to access to and control of resources; response to description of traditional roles in the total interaction set-up; search for new meanings of the relationships between man and nature; search for new meanings of the relationships between individual and society; search for new frontiers of identity; search for a more satisfactory system of control of resources; and search for a more satisfactory system of organization of community power at all levels. These responses, however, are neither mutually exclusive nor have all of them resulted in movements.

Roy Burman shows that, during British rule, alienation from land, due to faulty legislation pertaining to forest lands, and lack of understanding of the tribal social organization were responsible for tribal uprisings. Although they had diverse ideological overtones, the main theme was the millenarian—waiting for the day of deliverance from an acute situation of relative deprivation.

Roy Burman points out that tribal movements since Independence have been characterized by two features. There is a strong tendency towards establishing tribal ethnic identities. They find new meanings regarding the relationships between man and nature and individual and society by reinterpreting their own traditions and myths. The second major trend is in the direction of agrarian movements in the context of political ideologies, including the Naxalite one.

While Roy Burman considers the general characteristics of tribal movements in India, Joseph Troisi examines three specific movements among the Santals, namely the Santal Rebellion of 1855-57, the Kharwar movement and the Jharkhand movement. All the three movements combined traditional cultural elements and values with new themes in the framework of the millenarian ideology of the restoration of the golden age. The Kharwar movement, which emerged in the 1930s, however, was oriented towards reform in the direction of sanskritization. The Jharkhand movement took the Santals away from the process of Hinduization with increased ambivalence, involving them in the modern political processes in the 1940s and 1950s. The movement cut across different tribes and demanded a separate state for the tribals so as to be able to maintain their identity and autonomy.

Joseph Troisi emphasizes that these three movements should be looked at as three alternatives that the Santals adopted in overcoming their status of relative deprivation, and for improving their social, economic and political position. He shows how the penetration of Christianity in this area spread modern education and encouraged the emergence of a new leadership.

WOMEN'S MOVEMENTS

Women's movements form an important dimension of social movements connected with the renaissance. The status of women became the central concern of many reform movements, such as, the Brahmo Samaj and Arya Samaj in the nineteenth and the early twentieth centuries. The problems of women with which the leaders of these movements were concerned included sati, widow remarriage, divorce, female education, lower ritual status, *purda*, polygamy and dowry. The leaders of these movements formulated various programmes calculated to ameliorate the status of women. The freedom movement provided an impetus for collective mobilization under the leadership of Mahatma Gandhi. All these developments, together with the spread of a liberal egalitarian ideology under the British raj, created conditions for a social awakening among Indian women. A few leaders began to organize women for welfare work and political action in the freedom struggle. Several women's associations came into existence both at the regional and national levels. What kind of ideology did these early women leaders have? What is the nature of the new roles that they envisaged for women? What kind of symbols did they use in communicating their message to different sections of women?

Geraldine H Forbes raises these very questions in her essay on 'Women's Movements in India: Traditional Symbols and New Roles'. Forbes analyses the nature of women's movements between 1917 and 1947 on the basis of the profiles of two prominent women leaders—Saroj Nalini Dutt (1887-1925) and Sarojini Naidu (1879-1949). Forbes discusses two main themes in women's movements during this period—one that concerned social uplift and welfare and another that related to the involvement of women in the national movement. The two, however, were complementary, as the women leaders wanted to represent all women and to work for the uplift of all women. They argued that this amelioration work was essential to the national cause because women as mothers of children are agents of socialization as they inculcate new values and children are the future citizens. Thus, the leaders combined the modern with the traditional roles of women and made use of traditional symbols in the form of examples from myths to communicate their message. Forbes notes that the ideology of the women's movements in the pre-Independence period was far from being radical. It was an ideology which appealed to the middle-classes while still involving the women of the lower classes in the political awakening. However, these movements did succeed in bringing about reformative changes in the attitudes and status of women.

All the essays included in the two volumes have as their focus changes that have occurred in Indian society and culture as a result of social movements based on contradiction and conflict. Obviously, there is a need for more studies of social movements of diverse kinds in different regions so as to provide material with which to assess the nature of ideologies, and the direction of change in Indian society and culture.

Part 1

Part I

M S A Rao

Conceptual Problems in the Study of Social Movements*

IN RECENT YEARS social movements have attracted the attention of sociologists and social anthropologists in India. This paper does not aim to review the literature on social movements. Instead it attempts to outline the conceptual problems involved in a sociological study of social movements. One can identify five inter-related sets of problems. These are: (*a*) problems of definition and classification; (*b*) problems relating to the emergence of movements; (*c*) problems concerning the formulation of ideologies and establishing identities; (*d*) problems of collective mobilization, organization, leadership, internal dynamics and routinization; and (*e*) problems concerning the nature of the consequences for and changes in the wider society and culture.

It is necessary to distinguish a movement from a non-movement, and to identify the basic features which are characteristic of a movement. A social movement undoubtedly involves collective

*This paper is based on my book *Social Movements and Social Transformation: A Study of Two Backward Classes Movements in India*, which is in the press (Macmillan, New Delhi, expected late 1978).

This paper was presented at the Workshop on Social Movements. Later its revised version was presented as a Working paper in the panel on Social Movements at the XIII All-India Sociological Conference held at Chandigarh in December 1976. I am grateful to the participants of the Workshop as well as to those of the Conference for their comments.

action as distinct from individual action. However, only when the collective action is somewhat sustained, as distinct from a sporadic occurrence, does it take the form of a movement. This collective action, however, need not be formally organized, but should be able to create an interest and awakening in a sufficiently large number of people. Hence, a social movement essentially involves sustained collective mobilization through either informal or formal organization.

Secondly, a social movement is generally oriented towards bringing about change, either partial or total, in the existing system of relationships, values and norms, although there are efforts which are oriented towards resisting change and maintaining the *status quo*. The latter are more in the nature of counter attempts which are defensive and restorative rather than innovative and initiating change. They are the organized efforts of an already established, routinized order to maintain itself.

While there is considerable agreement among students of social movements regarding the two basic features—namely, collective mobilization and change-orientation—there are differences of opinion as regards including other criteria—such as, the presence of an ideology, method of organization and the nature of consequences—as part of the definition of a social movement.

Anticipating my argument in this regard, I consider ideology as an important component of a social movement as it distinguishes it from the general category of movements involving collective mobilization and orientation towards change. For example, a student strike involves collective mobilization and is oriented towards change. But in the absence of an ideology, a strike becomes an individual and isolated event and not a movement. On the contrary, if a strike is organized by a student organization with a defined ideology, it becomes an event in that student movement. Thus, a social movement is an organized attempt on the part of a section of society to bring about either partial or total change in society through collective mobilization based on an ideology.

While it is necessary to define the minimum criteria of relevance in identifying a movement, it is essential to define its limits. That is, when does a movement cease to be a movement? To anticipate the argument once again, when a movement becomes routinized with an established institutional procedure of recruitment and commitment and a code of conduct and sanctions for punishing deviants, it becomes part of the institutionalized system loosing its innovative features. Thus, when a movement with a defined ideology becomes a well established political party, it ceases to be a movement. However, the internal dynamics of the party may be such that it may lead to splinter movements. Hence, the main focus of a movement approach is to analyze the various processes involving a flow of activities and flux of norms and values in situational contexts.

The classification of a social movement is another definitional problem that must be tackled, for it helps to clarify its various dimensions. There have been several attempts to classify social movements using one or another criterion. Thus, on the basis of the criterion of the consequence of a movement, there are some movements oriented towards bringing about reform in some area of life or the other, involving new relationships, activities, norms and values. Other movements are oriented towards bringing about changes in super-ordinate and subordinate relationships which may be designated as transformative. Still others work towards bringing about revolutionary changes in all spheres of life and in all basic values.

The locus of a movement provides another criterion of classification. On this count, movements may be classified into linguistic, religious, sectarian, caste, peasant, worker, tribal, ethnic, faministic and student. Movements may also be classified on the basis of their scale and spatial spread. While some may be all-India, others may be regional and local. Another criterion of classification is the dominant issue of interest such as temperance, women liberation and a distinctive expressive art form.

It is necessary to emphasize that classification only helps to identify the main features of a movement; it does not fully explain its origin, growth, dynamics and consequences. Any classification is bound to remain inadequate, for a movement tends to acquire new features during its course and any classification can only be relative to a particular phase in its development. However, in classifying any movement I consider the criteria of ideology and the nature of consequences as critical in defining its nature and scope. The criterion of locus helps to identify the section of society which is involved in the movement. Thus, while locus provides the substantive aspect, the criteria of ideology and consequence provide the analytical foci of a movement.

Genesis of Social Movements

The problems of definition, including those of classification, pertain to the preliminaries of identifying a movement and operationalizing the problem of enquiry. One of the main issues in the study of any movement concerns its emergence. The relevant questions here are: what are the structural conditions under which movements emerge? What are the motivational forces? What are the theories which conceptualize the genesis of a movement? To what extent are they adequate?

Broadly speaking, there are three main theories which try to explain the structural conditions and motivational forces which give rise to a movement: These are theories of relative deprivation, strain and revitalization. The theory of relative deprivation has developed on two different lines: social mobility and social conflict. The former line of development is represented by Merton (1950) and Runciman (1966). Although the authors of the *American Soldier* (1949) were the first to use the notion of relative deprivation, it was Merton who systematically developed the concept in relation to reference group theory. Merton applied the concept to analyze social mobility. Later, Runciman, following Merton, developed the concept in relation to reference group and problems of inequalities and social justice. In this approach, relative deprivation is made the basis of a study of social mobility as occurring through emulation and positive reference group behaviour.

As against this approach, Marx and Aberle developed the concept of relative deprivation emphasizing the element of conflict. Marx and Engels (1973) recognized that dissatisfaction with the *status quo* was not determined by absolute conditions but by relative expectations. Aberle (1966), defining relative deprivation as a negative discrepancy between legitimate expectations and actuality, treated it as the bed-rock for a study of social movements. He analyzed relative deprivations in terms of material possession, status, behaviour and worth.

Gurr (1970) introduced several clarifications in the concept of relative deprivation. He considered relative deprivation not only in terms of expectations but in relation to perceived capabilities. He defined relative deprivation as a gap between expectations and perceived capabilities involving three general sets of values: economic conditions, political power and social status. The gap may be caused when expectations remain stable but capabilities decline (decremental deprivation); expectations rise but capabilities decline (progressive deprivation); and expectations rise while capabilities remain the same (aspirational deprivation).

A point that is conceded by relative deprivation theorists is that a position of relative deprivation alone will not generate a movement. The structural conditions of relative deprivation provide only the necessary conditions. Sufficient conditions are provided by the perception of a situation and by the estimate of capabilities by certain leaders that they can do something to remedy the situation.

The strain theory propounded by Smelser (1962) treats structural strain as the underlying factor leading to collective behaviour. Structural strain occurs at different levels of norms, values, mobilization, and situational facilities. While strain provides the structural condition, the crystallization of a generalized belief marks the attempt of persons under strain to assess their situation, and to explain the situation by creating or assembling a generalized belief. Both strain and generalized belief require precipitating factors to trigger off a movement.

Smelser's analysis of the genesis of social movements is in the structural-functional framework. Smelser considers strain as the impairment of relations among parts of a system leading to the malfunctioning of the system, and includes deprivation under strain. However, the relative deprivation theory emphasizes the conflict element which is productive of change, and does not consider conflict as leading to the malfunctioning of the system.

It may be asked whether social movements necessarily arise out of negative conditions of relative deprivation and strain. In this context, Wallace (1956) posited that social movements develop out of a deliberate, organized and conscious effort on the part of members of a society to construct a more satisfying culture for themselves. Wallace analyzed the dynamics of revitalization movements in four phases: period of cultural stability. period of increased individual stress, period of cultural distortion and consequent disillusionment, and period of revitalization.

The revitalization theory, however, propounds that adaptive processes are employed to establish equilibrium situations. Although social movements develop a positive programme of action, they tend to be double-edged. On the one hand they express dissatisfaction, dissent and protest against existing conditions, and on the other, they offer a positive programme of action to remedy the situation.

To my mind, the relative deprivation theory offers a more satisfactory explanation of the genesis of social movements for it is pivoted around conflict and cognitive change, motivating people and mobilizing them around certain interests and issues. Secondly, it offers the best explanation for the change-orientation of movements rather than to looking at movements as adaptive mechanisms restoring functional unity and equilibrium. However, the relative deprivation theory needs refinement in two directions. First, it is necessary to make the concept sociologically more relevant by eschewing individual and psychic deprivations. Such deprivations remain personal, arbitrary and even frivolous. For instance, it is hard to find anyone in the world who does not suffer from one kind of imagined or real deprivation or the other. The richest man may feel deprived of the peace of mind that a poor man has. Hence it is necessary to define deprivations in terms of collectivities and in the situational context of a differential allocation of rights and privileges in different spheres of social and cultural life.

Secondly, in considering areas of deprivation, Aberle, Glock (1964) and Gurr hardly include religion. It is necessary to note that deprivations in the religious sphere are as important as those in the spheres of economics, education, and politics. The participants in a movement, especially among the backward classes in India, view their deprivation in different areas—such as, religious, economic, educational and political—as interrelated, for they are different manifestations of inequalities and discriminations based on a differential allocation of diverse goods and services. The leaders of a movement simultaneously open up multiple fronts to attack the monopoly of the upper castes in various fields.

Ideology and Identity

Another set of conceptual problems in the study of social movements relates to ideology and the kind of identity the concerned groups establish. While Marx (1904) located ideology within the class structure, Mannheim (1960) considered it as a means of discrediting an adversary. In the context of the sociology of knowledge, his treatment of ideology acquired a perjorative connotation. However, Geertz (1964) lifted it out of this connotation by viewing it as a system of interacting symbols. As a symbolic system it acts as a bridge between source analysis on the one hand, and consequence analysis on the other. It interprets the environment and projects self-images. It codifies and organizes beliefs, myths, outlook, and values, defines aspirations and interests and directs responses to specific social situations. Thus it is not only a 'framework of consciousness' but also a source of legitimizing action.

The formulation of ideology is an important aspect of any social movement. The leaders work out different themes by which the concerned section in the movement attempts to improve its self-image, respect and honour. For instance, I have identified elsewhere (1977) a number of different themes in the ideology of backward classes movements: withdrawal and self-organization (as exemplified by the Sri Narayana Dharma Paripalana movement in Kerala and the Veerasaiva movement); claiming a higher *varna* status (Yadava movement) as a variation of the re-interpretation principle; and extolling the virtues of the Dravidian culture as against Aryan culture (DMK movement) and negating Hinduism altogether and embracing Buddhism (Mahar movement) as variations of the rejection principle. Then there is the Marxian ideology of class conflict combined with an anti-caste anti-Hindu bias (Dalit Panthers).

I would like to add two other themes based on relative deprivation. They are the Marxian ideology of class struggle without an ethnic component, and the millenarian ideology. Many peasant movements have the class struggle as their ideology. However, within this ideology one can identify several variations ranging from left radicalism to the extreme left position. At this point, peasant movements, like trade union movements, get affiliated with or involved in sharply defined political parties and movements.

The millenarian theme has been the dominant expression of relative deprivation among many tribal movements (see Fuchs, 1965). Here the future state of affairs to come (which will see a complete reversal of the present state of deprivation) acts as the motivating force for action in the present so as to prepare for the millenium. The millenarian ideology is the opposite of the ideology of the Yadava movement, in which the past glory of the Yadavas acts as a motivating force for action in the present. The millenarian ideology is characteristic of 'colonial' situations where deprived groups feel helpless in regard to their perceived capabilities in being able to alter the existing situation.

The leaders of a movement select different elements of relative deprivation and combine them in different ways to formulate an ideology. The organizational principles so selected depend upon the objective conditions of deprivation, the way the leaders perceive the situation in the centext of wider interacting forces, and the assessment of their resources or capabilities to meet the challenges. The ideology also provides the source of legitimization of the new values, norms and relationships envisaged by the leaders. It provides the basis of interest articulation and of establishing a new identity.

An important aspect of the ideologies based on relative deprivation is establishing identity in relation to other groups. The concerned deprived sections draw boundaries based on the ideology of their movement. While the boundaries tend to be soft with regard to cognate groups, they tend to be hard with regard to reference groups to which the deprived sections are opposed. I call the latter opposition reference groups.

Opposition reference group implies that the deprived sections do not just imitate the styles of life and adopt the privileged customs of the reference groups, but that they attack the monopoly of the reference groups in the use of economic, educational, political and religious goods and services. They attempt to take away these privileges from them. They not only attempt to lower the ceiling of the privileges enjoyed by the upper castes and classes but also raise their floor level through a conflict relationship with the privileged sections. It is not a situation of social mobility characterized by gentlemanly passing, but one involving confrontation and conflict which is a characteristic of the notion of opposition reference groups. Thus, although the Veerasaivas adopted many brahmanical customs, they were in conflicting relations with the Brahmins. The former attacked the monopoly of the latter and created a set of religious institutions parallel to that of the Brahmins. In so doing they did not seek legitimacy from the Brahmins but established independent sources of legitimacy through their priests and kings.

Collective Mobilization, Organization and Leadership

Collective mobilization, which is crucial in a movement, is not only related to ideology but to the nature of leadership and organization.

In the case of charismatic leadership, collective mobilization tends to be spontaneous. The process of recruitment, which is an important aspect of collective mobilization, tends to be highly diversified, depending on the talents of the people involved. While the traditional intellectual elite are drafted to formulate the ideology and to spread the message, others who do not have specific talents are recruited as volunteers for specific tasks.

Many social movements tend to be characterized by collective leadership with a division of labour among different types of elites. While the business elite gives donations supporting the various activities of the movement, the political elite takes leadership positions in the movement. Normally, social movements tend to develop a loose federal structure with central and regional associations being held together by relationships of local autonomy and external links based on common interests. This is different from the organization of political parties and trade unions where there is a centralized authority structure. Associations based on primordial ties or relations of production form the over-arching organizational framework of a movement.

One may identify different levels of commitment on the part of leaders and others, from faith to fanaticism. Commitment is manifest in the adoption of the belief system, willingness to volunteer in performing various tasks, readiness to take risks of different kinds. The more committed persons are rewarded in terms of higher status, honour, and tangible positions. In the process of collective mobilization, leaders tend to exploit the pre-existing kin, caste and linguistic ties of individual recruits and use the traditional institutional framework. They also operate through the idioms and symbols familiar to people, besides creating new units of organization.

Any social movement tends to develop an event structure over a period of time. A past event influences the choice of strategy in the events that follow in the context of interaction with other groups and opposition reference groups. Occasionally, an event within a movement gets connected with an event or events that occur elsewhere. A set of events centered round an issue constitutes a phase, and the course of a movement consists of several phases. It would be necessary not only to identify these events and phases but also to analyse why a movement takes a particular course and not another in the context of relevant alternatives.

When the organization of a movement becomes more formal and

rigid and when it accumulates property, there is a tendency for schisms to develop and splits to occur. One may identify three patterns of rifts that might occur during the course of a movement. While some conflicts are in the nature of personal rivalries, others are based on divergent ideological differences. Still other conflicts are based on complementary ideological differences, which generally lead to splinter movements.

Besides internal schisms, a social movement is subject to the process of routinization sooner or later. Often a protest movement starts off with a radical ideology but develops its own establishment in turn. A protest movement which rejects existing institutions will in turn attempt to codify its own belief system and provide institutionalized arrangements to enforce a code of conduct.

It is relevant to raise the question as to what happens to a movement after routinization in all areas of social life sets in. There are several possibilities: It might die a natural death; or it might lie dormant for some time and pick up new interests which will give it a new life; or it might develop internal contradictions that will throw up new forces directed towards increasing radicalization. In any case, the most crucial variable is the wider political context in which it operates. It is likely that the ruling or dominant party might absorb the radical elements present in the protest movement and render them ineffective by taking the lead in spearheading radical changes in society. In this context, the part played by the state in implementing radical changes becomes highly significant. The various programmes of the state may not be regarded as social movements, because these are aspects of established and institutionalized procedures to implement policies.

Social Consequences and Change

Any theory of social movement has to grapple not only with the dimensions of genesis, ideology, collective mobilization, organization and leadership, but with the conceptual problems relating to social change. In fact, the nature of the changes that a social movement brings about or intends to bring about is a crucial criterion in the classification of movements. The results of a movement bear a closer relationship with the ideology, interests and organization of a movement rather than with the structural conditions of relative deprivation. Aberle suggests that it is possible to establish an association between the social context of the deprived group and the type of movement based on the amount of change. However, it seems to me that there are two important sets of intervening variables between the structural conditions of relative deprivation and the consequential social changes of a movement, namely, the ideology-organization aspect, and the reaction of the opposition reference groups and the wider political context.

The social changes that result from a movement may be seen first in terms of the changes in the positions of the concerned section of a movement and secondly in terms of their impact on the wider society. In the context of the latter, a basic distinction has to be made between those social movements which have brought about either partial or wholesale changes in the structure of relationships and the values underlying them, and efforts which have resulted in marginal changes only aimed at maintaining the *status quo*. This distinction overlaps with Smelser's distinction between value and norm oriented movements. Values and norms, however, cannot be isolated from the positional picture; they have to be seen in relation to the social relationships and their linkages. Further, movements oriented toward changing values also bring about changes in norms specific to situations.

Normally, *status quo* oriented attempts—such as, those of the Kshatriya Mahasabha, the Kanya Kubja Brahmins and the Sanatan Dharma—spring up as a reaction to change-oriented movements. They are more in the nature of counter-efforts launched by the establishment. Here the first-class citizens (e.g., the Brahmins, Rajputs and Baniyas) feel disinherited and threatened by the radical movement. With a view to maintaining their position, they organize themselves and mobilize their caste men in an effort to reform customs which are considered outdated so as to catch up with the times. They form associations which tend to take up welfare and service functions, especially in urban areas, and act as pressure groups on certain occasions. For instance, the all-India Kshatriya Mahasabha pressed for the retention of princely privileges when the abolition of privy purses was being considered. Thus, it can be said that the privileged classes exhibit signs of counter efforts whenever they perceive their interests to be threatened. The bases of collective mobilization among the privileged groups are self-defence, self-help, correction of self-image and consolidation of status. In contrast to the *status quo* maintaining attempts which emerge among the dispossessed groups, social movements which originate among the deprived sections are oriented towards bringing about changes in the structure of positional arrangements, values and norms.

A distinction is normally made between structural and organizational changes; the former refering to the changes in the totality of relationships, relative positions and their arrangement, and values; and the latter signifying changes in the norms, activities and personnel from one position to another. I regard this distinction as having distorted our understanding of the nature of social change. For, in this framework, structural change is said to occur only when there is a black and white distinction; as, for example, when a society which is capitalistic becomes socialistic through revolution and rapid violent change. Structural change here is identified with the complete and total change of social systems. In reality, structural changes mainly occur in a discrete manner. They tend to be disjointed, discontinuous and partial. Many reform movements based on relative deprivation are neither aimed at a total and complete change in the social and cultural systems nor are they successful in bringing about such changes. Hence there is a need to define valid concepts so as to be able to analyze the different levels and kinds of structural changes. I have distinguished three levels of structural change: reform, transformation and revolution.

Reform movements may be identified with partial changes in the value system and consequential changes in the quality of relationships. Often reforms are associated with the belief system, world view, outlook, rituals and style of life of the affected groups. Indian history abounds with examples of reform movements. The devotional movements, which led to the formation of diverse sects in medieval India, revolted against the monopoly of certain sections of Brahmins over the various paths to salvation. These movements propounded that divine grace could be achieved through devotion which was open to all classes and castes. In so far as these movements abrogated the principle of birth which determined access to salvation through knowledge and ritual, they brought about structural changes in the religious sphere. The reform movements that emerged in British India, however, led to both doctrinal changes and to changes in the structure of social relationships.

In contrast, revolution is identified with radical changes in the totality of social and cultural systems. The changes are wholesale and sudden and are often associated with violence. Revolutionary movements are characterized by class conflict and are associated with political parties which operate on the basis of a carefully formulated ideology and a programme of action. The revolutions that occurred in Russia and China are examples.

Transformative movements aim at bringing about middle level structural changes in the traditional distribution of power and in the system of differential allocation of resources, rights and privileges by attacking the monopoly of the upper classes and castes in different areas of life including religion. The element of conflict in these movements acquires a sharper focus than in the reform movements. The nature of conflict in the case of transformative movements also tends to be different from that of the revolutionary movements. While in the case of the latter the conflict is based on the Marxist ideology of class struggle, in the case of the former, the conflict is more between ethnic groups though not without elements of class struggle being built into their ideologies.

A Methodological Question

In the end I shall raise a methodological question. It may be argued that a study of social movements belongs mainly to the domain of history and not sociology because a movement is discovered by the sociologist after it has come into existence, or when it is on the wane. A sociologist cannot do fieldwork while the movement is on either because he will not be aware of it or because it is difficult to carry out fieldwork especially when a movement is violent in nature.

As against this it may be said that social history is a legitimate field of sociological investigation. A movement no doubt has a time span and it is necessary for a sociologist to acquire the skills of a historian to collect historical data. However, the nature of interpretation remains sociological, and I have indicated in this paper some aspects of the sociological analysis of social movements. Secondly, it is not entirely true to say that sociologists cannot do participant observation in an ongoing movement. I had the good fortune to do fieldwork when the Yadava movement was at its peak and was demanding a separate Yadav regiment in the Indian Army. Similarly, Spevak (1975) was in the field when he observed all the three phases of the Navnirman movement in Gujarat: genesis, climax and the end.

The Kelloms, whose paper is included in volume two, studied a sect which was in the processes of being formed by Dada Sitaram in Banaras. Hence, if sociologists are on the look out, they can carry out fieldwork in an ongoing movement.

It needs to be recognized, however, that a researcher studying a social movement has to acquire training in the use of diverse techniques. The study of social movements requires somewhat different approaches from those required for the study of a village community or neighbourhood. In the former, the social space is wider and the time span longer. The field-worker faces the problem of handling diverse documentary data available in several languages. He has to travel a great deal to locate the documentary sources and interview people in different places and belonging to different generations. It involves attending conferences and meetings in different places, gathering data on different areas of the social life—religious, political, economic and educational—of the people involved in the movement, with a view to seeking interrelationships. In short, it involves the employment of such diverse techniques of gathering information as participant observation, survey method, historical and case history method, interview and content analysis, in a meaningful way. It demands the skills of building up of an event structure of a movement in relation to wider social and cultural forces. In order to handle problems of analyzing dynamic social processes over a period of time, we not only need to acquire diverse skills of techniques of gathering data but also to develop a conceptual framework to interpret and explain social movements. This paper is a step in this direction.

References

ABERLE, D.F. (1966) : *The Peyote Religion Among the Navaho*. Viking Fund Publications in Anthropology, No. 42. New York: Wenner-Gren Foundation.

FUCHS, STEPHEN (1965) : *Rebellious Prophets: A Study of Messianic Movements in Indian Religions*. Bombay: Asia Publishing House.

GEERTZ, CLIFFORD (1964) : 'Ideology as a Cultural System'. In David E. Apter (ed.), *Ideology and Discontent*. New York: The Free Press. pp. 47-67.

GLOCK, CHARLES Y. (1964): 'The Role of Deprivation in the Origin and Evolution of Religious Groups'. In R. Lee and M.E. Marty (eds.), *Religion and*

Social Conflict. New York: Oxford University Press. pp. 24-36.

GURR, T.R. (1970) : *Why Men Rebel*. Princeton, N.J.: Princeton University Press.

MANNHEIM, KARL (1960) : *Ideology and Utopia*. London: Routledge and Kegan Paul.

MARX, KARL (1904) : *A Contribution to the Critique of Political Economy*. Chicago: Charles H. Kerr.

MARX, KARL and ENGELS, FREDERICK (1973) : *Selected Works* (Three Volumes). Moscow: Progress Publishers.

MERTON, R.K. and ROSSI, ALICE KITT (1950) : 'Contributions to the theory of Reference Group Behaviour'. In R.K. Merton and P.F. Lazarsfeld (eds.), *Continuities in Social Research*. New York: The Free Press, pp. 40-106.

RAO, M.S.A. (1977) : 'Themes in the Ideology of Protest Movement'. In S.C. Malik (ed.), *Dissent, Protest, and Reform in Indian Civilization*. Simla: Indian Institute of Advanced Study. pp. 56-69.

RUNCIMAN, W.C. (1966) : *Relative Deprivation and Social Justice*. London: Routledge and Kegan Paul.

SMELSER, NEIL (1962) : *Theory of Collective Behaviour*. London: Routledge and Kegan Paul.

SPEVAK, M.L. (1975) : 'Nav Nirman Movement in Ahmedabad'. Paper presented at the Workshop on Social Movements, Department of Sociology, University of Delhi, 24-26 March 1975.

STOUFFER, SAMUEL A. *et al* (1949) : *The American Soldier: Adjustment during Army Life*. Vol. 1. Princeton: Princeton University Press.

WALLACE, A.F.C. (1956): 'Revitalization movements'. *American Anthropologist*, 58 (April): 264-281.

2

Partha N Mukherji

Naxalbari Movement and the Peasant Revolt in North Bengal

IT IS WITH a certain sense of reluctance and reservation that I have allowed myself to be drawn into writing this paper. Firstly, the study is still not 'completed' and is at the stage of field investigation. Hence, I have had to resort to certain generalizations which, perforce, may not be borne out by empirical realities. Secondly, unlike structural studies of caste, family, kinship and the like, the study of movements is very sensitive indeed. Any observation based on an inadequate or incomplete understanding of the phenomenon can be intellectually unethical. Finally, so fluid is the state of the movement at present that even to many participants the emerging patterns are not clear beyond a point. In spite of these formidable inhibiting factors, I have been compelled to respond to the pressures of the academic community to present some of my research material with the hope that it will stimulate those interested or engaged in the study of social movements. Under the circumstances, the tentative nature of my observations is inevitable.

I

The sudden spurt of interest in the study of social movements has clouded rather than clarified some of the theoretical-conceptual issues basic to the understanding of social structure and change. Most studies give no clear idea of their theoretical yield or the purpose for which the movements concerned are being studied. Yet they are useful and welcome insofar as they enable us to know more about social mobilization and its consequences. We are confronted with a variety of phenomena like student unrest, labour discontent, religious revivals, peasant revolts, urban tensions, and insurrections. Most of these phenomena purportedly relate to some kind of movement or the other. However, there appears to be a tendency to dub government or establishment initiated projects as movements. The movement label, it would appear, confers respectability and a sense of vigour (which may or may not be present) to the phenomenon, and hence its liberal use.

If we are to derive coherence out of the seemingly disparate material on social mobilizations we need to work towards a more meaningful theoretical framework which would enable us to differentiate between them. The relationship between social movement and social change (or resistance to change) is incontrovertible. Not to recognize this would be to lose the prime focus of any analysis of movements. Four basic premises follow from this (Mukherji, 1977:38):

1. Social movements are essentially related to social change and therefore to the social structure. This does not mean that a social movement is a necessary condition of social change; on the contrary, social change can take place independently of social movements through the operation of impersonal forces and factors. Nor does it mean that it is change-promoting—it can be, equally, change-resisting.
2. Social movements are products of a social structure and hence emerge out of certain conditions in the social structure.
3. Social movements themselves have a recognizable structure in terms of which they are rendered functional relative to their goals.
4. Social movements have consequences for the social structure of which they are the products.

These basic premises provide the perspective for relevant information on the phenomenon of social mobilization directed towards *some* change. Thus we are prompted to ask: what kind of change does the mobilization envisage? Or, what kind of change does it intend to resist? What conditions in the social structure have led to the demand for (or resistance to) change? What has been the impact of such a mobilization in terms of the intended changes? What has been the nature and composition of such a mobilization? Or is it that the mobilization is sporadic, spontaneous and lacking in any direction? All these queries, and numerous others emanating from these premises, become the *sine qua non* of any meaningful study of social movements and, through them, of our social reality and its vulnerability to and propensity for change. I make no tall claim that I have satisfactorily answered these questions in this small exposition.

Basic to any scientific enterprise is an attempt to classify the problematics of a study. Every scheme of classification has an analytical purpose. There is no single scheme of classification for any phenomenon, nor is any classification so sacrosanct that it cannot be replaced by a more efficient one. Analysts construct their own system(s) of classification so as to examine the details of the phenomenon under investigation. Thus, the same phenomenon can be classified in more than one way, by more than one researcher, and this is not only fair but desirable for a greater understanding of the same phenomenon. Classifications hardly, if ever, are wrong—they may be more or less efficient in the understanding of the phenomenon under investigation. However, without a system of classification we may be left with a bewildering mass of data which we are unable to absorb. Of course, it is possible to avoid classifying altogether if we confine ourselves to so microcosmic a field that it is not at all difficult to absorb the problem in all its descriptive opulence. But, then, not all phenomena can be subjected to such a microcosmic approach.

Scholars have propounded a variety of typologies to classify movements. For example, Turner and Killian's value-oriented, power-oriented and participation-oriented movements; Aberle's transformative, reformative, redemptive and alterative movements; Smelser's value-oriented and norm-oriented movements (Wilson, 1973:3-29); while Oommen refers to classifications based on locality, language, issues, social categories and sects (1977:14-37). It is my contention in this paper that a classification of movements by classification of change would be an efficient way of penetrating into the relationship between social movement, social structure and social change.

Logically, this leads us to the question of social change and its classification. A social system can be conceived of as consisting of 'structures which are interrelated'. Thus we can conceive of the family as a social system consisting of structures and relationships characterized by husband-wife relations, parent-children relations, inter-sibling relations, affinal-lineal relations, family-acquaintance relations and so on, in terms of reciprocity and exchange. Similarly, we can conceive of and identify the relevant structures that, in inter-relation, constitute the agrarian social reality. Social changes, therefore, can be viewed in following terms:

1. as changes occurring *within* given structure(s);
2. changes occurring from an *emergence of additional structure(s)*;
3. changes occurring due to the *elimination or loss of structure(s)*; and
4. changes occurring as a result of *replacement* of existing structure(s) by alternative structure(s).

Following the above classification of changes with respect to social systems, we can distinguish between *accumulative*, *alternative* and *transformative* changes. Changes of the first variety are accumulative; those of the second and third variety are alternative; whilst changes of the fourth type are transformative (Mukherji, 1977:43). Thus, changes taking place from a feudal system to a semi-feudal system may be largely alterative, but its culmination in a capitalistic or a socialistic system is certainly transformative. The establishment of soviets or peoples' committees (Jana Samitis) are in the same way alternative changes.

It will be clear therefore that social changes can be broadly classified in terms of changes occurring *within* structures, and of changes *of* the structures themselves with or without replacement, or by their qualitative change on account of the emergence of additional structures. Movements need to be classified by the changes they intend to bring about and/or by the changes that have already been accomplished. The critical discriminant for the classification of collective mobilizations, therefore, depends upon whether the goals are explicitly directed towards change (or resistance to change) of the structures, as against change within structures in the face of opposition against such a move. It is my contention that any collective mobilization for action directed explicitly towards an alteration or transformation of the structures of a system (or against an explicit threat to an alteration or transformation of a system), can be properly understood as a *social movement.* When the collective mobilization aims at effecting wide-ranging and far-reaching changes in the major institutional systems comprising the whole society, we can rightly term it a *revolutionary movement.* Collective mobilizations aimed at changes within a system are *quasi-movements.* The direction and rationale for such change is provided by the ideology of the movement. Thus there are movements galore but not many are social movements—most are quasi-movements, and very very rarely are they revolutionary movements. However, a revolutionary movement will presumably have to pass through the stages of quasi-and social movements before maturing into a revolutionary movement. Thus, such a framework attempts to move from a static to a hopefully more dynamic model of analysis of social movements. The corrollary of a movement countering a social movement—a counter-movement—is inevitable.

The question of values is wont to confound conceptualizations of social and revolutionary movements. A social movement is bound to have a positive valence for its partisans and a negative valence for those countering it, and vice versa. Both the Nazi and the Bolshevik movements were revolutionary in as much as they transformed the structures of their systems, but the valences were positive for the protagonists and negative for the antagonists. Likewise, counter-movements would also be both positively and negatively valenced. To dub a mobilization as a movement or a counter-movement solely on the basis of one's own value preferences would be to introduce an element of arbitrariness which would make any sociology of social movements counter-productive.

II

In this paper I shall confine myself to three aspects relevant to the understanding and appraisal of the movement under study. First, I shall make a macroscopic survey of the emergence of the new revolutionary party. Second, I shall describe the evolution of the peasant uprising in Naxalbari. And, finally, an attempt will be made to analyze and interpret tne substantive material presented.

A few observations on the methodology and the consequent limitations of the data collected to date is both desirable and necessary. Secondary source data is available mostly at the *initial* level, that is, they have been collected by agencies at the primary level for their own use but have thereafter not been further analyzed. Published work based on field data does not, to my knowledge, exist so far. Therefore, the data presented here has been obtained from available secondary sources as well as collected with the help of open-ended interviews with persons who, in the language of social anthropological fieldwork, are known as key informants. The key informants being themselves prime activists during the period of agrarian turmoil have provided information and knowledge about the movement in the style of oral history and ad hoc interpretations of events and processes. These materials are extremely rich. However, one has to exercise caution in the use of such data. They have to be cross-checked with interviews with co-activists who have participated in the same events. Further, they need also to be cross-checked with persons who were the targets of the activists and have thus shared the same experiences. I would like to warn my readers that this paper falls far short of the required rigour at the present stage of research. Therefore, an attempt has been made to interpret no more than what a judicious conservative restraint would permit.

Another point that needs to be underscored is that most of the interviews have been volunteered on the condition that the source of information is not revealed. Events have, therefore, been reported without revealing the source of information. But in most cases they are first-hand reports and hence can be accepted as valid data. The style of presentation of the data is narrative-descriptive. In the absence of more information about the universe of research, analytical tables have been avoided.

Finally, it should be borne in mind that a thorough study of the agrarian social reality, both in its historical and contemporary aspects has yet to be completed. The relationships between class, caste/tribe, faction and party; the penetration of market forces and their exploitative consequences; the various contradictions that are revealed in the social processes; and the operation of the manifest and latent levels of social reality—these have to await a more painstaking phase of research.

III

The 'left' movement in this country has been characterized by periodic splits. These splits have closely paralleled ideological rifts between dominant centres of international communism. The emergence of China as a major communist power in the East brought into existence a rival centre of Marxist-Leninist ideology which refused to accept the ideological hegemony of Soviet Russia in the world communist movement. Although this development had its reverberations in the Indian communist movement—first within the Communist Party of India (CPI), and then, subsequent to the Sino-Indian armed confrontation, in the form of the birth of the Communist Party of India—Marxists (CPI-M) in 1964—the movement, if it is to be properly understood, has to be examined in the context of the structural realities of our society and its propensities for change in the direction of a more egalitarian system (Sen Gupta, 1972:5). Peking hailed the new communist party.[1] The CPI-M decided to pursue as its immediate objective the establishment of a peoples' democracy under its leadership, while in the international sphere it was frankly critical of the Soviet Union and the CPI. It generally displayed its sympathy for China in its ideological warfare with Soviet Russia but refrained from an uncritical support of the Chinese position. But in spite of all this, it kept its international linkage with one or the other dominant centres undefined (Ram, 1969:11). Thus, the CPI-M took off from a pro-Chinese, anti-CPI, and anti-Soviet Union posture.

However, the CPI-M was born with a contradiction. Having adopted a pro-Chinese ideological stance it was unable to formulate clear guidelines for action in the concrete conditions of the Indian social reality. This ambiguity provided sufficient grounds for the extremists within the newly formed party to be critical of it. Persistent demands to clarify the party line was characteristic of the debates that raged within the Party until 1967 when it decided to join the election fray.[2] The CPI-M leadership acknowledged that the situation in India was not yet ripe for revolution and opted for participating in legislative politics with which, it argued, other kinds of struggles could be combined. A United Front government with CPI-M participation came into existence in West Bengal in February 1967, a situation which the United Front constituents certainly did not anticipate prior to the elections. This led to the emergence of a number of groups within the CPI-M which criticised the Party. The most articulate and active group was the Party wing of the Siliguri sub-division of Darjeeling district under the leadership of Charu Mazumdar, Kanu Sanyal and Souren Bose. Sushital Roy Choudhury formed an Inner-Party Anti-Revisionism Committee; Amulya Sen and Kanai Chatterjee formed the 'Chinta' group; whilst Swadesh Mitra led the Surjya Sen group (Roy, 1975:75).

There is sufficient evidence to believe that the pro-Chinese component of the top CPI-M leadership in West Bengal (particularly Hare Krishna Konar and also perhaps Promode Dasgupta) had actually encouraged the communist cadres in Siliguri sub-division to develop militancy on the peasant front. One of the leading activists of the Naxalbari movement claimed that in a Krishak Sabha meeting in 1964, Konar had argued forcefully that the parliamentary path was mere trickery (*bhowntabaji*), and that they should prepare for an armed struggle without which fundamental changes in the agrarian front cannot be achieved. Up to the time of the elections, the state level leaders did not discourage the arming of peasant leaders and cadres of Siliguri. It is even alleged that the state level leaders 'decided that the agitation would be launched immediately after the General Elections, due in March 1967, when the new Ministry would be sworn in (and as the party's calculation ran at that time, it would be the Congress Ministry once again back to power!)' (Roy, 1975: 69-70). However, finding themselves unexpectedly in power, and involved in eight coalition governments in other states in India, the CPI-M found itself in a new position of responsibility. It argued that the Congress defeat had ushered in qualitative changes in the political firmament, and as a revolutionary party in power it had to provide an example so that the process could engulf the entire country. Hence it argued in its Political Report adopted by the Central Committee that 'the fortunes of the entire party at the present stage of development are closely linked with the successful running of ministries . . .' (Roy, 1975:74). Or the same counts, leaders of the Darjeeling District of the CPI-M found this to be the most appropriate time for a peasant uprising. Thus the mobilization of peasants, meant to challenge Congress rule, in effect resulted in the embarrassment of the Party!

The Naxalbari peasant uprising exacerbated the existing schisms within the CPI-M and the extremist radical groups were either expelled or they dissociated themselves from the Party. The

Darjeeling District Committee had to be dissolved and as many as forty members were expelled from the Party (Roy, 1975:116-7). The Communist Party of China (CPC), which had been providing moral support to the radical dissenters within the Party, hailed the Naxalbari event as a 'spring thunder' over India, which according to them was a prelude to the revolutionary transformation ahead. Thus the stern disciplinary action taken by the Party against its dissenting members was more than compensated for by the revolutionary legitimacy conferred upon them by the Chinese testimonial. The zeal and enthusiasm of the breakaway dissenting groups was further reinforced by what they considered was a revolutionary cause. Further, they were aware of the support of many rank-and file members from within the CPI-M.

The most conspicuous among the breakway groups was the Naxalbari-o-Krishak Sangram Sahayak Samiti (Naxalbari and Peasant Struggle Assistance Committee—NKSSS) led by Sushital Roychoudhury. He was earlier editor of the CPI-M organ *Deshahitaishi* from which post he was removed forcibly. Thereafter, he started another paper, *Deshbarati*, which served as the mouthpiece of the NKSSS. Among other important splinter groups were the Commune group which advocated a guerilla type of revolution, patterned on the Cuban model of Che Guevara. This group operated clandestinely from within CPI-M. The Lokayan group (named after the paper), operating once again from within the CPI-M, while disfavouring the formation of a new political organization, advocated the replacement of the present leadership by the revolutionary leadership of the Party. Later on, they renamed their organ *Naya Yug*. The Maoist Communist Centre (MCC) was comparable in its militancy to the NKSSS. Its regular mouthpiece was *Dakshin Desh* and its other publications were *Istehar* and *Peoples' War*.

Apart from these groups, there were several other smaller but vocal groups of extremists who were critical of CPI-M policies. Thus the Surjya Sen group (also known as the Bolshevik group), the Purbadesh group, the Puber Howa group, the Red Flag group, the Kashthi Pathar group, the Nadia group, the Vitti group, the Kalpurush group, and the Biplabi Sanjog Sanstha group, all subscribed to a more explicit Maoist ideology and strategy for a radical transformation of the Indian social structure, more particularly the agrarian rural structure. The Presidency College Students' Consolidation, the students who articulated through the *Chhatra Fouz*, the Committee of

Revolutionary Students who identified with the Puber Howa group and the PGSF group constituted the militant Maoist groups within the student universe in Calcutta and elsewhere in West Bengal. All these different groups came under the general rubric of Naxalite politics.

It was at the initiative of the NKSSS—which had gained the recognition of the expelled members of the CPI-M of the Darjeeling District Committee under the leadership of Charu Mazumdar, Kanu Sanyal and Souren Bose—that the formation of the Coordination Committee of Revolutionaries (CCR) was spearheaded and came into existence by August 1967. This was before the Madurai meeting of the CPI-M Central Committee on 18 August 1967. The establishment of the CCR led to similar formations in the states of Bihar, Punjab, Maharashtra, Uttar Pradesh, Jammu and Kashmir, and Kerala. The extremists in Andhra Pradesh deferred the formation of a Coordination Committee until they were expelled by the CPI-M in their Burdwan plenum in April 1968. By November 1967, again at the initiative of the West Bengal Coordination Committee of Communist Revolutionaries (WBCCCR), the different state coordination committees resolved to form the All India Coordination Committee of Communist Revolutionaries (AICCCR). Thus, the extremists within the various states were organised with amazing rapidity and this was followed by their coordination at the inter-state level. By 22 April 1969, the process had reached its logical culmination with the formation of the third communist party of India on the birth centenary of Viadimar I. Lenin, the chief architect of the Russian revolution. The formation of the new party was announced by Kanu Sanyal at the May Day rally in Calcutta.

The birth of the Communist Party of India—Marxist—Leninist (CPI-ML) can be distinguished from the CPI-M on several counts. The latter came into existence as a consequence of a division within the CPI. It was a mobilization of protest within the Party which gradually led to the severance of ties from the undivided Party. A new party was born out of the womb of the agrarian struggle. Its period of gestation and maturity was irrevocably linked with this struggle. It took a definite form by stages. It also emerged as the result of the combined efforts of many groups and individuals fired by a common vision of the revolution. It was different in yet another sense—the new party attracted many recruits who were novices without any prior political socialization, and whose first political experience was becoming a member of the third communist party of India which promised a revolutionary transformation of society. However, the CPI-M, it should be remembered, was only one, though the major, constituent of Naxalite politics. There were others, like the MCC, who championed the cause of armed seizure of political power by the country's most oppressed.

Once the ideological and political bases of the Naxalite groups in different states were crystallized as the CPI-ML, they entered the political arena with renewed vigour. This time the programmatic content differed substantially from that of the peasant uprising in Naxalbari in 1967. From massive participation of peasants for forcible occupation of benami, vest land,[3] and *khas* land, emphasis was now placed on the liquidation of class enemies by a programme of annihilation through the use of guerilla tactics. Mass movements were rejected as revisionist, and secret and underground small-group squads replaced them with the aim of seizing political power. The programmes of strengthening base areas and preparing a Peoples' Liberation Army were not given any serious thought. In short, the Maoist strategy underwent a transformation in which Lin Piao's strategies during the Chinese guerilla offensive against Japan were invoked to legitimize the new strategies.

In the first flush of activity the movement spread fast and wide. Peking Radio announced on 2 April 1970 that there were forty-six places in India where the movement had struck[4] (Deshabrati, 1970:7). But it was in the states of West Bengal and Andhra Pradesh that its impact was maximally experienced, sufficient to call for the mobilization of police forces from outside the state and also to requisition the services of the armed forces. In Bihar, the Naxalite movement came face-to-face with the Sarvodaya movement, which had implications for both the movements at a later stage. The fact that all this could happen within three years of Naxalbari—no matter how miniscule the scale, intensity and spread, and the composition of the leadership and cadre—is sufficient reason not to dismiss the phenomenon as transient and ephemeral. Once again and with remarkable swiftness, the formal agencies of social control and mass media were able to deal it an 'effective' blow and suppress it. It appeared to many that with the death of Charu Mazumdar, their ideological mentor, the 'left adventurist' movement would meet its final denouement.

The brutal suppression of the movement by the ruling Congress

Party led to the unusual phenomenon of mass emigrations from a communist to a non-communist party—the Congress. This emigration took place partly on account of the newly acquired charisma of Indira Gandhi riding on the crest of a military and electoral victory; and partly because many of the cadres were a political or of the lumpen variety. In Naxalbari, quite a few took refuge with the CPI which has been in close alliance with Congress Party. This was facilitated by mass arrests, torture and indiscriminate liquidation of cadres. This brutal suppression was once again possible because of the conspiratorial means used to annihilate class enemies and the decision by the CPI-ML to establish the supremacy of red terror over white terror. This mis-interpretation of Maoism by Charu Mazumdar was communicated to him by the CPC some time in early 1971, but fearing the repercussions that such a critique of the policy from China would have on the leaders and cadres of the movement, it was neither released for discussion nor disclosed to the leaders until just before Mazumdar's arrest in July 1972. Mazumdar, however, tried to make quick but belated and futile attempts to undo the mistake by announcing in a hurry the formation of the Peoples' Liberation Army and the establishment of base areas. The CPC comment stated (*Mainstream*, 1972):

> Regarding the formulation that the open Trade Union, open mass organizations and mass movements is out of date, and taking to secret assassinations as the only way: This idea needs rethinking. Formerly we misunderstood your word 'annihilation'. We used to think that the idea is taken from our Chiarman's war of annihilation. But in July 1970 issue of *Liberation* (the organ of CPI-ML) we came to understand that this annihilation means secret assassination.

The arbitrary choice of targets left to the discretion of irrepressible and immature squad members of guerilla units encouraged the spread of violence of a kind which could not be controlled even by those who advocated it. By 1973, nearly 40,000 members or sympathizers of the Party were languishing in jails. The Party was banned and its publications confiscated.

Strangely enough the application of such force by the established ruling party did not lead to the dissolution and diffusion of the CPI-ML; indeed, it led to its 'multiplication'. For, from one

CPI-ML there emerged several CPI-MLs, each claiming to be the genuine party. Each has tried to consolidate itself, subjected itself to self-criticism, and forced itself to indulge in self-introspection. These groups are differentiated on the basis of 'pro-Charu liners' and those who are openly critical of Charu Mazumdar; while within the 'Charu-liners' they are differentiated as 'anti-Lin Piao' and 'pro-Lin Piao' groups, and those who remain basically pro-Charu Mazumdar without entering into the 'pro-Lin' and 'anti-Lin' controversy.[5]

Soon after the suppression of Naxalite activities in 1969-70, Naxalism reared its head again in Nadia (West Bengal) and Sahar (Bihar). In Sahar its impact continues unabated, with a firm base area established, although Nadia was 'tamed'. A period of relative lull was once again 'disturbed' by the remarkable victory of Santosh Rana in the General Elections of 1977 in a contest against both Janata and CPI-M candidates from the Gopiballavpur constituency of West Bengal. With the end of the Congress monolith came the enormous public pressure for the release of all political detenus, and a general amnesty was declared in West Bengal and Bihar. This again has reactivated the processes of unity and consolidation of the CPI-ML.

This is an extremely brief survey of a very complex phenomenon, which has been primarily undertaken to demonstrate the fact that the continued existence of the phenomenon, in spite of its repeated suppression, is the most significant aspect of this movement. The recurrence and repetitiveness of any phenomenon acquires a kind of meaning for the sociologist, requiring him to undertake a more searching study of the conditions in the social structure that generate it. It is in this perspective that I shall now examine the peasant revolt in Naxalbari up to 1972.

IV

Darjeeling is a frontier district of India. It is bounded on the North by Sikkim, on the North-east by Bhutan, on the West by Nepal, and on the South-east by Bangladesh. In 1971 it had a total population of 781,777 with an adverse female sex-ratio of 882, and a low density of population of 254 per sq. km. compared to the West Bengal density of 504. Interestingly enough, the literacy rate at 33.07 per cent compares marginally better with the average of 33.2

per cent for the state as a whole (*District Census Handbook*, 1973:v). The percentage of cultivators to total workers has declined from 37.5 in 1961 to 30.46 in 1971. But the percentage of agricultural labourers to total workers has increased from 2.9 to 9.12 within the same decade. Whether or not this is strongly suggestive of a downward mobile group from cultivators to agricultural labourers should form an important aspect of an economic analysis of this district. There is also a marginal decline in the scheduled castes and scheduled tribes population (13.18 per cent in 1961 and 12.57 per cent in 1971 for scheduled castes; 15.43 per cent in 1961 and 13.88 per cent in 1971 for scheduled tribes). One wonders whether the process of sanskritization is not causing the reduction in the respective categories (Mohanty, 1977:33).

The regions characterized by peasant revolt are the three police stations of Phansidewa, Naxalbari and Khoribari, covering an area of about 274 sq. miles with a population of about 1,50,000. There are 32 tea gardens in this area with a labour population comprising 30 per cent of the total population of the area. The terrain is scenic with forests and plantation. Cultivation is largely of paddy and jute. The area is of strategic importance. There is a narrow 'neck' which connects Eastern India with Dooars of Assam and Cooch Behar of West Bengal. The River Mechi, which is easily fordable except during the monsoon months, provides the boundary between India and Nepal. One principal feature of this region is the high percentage of share-croppers. Among those owning 5 acres or less, the percentage of share-croppers in Naxalbari, Phansidewa and Khoribari are 60.1 per cent, 65.0 per cent and 50.1 per cent respectively. These were the marginal peasants in the Tebhagha[6] movement as well as in the recent Naxalbari uprising who provided the main thrust of the movement. In comparison to the share-croppers, there are a few agricultural labourers in the area (4.6 per cent in Naxalbari, 6.1 per cent in Phansidewa, and 5.4 per cent in Kharibari). However, one has to understand the structure and historical background of the institution of crop-sharing associated with this part of Bengal in order to be able to appreciate the peasant mobilization that took place.

The Rajbansis are the most preponderant community in the population of this region and Jalpaiguri. They constitute nearly 25 per cent of the population of the entire terai region and certainly more than 50 per cent of the population in the regions of peasant unrest. It is said that this community is an aboriginal tribe earlier known as Koch. Around the fifteenth and sixteenth centuries under their leader Hajo they founded the Koch kingdom on the ruins of the ancient Hindu kingdom of Kamrup, with Kuch Behar as its metropolis. With the introduction of Brahminism two generations later, they abandoned the name Koch (which thereafter was despised) and adopted the name of Rajbansi, literally 'of royal kindred'. Obviously not all Kochs became Rajbansis so a hierarchy emerged. Many Kochs who were denied entry into the Rajbansi community opted for Islam. Thus the struggle for higher status led one section of the Kochs to become Rajbansis and another section to become Muslims. Those who remained Kochs therefore had to accept a lower status (Hunter, 1974:80).

The Oraons, Mundas and Santhals constitute a large proportion of the population in this region. Historically their immigration from the Chotanagpur and neighbouring regions seems to have been prompted by the need of the plantation owners to have a labour force which could clear forests and engage in efficient plantation labour. The tribals of this region were found most suitable and were presumably brought into the region as indentured labour. This aspect of the migration requires a more thorough study.

Unfortunately, readily available historical material on agrarian relations in this frontier forest region of North Bengal is dismally inadequate. What constitutes the districts of Darjeeling and Jalpaiguri was annexed by the British from Bhutan in 1865 'after a war into which we had been reluctantly forced by aggressions and insults' (Hunter, 1974:5). However, of the Jalpaiguri region the 'Report of Mr J. Tweedie, Deputy Commissioner of the Western *Dwars* on the land tenures of that part of the country, dated 11th September 1865', tells us that 'the Bhutias were foreigners in the *Dwars* and in this respect they and ourselves are equal. The inhabitants of the *Dwars* are Hindus and Mohammadans, with the exception of the migratory *Mechs* who live along the base of the mountains . . . ' (Hunter, 1974: 282). Hunter's statistical account unfortunately has less on the *jotedari* system of the terai regions of Darjeeling district than of Jalpaiguri district. But since both these tracts of land were annexed by the British from the Bhutanese, and both seemed to have had a predominantly non-Bhutia population more characteristic of the Indian communities, it may be profitable to examine the *jote* system falling within the purview of the Bhutan Subahs.

The agrarian hierarchy in the pre-British period in the Jalpaiguri region was headed by the Subah or the Bhutia Lieutenent-Governor who had no personal interest in the soil as landlord or tenant. His function was to transmit revenue collected from his area to the royal authority after retaining for himself a sanctioned portion. He was an appointed authority with no guarantee of permanency of position. "Under him were several tehsildars or *kathans*, 'who were of respectable birth, and of good repute in the country'." Serving as sub-collectors of revenue, they collected the rent from the entire territory and passed it on to the Subah, once again after retaining a sanctioned amount. Next in the agrarian hierarchy came the *jotedar*, 'a person who holds in severalty, joint, or in common, a piece of land for which he pays revenue directly to Government through his agents, the *tehsildars*'. The original *jotedars*, it seems, were settlers who would clear forest land, make it fit for cultivation, and then such lands would become their *jotes*. Thereafter the rule of succession would apply to the ownership and control of *jotes*. This process, in fact, was encouraged by Bhutia Rajas and governors who 'were wont to allow settlers to occupy unpopulated tracts of country for a term of five years, more or less, without payment of revenue. At the end of such term the settler became the *jotedar* of the land which he had brought under cultivation, paying thereon such Government revenue as might be fixed'. *Jotes* however could also be acquired by purchase or as gifts or grants from the Bhutia Raja.

The *jotedar* could operate as a peasant proprietor cultivating and disposing his produce in any manner he deemed fit. But the *jotedar* could also chose to play the role of a superior landlord in relation to the 'inferior estates, the tenants'. The *chukanidars* or *mulanidars* were those who entered into contract, for periods of more than one year, with the *jotedars* on fixed money rentals. The contract was temporary with no rights of sale or transfer except with the explicit permission of the *jotedar*. The *rayats*, in comparison, were yearly tenants paying annual money rents to the *jotedars*. The last in the hierarchy was the *praja*, or the tenant-at-will, who paid his rent in kind. Further, he was without capital and was dependent on the *jotedar* for his seed, plough-cattle, and implements of agriculture. The seed advanced was deducted at harvest time and the balance produce shared equally (Hunter, 1974: 280-6). Interestingly enough there was 'no tendency towards the growth of a distinct class of day-labourers in Jalpaiguri District, neither renting land nor possessing fields of their own' (Hunter, 1974: 279). However, there were those cultivating small patches of land who would also till the fields of others on the basis of equal sharing. These were the *adhiar* cultivators, who in the erstwhile Bhutia regions had to be given every kind of input by the *jotedar* and the only factor of production they could claim as their own was their manual labour. Undoubtedly, they must have been from the *praja* category of tenants-at-will, who, unable to meet their basic requirements, would become *adhiars* on a crop sharing basis.

The terai[7] region extending over the Himalayan foothills, we are told, was annexed in 1850 and the northern portion was attached to Darjeeling district. In this region the revenue collectors before the British were Bengali officers known as *choudharis*, who were not only the chief landholders and *jotedars* in their areas but also 'exercised civil and criminal powers'. When the British administration took over, they were retained 'with some alteration in their profits' but were stripped of their civil and criminal powers. However, by 1864 the institution of *choudharis* was abolished and the government entered into direct settlement with the *jotedars* (Baden-Powell, 1892:500). The *jotedars* in this region were on leasehold lands usually renewable on termination of the lease period. Initially, they were given three years contracts which by 1853 were increased to ten year periods.

Apart from the *choudhary* we find another variation in this region when compared to the agrarian structure in Jalpaiguri district. In addition to the *praja*, there were also *thikadars*. Instead of paying produce rent as the *prajas* did, the *thikadars* paid money rent and kept the entire produce (Hunter, 1974:103, 116-9). Also, although like in the Jalpaiguri region no class of day labourers could be discerned, 'children of ten years of age and upwards are commonly employed on agricultural labour only during the leaf-picking season in the tea plantations' (Hunter, 1974:103). Thus first indications of the advent of wage-labour in the form of child-labour can be noticed in the plantations.

This *jotedari* system of the nineteenth century steadily crystallized into a *jotedari-adhiari* system by the twentieth century. We have already noted the landlord-tenant configuration in which the structural position of the tenant-at-will (*praja*) was precarious. It has also been observed that this group of *prajas* did not own any of the means of production and had to engage in *adhiari* cultivation. Over a period of time the *adhiari* system became a necessary and inevitable complement of the *jotedari* system, presumably because the *jotedars* in general were not peasant proprietors who also tilled their own land. Hence the gulf between owners and tillers widened to the advantage of the owners. The *prajas* became *adhiars*.

By about the fourth decade of this century the agrarian system of exploitation had sufficiently crystallized all over Bengal to evoke the first major peasant revolt against the iniquitous relations of production. This crystallization of the *jotedari-adhiari* system was also expressed in physical terms. The residential pattern of each *jote* was mainly a *jotedar-praja* complex. Around the *jotedar's* establishment would be located the houses of his *adhiars* or *prajas*. This residential configuration constituted a *jote* named after the original *jotedar*. The *adhiar* seldom had a residence which he could claim as his own. It was the *jotedar* who provided the shelter and cattle-plough. But here the broad generalities end.

There were variations within the category of *adhiars*. The most preferred *adhiars* who gained precedence and favour over others were those who did not claim any share of the crop they produced. After harvesting, the entire paddy was taken to the landlords threshing floor (*khamar*) and nothing was taken by the *praja*. The condition of work followed the dictum, 'I will feed you (i.e., take care of you), you produce for me'. However, although the most preferred by the landlord, this was not the most pervasive form of *adhiari*, for the ration provided by the *jotedar* was hardly above subsistence level. Besides, this limited the freedom of consumption, whatever may be the meaning of such 'freedom' in real terms. The more prevalent form of *adhirai* was based on a system of share-cropping. On completion of harvesting the *adhiar* received his share of produce after certain standard, conventional deductions. The usual procedure followed a set pattern. The grain would first be stacked on the landlord's threshing floor, and the entire crop would then be divided into two equal parts. The *adhiar's* share would then undergo the following deductions:

1. If the cattle-plough had been provided by the landlord a deduction of 8 maunds[8] would be effected. This was known as *panudan*.
2. If the seeds were supplied by the landlord, twice the amount would be retrieved.
3. For every maund of crop weighed by the *sherwan* or *morol*

(paid servants of the landlord who perform the weighing operations), a deduction of 10 seers[•] would be made. Incidentally, the deductions so accumulated could not be by the *morol*. He would be paid a standard 10 to 15 maunds for weighing the total produce of 20 to 30 *adhiars*.

4. If the *adhiar* had borrowed paddy from the landlord as a consumption loan, one-and-a-half times the amount of paddy would be deducted, i.e., and interest of 50 per cent in kind.
5. If the *jotedar* needed to construct a granary (*gola*), he would deduct 10 to 20 seers of paddy. The landlord would exclaim, 'where will I put the paddy unless you construct the (*gola*)!' (*Dhanta Rakhobo Kothai, gola tairikorē dē*).
6. Anywhere between 2.5 seers to 5 seers would be deducted for the maintenance of the *jotedar's* stable, if he had one.

As a consequence of such extractions the little that the *adhiar* could take back home was grossly insufficient for his minimum needs, with the result that he would end up borrowing from the landlord. Thus continued the story of the ever-increasing burden of debt which kept the *adhiar* bonded in perpetuity.

While we have examined the *jotedar-adhiar* relationship in its structural aspects, it is also necessary to examine it in a dynamic, processual dimension. *Jotedars* would often want to clear forests and make them fit for cultivation so that they could augment their income. Often parcels of forest land would be given to persons free of rent—an arrangement colloquially described as *mufate khawa* (literally 'eating tree'). In about three to four years of hard and exacting labour the land (of say about 5 acres) would become fit for cultivation. No sooner would it start yielding a crop, than the *jotedar* would impose a *thika* or contract based on an assessment of the expected yield. If one 'hal'[10] of land was expected to yield say about 20 mounds, the contract bound him to a payment of say about 15 mounds annually. This would make him a *sarta praja*, meaning a *praja* under contract. He would then be given a plain paper receipt. As the yield would go on increasing and reach, say 50 to 60 maunds, he would be induced to accept rent receipts on the plea that this would give him the status of a permanent tenant who, therefore, could not be evicted. It is alleged that such 'rent receipts' would actually carry a declaration that he was an *adhiar* paying 15 maunds of paddy annually—the same amount he was paying in *thika*! After a lapse of a year or two the illiterate cultivator would suddenly be accosted by the *jotedar* for paying only 15 maunds when he was his *adhiar*! Thus unwittingly he would become an *adhiar*—from *thika*, to *praja* to *adhiar*. While this may not have been true for all *jotedars*, there is reason to believe that such tricks were widely prevalent.

Relationships of dependency and exploitation were not confined to the relations of production. The institution of *begar* or free labour prevalent in other parts of the country took the following forms:

1. The *adhiar* was expected to supply free labour for the *jotedar's* kitchen garden. This included cultivation of vegetables, etc., as well as such other work like erecting fences against stray cattle.
2. Periodic repairs to the *jotedar's* house was the responsibility of his *adhiars*.
3. If any marriage was finalized in an *adhiar* family, the *jotedar* had to be given a *bhent*, that is, some kind of a presentation in his honour. This could be a goat, or some rice, dal and vegetables, etc. The *bhent* invariably would be some article of food, sufficient in quantity for the *jotedar's* entire household—a functional equivalent of a marriage feast in which there was a status bar to their participation.

The *jotedar* also appropriated to himself the role of the judiciary at the *jote* level. He would not permit disputes to be taken to the formal institutions of justice, and pronounced his own judgements whenever necessary. Punishments for offences would range from fines payable in cash to the *jotedar* to beatings and expulsions from the *jote*. During popular festivals the *jotedars* would encourage the *adhiars* to accept food and meat articles to make merry. Later on, however, they would retrieve twice the amount supplied to them—a one hundred per cent interest on their merrymaking!

Thus the *jotedari-adhiari* system had perfected the exploitation of the labour of the *adhiar* by every conceivable means, keeping him utterly dependent on the *jotedar*. With no alternative occupational choices open to him, the *adhiar* became inextricably reliant on the *jotedar* for his very survival. This was the structure of relationships between the *jotedar* and the *adhiar*. This did not preclude, however, the existence of enlightened *jotedars*, who, operating within the exploitative system, gave evidence of humane considerations for their subjects. That is, they would exploit their labour within the framework of the system without becoming oppressive. But the fear and practice of oppression kept the system going.

V

A chronological unfolding of the communist penetration in the Siliguri sub-division is necessary for an understanding of the historical background to the Naxalbari peasant uprising in 1967 and the events that followed thereafter. The last waves of the Tebhagha movement died on the shores of North Bengal in a place called Patharghata in Siliguri. The famous Bose fraternity—Nripen, Biren and Atin—along with Bandhan Oraon, Taran Singh and numerous *adhiars* were arrested by the police as they stood on the threshing floor of *jotedar* Bhagwan Dayal Singh, a Rajput, to distribute the harvest. Soon after, the CPI was banned.

If the Tebhagha movement was dead in body, its spirit provided the beacon light for those who two decades later would create another peasant revolt in India. The slogans of Tebhagha and its front organizations—the Krishak Sabha (Peasant Association) and Krishak Samiti (Peasant Committee)—were the programmatic and organizational instruments with which activists like Panchanan Sarkar, Kanu Sanyal and others made their first entree amongst the exploited peasants. Some of the slogans used initially indicate the historical continuity of Tebhagha:

(*i*) We want the abolition of zamindari system (*Jamindari prathar uchched chai*).

(*ii*) Land to the tiller. One who owns the plough owns the land (*langaljar jamin tar*).

(*iii*) Tenant eviction will not be tolerated (*praja uchched cholbe na*).

(*iv*) 25 per cent interest for borrowed paddy (*karja dhaner soiya soodh*).

(*v*) Go on cultivating without surrendering (*dakhal rekhe chas karo*).

(*vi*) Defeat the Congress (*Congress sarkarer uchched chai*).

The earliest meeting in the rural areas of Siliguri sub-division were held in village markets (*hats*). From among those who flocked curiously to such meetings and showed some interest, came the first 'native' contacts. During this period the *jotedars* belonged mostly to the dominant community of Rajbansis. There were, however, poor Rajbansis as well who were ranked along with the tribal population of Santals, Oraons and Mundas (*mandeshias*). Right from the inception of political activities in 1951 and onwards, the *jotedars* and better-off peasants warned the others not to come under the evil influence of the 'red flag party'. The party cadres started politicizing the exploited sections of the rural community and urged them to become members of the Krishak Sabha. At first, the communist cadres did not find it difficult to enter into *jotes* but the *adhiars* who provided hospitality to them were later penalized and deprived of the cattle, ploughs and paddy loaned to them for consumption. This placed the activists in a moral dilemma.

In the first General Elections held in 1952 the two CPI candidates lost to the Congress. However, the CPI was able to field Bandhan Oraon of Tebhagha fame to contest from the tribal reserved constituency in Patharghata. Considering that Bandhan was a one-time Congress diehard this was an achievement for the CPI. The election was significant for the communist workers as they now clearly realized that effective work among the rural poor can only be done if one was rural-based, instead of being urban-based.

In the same year a conference of peasants was held in Ambari (P.S. Phansidewa). Kanu Sanyal was directed by the party to organize it. Nearly two thousand attended the conference which resolved not only to fight against exploitation but also to engage in active constructive work for the poorer sections of the society. They decided to open schools, help in providing drinking water and irrigation. A Coordination Committee was formed with Kanu Sanyal as the Coordinator. It was decided that Panchanan Sarkar and Jogen Mukherji would work in Khoribari, Chunilal Goala in Buragonj, Mujibur Rahman in Naxalbari, Khokon Mazumdar in Hatighisa and Keshab Sarkar is Champasuri. All decisions were arrived at by democratic consensus.

By 1953-54 the party was able to formulate its first programmes. They attacked the extraction of *panudan* and the 50 per cent interest on paddy loan. Agitations opposing these two modes of exploitation were carried on in Buraganj, Hatighisa, Tarabari, Phansidewa,

Ropandighi and several other places. I shall present four illustrative cases very briefly:

In Lakhijote (P.S. Khoribari) Choudhary Oraon, a *praja* of Kailash Giri, used to cultivate one 'hal' of land. The maximum amount that he had been able to take home from the *jotedar's* threshing floor at any time was six maunds. When he approached the Party, they intervened and he was able to take home 46 maunds of paddy. On paddy loans the *jotedar* had to remain content with 25 per cent interest and the *sherwan* who performed the weighing was given a fixed amount much less than what the *adhiar* used to be charged by the *jotedar*. Also, since the cattle-plough belonged to Choudhury he was able to demand an extra 8 maunds from the *jotedar*!

In Hariharasinghjote, Loos Oraon who used to do *thika* was threatened with eviction. The Party assembled an armed group in resistance and the *jotedar* was compelled to revise his decision.

In Hatighisa, a clash took place with a relatively small *jotedar*, Serket Singh. The peasants had declared that they would not give *panudan* unless the *jotedar* accepted tebhagha. Both sides sensed the possibility of violence and complained to the police. But Jangal Santhal's complaint against the *jotedar* reached the police earlier. Several people were injured in the clash that followed, including Babulal Vishwakarmakar who had to be admitted to the hospital. After a prolonged legal battle both sides got fed up and withdrew.

In Rangapami, the *jotedar*, Mitinlal, was confronted by nearly one thousand peasants who shouted 'no *tebhagha*, no *panudan*'. An armed clash ensued in which the police maintained neutrality. Later, however, the *jotedar* was able to get many of his peasants evicted.

Such early successes helped the Krishak Sabha to project an image of itself as an effective militant organization which worked against the exploitation of the *jotedars*. The membership started swelling as a consequence. But it was soon realized that the peasant struggle could become really effective only if the support of the plantation workers could be enlisted. It will be recalled that nearly a third of the population in the area was plantation labourers. This led to the formation of the Darjeeling District Cha Bagan Workers' Union, the first of its kind. The Union looked into several grievances of the workers relating to housing, water, ration, and through such small struggles the Union gained in strength. Again, because the need for a worker-peasant alliance was felt by the peasant leaders and because they had initiated the move to unionize the plantation labour, a healthy relationship developed between the workers and the peasants.

How strong the peasant-worker bond really was was amply demonstrated in the Bonus Struggle of 1955. Amongst the leaders of the Bonus Struggle were Jangal Santhal, Babulal Vishwakarmakar, Raghunath Vishwakarmakar, Kamalkan Singh, Mondol Karmakar, Punjab Rao and many other established peasant leaders. Three days before the declaration of the strike the houses of all the peasant leaders were raided by the police, but this pre-emptive move failed as all of them were able to elude arrest. Sangrami Samitis (revolutionary committees) were formed in each tea estate having a Union. The Krishak Sabha declared its unqualified support for the plantation workers and arranged to provide them with food during the strike. For seven days, massive worker-peasant processions rent the air with the workers' demands. Several thousands workers and peasants would join each procession. The demonstration that passed through Naxalbari was estimated at seven to eight thousand strong. The peasant leaders under warrant of arrest moved freely in the middle of the throng, as helpless policemen watched the massive protests in disbelief.

From 1950 till 1967, the demands of the peasants and workers lost neither their continuity nor their punch. After the West Bengal Estates Acquisition Act was passed in 1953, extensive mala fide transfers of land took place in order to escape the provisions of the law which imposed a land-owning ceiling of 25 acres. The legislation brought about an era of *benami* land-hoidings (i.e., control over holdings which were not owned directly). The Krishak Sabha addressed themselves to the task of discovering such *benami* lands and urged the peasants not to share their crop without satisfying themselves with documentary evidence of landownership.

The split in the CPI in 1964 resulted in most of the leaders of the Darjeeling District Committee opting for the more radical and peasant biased CPI-M. Many of the leaders were sent to jail and the *jotedars* once again stepped up their exploitation of the *adhiars* and landless peasants. When the leaders were released they were disillusioned by the ineffectiveness of legal means for the redressal of the grievances of the poor and exploited peasants. It was then that they started thinking more seriously of a revolutionary solution. After wide-ranging discussions at several levels, a general consensus seemed to emerge on the following points: *benami* and *khas* lands should be distributed among the peasants, and there was a need for a fundamental change in the landownership system. The Krishak Sabha gave its wholehearted support to these proposals but noted that it should be prepared to withstand the armed offensive of the state and the privileged sections of rural society. For this an armed preparation was felt absolutely necessary. The seriousness with which these revolutions were accepted is reflected in the large-scale mobilization of the peasants that took place in 1967 and the planned manner in which they spearheaded the movement. The administration noted that 'they have been getting ready for the agitation for quite sometime. The leaders have been able to organise a "militia" of about one thousand to two thousand Santhals armed with bows and arrows and other arms (not firearms). They have been given training in the use of the weapons they possess and are well disciplined'. This is quite a testimony for the peasants, coming as it does from the administration.

At this stage, it would be instructive to present the periodization of the evolution of the Naxalbari movement as seen by its principal architect Kanu Sanyal. He observes that 1951-54 was the organisational stage, in which 'the peasantry of Naxalbari, advanced through clashes to get them organized'. From 1953 to 1957 was the period of worker-peasant alliance and a 'united class of the workers and peasants'. Between 1955 and 1962, they responded to the call by the West Bengal Kisan Sabha 'to regain possession of *benami* land'. The experience of the Kisans proved the futility of such an effort within 'the four walls of law'. So the sub-divisional Kisan Samiti in Naxalbari 'gave the call to confiscate the entire produce of *jotedar's* land'. Sanyal lists the following items in the call: '(*i*) Reap and store the harvest at your own place and raise the red flag; (*ii*) *Jotedar's* to furnish proof of their ownership before the peasant committee, without which no share to them; (*iii*) arm yourself to protect the crop; and (*iv*) save your crop from the police'. During this stage, Sanyal reports, 'the fighting mood and the class consciousness of the peasants of Naxalbari was no lesser than that of 1967'. During the fourth stage (1962-64), in spite of the India-China war, the peasants refused to be infested by chauvinism (Sanyal, 1974). This gives us ample evidence that the Naxalbari peasant uprising has a historicity which dates back to and links up with the Tebhagha peasant movement in Bengal.

VI

There is a general impression that the origin of the peasant revolt in 1967 can be meaningfully traced to the 'six documents' circulated by Charu Mazumdar and the 'Siliguri group' (comprising Kanu Sanyal, Jangath Santhal, Khokon Mazumdar, Kamakshya Banerjee and others) in 1965-66 'calling for an instant armed peasant rebellion' for 'capturing power area-wise' (Roy, 1975: 66-7). It is also stated by Roy that the documents called for a partisan warfare within six months and 'it was actually within six months that the Naxalbari peasant uprising flared up in the spring of 1967' (p. 67). Such an analysis, besides being based on incorrect information, is fallacious for it presents a rather ahistorical explanation of the causes of the peasant movement. This is already amply clear from the historical exposition of the movement presented earlier.

At least two facts have to be put straight to avoid confusion. Firstly, the six documents were not 'brought out' between 1965-66 as contended by Roy. They were in fact released between March and September 1965. They may have, however, circulated between 1965-66 and beyond. Secondly, the 'Siliguri group' did not circulate this as the 'Siliguri group', with the exception of Charu Mazumdar and Panchanan Sarkar, was already behind bars. In fact the 'six documents' came to the knowledge of imprisoned members of the 'Siliguri group' when Panchanan Sarkar walked in with them. The initial reaction of the jail inmates was one of utter dismay as the contents of the 'six documents' were not discussed with them nor were they aware that such documents were being prepared for distribution. Also the manner in which Charu Mazumdar had elected to distribute these documents caused resentment. A few trusted and select followers of Charu Mazumdar were entrusted with the task of distributing and propagating the contents of the documents. In this selection, Mazumdar scrupulously avoided the peasant leaders who had worked with Kanu Sanyal, e.g., Panchanan Sarkar and his associates, who were till then not arrested. Two other documents were circulated around September 1966, but this time in consultation with Kanu Sanyal and Souren Bose. In these documents references have been made approvingly to the need for economic struggles. Sanyal writing much later observes (1974):

> CM (*Charu Mazumdar*, italics mine) sent 5/6 of his selected cadres

to the rural areas with these documents. These new young cadres went to the villages and made a futile attempt from 1965 to 1966 to propagate according to the documents. Meanwhile the cadres of Darjeeling District could know the contents of the documents after being released from jail in June 1966. Then the discussions on the basis of the documents started between them and CM

There have been basic differences on the much talked of six (and later eight) documents. The points on which an agreement was reached were the following: 'Chinese path is the path of liberation in India; agrarian revolution can be completed through armed struggle; to propagate the politics of the agrarian revolution among the workers and peasants and to organize them to build up a secret party organization'. The points on which Charu Mazumdar declined to agree were: 'the indispensability of workers' peasants' mass organisation and mass movements; necessity of inner-party ideological struggle inside CPI-M; political work and actions are not opposed to each other, on the contrary, action will be meaningless if politics are not put in importance and so political work is the condition of preparation; necessity of mass struggles through which organs of struggle are to be built up and necessity of mass organisations in urban areas' (Sanyal, 1974). It seemed that Mazumdar's ideas about forming secret combat groups to set fire to *jotedar's* house and to attack individual *jotedars*, in which action was given precedence over politics was completely out of favour with the Kanu Sanyal group. Sanyal points out that 'from the very start there were two distinct opinions which may be called confrontation between two lines' (1974).

Ultimately an agreement was reached between them on a 'division of territory'. The Naxalbari area was supposed to be guided on the basis of the agreed guidelines and the experiences of the peasant leaders and cadres, whilst Charu Mazumdar's eight documents were to be experimented with in Chater Hat Islampur in West Dinajpur. Assessing the Islampur experiment conducted on purely Charu lines, Sanyal comments (1974):

> Secret combat groups were formed, a little political propaganda was made and the work of action was started; that is efforts were made to set fire to *jotedars'* houses, some paddy were harvested in the night and plans for snatching guns failed. As politics was not

> given importance, as the necessity of building up mass organization and mass movements was ignored, the action based on combat groups became the assembly place for some lumpen elements. During the Naxalbari uprising in 1967 the *jotedars* of this area mobilized the entire peasantry behind certain political party and attacked the houses of some of the known combat group cadres.

Thus Sanyal's main criticism of the six documents was that they were ahistorical in as much as the peasant struggles prior to 1965 were not analyzed.

The Conference which was held at Buraganj sometime in April-May 1967 was the most crucial in terms of the decisions that led to further peasant mobilization. All the eight documents were discussed in the presence of nearly 5,000 peasants. Presumably the lines of agreement and disagreement mentioned by Sanyal figured in this Conference. The Charu-liners emphasized total appropriation of the lands of the big *jotedars*, disarming them of their lethal weapons appropriating their paddy, cattle and all other such property, establishment of a peoples' government, and annihilation of the *jotedars* and zamindars through armed revolution. The Kanu-line pointed out the imperative need of solving the land problem before contemplating an armed revolt. Once illegally held land in the occupation of the *jotedar* was seized, the question of defending it with all one's might will definitely arise, particularly if an offensive is mounted for the retrieval of such lands. Then the question of an armed revolt will become relevant. But if such developments do not take place and they can engage in a legal offensive, an armed confrontation need not be necessary. The following concrete decisions seemed to have emerged from the conference. The peasants were urged to (*i*) seize the lands of the *jotedars*; (*ii*) seize the lands of the plantation workers who had purchased land from poor peasants; (*iii*) cultivate lands held under (*i*) and (*ii*) and retain all the produce from lands appropriated from the *jotedars*, but share half of the crop produced on the plantation workers' lands; and (*iv*) where the *jotedar* is engaged in self-cultivation, such lands should not be seized.

We are now in a position to follow the actual Naxalbari peasant uprising in March-April 1967. Between September and December 1966, the tea gardens were rocked by strikes. Even more than the Bonus Struggle in 1955, it is contended by Sanyal, the solidarity of the workers and peasants was in evidence. It is after this experience that Charu Mazumdar was compelled by Sanyal and Bose to accept the need for economic struggle to strengthen the politics of agrarian revolution. The seventh and the eighth documents released by Mazumdar were subsequent to these events. The movement for seizure of crops had already begun in November-December of the same year and 'thousands of organized armed peasants harvested paddy and also snatched guns' (Sanyal, 1974).[11]

Meanwhile, the elections of March 1967 intervened. There were differences of opinion amongst the district level cadres as to their role in the elections. Some new cadres, presumably influenced by Charu Mazumdar, argued that participation in the elections would amount to advocating a parliamentary path which they rejected. However, the more predominant view—that the elections would enable them to further the politics of agrarian revolution—was ultimately accepted. Jangal Santhal, Souren Bose and Ratanlal Brahmin contested the Assembly elections from Phansidewa, Siliguri and Jorebungalow respectively. Arun Moitra and T. Wangdi, both of the Congress, won the Assembly seats from Siliguri and Phansidewa respectively defeating their nearest rivals Prem Thapa (AIGL)[12] and Jangal Santhal.

Although Jangal Santhal lost by a convincing margin of nearly 4,000 votes, it was claimed that the elections furthered the solidarity of workers and peasants in the Naxalbari region. It is a fact that the politics of agrarian revolution was the keynote of their campaign, which from the point of view of scoring an election victory almost certainly was not wise. For, such a campaign, instead of appealing to as many sections as possible, clearly and deliberately alienated a large section of the electorate. Thus, the campaign too followed a class approach. We know, for instance, that early in January 1967 meetings were being held where the cultivators were urged not to give any levy to the government, to gherao government offices if they demand it, and the *adhiars* were encouraged not to share their crop with the *jotedars*. The standing crop of one Safisuddin Ahmad of Rubvitta (P.S. Phansidewa) had already been removed prior to this meeting. In another meeting in Naxalbari on 26 December 1966, the Kisan Sabha asked their members to remain vigilant against the police which may come with search warrants to recover the paddy for the *jotedars*. In such an event they were to be prepared with bows and arrows to resist them. Thus the election theme continued to further the interests of the *adhiars* and poor landless peasants without much concern for how this would affect their election prospects.

Sanyal observes that during the election campaign the party cadres were mostly involved in political work. Hence political action had to wait until after the elections. Given the evolution of the movement and the steady build-up of agrarian revolt and protest it is difficult to see how the peasant leaders could have suddenly halted the process of mobilization and impending conflict, short of proving to be turncoats to the peasants whom they had mobilized! However, it is equally true that the emergence of the CPI-M as a major constituent of the United Front government was interpreted as fortuitous and their enthusiasm to carry on the struggle found an unexpected fillip. Thus between March and May 1967 more than a hundred cases of forcible cultivation and of dehoarding and confiscation of paddy stocks from *jotedars' golas* took place. It was argued by the peasant leaders and cadres that at a time when there was acute shortage of food they would not permit the *golas* of *jotedars* to be full so that they could trade with the misery of the people.

Describing their operations in the Naxalbari region, a peasant leader observed that they issued the following instructions to their cadres: (*i*) If the cattle-plough of the *adhiar* is taken away by the *jotedar* and sold in the market, go and appropriate their cattle and ploughs. (*ii*) How shall we cultivate if we have no food to eat? Go and ask the landlord for food. If he is reluctant, take away food by force and issue him a receipt if necessary. (*iii*) Then if the *jotedar* attacks with his gun, deprive him of his firearms. (*iv*) When you remove paddy from his granary, leave the amount that he would need for his family consumption. The rest should be distributed amongst landless peasants and *adhiars*. Separate receipts should be kept for each in duplicate. One would be handed over to the *jotedar* and the other would remain with the cadre who organizes the distribution. (*v*) The labourer will be given his daily wages in kind and the paddy consumed by him now will stand as loan from the landlord. The loan will be repaid by instalments from his daily wages in kind. No interest can be charged from him and he will return as much as he has consumed. (*vi*) The *adhiars* would return the paddy to the *jotedar* on 25 per cent interest instead of 50 per cent. More fieldwork is necessary to find out to what extent such a writ held or its spirit maintained.

The rate of escalation of activities was clearly indicative of a massive and a reasonably well worked out plan of operation. By the middle of May 1967, Hare Krishna Konar, CPI-M, the Land and Land Revenue minister in the United Front government, and also secretary of the West Bengal State Kisan Sabha, came to Siliguri post haste to use his personal influence to subdue his overzealous radical comrades. Konar engaged in wide-ranging discussions with the administration, the United Front constituents in Siliguri, his own party members, visited the field and came to the conclusion that the present problems arose out of faulty settlement of land and the undefined nature of land in many cases. He, however, agreed that this could be examined and settled by the administration only after normalcy was restored. He met Kanu Sanyal and Souren Bose individually and later in the presence of the Superintendent of Police (SP) at the Sukna Forest bungalow. The SP put forward three proposals which, if accepted, could lead to the solution of the immediate problem. These were (*i*) armed demonstrations should cease forthwith and complaints relating to land should be brought to the immediate notice of the Block Development Officer (BDO) or the Sub-Divisional Officer (SDO) who would expeditiously enquire and take suitable action. (*ii*) All those connected with the lawless activities in the Siliguri sub-division should submit themselves for arrest and not resist such operations of the police. (*iii*) Their proposed programme of dehoarding of food grains was welcome but it should be done by enlisting the cooperation of the police or any other responsible government officer and not by resorting to looting. It is stated that Kanu Sanyal did not appear to disagree personally with these proposals, but obviously he had to consult his comrades. However, Sanyal never showed up after this meeting.

It must be remembered that Konar and Sanyal had a long discussion *in camera* before the meeting which included the SP. In the absence of direct information from Sanyal, the impression one gets from those with whom Sanyal interacted is that Konar was at pains to explain the embarrassment caused to the CPI-M and the United Front government on account of their activities. He tried to convince him that it was in the long-term interests of the party that they ought to fall in line with their policies. He strongly urged them to surrender to the Court voluntarily on the basis of charges against them and it would be the party's responsibility to bail them out and pursue the legal battle. Sanyal is supposed to have replied that it was not for him to agree or to disagree to such a proposal and he needed to discuss these with his comrades before he could report back. For this he said he needed at least three days' time. Konar, however, was insistent that they should surrender by the next day. Sanyal, I am told, failed to give him any assurance. Predictably, Charu Mazumdar must have quashed the whole idea as a revisionist trap, a surrender and a betrayal of the revolutionary cause. Thus 18 May 1967 was the last day of contact between the CPI-M leader and its extremist dissidents.

The incidents that followed thereafter must necessarily be perceived from both the law-and-order and the movement ends. First let us describe the law-and-order view. Determined to restore law and order, a strong police contingent went to Barajharujote to effect the arrest of persons wanted in connection with a series of cases started over forcible ploughing of land. When they were confronted by nearly 300 men and women armed with bows and arrows, they waited until the arrival of reinforcements led by Inspector S. Wangdi. At this all the male members withdrew. When the police officers advanced a little ahead of their force, they were suddenly attacked by 200 to 300 men with bows and arrows. It is stated that the men kept their women in front and attacked from the rear. Both the Inspectors, Mukherji and Wangdi, were hit and the latter succumbed to his injuries in hospital. This occurred on 24 May 1967, barely a week after the Kanu-Konar talks.

The next day another police party under Inspector Alley found itself confronting a hostile mob, at least 1,000 strong. This prompted the SP Darjeeling and SDO Siliguri to take command of two police parties and advance towards the scene of tension. Whilst the SP's party met with no resistance, the SDO is reported to have been sandwiched between two menacing groups of men and women armed with bows and arrows. When repeated warnings failed to detract them from what appeared to be a definite offensive, the police had to resort to a total of eighteen rounds of firing, killing seven females, one male and two children.

To obtain a balanced perspective, it is also necessary to look at the peasants' view of the incidents. By 23 May 1967, the police had established their camps in Vijayanagar Tea Estate. The following morning they started combing the villages in search of CPI-M party cadres, starting from Raghujote. They reached Barojharujote by evening, but they found a deserted settlement. The police entered the empty houses and began destroying utensils and other belongings indiscriminately. The first resistance to this came from the womenfolk. They rebuked them for destroying their meagre belongings and asked them to withdraw since those whom they were looking for were not available. The police then withdrew to inform their superiors. Meanwhile Inspector Wangdi arrived with reinforcements. When the police once again advanced to the middle of the *jote*, the peasants sent a shower of arrows that injured both the Inspectors. The police fled leaving the wounded behind. It was the peasantry, they claim, that took the two bleeding Inspectors to the police van.

The same evening nearly 2,000 armed police entered the village and destroyed everything they could lay hands on. They found an empty village except for Banamali's pregnant wife. When she remonstrated with them for the rampage in which they were indulging she was kicked in the belly and fainted on the spot. Later, at the hospital, both the mother and child expired. There was another death—another woman, Fulchand's wife, who people say had the misfortune of witnessing the going-ons died from shock.

These events did not appear to cause any concern to the authorities. The peasants felt this to be a bad augury. They anticipated more repression to follow. Determined that these events should not be allowed to generate a psychosis of fear, the peasant leaders decided to counter the menacing developments by organizing village level meetings and processions to voice their protest. One such meeting was scheduled to be held in Prosadujote, largely at the initiative of the womenfolk who had reacted sharply to the death of two women the previous evening. At this juncture the SDO's police party was confronted by a babble of screaming women abusing them in unspeakable language. It is not clear what actually triggered off the actual firing, but it is clear that the police had felt agitated over Wangdi's death and the people confronting them, mostly women, were equally agitated over the two female mortalities. The overall impression that one gets is that the police insisted on going ahead and the women insisted on their returning back, fearing that otherwise their menfolk may be arrested. One point seems to be very clear—the demonstrating group did not expect the police would open fire on them. The place was an open space with very poor logistic support for the group to engage in combat with the police who sported infinitely superior firepower.

A couple of days or so later a poor Santal peasant was beaten up in Naxalbari market by some *jotedars* and Congress Party supporters. This exacerbated the already tense situation. The leaders concentrated in the Buraganj area, which was their best stronghold. Numerous processions, both large and small and which included 'small *jotedars*', voiced their protest against police repressions. The processions attracted between 5,000 to over 10,000 participants at times. The *jotedars* were requested to voluntarily hand over their firearms in preparation for the anticipated police offensive. It is contended that many *jotedars* voluntarily offered their guns but some who didn't were compelled to surrender them, which they did without offering any resistance. Thus within a very brief span of time the peasants in Buraganj acquired complete control over the area, where only their writ held sway.

For nearly three months—June, July and August 1967—the Buraganj area was declared a *muktanchal* or liberated area and a parallel government was established. It is claimed that during this period all petty thefts and anti-social activities came to a halt. In the face of grave external threat, the people were warned that no such activities would be tolerated. The exigencies of the situation saw the emergence and establishment of peoples' courts. Apart from Buraganj (P.S. Khoripari), peoples' courts also functioned in Choukpukri (P.S. Phansidewa) and in Sevdullajote (P.S. Naxalbari).

The core of the peoples' court consisted of five to six leading comrades of the area who first examined the cases before presenting them to an assembly of party members, sympathizers and others. The accused, after having heard the charges made against them, would be expected either to own their guilt or to defend themselves. The assembled members would thereafter discuss the cases and arrive at a verdict. Punishments would range from severe oral warnings to confinements for brief periods to beatings until guilt was owned and a promise was made not to repeat it, the misdemeanour, and so on. In some cases the guilty would be threatened with the death penalty should they indulge in anti-social activities again. The peoples' courts, it is claimed, had a remarkably sobering influence on so-called anti-social elements.

The liberated area of Buraganj, however, was never liberated from the fear of a police offensive, and even as the peasants exercised complete command over this small place, the police had cordoned off the entire area. One of the singular exceptions to the rule who floated the dictat of the 'peasant government' was Nagen Roychoudhury, a big *jotedar* of Nazirjote. He openly consorted with a police chowkidar named Bhusan Daffadar, and communicated with the police. When the peasants perceived a definite threat from his activities, they organized, a massive procession which went to his home and laid seige to it. An altercation with Roychoudhury ensued which infuriated the crowd. It is said that he then threatened them with his firearms which led the by now violent mob to brutally murder Roychoudhury and loot his property. Kanu Sanyal's report on the Terai gives some idea of the activities of the movement during this period (Sanyal, 1968; Mohanty, 1977: 42).

The murder of Roychoudhury on 10 June 1967 was interpreted as a climactic point of the peasant offensive. The police had already faced their first offensive in Barajharujote. In Prosadujote they had to open fire on women and children, but in Buraganj, in spite of their presence in massive numbers, Roychoudhury was beheaded by angry peasants. The news media in particular, and the various political parties, drew an alarming picture of the developments in this region in which the government remained a silent spectator. The national Parliament and the State Legislature took serious note of these events as the Chinese media heralded the advent of the 'spring thunder' over India. The West Bengal government was quick to send a Cabinet mission[18] to enquire into the affairs of North Bengal.

The Cabinet mission reached Siliguri within two days of the murder of Nagen Roychoudhury. The district administration, caught in the dilemma of what role it should adopt, presented its own understanding of the problem and sought the advice of the Cabinet mission. The officials had tried to evaluate how much the problem owned its origin to the social and economic grievances of the people. And, secondly, they had delved into the motivations of the peasant leaders by examining their economic status. Thus they were able to demonstrate (*a*) that the population increase in the rural areas had been far less than in the urban areas and that the density of population, compared to most other regions of West Bengal, was low; and (*b*) that the price of land was lower than in other areas of rural West Bengal. From these set of data they inferred that the pressure on land was relatively low and that, therefore, the hunger for land was also relatively less.

Their analysis of the economic status of sixty-nine peasant activists under custody also startled them. Only seven were agricultural labourers, fourteen were non-cultivators attached to plantations or engaged in petty business, and the rest were cultivators. Of the forty-eight cultivators, none cultivated an area less than 10 bighas[14] and there were at least ten who cultivated 10 bighas or more. These of course, included cultivation in share-cropping. On the basis of these facts, the administration argued that the people who were agitating or leading the revolt were not landless at all and nor were the people against whom the agitation was directed privileged persons. Further, the agrarian conditions in these areas were no different from those obtaining elsewhere in other states. The logical conclusion of these arguments was that the usual conditions which cause peasant unrest do not obtain here in as much measure as they obtain elsewhere in the state. However, they pointed out that if the intention of the movement was to bring about a radical change in the agrarian set-up, the laws of the land, and they stood then, would not permit it.

The conclusions that the officials arrived at are based on certain implicit and fallacious hypotheses based on the laws of linear proportions. For example, it would follow from the above observations that land hunger is a function of land prices. Thus, the higher the land prices the greater the land hunger. And the greater the land hunger or pressure on available land, the more likely the possibility of agrarian unrest. It follows therefore from such an argument that if those regions where land hunger and the pressure on land are high are not characterized by agrarian unrest, then surely in those regions where the pressures are relatively lower there is no justification for any such unrest. Hence it becomes a justifiable case to employ the law enforcement machinery. Such arguments are fallacious, dangerously simple, and betray an ignorance of social realities. The fallacies in such an argument lie, firstly and primarily, in treating the above variables as *the* crucial factors to the exclusion of other factors; and, secondly, in the use of simple structural comparisons ignoring the historicity of social realities, which come into being rather than just exist. In this case the contradictions that are inherent in the *jotedari* system and the role of the Krishak Sabha in unfolding them to the peasantry are two crucial factors that cannot be ignored in any analysis of the agrarian revolt in North Bengal. It is entirely possible that without the emergence of a strong Krishak Sabha, the revolt would not have fructified.

Rather than engage in an *a-priori* imputation of motives to the peasant leaders, it would be interesting to ask how it was that such a category of cultivators acquired leadership of the peasants who were engaged in a struggle for economic betterment. If we classify the data in a different way we get some interesting results (see Table 1).

Table 1
ECONOMIC STATUS OF MOVEMENT ACTIVISTS IN JAIL

Own Land (Bighas)	*Land in* Adhi *(Bighas)*							*Total*
	None	*up to 5*	*6-10*	*11-15*	*16-20*	*21-30*	*31 plus*	
None	21	—	—	16	1	—	—	38
up to 5				3	1		1	5
6-10	9		3	1				13
11-15	7	1	1			1		10
16-20	1							1
21-30	1							1
31 *plus*	1							1
TOTAL	40	1	4	20	2	1	1	69

As the Table shows, of the sixty-nine activists in custody, twenty-one did not cultivate any land. They were petty businessmen or plantation workers. Of the forty-eight who were cultivators, seventeen did not own any land of their own but engaged in *adhi* cultivation. Most of them cultivated land between 11 and 15 bighas in area, that is, roughly between 3.5 and 5 acres. The share that they would get in the crop would be anywhere between a half and a third of the total produce. If proper weightage is given to this factor, they could be said to be effectively cultivating between 1.5 and 2.5 acres, or even less. Then were twelve cultivators who had land of their own and were also cultivating in *adhi*. Thus, as many as twenty-nine were engaged in *adhi* cultivation. There were nineteen who cultivated their own lands only, most of whom had 5 acres or less. Considering that there are hardly any irrigation facilities in this region, multiple cropping is a rare practice.

Thus the economic status of most of the activists was not such as to suggest that they belonged to the privileged economic category. They were from the poor to middle peasant categories, the categories from which one would normally expect peasant leadership to emerge. Of the three who fall in the rich peasant category, the most outstanding example is provided by Panchanan Sarkar, whose credentials as a peasant leader can no longer be questioned. In fact, it is this whole range of peasant activists and leaders—from agricultural labourers, to poor and marginal peasants, to middle and rich peasants—that enabled such a massive mobilization. The strength of the Krishak Sabha lay also in this spectrum of leadership.

The Cabinet mission, while appreciating the facts, marshalled by the officials, had its own interpretation. It was of the firm conviction that the problem was essentially and primarily that of land and the subsequent lawlessness was mainly symptomatic of the disease. They therefore recommended a two-pronged approach to the problem. Firstly, the land problem would have to be tackled effectively and expeditiously. And, secondly, police action had to be taken, but on a low key so as to avoid heavy casualties. They then addressed a series of meetings in that region.

Five meetings were held in different parts of Siliguri in which the ministers aired their views on the urgency of the land problem and the need for restoration of normalcy to solve the problem. Both the reception meted out to the members of the Cabinet mission and the emphases of the mission members varied. In Naxalbari, Bishwanath Mukherji and others were gheraoed[15] from 3.00 P.M. till 10.00 P.M. on 13 June 1967 and were not 'released' until they gave some assurance of security of life and property. At other places, members of the Cabinet mission spoke more strongly against the 'lawless' activities and even urged them to repulse violent attacks.

The presence of the Cabinet mission and its unequivocal stand on the restoration of law and order led to an open confrontation with the rebel peasants. Even before they left, a series of incidents shook the area in testimony of the peasants' open defiance. On 14 June, paddy was removed from the houses of Ganesh Lohar and Kalia Rai and a similar looting was reported from Choupukhuria (P.S. Phansidewa). Processions and meetings were held in the Buraganj region which the police had now entered in strength and where they were carrying out surprise raids. But the main activists—Kanu Sanyal, Jangal Santhal, Kadam Mallik, Prem Lal Mallik and others—escaped after an armed encounter with the police. Tribeni Kanu of

Dhakuajote was killed after he attacked and killed a policeman who was allegedly attempting to rape his wife. In Bhatagoch, one Paulos Kujur (Oraon) had an altercation with some processionists and opened fire killing some militant peasants. In short, increased police efforts to arrest peasant leaders only resulted in a confrontation. In spite of their sincere efforts, the Cabinet mission failed to contact the activist leaders.

The Cabinet mission then called a press conference on 16 June and simultaneously released an appeal in Bengali and Hindi. Taking a forthright stand, the Cabinet mission appealed to the rebels to cooperate with them in solving the genuine problems. It reiterated its committment to work against the exploitation of the *jotedars*, zamindars, *mahajans* (moneylenders), and *bagichamaliks* (plantation owners). While appreciating the need for strong action, they warned that if such action is launched without due and rational consideration it becomes counter-productive. At the same time, the members of the mission appealed for cessation of rebel activities failing which, they said, the government would be compelled to take strong measures. The mission also announced the administrative steps it had taken to go into the land problem without delay.[18]

This clear and unambiguous appeal was followed by a quick succession of events, which are best presented in tabular form (Table 2). During this period a number of meetings took place in Lohasingjote (Khoribari), Mechijote (Naxalbari) and Fulbani Tea Estate (Khoribari).

Had the activities ot the rebels been confined to threats and expropriation of surplus foodgrains from the landlords, one would have interpreted this as a continuing defiance of their party and the government. But the rebels went much further and expropriated arms and ammunitions in preparation for an armed confrontation with the state machinery. This was indeed a serious matter verging on insurrection. Thus by 22 June we find the Cabinet mission issuing another appeal. This time they announced the formation of Land Reforms Committees at the Sub-divisional and thana levels (police station areas). They warned that any illegal activities from 22 June onwards would be sternly met by the iron-hand of the law. Any violent activity or attack in the name of self-defence was also forbidden and suitable police arrangements were assured. The signatories were Hare Krishna Konar, Bishwanath Mukherji, Nani Bhattacharya and Deoprakash Rai.

Table 2

EVENTS FROM 16 TO 21 JUNE

	Date	Target	Place	Activity
1.	16 June	Chandra Oraon	Kachumonijote (Phansidewa)	Unspecified harrassment
2.	17 June	Kamruddin Mohd.	Totaramjote (Naxalbari)	Pair of bullocks taken. away.
3.	18 June	Lawrence Pauna	Ganga Ram Tea Est. (Phansidewa)	Murdered. Noted criminal.
4.	18 June	Surendranath Ray	Chikanmanijote (Khoribari)	House raided.
5.	18 June	Narbahadur Gurung	Katiajote (Naxalbari)	House raided.
6.	18 June	Hembahadur Karki/ Dalbahadur Chetri	Nihaljote (Naxalbari)	House raided.
7.	20 June	Manoranjan Kar	Nihaljote (Naxalbari)	Threatened.
8.	21 June	Baneshwar Ghosh	Dayaramjote (Naxalbari)	Threatened.
9.	21 June	Gaishu Singh	Boromoniramjote (Naxalbari)	Demand for paddy.
10.	21 June	Mukundaram Singh	Boromoniranjote (Naxalbari)	Told to withdraw case against peasants.

This period also witnessed the formation of both political and non-political resistance parties and groups. Sampad Roy of the Samyukta Socialist Party (SSP) gave the lead in initiating resistance parties. Another resistance party came into existence under the leadership of a volatile Sikh, Bhag Singh, who had no known political affiliations. Meanwhile, unlawful activities like stray snatchings and even dacoities, quite unconnected with the peasant rebellion also started taking place. There followed a period of comparative lull, but no cessation, of rebel activities. On 27 June 1967, another appeal, the third within twelve days, was issued—this time by Bishwanath Mukherji, Amar Chakravarti and Deoprakash Rai—asking the extremists to surrender by 4 July 1967.

When by 5 July there was no response to the appeal, a Cabinet meeting authorized strong and appropriate action to bring the situation under control. Within four weeks of the Cabinet decision many arrests were made, including those of Majibur Rahman, Oli Mohammad and Jangal Santhal. Recovery of firearms was swift and satisfactory. 'Tangible progress' was recorded on the law and order front with the morale of the 'trouble shooters . . . completely shattered'. The West Bengal Governor, Dharam Vira's, visit to Naxalbari and Khoribari on 7 September 1967 probably signalled the end of law and order problems in the troubled region. However, one significant fact needs to be recorded. When the police operations were in full swing, thirty out of the thirty-eight tea estates in the Siliguri sub-division observed a day's token strike on 17 August 1967 in protest against police excesses in the Naxalbari area. This was yet another demonstration of the workers' solidarity expressed at a time when the peasant revolt was being curbed if not tamed.

VII

It will be recalled that the police began their offensive in a more determined way after the second appeal had been issued (22 June 1967). On the same day, the first meeting of Sub-Divisional Land Reforms Committee was held. It decided to take up those aspects of land reforms which could be tackled 'completely and quickly' and thereby restore confidence among the panic-stricken people in the affected areas. Thus the Committee decided that the following aspects should be taken up on a priority basis:

1. Licensing out of vested agricultural lands;
2. To study the feasibility, by undertaking a thorough survey, of increasing the amount of cultivable land from those areas which had hitherto been considered 'unfit-for-agriculture';
3. To inquire into specific cases of illegal eviction of *bargadars* (share-croppers) and to restore possession wherever possible;
4. To regularize the cases of encroachments on vested agricultural lands by (*a*) withdrawing pending eviction cases and (*b*) undertaking a fresh demarcation of such lands for allotment to eligible persons; and
5. To re-examine the eligibility of existing licenses. A licence fee of Rs. 10 per acre was charged from landless and poor

> peasant receipients of government vest land. This is not the same as 'distribution of land' for it does not "imply confirmment of title to ownership and all that is expected to follow from such proprietorship. There is also no guarantee yet that permission will continue to be given to the same person each year." (Basu, 1963:10).

The Thana Land Reforms Committee (TLRC) was composed of the BDO as its Chairman, the Junior Land Reforms Officer (JLRO) as its Secretary, the concerned member of the Legislative Assembly, representatives of political parties, the Anchal Pradhan and the Gram Adhyaksh. The members were told to bring to the notice of the Committee specific cases on any of the above aspects so that they could be enquired into. It was also decided that in discussing problems of a particular area, the Thana Committees would meet at their respective Anchals[17] for the convenience of the local people. However, the establishment of such committees is one thing and their functioning quite another. During the period of agrarian tension these Committees were boycotted by the CPI-M rebels who dominated the troubled area. It was soon evident that without their active cooperation these Committees could transact little business. In the meetings that were held in early July the non-official members were conspicuous by their absence. No illegal eviction of *bargadars* were brought to the notice of the Committee during this period. The list of licencees in occupation of government vest land was furnished before the Committee but none present questioned any of the names in the list.

The Khoribari Thana Committee meeting, which was held in Hatighisa Anchal on 3 July 1967, was attended by only two non-official members belonging to the RSP and the AIGL. These two and a member of the Panchayat complained that they were warned against attending these meetings. No villagers came before the Committee. The owner of the house where the meeting was scheduled to be held had locked his house and run away so that the meeting ultimately had to be held in the Anchal Panchayat office after the lock was broken open. The meeting ended without any concrete decisions as the two non-official members present had nothing to contribute.

The Buraganj Anchal meeting, scheduled for 4 July 1967, could not even be held. The Anchal Pradhan had fled from the village and expressed his inability to be of any help. The letters sent by the BDO to the panchayats could not be delivered as the postal peon could not enter the villages. The non-official members expressed their reluctance to attend the meeting without proper security. Thus it would appear that the rebel peasants were in almost total command of these thana areas where nobody was prepared to go against their writ either in willing conformity or in forced deference to their supremacy.

All these formidable obstacles notwithstanding, the bureaucratic machinery moved ahead with determination. By 7 July 1967, i.e., within a fortnight, they claimed to have distributed 76.05 acres to fifty-three people in the Hatighisa, Khoribari, Siliguri and Bandarjhuli areas. They claimed that in the week following they would make available another 51 acres for distribution amongst twenty to twenty-five persons in the Bandarjhuli area. A list of landless labourers had also been forwarded from Khopalashijote (Khoribari) and a survey would follow soon. By the first week of September, the administration who by now had the law and order situation under control, claimed that it had already distributed 984.22 acres amongst 686 persons through the TLRC. As many as sixty-six cases of eviction were brought to their notice of which thirty-five were settled amicably between the two parties.

It would appear that the performance of the TLRC was inversely related to the amount of control the rebel peasants exercised in the area. It is difficult at this stage to assess how much of this statistical data are an indication of a real fulfilment of the objectives for which the TLRCs were established. No doubt some of the land distributed by the TLRCs was given to deserving recepients. But it is universally acknowledged both by the bureaucracy and the peasantry that in course of time the functioning of the TLRC became counter-productive. The United Front government fell[18] and the Congress was saddled with four kinds of problems. Firstly, there were households which had occupied vest lands even before they were listed and declared as vested in the government. In this the CPI-M rebels had taken the maximum initiative. They had made a meticulous survey of land held in excess of the ceiling as well as lands which were clearly government lands. The entire movement of forcible occupation of land was based on the findings of a remarkably thorough study and perhaps the only one of its kind emanating from a non-governmental agency.

Thus the actual call for forcible occupation of surplus, *benami* and vest land was preceded by several years of arduous survey. In this sense, the preparation for the movement had a historicity which, so far, has been grossly underestimated by academics and ideologues alike. The credit for this goes to Kanu Sanyal and his team of dedicated workers. The impression one gets from the field is that, by and large, such lands were settled in favour of the occupants of the lands. But cases where *pattas* (settlement receipts) were given to non-occupants are not few.

The second problem related to households which were given *pattas* after the list of vest lands had been declared by the government. Such households acquired actual control over the lands allotted to them. Another problem arose out of a situation where peasants were given *pattas* but not actual possession of the land. This resulted in a conflict between those who were given *pattas* and those who were in actual possession of the lands allotted in the *pattas*. Those in actual possession of the land would file cases in the court pleading that since they were landless they should be permitted legal retention of the lands. The fourth category of persons were those who were entitled to vest land but were not listed at all.

With the advent of stability and peace, the restoration of law and order and the more efficient distribution of surplus land by the government, there emerged a group of *dalals* (brokers) who exploited the new situation created by the redistribution of land to the landless and poor peasants. They would approach those who were occupying vest land but had no *patta*. Among them, as noted earlier, were those who were actually in the category of landless and poor peasants, as well as those who had been able to manipulate a landless and poor peasant status for themselves. These brokers also found a happy hunting ground amongst those who were in possession of *pattas* but denied possession of the land defined in them. The nature of the 'fee' charged by such brokers ranged from a certain share of produce, usually half, to money, to the proposal that they be allowed to cultivate such land for a year or two. This 'fee' was not always contingent on the successful handling of the case. Often they would be demanded in 'advance'. Ironically, therefore, with the relaxation of tension and the return of 'normalcy', the situation once again veered in favour of exploiters and speculators.

The process of land alienation, resulting in the transfer of vest land from landless and poor peasants to better off landowners, also began to take place. Without cattle-ploughs and the necessary capital for seeds and manure, the poor recipients of vest lands found it more profitable to lease out their lands in exchange for a very moderate rent rather than let it remain fallow. This, repeated several times, usually paved the way for a permanent alienation of land. This process was probably accelerated after the fall of the second United Front government.

In another important sense, the agrarian problem is complex. The criteria determining who qualified for vest land was defined at the time of the abolition of zamindari in 1952. At that time, many Rajbansis were *jotedars* and prosperous peasants. Over a period of two decades the fortunes of many *jotedars*, Rajbansis, underwent catalysmic changes. Under the rapacious onslaught of migrant settlers, large areas of land went out of the hands of the Rajbansis many of whom became pauperized or were reduced to the status of *adhiars* and poor peasants. But even if a whole generation lived as paupers, they would not qualify for vest land as they were *jotedars* or better off peasants in 1952! Numerous Rajbansis, who experienced this steep downward mobility, constituted the backbone of the peasant mobilization in Naxalbari.

VIII

Quite contrary to the widely held view that consequent to the strong police action the Naxalbari movement was quickly brought under control, there is sufficient evidence to show that the rebel peasants and their leaders, whether in jail or outside, far from repenting their 'mistakes' and 'misdeeds', continued to be unswerving in their commitment to an agrarian revolution (Dasgupta, 1974:199-200). We have already noted the near-total strike of plantation labour in Siliguri sub-division. Meetings continued to be held in the plantations in sympathy and support of the Naxalbari movement. In this, R.B. Khatiwara took an active part.

No sooner had the agrarian tension been contained than urban unrest followed. Students in the colleges and in the North Bengal University (NBU) were divided against each other on the issue of the Naxalbari peasant revolt and the politics of agrarian revolution. In the first week of August 1967, Kisanlal Chatterjee, a brilliant student of the NBU, took a leading part in the disturbances in Siliguri which ultimately led to the arrest of Maidhan Das Agarwalla, owner of the

Bagdogra Tea Estate, on charges of hoarding food grains. Chatterjee was an ardent proponent of the peasant cause in Naxalbari.

The tension in NBU and in Siliguri was steadily mounting. Kisan Chatterjee, Deb Ranjan Bhattacharjee, Dilip Bagchi, Pabitra Pani Saha and Dipak Biswas were openly espousing the cause of Naxalbari revolt. They were successful in organizing dehoarding operations in Atharkhai and Tarabari (Phansidewa). This enabled them to build up a fairly strong base in these villages so much so that when the police approached these villages to apprehend some Naxalite extremists their efforts were successfully foiled. Utpal Dutt, the veteran theatre and film artist, visited the area and delivered fiery speeches commending the Naxalbari path. The situation in the NBU campus became increasingly tense as those students who opposed politics in the campus confronted the student activists. The violence in the campus arising out of this confrontation necessitated police intervention. Kisan Chatterjee, Dilip Bagchi and Pabitra Pani Saha were suspended by the Vice-Chancellor and they were arrested by the police shortly afterwards. Kisan was arrested in Suri on 24 September 1967.

The suspensions and arrests were followed by a wave of protest in NBU. A demonstration was organized in the beginning of November 1967 which demanded withdrawal of suspension orders on the three students, postponement of M.A. Part I and II examinations scheduled to commence from 6 and 7 November respectively, and withdrawal of the police from the campus. The M.A. examinations could not take place as no examinee turned up at the examination hall. The picketing outside the examination hall was reportedly peaceful and the examinations had to be postponed *sine die*.

A rival centre of activity, aimed at countering the extremist developments at NBU, was taking shape in Siliguri College. As early as 8 October 1967, a few students lead a procession in Siliguri town to protest against the 'high handedness' of the Students' Federation of NBU which consisted mostly of the extremists. They also demanded the continued detention of Kisan Chatterji. But the procession was poorly attended and fizzled out.

On 11 November 1967 a batch of about thirty students went in a procession carrying portraits of Mao Tse-tung, Ho Chi Minh and Lenin in Siliguri town. At the Station Maidan they called upon the *adhiars* not to share their produce with the *jotedars*. They pledged the unflinching support of the students in the struggle for land and its produce. This was followed by another procession on 28 November 1967 which was critical of the United Front and the ministry led by P.C. Ghosh. They emphasized that armed revolution was the only way to achieve socialism. As these urban protests gathered momentum, Charu Mazumdar, who was emerging as the main theoretician of the extremist group, and R.B. Khatiwara were arrested on 21 November 1967. However, because of ill-health, Charu Mazumdar was released on 7 December 1967. Soon after, he exhorted those who were not arrested or were on bail to go underground.

Probably the first meeting of the NKSSS under the leadership of Sushital Raychoudhury was held in Siliguri town on 29 March 1968. The meeting demanded the immediate release of peasant leaders and raised the slogan of land to the tiller and armed struggle to achieve it. The NKSSS started organizing branches in the various tea estates and villages and observed Naxalbari Shahid Dibas (Naxalbari Martyrs' Day) on 25 May 1968 in commemoration of those who had died on that day exactly a year ago. Posters and photographs provided vivid visual reminders of the events. The speakers in general were critical of the parliamentary path to socialism and expressed their belief in the Maoist path of an armed liberation struggle. They proposed a poll boycott and solicited support for an armed struggle. The function ended with the performance of a play entitled *Rakte Ranga* (Seeped in Blood) which was an enactment of the Naxalbari revolt against age-long exploitation and oppression.

By August-September 1968, we already find signs of renewed activity in the troubled areas. On 7/8 September 1968, the police were combing the houses for wanted persons and firearms in Hochai Mallikjote (Naxalbari) when they unexpectedly met with armed resistance from Babulal Vishwakarmakar who chose to die fighting rather than be taken captive. Babulal's martyrdom signalled the beginning of a new stage in the peasant revolt. Charu Mazumdar declared that henceforth the question before them was armed seizure of power; therefore arms had to be accumulated through *dakhal* (capture).

The government had to wait until the end of October 1968, i.e., for more than a year, to rope in Kanu Sanyal and Keshab Sarkar. But until their arrest, they moved freely, in and out of the area, frequently taking shelter in Nepal. The facility with which they continued to maintain contact with the people of this region at a time when the police were all over the area is ample evidence of the mass support of the peasants. This kind of support comes close to the requirement of a base area as envisaged in Maoist strategy. Such was the nature of peasant mobilization that even after several thousand arrests, the administration feared that the withdrawal of the massive police force deployed in the area may result in the recurdescence of the revolt. It is interesting to note that Khokon Mazumdar could elude arrest until January 1969, and Souren Bose continued to remain in command after Kanu Sanyal's arrest.

Meanwhile, the leaders arrested in connection with the peasant revolt refused to accept 'convict' status, demanded a 'political' status and a higher jail classification. 'Convict' Mujibur Rahman and under-trial prisoners, Kumar Kishan and Prem Kumar Bharadwaj, commenced a hunger strike on 18 October 1968. Jangal Santhal joined them on 26 October, whilst Kanu Sanyal and Keshab Sarkar joined them from the very day they were lodged in Darjeeling jail (31 October). Kanu Sanyal, Keshab Sarkar and three others were granted the status of Division I prisoners by 2 November 1968. When the cases of Mujibur Rahman and five others were under active consideration, Sanyal and Sarkar decided to call off their strike on 3 November.

On the same day that Sanyal and others called off their hunger strike, Kadam Mallick and others resorted to a hunger strike in Siliguri Special Jail to press similar demands. Four days later, another five convicts and seventeen under-trial prisoners joined them. By 10 November, the number of hunger strikers increased to thirty-four. On 11 November, Kanu Sanyal and Keshab Sarkar demanded the following: 'political' status and higher jail classification for all the persons arrested in connection with Naxalbari cases, their own transfer to Siliguri Jail, legal defence, and newspapers. They also asked the jail authorities not to handcuff or rope them while producing them before the court. By 20 November, Kanu Sanyal and three others had resumed their hunger strike. The number of hunger strikers stood at twenty-one on 20 November which increased to thirty-one by 7 December 1968. So weak had the hunger-strikers become that they could not follow the court proceedings. Also, forced nasal feeding and constant medical attention was required to keep them alive. This kind of fasting and non-cooperation continued until 26 February 1969, when Kanu Sanyal, Keshab Sarkar, Kamakshya Banerji, Mondol Karmakar, Khokon

Mazumdar and others broke their fast. However, the bail petitions moved on behalf of the Naxalites were rejected on 13 March 1969.

It is of interest to note that the CPI-M, which had lost power after the fall of the first United Front government, had consistently maintained a critical stand towards the rebels in their own party while at the same time advocating the release of all political prisoners. Thus when the CPI-M led United Front government assumed power for the second time with a clear electoral verdict, the government issued orders for the withdrawal of all the 114 cases started over the Naxalbari disturbances. Kanu Sanyal was released on 8 April 1969 from Darjeeling Jail.

It is therefore abundantly clear that the Naxalites did not at any stage succumb or surrender themselves before the superior power of the state. In prison or out of prison, their attitude was one of total defiance of the establishment. A shift however took place from the rural to the urban setting as the coercive apparatus of state strengthened its grip over the troubled region. To state that the strength of the movement was broken within weeks of effective police action in the Naxalbari region would, therefore, be to totally disregard the concurrent emergence of urban defiance. Rather than engineering a sudden collapse of the movement, effective police action in the rural areas resulted in the spontaneous spread of the movement to urban areas, particularly in the NBU, the railways, in the plantations and in some industrial establishments.

Given this situation it was not at all unexpected that the Naxalite leaders, once free, would redouble their efforts to make themselves more politically effective. Within months of the Naxalbari uprising in 1967, the revolutionary groups had been able to identify and coordinate themselves at the level of the states, and within two weeks of Sanyal's release the Communist Party of India (Marxist-Leninist) was formed on the birth centenary of V.I. Lenin. The suppression of rebel activities by the law and order agencies of the State and the total lack of any organizational support in their struggle were mainly responsible for the emergence of the new revolutionary party. Naxalbari had provided the context in which identities of interests got forged. It is as if a peasant movement such as this was needed to sort out the ideological wrangles that was plaguing the Communist movement in the country, more particularly the CPI-M. Naxalbari became the symbol of revolutionary ferment in India, whatever may have been its reality.

IX

The period following the release of the Naxalite leaders led to a situation quite different from that of the first phase of peasant rebellion in 1967. Now that the CPI-ML had come into existence, the CPI-M, and certain other parties like the SSP, AIGL, who commanded small enclaves of influence in the region, engaged in competitive militancy and extremism, in what seemed to be a game of one-upmanship in radicalism. By the end of June 1969, the CPI-M had stepped up its militant activities. On 16 June, members of the Kisan Sabha cleared parts of the Goke Forest and encouraged forcible occupation. At a later stage, however, this encroachment into the Forest Department's territory was withdrawn on government initiative. The incidence of *gheraos* of government officers at the village level (like the BDOs) suddenly increased. *Gheraos* were reported from Pulbazar, Phansidewa, Pathan, Naxalbari and the Sukna Tea Estate. The BDO at Phansidewa was held for nearly twenty-four hours, whilst the manager of the Sukna Tea Estate had to be rescued by means of a warrant issued by the Siliguri Court. The Siliguri Pavement Traders' Union pressed for alternative sites, whilst the Bagdogra Tea Estate had to remove some 'outsiders' whom they had employed, as 300 of their plantation workers went on protest strike. The Fulbari Pathan Tea Estate had to remove one of its labourers as 200 labourers went on strike. The National Union of Plantation Workers (NUPW) called counter-strikes in five tea estates demanding removal of some workers owing allegiance to the CPI-M.

In August 1969, protest activities in the plantations were stepped up by the CPI-M. Workers went on strike in many tea gardens on specific economic demands. At one place, the police had to open fire (Soom Tea Estate, 30 August 1969). Militant calls were given for occupying surplus land in plantations. Conspicuously enough, the activities of the CPI-M among the peasantry was hardly perceptible. This suggested that their erstwhile comrades, now under the banner of a new revolutionary party (CPI-ML), still held sway amongst the peasantry. However, two significant ideological floor crossings should be recorded here at this stage. Kamakshya Banerji and Phani Das, who had earlier played an overtly militant role with the extremists, joined the CPI-M. These were interpreted as 'desertions' by the CPI-ML.

Agrarian conflict resurfaced seriously only in November 1969 with the approach of harvest time. The CPI-M started organizing processions, with people armed with bows and arrows, in the Khoribari region in a style reminiscent of 1967. At a meeting held in Adhikarihat (P.S. Khoribari), the CPI-M speaker criticized the CPI-ML and lauded the role of the United Front government. In a meeting in Khaprail (P.S. Siliguri), they openly exhorted the *adhiars* not to share the produce from *benami* and vest lands with the *jotedars*. Sharing of crops, they urged, should be made contingent on the *jotedars* producing valid ownership documents. The party assured the support of their volunteers during harvesting.

The SSP also organized a series of demonstrations, led by Sampad Roy and Sovananda Das, in front of the BDO's office in Phansidewa demanding distribution of agricultural loans, etc. Later, the two formed opposing factions in the SSP. At a meeting held at Adhikarihat in July 1969, the Sampad Roy faction was critical of the Naxalites and urged people to locate *benami* and vest lands and occupy them. As harvest time approached, the Bangla Congress expressed their intention to organise a Shanti Sena (Peace Brigade), and the SSP appealed for peace. In December 1969, the RSP organized a Samyukta Krishak Sabha and nearly 100 persons armed with bows, arrows and spears demonstrated before the JLRO's office at Naxalbari demanding acquisition of surplus lands at Naxalbari and other tea gardens in the Siliguri sub-division.

In November-December 1969, we find the CPI, the Bangla Congress and the SSP each attempting to organize forcible harvesting of paddy from *benami* and vest lands. In each case, groups of people provided armed support for the harvesting operations. We hear of the CPI and the Bangla Congress attempting this at Kalanjote (P.S. Siliguri), and the Sampad Roy group in Gayabari and Dandagoch (both in Phansidewa). The RSP also organized armed processions voicing demands for occupation of surplus lands.

This period also witnessed many inter-party clashes in which the CPI-M seemed to have been pitted, in several contexts, with its other United Front constituents. The AIGL, unable to keep pace with the CPI-M's militancy in its own areas of dominance, declared the formation of a '*Dambar Fouz*'.

Thus, as has been observed, this was a period of matching militancy with militancy in which the CPI-M took the plunge, presumably to counter and offset the militancy of the CPI-ML. But, in effect, the whole environment became surcharged with this spirit of competitive militancy.

The Naxalites struck terror in the first week of December 1969 with three murderous attacks culminating in two deaths. Those attacked were Kamakshya Banerji, chowkidar, Bishnulal Singh of Jatrujote (P.S. Khoribari) and the Manager of the Singhuli Tea Estate, who escaped narrowly with severe injuries. The daffadar of Buraganj Anchal, a petty police official, and a member of the Home Guards in Hatighisa, were the next two victims in February 1970. The fifth murder took place in April 1970 when a *jotedar* belonging to Ghoshpukur was fatally injured in Kachumonijote (P.S. Phansidewa).

The decision of the Naxalites to open their account with a series of murders in rapid succession, seemed to have little direct relevance to the agrarian problems and were in the nature of retaliations against petty government officials and deserters. This was in sharp contrast to their earlier activities in 1967 which were based on forcible seizure of illegal *benami* land, a determined bid at dehoarding and a refusal to pay extortionate interest on paddy loans—all of which involved the mobilization of large masses of peasantry. The net result of their violent activities was that it set the police hounding after them and in August 1970 forty-four of them, including Kanu Sanyal, Kadamlal Mallik, Khodanlal Mallik, Panchan Sarkar, Kuru Murmu and other peasant leaders, were bundled in at Phansidewa. Jangal Santhal had been arrested earlier and, with the arrest of Punjab Rao on 26 September 1970, almost all prominent peasant leaders of any consequence were behind bars. There followed a lull in the activities of the Naxalites only to be broken by the murder of a *jotedar* in Telengajote (P.S. Khoribari).

Early in 1971 we find a sudden recrudescence of violent activities, including murders. The murders took place in Phansidewa P.S. in January 1971. The following month saw the death of a Sub-Inspector of Police in Siliguri town and two *jotedars* in Phansidewa P.S. A dacoity was also reported in the same month from the same region. In April, four murders were reported in Siliguri Sub-Division and dacoities were committed in Petki and Rupandingi (both in Phansidewa) and in Lalpool (P.S. Naxalbari). Those killed included Paulos Kujur (Oraon) of Bhatagoch (P.S. Khoribari) in retaliation for the death of two (or four?) Naxalites in an armed encounter in 1967, which has been referred to earlier.[10] In May 1971, two attempted murders at Phansidewa resulted in one death in Goabari. In July 1971, one person was shot dead and his brother injured in Utkaranjote (Naxalbari), whilst two murders were reported from the Bijoynagar Tea Estate. In August 1971, four more murders were reported from Phansidewa.

It is not unnatural to find that the Naxalites were often engaged in encounters with the police after December 1971. Such an encounter, in which both the police and the Naxals sustained casualties, took place in Birsingjote (P.S. Naxalbari). Premlal Mallik, a cousin of Kadam Mallik, was killed in an encounter with the police in the Tukurijhar forest (P.S. Naxalbari) in mid-February 1971. April 1972 saw another major encounter in Laxmijote resulting in losses on both sides—including one Sub-Inspector of police, a Home Guard and five extremists. By May 1972 the frequency of murders and dacoities had declined sharply.

There are certain clearly discernible patterns in the events of 1969 that stand out in sharp contrast to those that took place in 1967. Firstly, a sudden escalation in murders and the generation of a psychosis of terror invited swift and harsh police retaliation. Secondly, there was less visible conflict on direct agrarian issues and problems. For example, one does not hear of seizure of illegally occupied land under Naxalite leadership. Thirdly, much of these activities took place with the peasant leaders behind bars. Therefore, one wonders how much mass or peasant legitimation such activities carried. Fourthly, the earlier method of conflict was based on the mass involvement of the peasants, with several hundred armed peasants confronting their adversaries at a time. In contrast, the 1969 murders were conspiratorial and executed by secret guerilla squads. Even anti-social activities were endowed with revolutionary significance. Finally, whilst the 1967 uprising left an unquenched thirst for rebel activities whenever the opportunity arose even with thousands behind bars, the conspiratorial style of the activities of 1969 left the peasant masses guessing as to what all this would add up to! In helpless dismay, confused by ideological brainwashing, and cut off from their trusted leaders, they remained silent spectators to and unintended victims of a process in which they were neither participants nor decision-makers. In 1967, the mobilization by the peasant leaders was mass-based with thousands of peasants involved in a whole range of activities—from surveying *benami* and vest lands, to their forcible occupation when the call was given.

In 1969, the activists followed an elitist role emphasizing their intellectual and ideological superiority over the peasant masses, egging them on to activities whose significance they scarcely comprehended.[20] Not until this conspiratorial style was condemned by China was it given up; but by then it had already done irreparable damage and the party was in utter shambles.

X

There is another important difference between 1967 and 1969. In 1967, the revolt was based on peasant-worker solidarity, with the radical urban youth finding, at last, his source of revolutionary inspiration. In 1969, it was the urban-based youth and the party, whose zeal for revolutionary transformation transcended that of the peasant leaders and masses, who provided the leadership. Thus, this period witnessed a succession of violent activities both in the rural and urban areas. The emergence of the NKSSS and, above all, of Charu Mazumdar as the foremost theoretician and ideologue with unrivalled authority, directly contributed to the introduction of the urban-elitist-authoritarian-petty bourgeois bias in the conduct and style of operation of the movement.

During this period of resurgence of the movement, terror struck urban institutions equally, if not more vigorously, than the rural areas. Processions and demonstrations in urban areas were frequent and directed towards the administration and the police. But acts of violence and strikes rocked educational institutions, particularly the schools, and the police. Urban tensions began to build up at an accelerated pace from May 1970 onwards when NBU was again seized with trouble. The situation was grave enough to occasion the presence of the police outside the campus. The University had to be closed before the summer vacations after a murder was committed in Kochomonijote (P.S. Phansidewa).[21]

The closure of the university was followed by repeated attacks on educational institutions. The familiar pattern was—setting up red flags on the roofs of schools, exploding a few crackers to scare away the students, and then setting fire to records and furniture. In May 1970, as many as four schools were targets of such attacks. By July, Naxalite influence had penetrated amongst the railway employees in Siliguri. When the police arrested several persons, including a woman, in connection with an attack on a club located in the railway colony, the railway employees *gheraoed* the SDO Siliguri with unexpected speed, demanding the release of those arrested. To the stupefaction of the administration, the demonstrators included a senior railway officer. The *gherao* turned violent when somebody turned off the lights and a police official was stabbed under cover of the darkness. This led to more arrests by the police. Undaunted, the extremists were able to call a successful strike in all the schools in Siliguri, so much so, that students appearing for their half-yearly examinations were also unable to attend school. Thereafter followed a series of attacks on the police and on schools. Explosions of bombs and crackers were frequent. A bomb was also lobbed into the SDO's residence but, fortunately, did not explode. The climax was reached with the railway loco shed staff calling a lightning strike on 23 July 1970. Train services were disrupted on the Kishanganj-Alipurduar section, both in the meter and broad guagues. Meanwhile, bomb attacks on the police, arson, explosions, and attacks on educational institutions continued unabated. The Border Security Force was called in in large numbers and arrests continued. On 27 July, the strike was declared illegal under the Maintenance of Essential Services Act, 1968. This was followed by a call for a Siliguri Bandh on the 31st. Meanwhile, the Railway Minister declared that there should be no victimization of rail employees. The strike was ultimately called off on 2 August 1970. Thus, the months of July and August were characterized by great ferment and, it will be recalled, it was during this period that the peasant leaders were also arrested.

The reopening of the NBU did not restore calm. The hope that normalcy had been established was shortlived as six schools and the Siliguri Night College again became targets of attack in November 1970. This was followed by more arrests of students and, in turn, the police became targets of reprisal.

Following the arrest of some suspected extremists from the Telephone Exchange in Siliguri in December 1970, several government offices were attacked and a police jeep set on fire. In February 1971, the telephone employees of Siliguri and Bagdogra went on strike, demanding the release of their arrested colleagues on bail. They resumed work the next day, but disconnected the telephones of the magistrates and the police for a day. Attacks on schools, on the fire brigade and on the police continued unabated and bombs were freely used. During this period of utter chaos, sixteen extremists escaped from Siliguri Special Jail on 21 February 1971. It was in this well planned jail break that persons like Dipak Biswas, Shantilal Pal, Maniklal Singh, Ranjit Bhowmick, Punjab Rao, Dulal Chanda and others made good their escape, but some, including Punjab Rao and Dulal Chanda, were rearrested almost immediately. This resulted in some hard core Charu-liners rejoining their comrades, with the peasant leaders completely out of circulation.

March 1971 was perhaps one of the most disturbed months, with the CPI-M involved in clashes with the CPI-ML, INTUC[22], CPI, and the Congress (R) resulting in a number of injuries in every clash. Clashes between CPI-M and CPI-ML youths took a nasty turn, with murders committed on each sides. Educational institutions and the police were not spared by the extremists. Up to the month of February 1972, we find arson, bomb blasts on police targets, and attacks on educational institutions continuing, with the police trying to control a situation which it had never experienced since independence. However, by July 1972 we find a petering out of the acts of violence and a gradual return to normalcy.

Several important events took place which seem to have a direct bearing on the general reduction in militant and violent activities. First were the events in East Pakistan. A military regime rode roughshod over the popular sentiments of the people after denying them the fruits of an overwhelming electoral verdict. Considerable confusion prevailed within the Naxalite movement as regards how these developments which had led to the exodus of nearly ten million people into India, should be interpreted. The refugees brought with them harrowing tales of torture and of political and communal persecution, which stirred the emotions of millions in India but more particularly the people of Bengal. Therefore, any ideological interpretation dubbing Indian intervention as imperialist interference was considered renegade and totally unacceptable by many within the CPI-ML cadres. India's contribution to the liberation of Bangladesh was followed closely by the massive electoral mandate which the Congress Party received during the General Elections of 1971, testifying to the charismatic peak which Indira Gandhi had scaled and the halo of glory which now surrounded her. It is therefore no wonder that many, including those who had owed allegiance to the CPI-ML, began to be attracted to the Congress. People began to believe that the victor of Bangladesh could also vanquish *garibi*[23] equally effectively and expeditiously.

The Congress was returned from Siliguri and Phansidewa respectively. Many, including a large number of so-called anti-socials elements or lumpen, were able to cross over to the Congress, and thus avoid prosecution while also gaining political respectability and support. To no less a degree did the movement suffer when Charu Mazumdar died while in police custody. Although the movement was facing heavy weather in Bengal, Andhra and elsewhere, there was no one as competent as him in the leadership who could propound theories and evolve strategies, and integrate them convincingly in a Marxist-Leninist ideological framework. His death did not lead to violent reprisals as had been widely apprehended. The fact remained, however, that, for better or for worse, the movement was left without its foremost theoretician and tactician, a personality whose charisma was able to hypnotize even the most rational amongst them at times.

XI

What kind of an understanding or explanation can we arrive at with regard to the peasant revolt in North Bengal?

With the advent of the British, which also signalled the penetration of the money market economy into the rural areas, *jotedari* system crystallized into the *jotedari-adhiari* system. The introduction of the profit motive led to the gradual transformation of the feudal economy into one which bore marks of an increasing exploitation of labour aimed at retrieving the maximum produce and rents for the open money market. It was this contradiction between the money market with its profit motive on the one hand, and the feudal relations of production which enabled increasing exploitation of labour through debt bondage and bare subsistence wages, that was brought into a sharp focus by a group of communists who drew their inspiration from the Tebhaga peasant revolt which had rocked Bengal in the forties. The peasant mobilization went through a long process of maturation and eventually culminated in a revolt. However, as has already been observed, the revolt was not directed against the system but against its 'excesses'. Land to the tiller and a just sharing of crops between the cultivator and the owner remained its prime objectives. Even the relations of production were not sought to be altered or transformed—it was the exchange of goods between the producer and the owner that was sought to be properly regulated. But a movement which had been gradually moving towards revolt was suddenly required to launch a revolutionary onslaught against the landed interests and the state through guerilla warfare and violent methods. There was a natural cognitive lag between the requirements of a revolt and the demands of a revolution. This resulted in a contradiction between the actual subjective preparations for a revolt and the expected subjective preparedness for a revolution. This is clearly manifest in the difference between the active and meaningful participation of large members of the peasantry in 1967, and the bewilderment that overtook them over 1969-72. The events of 1967 were confined, by and large, to a revolt, whilst the events that ensued two years later were based on guerilla warfare and aimed at a seizure of state power.

The subjective preparation for any kind of movement involves an assessment of the quality and competence of the leaders and cadres and their relationship with the masses that they are expected to lead. Three kinds of leadership can be clearly distinguished in the Naxalbari movement. The indigenous rural leaders (e.g., Punjab Rao, Naresh Aich); the coopted rural leaders which had completely identified with their 'support base' by living with them, adopting many of their life styles, and sharing many of their privations (e.g., Kanu Sanyal, Panchan Sarkar); and the urban-based leaders, who may have evoked awe and reverence but not the unqualified trust of the simple peasants (e.g., Charu Mazumdar, Dipak Biswas). The legitimacy of the indigenous leadership with reference to its support base was unquestionable. The coopted rural leaders, by their transparent committment to the peasant cause, also enjoyed total confidence, even if they were 'different' from the peasants who had 'coopted' them. But their legitimacy was reinforced and maintained through the indigenous rural leadership which they had helped to create and which, in turn, depended on them. The urban-based leadership could gain 'entry' into the 'field' only through the legitimacy conferred upon them by the coopted rural leadership. Thus the urban-based leadership had to encounter two 'barriers' before it could penetrate the rural field.

Right from the very inception we notice a conflict between the urban-based and the coopted rural leadership. The urban-based leadership, armed with a revolutionary ideology, sought to enter the field directly by by-passing the coopted rural leaders, most of whom were then in prison. The six documents and the method of their propagation, as discussed earlier, is a clear evidence of this. In trying to effect this entry they were able to enlist the support of only a few intermediate level peasant leaders who were over-awed by the charisma of Charu Mazumdar. But such attempts didn't succeed. It is only at the Buraganj Conference held in Khoribari under the auspices of the coopted and indigenous peasant leaders that their ideology was heard by large numbers of peasants. And in 1967 the two lines of action were kept separate, with separate areas for their implementation. It is in 1969 that the coopted peasant leaders gave in to the superior intellect of the urban ideologues, keen to bring about a revolution in the countryside. The ill-conceived programme of guerilla warfare and the annihilation of class enemies which followed proved disastrous to the movement. Thus the breakdown of the channel of communication from urban-based to coopted to indigenous rural leaders resulted in a situation in which neither a fair assessment of objective conditions, nor the normal processes of subjective preparation could take place.

An analysis of the composition of the peasant leadership confirms Sanyal's claim in his Terai report of a range of participation which ran from rich peasants through poor peasants to landless labourers. The participants in the movement also reflected the same range of economic backgrounds, although a more thorough empirical enquiry is needed to assess the extent of actual participation of the different categories of peasants. The participation of cultivators, owning and/or cultivating land in share-cropping, does not necessarily imply that their motives in leading the movement were suspect. Considering that the main struggle was waged on behalf of the share-croppers, it was in the interest of those who were engaged in share-cropping (whether they owned land or not) to become partisans of the movement. However, whether the same group alignments for accumulative change would remain if the goal of the movement was alterative or transformative change is another question altogether.

While still on the question of the leadership of the movement, it is necessary to distinguish between two kinds of tendencies that had to contend with each other from time to time. On the one hand was the urban-based leadership which, cloaked in a more sophisticated ideology, claimed superior knowledge and status with regard to the manner in which the movement should be conducted. They would insist that the others follow the direction they gave and assured that the predicted outcomes would ensue. The coopted and indigenous leadership, on the other hand, always took their decisions as democratically as possible and involving the largest possible numbers. Whilst the former engaged in a one-way transmission of decisions already arrived at by a small group of movement leaders, the latter's decision-making process involved continuous feedback and participation from the various constituents. The former decisions were therefore generally biased in favour of theoretical-ideological considerations, whilst the latter were geared to the empirical-ideological. It is unfortunate that there was reluctance on the part of the former to give much importance to the latter, which, as has been observed, they often sought to by-pass.

This leads us to some important theoretical considerations. These two patterns of leadership behaviour are not typical to the Naxalbari movement alone and can be observed in a wide variety of situations. The leadership that is characterized by one-way transmission is typically elitist, because the basic assumption behind this approach is that the function of the leader is to lead the masses who are unable to do much otherwise. Thus there is a clear leader-mass distinction in such a conception of the leadership role. And this is the prime assumption in the elite theories.[21] In contrast, the leadership role which operates on a principle of continuous transmission-and-feed back with its base of support and at different levels of leadership is qualitatively different. Here the leadership role is based on collective responsibility with a sense of respect for the masses and their judgement and consequently is non-elitist. The elitist leadership is based on an organizational pattern which is highly centralized, with concentration of power at the apex. The non-elitist approach in essence is power 'deconcentrated' at several levels of leadership which reaches up to the masses. In Naxalbari, the elitism of Charu Mazumdar was not consistent with the non-elitism of Kanu Sanyal. Thus elitism can be present even in a movement based on a conflict between classes.

The central point around which the struggle in Naxalbari was conducted was that of class. It was clearly to further the interests of the labouring and peasant classes that the mobilization was organized. The social background of the participants in the movement ran from rich peasants through to the labouring classes, and also covered all ethnic and caste groups. It was not unusual that Paulos

Kujur (Oraon) was attacked by tribals, or that Rajbansis were pitted against Rajbansis.

The interpretative dimension of social mobilizations for change is perhaps the most difficult part of a study of movements. For here partisan values or prejudices are likely to interfere with an objective evaluation of the movement. Therefore, there is need for a dynamic (as opposed to a static) model of analysis and interpretation. Thus, if the interpretation is weak or superficial this would reflect the weakness of the model rather than the influence of value biases. In other words, we can have our value committments and yet not permit them, to the extent possible, to vitiate our interpretations.

I have presented elsewhere such a dynamic model of collective mobilizations for change (Mukherji, 1977:55). I shall briefly present the salient features of that model before attempting an interpretation of the Naxalbari peasant uprising. I have pleaded earlier for a classification of movements by the quality of change they bring about (or intend to bring about). This has led to the distinction between quasi-movements and social movements—the latter being concerned with changing the structure in contrast to effecting changes within the structure of societal systems. It is equally important to examine the means employed to achieve the goals. The means employed are an indicator of the degree of resistence to change in terms of the achievement of given goals. Thus, whether goals can be achieved by employing institutionalized means or by non-institutionalized means is a factor which cannot be ignored in any systematic analysis of movements. In the following model, means, goals, changes and movements have been brought together within a single framework of dynamic analysis (see Fig. 1).

It will be clear from the framework of analysis that quasi-movements need not always indicate a stable situation. Demands for a bonus hike, or a wage increase, or a reduction in working hours may require mass protests by system participants through accepted, legitimate and institutionalized channels like workers' unions and strikes. There follows a period of bargaining and settlement. The structure remains unaffected, and a redistribution of rewards and facilities take place. Such a situation is stable. Consider now a situation in which there are no adequate institutional mechanisms to regulate intra-systematic changes. In that case, intra-systematic changes would have to be brought about through non-institutionalized means. For example, coups abound in societies where legitimate

Figure 2.1

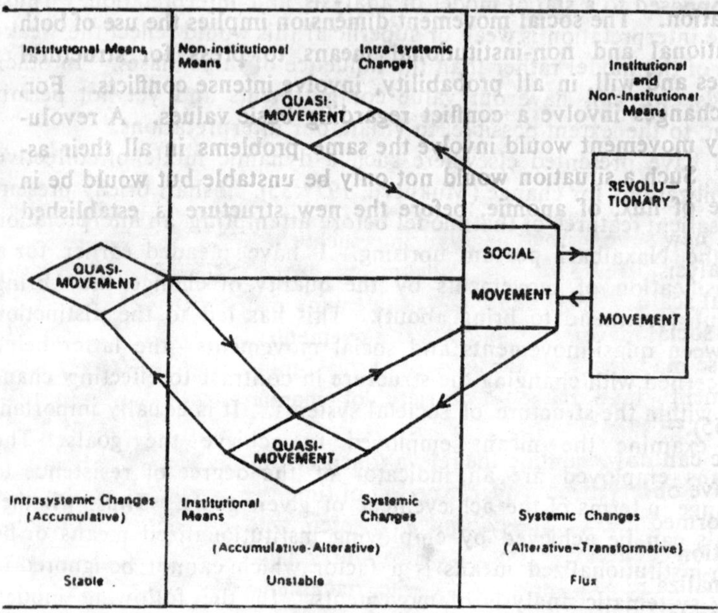

Institutional Means
Non-institutional Means
Intra-systemic Changes
Institutional and Non-Institutional Means
QUASI-MOVEMENT
REVOLUTIONARY MOVEMENT
QUASI-MOVEMENT
SOCIAL MOVEMENT
QUASI-MOVEMENT
Intrasystemic Changes (Accumulative)
Institutional Means
Systemic Changes
(Accumulative-Alterative)
Systemic Changes
(Alterative-Transformative)
Stable
Unstable
Flux

institutions for the circulation of the elite without conflict do not exist. It is also conceivable that systematic changes can be brought about by persistent struggles through the institutions of protest and power that already exist. In either of those situations, the conditions are no longer stable, for the system gives clear evidence of a need for structural change(s). Frequent coups may be symptomatic of the need for a structure which provides for a smoother elite circulation. The social movement dimension implies the use of both institutional and non-institutional means to press for structural changes and will, in all probability, involve intense conflicts. For, such changes involve a conflict regarding basic values. A revolutionary movement would involve the same problems in all their aspects. Such a situation would not only be unstable but would be in a state of flux, of anomie, before the new structure is established with a new set of values legitimizing such changes. In this scheme of analysis, 'revolutionary movements are social movements of societal scale. A revolutionary movement may encompass a variety of social movements and quasi-movements; a social movement, likewise may give rise to a variety of quasi-movements; and a quasi-movement may have a variety of manifestations' (Mukherji, 1977:55).[25]

We can now examine the relevant aspects of the Naxalbari revolt. We have observed how over a period of time the jotedari system was transformed into the *jotedari-adhiari* system with an increasing contradiction between capital and labour. This led to the growing marginalization of the peasant who remained a cultivator without any capital, without ownership of the means of production, and in perpetual 'bondage'. In addition, we find a steep downward mobility of many erstwhile *jotedars* who were reduced to the status of marginal peasants in bondage. Thus we find two sources or streams of marginal peasants, each stream in interaction with the other building up a context of discontent. It is therefore not surprising that the demands of the Tebhaga movement found more appropriate soil here than presumably in places where the movement had raged. For, the proportion of landless labourers was insignificant here and the predominant mode of production and exploitation involved the marginal cultivator-peasant and his landlord.

The function of the process of political socialization which the communist cadres undertook was to make the *adhiars* understand this contradiction explicitly. Once this process started, the vehicle for action, the Krishak Sabha, was pressed into action. The Krishak Sabha organized itself at the grass root level and became entrenched. It kept on fighting for numerous small economic demands and for the redressal of grievances. It was able to recruit many peasant cadres, and develop a militant peasant leadership, particularly at the intermediate levels. Above all, it was able to give the lead in establishing a workers' union among the plantation labourers.

The plantation labourer, it should be borne in mind, is quite different from the industrial worker with whom he may have certain similarities. The plantation labourer works in the rural milieu, handles plants which are cultivated, carries and conserves his cultural heritage, lives in a community and so on. The solidarity that was forged so easily between peasants and workers was on account of the greater commonality between the two and their close physical proximity.

And yet in a very fundamental sense the problems of the worker and the marginalized peasant differ. The worker is located in a system of centralized production where the relations of production are quite different from the dispersed units of production that characterizes the *jotedari* system. The numerous workers have to confront a few owners of the means of production, whereas the numerous peasants have to deal with many *jotedars*. Thus, by the very nature of the feudal system of production and distribution, a great deal more organization and a capacity for a sustained struggle are required for social mobilization. Further, the centralized production system has a much simpler stratification clearly differentiating those who are exercising authority and those over whom the authority is being exercised. Not so with the feudal system where the agrarian hierarchy is blurred by norms of ethnic, kinship, caste and factional ties, all of which get mixed up in the feudal context. This is one reason why it has not been possible yet to evolve a structure in an agrarian milieu parallel to the workers' unions characteristic of industrial structures. Thus, while there have been peasant organizations (Krishak Sabhas), they have not been able to grow into organizations which could claim a statutory legal or bargaining status.

Since the early fifties, the kind of mobilization that was being organized was precisely in the nature of bargaining structures. The Krishak Sabha did not contemplate bringing about structural or systematic changes in the feudal system—it was merely trying to get for the marginalized peasants a better share of the produce; and where he was being denied a share of the surplus land, it tried to give him a patch of land, even, if need be, by force.[26] The old slogan—'land to the tiller'—still held good for the government and the Krishak Sabha alike. What gave such mobilizations a 'revolutionary' colour was the adoption of non-institutionalized means for the achievement of intra-systemic changes. Since no institutionalized mechanism for bargaining was available in the semi-feudal set-up, even to bring about intra-systemic changes directed towards a reallocation of rewards within the system required the use of non-institutionalized means. Thus, the Krishak Sabha tinkered with the problems of relations of production without questioning the institutions related to the ownership of the means of production, nor demanding for itself a permanent statutory bargaining status. In either of these situations it would have acquired the status of a social movement, for, to challenge the institution of the ownership of the means of production would have meant a frontal attack on the feudal system, and the claim to a permanent bargaining status for itself would have meant the institutionalization of an additional structure.

It goes to the credit of Charu Mazumdar that he realized that nothing short of a systemic change could end the exploitation and oppression inherent in the semi-feudal system.[27] He therefore sought to wrench the power of oppression from the *jotedars*, so that systemic changes could be introduced by the landless and poor peasants in alliance with workers and other sympathetic sections of the agrarian structure. Mazumdar, however, never elaborated on the system that would replace the existing system. He felt that the cumulative impact of the numerous open, mass struggles had resulted in very narrow economism. 'Land to the tiller' had only aroused in the landless and marginal peasants the insatiable urge to acquire property in the manner that the system provided—it did not socialize the peasants against the system itself. It is presumably this that made him overreact against open, mass struggles on narrow economic demands, which he dubbed as revisionism. He, therefore, shifted the focus of the struggle from narrow economic demands to the capture of power by force. In this also he relied more on a small group of highly socialized cadres rather than on peasant leaders steeped in the tradition of economic struggles. Finding himself faced with a situation without precedent, he tried to evolve a methodology of action that would enable the achievement of his objective. He found Lin Piao's system of guerilla warfare, tried and tested against Japanese imperialism, to be the most appropriate. To this he added his own formulation of annihilation of class enemies, which in essence was indistinguishable from secret assassinations. As a result, he drove the movement completely underground.

Mazumdar's logic had several implications. Firstly, the large masses of peasantry trained and brought up in open militancy suddenly found themselves confronted with a task to which they were badly attuned. From seizure of crops and forcible harvesting to annihilation of class enemies was a shift which the militant peasants found difficult to absorb. In 1970 there were no longer any 'cadre groups', there were only 'guerilla groups'. In this too the leadership passed into the hands of urban cadres were the only ones who 'understood' what was to be done—the 'ignorant' peasants had merely to follow. The result was the quick erosion of the strength of the Krishak Sabha which suddenly found itself declared 'obsolete'. In the absence of peasant leaders like Kanu Sanyal, Panchanan Sarkar, Jangal Santhal, Punjab Rao and others who were in prison, the Mazumdar formula was applied without resistance. Secondly, with the Krishak Sabha out of circulation, the plantation workers were also not clear as to what would be their role now. Except for a day's strike in sympathy, it is not at all clear what role they adopted in the new circumstances. In short, the new, urban-based leadership usurped the field of the peasant leaders and at the same time introduced a vastly different programme for which the 'field' was hardly prepared.

What in effect happened was that a revolutionary movement was launched by inactivating the quasi-movements that had been operating in an already unstable situation. Therefore, not only was the call for revolutionary action premature, it in addition neutralized the very infrastructures without which no revolutionary objective can be achieved. Rather than strengthen these infrastructures with revolutionary politics, it by-passed them for fear that they may resist it. The Krishak Sabha was maturing gradually through experience. The first stage of maturity was reached when it realized the need for organizing the plantation workers to make the peasant struggle mere effective. The second stage was being reached when they began to realize that the problems of the peasants could not be solved within the 'four walls of law'. A natural extension of such experiences should have led to the analysis of the system itself and the possibility of altering it. Thus, it is not sufficient that objective conditions for social transformation exist; it is more important that the actors in the system internalize the contradictions through experience before subjectively preparing for the struggle. For, the implications of such struggles, the 'sacrifices' that one must expect and anticipate, should be clear to the rank and file of the participants. This enables preclusion of adventurism from revolutionary action.

It will not be out of context to compare the Gandhian Sarvodaya movement of *gramdan* with the Naxalbari movement. Charu Mazumdar's reaction to an economism geared to narrow material values is comparable to the concept of *aparigraha*, or 'wantlessness', put forward forcefully by Gandhi. The Naxalbari experience enshrined the progressive cumulation of countless struggles, not for a change of the system but for a reallocation of the rewards within the system in which individual ownership of landed property remained a basic feature. The *gramdan* movement attempted to reorient the system by replacing individual ownership of land with communal ownership. While the Naxalbari movement in its period of maturation found it necessary to struggle for even the very minimum and just demands, the Sarvodaya movement relapsed into a mystic trust in a change-of-heart that would usher in a new society.

Thus we are faced with a curious paradox where, on the one hand, a movement found it necessary to engage in constant struggle to realise even the simplest demands of the poor and labouring classes, while, on the other, a situation in which a revolutionary transformation is expected to take place by abjuring any kind of conflict in the name of non-violence. It is only lately that this fallacy in the Gandhian movement has been exposed.

The re-thinking, the self-criticisms, in the several political groups that exist today in the name of Naxalite politics are enough evidence that movement activists are busy analyzing their own performance. There is little doubt that such introspection has made the ideologues and activists less doctrinaire than before. There is a genuine spirit of enquiry in which the empirical realities of societal structures and the constraints they impose on bringing about a radical transformation are appreciated. A group is definitely emerging who want to utilize parliamentary institutions for furthering the revolutionary cause. Others interpret this as an abdication in favour of revisionism. The search for a radical transformation is on, both among Naxalites and those who subscribe to a radically different methodology of militant struggle. It remains to be seen whether the breakthrough point is reached, by whom, and how.

Appendix

TEXT OF APPEAL ISSUED ON 16 JUNE 1967 BY THE CABINET MISSION

1. For a real and satisfactory solution of the problems of land, maintenance of peace and the cooperation of the people was absolutely essential.

2. The U.F. government was fully aware of the history of exploitation by *jamindars*, *jotedars*, *mahajans* (moneylenders) and *bagicha maliks* (plantation owners) and their oppression of the poor peasantry. The government is aware of the problems of *benami* lands, of land redistribution and eviction of the poor peasants by big landowners. The government is committed to help them within their limited powers. In the past the peasants have launched movements against such exploitation and oppression and it is but natural that they feel more encouraged and hopeful now that the U.F. government is in power. The government has welcomed powerful movements which have been launched after due and rational consideration by peasants, workers and other people, for they have enabled the strengthening of democratic movement for the solution of peoples' problems.

3. If, however, such a movement based on legitimate problems are wrongly directed against the progressive government of the people, if terror is created in the minds of the common people, if in the name of movement looting and even murder is encouraged, then this leads not only to an uncalled for violence but it adversely affects the interests of the poor and struggling peasantry. No progressive force can allow itself to fall to such a trap in a fit of blind protest. This unfortunately is precisely what is happening and the reactionary forces are finding an opportunity to sabotage the efforts of the government.

4. Just as it is the duty of the U.F. government to satisfy the legitimate demands of the peasants and their movement, it is expected in the interest of the common man that peace is maintained and security of citizen's life guaranteed. Keeping these two duties in view we propose the following for the speedy restoration of normalcy:

(*i*) A high ranking officer has already been appointed to go into the problems relating to land. Further, an advisory committee consisting of members representing different political parties and organisations is being established to inquire and assist the government in problems relating to land.

(*ii*) We are appealing for the restoration of peace and normalcy in the region. Peasants and leaders are generally requested to desist from anti-social activities. The government clearly states that it will not harbour any retaliatory or violent attitude for their past activities. Even in the matter of legal cases the attitude will remain the same.

(*iii*) In the meantime steps have been taken to ensure security of the citizens' lives. If unfortunately any part of the peasant movement does not respond to our appeal and continue in their anti-social activities, then there will be no other alternative but to take even stronger steps to restore normalcy. Although this will be an extremely painful step to take, their would be no other way left for the government but this.

It is our appeal that no one should push the U.F. government to such a situation. Nobody should get excited and make the complex situation even more complex. All should help us in translating our above decisions into actuality. Defeat the reactionary forces at sabotage.

15 June 1967
Siliguri

HARE KRISHNA KONAR
BISHWANATH MUKHERJI
SUSHIL DHARA
NANI BHATTACHARYA
AMAR CHAKRAVARTI
DEOPRAKASH RAI

Notes

1. The Peking Review, 22 January 1965, hailed the new party as 'the end of the first stage of the struggle against bourgeois-reformist policies and disruptive organizational practices adopted by the Dange group'.
2. 'For three years the party had put off taking a stand on the ideological issues that divided the CPSU and the CCP; linked with these issues were the strategic-tactical lines most suitable for the CPI(M) itself . . . . The party leadership during this period had moved considerably toward the right, with equivocation on the question of peaceful or non-peaceful struggle and, finally, with a return to parliamentarism' (Sen Gupta, 1972: 324).
3. "Vest land" refers to surplus land vesting in the state. Such vest land is composed of (a) surplus land available from implementation of land ceiling legislation and (b) surplus available in the form of land already under the ownership of the state which generally is not under cultivation. Act 4 Section (1) Chapter II of the West Bengal Estates Acquisition Act passed on 5 May 1953 states: "The State Government may from time to time by notification declare that with effect from the date mentioned in the notification, all estates and the rights of every intermediary in each such estate situated in any district or part of a district specified in the notification, shall vest in the State free from all incumbrances."

   The Act at the same time imposed a ceiling on landholding. "An intermediary, however, was given the right to retain ownership of certain types of land including non-agricultural land in khas possession not exceeding 20 acres and agricultural land in khas possession not exceeding 20 acres and agricultural land in khas possession not exceeding 25 acres." (Basu, 1963:94, 8).

4. These were Kangra (Himachal Pradesh), Hoshiarpur, Jullundur, Bhatinda, Sangrur, Patiala and Rupar (Punjab); Nainital, Moradabad, Lakhimpur-Kheri and Unnao (Uttar Pradesh); Champaran, Muzaffarpur, Monghyr, Darbhanga and Singhbhum (Bihar); Darjeeling, Jalpaiguri, West Dinajpur, Maldah, Birbhum, Murshidabad, Nadia, Purulia, Burdwan, Hooghly, Howrah, 24-Parganas and Midnapore (West Bengal); Ganjam and Koraput (Orissa); Goalpara (Assam); Tripura (Tripura); and East Godavari, Vishakapatnam, Krishna, West Godavari, Khammam, Warangal, Karimnagar, Nalgonda, Anantpur, Guntur and Nellore (Andhra Pradesh).
5. Mohanty provides a comprehensive list of major groupings. They are (*i*) CPI-ML (Charu-Mazumdar group, pro-Lin Piao faction); (*ii*) CPI-ML (Charu Mazumdar group, anti-Lin Piao faction); (*iii*) United CPI-ML also known as Central Committee CPI-ML (S.N. Singh-Chandrapulla Reddy group); (*iv*) Andhra Pradesh Communist Committee (Revolutionaries) (T. Nagi Reddy group); (*v*) CPI-ML Central Organising Committee (Suniti Ghosh-Sharma faction); (*vi*) Eastern India Zonal Consolidation Committee of CPI-ML; (*vii*) The Maoist Communist Centre; (*viii*) The Mukti Yuddha group; (*ix*) Unity Centre of Communist Revolutionaries of India—ML; and (*x*) Centre of Indian Communists (1977:xxi).
6. Between September 1946 and May 1947 the peasants in many parts of Bengal rose in protest against the prevailing produce rent in share-cropping. The peasants responded to the call for a revolt against the extortionate fixed rate of rent of 50 per cent of the produce (excluding charges for agricultural inputs, implements and other charges which were further deducted from the 50 per cent) by the Bengal Provincial Kisan Sabha (BPKS)—the Bengal wing of the All India Kisan Sabha (the national level peasant organisation) (Sen, 1971:4-7; Sen, 1972:36-7). The demands which the BPKS had formulated were not only confined to crop-sharing but also to wider issues involving the peasants. These were: (*i*) two-thirds share of the standing crop to the share-cropper; (*ii*) tenancy rights of the share-cropper on the land he tills; (*iii*) interest on paddy loans should not exceed 12.5 per cent; (*iv*) no other demands should be made by the landowners on the share-cropper as deductions from produce rent; (*v*) no payments of produce rent will be made without receipts; (*vi*) cultivable fallow land must be put to cultivation and (*vii*) the harvest will be stacked in the share-cropper's threshing floor and not on the landowner's (Omar, 1963:151).
7. The region along the Himalayan foothills is known as the *terai*.
8. 1 maund is equivalent to 82 pounds.
9. 1 seer is equivalent to 2 pounds.
10. A hal is that quantity of land which can be brought under cultivation with one plough. This ranged between 2 to 6.5 acres.
11. The veracity of Sanyal's claim cannot be easily doubted. There is enough evidence of frequent strikes and lockouts in tea plantations during this period. We know, for instance, that the Upper Fagu Tea Estate and the Somabeong Tea Estate were under lock-out, and the Singell Tea Estate, the Teesta Valley and Fulbaria Tea Estate, the Rangaroon Tea Estate, the Belgachi Tea Estate, the Putnibari Tea Estate, the Government Cinchona Plantations and the Runganeet Tea Estate, to

mention only a few, were constantly faced with the demands of their labour and strikes in support of their demands. The demands centered round the irregular supply of weekly rations, irregular payment of wages and on non-payment of bonus as per the government award. All these events took place between December 1966 and January 1967.

12. AIGL is the All India Gurkha League.
13. The composition of the Cabinet mission was as follows:

Name	*Party*	*Portfolio*
Hare Krishna Konar	CPI-M	Land and Land Revenue
Bishwanath Mukherji	CPI	Irrigation and Waterways
Sushil Dhara	Bangla Congress	Commerce and Industry and Community Development
Nani Bhattacharya	RSP	Health
Amar Chakravarti	FB	Law and Excise
Deoprakash Rai	AIGL	Tribal Welfare

14. In North Bengal 1 acre is 3 bighas.
15. Gherao is a type of 'arrest' in which a group of persons, having some grievance which they feel has not been heard to their satisfaction through normal channels, decides to surround and keep captive the decision-makers until some assurance regarding their grievance is given.
16. The text of the appeal has been provided in an Appendix to this paper.
17. Anchals are the first level of local self-government in the Panchayati Raj scheme in force in West Bengal.
18. The first United Front Government in West Bengal came to power on 2nd March 1967 and fell on 21st November 1967. The second United Front government came to power on 24th February 1969 and fell on 16th March 1970 with the resignation of the Chief Minister Ajoy Mukherji.
19. Actually it is not very clear whether two or four persons were killed in the encounter. Both the figures are from separate government reports. Field data suggests that the figure is four killed. However, it is certain that the figure ranges between two and four.
20. It is alleged that the guerilla squads that operated amongst the peasants, while their leaders were in prison, sought to discredit the leadership of Kanu Sanyal labelling him and his group revisionists.
21. Phansidewa, it may be noted, is within walking distance from NBU.
22. INTUC (Indian National Trade Union Congress) is the trade union led by the Congress Party.
23. *Garibi* means poverty.
24. The theory of elites suggests that persons occupying the highest indices in their branches of activity are the elites, and they occupy such positions because of their superior abilities and merits (Pareto, 1935:1433). Thus, society needs elites—the organized and competent minority—to rule the masses who apparently cannot be so organized (Bottomore, 1971:31). The catch in such theories lie in the following problems: (*i*) the 'merits' of those in elite

positions do not necessarily correlate with excellence (i.e., the occupant of a privileged position need not be the most competent); (*ii*) the positions requiring the greatest competence are not necessarily the most privileged positions (e.g., an engineer is less privileged than an administrator and more privileged than a school teacher); and (*iii*) the very definitions of competence, and the attendant rewards that go with it, are based on value preferences which are constrained by structural realities (e.g., a school teacher's role is devalued although he is society's prime socializer). Such theories stipulate a circulation of elites from the masses to the non-governing elite, and from there to the governing elite, without which there will be discontent and the possibility of a revolution (Mosca, 1939:337). But recruitment from the masses is always a trickle compared with the torrent from amongst the elites (Miller, 1960:895; Wence, 1969). Pathy makes an excellent study of the elite-class relationship which has been ignored in elite studies and class studies alike (1977).

25. Another important theoretical dimension of social movements that needs to be explored empirically is the 'surfacing' of latent structures in the wake of a conflict in the movement dimension. Societal structures in ongoing systems are manifest and can be mapped at any time during the existence of such systems. Social movements provide a context of conflict in which the structures are in a different configuration. With the ebb of the movement or its termination such structures may not be 'visible'. The contradictions between the manifest and latent structures would indicate the direction of change. However, such an analysis has to await further research.
26. In this sense the Sarvodaya concept of *gramdan* in its original formulation was revolutionary as it replaced private ownership of the means of production with the collective ownership of the *gramdan* community.
27. It is necessary to distinguish between oppression and exploitation. It is possible for a system to be exploitative, as most systems indeed are, and yet not all those who are in a position to exploit need be oppressive. Exploitation is an objective definition of a system of asymmetrical exchange, whereas oppression lies in the articulation of power to punish, to inflict injury, even arbitrarily, to maintain one's political superiority. In fact, it is precisely because exploitation and oppression do not easily coterminate that mobilization against changing an exploitative system is so difficult. Often it is far less difficult to mobilize against oppression than against exploitation.

Acknowledgement

In 1973 the Center for the Study of Social Systems, Jawaharlal Nehru University, initiated the Movements Study Programme in which several members of the Faculty elected to study certain movements. The present study has been in the making since then. Realizing that proper justice to such research cannot be done unless the enquiry was taken to the level of field investigation, the Indian Council of Social Science Research kindly granted my request for a fellowship so that I could pursue full time research. Therefore, thanks are due both to the Council and the Center for making this work possible. For research of this nature to be objective, the cooperation of the Home Ministry is absolutely vital. In full realization of this they have kindly extended their cooperation particularly at the level of the states. I am more than grateful to the simple peasants, activists and officials in various administrative hierarchies for the trust they have reposed in me. I only hope that by a truthful projection of the reality I shall prove worthy of their trust. I realize that in many ways Amit Gupta's assistance has become a necessary condition for the conduct of this research. I thank him and look forward to his continued cooperation. For providing me with efficient secretarial assistance, ever cheerfully, I thank A.N. Kunjunny. Finally, I am grateful to Goparani Mukherji for her quiet contribution as a perennial source of mental and moral strength to me.

References

BADEN-POWELL (1892): *The Land Systems of British India.* Vol. 1. Oxford: The Clarendon Press.

BASU, S.K. and S.K. BHATTACHARYA (1963): *Land Reforms in West Bengal.* New Delhi: Oxford Book Company.

BOTTOMORE, T.B. (1971): *Elites and Society.* Harmondsworth: Penguin Books Ltd.

CENSUS OF INDIA (1971): Series 22, *West Bengal.* Part X—A+B. Directorate of Census Operation, Government of West Bengal.

DISTRICT CENSUS HANDBOOK (1973): *Darjeeling.* Calcutta: Government Press.

DASGUPTA, BIPLAB (1974): *The Naxalite Movement.* Calcutta: Allied Publishers.

DESHABHARTI (1970): Broadcast made on 2 April. Reproduced in *Special issue on Lenin Centenary*, 23 April.

HUNTER, W.W. (1974): *A Statistical Account of Bengal.* Vol. X. New Delhi: D.K. Publishing House.

MILLER, S.M. (1960): 'Comparative Social Mobility', *Current Sociology.* IX(1), p. 895.

MOHANTY, MANORANJAN (1977): *Revolutionary Violence*. New Delhi: Sterling Publishers Pvt. Ltd.

MOSCA, G. (1939): *The Ruling Class*. New York: McGraw Hill.

MUKHERJI, PARTHA N. (1977): 'Social Movement and Social Change'. *Sociological Bulletin*. Vol. 26(1), (March), pp. 38-58.

OMAR, O.B. (1963): *Chirasthayee Bandobabaste Bengal Krishak* (Jaista 1370, in Bengal). Dacca: Maola Brothers.

OOMMEN, T.K. (1977): 'Sociological Issues in the Analysis of Social Movements'. *Sociological Bulletin*. Vol. 26(1) (March), pp. 14-37.

PARETO, V. (1935): *The Mind and Society*. Vol. 3. London: Jonathan Cape.

PATHY, JAGANATH (1977): 'Political Elite of Orissa'. Unpublished Ph.D. dissertation. Jawaharlal Nehru University, New Delhi.

PEKING RADIO (1970): 'Sashastra Saktir Madhyame Rajnaitik Khamata Dakhaler Bijopathe Bharatiya Janganke Agiye Nichchen'. Broadcast made on 2 April. Reproduced in *Deshabrati*. Special issue on Lenin Centenary, 23 April.

RAM, MOHAN (1969): *Indian Communism: Split within Split*. New Delhi: Vikas.

ROY, ASHIS K. (1975): *The Spring Thunder and After*. Calcutta: Minerva Associates (Pvt.) Ltd.

SANYAL, KANU, *et al*. (1972): *Mainstream*. Vol. XI(8). 21 October, pp. 133-34.

— ——(1974): 'More About Naxalbari'. *Proletarian Path*. May-August, Vol. II, Nos. 4 and 5, pp. 21-27.

——————(1968): 'Report on the Peasant Movement in the Terai Region'. *Deshabrati*. 14 October.

SEN, SUNIL (1972): *Agrarian Struggle in Bengal, 1946-47*. New Delhi: Peoples' Publishing House.

SEN, SATYEN (1971): *Gram Banglar Pathe Pathe*. Calcutta: Vishwabani Prakashan (in Bengali).

SEN, GUPTA BHABANI (1972): *Communism in Indian Politics*. New York: Columbia University Press.

WENCE, R. (1969): 'Electoral Participation and the Occupational Composition of Cabinets and Parliament'. *American Journal of Sociology*. Vol. 75(2) (September), pp. 181-192.

WILSON, JOHN (1973): *Introduction to Social Movements*. New York: Basic Books.

3

Rajendra Singh

Peasant Movements in Uttar Pradesh: A Study in the Politics of Land and Land Control in Basti District, 1801-1970[1]

Introduction

THE PART THAT collective actions, through conflict and opposition, rebellion and revolt, have played in bringing about radical social changes in various aspects of society has been a relatively neglected field of sociological study (Coser, 1956:197; Gurr, 1970:ix; Dahrendorf, 1959:159; Gusfield, 1970:vii; Killian, 1964:226). Further, the peasants' potential for protest and uprisings has suffered from even greater neglect. The latter specifically relates to the prophet of revolution, Karl Marx, who found both European (Marx, 1971: 229-31) and Indian peasantry (Marx, *New York Daily Tribune:* 25 June 1853) perenially resigned and apathetic to injustice and quiscent to oppression and exploitation.

However, this most pervasive, persistent and largest section of human population, whom Marx attributed passivity to and at whom he sneered for being devoid of revolutionary power and dubbed them as a 'sack of potatoes' (Marx, 1971:231), gained revolutionary status in the writings of Lenin (1970:502), Mao (1954:21) and Fanon (1974:47). Historians' data concerning India (Habib, 1963:333-38) have demonstrated the fact that Marx's contemptuous characterization of the Indian peasant was historically false.

The capacity of peasants to organise against societal opposition and repressive political measures, and to rebel and revolt against injustice, oppression and an exploitative social order has become an inescapable reality. A large number of studies, consequently, have examined the role of peasant protests in relation to social change and development. (Moore, Jr., 1967:x; Landsberger, 1974:ix; Shanin, 1971:11-14, & 1973:39-40; Wolf, 1971:xi). Among the third world societies, peasant uprisings are becoming more acute (Worsely, 1964: 119-70; Shanin, 1973:42). Peasant movements, uprisings and revolts have come to be treated as consequences of the process of modernization (Pye, 1964:163-65; Moore Jr., 1967:453; Hobsbawm, 1973: 3-6) which began after these societies had thrown over their colonial past.

In India, while peasant uprisings were not rare during the late Mughal period (Habib, 1963:340-41 & 346; Nehru, 1945:319), their frequency and intensity increased with the increasing rate of politicization of the peasants. They reached their height around and after Independence in 1947. The peasant movements of Telangana during 1946-51 (Sundarayya:1972), Tebhaga in Bengal during 1946-47 (Sen:1971), Naxalbari which began in 1967 (Das Gupta:1974), and the land-grab movement of 1970 (Singh:1974), have not yet come to an end. However, there is need for a systematic classification and definition of peasant movements. For, in the absence of such classification, any field study on the subject will suffer from want of validity and reliability. Hence, before I present my data on peasant movements in Uttar Pradesh, I shall deal with the problem of classification.

Peasant Movements in India: The Problem of Classification and Definition

Relying solely on empirical rationality, science is an attempt at a systematic causal explanation of phenomena. One of the cardinal principles of science and scientific inquiry is its emphasis on classification. It is through the categorization and classification of phenomena—otherwise in a state of chaos—that a scientist seeks to delimit his field of inquiry and to add shreds and patches of reality into an orderly system. Definition can be seen only as an extension and outcome of the process of classification.

This rule of science has been bypassed by some social historians (for example, Malaviya, 1956:184) as well as social scientists (for example, Gough, 1974: 1391-92). In their attempt to present an account of peasant movements and uprisings in India, they have shown an indiscriminate zeal in lumping together almost all types of collective mobilizations involving protest, rebellion and revolt into an all-inclusive category of peasant uprisings.

The questions and issues arising thereof, which bear directly upon such a tendency, will hopefully help in solving the problem of the classification and definition of the subject as indicated below:

1. What were the foci of protest and conflict? This question pertains to the issue of locating the axial factors—such as, land and its produce, communal, religious, cultural and political factors—around which mobilization took place.
2. Who were the participants in such mobilization? Which section or sections of a community were they drawn from? This relates to agrarian categories of small cultivators and agricultural labourers on the one hand and the erstwhile rent and revenue collecting class of rajas, talukdars and zamindars on the other. Socio-territorial categories of tribe and other ethnic groups among the Hindus and Muslims are also crucially related to this question.
3. Finally, against which group or class of society, or against which societal institution, was the conflict launched?

A study of the foci, the participation and the target provides sufficient bases for distinguishing peasant movements from other types of movements in society.

Gough (1974:1391) defines peasants as 'people who engage in agriculture or related production with primitive means and who surrender part of their produce . . . to landlords or to agents of state'. Implicit in this definition is the 'underdog position or peasantry who have a relation of subservience to the state of intermediary landlords. In India, the latter constitute the class of rajas, talukdars and zamindars, who stand out as a distinct category separate from the category of peasant. The separating line is the nature of ownership of and control over the land and its produce.

By keeping in view the foci of the movement, the nature of the composition of its participants and the target against which it was launched, we will not only be able to narrow the scope of our study but will also be in a position to separate much of the chaff which abounds in the reporting of peasant movements and uprisings in India. An examination of a few instances will illustrate our point.

Malaviya (1956:183-84) treats the Hindu Satnami movement, which had a purely sectarian focus, as a peasant uprising. The tribal rebellion of the Santals is characterized by both Malaviya and Gough as a rebellion of the peasantry. In this case, the socio-territorial categories of tribe and village have been merged without any statement of the principle of resemblance. Violating the rule of participation, Gough pushes the nativistic movements of Raja Chait Singh of Oudh and Vizier Ali of Gorakhpur during 1778-81 and 1799 respectively into the category of peasant movements. Similarly, Gough (1974:1391) and a few historians (Habib, 1975:36; Chaudhry, 1957:32) treat the Mutiny of 1857 as a peasant uprising *par excellence*.

In the erstwhile state of Agra and Oudh, the 1857 Mutiny was a raja's and zamindar's movement which was launched against the British on account of their revenue exaction policy. The data from Aligarh (Stokes, 1970:20) as well as from Basti amply substantiate the apprehension expressed above. As in the case of Stokes' study, in Basti too it is found that the Mutiny rebels were only the rani, raja and thakur zamindars of the district. Rani Jugatraj Kunwar, widow of Raja Jang Bahadur Singh of Amorha (Government of India, 1907:92), Raja Udai Pratap Singh of the Nagar estates and the Thakurs of Bakhira were the ones who revolted against the continuation of British administration. Their estates and property and those of their kinsmen were confiscated. Some of them committed suicide and others were hanged by the British. Thus, the rebellion of the rajas, ranis and thakurs can hardly be called a peasant movement.

Gough's attempt (1974:1399) to search for an European model of banditry (Hobsbawm: 1959) in the institution of thuggee in India is too far-fetched in relevance as well as in application. Similarly, the fifty-one Moplah communal outbreaks, which took place over a century from 1821 to 1921, have been listed to add to the statistics of upsurgencies of Indian peasants (Malaviya, 1957:183-84; Gough, 1974:1397). Sitaramayya, a Congress Party historian, states on the contrary, 'The Moplahs were guilty of acts of compulsory conversion (of Hindus), looting of *Hindus*, arson and murder . . . (emphasis mine, Sitaramayya, 1946:220). For him, the Moplah revolts were Muslim communal uprisings (1946:1294). The communal fanaticism of the Moplahs, which remained a consistent and overriding factor in all the Moplah outbreaks, is further supported by an enthnographer (Miller, 1976:109) on the basis of his field data. All the fifty-one rebellions of the Moplahs exhibited the following tendencies: (*a*) to become *shahid* (religious martyr); (*b*) to go to (Muslim) shrines for blessings; (*c*) to attack Hindu families and destroy their temples; and, finally, (*d*) to express the belief that death in the cause of the faith (Islam) brought a blessed end.

How can a movement consisting of only Moplah Muslims attacking only Hindu families, their temples and property in an effort .o become *shahid* in the expansion of the Islamic faith be treated as a peasant movement?

Thus far we have shown that the efforts of certain Marxists to treat all types of protests and revolts as peasant movements are not accurate. Our purpose in the formulation of questions and issues regarding peasant movements was twofold. One was to highlight the methodological difficulties of classification, which, as illustrated above, challenges the validity of most studies of peasant movements. The second purpose is to pinpoint indices and criteria for typifying peasant movements as a genera distinct from other movements in general. The latter purpose can best be served by spelling out the sense in which the term 'peasant' and the concept 'peasant movement' are being employed in this study as also by indicating the method of the study.

Concepts and Method

In our study of peasant movements in Uttar Pradesh, with a special focus on Basti district, the term 'peasant' will exclude the following two sections of society: (*a*) The erstwhile rent and revenue collecting class of rajas, talukdars and zamindars, who were generally related to the peasant by ownership relations rather than by productive relations; and (*b*) the class of traders whose main source of subsistence is the purchase and sale of rural commodities rather than direct involvement in land and agriculture.

The nearest local equivalent of the term 'peasant' is kisan and khetihar mazdoor in Uttar Pradesh, and we can residually identify the following categories of population as belonging to this section:

1. All the ex-tenant cultivators who were paying rent or revenue to zamindars because they had inferior proprietory rights over the land they tilled before the abolition of the class of intermediaries.
2. All the khetihar mazdoors (agricultural labourers) who either have no land or have such small holdings that they cannot support themselves and, as such, are compelled to work on others' land on a daily wage.
3. Most of the village artisans, like lohar (ironsmith) barhi (carpenter), nai (barber), dhobi (washerman), etc., who, on the basis of the local norms of jajmani get a share, known as *mandi* (a twenty-fourth part of a bigha)[2] crop or land to cultivate in exchange for the services they render to other sections of the rural population.
4. Finally, it will include the most numerous section of rajas, talukdars and zamindars who have suffered a loss of land ownership and a radical reduction in their control over land on account of the abolition of zamindari in 1952. A rent and revenue collecting class has, in general, become a cultivating class with small land-holdings.

These indices for the exclusion from and inclusion in the category of peasants (kisans) have been evolved primarily in view of the existing agro-social situation in Basti and adjoining districts of eastern Uttar Pradesh. Local, regional and national variations in tenurial systems and agrarian relations are so far and wide apart that at the present stage of our limited knowledge about them it will do more harm than good in terms of a scientific enquiry to fence a community into the close confines of a definition. Hence, the above indices will be used only, to borrow Gusfield's phrase (1970:4), as 'road signs pointing to a direction. . . .'

We define a 'peasant movement' as a *relatively organized and continuous collective action involving violence, or the threat of violence, for securing more share in the control or ownership of land and its produce and to abolish injustices which have arisen thereof*, and which involves kisans and khetihar mazdoors as defined above. We recognize that kisans and khetihar mazdoors, who make up the category of peasants, do not make peasantry a homogeneous category. Indeed, they stand at variance with each other in the agrarian social structure of Basti. However, both of them share a common interest in securing a greater share in the control and ownership of land and its produce.

The term 'control' is not used here as a synonym of the term 'ownership', as some scholars are apt to do (Frykenberg: 1969:xiv), nor do we use it to avoid technical difficulties as suggested by a few social scientists (Kumar, 1972:63). Instead we use it explicitly to cover the following situations.

First, there are instances of concealed land holdings wherein the owner is a dummy on the patwari's (village land record keeper) *khasra* (land record file), while the land is actually held, controlled and tilled by someone else. The purpose of such concealment is to defeat the implementation of ceiling on land holding, through *niwasa* (inheritance of ownership of land by a married daughter at the death of her parents who had no male issue). Here the land is actually controlled and cultivated by members of the family of orientation of the daughter. Secondly, there are instances where ownership over pasture, pond and *dahar* (bullock cart track land) is joint among the maliks but is actually controlled by one or a few of them. Maliks, who will be discussed in detail later, were the traditional landlords in Basti. The term 'injustice' along with other descriptive terms used above, shall be explained in detail in subsequent sections of this paper.

The problem of method in science is logically linked with the problem of study and the nature of its subject matter. In order to bring the latter into sharp focus, we intend to identify two analytically different but empirically interdependent sets of variables which materially bear upon the description, analysis and explanation of peasant movements in Basti. Following Eckstein (1964:4-5) the first set of variables refer to structural situations. This will involve an examination of caste/class relationships with the corresponding mode of agrarian relations in a dynamic perspective. A crucial element in such an examination is the study of the system of land control and its ownership. Since the situations which prevailed in Basti district during the thirties had roots in the past, we shall draw data covering a period from 1801 to 1970 to show the ramifications, these categories underwent in Uttar Pradesh in general and in Basti in particular.

The second set of variables refers to processes which may or may not have logical connections with the first set, but which emerge and operate as collective actions. The manifestation of collective actions in Basti varied from sporadic protests and violent rebellions to relatively more organized, sustained and continuous movement of Nijai Bol (declaring ownership over malik's land) and land-grab. I have discussed the latter movement in detail elsewhere (Singh, 1974) and I will only refer to it here for purposes of analysis and comparison. A historico-sociological analysis of the above mentioned movements materially bear upon their linkage and correlation to two sets of variables. These variables are the culture of inequality and the process of politicization. We shall apply Stuart Mill's logical method of agreement and difference in a historically comparative perspective. The question is why the peasants during 1801-1930, when the relative oppression was high, remained quiscent, but when the oppressions started declining during 1930-1970, they became upsergent. We can look at it as an encounter between—two cultural forces—traditional culture of inequality and the modern culture of equality. While the traditional leadership buttressed the former, the modern political elite helped promote the latter.

Keeping in view the broad outline stated above, we shall employ historiographic methods to reconstruct the structural situation. (For sociologists, historiographic materials are important only to the extent that they illumine behavioural data drawn from field studies concerning existing situations.) We therefore use both historical as well as field study methods in our inquiry. Much of the data collection was carried out during one year's field investigation in Basti district in the late sixties. Subsequently, intermittent visits to the field have helped in recording the sequence, processes and modalities of change. References to cases of peasant unrest in other parts of Uttar Pradesh will be presented only for contextual purposes. We start our analysis by presenting below some relevant facts concerning Basti district.

Basti: Some Salient Features

In 1801, the Nawab Wazir of Oudh surrendered a part of his territory to the East India Company. This part was referred to as the 'Ceded Districts'. Gorakhpur, the parent district of Basti, was one such Ceded District (Government of India, 1907:68-155). The districts of Bundelkhand division were known as 'Conquered Districts'. Ceded and Conquered Districts made up the erstwhile North-Western Provinces of the East India Company. The tenurial status of the districts of the above Province was different from some of the remaining parts of Oudh which remained under the Nawab. The latter had the system of talukdari tenure. In 1856, the Company annexed the remaining territory of the Nawab of Oudh. The state of the United Provinces of Agra and Oudh was the product of an amalgamation of the North-Western Provinces and Oudh which took place in 1902 (Neale, 1962:13).

Basti became an independent district, distinct from the district of Gorakhpur, in 1865. Basti is bounded by the districts of Gorakhpur and Gonda in the East and West respectively. The kingdom of Nepal lies on the North and the river Sarju divides it in the South from the district of Faizabad. It has six tehsils—Basti, Harriya, Khalelabad, Domarisganj, Bensi and Naugarh. At present it has a population of 26,27,061 living in an area of 2,821 sq. miles. Consequently, there is a very high density of population in Basti. As against an average of 648 persons per sq. mile for the state of Uttar Pradesh as a whole, this district has 926 persons in the same area (Government of India, 1961:21). Its only town, Basti, is the administrative headquarters of the district. Being predominantly a rural district, 95.5 per cent of its population lives in 7,653 villages. Basti is a typical agrarian society. 91 per cent of its population subsists directly upon agriculture and agricultural employment.

In terms of religious composition, Hindus account for 81.00 per cent and Muslims for 18.00 per cent of the population. Other communities (the Sikhs, Christians and others) form 1.00 per cent (Government of India, 1961:522-23). While its territorial and total cultivatable area remained by and large static, its population had shot up by 62 per cent by the end of the sixties compared to 1901, leading to a tremendous pressure on land. The scheduled castes, who account for 20.1 per cent of the population (Government of India, 1965:viii), are mostly agricultural labourers. Despite the fact that Mahatma Gandhi and Jawahar Lal Nehru paid their first visit to Basti in 1919, the District Congress Party was formally established only in 1920. The situation of animation remained till around 1930 when local educated youths, under the growing influence of Mahatma Gandhi, entered the Congress Party. The second visit of the Mahatma in 1935 invigorated and strengthened its organization. The Congress by that time had become an agent of the down-trodden in Basti.

Against this background of bare facts and figures, we shall attempt first to describe and then analyse the data on the structural situation of Basti.

Social Structure in the Colonial Situation: Caste, Class and Land Control

During the colonial period (1801-1947), the social structure of Basti corresponded, by and large, to the structure of land relationship. The placement of individuals and groups in the status hierarchy of castes, generally overlapped with and corresponded to their class hierarchy. Caste as an institution based upon the concept of inherited inequalities of power and privilege, purity and pollution, gave rise to a still greater inequality in the distribution of material resources (Singh, 1974:47). High and low caste divisions in Basti ran parallel to the high and low access of groups and individuals to control over land and water resources. Since caste and class groupings coincided with each other during the colonial period, we shall deduce classes from their caste base for analytical purposes. We are doing so with the full awareness that, as opposed to the relative permanence of castes, classes in Basti have been found to have an episodic origin and die with the death of the issues around which they emerge (Singh, 1974:68). The field data generated by Yogendra Singh (1970:63; 1968:165-86) relating to a village of Basti district, lead him to a similar conclusion in regard to caste and class as categories for sociological analysis.

The easily discernable classes were the maliks, who were lords of the land, and the Prajas who were subjects of the landlords. We shall portray the position of each of the two classes in relation to land, and the way these relations underwent changes in the direction of agrarian modernization, i.e., towards the slow re-distribution of land in favour of many rather than its concentration in the hands of a few during subsequent periods of British rule in Basti. In doing so, we intend to demonstrate the nature of contradictions that existed between property relations and production relations, and the way these contradictions underwent a sea-change over time, especially after Independence. The Muslim population, which belonged to the class of prajas, will be discussed at appropriate places as their ethnicity reflected upon the situation of agrarian unrest in a specific way in Basti.

THE MALIKS

Between 1801 and 1842, the class of maliks, consisted primarily of Rajput rajas and Thakur zamindars. Both belonged to the Kshatriya (warrior) caste. In most cases, a raja was the clan-head of the Thakurs in Basti. The Census of 1901 divides them into twenty-four exogamous clans. The dynastic clans were the Suryavanshis, Sarnets, Kalhansas and the Gautamas (Morgan, 1901). The chiefs of these clans were known as rajas (Government of India, 1907:78 & 142-54). In the absence of the rule of primogeniture in the region of East Uttar Pradesh, the rajas and their kinsmen used to have the same type of proprietory rights over land. Most of the clans came from far off places and suplanted the aboriginal population of bhars, tharus, doms and domkatars (Government of India, 1907:144) and established their control over land, ponds, rivers and forests. The non-dynastic Rajput zamindars, like other kinsmen of the rajas, were either zamindars or held birta (grant) from them in return for their soldierly services.

The division of land and its resources within the clans and caste of Rajputs was based upon the systems of zamindari, pattidari, and *bhaichara*. In Basti, the three systems operated together. As shown in Table 1, the proprietory rights of land in Basti towards the close of the nineteenth century was concentrated, with a few exceptions, in the hands of one caste, which made up the class of maliks.

Table 1

NATURE OF PROPRIETORY RIGHTS BY NUMBER OF VILLAGES IN BASTI IN THE BRITISH COLONIAL PERIOD

	Single Proprietorship	*Joint Zamindari*	*Pattidari*	*Bhaichara*	*Revenue Free and Others*	*Total*
No. of Villages	786	1451	5254	10	137	7638

SOURCE: Government of India, 1907:86-116.

In actual practice, the distinction between the zamindari and pattidari villages was not maintained, as the pattidari system, along with *bhaichara*, emerged out of the system of zamindari as a result of the portioning of property and dissension among families (Neale, 1962:41). Being based on the concept of joint ownership by a clan, these systems were in effect the same. The caste of Rajputs, who accounted for only 3.12 per cent of the population (Government of India, 1907:78) in 1901, made up the class of maliks and exercised almost absolute control over land and its produce during that period. The actual production was carried out by the prajas, but the latter had no proprietory rights in land.

The power structure was based upon the capacity of the caste to control land. As land was a formidable instrument for the control of people and communities, the rajas of dynastic origin or influential Thakurs belonging to non-dynastic clans used to act as centres of an influence-zone, around whom their clan members (collaterals), in alliance with other clans through affinal relationships, used to gather thus creating a large area of influence which they maintained by reinforcing each other's power. Kinship ties produced tentacles which tenaciously held Basti peasants fast under their grip.

Holt Mackenzie, who was the Secretary of the Board of Commissioners, North-western Provinces during 1818-1820, writes: 'Nothing but violence appears to have disturbed the tenure of the village zamindars; neither the furthest exile, nor the longest absence, dissolved the tie that bound them to the field of their ancestors, nor destroyed their right to resume possession when they returned.' He further comments: 'In almost all the districts the largest proportion of land belonged indisputably to village zamindars . . . .' (cited in Government of India, 1948: Vol. I:83). Powerful as they were, the class of Rajput maliks, sitting on top of the sharply conical social pyramid of Basti, exercised the following types of controls, firstly, over land and its produce and, secondly, through the land, over the class of prajas.

The Traditional System of Land Control

To begin with, the maliks exercised the exclusive right to sell, purchase and mortgage of land.

Second, no one could cultivate the land or make use of it in any way without the permission of the malik and he retained the right to evict the cultivator from the land at any time, at his wish.

Third, all the *banjjar* (wasteland), *usar* (alkaline land), *abadi* (village land) and *charagah* (pastures) were made available to others only by the consent of the malik.

Finally, forests, ponds and ferries were directly under the hold of the malik. This, and the third point listed above, provided *savar* (peripheral and supporting) income to the malik.

The general tenurial patterns and practices on which the system of land control was based in Basti were of the following types:

1. *Khud kashat* or *seer* land
2. *Patta* land
3. *Birta* land
4. Land on *malguzari* or *lagam* (tax or revenue)
5. *Adbatai* land (share-cropping land)

Seer land used to be under the direct *joi* (cultivation) of the malik's *hal* (plough). Since the malik castes observed taboo in touching the plough, they relied mainly on the local system of *bhataits*. The *bhatait* system was a traditional mechanism for economic symbiosis in Basti. According to this system, the chamar families living on the *abadi* land of a malik pooled all their labour force to cultivate the malik's land and in return received one-sixth of the agricultural produce from each harvest. The *patta* system, on the other hand, involved cash or cattle exchange between the malik and the pattedar (holder of the lease). In Basti, *patta* was usually given only to the members of one's own clan or near affinal relations.

The *seer* land and the *patta* land were lands of the malik which used to be directly under his plough or control. Land was made available to the class of prajas on the basis of *birta*, *malguzari* and *adbatai* types of tenurial patterns.

Birta (grant) was made to any other caste and family in return for services. This was exercised generally in favour of Brahmin and fellow Rajput castes. Brahmins, being priests, teachers and councillors to the maliks, used to get village or land grants from the maliks in return for their services. The same was given to the Rajputs in appreciation of their soldierly or administrative services. The holders of such grants were known as *birtiyas* of a particular malik family or of his clan. With the exception of the Brahmin families of Jagdishpur, Kalayanpur and Belbharia in Harriya tehsil, who received land directly from the Imperial Muslim rulers, nearly the entire population of Brahmins in Basti (11.31 per cent) were either Rajputs, *birtiyas* or just simple *assami* or prajas. Like any other group from the class of prajas, the *birtiyas* too had to pay *malikana* (tax due to the malik).

Adbatai was based on the practice of the malik and the cultivator sharing the harvest equally. The difference between *bhatait* and *adbatai* was that in the former case the maliks put in all the investments in the form of seeds, manure, plough, etc., while in the case of the latter it was done by the cultivator. Secondly, *adbatais* usually belonged to caste Hindu groups unlike the *bhataits* who predominantly belonged to the exterior caste of chamars in Basti. *Malguzari* or *lagan* land remained with the caste Hindu or Muslim cultivators who paid a fixed revenue to the malik in return for the right to cultivate the land. This right, however, was subject to the approval of the malik.

Uncultivated land—like *usar*, *banjjar*, *charagah* and *abadi* land—were given to the prajas for such use as grazing and herding of cattle and *khaliham* (threshing floor) in return for a fixed amount of milk, *charwahi* (grazing the cattle of malik free of any charge) and *begar* (unpaid labour). *Abadi* land was given for house-sites. Any one who grew *singara* (water-nut) in the pond or vegetables on its banks had to surrender half the produce to the malik. Similarly, there was a tax on crossing the river and one had to pay ferry charges for doing so.

In addition to the above, there used to be a ritualized subsidiary system of economic exactions of praja by the maliks. This was not like the system of malikana, which referred to the wide practice of payment to the lord by the subject in a secular sense as the latter tilled or used the lord's land. There seems to have been an element of economic rationality in the system of malikana. But the subsidiary practices which involved economic factors were predominantly ritualized and an element of religion was added to them. Among these subsidiary practices were *biahu* which refers to a payment in cash or kind to the malik whenever a daughter in the malik's family gets married; *hathiahi* and *ghorahi*, which refer to a practice of making payment to the malik at the time he purchases an elephant or a horse; and *pujahi* which involved making a contribution to any religious function that the malik may hold.

Thus, in the total economic sphere of the land-based community of Basti, the malik enjoyed an all pervasive influence and appeared to have unbridled power to demand a share in the produce of the prajas. In practice, therefore, control over land also meant control over people.

During the earlier half of the nineteenth century, despite all that we have described above concerning the different types of exactions, there was not a single recorded case of peasant protest or uprising against the maliks in Basti. On the contrary, the maliks were exalted by the prajas as their *sarkar* (law-incarnate), *deo-bhagwan* (God-incarnate) and *mai-baap* (parents). The explanation for this lies in the presence of an active and specific type of culture —the culture of inequality, which we shall discuss later.

Based upon the traditionally accepted concept of hierarchy, established and reinforced by the culture of inequality, the social harmony between the classes of maliks and prajas underwent a change after 1842. In the beginning, the changes were seemingly slow and relatively imperceptible. They were, however, effective in sowing the seeds which led to far-reaching consequences in Basti during the twentieth century.

It is historically false and factually misleading to blame the British for the creation of a class of maliks (the intermediary class) in India. On the contrary, all revenue policies adopted in Basti and land settlement acts enacted by the British, were essentially anti-malik in nature. These policies and leglslations not only materially affected the traditional tenurial structure of the district but also initiated a process which attacked the Rajput maliks' monopoly over land and people.

During the first three years (1801-03) of the British occupation of Basti, its revenue system was based on the talukdari pattern, wherein the maliks paid a fixed lumpsum amount to the British. In 1803, this netted a total of Rs. 2,26,660. In 1889 the revenue from the district was Rs. 19,91,195 (Government of India, 1907:115-20). This increase of approximately ten times was possible only on account of a change in agrarian policy. A brief review of this policy will illustrate the point.

The temporary Land Settlements of 1803, 1806 and 1809 reduced the revenue-free villages in the possession of the maliks, and levied increased taxes upon them. The revenue demands were becoming so oppressive, that at some places the maliks started quitting their villages (Government, of India 1907:23). The most significant attack, however, came from the Fifth Land Settlement Act of 1842. This Act cut off the tenurial nexus of superordination and subordination that existed between the *birta*-holders (grantees) of the class of prajas and the Rajput rajas and zamindars who were their grantors. This was done by upgrading the inferior tenurial position of the *birtiyas* which brought them on par with the traditional tenurial rights enjoyed by the maliks.

Stokes (1970:26) noted the same process in various districts in Western Uttar Pradesh. The net impact of this act was the broadening of the too narrow apex of the social pyramid of Basti which expanded to accommodate the Brahmin caste of *birtiyas* among the maliks and which had hitherto been peopled only by the caste of Rajputs. The rate of expansion of the class of maliks is actually also an index of the rate by which Rajput power over land and people decreased. The rise of mahants (Brahmin priests) to the class of maliks was at the cost of the Rajputs who alone had so far enjoyed the privilege of being maliks.

While the Settlement Act of 1842 devalued the status of maliks by creating more maliks, the acts of 1889 and 1929 reduced the control of the maliks over the prajas. In 1889, the cultivators, who were generally from the lower middle castes, were given inevictable occupancy rights over the land under their cultivation. In Basti, they were made *dhakhilkars* and *pokhetedars* and had to pay only a fixed revenue to the maliks.

Two tendencies are clearly discernable: First, there was a dilution of the class of zamindars with the creation of more zamindars from other castes where there were previously only a few belonging to the Rajput caste only. Secondly, there was an ascendancy of a secure lower middle caste peasantry with occupancy rights as *dhakhilkars* or *pokhetedars*. Both the tendencies were the outcome of the British revenue and agrarian policies. However, enormous disparities existed between the class of maliks consisting of the two highest castes—the Rajputs and the Brahmins—on the one hand, and the remaining castes on the other. In 1901, the extent of the land disparity was as given in Table 2.

While previously no other castes except the Rajputs were maliks, the British promoted the Brahmins so that they shared the power of zamindari control over land and people along with the Rajputs. Similarly, while previously the peasants had no tenurial security

Table 2

LAND DISPARITY BY CASTE GROUPS

Caste Groups	*No. of Castes*	*Percentage of Population to the Total Population of the District*	*Percentage of the Agricultural Land Owned*
UPPER CASTES	2	14.4	64
OTHER HINDU CASTES AND MUSLIMS	63	85.6	36

SOURCE: Government of India, 1907:88.

except the one which rested on the good wishes of the malik, the British snatched at least 36 per cent of the agricultural land in Basti (Charan Singh, 1959:67)—and 33 to 40 per cent in Uttar Pradesh in general—from the maliks in favour of creating a secure peasantry (Government of India, 1948:603). The British carried their egalitarian agrarian policies further and abolished in 1929 the tenurial institutions of tenants-at-will and delinked such peasants from the will of the malik by making their tenure (such as that of the *dakhilkars*) secure and unevictable.

THE PRAJAS

Subordinate as they were for land and livelihood to the maliks, the traditional position of the prajas corresponded to the general underdog position of peasantry elsewhere (Shanin, 1971:17). In Basti, 'peasantry' refers to the categories of cultivating ex-tenants and agricultural labourers who belonged to the general class of prajas (see Table 3). In comparison to the nature of peasantry in other societies, the uniqueness of the peasantry in Uttar Pradesh in general, and in Basti in particular, lies in the extent to which they are internally divided. The Hindu principle of hierarchy differentiated, and still continues to differentiate, the peasantry by setting them apart in numerous capsules of castes that are arranged neatly and vertically, one upon the other, in the social structure. Considerations like high and low, superior and inferior in terms of purity and pollution, ritual status and proximity to upper caste groups are reflected in the structure of Hindu peasantry which is unparalleled anywhere in the world with regard to its internal divisions.

Table 3

DISTRIBUTION OF THE HINDU POPULATION BY THEIR CASTE STATUS, CLASS AND OCCUPATIONAL POSITION*

Class Position	*Caste Status*	*No. of Castes in the Group*	*Occupational Position*	*Per cent of the Total Hindu Population*
THE MALIKS	Upper Castes	2	Zamindar Landlords	14.45
THE PRAJA	(*a*) Middle Castes	8	Trade and Business	7.16
	(*b*) Lower Castes	38	Cultivating Ex-tenants	57.36
	(*c*) Untouchable, Exterior Castes	10	Landless Agricultural Labourers	20.43
	(*d*) Others	6	Nomads and Unspecified	0.60
TOTALS		64		100.00

SOURCE: Government of India, 1931: Vol. XVII:500-20.

* 82.56 per cent of the Hindu Caste figures are projected on the basis of the 1931 Census.

Besides the 17.4 per cent Muslim population, the Census of 1931 reports the existence of no less than 62 castes belonging to the class of prajas. Just below the upper caste maliks there were eight trading castes, like halwais, baniyas and sonars, who constituted the rural merchant group. The Kayastha caste, which was relatively more literate, provided palwani's and munshis (record-keepers) to both the government and the maliks. As prajas of the maliks, these merchants paid *gharahi* (tax for building house and opening shops) to the latter. Whenever the merchants carried on trade in the weekly bazar held on the land of the malik, they had to pay an additional tax called *tehbazaari* on each such market day.

The majority of the cultivating ex-tenants belonged to the lower caste group. They are clean and touchable caste Hindus who have closer ritual proximity to the ex-maliks. They are represented by as many as 38 different castes. Castes like ahir, kurmis, pasis, kahars kalwars, gadarias, barais, barhais, muraos, kueris, nais, kumahars, thatheras, tamotis, malis, dhobis, faquirs, lohars, korias, khiks, and a few more insignificant castes belong to this group. Numerically dominant among these castes are the ahirs and the kurmis with a population of 11.8 per cent and 8.71 per cent respectively. These two are key peasant castes and their role in relation to land and its control is central to our study. Despite the imposition of different types of exactions by the maliks as mentioned earlier, the Ahirs and kurmis survived as the two most important castes who received the maximum benefits from land reforms both during British period as well as after Independence. For, these were the castes that secured under-proprietory tenurial rights on the land after the Land Settlement Acts of 1883 and 1889 during the early part of British rule. On account of these Acts, they were the first to gain the status of *dakhilkars* and *pokhetadars* (occupancy tenants) in Basti. These two castes possessed 4 per cent of the total agricultural land in 1901 under inevictable occupancy rights. In addition they used to till land as *adbataidars* (share-croppers), tenants-at-will and also on the payment of *lagan* (revenue). It is important to note that being numerically preponderant and in a relatively better financial position, these two castes were easily able to offer *begar* on the one hand and pay taxes, like *biahu*, *hathiahi* and *ghorahi*, to the malik on the other. Their financial strength enabled them, as compared to other castes of this group, to be the real men-behind-the plough. The Land Settlement Act of 1929 further strengthened their hold on the land and equipped them potentially to reap the maximum benefits from the agrarian reforms which were implemented after Independence.

Untouchable exterior castes were the wretched of Basti in the real sense. Of the various castes of this group—like, mochis, bhangis, doms, dausadhs, koris, badhiks, bahelias, bayars and barwars—the chamars have been most preponderant in number. They alone constituted almost 17 per cent of the Hindu population (Government of of India: 1931:XVII:500). It is an unbelievable fact that the chamars, even though they were numerically stronger than the Rajputs and Brahmin maliks of the upper caste group, together owned just 29 acres of land in the entire district in 1901. The severity of the structural polarity which existed between the maliks and the chamars, bhangis and other untouchables of this group can be summed up in one sentence: They were persona non-grata in relation to the caste Hindus and especially to the maliks. For, their mud dwellings were on the malik's land. The timber and straw used for the roofing of their dwellings were supplied by the maliks. Traditionally, they and their family members were brought to that hut under the cover of darkness from a distant village of another malik of a different clan. The food that they consumed was also provided by the malik. In return, the malik received the entire labour of that family. The total relation of super- and subordination between a chamar and a malik could not be broken either by the latter or anyone else on his behalf except by the malik who had the right to throw out the chamars at his wish from his *abadi* land.

Being placed at the extreme bottom in the Hindu hierarchy, the severity of proscription and prescription and prohibition for this group were equally extreme in nature. These deprivations were in the order of inverse relation with the capacity of a caste to own and control land. Thus, on the scale of proscription and prohibition, while the right to worship in the temple, to obtain education, to use gold and silver ornaments and alloy utensils, and the importance of the chastity of womenfolk were part of the malik's *sayak* (countenance), the same had a diminishing tendency as one went through the middle and lower caste-groups of prajas, down to the groups of untouchables among whom the total absence of these moral, religious and materialistic standards characterized their caste attributes. I have tried to explain this specific scale with the help of a tentative concept of the culture of inequality (Singh, 1974:48).

Culture of Inequality

Despite their wretched conditions and an abject subordination to the maliks, the prajas, especially the untouchables who were nothing more than serfs and slaves, continued to live within an apparently harmonic agrarian system in Basti. Between 1801 and 1930, we do not know of a single recorded case of an organized attempt to improve their conditions on the part of the peasant castes. The numerically large caste of chamars and other castes of the untouchable group were down-trodden and suffered most under the maliks. Yet, they too did not resort to protest to obtain social justice in Basti. The same untouchables, however, in alliance with the other peasant castes, became rebellious after the thirties of this century.

The utter quiescence of all the peasant castes, including the untouchables, during a period when the objective conditions for collective protest and conflict were most mature and ripe can, perhaps, be explained within the framework of an all-pervasive cultural ethos of the hierarchical Hindu society. We have used the term, culture of inequality, as an explanatory concept earlier (Singh, 1974:48) to analyse the idea of peasant deviation and conformity in relation to the class of maliks. Rudimentary as it was in formulation, its conceptual meaning needs further elaboration.

From an ethnoscience point of view, each caste used to be (and in varying degrees, this is still so) a distinct semantic domain (Tyler, 1969:7-8) in itself. Each such domain evoked a series of attributional and behavioural images specific to a caste or group of castes. The hierarchical caste system of the Hindus specified *jati-dharma* (religion specific to caste), *jati-karma* (behaviour specific to caste) and went to the extent of assigning *jati-gur* (psychological disposition to behavior specific to caste) to individuals who belonged to various categories of this system. The caste name Brahmin is also a linguistic symbol which identified a class of people who, on account of their religion, behavior and dispositional attributes, were thought to be closer to 'Brahm': the Hindu symbol of Supreme God. Since God is supreme and purest, those who were most proximate to that symbol were, therefore, highest on the cognitive map of Hindu hierarchy. The Kshatriyas (the Rajputs) are next to the Brahmins in the ritual hierarchy but at the top in terms of their material power. Their caste name therefore symbolized a protective umbrella for all the castes. Being a warrior caste, the symbol of an umbrella for the caste of Kshatriyas was appropriate.

The peasant castes belonged, in general, to the Sudra category which symbolized the behavior and attitude of people predisposed to render service to the Brahmins and Kshatriyas. The untouchables in fact were prisoners of Hindu symbolism which produced a language that conditioned thought, and the thought in turn went a long way towards shaping the culture of the caste community of Basti.

Thus, the name symbols of untouchable castes, such as chamars, bhangis, badhiks and bahelias, evoked a series of attributional and behavioral images which related to things and objects held extremely impure and profane by Hindu society. Chamars were the ones who used to skin dead animals and eat carrion, deal in raw hides and are devoid of any disposition for intellectual activity. The people of

Basti suspected the morals of a chamarin (female chamar) or the brilliance of a chamar student, as these qualities were held to be unusual for members of this caste. Similarly, badhiks and bahelias were those who were assigned the disdainful function of killing and trapping animals and birds. The caste of bhangis is linked with dirt, filth and their hands are smeared with night soil. By and large dark-complexioned with a predisposition towards being mentally dim and morally weak, their function was to obey and accept the demands of the maliks in Basti. Their *jati-dharma*, *jati-karma* and *jati-gur* had ordained them not only to do so but to remain so.

The principle of hierarchy was so elaborate and pervasive in Basti that, as reported elsewhere, the model of caste stratification had been extended to classify animals and plants too. In Basti, the bull is thought to be a male Brahmin and the sacred cow a female Brahmin. Lions are Kshatriyas, and untouchables are pigs. The shrub of mehndi is chamar and the peepal tree is Brahmin. The principles of purity and pollution that are attached to these animals and plants are the same as those that are attached to different segments of Hindu society. Contemporary sociologists in India have not examined the symbolic aspects of caste in India. Henle's (1968:421-25) elaboration of the *Sapir-Worf* hypothesis in this direction, can provide useful insights into a further analysis of caste inequalities in India. For, the Hindu's cognitive scheme divides empirical realities into high and low orders and ranks.

In the light of the foregoing discussion, the *culture of inequality* can be said to refer to values and norms commensurate with a socio-cultural system in which equality was justified and oppressions arising from it were tolerated by the people. The peasant's *jati-dharma* sanctioned, their *jati-karma* rationalized and, finally, their *jati-gur* reinforced not only a passive acquiescence to the maliks' superiority but also demanded an unflinching loyalty and an active support to perpetuate his power over them. Values and norms upheld the principle of hierarchy. The principle of *Homo-equalis* was deemed to be a deviation and hence it was actively avoided. All the exceptions made by the maliks from among the prajas, which we enumerated earlier, failed to sharpen the deprivations as they were absorbed by the sponge-like action of the culture of inequality in Basti.

The period of this culture was a pre-political period. Basti continued to remain a tolerant agrarian society as long as that culture held people effectively (Beteille, 1974:197).

We are not suggesting that during this period peasant deprivation and discontent did not exist or peasants had no capacity to protest. On the contrary, our data refute the notion entertained by a few social scientists (Joshi, 1974:57; Dumont, 1969:46; 1973:238) that the conditioning to fatalism or passivity, considered to be typical to the Indianness of the Indian peasant, puts limits to their own efforts at self-preservation. Moore's judgement concerning the constraining influence of caste on organised protest (1967:335) is equally refuted. For, the peasant uprisings of the forties and seventies did not emerge after supplanting caste or after a rooting out of the fatalistic tendencies of the peasants.

What we intend to suggest is that, given a state of deprivation and given a capacity to protest, the sponge-like culture of inequality as a pre-political culture of Basti did not make the peasantry conscious enough first to articulate their deprivation and discontent in an organized manner; second, it did not make them feel the need and urgency to abolish these deprivations through collective effort; and, finally, it did not help them to identify any class or caste, including institutional practices, to blame and to hold responsible for the injustices done to them. Culture is not a kulak, nor is it a few percentage of population that make up a ruling caste or class. The culture of inequality was a way of life. One could attack a way of life only by offering a better alternative. And this was exactly what the process of politicization brought to the peasantry of Basti.

Politicization and the Rise of the Political Elite

The politicization of the peasantry during British rule in India was linked with the growth of the independence movement spear-headed by the Indian National Congress. The revolt of Chauri-Chaura near Gorakhpur in 1920 and the No-Rent and No-Tax compaigns of the Congress against the British in 1930 involved both the zamindars and the peasants in Uttar Pradesh (Sitaramayya 1946:235, 325, 415). As the peasants constituted the majority of the population, the Congress paid special attention to introducing them to various techniques of agitation against the British. Subsequently, however, especially during the thirties and after, the peasants began to use the same techniques against the zamindars as well. In fact, the history of the Congress during the pre-Independence period was a history of mass satyagraha (passive resistence), civil-disobedience, non-cooperation, bycotts, picketting, hartals (strikes) and marches.

The politics of agitation launched by the Congress, its self-asserting innovations and its ensuing socio-political consequences were of far-reaching significance for the peasantry in Uttar Pradesh. Its importance lay in the impact that it made upon the peasants. It accelerated the spread of democratic egalitarian values in the countryside where the rules of inequality used to prevail. The major contribution of the Congress, besides winning freedom from colonial rule, can be seen in terms of its repeated efforts to arouse the hitherto dormant peasants to try and alleviate their conditions. One of the objectives of the Indian National Congress during the pre-Independence period was to introduce the peasants to modern political and economic concepts and to the essence of democracy and socialism (Sitaramayya, 1946:141, 295). In the process of doing so, it tapped the peasants' potential for collective action by providing them an aspiration for equality, an organization and ideology in consonance with these projected aspirations, and, finally, by making available a grass-root leadership which helped them to identify the targets to attack in Basti. During the thirties and forties a class of educated, self-employed Congress recruits began to emerge in the district. They came mainly from the following communities: mukhtars (indigenous advocates), vakeels (lawyers), and shastris (graduates trained at the Congress run educational institution of Kashi Vidyapith, Banaras). A brief description of their role in peasant mobilization is being presented below.

Following upon the first visit of Mahatma Gandhi and Jawahar Lal Nehru in 1919, the Congress Party came into being in Basti in 1920. However, it remained in an embroynic state till 1930 when a group of educated young men took over its leadership. These educated men were either shastri degree holders from Kashi Vidyapith or held the certificate of mukhtars. Out of the five dominant mukhtars, three were from the caste of Kayastha and two from the Brahmin caste. The shastris belonged to the Brahmin caste only. The Muslim community provided two Aligarh University trained advocates to the local Congress leadership.

With the exception of the Muslim advocates who held large tracts of land in the district, all the mukhtars and shastris came from families of munshis (record-keepers)—managers and administrators who were the paid employees of the maliks, especially of the Rajput maliks. In most cases, the education of the mukhtars and shastris had been financed by the malik who also employed their parents. The Kayastha caste was, traditionally, relatively more literate and as such the jobs of village patwari, the maliks' munshis (or managers) were held by the members of this caste. Educated Brahmins who joined the Congress had received too small a *birta* from the Rajput maliks to live independently.

In the case of almost all the mukhtars and shastris, it was found that their parents came from families patronized by a rich malik, had close relation with the malik's family and were exposed to the oddities of servitude usually demanded from them by their patrons. Being equal, or almost equal, to the maliks in ritual status, their education sensitized the sons of these families to their relative deprivation. Actually, education and politics were the only weapons in the hands of this class which brought them on par with the maliks after 1947. They used these weapons effectively.

The educated political elite toured throughout the district exhorting the villagers to organize themselves against the British as well as their agents—the local zamindars. While the millenarian utopia of Ram-Rajya (the Hindu concept of the ideal state) when the rivers would flow with milk was offered to the peasantry, they insisted that such a time would come only after the land had come under the plough of the tiller permanently. Village fairs, weekly markets and other public places were transformed into schools of socialism and democracy by these mukhtars and shastris of Basti. Their educative effect on the spread of modern political socialization was deep and wide.

Any assessment of the sequence and occurrence of peasant rebellions and movements in Basti should follow upon a discussion of the legal and agrarian consequences of the pro-peasant policies of the Congress. This is worth examining because, while the district level Congress leadership was stirring up the wrath of the peasantry against the zamindars, its national and state leaders, like Jawahar Lal Nehru and Pandit Govind Ballabh Pant, were exerting pressure upon the government of the time to institute pro-peasant agrarian laws.[3] It instituted several enquiry committees to record the grievances and discontent of the peasantry against the zamindars and talukdars of the United Provinces (Sitaramayya, 1946:500-1). The

Special Agrarian Enquiry Committee, known as the Pandit Committee and headed by Pandit Govind Ballabh Pant, submitted its report in 1931. Alavi's (1965:262) charge that 'Gandhi . . . played a vital role in mobilizing peasant's support for the National Congress. But if he made the peasant speak for the Congress, he did little to make the Congress speak for the peasant', is untrue. Gandhi took the problems of the peasants of the United Provinces and placed them before the Viceroy at Simla in 1931 for remedy and threatened to launch a satyagraha if nothing was done to ameliorate their conditions. Actually, Gandhi had been the prime mover of the pro-peasant policies of the Congress (Sitaramayya, 1946:501).

From the thirties to the mid-forties the Congress in the United Provinces continued to pressurize the government, sometimes alone at other times in alliance with left-oriented organizations such as the Kisan Sabha and the CPI—which were gradually emerging. The All-Parties Conference held at Lucknow in 1936 (Malaviya, 1956: 200; Rasul, 1974:3-4) was the outcome of such alliances. Up to 1947, the Congress was sufficiently left oriented to keep the CPI and the Kisan Sabha relatively subdued in the United Provinces.

The radicalism of the Congress emerged because of two main factors. As they had nothing to loose, the peasantry were more disposed towards joining the Congress mobilization against the British, provided they could get land from the local maliks. They formed the majority of the population as compared to the minority population of zamindars and talukdars.. The Congress promised land to the landless and, to those who had land, security over their holdings. Secondly, the Congress leadership had an ambivalent relationship with the rajas, zamindars and talukdars in general. The ambivalence of the Congress leadership had roots in the past subordination of their families to the privileged class. With some justification, it can be stated that the parents and grandparents of even leaders like Mahatma Gandhi and Jawahar Lal Nehru had been diwans and managers or munshis of the rajas and zamindars in India. The entry of these leaders first into the practice of law after education, and then into politics was partially caused by a reference group behavior arising out of their deprivations which were exposed in contrast to the relative affluence of the rajas and zamindars. Parallel to this process was the equally ambivalent attitude of the latter towards the Congress leaders. The rajas and zamindars underestimated the potentiality of both the peasants and the Congress leaders.

The Nijai Bol (1946) and Land-grab (1970) Movements

The structural conditions and cognitive perceptions of the political elite as discussed above had a bearing upon the incidence of peasant protests and uprisings in the Basti district. Thousands of kisans and khetihar mazdoors from hundreds of villages participated in the pre-Independence movement of Nijai Bol (declare ownership of land) and the post-Independence movement of land-grab. These movements were preceded and followed by a number of relatively unorganized and sporadic peasant rebellions against the maliks. Over a period of 35 years (1935-70), our field investigation reveals no less than thirty violent peasant rebellions. Eleven major rebellions resulted in the murder of nine influential maliks and five peasant leaders in open encounters. Several hundred maliks and kisans received injuries.

The figures mentioned above exclude several cases when kisans and mazdoors were disposed off by the maliks on reasons emanating essentially from the issue of land and its control but which were cautiously camouflaged and 'officially' dubbed as incidents of either dacoity or caste and communal riots.

Movements which appear to be sudden and dramatic are not actually so in their origin and growth. The field data presented below demonstrate the fact that, quite often, as it was with the case of Nijai Bol, organized movements are culminations of amorphous and unorganized stages in the career of the movement. Under conditions of sustained politicization and an effective leadership, episodic issues of conflict, long-term grievances and discontent, and even random cases of complaints and conflicts, tend to be pieced together into a full blown movement with an organizational structure, ideology and collective goals.

In Basti, there used to be issues like eviction of tenants from the land; extortion of *begar* and *malikana* from them; the sexual exploitation of their womenfolk; and the maintenance by high caste maliks of concubines, who were mainly enlisted from among lower caste females. The earlier tolerance of these practices which were considered to be part of the institutional apparatus of the culture of inequality, was transformed by politicization into a set of critical issues which unleashed violent rebellions resulting in murders and bloodshed.

Before we present the details of the peasant rebellions and

movements of Basti, a few elementary clarifications need to be offered. The pre-Independence movement of Nijai Bol, following the clue from Wilson (1973:12-13), is being treated as a specific movement; for, its organization, ideology and goals were part and parcel of the general movement of the freedom struggle led by the Congress. Land-grab, on the other hand, was a general movement which was an independent mobilization in itself. Nijai Bol was confined to the northern part of Basti, while the Land-grab movement had an all-India basis. We shall refer to Nijai Bol as a pre-Independence peasant movement and the latter as a post-Independence peasant movement. Similarly, cases of rebellion, in so far as they are related to the two movements under our study, will also be discussed. We shall confine our data to (*a*) the foci of rebellions and collective mobilization; (*b*) the sections of the population involved; (*c*) the targets for or against which the conflict and mobilization took place; and, finally (*d*) its consequence on the social structure. In doing so we shall highlight aspects of organization, ideology and leadership. An attempt will be made to understand the agro-social consequences of collective action on the caste and class structure and the changes that took place in the property and productive relationships in the district.

Pre-Independence Peasant Rebellions and the Nijai Bol Movement

The Cases of Rebellion

Of the thirty total rebellions, twenty-three took place around Nijai Bol. A majority of them preceded the movement. A few took place as its backlash. We are presenting six representative case studies which illustrate the rebellions that preceded the movement. For obvious reasons, we shall not identify the key persons involved nor the villages where these rebellions took place.

Cases of Rebellions in which Maliks were Killed

Case No. A-1: In 1937, a zamindar of Rajput caste, Mr. M of V village, was attacked by 150 tenants over the issue of eviction of land. Mr. M had forcefully evicted a tenant of the village with the help of his kinsmen and sepoys. Field investigation reveals that he used to exact heavy *begar* and *malikana* from his subjects—the cultivating tenants and farm labourers belonging to such castes as ahirs, kurmis, and chamars. He used to pay only half of the current wage rate to his mazdoors. No family of the praja class could resist his demands. Opposition to his demands used to lead to physical torture, the burning down of their thatch-huts and the humiliation of their womenfolk.

The tenants had heard the name of Mahatma Gandhi and were aware of the Congress Party. But they had not met any of the district Congress leaders. They however knew that the Congress was uniting the kisans and the mazdoors to abolish the injustices of the maliks. One day in December 1939, when Mr. M let loose his lathi-weilding kinsmen and sepoys to force three more tenants not to plough the land that was previously given to them to cultivate on the basis of an annual *lagan* (rent or tax), the tenants withdrew from the fields. They held a meeting that night where they decided that this eviction was unjust as they had been paying the *lagan* regularly to the zamindar. The tenants jointly agreed to reoccupy the land the next day. After taking this decision, the tenants sent emissaries to their relatives living in neighbouring villages.

Next morning, the zamindar being partially aware of what was brewing among the tenants in the village, waited for the peasants to come to the field. And the peasants not only went with their ploughs but were armed with spear and lathis and were accompanied by their womenfolk. An encounter took place between fifty men of the zamindar and 150 men and women tenants, resulting in the murder of Mr. M. After the rebellion, the menfolk left their villages but the women held their hold on their huts as well as on the land. Fifty persons suffered serious injuries.

Case No. A-2 : Mr. M-1 of V-1 village, a Brahmin zamindar of considerable local influence, was killed by his tenants in the summer of 1938, over the issue of the use of tank water for irrigation. Before the abolition of zamindari, water resources were in the possession of the zamindars. Summer crops of wheat, barley and sugarcane are based solely upon irrigation from the village ponds. The zamindars used to coerce tenants by denying them water for the irrigation of their crops. They could destroy the tenants' crop by refusing them water. But such refusals were rarely used for the collective coercion of the tenants of five or six villages.

Mr. M-1, besides demanding the usual *malikana*, *begar*, and *lagan*, had raised a demand for *hathiahi* (tax to purchase elephant) on the tenants of the surrounding villages over which he had zamindari rights. The praja, consisting mainly of kisans and mazdoors, was finding it impossible to pay still another tax as they had made an additional payment of *biahu* (tax at the marriage of zamindar's daughter) only a month earlier. The villagers collectively decided not to pay *hathiahi*. This denial aroused the wrath of Mr. M-1 and he ordered his men not to give water to any kisan for irrigation from any of the village ponds.

The kisans had only two alternatives. One was to pay the *hathiahi* and prevent the crop from drying up and the other was not to pay the *hathiahi* and let the crop perish. The latter was a more heavy punishment than the former, as their livelihood depended upon the harvest of the crop.

The village where this episode took place is close to the headquarters of the district—the town of Basti. Unlike those of village V, most of the kisans of this village had direct contact with the vakeels and mukhtars of the Congress Party of the district. It is reported that resistance, including the use of violence, was the counsel of the Congress leaders as the relations between the Congressmen and Mr. M-1 and the maliks in general was not compromising.

Politically backed by the local Congress leaders, thousands of kisans of all the praja castes, including Muslim cultivators, planned to hide themselves in a mangoe groove near one of the ponds. According to the strategy, about a dozen of them started taking drawing water from the pond. Mr. M-1, followed by hundreds of hired supporters and kinsmen, came to the pond to stop this. The kisans who were disobeying the order of the zamindar, tactfully stopped taking water and with folded hands approached the malik as if to touch his feet (a respect usually shown to all maliks by those belonging to the praja class in Basti).

Mr. M-1's followers could not read the designs of the tenants. While these twelve kisans, including five women thus managed to encircle Mr. M-1, his followers heard shouts from the groove. While Mr. M-1 was held firm by his feet, the hiden rebels came out from the groove with lathis, spear and hatchets shouting slogans. The Malik's followers could not save Mr. M-1, who had been killed by then, as they themselves were outnumbered by the onrushing body of kisans.

After killing Mr. M-1, the rebels drove away the malik's men and then attempted to mount an attack on his *haveli* (residence) inside the village. The malik families in the village were terrified. The rebels were trying to put their *havelis* on fire. However, at the intervention of an elderly kisan, no further damage was done. After dropping the malik's body at the gate of his *haveli*, thousands of kisans withdrew to their respective villages with a threat that any future demand for *malikana*, *hathiahi* or *biahu* would result in the death of more maliks.

Case No A-3: Mr. M-2, a Brahmin zamindar of village V-2, was killed by kisans and mazdoors in the winter of 1944 on account of his oppressions which bordered on sadism. Mr. M-2 controlled 52 villages under the joint zamindari tenure of his clan and was the largest holder of zamindari rights among the clan families. His power and influence spread far wide and his conduct towards the tenants was despotic.

For instance he used to collect all his Muslim tenants at one place and make them sit in the duck posture. His effronts did not stop there. He used to force the Muslims to recite aloud the name of the Hindu diety, Lord Rama, for hours in a chorus. Fanatic as he was, he did not permit them to cut down the volume of recitation and insisted that the recitation be rhythmic and musical. Any Muslim who faltered was stripped naked and his face smeared with pig dung (anything pertaining to a pig is a taboo in Islam). The unfortunate Muslim was then taken round the village on a donkey. Mr. M-2's men followed the Muslim lashing him with a whip till he fainted.

Further on, praja family could not drink or sell the milk of his cow, eat the vegetable he had grown or reap the harvest raised by him without the permission of this Brahmin malik. Once he forcefully deployed hundreds of chamars to weed out the paddy plant instead of the paddy weed from the farm of a tenant.

Physical torture, religious persecution, and mindless oppressions of newer and newer types—the two mentioned above had occurred nowhere else in Basti—created a sense of utter insecurity of life and property among the kisans. The eviction of tenants from land, the extortion of *malikana*, and non-payment of wages to mazdoors, were relatively milder punishments that M-2 inflicted. It is reported that he had murdered a few kisans earlier and had those cases suppressed from the notice of the police and district officials.

Kisans and mazdoors, irrespective of their caste and community, and especially the Muslims and the Hindu chais and chamars, of V-2 village in collusion with the same sections of the community from the neighbouring villages united among themselves. Money was raised by voluntary contributions by all the kisans to help the members of the squad who were to lead the rebellion against Mr. M-2. All this was done spontaneously by the kisans in utter desparation to get rid of their oppressor. One night, when Mr. M-2 was camping in a village near V-2, the rebels surrounded his dwelling. His escorts and sepoys (mercenaries) were belaboured and driven out of the village. M-2 hid himself in a room from where he was pulled out and hacked into pieces. It is reported that, a few days before the rebellion, he had sent his messengers to different villages to forcibly collect *malikana.*

No political leader of the district can be directly linked to this incident, though the general awakening of kisans—that they had a right to till the land and live respectfully—could be said to be at the root of it. They were, however, amply conscious of the future for which Mahatma Gandhi and the Congress were struggling for.

Case No. A-4: Mr. M-3 of a zamindari of village V-3 was killed by kisans and mazdoors in the summer of 1945. He belonged to the family of Chowdhry of Dhekhari who were the only kurmis in the entire district to have zamindari rights over land. In fact, the Raja of Bansi had given a number of villages as *birta* to this praja family during the early nineteenth century in return for their exemplary loyalty and services. In 1842, when *birtà* tenure was upgraded into zamindari tenure, the kurmi family gained zamindari rights over the granted villages.

Mr. M-3 traditionally came from the class of the oppressed. With the exception Mr. M-2, Mr. M-3 excelled the high caste maliks in oppression over his tenants. His major and unique technique of exploitation, in addition to the generally prevailing extortions noted earlier, was sexual perversions. He maintained concubines in each village where he had zamindari right. These concubines, who were mainly kisan women, were constantly replaced as they grew older.

He used land and its resources to compel the kisans, mainly from the caste of chamars, to help him in recruiting concubines. Resistance against his wishes resulted in eviction from land, burning of huts, excommunication from the village and prohibiting the use of grazing land to their cattle.

The general winds of change fanned by a local Congress leader, had already introduced the kisans to the values of self-respect, equality before all and the means of agitation to resist oppression and exploitation. Becoming aware of their deprivations, caste Hindu kisans, untouchable chamars and Muslim peasants organized themselves against Mr. M-3. It so happened that Mr. M-3 was evicting a chamar from his home at about this time. The reasons for this action was no secret to the villagers. Mr. M-3 was demanding the newly-wed wife of the chamar mazdoor as a concubine.

Five hundred prajas belonging to different castes and including untouchables and Muslims, stormed village V-3 and caught hold of Mr. M-3 and his men numbering forty. Mr. M-3 was cut asunder by the neck, his men were beaten up severely, and his property was looted by the rebels. The ghastly scenario portrayed by my informant resembled the plot of Emile Zola's *Germinal.*

Cases in which Rebels were Killed

Case No. B-1: In October 1944, 500 kisans and mazdoors, armed with lathis, spear and choppers, mounted an attack on the *kothi* (residence) of Mr. M-4, an influential Rajput zamindar of village V-4. The rebels were backed by approximately 1,500 men, women, and children who were shouting slogans and abuses. Their slogans were: *Zamin-ka-Badla Jaan-se-Lenge* (we shall take life in return for land), *Attayachar nahi Challega* (exploitation will not be permitted), *Khoon Choosene Wale ko Ham Mitti me Milainge* (we shall humble the blood-sucker).

The leader of the rebels was a caste Hindu tenant who was an active village worker of the Congress party. As a result, the rebellion had distinct overtones of the radical egalitarian ideology of the then Congress party. The rebels were well organized under the recently emerged organization of kisans and were led by their own political leader. The leader was literate and could read and write Hindi. In fact, his primary education had been encouraged and supported by Mr. M-4.

The issues at hand was possession of land and the use of pond water for irrigation which Mr. M-4 was denying to the kisans. Around these central issues, the kisans had gathered allied charges, namely, beating up of a farm labourer, the humiliation of a lower caste female farm labourer at the hands of Mr. M-4's servants, among others.

The tenant leader was in league with one Mr. Ram Mohammed Singh who attempted to unify Hindu and Muslim peasants. He tried to do so by adding the Hindu Lord Rama to the Islamic prophet Mohammed in his name, and claimed to be the representative and leader of the Muslim as well as Hindu peasantry. The peasantry in this area were divided on the lines of religion into Hindu and Muslim. It is worth noting that Ram Mohammed Singh was a new settler in Basti and his antecedents were little known to the people. It was reported that he was a follower of Subash Chandra Bose—the militant revolutionary leader who had organized the Indian National Army (INA) to fight the British outside the country for India's freedom. Ram Mohammed Singh was a soldier of this army and had just returned from Burma after the breaking up of the INA. It is reported that he formed a local Peasant Revolutionary Party of which he himself was the leader.

Mr. Mohammed Singh was supported by a local Hindu sadhu whose temple used to be the office of his party. The sadhu used to sound his bugle to call the peasants from the neighbouring villages for meetings and to plan a revolutionary purge of the district zamindars. (His diary, it is alleged, indicated the names of the zamindars to be killed. This diary was discovered when he was arrested by the police in 1950 after the rebellion of Bhanpur in which two brothers of a Rajput zamindar family were killed.) Mr. Mohammed Singh had organized the peasants of approximately five hundred villages. The villages of Karmaihya, Bhanpur and Itahya, where rebellions took place, were among the villages over which he exercised his influence.

Supported by the followers of Mr. Mohammed Singh (who himself was absent from the scene of rebellion) the tenants swarmed around the *kothi* of Mr. M-4. The zamindar had a double-barrel shot gun with only one cartridge in it. His men had deserted the *kothi*. Left alone with his family members, he bolted the doors of his house from inside and placed himself at a window from where he could see the rebels.

Five hundred armed men, backed up by 1,500 men, women and children, hesitantly attempted to break down the door. Their hesitation was dispelled by their leader who exhorted them to force open doors. The moment he struck his *kulahri* (hatchet) on the door, a shot was fired from the nearby window of the house killing him on the spot and paralysing five others. The crowd thought that any further attempt to force open the door would result in the fate suffered by their leader.

On the contrary, without a single cartridge in his gun, Mr. M-4 came out of the house and threatened to carry on shooting if the rebels did not vacate his *kothi* premises. The rebels, being unaware of the fact that the gun was empty, ran helter and skelter to save their lives. However, before this incident took place, the rebellious crowd had already burnt down the malik's cattle shed and had set fire to his granery.

Case No. B-2 : Major M-5, an army officer and a well-to-do Rajput zamindar of village V-5, shot dead his kayastha caste farm employee in December 1945 in order to save his life from the rebellion led by the latter to take possession of his land. Being posted in the army, Major M-5 used to be far away from his zamindari villages and *seer* farms for long spells of time. His elder brother used to stay at home in the village. But he was blind. The Major had recruited a person belonging to the kayastha caste from among his tenants to look after his farm and zamindari property. In return, the caretaker tenant was given rent-free land.

The revolutionary zeal of Mr. Ram Mohammed Singh and the radical favour of the organization he had formed (see case B-1) combined with the general uprisings that were taking place, influenced the caretaker to become disloyal to the Major and join hands with the restive kisans. The uprising described in case B-2 above had taken place only a few miles away from village of V-5 and the tremor created by that rebellion was still reverbating in the region.

The kayastha caretaker proceeded to distribute all the *seer* land belonging to the Major to kisans and mazdoors, parcelling the land into hundreds of units. Further, he distributed the land to the peasants without imposing any conditions for the payment of tax or revenue. In fact, it is alleged that he wanted to develop some sort of a commune of kisans in village V-5 and the adjoining villages. His attack was on the *seer* and zamindari rights of the absentee zamindars.

Major M-5 was informed about this act of 'socialism' involving his land and the refusal of the kisans, who were his praja under different formal and informal tenurial rights, to pay rent. The Major returned to his village and found the situation tense and explosive. He could not believe that his caretaker had been disloyal. He started taking a round of his *seer* farms and zamindari villages to assess the situation. While he was in a small hamlet near the village, threatening a tenant about the possible forceful eviction of kisans from his *seer* land, about seven hundred kisans led by the caretaker surrounded the hamlet. Major M-5 had only fifteen men with him. Sensing trouble one of his personal servants ran back to the village where the Major resided, and brought a shot gun back. Meanwhile, the rebels had closed in upon the thatched mud house of one of his tenants where the Major and his fourteen supporters, including three relatives, had taken shelter. An encounter ensued in which fifty rebels received head and limb injuries while the Major's supporters were all injured. After incapacitating these men, the rebels encircled the mud house to which the Major had now retreated. It is reported that the servant who had left for the village to fetch the shot gun, finding his master unarmed and surrounded, hid the gun and the cartridge belt under his woollen wrapper. The rebels had, in the meantime, decided to set fire to the thatched roof of the mud house, either to smoke the Major out or to roast him alive.

The loyal servant, a bavi by caste, pretended to be upon the side of the rebels and climbed upon the wall surrounding the hut. He then pushed aside the thatching making a hole wide enough for him to able to drop the gun inside. Armed with a gun and enough cartridges, the Major came out of the house and shot the kayastha leader, who was at the forefront of the blood-thirsty crowd of kisans. The leader died on the spot. He fired a few more shots, but besides receiving bullet injuries in their legs and arms no one was fatally wounded.

Meanwhile, news of what was happening reached the maliks of neighbouring villages who decided to go to the rescue of the Major. Rajputs and Brahmins rushed to the hamlet and chased the fleeing rebels and beat them up. Some of the peasants died later on, as they did not receive proper medical attention.

FURTHER DEVELOPMENTS

Pandit Nehru visited Basti in 1946. In view of the rebellious situation in the district, the local Congress leaders had been pressing the Central and State Congress leaders to take immediate remedial measures against the oppressive agrarian structure of Basti which was becoming tense and explosive. In all the cases of rebellion described above, the local Congress leaders had provided moral support. This support was explicit and direct in most of the cases, but where their involvement was not direct, they made use of both types of cases—i.e., where the peasants attacked the maliks and vice-versa. Their speeches and the examples of rebellion cited by them provided a politico-moral basis for the kisans' uprisings. Twenty-three rebellions, eighteen of which took place between 1935 and 1946, involved sporadic attacks on the rajas of Mahson, Basti and Shohrat Garha. The Rajput zamindars of Dokam, Karmaihia, Bhanpur and the Brahmin zamindars of Gadawar and Narharia were attacked by kisans. Thousands of cases involving charges such as tresspass, causing physical injury, murder and attempt to murder, were registered in the district courts. The vakeels and mukhtars, who had rallied behind the Congress, were reportedly encouraging the kisans to rebel and confront the maliks.

Ram Mohammed Singh was encouraging rebellions while at the same time consolidating his following in the central part of the district. In the mid-forties, beneath the dust of random rebellions and sporadic uprisings, one issue began to emerge as the single most important one. And this was the peasants' contention that the village land records were a farce and that the records must be urgently corrected to ensure that the name of the cultivator who actually tilled and possessed the land was recorded as the 'owner' instead of the original owner who neither tilled nor actually possessed the land. This was a radical demand which questioned the then existing structure of land property rights. This demand of the peasants of Basti was, in fact, consistent with the general Congress slogan that land must belong to the actual tiller.

Pandit Govind Ballabh Pant, who was the Chief Minister of the then Provincial Government of the United Provinces, also headed the State organization of the Congress. He took up the demands of the peasants and instituted a Record Operation on Land in Basti.

The politicization of the peasantry and their rebellion against the maliks led to the corrosion of the culture of inequality. With the decline of that culture a relatively organized and broad-based kisan mobilization became almost inevitable. For, all the factors of necessary conditions (see Rao, Chapter I) had begun to manifest themselves for such a mobilization. In the central part of the district, Ram Mohammed Singh had formed his own local Revolutionary Party. Despite the fact that he was successful in organizing hundreds of villages against the maliks, he had no links with any other political organization in the State. The Record Operation, which theoretically meant correction of land records at the village level, was in fact a measure that involved on the spot verification of land-possession and transfer of ownership right from the person who legally owned but did not possess (till), to the person who actually tilled the land but did not legally own it. This was an extremely radical measure as it went a long way towards narrowing the gap which existed between the property and the productive relations in the agrarian social structure of Basti. The following are the details of the moment which emerged around the Record Operation. We shall present the facts around their foci, section of population involved, the targets of attack and finally the changes that followed in the social structure of Basti.

Nijai Bol Movement

Foci of the Movement

The local term Nijai Bol means the declaration of the actual possession of land by the kisan (the term 'Niji' in the local dialect stands for 'self' or 'personal'). Its main thrust centred around such issues of structural contradiction in the agrarian situation of Basti as :(*i*) the right of ownership of land (property right) was vested in a minority population of Rajput and Brahmin maliks; (*ii*) the maliks did not actually till the land and, hence, did not have a direct productive relationship with the land; (*iii*) land resources like pastures, wood and water were owned and controlled by the maliks as opposed to the actual users, the kisans; and (*iv*) agriculture being the only source of subsistence, a majority of the actual tillers and users of land resources were exploited, oppressed and subjected to coercion and humilation by the minority maliks through their denial, or threat of denial, of the land and its resources.

The peasants organized agitations and meetings at each thana (police station), tehsil and district headquarters to press for their demands. The Congress party men took a lead in organizing these meetings. Hartals were launched throughout the district and at some places incidents of violence also occurred. Zamindar maliks, patwaris, tehsildars and district collectors were named and denounced.

The perception of these agrarian contradictions by the kisans and their awareness of their real position vis-a-vis the maliks in the overall social structure of Basti, was an outcome of a long political praxis. This perception provided sufficient conditions for the emergence of the movement. The entire effort of the Congress organization in Basti during the thirties and forties and uptil 1947 when India became independent had been to inculcate in the peasants an awareness of their deprivations which were demeaning their identity in society. There was a deep sense of alienation from the source of production. This search for identity and selfhood was linked with the problems revolving around the contradictions that existed between ownership and control of land on the one hand and the actual possession of production from land on the other. Non-owners of land, even when they actually possessed the land, were subject to the owner's control as they could be evicted by the malik at his wish.

Hence the main object of the Nijai Bol movement was to rectify these structural contradictions which actually meant doing away with the institutions and norms which sustained the culture of intolerance and inequality. They were told by the leaders that it must be replaced by the culture of equality. The peasants felt that the aim of bestowing the legitimate right in the land to the tiller, was the axial factor which, if achieved, would automatically take care of the other oppressions.

The peasants did not trust the village patwaris, tehsildars and district collectors. The peasants considered them to be in league with the maliks. Consequently, the peasants demanded that the land ownership records maintained by the patwaris should be corrected as the ownership records did not register the name of the tiller. They charged that land records were in favour of the malik who continued to be the legal owner of the land in the records even though he did not actually till the land. The various rebellions and the general and growing mobilization of the peasants ultimately forced the State to institute Record Operation measures in Basti. The so-called Record Operation was in fact a record correction operation, wherein an officer of district collector's rank, other than the district collector of Basti, was deputed by the State to go to each village and inspect each plot to verify the possession of land and record the name of the claimant as the owner of that plot.

Sections of Population Involved

The Record Operation officer was deputed in 1946. It was the usual practice of officers in the British administration to move around with their tents and to camp at different villages to keep in touch with people. Accordingly, the Record Officer pitched his camp in a grove near village Dengha beside the road which connects Basti district headquarters to the border town of Jhande Nagar in Nepal. Village Dengha falls in the trans-Rapti river area of the northern part of the district.

In his first assignment, the officer had to cover around 500 villages of that area to record the name of any peasant who claimed possession of a plot of land. When a malik disputed the claim of a kisan, the officer relied upon on-the-spot oral witness of any one of the crowd of kisans and maliks that followed the officer from plot to plot in each village. The officer's decision invariably went in favour of the kisans as they outnumbered the maliks in terms of producing witnesses.

Several thousand prajas, both from the Hindu and Muslim communities, were involved in this operation, which took the form of a moment that lasted till 1948. The after-effects of this operation reverbated till 1953.

The Hindu section of the praja included such 'clean' castes as kurmis, ahirs, gadaiva, chai, pasi, murao, and mali. Almost the entire section of untouchable castes of chamars and bhangis rallied behind the caste Hindu praja. In villages where a minority group of Muslim peasants lived side by side with the Hindu praja, both communities united themselves into one class against the maliks. However, the same was not true in the case of those villages where the Muslims predominated over the Hindu praja in numbers. We shall in the following section highlight the communal streak which persisted in Basti from the Nijai Bol to the land-grab movements.

The mobilization of the praja to obtain ownership rights over the land that they tilled took such an anti-malik turn that at the instance of their leaders they decided to use this opportunity to take possession of the *seer* land of the maliks which, in fact, was in most cases possessed and cultivated by them. An indiscriminate campaign grew up to *bol* (declare) possession in order to claim ownership. At the instance of their local leaders (the Congressmen), the kisans and mazdoors organized meetings in each village where the Record Operation officer was paying a visit to press their demands.

In these meetings, the kisans decided among themselves to take over all the land of the maliks. Meetings were regularly held to conduct their campaign in an orderly fashion. It needed a clear understanding among the kisans and mazdoors as to who was going to claim which plot of land belonging to the malik and who were going to be the witnesses if the malik challenged the claim. In some villages which were peopled primarily by non-cultivating castes like halvais (confectioners), banias (trading caste) and sonars (goldsmiths), the inhabitants mobilized the peasants and extended their support to them in return for a share of the gains from the land.

However, signs of dissension soon began to appear within the organized class of prajas, which had been cemented only temporarily. The disagreements centred around three issues: (*a*) Caste Hindus like kurmis and ahirs manipulated the situation more in their favour than in favour of the untouchable castes and Muslims. Poor, landless and handicapped as they were, the chamars and bhangis were discouraged from declaring their claim over bigger plots of land on the argument that they did not previously possess any land as compared to the cultivating castes such as the kurmis, ahirs, murao and gadarias. Besides, the two untouchable castes were in a minority position being scattered over the villages of the entire area, numbering five to fifty families in each village. (*b*) The Muslim population in villages with a mixed population were, on account of the general political situation prevailing in those days, divided within their own community—one for the Congress, the other for Mr. Mohammed Ali Jinah and the Muslim League party led by him. The latter group showed no interest in what was going on in Basti with the support of the Congress as their heart lay in Muslim League party. They were part of the general separatist movement of the Muslim League, the macro-picture of which had been admirably analyzed by Paul Brass (1970:1-2).

Those Muslims who were in the Congress or were its sympathizers, ranked below the clean Hindu caste as far as the ownership of property was concerned. The situation with regard to the Muslim population can be explained with the help of the following case studies.

Case No. C-1: Village Bijaura, lying at the north-western boundary of the district, was a zamindari village of the maliks of the kalhans clan. The predominant population was (and continues to be) of Muslim cultivators. The maliks were absentee zamindars who used to control the land from a distance of ten miles where they resided (and continue to live). All the land was actually possessed and tilled by the Muslim kisans.

When the Record Officer (who himself was a Muslim) arrived in the village and asked for the declaration, the Rajput maliks went around the adjoining villages, which had predominant Hindu populations, declaring that the Muslims of Bijaura village were going to build a Pakistan in Basti with the connivance of a Muslim officer, by taking over the land owned by the Hindu malik. The ruse worked, and a riot took place in which unusually all the brahmins, kurmis and ahirs forgot their class differences to rescue the Rajput maliks from the Muslims who were 'going to make a Pakistan in Bijaura village'. Muslims were beaten up by the Hindus and the maliks retained their ownership as no Muslims dared to declare possession of a plot. This case happened on the eve of the operation in Basti.

Case No. C-2: In village Rudraulia, on the other hand, same kalhans clan maliks actually cultivated their *seer* land. The predominant population of this village was (and continues to be) composed of clean Hindu caste kisans. The Muslims were in a minority. Hindu and Muslim kisans were in unision. In contrast to Case No. C-1, the Hindu and Muslim kisans united together to declare possession over all the malik's land, including the *seer* land. The Hindu malik in this case was pitched primarily against the Hindu kisans.

Finally, there is a case which pertains to the primordial loyalties of some non-politicized sections of the praja that held the traditional culture and the malik dearer than the demands for land and equality of status. One group consisted of the immediate servants like halvaha (chamars who tilled the maliks *seer* land on wages), goriet (head halvaha), bhataits (halvahas who got a one-sixth share from the harvest from the malik's land), and functionary jajmans like kanhar, bari, nai (barber) and dhobi (washerman). These were traditionally bound symbiotically to the maliks and entertained an objectively false but conscious feeling of satisfaction with their position. Psychologically, they had a sense of identity as their identity was organically linked with the identity of their Maliks.

Alienation in this section of population was comparatively low.

The other group consisted of those who got estranged from their fellow class members on the issue of competing with them for either getting their approval for declaring ownership over more land or over better land. Such failures created disaffection among different sections of the praja and these disenchanted groups even started going back into the fold of the malik at some places.

Despite the growing divisive tendency, the involvement of praja in this movement exhibited certain organizational characteristics. Peasants had informally chosen village leaders—illiterate kisans and mazdoors from each village. The function of these leaders were: to keep in touch with other village leaders of the area and keep informed about the happenings around; and to keep the district Congress leaders—the mukhtars and vakeels—informed about their activities and to seek advice in case of any doubt. They had also set up a group of lathi-weilding mobile squads of peasants which could go to any village at the request of the village leader. But the structure of this organization underwent a slow dissolution in the end.

Target of Mobilization

The maliks and zamindars were the target of the movement as they were being blamed for the past fifteen years first by the Congress leaders and subsequently by the kisans of Basti. The utopia of Rama Rajya, of equality and the promise to abolish oppressions and exploitations, that were raised as slogans by the Congress during the course of the freedom struggle, inculcated a new set of economic and political aspirations. The hurdle against the realization of such aspirations were the British and the class of zamindars. The kisans were told that by getting rid of these two institutions they would actualize prosperity and justice.

The schooling of kisans in the politics of agitation and optimism had started crystallizing around the maliks as the class responsible for their poverty, abject humiliation and various kinds of institutionalized oppression. Sporadic agitations, protests and rebellions between the mid-thirties and mid-forties were the links between the extending chain of slow identification of class institutions and practices which were held ultimately responsible for the wretchedness of kisans in Basti.

The institution of zamindari and the class of zamindars, the oppressive practices of *malikana*, *begar*, *hathiahu*, *biahu*, *ghorahi* and payment of low wages to mazdoors, and the eviction of tenants from the land which emerged from the system of zamindari and the class of zamindars were isolated, blamed and held responsible for all the problems of kisan.

Consequently, there was not a single case in Basti where declaration of ownership in the course of the Record Operation was effected on the land of a kisan by another kisan. Invariably, the arget was the malik and his land, irrespective of the fact whether it vas the malik's *seer* land or land on *lagan*. In fact, despite internal issions within the class of praja and the growth of defections and he formation of splinter groups, the Nijai Bol movement cohesed nd articulated its grievances and sources of deprivation into one 'ass ideology—the ideology that land should go to the actual ıltivators. The sharpening of the class solidarity of the prajas led) the focussing of their mobilization against the class of maliks. The rise of the class situation as far as the prajas were concerned was inversely correlated to the process which led them to identify the other class as the cause of their problems.

Structural Consequences of the Nijai Bol Movement

The organized movement of kisans and mazdoors against the maliks to procure initially ownership right over land they possessed and tilled and its subsequent expansion to take over all the cultivable land of the maliks, led to both short term and long term consequences.

The following were the immediate and short term consequences: (*a*) rise in the frequency of litigation between the maliks and the prajas; and (*b*) violence, unrest and agrarian tension resulting in further rebellions of kisans against the maliks. The maliks challenged the kisans' declaration of possession over their lands and they also challenged the decision of the Record Officer to accord ownership to the kisans at the instance of oral and on-the-spot witnesses. One Rajput zamindar alone had filled as many as five hundred cases in the court of the Munsif Magistrate at Bansi (sub-court of the district dealing with property cases, located at the Bansi tehsil of Basti). Most of the zamindar families had an average of 300 cases filed against the kisans.

This spate of litigation past led to further rebellion and violence.

For instance, two brothers of Bhanpur village, who belonged to the family of a zamindar, were attacked by 1500 kisans led by Ram Mohammed Singh and were killed by the rebels (Case No. B-1). In another rebellion in Dokam village, a Muslim kisan was killed by the malik.

Another immediate consequence was the disappearance of what Freire calls the 'Culture of Silence' (1975:10) which seems to have been the by-product of the culture of inequality in Basti. Class consciousness emerged among the kisans and led to the organization of the masses into one class in opposition to the class of maliks. A sense of emancipation, of being independent of the malik, of being capable of effecting intended changes in their lives and of realizing their dormant capacity to mould the situation in their favour even if it involved the use of force, violence and bloodshed, were indeed developments of great historical importance in Basti.

The long term consequences of this movement were of far-reaching structural consequence and have had crucial impact upon the emergence and decline of the land-grab movement in 1970, after approximately twenty years of peace in Basti. It also relates to the structural situations which prevail at present as well, namely, the caste or class relations which exist today were, to a great extent, shaped and determined by the first movement of Nijai Bol.

Some of the most significant consequences of this movement on the social structure were as follows:

(*a*) There was the beginning of the pauperization of zamindars. Their land was under the kisans' possession, *lagan* and tax were not being paid to them and they had to spend their remaining financial resources in litigation to get back the lost land. They did get back some part of their land in many cases but only after losing a large part of it to the kisans.

(*b*) There was the transfer of land from upper caste maliks to lower caste cultivators and the consequent smoothening of the upward socio-economic mobility of these castes.

(*c*) The untouchable Hindu castes and the Muslim community failed to keep pace with the clean Hindu castes as they neither had the numerical strength nor a history of possession of land on the one hand, while factors of a sectarian and communal nature (specifically in relation to the Muslim population) operated against them on the other.

(*d*) Finally, the kisans were able to build up a pressure group in the government after Independence which led to the Abolition of Zamindari Act in Uttar Pradesh and the fixation of a ceiling on holdings of land. This further accentuated the process of the emergence of a peasant middle caste in Basti during the fifties and sixties.

Land-Grab Movement (1970): A Brief Summary

Presented below are the bare minimum relevant facts concerning the land-grab movement of 1970 in Basti. My purpose in this presentation is two-fold. One is to construct the causal and sequential unfolding of the social reality through time. Following the first, the second purpose is to attempt a comparative historical analysis of the two movements—Nijai Bol and land-grab. The changed historical contexts have had great significance in illuminating not only the structural bases of peasant movements in Basti but far more significance in determining the success and failure of these movements as well.

Historically, Nijai Bol had a convulsive birth. It struggled out of the long and deep-rooted traditional culture of inequality in a colonial situation through a spurt of rebellious mobilization. It converged upon the foci of the Congress party which was fighting the struggle for freedom. The Congress was seeking emancipation from the British as well as the upliftment of the kisans and mazdoors. The peasants of Basti were seeking emancipation from the zamindars and the oppressive institutions and practices that they used against them. In 1947, the Congress won independence for the country and in 1952 they abolished the institution of zamindari in Uttar Pradesh. The structural consequences were radical: large-scale upward class mobility of clean Hindu castes and the downward fall of upper castes giving birth to a strong middle class peasantry consisting primarily of caste Hindus. Left behind were the untouchables and the Muslim peasants.

By the sixties of this century, the above processess were well under way and under the Congress rule Basti remained peaceful till 1970 when left-oriented parties dug out the same issues which the Congress had raised in the colonial context against the zamindars. Land-grab had no convulsive birth and had a background of relative peace and middle class prosperity. But this time, while the movement was against the Congress and the ex-zamindars at an all-India level, the mobilization and the involvement of peasants in Basti was far more limited. Out of nineteen attacks, only seven resulted in face to face encounters (Singh: 1974). It was mainly the caste of untouchables and the Muslims who participated. The targets included even ex-praja caste kurmis. The leaders were by and large imported to Basti from outside. The participation of chamars and Muslims and the slogan '*Muslim Harijan Bhai Bhai, Hindu Jati Kahan Se Aai*' galvanized anti-left forces in which all the caste Hindus participated to crush the uprising of untouchables and Muslims in the district.

The emergence of communal forces and the government's interventions aborted the land-grab movement in the district. Unlike the enormous structural changes that followed Nijai Bol, the land-grab movement could not make even a minor dent on the existing caste and class relations in Basti. This, on the contrary, made the peasants suspicious of the role of the leftist political parties in Basti.

The peasants of Basti are not romanticists—they are hard realists. They rose in unison when their 'peasant-rationality' impelled them to 'see' the objective existence of land surplus, and its denial by zamindars who misused the land for oppression. They rose to rebel and launch the Nijai Bol movement. But in 1970, despite all recitations of Marx and Mao by the leaders of the opposition (exceptions were right-oriented parties like the Jan Sangh and Swatantra parties), only the untouchables and Muslims reacted favourably Their organized potential to bring about the intended changes through the movement was insignificant. And the land-grab, all-India movement totally failed in Basti.

Analysis and Conclusion

We have tried to place Basti in a broad perspective of time covering a span from 1801 to 1970 of two entirely different historico-political contexts—the contexts of colonial and independent India. Our attempt has been to combine historiographic and field study materials for a comparative analysis of the social structure and the emerging social processes along the two contexts in a dynamic agrarian setting. The two peasant movements of Nijai Bol and land-grab belong to the colonial and post-Independence periods respectively. The social structure has been operationalized in terms of such empirical referents as caste, class and their relation to land and its control. Categories of structure and processes are analytical in nature. The introduction of the culture of inequality and the process of politicization in relation to the former two categories of our logical schema has been done with a specific purpose. It helps explain the modalities of persistence and change of structure and process in Basti. Taken together, in their different combinations, they highlight not only the contextual structural bases of absence and presence of peasant mobilizations but—and this is important to note—when they did manifest, their combination throws light on the genesis of such manifestations, their growth, success, failure and the impact that they could or could not make on the larger society.

In view of the above perspective, the Basti data helps not only in giving a lead towards the formulation of a working sociological frame of reference for the study of movements and change among the peasantry in India, but helps us to re-examine some of the concepts and notions with regard to the above subject also. For, faulty perspectives tend to lead to false inferences.

A comparative overview of the pre-Independence and post-Independence peasants movements in Basti (Nijai Bol and land-grab respectively), strengthens our contention that the explanation of movements cannot be complete unless their structural bases are analysed. Both movements and the series of rebellions preceding and following the first were the collective attempts of peasants to resolve actual or alleged contradictions of the social structure which was held responsible for adversely affecting the lives of kisans and mazdoors. Viewed in the above perspective, peasant movements tend to be processes which struggle for creating an anti-system (Eisentadt, 1964:335-47) of the established system and an anti-structure (Tirykian, 1970:112-35) of the structure of the time which prevail in society.

However, the mere objective existence of structural contradictions is not enough to generate processes for its negations. These contradictions have to be perceived as being responsible for oppressions and exploitations, injustice and the humilation of a majority population and this feeling has to be transmuted into a shared collective disenchantment. Deprivations and denials emanating from the structure thus have to first manifest themselves in and agitate the minds of people before they manifest and agitate their behaviour. Such a mental and behavioural crisis takes place only when the afflicted and oppressed section of the populace is exposed to norms and values other than the ones which traditionally govern their wretched life, which can provide the standards of estimation of not only why they are what they are but also to help in realizing what they ought to be.

Such a praxis in the case of Basti was not a spontaneous phenomenon. From 1801 to 1930, till the political elite came on the scene, the class of prajas endured all types of oppression and injustices at the hands of the maliks with a total quiescence. For, the normative contraption of the culture of inequality sponge-acted all the possible precipitations of deprivations and went one step ahead to accord traditional legitimacy and institutional approval to such an exploitative nexus which existed between the two classes. How else can one evaluate the semantics of such exalting referential phrases for maliks as *mai-bap* (parents), *deo-bhagwan* (God incarnate) and the *sarkar* (rules of conduct incarnate) used by the prajas to relate themselves to the maliks except that these symbols were the integral element of a dominant culture which structured their cognitions and determined their behaviour. No wonder that Hindu religion provided an easy pedestal for the installation of this culture.

The essential point to note is that the encompassing cultural idiom generates its own rationality. Before 1930, if the peasants showed tolerance and obesiance towards the maliks, this was not on account of their fatalistic world view or on account of their utter passivity as suggested by a few (Joshi, 1974:57; Dumont, 1969:46; 1973:230). Instead, in the absence of an alternative culture or system of other evaluative standards, their quiescence was a rational and meaningful act. Field experiences show that the peasants are hard realists with an innate sense of cunningness.

In the case of Basti, the perception of objective structural contradictions and the ensuing process of concretization of disenchantment and blaming of the system responsible for injustice and exploitation, was linked with the introduction of the peasantry to the political ideology of egalitarianism. Political ideology thus provided a locus around which mute disaffection was transformed into a loud protest. Conciousness is by and large a consequence of a new process of socialization.

The peasants' conciousness of relative deprivation which led to the rebellions and movement of Nijai Bol during the colonial period, had grown out of the sustained efforts of the local Congress leaders to politicize the masses in an endeavour to mobilize the peasants against the British as well as the zamindar maliks. They not only infused a capacity among the peasants to evaluate their own miseries and wretchedness but helped them also to identify the class and system responsible for their conditions. In the case the of land-grab movement in the post-Independence period, this process was spearheaded by the left-oriented political parties. While Nijai Bol was a specific movement which formed part of the general movement of the freedom struggle, land-grab was the general movement in itself. Both movements were backed and supported by different ideologies and political parties.

The role of the political elite in these movements was crucial. They attacked the traditional culture which legitimized oppression and, in the process of doing so, mobilized the peasants against the beneficiaries of that culture—the zamindar maliks and the system of zamindari. Political ideology and politicization provided new standards of rationality, a premise which proved traditional rationality irrational and therefore worth rejecting. Such a process was not abrupt—it involved the creation of sustained anxiety and consciousness of deprivation (see paradigm).

In Basti, the two movements were not sudden and did not have a dramatic origin. Each one was the culmination of a long series of actions and reactions, some time followed by episodic issues and sporadic rebellions as was the case with the Nijai Bol movement. In the case of land-grab, however, agitational politics was the main strategy.

While the presence of an ideology and the support of political organizations constitute the essential pre-requisites for the birth of peasant movements, the success or failure of such a movement is subject to the nature of the social structure. Unless the social structure is perceived to be adversely affecting the majority of the sections of the peasantry, rigorious ideology and an active political party cannot succeed in launching a movement with worthwhile results. For, the awakening of the minority sections of peasantry initiates a counter-process amongst the majority sections to organize themselves against the former, thus aborting the original movement which fails to bring about any structural re-alignments in the larger society. Politics and

Paradigm

Approximate Periods	*Nature of Social Structure*	*Objective Conditions*	*Intervening Factors*	*Types of Processes and Consequences on Structure*
1. BRITISH 1801-1930	Classes of maliks and prajas	High oppressive relation between the two classes	Culture of inequality dominant	Absence of peasant conflict and movements; status-quo maintained
2. TRANSITIONAL 1930-1952	Tendency towards the decline of maliks	Reduction of oppressions	Politicization by the Congress and decline of culture of inequality	Peasant rebellions and movement of Nijai Bol. Radical changes in class structure
3. INDEPENDENT 1952-1970	Decline of maliks and rise of Prajas. Formation of middle class peasantry	Tendencies towards oppression of lower class peasantry by the middle class peasantry	Politicization by the left-oriented political parties	Land-grab movement. No change in class structure, due to communal factors

ideology, divorced from a structural understanding of society on account of the above reasons, remain as rhetoric and not as reality.

Let us elaborate the above point in the light of the Basti data. The foci of the two movements, the involvement and mobilization of peasantry, the target of attack, and, finally the changes that followed or did not follow from them, were subject to a large degree to the enormity of the structural contradictions at the time of their occurrence.

During the British period—when the system of zamindari was in force and the maliks were at their zenith—the actual contradiction between ownership of property and productive relations and the oppressions inflicted by the maliks on the prajas, did generate rebellion and mobilization under the catalytic impact of politicization. The spate of murders, violence, and litigations which flowed from them brought about radical changes in the land relationship of Basti. The peasants united against the minority maliks and snatched away not only the land they themselves tilled but also the land 'tilled' by the maliks. The echoes of this movement subsided only after the abolition of zamindari in 1952. During this movement, ideology, political party and the peasantry as a coherent class had a logical convergence. The decline of the maliks and the rise of caste Hindu in the form of a strong middle class peasantry was a great structural change in Basti.

However, the same was not true in the case of the land-grab movement of 1970. The ideologies of Marx and Mao were pitched against the secure position of the original maliks and the new rich mahton (rich peasants of lower caste) by the left oriented parties (Singh, 1974). This movement ended only in the histioronics of agitation rather than in a meaningful movement. The reason for this was that ideology and politics could only make inroads into the untouchable sections of khetihar mazdoors and the Muslim population. They were the ones who got the least of the benefits that flowed from the agrarian reforms that were implemented in the fifties. Being in a minority, they could only evoke the wrath of caste Hindus who comprised the entrenched middle class, rather than bring about any change in their wretched conditions.

The middle class peasantry in Basti is conservative, mainly consisting of upper caste ex-maliks and clean caste ex-prajas. It has emerged slowly, but after its emergence it has come to reassert the discarded culture of inequality to dominate over the untouchables and the Muslim population. The atrocities committed against Harijans are manifestations of the reincarnation of that culture.

The explanation of the above situation bears directly upon the organizational aspect of the land-grab movement and on the involvement of various categories of peasants in the mobilization for or against the movement.

When the foci of a movement is logically linked with the dichotomies of structure and if this dichotomy is shared by the majority of peasants, then the organizational aspect of the movement grows spontaneously with mass participation. Such a spontaneous organization is too loosely structured to be called a formal organization. Grass-root leaders tend to play a crucial role in its mobilization, maintaining a link with the leaders of the backing parties. However, if these logical connections are absent, the organizational aspect of the movement by and large remains only a political party affair. Nijai Bol had the organizational character of the first type while the land-grab movement did not have it.

The mobilization and strategy of a movement depend upon the degree of internal cohesion or division among the participants in the movement and their structural relation with the sections of population or class, or institution and practices blamed and attacked. An inquiry into this aspect of the movement in Basti necessitates an analysis of the peasantry and their relationship with the rest of the society.

The peasantry of Basti, consisting of kisans and khetihar mazdoors, is hardly a neat homogeneous group. Its internal divisions are perennial and, as such, cleavages in the peasantry vary along the primordial ties of caste and communal groups (Alavi, 1973). Encapsuled as they have been (and are), the peasantry is sub-divided into no less than sixty Hindu castes—each one unequal to the others in social rank. On top of it, occasional reference to sectarian and communal issues set apart the Hindu peasantry from their Muslim counterparts. I have summed up the axiomatic, hypothetico-deductive statements of social scientists divorced from the field situation about the alleged polarization of contending classes in the countryside of India, elsewhere (Singh, 1974:45-46). In fact, classes are not a structural reality to which some degree of enduring permanence can be attributed. Class formations and the emergence of a movement are episodic and die with the resolution of the issues around which they emerge.

The structural nature of the peasantry shapes the mobilization and strategy of the movement. For instance, while in the case of the first movement almost all sections of kisans and mazdoors arose as a cohesive class against the zamindar maliks and adopted a well planned strategy to defeat them, the latter movement could not unite the untouchables and Muslims in Basti. The communal element did manifest itself during the Nijai Bol movement, but it had a limited and localized effect; the same element proved disastrous to mobilization in the land-grab movement. It is in the above context that Hobsbawm's (1973, 12) observation proves to be valid and meaningful.

The foregoing analysis offers us an occasion to re-examine the prevalent concepts and notions with regard to peasants and peasant movements in India. The Nijai Bol movement goes against the contention that the division of peasantry along caste and communal lines reduces the potential for peasant movements in India (Moore Jr., 1967:202). Gough's (1974:1391) contention that caste is no hurdle for peasant uprisings is supported by this study. When the objective contradictions are actual and realized and when they affect the lives of the majority population, caste does start behaving like a class. But no sooner has the class formation rendered benefits to the majority, it relapses back into its caste locus. When surplus land does not actually exist and when land is shared by the majority section of the peasantry, perpetual exhortation for the class formation to carry out a struggle remains more academic in reference. The peasants are realists and this adversely affects the future chances of the emergence of any movement in Basti along class lines. For, land has already gone through the processes of reduction from large to small from small to still smaller holdings. It has reached the saturation point and unless one makes it elastic, further reduction in the size of holdings for distribution among the untouchable mazdoors will, in all probability, unleash a movement whose focus will not be land but caste or communalism. Instead of transferring the landless population to meaningful occupations, the political culture of the dominant party injected false promises, dissension and conflict among the various peasant sections. The solution to the problems in Basti will not come through a third peasant movement but by creative planning for the poor.

Notes

1. This is the revised version of a paper presented to the Workshop on Social Movements in India, organised by Prof. M.S.A. Rao in March 1976. I express my thanks to Dr. Anand Chakravarty who had seen an earlier draft of the paper and offered useful suggestions. However, the credit for the completion of the paper goes to Prof. M.S.A. Rao whose patient persuasions and encouragement impelled me to expedite its completion. I express my heartful thanks to him.
2. In Basti, a bigha is equivalent to one-third of an acre.
3. I am producing below three political statements which, by and large, reflect the general Congress policies in relation to the peasantry and agrarian reforms in India. In a historical sequence, the statements belong to two Congress Prime Ministers of Independent India who held that office for almost more than three decades and had all the resources at their command to translate their intentions into actual reform.

    1. Pre-Independence (1936)—NEHRU: 'The dark shadow of the peasant covers the Indian landscape and introduces itself into each one of our problems, political and economic'. Foreword to Z.A. Ahmed's 'The Agrarian Problem in India', A.I.C.C., 1936.
    2. Post-Independence (1954)—NEHRU: 'We have done away with the big

Zamindars and Jagirdars, they are all over'. *A.I.C.C. Economic Review*, 1 May 1954.

3. Post-Independence (1970)—INDIRA GANDHI: 'Land reform is the most crucial test which our political systems must pass in order to survive'. Inaugural address, Chief Ministers' Conference on Land Reform, New Delhi, September 1970.

References

ALAVI, HAMZA (1965): 'Peasant Movements'. *Socialist Register*.

———(1973): 'Peasant Class and Primordial Loyalties'. *The Journal of Peasant Studies*. I(1).

BETEILLE, ANDRE (1974): *Studies in Agrarian Social Structure*. Delhi: Oxford University Press.

BRASS, PAUL R. (1970): 'Muslim Separatism in United Provinces', Report from *Economic and Political Weekly* V (3, 4 & 5), Annual Number (January).

———(1975): *Language, Religion and Politics in North India*. New Delhi: Vikas.

CHAUDHRY, S.B. (1957): *Civil Rebellions in the Indian Mutinies*. Calcutta: World Press.

COSER, LEWIS (1956): *The Functions of Social Conflict*. London: Routledge and Kegan Paul.

DAHRENDORF, RALF (1959): *Class and Class Conflict in Industrial Society*. London: Routledge and Kegan Paul.

DASGUPTA, BIPLAB (1974): *The Naxalite Movement*. New Delhi: Allied Publishers.

DUMONT, RENE (1969): *The Hungry Future*. London: Andre Deutsch.

———(1973): *Socialism and Development*. London: Andre Deutsch.

ECKSTEIN, HARVEY (1964): 'Introduction'. In Harry Eckstein (ed.), *Internal War*. New York: Macmillan.

EISENSTADT, S.N. (1964): 'Institutionalization and Change'. *The American Sociological Review*; 29:335-347.

FANON, FRANTZ (1974): *The Wretched of the Earth*. Harmondsworth, Middlesex: Penguin Books Ltd.

FREIRE, PAULO (1975): *Pedagogy of the Oppressed.* Harmondsworth: Penguin Books Ltd.

FRYKENBERG, ROBERT E. (ed.) (1969): *Land Control and Social Structure in Indian History.* London: The University of Wisconsin Press.

GOUGH, KATHLEEN (1974): 'Indian Peasant Uprisings'. *Economic and Political Weekly*, IX (33 & 34); Special Number (August).

GOVERNMENT OF INDIA (1907): *District Gazetteer of the United Provinces of Agra and Oudh.* Vol. 32. Allahabad: Superintendent of Printing and Stationery.

———(1931): *Census of India. United Provinces of Agra and Oudh*, 17(2). Allahabad: Superintendent of Printing and Stationery.

———(1948): *Report of the United Provinces Zamindari Abolition Committee.* Allahabad: Superintendent of Printing and Stationery.

———(1961): *Census of India.* 15(2-a). Delhi: Seperintendent of Printing and Stationery.

———(1965): *District Census Hand Book.* 46—Basti District. Allahabad: Superintendent of Printing and Stationery.

GURR, TED R. (1970). *Why Men Rebel.* Princeton, N.J.: Princeton University Press.

GUSFIELD, JOSEPH (*ed.*) (1970): *Protest, Reform and Revolt: A Reader in Social Movements.* New York: John Wiley and Sons Inc.

HABIB, IRFAN (1963): *The Agrarian System of Mughal India.* Bombay: Asia Publishing House.

———(1975): 'Colonization of the Indian Economy, 1757-1900'. *Social Scientist*, III (8).

HOBSBAWM, ERIC (1959): *Social Bandits and Primitive Rebels.* Glencoe, Illinois: Free Press.

———(1973): 'Peasant and Politics'. *The Journal of Peasant Studies*, I (1).

HENLE, PAUL (1968): 'Language, Thought and Culture'. In Robert A, Mannes and David Kaplan (eds.), *Theory in Anthropology.* London: Routledge and Kegan Paul.

JOSHI. P.C. (1974): 'Indian Marxism'. *Seminar*, June.

KILLIAN, LEWIS (1964): 'Social Movements'. In Robert E. Faris (ed.), *Hand Book of Modern Sociology.* Chicago: Rand McNally.

KUMAR, DHARMA (1972): 'Review' of Robert E. Frykenberg (ed.), *Land Control and Social Structure in Indian History. The Indian Economic and Social History Review*, IX (2).

LANDSBERGER, HENRY A. (*ed.*) (1974) : *Rural Protest: Peasant Movements and Social Change.* New York: Macmillan.

LENIN, V.I. (1970) : *Selected Work.* Vol. II. Moscow: Progress Publishers.

MALAVIYA, HARSH DEO (1956) : *Village Panchayat in India.* New Delhi: All India Congress Committee.

MARX, KARL (1853) : *New York Daily Tribune.* New York: 25 June.

MAO TSE-TUNG (1954) : *Selected Works of Mao Tse-Tung.* Vol. I. New Delhi: Orient Longman.

MILLER, E. ROLAND (1976) : *Mappila Muslims of Kerala: A Study in Islamic Trends.* New Delhi: Orient Longman.

MORGAN, T. (1901) : *Manuals of Title Holders: United Provinces of Agra and Oudh.* Allahabad: Superintendent of Printing and Stationery.

MOORE JR., BAVINGTON (1967) : *Social Origin of Dictatorship and Democracy.* Boston: Beacon Press.

NEALE, WALTER C. (1962) : *Economic Change in Rural India: Land Tenure Reform in Uttar Pradesh, 1800-1955.* New Haven and London: Yale University Press.

NEHRU, JAWAHAR LAL (1945): *Glimpses of World History.* London: Lindsay Drummond.

PYE, LUCIEN (1964) : 'The Roots of Insurgency and Commencement of Rebellion'. In Harry Esklein (ed.), *Internal War.* New York: Macmillan.

RAO, M.S.A. (1976) : 'Some Conceptual Problems in the Study of Social Movement', chapter 1 in this Volume.

RASUL, M.A. (1974) : *A History of All India Kisan Sabha.* Calcutta: National Book Agency Private Ltd.

SEN, SUNIL (1971) : *Agrarian Struggle in Bengal, 1946-47.* New Delhi: People's Publishing House.

SHANIN, THEODOR (*ed.*) (1971) : *Peasants and Peasant Society.* Harmondsworth, Middlesex: Penguin Books Ltd.

————(1973) : 'Workers and Peasants in Revolution'. *Spokesman*, No. VI.

SINGH, BALJIT AND MISRA, S. (1964) : *A Study of Land Reform in Uttar Pradesh.* Calcutta: Oxford Books and Stationery Co.

SINGH, CHARAN (1959) : *Joint Farming X-Rayed.* Bombay: Bharatiya Vidya Bhavan.

SINGH, RAJENDRA (1974) : 'Agrarian Social Structure and Peasant Unrest: A Study of Land-Grab Movement in District Basti, East U.P.'. *Sociological Bulletin*, XXIII(1).

SINGH, YOGENDRA (1968) : 'Caste and Class: Some Aspects of Continuity and Change'. *Sociological Bulletin*, XII(2).

————(1970) : 'Chanukhera: Cultural Change in Eastern Uttar Pradesh'. In K. Ishwaran (ed.), *Change aud Continuity in India's Villages.* New York: Columbia University Press.

SITARAMAYYA, P. (1946) : *The History of the Indian National Congress.* Vol. I. Bombay: Padma Publications Ltd.

STOKES, ERIC (1970) : 'Traditional Elites in the Great Rebellion of 1857: Some Aspects of Rural Revolts in the Upper and Central Doab'. In Edmund Leach and S.N. Mukerjee (eds.), *Elite in South Asia.* London: Cambridge University Press.

SUNDARAYYA, P. (1972) : *Telengana Peoples Struggle and its Lesson.* Calcutta: Communist Party of India Publications.

TIRYKIAN, EDWARD A. (1970) : 'Structural Sociology'. In John C. McKinney and Edward A. Tirykian (eds.), *Theoretical Sociology: Perspective and Development.* New York: Appleton-Century-Croft.

TYLER, STEPHEN A. (1969) : 'Introduction'. In Stephen A. Tyler (ed.), *Cognitive Anthropology.* New York: Holt, Rinehart and Winston.

WILSON, JOHN (1973) : *Introduction to Social Movements.* New York: Basic Books Inc.

WOLF, ERIC (1971) : *Peasant Wars of the Twentieth Century.* London: Faber and Faber.

WORSELY, PETER (1964) : *Third World.* London: Weidenfeld and Nicolson.

4

K Ranga Rao

Peasant Movement in Telangana

DESPITE OBVIOUS structural constraints, traditional India has experienced a number of peasant uprisings before and after Independence (Desai, 1969:390-7). The Communist-led armed insurrection between 1946 and 1951 in the Telangana region of the former princely state of Hyderabad certainly stands out as the most important one. The present ideological and organizational split in the Communist Party of India can be traced back to the differences in the thinking of the Party's leadership during the last phase of the Telangana uprising. Today we find the Communist Party divided into three distinct ideological groups: the Communist Party of India (CPI), the Communist Party of India-Marxist (CPI-M) and the Communist Party of India-Marxist-Leninist (CPI-ML). The viewpoint of each of these groups has been presented in recent publications by the respective parties. The CPI considers the armed struggle in Telangana, which took place after the accession of the state of Hyderabad to the Indian Union in September 1948, as undesirable (R.N. Reddy, 1973; Ch. Rajeswara Rao, 1972). The CPI-M supports the continuation of the struggle after the accession as a partisan peasant struggle but not as a liberation struggle against the Indian Union government led by the Congress party with Nehru as the Prime Minister (P. Sundarayya, 1972). The Revolutionary Communist Party, however, firmly justifies the armed struggle and in fact considers the methods utilized as being appropriate for bringing about the needed revolution even today (D.V. Rao, 1971). The revolutionary group is further divided on the subject. Notwithstanding the ideological debate concerning the implications of the peasant movement for a strategy of revolutionary change in India, the nature of the Telangana peasant uprising, the historical and structural conditions which led to its growth, and its consequences deserve a sociological analysis.

Peasant uprisings form part of several social movements in Telangana. Smelser categorized social movements as being either 'norm-oriented' or 'value-oriented'. While the former are generally reformatory, the latter are revolutionary in orientation. A norm-oriented movement may in due course develop into a value-oriented movement or vice-versa. At a particular point in a movement a situation could develop which contains elements of both. Which form would subsequently become dominant and continue would depend on the objective conditions on the one hand and the subjective feelings of the participants and the ideology put forth by the leaders on the other. Smelser's 'value added approach' is useful in the understanding of different stages of a movement. According to him 'the value-added logic implies a temporal sequence of activation of determinants, that many or all of these determinants may have existed for an indefinite period before activation' (Smelser, 1962:19). A social movement may start as a protest and take on different forms as it grows (P.N. Mukherji, 1977).

In what follows, the Telangana peasant movement, which took place over the years 1946-1951, is analyzed as part of different social movements and as such the nature and characteristics of each of the stages preceding and succeeding it are brought to light. This paper is based not only on secondary sources but also on fieldwork. As a backdrop, an account of the socio-economic structure of the erstwhile state of Hyderabad is presented.

Socio-economic Structure of Hyderabad State

The state of Hyderabad was ruled by the Nizam, a Muslim, from around 1720. It was a multi-lingual state consisting of three linguistic areas: Telangana (eight districts), Marathwada (five districts) and Karnataka (three districts). The Telangana region comprised almost half the area of the state. Muslims lived in the urban areas including the city of Hyderabad. Owing to the influx of Muslims from other states in India and the proselytization of Harijans and other backward classes, the percentage of Muslims is estimated to have risen from 10 per cent in 1901 to 14 per cent in 1948. An organization called Anjuman-e-Tabligh-ul-Islam was carrying on proselytization activities. In 1948, urban growth was slow—only six out of every 100 persons in the state were living in urban centres. Not more than 10 per cent were literate. The medium of instruction was Urdu which was the spoken language of the Muslims. The number of newspapers was limited and Urdu newspapers had larger circulations than other papers. In 1931 about half of the police force consisted of Muslims.

Agriculture was the main occupation of 85 per cent of the population. Industrial growth was very little and 90 per cent of the industries were owned by Muslims. About 60 per cent of the land in the state was under the Rythwari revenue system and the remaining 40 per cent was under the direct control of the Nizam, the overlord, and the sub-feudal lords such as jagirdars and *maktedars*. Even in the non-jagirdari areas, almost every village was under the control of landlords—locally called Deshmukhs and Deshpandes—and the village hereditary officials. These landlords owned major portions of the lands in the villages. All this gave rise to absentee-landlordism and an oppressive system of land tenure (Socialist Party, 1948; P. Sundarayya, 1972). Of course, the conditions in the jagirdari areas were worse. While many jagirdars were Muslims, the landlords were mainly Hindus and mostly belonged to the Brahmin and dominant agricultural castes such as Reddis, and Velamas. It was estimated that between 1910 and 1940 land alienation took place on a large scale and many cultivators became tenants-at-will, crop-sharers and landless labourers. Side by side, owing to the increase in the cultivation of commercial crops, owner-cultivators became rich. But during the period of economic depression (1929-34) and for some time after, the price situation was not favourable to the cultivators in general and to small cultivators in particular. Around the Second World War, prices increased and this was advantageous to the rich peasants but not to the poor. As the wages did not increase corresponding to the rise in prices, labourers were affected adversely (for details see Dhanagare, 1974). The estimated average per capita income around 1940 was Rs. 18 per month and obviously there were wide discrepancies in the levels of living.

In the countryside, the jagirdars, landlords and government officials were exploiting the people in a number of ways. The *vetti*, or the practice of free and forced labour and exactions, was in vogue in the state of Hyderabad in general and in Telangana in particular. Under the feudal system in each village the service castes were granted partially rent-free lands and the families holding these lands were expected to serve the officials visiting the villages for some nominal payment. But in practice they were paid nothing and were treated no more than slaves. The Harijan leather-workers, the washermen, potters, barbers as also carpenters and blacksmiths served the Deshmukhs and officials for no payment. Harijans virtually acted as watchmen of the houses of the jagirdars, Deshmukhs and village officials. This practice also enveloped the merchants who were expected to supply provisions free of cost to the visiting officials. The Brahmin purohit was also not exempt from the system of free services.

Early Social Reform Movements

It is necessary to note that the early social movements in the state of Hyderabad originated in the city of Hyderabad, which was a part of the Telangana region. In the initial stages, the movements were cultural and literary in character, supported and led by the upper-middle class Hindu intellectuals largely belonging to the Brahmin caste followed by the Reddis. In the beginning of the twentyeth century, a Telugu literary movement was started and efforts were made to establish libraries in different towns of Telangana. It was in 1901 that the first literary association (Sri Krishnadevaraya Bhasha Nilayam) was established in the city of Hyderabad under the leadership of K. Lakshmanna Rao. A concerted effort, however, may be said to have been made only in 1921 in the form of an association called the Andhra Jana Sangham. It is of interest to note that at the Hindu Social Conference which took place in 1921, a lawyer from Telangana tried to speak in Telugu but the audience objected and he was asked to speak either in Urdu or Marathi. This was a direct insult not only to the speaker but also to the Telugu language (D. Ramanuja Rao, 1964; R.N. Reddy, 1973). This incident made a few of the local Telugu-speaking elite think seriously about their language and culture and the need for maintaining the self-respect of Telugu-speaking people. The idea slowly gained strength, and on 12 November 1923, the Andhra Jana Sangham was inaugurated. The objectives of this association were: establishment of libraries, felicitation of Telugu pandits, development of research in Telugu language and culture, and spreading education among the people. Influenced by the Indian National Congress and the various social reform movements then taking place in other states, the Sangham also included help to destitutes as one of its objectives. The development of the arts was also one of its aims. The Sangham soon began to take interest in the abolition of social evils such as the system of forced labour (*vetti*). The merchants also went into action and formed an association which demanded the abolition of the practice of free supply of provisions to government officials. These programmes gave a spurt to the reform movements in the Telangana region in general and in the districts of Nalgonda and Warangal in particular. In 1922, two Telugu weeklies were also started. Thus, the Jana Sangham, which was started primarily as an association for the cultural development of the Telugu-speaking people and as a protest against the dominance of Urdu, became an important social and cultural reform organization. As a reaction to this, the Muslims formed an association called the Majlis Ittehad-ul-Muslimeen. Its aim was to organize the Muslims as a united force against the Hindus and to lend support to the Nizam of Hyderabad. Each Muslim declared himself 'Anar Malik' meaning 'I am the head'.

The Arya Samaj was active in the city of Hyderabad and in Marathwada. The elite of Telangana as also of Marathwada and Karnataka were alarmed at the growing Muslim domination in the state. The Samaj opposed the proselytization of Hindus and was busy purifying and reconverting converted Muslims to Hinduism. This led to Hindu-Muslim conflicts. There was a demand for the proper representation of Hindus in the government and in the administration. But no political meetings could be held in the state itself. Hence the first political meeting (1928) was held in Akola in the province of Berar. However, its impact on the government was insignificant.

The Telangana leaders in Hyderabad then felt it necessary to intensify their social reform activities as also to spread the message to different parts of Telangana. In 1930, the Andhra Mahasabha was formed with the main purpose of educating the people against forced labour, untouchability, and other social evils and to impress upon the government the need for the abolition of such undesirable practices. The meetings of the Sabha concentrated on social evils such as purdah, child marriage and the taboo on widow-remarriage. They propagated the entry of Harijans into temples and requested the government to lift the prohibition on cultural meetings. Organization of Mahila Sabhas and exhibition of physical exercises were a regular feature of each of the Sabha meetings. The Andhra Jana Sangham slowly became defunct and all its members joined the Andhra Mahasabha. M. Hanumantha Rao was the moving spirit behind the Mahasabha.

In the beginning, the Nizam's government responded well to the demands of the Andhra Mahasabha and issued orders prohibiting forced labour—however, these orders were never really implemented. Soon the Muslim organizations and the government came to suspect the motives of the reformers and began to create a number of hurdles in the functioning of the Mahasabha. It became difficult for the Mahasabha to conduct meetings every year. The first two meetings were held in 1931 and 1932, while the third meeting was held in 1934. It is important to note that the Andhra Mahasabha also came in for criticism from the orthodox sections of the Hindu population. Many orthodox people felt that what the Mahasabha was doing was against Hinduism. This gave a chance to the government to forbid the Mahasabha, under one pretext or the other, from conducting its meetings regularly. In fact, in 1936 Ali Yavar Jung, then in-charge of press and publications, expressed the opinion that the Andhra Mahasabha might in due course fight for the union of Telangana with the adjacent Andhra region which was a part of Madras Province! One good feature, however, was that the government considered the Mahasabha to be a secular and not a religious organization (M. Hanumantha Rao, 1950).

A section of the elite of the state of Hyderabad revived the demand for equal rights for Hindus along with Muslims, and also for responsible representative government in the state. Accordingly, an organisation called the Nizam Subjects League was formed in 1935 and a number of nationalistic Muslims joined it even though the government soon declared it illegal. It was, therefore, given to the Andhra Mahasabha to take the lead. By this time a number of middle class youth had joined the organisation and they too felt the need for political reform in the state. The sixth annual conference of the Andhra Mahasabha was held at Hyderabad in 1937. This meeting passed a resolution requesting the political reforms committee appointed by the Nizam to recommend the establishment of responsible government in the state. Thus by 1937 the Andhra

Mahasabha had become a political organisation as well.

From 1938 onwards, important political developments took place in the state in quick succession. The Hyderabad State Congress was established and many from among the younger generation joined. The Nizam's government objected to the name of the organisation as it sounded like a state branch of the Indian National Congress. Consequently, it was renamed the Hyderabad National Conference. Even so, the government used its iron-hand and banned the organisation on the plea that it did not represent Muslims. Govindarao Nanal, Ramananda Tirth and others were the Congress leaders. The Congressites along with members of the Andhra Mahasabha took part in the satyagraha which was launched against the autocratic rule of the Nizam's government. Workers from the Arya Samaj and the Hindu Mahasabha also participated in this satyagraha. Slowly the Vandemataram movement gained momentum. The students of Osmania University also supported it. In those days in colleges and schools, students had to sing a prayer for eternal life of the Nizam. The students of Osmania University decided to sing the patriotic national song, Vandemataram. It was around this time that communal conflicts began to break out.

In 1939, Ravi Narayana Reddy, an influential young leader, came under the influence of the Communist Party of India and became its member. He was an active member of the Andhra Mahasabha and also took part in the Congress-led satyagraha in 1938 (S.R. Tirth, 1967). The seventh annual meeting of the Andhra Mahasabha was held in 1940. For the first time, speeches were made on national and international politics and a resolution was passed to boycott the pro-Muslim and pro-landlord political reforms proposed to be introduced by the Nizam's government. This resolution, which was moved by R.N. Reddy, created a controversy between the elders and youngsters, or between the conservatives and radicals. The eighth meeting of the Andhra Mahasabha was presided over by Ravi Narayana Reddy himself. He talked at the meeting about capitalism and its problems as also the problems of the Muslims and the Ittehad-ul-Muslimeen—subjects which had never been discussed before. It was also soon after this meeting that a section of the Andhra Mahasabha identified itself with R.N. Reddy and his ideas. They began visiting the villages in the interior and discussing the economic and political problems of the day.

The subsequent annual meetings of the Andhra Mahasabha witnessed the emergence of different factional groups and by 1942 the envitable split had taken place. The eleventh meeting was held at Bhongir in 1944, again under the presidentship of Ravi Narayana Reddy. This meeting almost turned out to be a gathering of Communists, with the old stalwarts and the nationalist, Congress-minded youngsters missing altogether. A number of Communist volunteers from Vijayawada (Andhra) attended the meeting and in a way the Andhra leaders led the deliberations. As Ravi Narayana Reddy put it: 'The Bhonagir Conference which demoralised the rightists and created great enthusiasm and determination among the youth turned the history of Telangana on to new paths. It left a deep impact on the struggle of the people of Hyderabad State' (R.N. Reddy, 1973).

In 1945, there were two rival meetings of the Andhra Mahasabha. One was held at Warangal and was attended by non-Communists. The other was held at Khammam and was attended by Communists and their sympathisers. Both the groups discussed the problems of popular government, representation for different religious groups, problems of peasants and agricultural labourers, etc. It must be noted that these were also the last important meetings of the two wings of the Andhra Mahasabha. While the liberals slowly became a part of the state branch of the Indian National Congress, the radicals joined forces with the Communist party. Of course, within the Congress there were two groups as well—one consisting of liberal-conservatives and the other of progressive-nationalists (K. Narayana Rao, 1972).

From Reform to Revolution

We have noted that the Communists took control of the Andhra Mahasabha from about 1940. The Mahasabha slowly gained strength and popularity in the rural areas. Step by step the movement took the form of a peasant upsurge culminating in a major uprising between 1947 and 1950. This period of upsurge could be conveniently analysed in three phases.

The first Phase: Mass Resistance and Upsurge

We have earlier described the socio-economic structure of the state of Hyderabad and the oppression to which the peasants were subjected, and how the middle classes as well as the lower classes in the rural and urban areas were made conscious of the injustice meted out to them by the Nizam's government and the feudal lords.

These were the days of Second World War. There was food shortage all around. The government introduced rationing on commodities such as sugar, cloth, wheat, rice and kerosene. A system of levy on foodgrains was introduced. Under this system, each cultivator was required to give a certain quantity of foodgrains per acre to the government. While every cultivator was expected to perform this duty, the landlords managed to escape somehow or the other and the burden fell on the ordinary peasants. The price paid by the government was less than the market price. Merchants hoarded the daily necessities of life and sold them in the black market at a higher price. The government also forcibly collected money towards the war-fund. All these measures seriously affected the peasants. At the same time, the big landlords and deshmukhs continued their exploitation of the tenants, agricultural labourers and other service castes. Forced labour still continued. However, the masses were no longer as subservient as before and began to resist these exploitive measures.

The large-scale discontentment that gripped the middle classes and the poor peasants and workers was naturally favourable to the growth of the Andhra Mahasabha and the Communist Party. In many villages of Nalgonda district, struggles between the peasants and the propertied classes began to take place. The big landlords and the police joined hands with one another to resist this onrushing tide of resentment. But the masses fought the police and the goondas hired by the landlords. Attacks by armed police on villages in the Nalgonda district became a regular feature. The houses of important Andhra Mahasabha leaders were raided and many were arrested. Sundarayya and Ravi Narayana Reddy have provided detailed accounts of the methods which were adopted by the people to fight the Nizam's police and the types of clashes that took place in different villages (P. Sundarayya, 1972; R.N. Reddy, 1973). It would be sufficient to say here that during this period the Andhra Mahasabha and the Communist party trained many volunteers to fight the police with lathis and slings. Women volunteers used to throw chilli powder, stones and boiling water at the police. Sundarayya writes that it was "only when under the incessant armed police attacks, the first upsurge of the peasant masses was suppressed and our cadre were forced to scatter, and the police and their landlord agents started combing villages and fields widely, that the party, with the sanction of the Politburo, allowed our cadre to arm themselves with muzzle-loaders and seize fire-arms (sporting guns, revolvers, and rifles) and allowed them to go in for armed self-defence. It was only then some elementary training in handling small arms, and some elementary field-craft, use of explosives for mining and bomb-making and tactics to attack enemy targets, etc., were taught to a limited cadre" (P. Sundarayya, 1972:40).

Nonetheless the masses could not continue their fight against the army which established camps in many villages. The Nizam's government also banned the Communist party in November 1946. Thus the mass upsurge against the big landlords and the government came to a halt. But the ban on the state Congress unit had, however, been lifted by that time.

THE SECOND PHASE: LIBERATION STRUGGLE

Soon after the ban was lifted in April 1946, the State Congress began to mobilise people in favour of a struggle for the freedom of Hyderabad State (N. Ramesan, 1966). It began to pressurise the Nizam of Hyderabad to join the Indian Union in the event of the British granting independence to India. On 11 June 1947 the Nizam announced his desire not to join either the Indian Union or Pakistan and to remain independent. He also imposed a ban on the hoisting of Indian National flag in the state of Hyderabad. The State Congress adopted a resolution moved by late Sri Burgula Ramakrishna Rao protesting the decision of the Nizam and decided to launch a State-wide satyagraha. On 7 August 1947 national flag was hoisted all over the state of Hyderabad. Thousands of satyagrahis were arrested. India became independent on 15 August 1947 and on 27 August 1947 the Nizam declared his independence. People of all sections were deeply disappointed by this decision of the Nizam. While all the political parties supported the accession of the state of Hyderabad to the Indian Union, the Ittehad-ul-Muslimeen was opposed to this move. The Ittehad-ul-Muslimeen developed a cadre of volunteers who were called Razakars and these Razakars began to rouse the feelings of Muslims against Hindus. The Razakars also ran a school of espionage and propaganda (K.M. Munshi, 1957). Under these circumstances political parties of all shades united under the leadership of the Congress led by Ramananda Tirth and planned statewide non-cooperation and civil disobedience campaigns. Except for a small number of Hindu feudal-lords all the Hindus and some Muslims supported these activities. The Communists, Congressites as also Socialists led the campaigns such as refusal to pay taxes on land and on palm and date trees, boycott of toddy shops and non-payment of customs tax. Customs check-posts on the borders were burnt down. In view of the government's ban on it, the Communist Party functioned from Vijayawada. The army and the Razakars resorted to large-scale terrorism and even took to methods such as murder, arson and rape. In the beginning, the Congress and Communist squads worked hand in hand. The Congress set up its camps on the borders and from there made counter-raids on the police and the Razakkars. While the Communists squad mainly worked from within the state, a few were set up on the borders and particularly in the Munagala enclave situated in the district of Nalgonda. Students boycotted schools and colleges, many village officials ceased to cooperate with the government, and clashes between the people and police became frequent. During the day, the Razakars and police forced the people not to cooperate with the Congress and the Communists and in the night the Congress and Communist volunteers would force the villagers not to cooperate with the government. Not being able to put up with these pressures and counter-pressures, some big landlords migrated to towns and others migrated to neighbouring states of the Indian Union. Those who remained in the villages were mostly from among the middle class and the peasantry. The Communists took the later categories of people into confidence and with their help intensified attacks on the police. In fact, the Communist leadership made a study of the whole situation and arrived at the conclusion that the field was fertile for armed insurrection and guerilla type of warfare. They procured arms from various parts of the country and established regular armed squads all over Telangana.

In addition, in keeping with its ideology, the Communist Party raised the slogan 'land to the tiller' and began to work against the landlords. Tenants were asked to occupy lands and government-owned waste land was distributed among the landless. The Andhra Communist Party extended its support to the Telangana movement in all possible ways. In a way, the Andhra leaders were really guiding the movement. By the end of 1947, it was estimated that the Communists had succeeded in distributing the land of the rich landlords among the poor and established local rule in about 3,000 villages. Munshi refuted this claim but felt that the number of liberated villages could not be less than 2,000 (Munshi, 1957:154).

This full-scale armed revolt was not supported by the Congress Party leadership both at the national and state levels. In January 1948, Ramananda Tirth dissociated the Congress from the armed clashes. Naturally, the talk of radical land reform and the sectarian policies of the Communists antagonised the landlords. The Congress was in favour of agrarian reform but was certainly not in favour of a class-conflict in any form. Consequently, the Congress, which initially worked along with the Communists in resisting the Nizam, withdrew and left the Communists all alone in the field. In fact, the Communists and the Congress were involved in some kind of infighting. They even began to throw bombs at one another's camps. Despite this, the way in which the Communists increased the number and the strength of their squads is note-worthy. Village squads 'with about 10,000 members and regular guerilla squads with more than 2,000 members were formed' (Sundarayya, 1972:60). A field survey of eight villages in Suryapet taluk revealed that in each village between three and twenty-three members joined the village Communist bands and a majority of them belonged to the lower caste peasant groups. Some also belonged to the locally dominant Reddi and Brahmin castes. In the liberated villages, Gramraj was established.

By about June 1948, civic life in Hyderabad state virtually came to a standstill. The Razakars terrorised the people. They killed a number of villagers who were suspected of anti-government activities. In one village, '19 Hindus were made to stand in a line and (were) shot dead by the police' (Munshi, 1957:76). Similar incidents took place in many villages. According to the data collected by this author, fifteen people were shot dead in one village on the same day (K. Ranga Rao, 1976:288); and in four villages of Suryapet taluk of Nalgonda district thirteen persons were killed. It was estimated that 'between April 1947 and March 1948 approximately 250 villages in the state had been looted or burnt. Four thousand houses set on fire, 500 persons killed or wounded and 450 women molested' by the Razakars (Munshi, 1957:137).

In the villages, the Communist inspired revolutionary spirit was on the increase and the influence of the Congress had waned. The Communists killed seventeen persons in the seven villages studied by the author. All those killed were either rich peasants or supporters of the Nizam's government. Three out of the seventeen were Razakars. In all the villages, the landlords left villages and took refuge in the towns or in the border villages. In three villages, the lands belonging to the landlords were distributed among the tenants and poor peasants. A government report said that 'From the 15th August 1946, to 13th September 1948, they (the Communists) brutally murdered nearly 2,000 persons, attacked 22 police out-posts, seized and destroyed village records, manhandled a large number of village officials, burnt 'chawdis' and customs out-posts, captured 230 guns, looted or destroyed paddy and robbed cash and jewellery worth more than a million rupees. They attempted large-scale disruption of communications and lines of supply and transport and steadily and systematically adopted the technique of guerilla fighting with the arms and resources at this disposal' (Munshi, 1957:128). Even so, the Hyderabad government lifted its ban on the Communists and put many Congress leaders behind bars. This further led to the growth of Communist power in the countryside. It was under these conditions that the Union government took police action in September 1948 against the Nizam, and made the state of Hyderabad a part of the Indian Union.

THE THIRD PHASE: ARMED STRUGGLE AND PARTISAN RESISTANCE

It is now clear that during the first phase the peasant movement came under the influence of the Communist Party and the Communist-led Andhra Mahasabha; and in the second phase, after Independence in 1947, the Communists and the Congress parties put up a joint front against the Nizam but soon the upsurge against the Nizam and the Razakars turned into an armed struggle against the Nizam's government led by the Communists, while the Congress and the Communist Parties fell apart. The anti-Hindu behaviour of the government was also a factor which encouraged people of all classes to support the united front of the Congress and the Communists. In both the phases, the Communist-led upsurge turned into a class struggle and this slowly alienated the Communists from the landlords as also from rich peasants. It was also evident that the Congress government at the centre looked upon the Communist-led armed struggle with resentment.

After the police action, military rule was established. The Razakar menace was curbed and the Razakar leaders, Kasim Razvi and others, were put behind bars. People supported the army in arresting the Razakars. Those who had temporarily migrated to the towns and border areas settled back in the villages. Landlords made efforts to take back their lands which the Communists had distributed among the poor. The Congress Party was the main adviser to the military government and participated in the civil government established sometime later. This naturally went against the Communists and their activities. Landlords and rich peasants and other sections of the population began to support the Congress.

All these developments went against the gains made by the Communist Party so far and the Party, therefore, found itself in a strange situation. After serious deliberations, the Communist Party decided to revitalise its armed struggle against the new government with the avowed aim of consolidating the gains of their struggle in favour of the poor peasants and the rural labour force. Guerilla warfare again spread to different villages and Communist squads took shelter in the villages in the plains and slowly moved to the forest-tribal areas as well. Consequently, the landlords and the village officials again moved to towns and cities for shelter. But slowly the guerilla squads found themselves in a helpless situation. The army made large-scale arrests and killed the Communist guerillas and their supporters in the villages and tribal areas. The Congress and the local leaders openly supported the army in its raids on Communist hide-outs and the arrest of Communist leaders. The army intensified combing operations and tortured the Communists and their supporters. The Communist Party had taken arms from the Razakars when they were surrendering themselves to the Indian army but the quantity was not sufficient for their task. Hence the Communists established their own centres of production of arms in the forest areas. However, as the pressure from government increased and the people began to withdraw their support, it became impossible for the Communist Party to continue the armed struggle. Ravi Narayana Reddy writes that

The party was in a state of disarray as a result of these large-scale arrests. Thousands of Comrades were either arrested or they resigned from the party unable to withstand cruel torture. Those who resigned were all put behind the bars. With a membership of thousands the party strength dwindled to hundreds by the end of 1948. Fifty to hundred members were left in each taluk. They were not able to face the army in the plains and as such it became essential to move into forest areas for self-defence. (R.N. Reddy, 1973:60-1).

Sundarayya presents a vivid picture of the atrocities committed by the military and the activities of the Communist squads during the period (Sundarayya, 1972).

The Communist leaders began to differ on the question of the continuation of the armed struggle, its nature and the strategy to be adopted. Discussions were held for and against adopting the Chinese path and on the character of the struggle in Independent India (for details see Sundarayya, 1972). A delegation of the Communist Party also met the Communist Party of the Soviet Union and Comrade Stalin. It was observed that as the support of the people became less and less, the armed struggle was getting transformed into acts of individual terrorism and, therefore, it was decided that the armed struggle be withdrawn. It was clear that fighting the powerful Indian Union was not the same thing as fighting the crumbling regime of the Nizam which was supported only the minority religious community. Before making an open declaration of the termination of the struggle, the Party tried to bargain with the government and obtain some concessions in favour of its leaders and the guerilla volunteers. In the face of an uncompromising attitude on the part of the government, the Party unilaterally declared, in October 1951, to withdraw the armed struggle unconditionally. The Party also took a decision to take part in the general elections of 1951-52. Since there was a ban on the Party, the Communists joined hand with other political elements and took part in the elections under the banner of People's Democratic Front. The Front won a big majority of seats in Nalgonda and Warangal districts. Thus, the Communist Party of India entered the era of parliamentary democracy in India.

After the police action, the Congress Party tried to spread the message of Gandhiji in different parts of the state of Hyderabad.

As a part of this programme, Ashrams were set up in some villages. Outside the state, Acharya Vinoba Bhave was propagating the Sarvodaya philosophy. In April 1951, a Sarvodaya Sammelan was conducted in a village near Hyderabad to which the Acharya was invited. After the Sammelan was over, the Acharya decided to undertake a two-month *padayatra,* and visited villages which had experienced the Communist-led armed struggle. People in the countryside were surprised to see him and his followers walking through the villages across the hilly terrain without any fear of the army or the Communists. He also took every opportunity to meet the Communist leaders and wean them away from the path of armed struggle. On 18 April, the Acharya camped at Pochampalli village where some local villagers had been killed by the Communists. In a prayer meeting which was attended by the villagers, the local Harijans requested his assistance for obtaining some land for cultivation. This request of the Harijans made Vinobaji realise the importance of the problem of land in any effort to drive the peasants and labourers away from the path of violence. Instantaneously he immediately requested his audience to come forward with *bhoodan* to the Harijans. One rich farmer by the name of Ramachandra Reddi announced a donation of hundred acres of land. Encouraged by this response, Vinobaji took up the Bhoodan movement and spread it all over the country. U. Kesavarao, a long time worker in the Bhoodan movement, explained the significance of 18 April and the Bhoodan movement. According to him the number eighteen is associated with a number of events in Hindu culture. The Bhagavadgeeta has eighteen chapters and the Kurukshetra war was fought for eighteen days with eighteen *akshownee* of troops. It is not our concern here to discuss the merits and demerits of the movement. What is, however, significant for us to note is the fact that a non-violent movement emerged out of the ashes of a violent revolution. The Bhoodan movement presupposes a change of heart on the part of the landlords. Even though Ravi Narayana Reddy did not agree with this ideology, he rightly claims that 'the peasant struggle for land was a prelude to the Bhoodan movement' (R.N. Reddy, 1973:78). Oomen rightly says that the Telangana peasant revolt provided 'the womb to the non-violent Bhoodan-Gramdan movement' (Oommen, 1977:27).

It is difficult to pass any judgement on the failure or success of the Telangana armed struggle. The judgement depends on the indices we adopt for measuring its success or failure. One thing is clear—the Congress government could not be blind to the movement if it were to gain legitimacy and public acceptance. The objective conditions were of exploitation and underdevelopment, and the maldistribution of land was the most important of all the problems. Accordingly, the governments which were formed after the 'liberation' of Hyderabad state took reformative measures one after the other. The jagirdari system was abolished and progressive land reforms were enacted. Despite many loopholes in the implementation of the acts, the land reforms gave security to the tenant, and many became 'protected tenants' and subsequently became owners of the lands under their cultivation. The Communist-led peasant movement, with its ideology of class-struggle, definitely made the landlords feel that it would be difficult for them to continue to maintain large holdings, and encouraged them to dispose off a major portion of their lands. This measure also indirectly benefited the poor and the landlords.

Conclusion

We have analysed the class composition and ideological foundations of the Telangana movement in its different phases. The antecedents and consequences of the armed struggle have been noted. Sundarayya presents a comprehensive analysis of the causes for the withdrawal of what he calls the 'Telangana armed partisan resistance' (Sundarayya, 1972). Dhanagare also presents a sociological analysis of the peasant insurrection (Dhanagare, 1974). Consequently, there is no need to dilate on these aspects. However, in conclusion, the following remarks seem to be worth making.

The peasant movement led by the Communists with a revolutionary ideology of class struggle has to be seen in relation to other movements which sprang up in Telangana in the beginning of the twentieth century. The Telugu literary movement introduced ideas of renaissance and was against the Nizam's establishment. Under the influence of the Indian National Congress and the Arya Samaj, the Telangana elite gave a new direction to the activities of the Andhra Mahasabha in the 1930s. They mobilised the public for the abolition of forced labour, untouchability and other social evils. They also demanded equal educational and economic opportunities, and equal political representation for the Hindus.

In the 1940s, the Andhra Mahasabha split into two factions—one dominated by the Communists and the other by non-Communists. This was the beginning of the peasant movement organised by Communist leaders on the ideology of class conflict. We have shown how the movement was marked by violence between 1947 and 1950. The Andhra Communist Party supported the movement and its ideology provided the main motive force for massive collective mobilisation.

In sociological literature there is a controversy as to the role of economic conditions in a revolution. Marxian and Tocquevillian notions present two contrasting viewpoints (J.C. Davies, 1968). Ravi Narayana Reddy poses a relevant question. He states that 'the feudal conditions in Hyderabad state were in no way special and peculiar to it, far worse conditions prevailed in the state of Rajasthan and Madhya Pradesh' and then asks 'why did not similar intense struggles take place there?' (R.N. Reddy, 1973:62; also see Moore Jr., 1967:381). He himself answered the question by saying that the presence of a ruler from a minority religious group, lack of civil and religious liberties and the correct understanding of the socio-economic situation pertaining in the state of Hyderabad by the Communist Party were the main causal factors. While this is true, we have to note that among other structural factors it was the objective improvement in the economic and social conditions of the people of the state just before the outbreak of the Second World War which was followed by a period of reversal and oppression that made the peasants, rich and poor, take part in the campaigns of non-cooperation against the Nizam's government during the days of the levy of food grains, etc., under the collective leadership of the Congress and the Communist Parties and the combined Andhra Mahasabha. Probably the mere existence of adverse economic conditions without the upward and then downward changes would not have given rise to the uprising. It therefore looks as though 'the actual stage of socio-economic development is less significant than the expectation that past progress, now blocked, can and must continue in the future' (Davies, 1968: 407). Of course, ideology and the political leadership are crucial in assessing the objective conditions and subjective feelings of the people correctly.

The consequence of the movement will have to be judged in terms of the nature of social changes brought about as compared to the conditions and value system that were prevalent in the pre-movement stage. Many progressive land reform measures were enacted in the 1950s and these helped the tenant cultivators and landless labourers. The rich landlords realised that they can no longer exploit the tenants and impose forced labour. The movement did bring about a change in the traditional distribution of power which M.S.A. Rao calls social transformation (1977). However, the Communist-led peasant movement fell short of bringing about a social revolution. There were serious differences of opinion among the leaders and they also changed their views after the police action. The revolutionary ideology was softened and the Communist Party, which had led the movement, became part of the democratic system. Thus, the peasant movement in Telangana succeeded to a great extent in bringing about social transformation if not revolution.

References

DAVIES, J.C. (1968): 'Toward a Theory of Revolution'. In Lindenfeld (ed), *Reader in Political Sociology*. New York: Funk and Wagnalls.

DESAI, A.R. (1969): *Rural Sociology in India*. Bombay: Popular Prakashan.

DHANAGARE, D.N. (1974): 'Social Origins of the Peasant Insurrection in Telangana (1946-51)'. *Contributions to Indian Sociology*. (New series), 8, pp. 109-134.

HANUMANTHA RAO, M. (1950): *Telangana Andhrodyamamu* (Second Part) Hyderabad: Sri Vani Mudralayam.

MOORE JR., BARRINGTON (1967): *Social Origins of Dictatorship and Democracy*. Boston: Beacon Press.

MUKHERJI, P.N. (1977): 'Social Movements and Social Change'. *Sociological Bulletin*. 26(1), pp. 38-59.

MUNSHI, K.M. (1957): *The End of an Era*. Bombay: Bharatiya Vidya Bhavan.

NARAYANA RAO, K. (1972): *Hyderabadu Swatantrodayamamu. Andhra Patrika* (Aug. 15) Vijayawada: Andhra Patrika Publication.

OOMMEN, T.K. (1977): 'Sociological Issues in the Analysis of Social Movements in Independent India'. *Sociological Bulletin*, Delhi, 26(1).

RAJESWARA RAO, CH. (1972): *Charitratmaka Telangana Poratam*. Vijayawada: Visalandra Publishing House.

RAMANUJA RAO, D. (1964): *Telanganalo Jtiyodyamalu.* Vijayawada: Desi Book Distributor.

RAMESAN, N. (1966): *The Freedom Struggle in Hyderabad.* Hyderabad: The A.P.S. Committee.

RAO, D.V. (1971): *Viplava Communistulu Karyakramam.* Vijayawada: Janasakthi Publication.

RAO, K. RANGA (1976): 'Social and Political Changes in a Telangana Village, 1946-1968'. In M.N. Srinivas *et al* (eds.), *Dimensions of Social Change in India.* New Delhi: Allied Publishers.

RAO, M.S.A. (1977): 'Themes in the Ideology of Protest Movements'. In S.C. Malik (ed.), *Dissent Protest and Reform in Indian Civilization.* Simla: Indian Institute of Advanced Study.

REDDY, R.N. (1973): *Heroic Telangana.* New Delhi: Communist Party Publication.

SMELSER, J.N. (1962): *The Theory of Collective Behaviour.* London: Routledge and Kegan Paul.

SOCIALIST PARTY (1948): *Hyderabadu Samasya: Bhavi Kartavyamu.* Hyderabad: Socialist Party.

SUNDARAYYA, P. (1972): *Telangana People's Struggle and its Lessons.* Calcutta: Communist Party of India (Marxist).

TIRTH, SWAMI R. (1967): *Memoirs of Hyderabad Freedom Struggle.* Bombay: Popular Prakashan.

5

Chandrashekhar Bhat

The Reform Movement among the Waddars of Karnatak*

SOCIAL MOVEMENTS ARE an essential part of societies. While in some societies they are more pronounced and apparent, in others they are latent. The study of social movements is primarily a study of the social or cultural change of a social order as well as of values and norms (Evans, 1973:11). Herbert Blumer refers to social movements as '. . . collective enterprises to establish a new social order of life'.[1] In brief, a social movement may be considered to be an organized attempt on the part of a section of society to bring about either partial or total change in society through collective mobilization based on an ideology.[2]

For many sociologists the structural basis of social movements lie in 'discontent' arising out of 'relative deprivation' and these movements may take any form—from a slow and gradual reform movement to a radical and revolutionary one. Rao[3] suggests the possibility of classifying movements on the basis of their consequences. A further distinction is made on the basis of the nature of change and the ideology of the movement: movements can be aimed at reform in one or another aspect of social life, or oriented at bringing about changes in superordinate and subordinate relation-

*This paper is based on fieldwork carried out between September 1970 and March 1971. It forms part of my Ph.D. thesis submitted to the University of Delhi in 1977. The research work was carried out under the guidance of Professor M.S.A. Rao.

ships (these being referred to as transformative movements) and, finally, those oriented towards bringing about revolutionary change in every sphere of life and in basic values. Emphasizing on the means adopted by change oriented movements, reform movements are described as those movements that utilize legitimate means. In these movements, changes are sought to be brought about within the given framework of a society and the means adopted are consistent with the social norms and values of that society. Radical or revolutionary movements are characterized by the rejection of existing legitimate means and by the adoption of means that are considered improper by the establishment in their attempt to achieve change in all spheres of life, including basic values. This paper is an account of the reform movement among the Waddars of Karnatak, who form part of the scheduled castes.

The Socio-political Background

The social movement which took place among the Waddars may be treated as a part of the broader process of the Backward Classes movement in Karnatak which began during the later days of British colonial administration. The origin of Backward Classes movement in Karnatak coincided with the beginning of the non-Brahmin movement (around 1918), which also marked the decline of Brahmin power in the erstwhile princely state of Mysore with the resignation of Sir M. Visveshwarayya from the Diwanship. In the same year, a deputation of non-Brahmin leaders met His Highness the Maharaja to protest against the discrimination practised against non-Brahmins. His Highness appointed a committee headed by Sir Leslie Miller to go into the problems of the non-Brahmins. The report was presented for discussion in the Representative Assembly in 1919. The Government passed an order on the recommendation of the Miller Committee Report for equitable communal representation in the public services (Hettne, 1974). This had the effect of further encouraging the non-Brahmin movement.

The non-Brahmin movement in Karnatak was spearheaded by the Vokkaligas and Lingayats, the two dominant castes of this region. In fact, the Vokkaligas as well as the Lingayats constituted a number of distinct caste before 1900. But the 1901 Census listed them as single castes without subdivisions. While the different cultivating castes forming the Vokkaliga category had little in common in the social context, the Lingayats had a common religious background of Virasaivism. However, this categorization provided the leaders of the non-Brahmin movement with a significant base for collective mobilization. An interesting development that followed the emergence of these categories was the starting of caste associations for effective mobilization. Thus, the Lingayats established the Mysore Lingayat Education Fund Association in 1905, and, in 1906, the Vokkaligas formed the Vokkaligara Sangha. The non-Brahmin connection provided them with a common platform and held these groups together as long as there was Brahmin dominance.

The non-Brahmin movement finally merged with the Congress movement in the state in 1938 when the latter was emerging as a national force. During the 1930s and forties, the non-Brahmin groups began to loose their cohesion and each caste category began to demand separate representation for itself both in the Representative Assembly and in government service. The non-Brahmin movement took the shape of a Backward Classes movement from the 1940s onwards. The two dominant groups of castes, namely the Vokkaligas and the Lingayats, began to fight between themselves for a share of political power in the newly emerging representative political system. The new constitution of India came into force in 1950, following India's Independence in 1947. Besides the statutory safeguards, the Constitution also provided the Backward Classes with certain benefits such as reservation of seats in the fields of education, employment and politics, and in welfare schemes. Both the Vokkaligas and the Lingayats enjoyed constitutional benefits as Backward Classes and thus began to develop a vested interest in their 'backwardness'. These benefits have, in turn, facilitated reforms in their rituals and enabled them to gain a better status in society.

The scheduled castes form one of the important sections among the Backward Classes. In fact, when the communal issue gained importance and generated the non-Brahmin movement, there was no reference to scheduled castes. It took some time for the scheduled castes to organize themselves and acquire political prominence. With the coming of parliamentary democracy and with the reservation of seats for them at different levels of the political machinery, the scheduled castes emerged as a significant support bloc to different political parties (Misra, 1976). They employed their new-found bargaining power to obtain a better deal in terms of socio-economic development and upliftment. We shall now discuss the reform movement among the Waddars, a scheduled caste, against this wider socio-political context. However, before we discuss the origin of the reform movement, we shall note who the Waddars are.

The Waddars

The Waddars are a category of castes engaged in occupations like earthwork and stone-breaking in different parts of India. They are largely found in the states of Andhra Pradesh, Tamilnadu, Maharashtra and Karnatak. They are scattered both in rural and urban areas and a large number of Waddars are migrant labourers. Early accounts of the Waddars mention that they were a wandering and unsettled or nomadic tribe.[4] In some areas of Madras, Andhra Pradesh and Karnatak they are even today classified as a wandering tribe or wandering and criminal tribe.[5] In the state of Maharashtra they are classified under depressed classes. They are also listed under scheduled castes as per the Scheduled Castes and Scheduled Tribes Modification Order, 1956, throughout Karnatak except Coorg, Belgaum, Bijapur, Dharwar, North Kanara, South Kanara, Gulbarga, Raichur and Bidar districts and Kollegal Taluk of Mysore district. In other words, the Waddars were placed in the list of scheduled castes in the erstwhile princely state of Mysore. Today, the Waddars are found at varying stages of nomadic and settled life, irrespective of whether they are classified under scheduled castes or depressed classes or denotified tribes. According to a recent estimate,[6] their population in Karnatak state is 4,58,560.

The Waddars claim that they had a number of sub-castes of which only nine are known today. They are Kallu Waddars (stone-breakers), Mannu Waddars (earthworkers), Uppu Waddars (salt traders), Bandi Waddars (cart users), Girini Waddars (grindstone makers), Raja Waddars (employed by royal families), Aragu Waddars (lac-sellers), Tudugu Waddars (thieves) and Oru Waddars (town-dwellers). All these sub-castes appear to have been named after their traditional occupations. The first three subcastes—namely, Kallu, Mannu and Uppu Waddars—form the bulk of the Waddar population in Karnatak state.

The Kallu Waddar sub-caste has the largest population among

the Waddars of Karnatak. The name of this sub-caste is derived from their traditional occupation of working on stone. They are mainly employed in stone quarries, building constructions, road-metalling and in cutting grindstones. Though the Kallu Waddars are spread all over the state they are more numerous in the districts of Bangalore, Bellary, Chitradurg, Kolar and Shimoga. The next group in terms of numerical strength is the Mannu Waddars. They are largely found in the districts of Mandya, Mysore, Gulbarga and, to some extent, in Chitradurg and Shimoga. They are known for working with earth—such as in sinking wells, constructing railway tracks, irrigation canals, tanks, dams and bridges, and in repairing all these types of constructions. The Uppu Waddars are numerically the third prominent sub-caste among the Waddars. They are so called due to their traditional occupation of trade in salt and tamarind. They pursued their traditional occupation till the beginning of this century and later gave it up since trade in salt and tamarind could no longer earn them a livelihood. They migrated to cities in search of work where they were forced to take up menial jobs like sweeping and scavenging. The Uppu Waddars are found in Bangalore, Kolar, Tumkur and Chitradurg districts.

The Waddars believe that they originally formed a single endogamous group but that the differences in occupations led in due course to the emergence of a number of separate endogamous groups. The segmentation of the caste into smaller endogamous units, which may be termed sub-castes, seems to have occurred during the early or mid-nineteenth century. The rules of endogamy were flexible till almost the end of nineteenth century which is evident from the writings of Nanjundayya and Ananthakrishna Iyer. Referring to the endogamous nature of the Wadder caste, Nanjundayya and Iyer (1931:661) wrote '. . . by changing the line of their work into that of stone, earth (Mannu) Voddas may be allowed to marry a girl of Kallu Vodda section'. Today these endogamous groups are hierarchically ranked and each sub-caste claims superiority over the other. However, the Kallu Waddars enjoy a high status and claim superiority over the other sub-castes on the basis of their occupation. Among the occupations pursued by the different sub-castes, working on stone is considered to be the most respectable. The Mannu Waddars stand next to the Kallu Waddars because working with earth is considered to be lower than stone work but higher than the other occupations. The Uppu Waddars are considered to be the lowest in the status hierarchy of the Waddar sub-castes.

There are different opinions concerning the position of the Waddar community in the caste hierarchy. Some of the early accounts of the Waddars describe them (or at least some of their sub-castes) as untouchables. For instance, the *Gazetteer of Bombay Presidency* (1884) mentions that the Waddars were '. . . living in small huts of bamboo matting and thatched roofs on the border of towns and villages'. Thurston (1909:422) wrote that '. . . numbers of Odde (Voddas) are now permanently settled in the outskirts of large towns, where both sexes find employment as sweepers, etc., in connection with sanitation and conservancy'. In a recent study, Scarlett Epstein (1962:161-62) observed that the Waddar's '. . .migration in search of work has led them to performing tasks which degraded them to untouchables'. Their efforts to achieve a higher status, however, have met with considerable success in Karnatak where they now occupy a position higher than the one enjoyed in the past. It is through a gradual and persistent social movement that the Waddars realized their present status in society.

Sedentarization and the Contextual Base

The social movement which took place among the Waddars has certain unique features which distinguish it from the social movements launched by other castes in Karnatak. The Waddars were largely leading a nomadic existence till recently and, hence, the sedentarization of the Waddars formed the first step in providing a contextual situation for any social movement to occur. The establishment of an ethnic identity (Barth, 1969) in the new contextual situation and the final incorporation into community life provided the situation for the movement in a new social system. As nomads, the Waddars remained peripheral to the social system and the above-mentioned processes—sedentarization, establishment of ethnic identity and incorporation—provided them with a base in the system so as to initiate a movement. In a way, these processes too form part of the social movement, but without which the movement would have had no contextual situation or base and would have also lacked any focus.

The process of sedentarization among the Waddars was largely encouraged by two factors. As Barth (1965:110) observed, nomads generally acquire land when they accumulate wealth and are motivated in that direction (since wealth alone is not a sufficient criterion for such a process). The motivation to settle down when sufficient wealth is accumulated comes from the possible advantages in terms of opportunities in education, political participation, stable life and such other benefits of sedentary life. Second, sedentarization may also be motivated by external factors such as government schemes, social reformers and well-wishers. Both the internal and external factors were at work amongst the Waddars who began to settle in different parts of Karnatak.

The process of sedentarization does not end with merely settling down in a locality. The newly settled population interacts with the community around it and attempts to establish close social, economic and political ties. The success of sedentary life depends upon the degree to which the new settlers are incorporated into community life. The establishment of an identity is another dimension of the process of sedentarization. The new group, hitherto unknown in the local or regional social system, has to establish its identity and carve out a place for itself in the system. First of all, the new group has to identify itself as a unit, similar to other units in the society, and locate its position in the system. In the case of the Waddars, they had to identify themselves as a caste and establish a position in the system of castes of the locality or region in which they settled.

The migration of Waddars into Karnatak, at different points of time and to different areas, rarely led, if at all, to competition with local groups in terms of occupational pursuits and other interests. With regard to their ecological adaptation and adjustment, the Waddars' traditional occupations had ample scope in Mysore. They capitalized on a different 'niche' of nature than the ones exploited by local occupational groups or castes. Thus, there was no opposition when the Waddars began to settle down in Karnatak. Though the Waddars consist of different occupational and endogamous groups, they possess certain features in common—all Waddars speak the same language (Telugu), they believe in common myths, and their rituals and religious beliefs, political institutions and so on are fairly similar. In addition to a common name, these common features have given all Waddars a single ethnic identity, cutting across occupational and endogamous boundaries and distinguishing them from others. Another important feature encouraging an ethnic unity and identity among the Waddars is that they are identified as a single ethnic group by the non-Waddars—an important factor in an understanding of the way they were incorporated in the system of 'polyethnic' groups. They represent a group possessing certain identifiable criteria; they are known for their hard-work on the positive side and an 'ignorance and roughness' in their behavioural aspect on the negative side. They have been able to establish an ethnic identity and a position in the system of castes following their sedentarization. Initially, they occupied a position just above the line of untouchability. Besides facilitating a place in the local caste hierarchy it also provided them with opportunities for participation in the economic, political and religious life of the region. Above all, they were absorbed in the community life of their localities. Incorporation in community life forms a highly significant stage in the course of the upward mobility of a once nomadic group. It provides the social base for further mobility in the existing system of castes.

The process of sedentarization of the Waddars in rural and urban locales had different social consequences in the context of the Waddars' social movement. The Waddars settled in urban areas have greater opportunities in terms of education, employment, political participation and life styles than those living in rural areas. As a result, there is a greater social awakening and collective mobilization among the Waddars in urban areas which provide the requisite leadership and organizational structure oriented towards a change in social status.

Sedentarization, establishment of identity and incorporation into the community life by carving out a place for themselves in the local or regional social system form only the first phase of their efforts at upward social mobility. Efforts to achieve a status higher than they initially enjoyed, through both ritual and secular means, constitute a part of the reform movement. Herein it is possible to locate certain characteristics common to social reform movements in general, such as collective action or collective mobilization, change orientation and ideology.

Reformers and their Reforms

The reform movement among the Waddars began with individual instances and gained popular support at a much later stage. Following their sedentarization, those Waddars who could afford it availed themselves of the opportunity of education. They realized that their low position in society and relative deprivation were the result of certain distinctive practices of their castes. This realization of their degraded position coupled with the optimism of the educated Waddars who felt that they could do something to raise their status, initiated the second or the later phase of their movement. The origin of this movement may be traced to the 1930s when a few educated Waddars organized informal meetings of the caste elders to discuss the changes that ought to be brought about in certain aspects of their life. Kolar and Chitradurg were the centers of this awareness wherefrom the movement emanated and spread to other parts of Karnatak.

The Waddars believed that their low social status was due to their dietary habits and age-old customs and ritual practices. Their first attempt to improve their image in the eyes of the non-Waddars began with reforms in their eating habits. A step in this direction was their self-imposed ban on the eating of rats which, they believed, was one of the reasons for their low status. The next important change they sought was to initiate their women to wear bangles and blouses. Traditionally, Waddar women wore only one brass bangle on the left wrist and no blouse or brassieres. The institution of marriage was also subjected to certain reforms. Not merely did they differ in their marriage rituals from the rest of the population but even the very timing of their marriage rites distinguished them from other Hindu castes. First, they sought to change the time of marriage from midnight hours to an auspicious hour of the day, in consultation with a Brahmin astrologer. Next they tried to acquire the ritual services of a barber a washerman and a Brahmin priest. Thus, reform activities were not merely confined to bringing about changes in their dietary habits and dress but, more than these, in their traditional customs and practices.

Among the few educated Waddars who set out with a missionary zeal to change Waddar society were Smt. Yellamma of Kolar and Sri Manjari Hanumanthappa of Chitradurg district. Yellamma was the first lady to be educated up to lower secondary, followed by teacher's training. In this process she came into contact with people belonging to higher castes and was influenced by their ways of life. She was not only eager to acquire knowledge of their ritual practices but also went through some of the religious texts on Hinduism. She started her career as a teacher in 1932 and, in addition, took up active social service for the amelioration of the conditions of members of her community. She undertook a tour of all villages of Kolar district towards the end of 1939, and visited other parts of Karnataka in 1940 where Waddars were found in large numbers. Her primary aim was to approach women who had hardly known any *nagarikatana* (civilized ways of life). Along with instructions on material and dietary aspects of life, she also convinced them about the need to change their outdated ritual practices. She propagated a sanskritized version of their religious affiliations, caste structure (*kulas* and *gotras*), deities of worship, modes of ritual observances during the rites of passage, fairs and festivals and their cultural heritage (Yellamma, 1948).

Another important member of the Waddar community who tried to bring about changes in their material and social life was Manjari Hanumanthappa. While Yellamma stressed the need for bringing about changes in the religious life, Hanumanthappa worked for their upliftment mainly through education. He began his career as a primary school teacher and his proficiency in music made even some Brahmins invite him to teach music to their children—which was unimaginable in the 1930s. He was exposed to the styles of life of the higher castes which made him realize how ignorant and illiterate his kith and kin were. He arranged a few meetings of the prominent members of his caste at Chitradurg during the later part of the 1930s. In 1940 he started a hostel for Waddar boys by raising contributions from members of the community and by obtaining a government grant. Spurred on by the success of the first community hostel he directed his efforts towards establishing more hostels, both for boys and girls. Thus, for the first time, a hostel for girls was opened in Chitradurg in 1942. To start with, there were fifteen girls. Even though many of them left the hostel within a short period, Hanumanthappa somehow managed to avoid closing it down. From 1946 onwards, a number of Waddar hostels were established—at Shimoga, in 1946, at Tumkur in 1947 and at Challakere and Bangalore in 1948. Five more hostels were started in 1950 at Hiriyur, Hosdurg, Holalkere, Jagaloor and Malur. Today there are in all sixteen hostels for boys and two hostels for girls.

The success of the early social reformers depended on their ability to mobilize members of their caste. This mobilization began with their reform activities and was confined only to certain areas. It was also sub-caste oriented in the initial stages—the sub-caste to which the social reformers belonged tended to get much more involved than other sub-castes. The establishment of hostels led to closer contacts between the various sub-castes, since these hostels admitted students from all Waddar sub-castes. Another significant aspect of collective mobilization among the Waddars was the formation of caste associations.

Caste Associations and Collective Mobilization

The reform movement among the Waddars gained momentum during the early 1940s and led to the formation of caste associations at Chitradurg and Kolar in the first instance. The first caste association was started at Chitradurg in 1940 with fifteen members and is known as the Chitradurg District Waddara Sangha. For the first time, important members of different Waddar sub-castes were brought together in one forum. It continues to operate as a district association.

The Waddars of Kolar district followed the Waddars of Chitradurg by establishing the Kolar District Waddara Sangha in 1942. The Kolar and Chitradurg Waddar associations jointly organized the first ever conference of the Waddar community in 1942 at Mudu Madugu, situated in Srinivasapura taluk of Kolar district. They invited not only the Waddars of Karnatak but also those of Andhra Pradesh and Tamilnadu. The main purpose of the conference was to bring all the Waddars together so as to formulate plans for the upliftment of their community. The conference also felt that there was a need for changing the caste name.

They organized another conference—the biggest ever in the history of Waddar conferences—in 1944 at Davanagere. Changing the caste name was one of the major issues discussed at this conference. The Waddars were aware of many instances of castes changing their name: for instance, the Adikarnataka, Adidravida and Cheluvadi had changed their names of Harijans, Goldsmiths to Viswakarmas and Lambanis to Banjaras. They felt that the word Waddar had become such a degrading usage that the non-Waddars were using it as an abusive term. Some Waddars (the Uppu Waddar sub-caste) had taken to sweeping and hence they were also considered to be untouchables. As a result they found it difficult to rent houses in towns and cities. The Waddar leaders thought that the only way out of this situation was to change the caste name. With regard to the choice of a new name, there were three suggestions: some suggested that they should be called 'Wadeyaraju' and a few others suggested it should be only 'Raju'. These names were suggested because they would at once indicate that the Waddars had a royal heritage and that therefore they should be considered to be Kshatriyas. In one of their pamphlets they have even claimed Kshatriya status by calling themselves 'Wadeyaraju'. The conference, however, thought that these names were too high sounding and decided in favour of the name 'Bhovi', which was already in vogue as a surname for their traditional caste panchayat leaders. They believed that this term would enable them to acquire a better status in society since it is referred to in the *Mahabharata*. The *Mahabharata* mentions that there were people called Boyas or Bhovis who had the privilege of carrying the King's palanquin. Thus, the Conference passed a resolution requesting the central and state governments to change the name of their caste. Both the state and the central governments conceded their request and approved the new caste name.[7]

The Conference also offered them an opportunity for establishing closer ties between the various sub-castes. The two caste associations organized further meetings—at Haveri in 1945 and at Shahabad in 1954. The main purpose of these meetings was to plan the various measures to be taken for the amelioration of their conditions.

The Waddars of Bhakshi Garden in Bangalore started a separate association exclusively for the Uppu Waddars in 1946 and called it the Bangalore City Raja Boyila Sangha. Later in the same year they renamed it the Akhila Mysore Raja Boyila Sangha for the purpose of including all the 'Raja Boyis' of Karnatak. The Uppu Waddars wanted to be known by this name. But this Sangha had no connection with the Waddar associations of Kolar and Chitradurg. Their traditional panchayat, the *dharma sabha*, was asked to conduct its deliberations under the auspices of the Sangha. In 1959, they changed the name of the association again to Akhila Mysore Boyila Sangha, omitting the word 'Raja'. But all these associations remained local in nature and the Waddars had no single and effective caste association at the state level for a long time. It was only in 1956 that the Vishala Mysore Waddara (Bhovi) Sangha was established in Hubli. Its twin purposes were to undertake social reform among the Waddars, irrespective of their sub-castes, and to safeguard the interests of the community.

The efforts of individual social reformers and of the caste associations have succeeded in improving the Waddars' status to a considerable extent. The adoption of caste Hindu rituals and their belief in the notion of ritual purity and pollution has given the Waddars the opportunity to claim a superior status in the hierarchy of castes. Again, by accepting to serve the Waddars, the barbers and washermen have apparently conceded their claim to a higher status. But neither the barbers nor washermen consider the Waddars in any way superior to them, whether in ritual ranking or otherwise. They do not accept any food from the Waddars. The Waddars, on the other hand, have now begun to claim superiority over barbers and washermen. They support this claim on the basis of non-acceptance of cooked food from the latter. However, non-acceptance of food always leaves room for ambiguity with regard to the relative position of a caste in the caste hierarchy. The Waddars were generally clubbed along with the Korachas, Koramas and Lambanis who form a cluster of castes occupying a position just above the untouchable castes. But the Waddars have moved upwards to equal or surpass the castes of washermen and barbers as a result of their efforts to rise in the hierarchy. Indeed, the fact that Brahmin priests are prepared to conduct Waddar rituals along sanskritic lines is a clear indication that the Waddars do enjoy a higher status than before.

The Waddars have tried to raise their ritual status in the hierarchy of castes through reforms in their rituals and ritual interactions. In these ritual interactions the higher castes—such as, the Vokkaligas, Lingayats and Brahmins—are taken as the positive reference group. These castes may be regarded as the normative reference group too, since they provided the Waddars with norms or standards of behaviour as a frame of reference. On the other hand, the castes of Koracha, Korama, Lambani, Jadamali and Madiga constitute the negative reference group in the course of the Waddars' upward mobility. On the ritual plane, the Waddars compared themselves with members of these castes while claiming a higher ritual rank than the latter. But the Waddars faced certain opposition from members of the castes of washermen and barbers. Though the latter agreed to serve the former, they consider the Waddars to be inferior to them in status. Therefore, members of the washerman and barber castes do not accept any cooked food from the Waddars. They are paid either in cash or in kind (grains, coconuts and fruits) for the ritual services they perform for the Waddars.

Ideology and Ethnic Identity

Various myths and legends shared by all the Waddars provide them with both ideology and identity—essential characteristics of any social movement. Thurston (1909:425-27) has recorded a few myths and legends which trace their descent and give legitimacy to the various occupations they pursue. One such myth connects the Waddars to Shiva and his wife, Parvathi. According to this legend, Shiva and Parvathi came to Bhuloka (the earth) on a summer day. Thanks to the intense heat they began to perspire and feel thirsty. Shiva transformed the drops of his perspiration into a man with a pickaxe and crowbar, while those trickling from Parvathi's body were transformed into a woman carrying a basket. The man and the woman were ordered to sink a well till they obtained water. This they did and Shiva and Parvathi bestowed various gifts on the man and the woman as a reward. However, the man and the woman expressed their unhappiness over the gifts saying that they were too small a recompense for their labour. This so infuriated Shiva that he cursed them, saying that they and their descendants would live by the sweat of their brow. Besides suggesting divine origin, this myth also sanctifies one of the main Waddar occupations.

Another legend connects the Waddars to Bhagiratha, a Kshatriya ruler. When there was a severe drought, so runs the legend, Bhagiratha's brothers began digging in their quest for water. In the process they reached Pathala, the seventh world below the earth according to Hindu mythology, where they found a *muni* (ascetic) meditating. The latter's meditation was disturbed by Bhagiratha's brothers. The enraged *muni* burnt them to ashes and cursed their descendants to be earth-diggers. Bhagiratha, finding his brothers missing, trekked his way to Pathala and, to his dismay, found their ashes. When he approached the *muni* for the lives of his brothers, the latter asked him to bring down the heavenly river Ganga to Pathala in order to revive his brothers. Though Bhagiratha could succeed in reviving his brothers back to life, the curse on the descendants continued. The Waddars claim that they are the descendants of Bhagiratha's brothers and hence had to pursue the occupation of digging due to the *muni's* curse.

The sociological significance of such myths and legends, as mentioned above, is that they give legitimacy to their manual occupations of digging wells and working with earth. They give the Waddars, as a whole, an element of self-esteem that they are following these occupations as a result of a divine curse. These myths and legends implicitly support their claim to a Kshatriya status, thereby also providing an ideological locus for their movement. They also serve as a heritage common to all sub-castes, thus emphasizing a single ethnic identity. Their ethnic identity is further strengthened by their belief in a common origin and a realization that the sub-castes had come into being merely as a result of varying occupations which developed over time. This and the earlier myths play a very important role in establishing and maintaining an ethnic identity, which is a crucial element in collective mobilization.

Political Emancipation and Collective Action

While the myths and legends current among the Waddars formed the basis of their unity, the objective socio-political conditions promoted it. The fact that they were listed as a scheduled caste, as mentioned earlier, in the erstwhile princely state of Mysore, brought them closer together for collective action so as to reap the fruits of constitutional benefits and safeguards. In other words, the Waddars formed a single group *vis-a-vis* the other scheduled castes. The Waddar caste associations, which had earlier aimed only at social reforms, extended their activities to avail themselves of the opportunities and benefits afforded them by the new Constitution. Along with instructing the masses on *naveenachara* (new practices for bringing about social reform) these associations educated the Waddars on the various facilities they could obtain from the government through the special schemes that it had launched in education, employment, financial assistance and so on for the welfare of the scheduled castes.

The newly formed state level association, namely, the Vishala Mysore Waddara (Bhovi) Sangha, gradually acquired a certain political complexion soon after its inception. It took up the issue of the inclusion of the Waddars of the newly integrated parts of Karnatak in the list of scheduled castes. The Sangha decided to urge the state and central governments to remove the territorial restrictions and to consider the Waddars of the reorganized state of Karnatak as a scheduled caste, thereby to extend the benefits enjoyed by the

Waddars of the erstwhile princely state of Mysore to those living in Karnatak (following States Reorganization in 1956). In 1956, the Sangha invited the then Chief Minister of Mysore, Sri S. Nijalingappa, and requested him to recommend their case to the centre. When they found that no response was forthcoming, they organized another meeting at Belgaum in 1958 under the chairmanship of Sri B. N. Datar, the then Central Minister for Home Affairs and Backward Classes. He assured them that necessary arrangements would be made to remove area restrictions if the centre received an appropriate recommendation from the state government. In 1958, the Sangha also sent deputations to meet the then Chief Minister of Mysore, Sri B. D. Jatti, the Minister for Social Welfare, Sri N. Rachaiah, the Deputy Minister for Home Affairs, Sri Basavalingappa, and the Minister for Education, Sri Anna Rao Ganamukhi. The Vishala Mysore Waddara (Bhovi) Sangha also pressed this issue at its subsequent meeting at Bangalore in 1959. In 1962 they invited Mrs. Yashodra Dasappa, the then state Minister for Social Welfare, to preside over their caste conference and sought her help for the inclusion of the Waddars of the newly integrated parts of Karnatak in the list of scheduled castes. However, they met with no success and their consistent failure in this regard detered them from holding any caste association meeting for a long time. Except for meeting on a routine basis for the election of office bearers, the Sangha remained almost inactive for the next few years.

While the Waddars singularly failed to remove area restrictions, they did succeed in securing a few of the Assembly seats reserved for scheduled castes during the elections of 1962 and 1967, by defeating some prominent Harijan leaders. The Waddars have an edge over Harijans as they are not untouchables. Hence a Waddar would in all probability, be preferred to a Harijan by members of all the clean castes. This led to tensions between the Harijans and the Waddars, as the latter posed a potential threat to the Harijans. They thought that if they were clubbed together with the Waddars it could jeopardize their political future.

During the 1962 elections to the legislative Assembly, a well-known Harijan leader, who belonged to the Congress Party and was a Deputy Minister in the State Ministry—Sri B. Basavalingappa—was defeated by a Waddar, Sri D. Munichinnappa, in the Bangalore South Constituency reserved for scheduled castes. Basavalingappa filed a case against Munichinnappa in the Election Tribunal,

Bangalore, that the latter did not belong to any scheduled caste. Munichinnappa had mentioned his caste as 'Bhovi (Waddar)' in his nomination form for the election. The petitioner maintained that the Waddars as a whole were not included in the list of scheduled castes but only the Bhovi sub-caste of the Waddars. Munichinnappa argued that Bhovi is not a sub-caste but the new caste name adopted by the Waddars which has been duly accepted by both the state and central governments. Though he lost the case in the Election Tribunal, Munichinnappa's election was upheld by the Mysore High Court. This incident served to intensify the antagonism between the Harijans and the Waddars. The Harijans took the issue to the national level and demanded that the Bhovis or Waddars be deleted from the list of scheduled castes during the Scheduled Castes and Scheduled Tribes Amendment Order Bill introduced in Parliament in 1967, on the plea that the latter are not untouchables. This development not only rejuvenated the Vishala Mysore Waddara (Bhovi) Sangha but also gave birth to another state level association—the Vishala Mysore Bhovi (Waddara) Junanga Sangha (set up in 1966 with Bangalore as its headquarters). These associations had to prove that the Waddars were down-trodden people who bore the stigma of untouchability if the caste was to be retained in the list of scheduled castes. They formed committees to approach all the concerned authorities to recommend the continuation of the Waddars in the list of scheduled castes. They met the then Chief Minister of Mysore, Sri Nijalingappa, in April 1966 and persuaded him to advise the Government of India to retain the Waddars of integrated Karnatak in the list of scheduled castes. They obtained certificates from Town Municipal Councillors, Municipal Presidents, Block Development Officers and the Commissioner of Bangalore Corporation, to the effect that the Waddars are employed as sweepers and scavengers and suffer from the social disability of untouchability. They also published pamphlets giving details of their pitiable socio-economic conditions and provided statistics showing how the Harijan's enjoyed the lion's share of benefits among the scheduled castes and to prove that they are more backward—educationally, socially, economically and politically—than the Harijans.

Besides the above-mentioned efforts, the Waddars also contacted other minority communities among the scheduled castes in Karnatak, particularly the Banjara (Lambani), Koracha and Korama, who were placed in a similar social situation. The outcome of this was a Conference of the Mysore State Bhovi (Waddar), Banjara (Lambani), Koracha, Korama and other Scheduled Castes, which was held at Bangalore in June 1966. This Conference resolved to request the government to retain the Bhovis, Banjaras, Korachas, Koramas and others in the list of scheduled castes in the integrated state of Karnatak by removing the area restrictions.

The Waddars partially succeeded in their objective. The Scheduled Castes and Scheduled Tribes Order (Amendment) Bill, 1967 was introduced in Parliament on 12 August 1967 and the Bhovi community was continued in the list. But they did not succeed in persuading the government to remove area restrictions.

Conclusion

The foregoing account of Waddar caste associations and their activities throws light on the nature and extent of their caste movement. The Waddar caste movement is highly significant in terms of ethnic identity, opportunity structure, and politicization. The establishment of Waddar caste associations in different parts of Karnatak brought many of the sub-castes in the respective regions together. Subsequently, the state level associations, one at Hubli and the other at Bangalore, led to the further unification of different sub-castes all over the state for political and economic purposes. Such unification not only gave rise to closer communication between the Waddars but also fostered a common identity, cutting across sub-caste and regional differences. As part of the reform movement, the caste associations played an important role in bringing the Waddars of diverse occupations and sub-castes together and giving them an ethnic identity. They made the Waddars aware of the various opportunities open to them for their all-round development. These associations are primarily responsible for obtaining multiple opportunities in the fields of employment, education and politics by having accomplished the retention of the caste in the list of scheduled castes. Further, the movement also facilitated the politicization of the Waddars. It afforded opportunities to the Waddars to participate in politics at the local, regional and state levels.

A social movement emerges into prominence in situations of conflict and confrontation, and the Waddars' case amply illustrates this contention. The tension between the Waddars and the Harijans has provided the Waddars with a definite locus for their collective mobilization. It tended to merge all sub-caste identities and foster a single ethnic identity. Thus, one of the major consequences of the reform movement among the Waddars is the formation of an ethnic group with a defined ideology.

In the political context, the Waddars compared themselves with the Harijans to show that they are more backward than the latter in all walks of life. But the purpose of taking the Harijans as a comparative reference group is not to emulate them but to compete with them for political gains and for benefits in the fields of education, employment and financial assistance which have been earmarked for the scheduled castes. However, the Harijans opposed the Waddars' move on the grounds that the latter were not untouchables. In this context, the Harijans formed the opposition reference group for the Waddars in their effort to bring about change along the secular axis.

The Waddars' political mobilization, through the caste associations and their activities, is closely related to their social reform movement. By political mobilization, the Waddars could avail themselves of the secular benefits which are channellized towards achieving social mobility. The movement among the Waddars may be best described as a social reform movement, which brought about social mobility and change in the existing social and cultural system.

Notes

1. Cited in Evans (1973:11).
2. M.S.A. Rao, *Social Movements and Social Transformation* (forthcoming).
3. *Ibid.*
4. *Census of India*, 1881, *Mysore: Report*. Bangalore: Superintendent of Census. *Gazetteer* of Bombay Presidency, Vol. XXVIII, *Bijapur District*, 1884.
5. *Census of India*, 1961. Vol. I, Part V-B(ii).
6. Havanur, L.G., *Karnataka Backward Classes Commission Report*. Vol. 2, Bangalore: Government Press, 1975, p. 94.
7. Vide G.O. No. M81 Y 3-206-GM-20-44-15 dated 2 February 1946.

References

BARTH, F. (1965): *Nomads of South Persia*. Norway: Universitetsforleget (First published in 1961).

BARTH, (ed.) (1969): *Ethnic Group and Boundaries*. Boston: Little, Brown and Company.

BHAT, CHANDRASHEKHAR (1969): 'Ethnographic Study of the Waddars of Mysore with Special Reference to their Nomadism'. *Bulletin of the Anthropological Survey of India*. 18(4): 255-310.

EPSTEIN, SCARLETT (1962): *Economic Development and Social Change in South India*. Bombay: Oxford University Press.

EVANS, R.R. (ed.) (1973): *Social Movement*. Chicago: Rand McNally College Publishing Company.

GAZETTEERS OF INDIA (1884): Bombay Presidency: Vol. XXIII, *Bijapur District*. Bombay.

HETTNE, B. JORN (1974): *Mobilization and Political Change in Karnataka*. Department of Peace and Conflict Research, University of Gothenburg (mimeo).

INSTITUTE FOR DEVELOPMENT RESEARCH (1975): *Socio-Economic Development and Regional Planning in Karnataka*. Mid-term Report (Mimeo).

IRSCHICK, EUGENE F. (1969): *Politics and Social Conflict in South India: The Non-Brahmin Movement and Tamil Separatism 1916-1928*. Bombay: Oxford University Press.

KIDDER, ROBERT L. (1974): 'Litigation as a Strategy for Personal Mobility: The Case of Urban Caste Association Leaders'. *Journal of Asian Studies*. 33(2): 177-91.

MERTON, R.K. (1957): *Social Theory and Social Structure*. New York: The Free Press.

MISRA, P.K. (1976): *The Harijan Issue in Karnataka*. (Mimeo).

NANJUNDAYYA & ANANTHAKRISHNA IYER (1931): *Mysore Tribes and Castes*. Vol. 4. Bangalore: Government Press.

RAO, M.S.A. (1970): *Urbanization and Social Change*. Delhi: Orient Longmans.

————(1973): 'Role Analysis and Social Change with Special Reference to India'. Paper submitted to the IX International Congress of Anthropological and Ethnological Sciences. Chicago. (Mimeo).

————(1976): "Some Conceptual Problems in the Study of Social Movements". Paper presented at the XIII All-India Sociological Conference, Chandigarh. (Mimeo). Chapter 1 in this Volume.

————(Forthcoming): *Social Movements and Social Transformation*. A Study of Two Backward Classes Movements. New Delhi: Macmillan.

THURSTON, E. (1909): *Castes and Tribes of Southern India*. Vol. 5, Madras: Government Press.

YELLAMMA, K.C. (1948): *Bhovi Jananga Kula Samme Charitre, Gothravali Mathu Neveenacharagalu* (Kannada). Kolar: K.C. Yellamma.

6

M S A Rao

Social Movements among the Backward Classes and the Blacks: Homology in the Sources of Identity

DEPRIVED SECTIONS OF society in different parts of the world have organized themselves into protest movements to fight against discriminations of various kinds based on colour, religion, caste and tribe. Their problem, however, has been one of establishing a new identity —the kind of image that they want to protect in order to gain self-respect, honour and status. While the question of identity has been common to all the deprived sections, the answers that they have sought to provide have been different but homologous. This paper* is an attempt to provide a classificatory scheme, at an abstract level, for the analysis of the homology in the sources of identity among the Backward Classes and Black movements, which have arisen under diverse social and cultural conditions such as India and the United States of America. The paper does not deal with the question why and under what circumstances certain movements choose one source of identity rather than any other,[1] because such a question can be answered only by a detailed empirical examination of the event structure and cognitive response of the concerned group in the wider economic and political contexts. I believe such

---

*I am grateful to Professor Nathan Glazer for his valuable comments on an earlier draft of this paper. However, I alone am responsible for the views expressed.

an enquiry should follow the analysis of logic of forms and homology between them.

The social movements that have occurred among the Backward Classes in India and the Blacks in the United States have undoubtedly arisen under diverse social and cultural circumstances. The differences are too apparent. For instance, while Indian society is characterized by the caste system, American society is characterized by class, race, and ethnicity. The Indian and American systems of hierarchy and control are different. The latter is a developed nation, whereas the former is a developing one. Nevertheless, as we shall point out later, the ways in which the Backward Classes and Blacks have sought to establish new identities are homologous, at an abstract level, and not similar.

The problem of identity is crucial in the formation of protest groups and for collective mobilization. The existing groups project a different image of themselves *vis-a-vis* other groups and define their internal and external relations in the light of this self-image. Identity is, however, a dynamic phenomenon—old identities are discarded and new ones are assumed. The self-perception of the group changes in the context of the current objectives to be gained and interests to be pursued. In the context of social movements among the deprived sections, the element of conflict becomes prominent, sharpening the criteria of incorporation and exclusion.

The problem of identity is intimately related to ideology which is a symbolic system. An ideology provides a set of beliefs and symbols in relation to the aspirations of the concerned group and its response to reality. It helps the codification of beliefs, interprets the surroundings and legitimizes action. It also develops symbols and codes. It is necessary to stress that the ideology of social movements among the deprived classes tends to be double-edged. It not only provides self-defence against powerlessness but also acts as a guide to aggressive action.

In order to understand the formation of ideologies it is necessary to analyze the structural situation of the Backward Classes and the Blacks in terms of relative deprivation. However, the position of relative deprivation provides only the necessary conditions for the formation of a protest ideology. The sufficient conditions are supplied by the self-perception and the ideology of the concerned group, on the basis of which a new identity is established.

Position of Relative Deprivation

The position of the Blacks and the Backward Classes[2] in their respective social and cultural systems is characterized by relative deprivation. To take the position of the Blacks, the American Negroes, who first landed in Virginia in 1619, had the status of indentured labour but were later made slaves. Chattel slavery was soon institutionalized. The slaves were denied both civil and political rights. Husbands, wives and children could be separated, and children often derived their status from their mothers. The slaves were awarded as prizes in lotteries and raffles. They were wagered at gambling tables and horse races (Stampp 1956:201). They were whipped for minor crimes, mutilated for harsher crimes and killed for striking a white.

The slaves worked from dawn to dusk under the supervision of a whiteman. While the old men tended gardens and looked after the animals, old women did domestic work. They lived in small huts, or slave cabins, which had no amenities. They were not allowed to retain their culture, language and religion. They were converted to Christianity and were told by the white ministers how to adjust to their conditions of servitude which was ordained by God. Bishops and other religious leaders frequently owned slaves themselves (Franklin, 1948:200). This situation lasted for about two-and-a-half centuries till the end of the Civil War in 1865.

Among the Backward Classes in India, the category that has now come to be identified as the scheduled castes, which includes the ex-untouchables or Harijans, had a status in the traditional social system before British rule which was more or less homologous to that of the Blacks. Verba, Ahmed and Bhatt (1971: Chp. III) have systematically compared the contemporary social and economic positions of the Blacks and the Harijans. We shall consider the parallels only in the traditional social systems, to enable us to understand the structural conditions in the emergence of social movements.

Serfdom and slavery existed in parts of India, where agricultural labourers were recruited from among the untouchable castes and, in some cases, from among the tribes. For instance, in Kerala (Rao, 1957:37), the Pulayas, Cherumas and Panas (a tribe) belonged to the category of agrestic slaves. They were governed by three types of tenures, the degree of severity being highest in the first type. In this they were the property of their masters, being bought, sold and transferred like any other commodity. But unlike the Blacks, the husband and wife were never separated. They lived in huts on the farmstead, had their own family life, followed their own religion but always worked for their masters.

The untouchables suffered from many kinds of religious and secular disabilities. On the religious side they were not allowed to study the sacred scriptures nor to worship at the temples of the caste Hindus. Their touch was considered defiling by the caste Hindus. Hence, they were not allowed to use the tanks and wells of the latter. Extreme forms of discriminations existed in Kerala. There was not only touch pollution, but also distance pollution. The unapproachables were forbidden to build houses of bricks, to use an umbrella or footwear. Their women were obliged not to cover their breasts. Any violation of the customary norms of behaviour was rewarded with very severe forms of punishment—from decapitation to multilation.

Thus, both the Blacks and the scheduled castes suffered from intense forms of relative deprivation in the fields of religion, education, economics and politics. They were discriminated against in the dress they wore, their speech, the houses they built, the way they carried themselves and the manner in which they interacted with the privileged. The latter zealously guarded their privileges and brutally punished those who violated the customary laws.

Until the beginning of the nineteenth century, the scheduled castes and the Blacks largely accepted their lot. Some of them rebelled against their helplessness, but the vast majority believed that their real chances lay in obedience and hard work as there was some reward for these 'virtues'.

First Awakening

While the presence of structural conditions of relative deprivation provided only the necessary context for the genesis of protest movements among both the Blacks and the Backward Classes, certain external influences provided the sufficient conditions to create an awakening among them. The first signs of an awareness of the extremely deprived status that they occupied occurred under diverse circumstances in the two cases. The Christian missionaries were about the first group to organize a programme for the scheduled castes, who were then referred to as the depressed classes. The missionaries not only converted them to their respective denominations but initiated a broad-based programme involving English education, and the setting up of orphanages and other special welfare measures. Those of the depressed classes who were converted to Christianity soon developed a different life style from their contemporaries. They received English education and were recruited to various government jobs.

Those of the depressed classes who had not embraced Christianity were quick to perceive the difference between their status and that of their converted brethren. The perception was one of the factors which led to an awareness among the non-converts. A further impetus was provided by the national movement which provided an ideology of egalitarianism and supported social movements which revolted against discrimination of any kind. Then there were the reform movements organized by the upper castes which initiated programmes of education and welfare for the Backward Classes, especially the depressed classes. These movements, being liberal, were against many orthodox brahmanical practices, including their attitudes towards the untouchables. Finally, the British abolished slavery and introduced an egalitarian system of law, liberal education and notions of representative government. All these developments provided a favourable climate for the genesis of social movements, with distinct ideologies and leadership, among the Backward Classes.

Among the Blacks, social awakening was initially brought about by the efforts of the Quakers in 1775 when they founded the Pennsylvania Abolition Society. This was the first organization in the United States which adopted an anti-slavery stance and advocated schooling for the Blacks (Bennett, 1970:362). Thus the first awakening occurred in colonial America before it became independent in 1876. Soon after, some states—such as Vermont, Massachusetts and Pennsylvania—abolished slavery. Blacks became more and more awakened to their slave status and there were many slave insurrections in the early nineteenth century. Some of the major ones occurred in Richmond (1800), Charleston (1822) and Southampton (1831).

Not all Blacks were slaves. There were also free Blacks who had migrated from Africa in the middle of the seventeenth century and who numbered about 60,000 by the end of the eighteenth century. They were mostly concentrated in the Northern part of the United States and enjoyed certain benefits which their brethern in the South did not. For instance, they were admitted to universities and several of them rose to positions of eminence in the fields of education, journalism and literature. It was this modernized section of the Blacks that provided the leadership in the anti-slavery movement which led to the Civil War in 1861 (Pinkney 1969:16).

The Whites of the North took a leading part in the Civil War. Under the leadership of Abraham Lincoln, a Union Army was formed which fought against the Confederate Army. On 1 January 1863, President Lincoln issued the Emancipation Proclamation and more Blacks joined in the ongoing Civil War. They were mostly recruited to the United States Coloured Troops. The Confederate Army surrendered on 1 April 1865, and Lincoln was assassinated on 14 April. In the same year, slavery was abolished in America while the Civil Rights Act of 1866 gave the Blacks equal political rights.

The victory of the North in the Civil War was more ideological than real. The Southern States continued to practise varying degrees of racial discrimination and the 'Jim Crow Laws', a watchword for racial segregation, reappeared restoring white supremacy. In 1883, the Supreme Court declared the Civil Rights Act of 1875 to be unconstitutional. Between 1880 and 1900, thousands of Blacks were lynched by the Ku Klux Klan in the South, and there was mass migration of the Blacks to the North.

Myrdal (1944:587-588) notes that the various measures of segregation and discrimination against the Negroes assumed a discending rank order centering round white man's aversion to amalgamation: (*i*) ban on inter-marriage and other sex relations; (*ii*) all sorts of taboos and etiquettes in personal contacts; (*iii*) segregation in schools and churches; (*iv*) segregation in hotels, theaters and public conveyances; (*v*) discrimination in public services; (*vi*) inequality in politics; (*vii*) inequality in justice; (*viii*) inequality in bread-winning and (*ix*) inequality in relief. The Blacks attempted to organize themselves more systematically to fight against such discriminations.

It is against this background of a fluctuating fate—of an early awakening and some gains—that organized movements arose among the Blacks and the Backward Classes by the turn of the present century which attempted to establish new identities on the basis of defined ideologies.

New Identities

BACKWARD CLASSES MOVEMENTS

The Backward Classes, who suffered from different degrees of relative deprivation, became aware of their status with the spread of new liberal ideas and alternate sources of legitimacy that were ushered in by British rule and the Indian national movement. They began to organize themselves in different parts of India, establishing new identities based on diverse ideologies. Our concern is more with these ideologies rather than with empirical details. One may identify three kinds of ideologies (Rao, 1977). First, many castes belonging to the other Backward Classes claimed a higher *varna* status through a reinterpretation and recasting of appropriate mythologies of origin. For instance, several cognate castes—such as the Ahirs in many parts of North India, the Gopas in Bengal, the Gaulis in Maharashtra, the Gollas in Andhra Pradesh and Karnataka, and the Konars in Tamilnadu—claimed descent from the Yadu dynasty (a famous Kshatriya dynasty in Hindu mythology) to which Lord Krishna belonged. In the second decade of the present century they organized themselves into an All-India Yadava Association. In parts of North India, especially Bihar, the Yadavas came into direct conflict with Bhoomihar Brahmins, when the former donned the sacred thread (symbol of the twice-born) in public.

The idea in such attempts to claim a higher *varna* status was to establish a new identity so as to gain self-respect, honour and esteem. This was not a process of imitation but a language of aggression by which sections of the Backward Classes challenged the monopoly of the upper castes in terms of access to the rituals and religious services of brahmanical Hinduism from which they had been barred for centuries. Thus, when the Yadavas donned the sacred thread, the symbol of highest ritual status, they were not imitating but challenging the monopoly of the twice-born caste Hindus which was borne out by the ensuing confrontation where the latter attempted to beat up the former in order to maintain the *status quo*.

Another variation in this approach of reinterpreting Hindu religion in search of self-determination, was developed by the Sri Narayana Dharma Paripalana Movement ('Movement for the Propagation of Sri Narayana Guru Swamy's Philosophy') among the

Izhavas (toddy-tappers) of Kerala. Until 1935, the Izhavas belonged to the scheduled castes category. They were considered to be unapproachables by the clean castes. The Izhavas, who formed about twenty-six per cent of Kerala's total population, suffered from many religious, economic, educational and political disabilities. Around the turn of the present century a charismatic leader, Sri Narayana Guru Swamy, gave them a new religion of one God, one religion and one caste which transformed their life styles and outlook. He established a set of religious institutions (temples, priests, monasteries, monks, household disciples) parallel to that of the teetotalarian and vegetarian variety of brahmanical Hinduism. Thus, although the Izhavas were not born in the upper castes, they could acquire the religious goods and services of the upper castes—something which had been denied to them for centuries. This helped the Izhavas both to gain self-respect and to adopt a protest ideology to challenge the religious, economic, educational and political supremacy of the upper castes.

A second variety of protest ideology was based on the rejection of the brahmanical Aryan religion and culture. The Dravida Kazhagam Movement in Tamilnadu idealized the Dravidian culture and religion and attacked the Aryan culture and religion. For the followers of the D. K. Movement, Ravana was virtuous whereas Rama (an incarnation of God) was wicked. The Self-Respect movement started by Ramaswamy Naicker advocated that his followers should have their own priests. The movement drew its main support from the low-castes/classes. Its leaders worked hard to escape the tyranny of the Brahmins and their culture, and to extol the virtues of the Dravidian culture and religion. In its extreme form, the Dravida Munnetra Kazhagam advocates the separation of Tamilnadu from the Indian Union.

The Mahar movement under the leadership of Ambedkar exemplifies a variation of the principle of rejection in protest ideology; namely, abandoning Hinduism altogether and embracing another religion (in this case Buddhism). The Mahars formed an important section of the scheduled castes of Maharashtra, constituting about ten per cent of that state's population. They served as village watchmen, messengers, and removers of cattle carcasses. These services were hereditary and were paid for in kind. The Mahars were also weavers, petty traders, carpenters and cultivators. Thus, they occupied a low position in the caste and occupational hierarchy, and as such suffered from many religious, economic, educational and political disabilities. In the third decade of the present century, the Mahars organized themselves under the leadership of Dr. Ambedkar. Dr. Ambedkar vacillated between adopting one of two themes of identity to fight against the discriminations imposed by the upper castes—whether to stay within the Hindu fold or to abandon Hinduism altogether. He finally resolved the dilemma in 1956 by accepting Buddhism and abandoning Hinduism which also meant giving up caste. A large number of his followers embraced Buddhism which upheld egalitarian values and was also, at the same time, within the Indian tradition (Patwardhan, 1973:105-69).

Thus the ideology of the Mahar movement reflects a total rejection of the religion of the caste Hindus which was identified with hierarchy and inequality. It also reflects the message of new identity—that the Mahars now belong to a religion which stands for egalitarian values and hence they are superior to the caste Hindus. This is another strategy to gain self-respect and esteem on the one hand and to negate or protest against the religion of the upper castes on the other.

While these two types of ideologies—reinterpretation and rejection—have, in one way or the other, a religious dimension, the ideologies of civil rights and class-conflict are secular in character. The civil-rights ideology, based on democracy, motivated the Backward Classes to evolve campaigns to fight for equality in educational, economic and political opportunities. Thus, the leaders of the SNDP and the Mahar movements agitated for their basic civil rights. In this they also incorporated the religious-cultural ideology in this approach in seeking to gain self-respect and honour.

The ideology of class conflict provides another secular source for establishing a separate identity as the exploited class. The Dalit Panther movement, fashioned after the Black Panthers of America, emerged among the Mahars of Bombay and Poona in 1972. Its spokesmen were Namdeo Dhasal, Raja Dhale and J.V. Power, all eminent literary men. It cashed in on the frustration that the urban youth were experiencing when faced with diverse forms of discriminations against the untouchables and the oppressed. According to its manifesto, the Dalit Panthers included all the revolutionary parties seeking to destroy the Hindu caste system. Its declared enemies were the landlords, capitalists and money-lenders. It aimed at an all round revolution. It is significant to note that the Panthers' ideology is akin to Fanon's (1973) view that colonialism cannot be separated from race. In the ideology of the Dalit Panthers, class struggle cannot be separated from an anti-caste Hindu attitude.

Thus, the protest ideologies of the Backward Classes movements reveal four organizing principles: (*i*) reinterpretation of myths of origin or of one's own religion; (*ii*) rejection of Hinduism and Aryan religion and culture; (*iii*) civil rights; and (*iv*) class conflict.

Protest ideologies, as discussed above, have been dominant in establishing new identities among the Backward Classes, characterized by conflict with the dominant groups. One may, however, point out that there have been attempts on the part of certain sections of the Backward Classes to move up the social ladder not by claiming equality with the dominant groups but by adopting certain elements in the life styles of the upper castes without courting conflict with them. For instance, the Chambhars, an untouchable caste of Maharashtra, accepted their position as leather workers, and gained upward mobility without coming into conflict with the dominant groups, the Marathas and the Brahmins. The Chambhars' larger identity was with the Hindus (Patwardhan, 1973:18, 49). Their self-image was to be 'good boys' in the eyes of the dominant groups and to gain access to modern economic and educational opportunities through request, acquiescence and good conduct. However, this approach or ideology has not resulted in any recognized social movement, but has remained largely at the level of individual effort. As we shall see later, the acquiescent ideology is logically opposed to the protest ideology.

Black Movements

The ideological underpinnings of the Black movements have been wide ranging—from acceptance and accommodation to extreme forms of nationalism. The acquiescent ideology was systematically developed and practised by Booker T. Washington. Washington was a 'pussy footing' uncle Tom accommodationist. He advocated the uplifting of the Blacks through industrial education and economic self-help. He founded the Tuskegee Institute to train Black workers in agricultural and industrial vocations. He also founded the Negro Business League (NBL) around 1900 and was prepared to forego Black participation in politics and to accept segregation as the price to be paid for white financial support for his educational and economic efforts.

While Washington tolerated Black suppression, Du Bois demanded full fledged civil rights on the basis of a protest ideology. In the Niagara Movement which he organized in 1905, Du Bois counteracted Washington's moves and argued for male suffrage, full civil rights, economic opportunity and the education of Black youths. He established the National Association for the Advancement of Coloured People (NAACP) in 1910. He also developed an interest in pan-Africanism, and was influenced by Marxism. But he maintained that race was stronger than class. Du Bois vacillated between Marxism and a middle class ideology and the latter eventually got the better of the former in him (Allen, 1970:98-9). This was the strategy that he adopted in fighting for the basic civil rights, and he came to be regarded as the father of the civil rights movement.

Besides NAACP, the other civil rights organizations were the National Urban League (NUL) and the Congress of Racial Equality (CORE). The NUL was established in 1910 for the purpose of easing the transition of the Southern rural Negro into an urban way of life in the North. The CORE was established in 1943 to work out a programme of direct action against racial segregation. All these organizations were democratic, inter-racial in composition and protest-oriented in their ideology.

Another moderate ideological position was adopted by Martin Luther King, a Baptist preacher. King practised non-violent direct action, on the model established by Gandhiji, and led many successful marches. He moved the Negro struggle from the courtroom to the streets and from law libraries to the pews of the church. In 1957 he organized the Southern Christian Leadership Conference (SCLC) which led numerous economic boycotts, desegregation and voter registration campaigns. This was the first civil rights movement to start in the South. King was working in a situation of violent racial riots in the 1960s but advocated a non-violent approach. He was assassinated in 1968.

While the civil rights ideology of Du Bois and King were based on moderate protest, there was another set of ideologies which advocated Black nationalism in different degrees, based on different theological interpretations of Christianity.

Marcus Garvey was the key figure in the mass movement. He emphasized withdrawal and self-organization on the basis of a new interpretation of Christianity, a principle that was adopted by the leaders of the SNDP movement. Born in 1887 in Jamaica, he came to be called the Black Moses giving the American Blacks a sense of racial pride based on their African heritage. He established the Universal Negro Improvement Association in 1914 in the USA, which had a membership of over two million by 1920. Garvey aimed to liberate the Blacks by developing a distinct racial type of civilization—that is, the African one—by rejecting American culture and society and by advocating the migration of the Blacks to Africa (Bracey Jr. *et al*; 1970:158-60).

The movement launched by Garvey also concentrated on Christian regeneration, and the educational and economic development of the Blacks. Garvey created a new religion—the African Orthodox Church—which was a fusion of elements of the Greek Orthodox and Episcopalian faith. One of the fundamental tenets of the new faith was the characterization of Christ as a blackman. Bishop McGuire announced that henceforth the Negro's devil would be white, and the Negro will have his own illustrated Bible with pictures of Negro saints and angels. Marcus Garvey was depicted as one of the saints stressing one God, one Aim, and one Destiny (Allen, 1970:100).

Following Marcus Garvey, a more systematic reinterpretation of Christianity provided a powerful militant ideology for the Blacks in the first and second decades of the twentieth century. The Negroes had earlier developed a Christ-like image of themselves to rationalize their self-respect and which was based on their slave morality—patience, humility and good nature. However, as more Negroes gained relative independence, the Christ-like image was turned into a mechanism challenging the Whites' interpretation of Christianity. The Negroes compared their Christ-like image with the inhuman Whiteman who was unlike Christ. The Christ-like image of the Negro suggested a mission to undertake reforms in this world. Thus, the ego-defence image was turned into a weapon of militancy, and a few important clergymen were pushed into this worldly fight for civil rights. Around 1915, both R.R. Wright Jr., editor of the *Christian Recorder*, and Reverdy C. Ranson, editor of the *AME Church Review*, transformed the slave religion into a religion of militancy. Their religion penetrated the class-rooms of the Negro universities and colleges, and became the sociological dogma taught to thousands of students. It set the Negro up as the moral arbiter of American civilization (Fullinwider, 1969:28, 41, 72).

Marcus Garvey's formulation of Jesus as the God of the oppressed and the theme of the double-edged Christ-like image of the Negro, were systematically developed later by Black Christian theologists in the context of Black power which emerged in the 1960s (Cone, 1970). The argument of Black theology runs as follows: Christian theology as developed by the Whites is the theology of the White oppressors giving religious sanction to genocide and enslavement of the Blacks. It is compatible with White racism. On the contrary, Black theology has emerged as a theology of liberation, identifying itself with the oppressed Blacks of America. It sees God of the Biblical tradition as being not neutral in human affairs, but as being on the side of the oppressed. He is not colour blind in the Black-White struggle, but takes the side of the Blacks, the oppressed. Therefore, the movement for Black liberation is the work of God Himself. All acts which impede the struggle of Black self-determination are anti-Christian, the work of Satan.

Black theology thus restructures the Christian belief system to serve as an instrument of Black liberation. It is the theological expression of a people who lack social and political power. It is the idiom of Black consciousness. Theology is used to uncover the racial biases of White Christianity. For instance, St. Paul asked the slaves to obey their masters. Because of the curse of Ham, Blacks had been condemned to be inferior to Whites. Similarly, Calvin and Wesley did not say anything against slave trading. On the other hand, the Black theologians—like Richard Allen, Danial Payne and Highland Garnet—revealed the incompatibility of White Christianity as the religion of liberation of the Blacks (Cone, 1970:73). Black theology reinforced the secular ideology of the Black power movement which we shall discuss later.

While Black theology provided a radical theme within the framework of Christianity, the adoption of Islam by a section of the Blacks was a revolt against the integrative influence of Christianity, the religion of the Whites. The principle of rejection of the religion and culture of the oppressor as a form of identity was also adopted by the Mahar and Dravida Kazhagam movements among the Backward Classes in India.

The Black Muslim movement was started by Timothy Drew who became Noble Drew Ali. He established the first Moorish Science Temple in New Jersey in 1913. The new Prophet, Drew Ali, gave the Black Americans an Asiatic origin. He translated the Holy *Quran* into English, and founded temples in different cities. The movement, however, gained momentum under the leadership of Elijah Muhammad (Robert Poole) who was born in Georgia in 1897. Under his leadership, the membership increased significantly. Elijah Muhammad eschewed all that was White. He asked his people to give up slave surnames. For instance, he changed the name Sam Washington to Sam X. The Muslims rejected Christianity as the Whiteman's religion, and Allah was seen as the supreme Blackman (Lincoln, 1961:76-7).

Malcolm X joined the Black Muslim Nation in 1953 and worked as a Minister in a temple. He rose to fame very quickly and became the nation's first National Minister in 1963 because of his personal charisma. He was a man of action and an undaunted speaker. He went to many Muslim countries in Africa and the Middle East and visited Mecca. He gave the Black Muslims an Afro-American identity and sang the glories of Black civilization. He was the spokesman of the American Blacks in international forums and strengthened the ideology of Black nationalism in America.

The Afro-Asian ideology reinforced Black nationalism in more ways than one. First, there was the search for identity based on specific genealogical connections with the home country. Secondly, there was an element of pride in claiming that the Blacks were the founders of such ancient civilizations as the Sumerian, the Egyptian, the Dravidian and Carthage (Malcolm X, 1970). This promoted not only a sense of belonging but also a feeling of self-respect. Thirdly, the ideology of African descent led to the adoption of many symbols and styles in dress and hairdo which enabled them to maintain an African identity. Fourthly, the Afro-Asian ideology did not remain only at the level of symbols but had concrete manifestations of international cooperation. At this level, however, the Black world was seen in terms of Islamic identities.

While Black theology and the Black Muslim movements stemmed from religious ideas, the Black power and Black Panther movements established new identities on the basis of Marxist ideology, which has a parallel in the Dalit Panther movement. Although Malcolm X was the ideological father of the Black power movement, it was Carmichael who spearheaded it. He was the Chairman of the Student Nonviolent Coordinating Committee (SNCC) founded in 1960. In '966, James Merdith's individual act of heroism (walking through and surviving bullet injuries) precipitated a major new development of emphasis in the long struggle for racial equality in America. It was in this 'March Against Fear' that the slogan 'Black Power' emerged. The ideology of Black power was contrary to the civil rights phase of the Black liberation movement which had more or less ground to a halt. Although the Civil Rights Law of 1964 and the 1965 Voting Rights Act were passed, there were considerable difficulties in enforcing them effectively. The SNCC addressed itself to this task. It also showed that civil rights did not mean anything to the poor. Only the educated and qualified could get jobs and secure effective voting rights through this approach. The de facto racial injustices of sprawling urban America—the systematic separation of life with the Negroes occupying decaying areas in the centre of cities and the Whites living in comfortable middle class suburbs—were considered to be the real problems (Feaver, 1970:143). The under-privileged Negroes in the urban ghettos of the North gained least from the civil rights movement. Carmichael, born in Trinidad, graduated from Howard University in 1964, was successful in injecting an element of self-determinism into the Black movement and in taking it away from the civil rights approach which the integrationists had adopted. Black power meant different things. But mostly it meant fighting for political representation and the creation of power bases for the Blacks.

The basic premise of Black power is 'before a group can enter the open society, it must first close ranks' (Allen, 1970:50). Blacks are not like other ethnic groups in American society. Carmichael characterized the Black communities as exploited colonics of the United States, and, following Fanon, identified the Black struggle with anti-colonial movements in the Third World with the consequent revolutionary implications. Black power was conceived as the politics of liberation in the Third World. Carmichael and Hamilton (1967) argued that the White-inspired private and public 'uplift services' imposed a dehumanizing paternalism on the Blacks, and that this perpetuated the pattern of colonial relations. Hence, the Blacks should give priority to the political goals of Black determination, Black self-identity and Black racial solidarity.

The Black power movement was later endorsed by the Congress of Racial Equality (CORE) which, until then, had followed a policy of integration relying on non-violent action. In 1966, CORE defined Black power as effective control and self-determination by men of colour in their own areas, while power was total control of the economic, political, educational and social life of the Black community from top to bottom. It also maintained that the exercise of power at the local level is simply what all other groups in American society have done to acquire their share of total American life. CORE's Black power resolution eliminated the ideology of racial integration as the group's goal and replaced it with the goal of racial co-existence through Black power (Allen, 1970:69).

Around 1966, another extremist development occurred—the Black Panther movement, organised by two students at Merritt College in Oakland, Newton, and Seale who were inspired by Fanon, Mao and Guevara. The Black Panther Party for self-defence was meant to arm the Black people so that they could directly protest against the attacks of the police and their brutalities and harassment. Newton and Seale also established the Community Alert Patrol (CAP) to curb police excesses on ghetto residents. Another eminent Panther was Eldridge Cleaver, who came into prominence in 1968. He declared Fanon's book, *The Wretched of the Earth*, to be the Bible of the Black Liberation Movement in America, for it legitimized the revolutionary impulse (Feaver, 1970:168).

The Panthers emphasized revolutionary nationalism rather than cultural nationalism. They were more militant and radical, and were able to penetrate into the poor working class of the urban ghettos.

Homology in the Sources of Identity

Against the foregoing account of the ideologies of different social movements among the Backward Classes and the Blacks, we may analyze the homology in their attempts to establish new identities. Figure 1 provides the classificatory scheme of the sources of identity.

Broadly speaking, two alternatives were open to the Backward Classes and Blacks to meet the challenges facing them. One was to adopt a position of non-confrontation, accepting their low position but requesting the dominant groups to allow them to have access to modern opportunities of education and employment so that they might serve better. The dominant groups, out of generosity, compassion and pity, granted them certain benefits as rewards for their good conduct. The other alternative was to protest against their

Figure 6.1

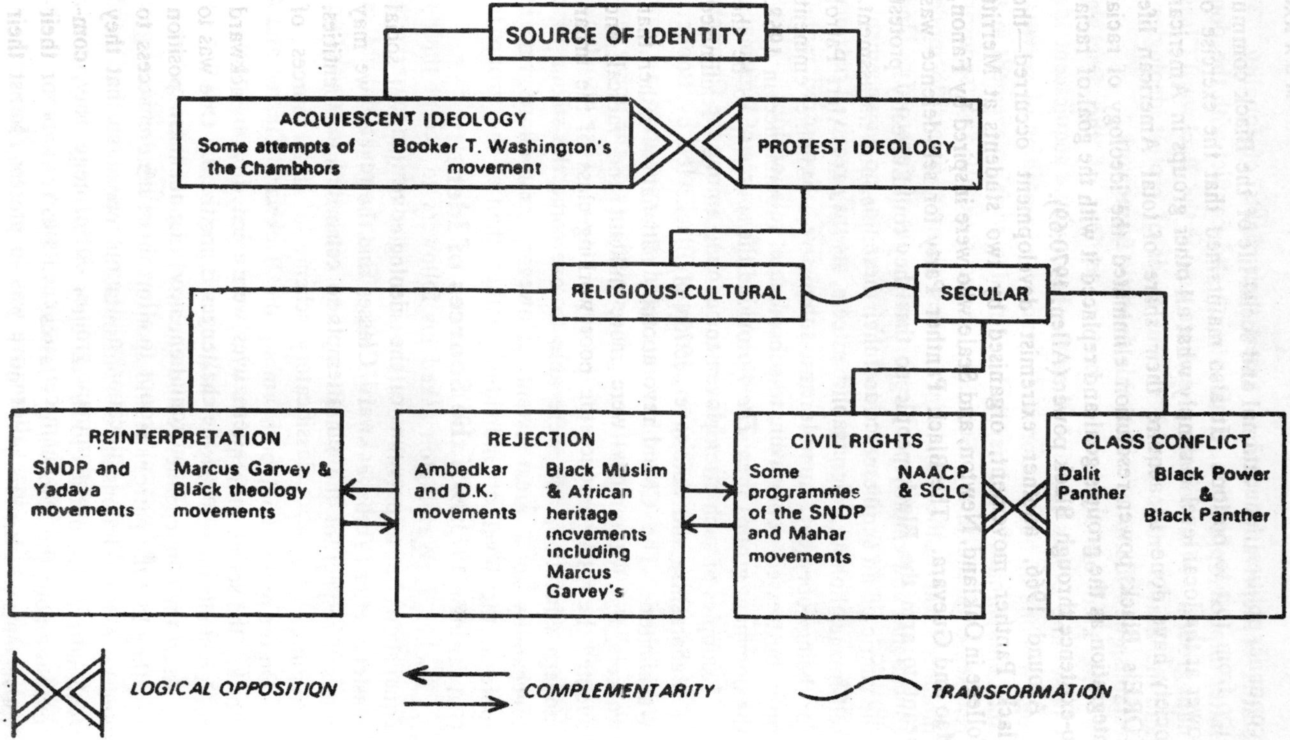

SOURCE OF IDENTITY
ACQUIESCENT IDEOLOGY
Some attempts of the Chambhors
Booker T. Washington's movement
PROTEST IDEOLOGY
RELIGIOUS-CULTURAL
SECULAR
REINTERPRETATION
SNDP and Yadava movements
Marcus Garvey & Black theology movements
REJECTION
Ambedkar and D.K. movements
Black Muslim & African heritage incvements including Marcus Garvey's
CIVIL RIGHTS
Some programmes of the SNDP and Mahar movements
NAACP & SCLC
CLASS CONFLICT
Dalit Panther
Black Power & Black Panther
LOGICAL OPPOSITION
COMPLEMENTARITY
TRANSFORMATION

status of deprivation and to assert their rights of equality. The latter implied opposition, confrontation and conflict with the dominant groups. Most social movements among the Backward Classes and the Blacks made use of various kinds of protest ideologies to establish new identities within this dualistic framework.

The kind of identity that certain sections of the Backward Classes and Blacks established on the basis of the acquiescent ideology was one of humiliation as they accepted a position of servitude. Such an approach could hardly be termed a social movement in the real sense of the term. Secondly, it was a situation of 'sponsored mobility' where the dominant groups granted access to modern educational and employment opportunities out of generosity. Under the rubric of an acquiescent ideology, there was no enhancement of self-image, honour, dignity and esteem, as they received patronage for being obedient, humble and submissive. Sponsored mobility only buttressed superordinate-subordinate relationships. Thirdly, the dominant groups themselves provided the source of legitimacy.

Examples of such attempts are to be found among the Chambhars of Maharashtra and among a section of Blacks led by Booker T. Washington. The Chambhars accepted their position as leather workers, and, without challenging the superiority of the upper castes, adopted the ritual practices of the upper castes. They also took to modern education, and were able to overcome the stigma of untouchability to a great extent. However, these efforts remained more at the level of individuals rather than at the group level (Patwardhan, 1973:49-51, 194).

Booker T. Washington asked his followers to accept their unequal status but to pursue vocation-oriented education to serve their masters better (Verba *et al*, 1971:69). This, however, did not raise the self-respect of the Blacks as they consented to a position of servitute.

On the other hand, both among the Backward Classes and the Blacks, the social movements which were based on an ideology of protest, built up self-respect, honour and prestige by enabling them to assert their independence and equality. Under these circumstances, they lost the patronage and sponsorship of the dominant groups and were in a relationship of confrontation, opposition and conflict with latter. In contrast to the acquiescent ideology, the concerned groups among the Backward Classes and Blacks involved in those movements which were based on a protest ideology had their own sources of legitimacy, independent of the dominant groups. Thus there is a logical opposition between the identity based on an acquiescent ideology and that based on a protest ideology.

Verba *et al* (1971: Chap. II) have compared the social movements that took place among the Blacks and the Harijans. They have drawn parallels between the Mahar movement on the one hand and Booker T. Washington's movement which they characterize as having a goal of 'separate but not quite equal'. They also consider Dr. Ambedkar's movement as parallel to Marcus Garvey's and the Black Muslim movement under the 'rejection of the system' goal. While I am in agreement with their second parallel, I do not think that it is appropriate to treat the Mahar movement as having an accommodationist ideology, given of the element of confrontation and conflict that has marked it. It was essentially a protest movement claiming equality and not accepting unequal status as the Chambhars or Booker T. Washington did. The Mahars protested against their status of relative deprivation as long back as 1890 and fought long for the abolition of discriminations (Zelliot, 1970:404).

We shall now consider the homology in the themes of protest ideology and the kinds of identities that were established on their bases among the Backward Classes and the Blacks. The protest ideology has two main themes: religious-cultural and secular. The religious-cultural theme manifests itself in the principle of reinterpretation of scriptures, myths and rituals, and in the principle of rejection of the religion and/or culture of the dominant group. It may be asked why certain sections of the Backward Classes and the Blacks choose religious ideas in order to protest and establish a new identity. There are two main reasons for this. First, religious ideas form an effective source of legitimacy, which the dominant group often use to uphold their superior status. The deprived groups can reinterpret the same ideas in a different way so as to legitimize their claim to equal or superior status *vis-à-vis* the dominant groups. Secondly, myths, beliefs and rituals provide the language of protest against the dominant groups. They are double-edged weapons which attack the monopolistic position of the dominant groups and also provide the basis of a new identity.

Viewed in this light, the SNDP movement exemplifies the principle of reinterpretation as a theme of the protest ideology. The Izhavas of Kerala suffered from conditions of acute relative deprivation within the framework of the caste system as characterized by the principle of purity-pollution. This principle was legitimized by the priests of orthodox Hinduism (Brahmins) and by the kings who wielded secular authority. During British rule, these two sources of legitimacy were undermined to a great extent, and new sources of status were established, based on occupation, income, education and an egalitarian value system. Under such conditions, the leaders of the deprived sections were awakened to alternative sources of identity. Two ways of protest were open to them. One was to reinterpret Hinduism and claim a new identity within its fold, and the other was to abandon Hinduism and embrace another religion and culture. The Izhavas chose the former, although they did make several attempts to choose the latter, because of the presence of a charismatic leader, Sri Narayana Guru Swamy, among them.

Sri Narayana Guru Swamy established a new identity for the Izhavas based on a reinterpretation of orthodox Hinduism. He denied the existence of a plurality of Gods, religions and castes. He argued against the criterion of birth as the basis of differential access to the highest forms of spiritual knowledge, and demonstrated the efficacy of training in gaining this knowledge. He was also against superfluous and expensive rituals. He established a set of beliefs, rituals, temples and priests which was parallel to that of the upper castes. The world-view of his reinterpreted Hinduism was both enlightened and simple, on the basis of which Izhavas were able to claim a new identity with honour, esteem and self-respect.

Similarly, the Ahirs and other cognate castes systematically reinterpreted the Yadava myth of origin of their castes in legitimizing their superior status. This was a language of protest against the status that was accorded to them by the dominant groups. They not only achieved self-respect and honour, but also gained access to the religious goods and services of the twice-born castes which they had long been denied.

The same principle of reinterpretation of religious ideas was adopted by a section of the Blacks. They were able to establish a new identity on the basis of a reinterpretation of Christianity. Marcus Garvey created a new Christian religion which characterized Christ as a Blackman and as the God of the oppressed. There was a move to prepare a Black Bible with pictures of Negro saints and angles. But a more systematic interpretation of Black Christianity uncovered the racial biases of White Christianity. Black theology emerged as the theology of liberation identifying the Blacks as the oppressed and the whites as the oppressors. Christ was always on the side of the oppressed. Hence the movement for the liberation of the Blacks was considered as the work of God Himself. The Black Christian theology which ran parallel to White Christianity gave the Blacks a new basis of identity, legitimizing their efforts towards self-determination and their efforts to gain honour and prestige. Black theology was the language of 'revolution' against White supremacy and provided a double-edged ideology for the Black movement.

Thus, certain sections of the Blacks and Backward Classes reinterpreted Christianity and Hinduism respectively. The new ideology provided the language of protest and aggression against the opposition groups. The Blacks and the Backward Classes are far removed from each other in terms of their society and culture. But in their attempts to organize protest movements they made use of the same ideology of reinterpreting the religions to which they belonged in order to gain self-respect, honour and esteem and to fight against the opposition reference groups.

Certain other sections of the Blacks and the Backward Classes worked out another type of response to 'oppression'. They abandoned the religions to which they belonged and embraced a different religion. A section of the Blacks gave up Christianity in utter frustration; identifying it with White domination, and embraced Islam. The leader of the Black Muslim movement, Elijah Muhammad, rejected Christianity as the Whiteman's religion and eschewed all that was White, including White surnames. Thus, the Black Muslim movement established a new identity for Black self-determination on the one hand, and served as a form of protest against the religion of the Whites on the other.

Under the leadership of Malcolm X, Black Muslim ideology was linked with African nationalism and Black civilization. The establishment of an African heritage served to establish a new identity, which was different from the Western civilization complex. The glorification of African symbolism by the Blacks meant rejection of the White civilization and an assertion that their civilization was more ancient than and superior to Western civilization. African heritage as a source of new identity was also emphasized by Marcus Garvey and Du Bois.

Marcus Garvey's movement may be seen as combining the two themes of protest ideology, namely, reinterpretation of Christianity and rejection of American society and culture, and adoption of the

African heritage. It is necessary to point out that one theme in the protest ideology can complement another as they are logically compatible with each other under the rubric of protest. Whereas an acquiescent ideology cannot be combined with a theme of protest ideology as there is a logical opposition between the two. If, in any particular case, a movement starts with an acquiescent ideology and gives it up and develops a protest ideology, the two should be considered as separate movements and not as different phases of the same movement, because the two identities are different in kind.

The principle of rejection was also followed by a section of the Backward Classes led by Ambedkar, the leader of the Mahar movement. He abandoned Hinduism, which he identified with brahmanical and upper caste domination, and embraced Buddhism which was the symbol of egalitarianism. Similarly, Ramaswamy Naicker, the leader of the D.K. movement, abandoned all that was Aryan religion, language and culture, and adopted the Dravidian religion, language and culture. This new identity provided the basis for establishing self-determination, respect and hohour on the one hand, and for protesting against the domination of the upper castes on the other. Thus, both the Blacks and the Backward Classes adopted the same principle of rejection of the religion and culture of the oppressors in establishing new identities. They adopted new religions which were symbolic of freedom from oppression.

New identities are established not only on the basis of a religious-cultural ideology but also on the basis of a secular one, with civil rights and class-conflict themes. The former, when viewed as an attempt to claim equality of status through democratic means, is exemplified by many backward classes movements fighting for basic secular rights such as right of admission to schools, right of recruitment to government jobs and right of adult suffrage. For example, these programmes were part of the SNDP and Mahar movements. A point to be noted here is that the leaders of these movements adopted both religious-cultural and civil rights ideology simultaneously in their efforts to attain equality of status with the dominant groups on the ritual and the secular planes.

Among the Blacks, the adoption of a civil rights ideology as a form of protest was used by the leaders of the civil rights movements—Du Bois (NAACP) and Martin Luther King (SCLC). While Du Bois also made use of the cultural symbolism of pan-Africanism and Negro identity to spearhead his legalistic programmes, Martin

Luther King used the Black Church as the basis of organizing non-violent civil struggles. Thus they combined both religious-cultural and secular civil rights ideologies.

While the civil rights ideology operates within the framework of democracy, the class-conflict ideology is part of communism. It drives a wedge between the deprived sections and the dominant groups. As members of the exploited class, the former wish to achieve liberation through class struggle. The secular ideology of class conflict was adopted by the Black Power and Black Panther movements. The ideological basis of both movements came from Frantz Fanon who considered racism not as an independent phenomenon but rather as being dependent upon hierarchical relations imposed by a group with a technical advantage over another. Fanon (1971:31) extended Marx to consider the relations of production themselves as forming a superstructure of exploitation and which would disappear only through a struggle for political liberation (Zolberg, 1970:174). Thus it was relations of production plus racism which provided the ideology for a section of the Blacks. In this approach, the Blacks were doubly oppressed—they not only formed part of the proletariat but were victims of racial discrimination. It gave them a new identity to fight against White colonialism and capitalism.

Among th: Backward Classes, the Dalit Panthers adopted the ideology of class conflict and anti-caste Hindu feeling. The new identity that emerged based on these two principles enabled the young urban Mahars to attack the upper caste Hindu capitalists. Thus, a section of both the Blacks and the Backward Classes used the principle of class-conflict along with an ethnic element to establish new identities. While the former belonged to the secular domain, the latter was part of the religious-cultural syndrome as we have seen earlier. With this new identity they could attack the double-faced enemy, the white-capitalist and the caste Hindu-capitalist.

This shows that the two seemingly opposite principles—secular class conflict and religious-cultural—can be seen as transformations. The secular ideology can be recoded into the religious-cultural one and vice versa. At a higher level of abstraction, the opposition is overcome through transformation. The secular and the religious principles can be made to achieve the same end, namely, that of establishing a new identity for self-determination and for attacking the monopolies of first-class citizens over religious, economic, educational and political goods and services.

Notes

1. An explanation in this direction has been indicated with reference to the SNDP movement.
2. The general category of Backward Classes consists of three specific categories: scheduled castes, scheduled tribes and the other backward classes. The first two are scheduled in the Constitution and are entitled to economic, educational and political privileges (Moorthy, 1975). The third one, generally consisting of lower and middle level clean Hindu castes, are entitled only to economic and educational privileges based on economic criteria of backwardness. But there is considerable variation, in respect of groups receiving the benefits, from one state to another. For the purposes of this paper, scheduled tribes are left out. The scheduled castes form the main focus. The other backward classes are also referred to wherever they are relevant. While the scheduled castes constituted 14.6 per cent of the total population of India in 1971, the Blacks formed 11 per cent of the total American population in 1970.

References

ALLEN, ROBERT L. (1970) : *Black awakening in Capitalist America.* New York: Doubleday.

BENNETT JR., LERONE (1970) : *Before the Mayflower: A History of the Negro in America 1619-1964.* Baltimore : Penguin.

BRACEY JR., J.H., AUGUST MEIER, & E. RUDWICK (1970) : *Black Nationalism in America.* Indianapolis: The Bobbs-Merrill Company.

CARMICHAEL, S. & C.V. HAMILTON (1967) : *Black Power.* New York: Random House.

CONE, JAMES H. (1970) : *A Black Theology of Liberation.* Philadelphia: J.B. Lippincott.

FANON, FRANTZ (1973) : *The Wretched of the Earth.* Harmondsworth: Penguin.

FEAVER, GEORGE (1970) : 'Black Power'. In Maurice Cranston (ed.) : *The New Left.* London: The Bodley Head.

FRANKLIN, JOHN HOPE (1948) : *From Slavery to Freedom.* New York : Knopf.

FULLINWIDER, S.P. (1969) : *The Mind and Mood of Black America.* Illinois: The Dorsey Press.

LINCOLN, C. ERIC (1961) : *The Black Muslims in America.* Boston: Beacon Press.

MALCOLM X (1970) : *Afro-American History.* New York: Pathfinder Press.

MOORTHY, O.K. (1975) : 'Development of Scheduled Castes: An Appraisal'. *Journal of Social Science Research.* 18(2):29-50.

MYRDAL, GUNNAR (1944) : *An American Dilemma: The Negro Problem and Modern Democracy.* New York: Harper and Brothers.

PATWARDHAN, SUNANDA (1973) : *Change among India's Harijans.* New Delhi: Orient Longman.

PINKNEY A. (1969) : *Black Americans.* Ethnic Groups in American Life Series. Englewood Cliffs, New Jersey: Prentice-Hall.

RAO, M.S.A. (1957) : *Social Change in Malabar.* Bombay: Popular Book Depot.

——— (1977) : 'Themes in the Ideology of Protest Movements'. In *Dissent Protest and Reform Movements in Indian Civilization.* S.C. Malik (ed.) Simla: Indian Institute of Advanced Study.

——— (forthcoming) : *Social Movements and Social Transformation; A Study of Two Backward Classes Movements in India.* New Delhi: Mac millan.

STAMPP, K.M. (1956) : *The Peculiar Institution.* New York: Knopf.

VERBA, SIDNEY, BASHIRUDDIN AHMED & ANIL BHATT (1971) : *Caste, Race and Politics.* Beverly Hills: Sage Publications.

ZELLIOT, ELEANOR (1970): 'Mahar and Non-Brahmin Movements in Maharashtra'. *Indian Economic and Social History Review,* Vol. 7, pp. 397-415.

ZOLBERG, A.R. (1970) : 'Frantz Fanon'. In Maurice Cranston (ed.): *The New Left.* London : The Bodley Head.

7

Kenneth W. Jones

Social Change and Religious Movements in Nineteenth Century Punjab

COMPETITION AMONG DIVERSE religious movements became an increasing feature of nineteenth century India, particularly in Punjab. Although this phenomenon has been widely discussed and often condemned, it is not yet fully understood. For many periods and places, there is a lack of detailed historical narratives which would provide an exact knowledge of what happened: when, where, and by whom. Scholars also need a more sophisticated conceptualization of the interplay of forces which created and sustained competition and conflict between religious movements. We must take into account three sets of forces which interacted upon each other to produce religious conflicts in nineteenth century Punjab: first, the traditional world of pre-annexation Punjab; secondly, the forces of modernization which changed that traditional world in the second half of the nineteenth century; and, lastly, the policies and actions of the British colonial administration. Each of these three interacted with the other two. Nothing was stable, fixed or stagnant. Nor had it ever been. Indian society has always been in a state of movement and dynamism. During the nineteenth century, the rate of change may have increased but this cannot be taken to imply a pre-1849 period of immobility. Here we will emphasize the forces of modernization, particularly social and psychological factors which have tended to receive little attention in past scholarship. This is not to claim that these forces should be given precedence over all other contributing factors, but that they should be given serious attention by those who wish to understand the changes which took place in Punjabi society during the years prior to World War I.

Before examining the forces of modernization, it is necessary to note two features of the traditional Punjab prior to the British conquest. Punjab had long been an area of religious ferment. Buddhism had made inroads into the parent Hindu community only to be almost totally destroyed with only a remnant left in the high valleys of the Himalayas. Islam had, through immigration and conversion, become the largest religious community accounting for nearly half of the population of Punjab. The rise of Sikhism added a new dimension to the religious composition of the Punjab. With Islam and Sikhism, violence and conflict became firmly associated with religion. Hinduism in the meantime shrank to a minority community which had lost both political power and numerical dominance.

An understanding of the interrelations between the religious communities of the Punjab, necessitates the realization that these religions are not historically comparable, but represent two different types of religions—the evolutionary and prophetic. Evolutionary religions are those systems of belief which have no definite beginning in time, but grow with the social and cultural system of a particular people. They have no founding prophet and do not convert. Membership is ascriptive—that is, based on birth and not on belief. These are the parent religions of mankind. Prophetic religions, by contrast, begin with one man and his message. They are initially cults centered around a prophet. If they succeed, and very few do, they gradually split off from the parent religion. New prophetic faiths may in turn develop from the base of either an evolutionary religion or a prophetic religion. They develop their own sets of rituals and their own sense of identity. Authority is based on a new text or texts. Membership is by belief, by the acceptance of a new prophetic message, and, therefore, all prophetic religions proselytize. They seek to convert and in fact claim universal appeal for their faith. They would convert the world. Since membership in a prophetic faith requires belief, one can leave that faith by rejecting its ideology. Membership of an evolutionary religion cannot be lost by the lack of belief, but only by conversion to a prophetic religion.

The two best examples of surviving evolutionary religions are

Hinduism and Judaism. Both have been parent religions to many cults and a few successful prophetic faiths such as Islam, Christianity, Buddhism, Jainism, and, if one considers it to be a separate religion, Sikhism. Initially, all these were religious and sectarian movements. The historical pattern is clear. Christianity began as a Jewish cult, gradually converted from within Judaism, then from the Roman world beyond, and in the process became a separate religion. Buddhism and Jainism developed in much the same manner as Christianity, while Islam grew as a syncretistic faith, drawing on Judaism, Christianity and the pre-Islamic sects of the Arabian Peninsula. Similarly, Sikhism developed out of an interaction between Islam and Hinduism. The long, bitter religious-political struggle of the Sikhs against the Mughal state tended to foster and maintain a close affinity of Sikhs and Hindus in the Punjab.

By contrast, the events and forces of the nineteenth century heightened Sikh awareness of their own identity and thus pulled them away from the parent Hindu community. Pre-conquest Punjab thus had one evolutionary religion—Hinduism; and two prophetic faiths—Islam and Sikhism. The British added a third prophetic faith, Christianity. In order to understand the relations between religious communities, we must keep in mind the faiths that are present and the type of religious community with which we are dealing.

Religous conflict in tarditional Punjab stemmed from intolerance on the part of the dominant community such as was exhibited during the early days of the Islamic conquest or later by occasional rulers. This might take the form of forced conversion, the destruction of temples, or discriminatory governmental policies. Conflict also rose from inherent points of tension between different religious communities. The slaughter of cattle by Muslims, particularly during religious festivals, or the playing of music in front of a mosque by Hindus, are examples of these inherent points of tension. The degree of inter-religious violence created by such events still needs to be determined by historians. We are often given a picture of religious peace and tranquillity in the pre-British era, particularly during the period of Sikh dominance; however, this vision of the past is not substantiated in fact. There still needs to be a careful detailed analysis of inter-religious relationships during the Sikh period. Until such research is completed we will not be able to fully assess the impact of traditional social dynamics on the years after annexation.

The British conquest ushered in a period of change, of interaction with intrusive Western civilization that would ultimately affect all segments of Punjabi society, though not evenly. Cultural change was highly selective. First to be drawn into the newly-established colonial world were those groups in Punjabi society which were already literate and living in the towns. They learned English, accepted some of the external cultural traits of the English, and found employment either directly with the new government or indirectly in occupations related to that government (such as, teaching, journalism or law). In Punjab, as elsewhere, these were primarily Hindus of the Brahmin or Vaishya *varnas*—Saraswat and Gaur Brahmins; and among the Vaishyas, khatris, aroras, baniyas, and suds. An education in English was the key to financial success. By the 1880s, a college education became increasingly necessary for higher positions in government service and the professions; as a result, young men from throughout the Punjab began to trek to the Government College, Lahore. Here they received a higher education in English and also imbibed the culture of Lahore which they would in turn spread throughout the Province. Punjabi Hindus led in this development, since that community traditionally possessed the largest number of literates. Sikhs and Muslims followed and began to develop their own English-speaking elites. The pattern of anglicization in the Punjab was not dramatically different from other parts of British India, with the Hindus leading and other communities following behind.[1]

The acquisition of an English education, especially higher education, was not for the Punjabis or other Indians a culturally neutral act. It produced individuals affected by both alienation and marginality. By alienation, we mean the distance that exists between a person or group of people and the norms of their own society. This process is often seen in relation to higher education and takes place within one civilization. As they proceed through the educational process, especially at its higher levels, students change and grow. They develop concepts, habits, tastes and life-styles that are often at variance with the norms of their society. This is particularly so when students leave their home community for higher education in an urban environment. For many individuals, such alienation is not severe, but it does make them uncomfortable with the social world of their childhood. Higher education and a professional or intellectual occupation can produce a strong sense of separateness from the cultural norms of society, creating what is so often termed the 'alienated intellectual' of Western culture.

Involvement in a culture other than one's own can produce a degree of marginality, a feeling of affinity to another dramatically different way of living and thinking. In a colonial milieu, both the rulers and elements of the ruled classes are affected by the opposing culture, changed, and made marginal to their parent culture. Mastery of an English education and the English language provided individuals with a new set of terms and concepts in which they could think and view their traditional world. They would inevitably think differently than non-English speakers around them. Anselm L. Strauss, the noted social psychologist, has observed that

> in coming to new terms a person becomes something other than he once was. Terminological shifts necessitate, but also signalize, new evaluations: of self and others, of events, acts, and objects; and the transformation of perception is irreversible; once having changed there is no going back. One can look back, but he can evaluate only from his new status.[2]

With the new perspective provided by English education, young Punjabis looked out at the traditional world around them. They felt ill-at-ease with many of the customs accepted by their fellows and yet could not express that sense of alienation. Ruchi Ram Sahni, recalling his student days at the Lahore Government College, felt that he and others like him existed in an unprecedented situation to which the traditional patterns of behavior no longer applied. 'Situated as we of the first generation of University students were, practically without guidance from our elders, even as to the choice of our subjects or future careers, we were largely like a boat without a steers-man—at the mercy of the current that might be flowing at the time.'[3]

The sense of alienation created through the educational process was heightened and maintained in the years that followed by participation in the anglicized world of the British. Those who worked directly or indirectly for the British found it necessary to adjust themselves, at least in part, to British norms of behavior. The office provided an anglicized environment, even if the home remained traditional.

Anxiety among educated Punjabis also arose from the fact that they were under attack from two groups—Christian missionaries and indigenous reformers. The Christians condemned all religious communities claiming that each was an untrue faith filled with superstition and error. They used a wide variety of techniques: tracts, journals, street preaching, *zenana* missions, medical missions, and Bible lessons in their extensive school system—in short, all the modern methods of proselytization.[4] Criticism was also levelled against traditional beliefs from within each religious community. Among the Hindus, this meant the Brahmo Samajists who had been active in Lahore since 1863 and individual critics such as Munshi Kanyalal Alakhdhari.[5] For those who felt completely secure in their religious beliefs and social customs, such criticism had little impact. But for individuals already uneasy, who doubted the validity of their traditional world, these attacks could not be ignored.

The presence of the British *Raj* and its associated cultural changes necessitated some kind of response, ranging from total acceptance of British cultural norms to total rejection. Individuals who did not have to interact with the British could attempt to ignore them, in the hope that they, like other conquerors, would either leave or become Indianized. This position became increasingly difficult to maintain, since the British did not leave nor did they acculturate to an Indian norm. At the opposite end of the spectrum lay total acceptance, which in practical terms meant adopting British dress, diet, language, and religion. It meant conversion to Christianity and an attempt to become British. Such a step demanded the cutting of all ties with one's friends and relatives, while rejecting all or nearly all Indian tradition and heritage. But no matter how successful the process of anglicization, one could not become British. Their racism precluded that and barred the entry of Indians into British society. As a result, few educated Indians converted to Christianity or sought to join the ranks of the conqueror's world. Instead, they sought a middle solution somewhere between acceptance and rejection.

The alienation and marginality of the English educated classes provided a basis for a series of social and religious movements throughout the subcontinent. These movements—the Brahmo Samaj, the Prarthana Samaj, Ahmadiyas, Singh Sabhas, and the reforms of Sayyid Ahmad Khan, to name but a few—shared similar suppositions and goals. All considered that their parent religious community was degenerate, filled with superstition and evil social practices. This sense of degeneracy arose from the fact of British conquest (all communities were defeated communities), and it also rested on a sense of alienation present among the educated elites of each community. Each movement developed its own explanation for this degeneracy and each called for a return to the past in order to create a new 'golden age' for their religious community. The religious and social systems advocated by these movements were modernized and appealed to the educated elites. Here they found a set of beliefs and practices with which they could be comfortable, in which they could believe, and thus could defend from criticism, be it internal or external. Membership in these new movements eased the sense of alienation and marginality which haunted many of the educated elites. They had found a refuge, a middle ground between their traditional society and the new intrusive culture of the colonialist.

In the Punjab, a series of social and religious movements arose during the second half of the nineteenth century. Three of these—the Arya Samaj,[6] the Singh Sabha,[7] and the Ahmadiyas[8]—will provide us with excellent examples of such movements. We will not attempt here to trace their historical development in detail, since that would be beyond the scope of this article, but will instead use them to examplify an historical process. Each of these movements provided its followers with an ideology which explained both past and present, while promising a future return to eminence. Swami Dayanand placed the beginning of the Hindu downfall in the ancient past as a result of the *Mahabharata*. After this great war, the Hindus lost the correct knowledge of the Vedas, truth was no longer taught, and Hinduism sank into superstition and ignorance. Mirza Ghulam Ahmad called for a re-interpretation of Islam based on his claim to be a new prophet, first of Islam, then later of Hinduism, Judaism, and Christianity. He would, through his prophetic message, return to a purer and more correct Islam. The Singh Sabhas wanted to restore the Khalsa to true Sikhism and in the process began to cut the bonds which existed between Hinduism and Sikhism. A restored Sikh identity meant a separate Sikh identity.

Each religious community entertained a sense of failure due to British domination and each demonstrated the attitude of a suppressed minority. The Sikhs were, of course, a minority in Punjab and throughout British India. The Punjabi Muslims were a majority and a growing one in their own Province. They were a minority in India, but were part of a world community of Islam. Their status—minority or majority—depended on the context in which they were viewed. The Hindus had somewhat of a similarly ambiguous position. A declining minority in the Punjab, they were members of an overwhelming majority on an all-India basis. Still, they did not act as members of a majority community, but as a frightened minority. The key to this attitude lay in the nature of Hinduism, in the fact that it was an evolutionary religion and as such did not convert.

The Punjabi Hindus looked back to the golden age when all of South Asia was Hindu. They had fallen from that position. Islam converted from among them, and after the annexation of the Punjab so did the Christian missionaries. They had no way to counter this threat and could only meekly await a future decline in the size and strength of the Hindu community. The majority status of the Hindu community did not relieve this anxiety, since the Hindus had little hope of retaining that status. Sooner or later they would be overwhelmed by the prophetic faiths which surrounded them. One other aspect of the issue of majority versus minority status stemmed from the dominance of a foreign power. An effective majority meant the British plus one. Any group who managed to acquire the support of the British administration immediately became a threat to all other communities. Thus, the British could and did manipulate one community against the others, and at the same time the leaders of the different religious communities tended to compete rather than to cooperate with each other. Real power rested with the British, so why talk to the other communities. Competition dominated over cooperation.

Once the new ideologies of Aryas, Ahmadiyas or Singh Sabhas found supporters, conflict followed immediately. The adherents of these movements found in them a relaxation of the tensions produced by alienation and marginality. This in turn produced the need to proselytize and defend their new sense of well-being and the movements which produced that well-being. All of these new organizations had a message to preach and did so with vigour. Their most fundamental enemies were the orthodox leaders within their own communities. Here bitter conflict ensued, as each movement sought to establish itself at the expense of the traditional faith. Conflict also arose between the new movements and the older associations dedicated to change. The Aryas challenged the Brahmo Samaj—which had been brought to the Punjab by emigre Bengalis—in a contest to decide which movement would dominate among the educated Punjabi Hindus.[9] They also struggled with the Dev Samaj, led by the ex-Brahmo Pandit Shiv Narayan Agnihotri.[10] The contests with the Dev Samaj and Brahmo Samaj soon ended, as the Aryas grew in strength. Arya-Sanatanist struggles, however, continued well into the twentieth century.[11] Even the bitterest conflict did not preclude occasional cooperation against a common enemy: all Hindus against Muslims, or all against the Christian missionaries. But the world of Punjab was becoming more complex and more combative.

The initial struggles within each religious community expanded into conflicts between different religious communities. New ideologies had to be protected from external criticism. The Aryas began an extensive campaign against both Christianity and Islam. They adopted all the techniques introduced into the Punjab by Christians and Brahmos. Tracts, journals, paid missionaries, and street preaching—the necessary infrastructure to support such activities was also created. Arya missionaries used traditional forms as well—*shastrarths*, and Hindu *melas*—to spread their message. The Ahmadiyas paralleled developments within the Arya Samaj. They too attempted to proselytize and also became locked in a vicious struggle with the Arya Samaj. This was led by Mirza Ghulam Ahmad and Pandit Lekh Ram. Both sides produced a stream of tracts aimed at discrediting their opponents. This conflict functioned on three levels. It was highly personal between Mirza Ghulam and Lekh Ram; it was bitter contest between the two movements; and each side also took on the task of speaking for their respective religious communities, Muslims and Hindus. The height of this conflict was reached in 1897 with the assassination of Pandit Lekh Ram. The resulting chaos provided a brief preview of the partition agony of 1947.[12]

The Aryas—with their new prophet, their sacred text, the *Satyarth Prakash*,[13] and their new ideology—made one significant institutional change in the Hindu religion. Through the adaptation of *shuddhi*, a rite of purification, the Arya Samaj transformed Hinduism into a conversion faith. Using *shuddhi*, individuals who had been converted from Hinduism could be reconverted and restored to their parent religion. The Aryas expanded the use of *shuddhi* to encompass those whose ancestors had once been Hindus and finally applied it to anyone regardless of their parentage. All could become Aryas and thus Hinduism could and did possess a universal doctrine equivalent to a prophetic religion. In this way, the Aryas sought to meet the challenges of the prophetic religions and end the drain of their numbers to other faiths. The introduction of *shuddhi* tended to heighten religious competition, as Muslim and Christian leaders found themselves faced with a new, aggressive Hinduism, which could and would convert. Since the Aryas clearly laid claim to all those who had once been Hindus, this seemed to threaten the vast majority of the non-Hindu communities. All sides escalated their attempt both to convert and to win back members of their own community.

Shuddhi also played a key role in relations between the Aryas and the Sikhs, and on a broader basis between the Sikhs and the Hindus. The story of Arya-Sikh relations is complex.[14] Initially, many young educated Sikhs were attracted to the Arya Samaj. It seemed to be a movement compatible with the best of Sikhism and to contain in it many of the Sikh criticisms of orthodox Hinduism. By the late 1880s, however, most of this group of Sikhs had left and joined the Singh Sabhas. The Aryas had condemned orthodox Sikhism in the same terms as they had used for orthodox Hinduism. The Sikhs responded to this as criticism, emanating from outside of their community, as anti-Sikh. During the 1890s the Sikhs and the Aryas both fought and cooperated. *Shuddhi* campaigns were often conducted jointly by the Arya Samaj and the Singh Sabhas. Both sought to win back converts to Islam and Christianity. By 1900, this cooperation came to an end. The Aryas had begun to use *shuddhi* to purify outcaste groups, transforming them into pure-caste Hindus. This step was aimed at slowing Christian conversion among outcastes and was also a radical form cf social uplift. A group of Rahtias from the Jullundur Doab approached the Singh Sabhas for help in removing the disgrace of their untouchability. The Singh Sabha leaders sympathized but offered little concrete help, so the Rahtias turned next to the Arya Samaj. Lala Munshi Ram (Swami Shraddhanand) offered to perform a *shuddhi* ceremony for all Rahtias who were willing to submit to it. The ceremony was carried out in Lahore on 3 June 1900. The Arya ceremony began with a shaving of both hair and beard, followed by a series of other steps. The public shaving of the Rahtias outraged the Sikh community. It was not only a sacrilege, but, on a practical level, the purified Rahtias had not only been uplifted but transformed from Sikhs into Hindus. This act brought an end to cooperation between Sikhs and Aryas, and also intensified the Sikh drive to find their own identity.

With the close of the nineteenth century, the competition between religious movements generated by social and psychological forces became intermeshed with economic competition. During the 1870s and 1880s, a new, anglicized Hindu elite came to dominate those occupations which demanded a knowledge of English. By 1890, the Vaishya and brahmanical castes of the Hindu community dominated both the student and literate groups—the learned and learning. Khatris, baniyas, aroras and Brahmins accounted for 82 per cent of the English literate among the Hindus.[15] The urban Hindu elite led within the Hindu community and also without. They remained far in advance of any group within the Sikh or Muslim communities. They formed an educated elite firmly entrenched in government service, education, journalism, law and non-agricultural business.[16] This position of economic dominance did not remain unchallenged, or unchanged. By 1900, new groups both within and beyond the Hindu community came to challenge the position of the urban Hindu. Within the Hindu community the more well-to-do agricultural classes led by the Rajputs and Jats began to receive education on a growing scale. They would challenge the older elite from within. Outside of the Hindu community the most serious competition came from a growing Muslim educated elite led by Sheikhs, Kalals, and Sayyids. The Muslims moved steadily into law and business.[17] By 1911, the Sheikhs stood third in non-agricultural wealth and fourth in industrial ownership.[18] Urban Hindus saw competition from new groups both within and beyond their community. The ideological struggles already in full flower were now heightened. Economic competition followed ideological struggles and interacted with them to create further inter-communal conflict.

By the end of the century, competition between religious movements had become an institutionalized part of Punjabi life. Each religious community possessed one or more aggressive movements. The commitment to these movements rested on educated Punjabis and their sense of alienation from traditional society. The greater the alienation, the greater the commitment to a new ideology, and the more imperative it was to defend that ideology. Punjabi culture was typified by an atmosphere of *mandan-khandan*, of conflict, of tract and pamphlet wars, as each side hurled insults at the other. The dynamics of conquest and modernization created the need for new ideological movements, and, once these movements came into existence, they developed according to their own dynamics. Religious competition was not the result of a moral failing or an evil foreign plot, but an outgrowth of the colonial experience and the nature of pre-conquest society. This is not to argue against a British contribution to the worsening of inter-religious relations, but to recognize other forces which also contributed to the process.

We will not examine in detail the British role in religious conflict but will use a few points to illustrate the various ways in which they contributed to religious competition in Punjab. To begin with, the British arrived in Punjab with a mature imperial ideology. Christianity, along with white racism, was an integral part of this ideology. The Punjabis did not differentiate between soldier, administrator and missionary. The British appeared determined to conquer, administer and convert. During the late eighteenth and early nineteenth centuries in Bengal it was possible to see the government and the Christian religion as two separate entities. It was not possible to see that in Punjab. Militant and aggressive Christianity backed by a dominant political power was met by militant religious movements in all the three Punjabi communities. Thus, the arrival of the British set the stage for religious conflict and also introduced the Christian missionaries—exponents of another prophetic faith armed both with modern techniques of proselytization and the assistance of a new government. The British government may have been religiously neutral as regards non-Christians, but not in relation to Christianity.[19]

British policy oscillated between deliberate attempts at divide and rule and a general desire to limit religious controversy. The key factor here seemed to be their own sense of security. In the immediate aftermath of the Mutiny, the British deliberately reorganized their military forces on a policy of ethnic regiments. They consciously attempted to create a military structure in which each community was divided from all others. Such a divisive policy appears to be absent during the 1860s and through to the 1880s. Often British administrators reacted to religious conflicts with a concern for law and order—the classic mentality of the police and the bureaucrat. This was, of course, during the period when the British were most confident and secure in their own dominance. With the 1890s, their position began to deteriorate and they responded with increasing attempts to maintain control through a policy of divisiveness. In the Punjab, educated Muslims were given preference over

Hindus and the Punjab Land Alienation Act (1900) was aimed deliberately at the Hindu urban classes. The twentieth century would see an escalation of attempts to maintain the staus quo by the manipulation of class and religious differences.

What should also be given careful attention are those acts of the British which contributed to religious competition, even though there was no deliberate attempt to do so. The best example of this can be found in the effects of the decennial census. The census is a normal function of government, usually done to make taxation more effective. It is highly unlikely that the the British intended to divide one group from another, to accelerate caste consciousness or religious competition through the introduction of the census. Yet, few institutions have had such a widespread impact as this one. The census reports became tally sheets recording the progress or decline of each religious community and of individual movements. They were eagerly awaited and very closely read. Hindu leaders saw themselves slipping in numbers decade by decade. They declined steadily. U.N. Mukherjee, in a series of articles under the title 'A Dying Race', predicted the extinction of all Hindus, province by province, as he projected statistical trends in the census report into the future.[20] The Muslims and Sikhs advanced, but all communities faced a common threat from Christian conversion. The numbers of Christians were not significant, but their percentage increase was truly frightening. In 1881, Christian converts numbered 3,912. In ten years they reached 19,750—a rise of 410 per cent. In 1911, they had nearly doubled to 37,980 and in 1921 they more than tripled to 163,994[21]. Projected into the future, this pattern of increase could frigthen even the staunchest leaders of the religious communities in the Punjab.

The census reports also recorded the rise of the new movements, their relative strength as compared both to each other and to their parent communities. By labelling people as Sikh, Hindu, Muslim, etc., the census also contributed to a hardening of religious lines. Each individual belonged to a distinct group, clearly laid down in print, categorized, and numbered. Lastly, and most importantly, the census reports heightened an awareness of numbers—they created a contest of numbers. In fact, numbers became the prime symbol of success. To grow in numbers meant progress, to shrink in numbers meant decline. This attitude still persists and can be traced to a 'census mentality' created during the nineteenth century as an outgrowth of the British administrative structure. The British would deliberately play the numbers game during the twentieth century, but they did not do so in the nineteenth.

The British, then, contributed to religious competition both deliberately and inadvertently. Both aspects of British administration need to be given careful attention in order to understand the dynamics of competition between the religious movements. The question of British divide and rule tactics exists in the realm of objective reality—what they did; but there is another type of reality which may be of much more significance, this is 'subjective reality'—not what the British did, but what people believed the British were doing. For instance, educated Punjabi Hindus firmly believed that the British government was hostile to their community and was determined to limit the growth of the educated Hindu elite. They acted accordingly. By the late 1890s, this belief was well grounded; in fact, before this it had much less of a factual basis, but whether the belief was or was not justified made little difference. People act on what they think is true, and it is their perception that counts.

To conclude, several points need to be reiterated. Above all else, an understanding of the social, religious, and cultural changes which took place in the nineteenth century must be based on a consideration of a number of inter-related events. Here we have attempted to group these events and forces around three poles—the traditional framework of Punjabi society, the forces of social change within that society which developed after the annexation of Punjab in 1849, and the policies and actions of the British raj. The middle of these three—the forces of social change, of modernization—have been highlighted here since they have been neglected elsewhere, in order to understand the competition and conflict among the religious movements. This is essentially a way of looking at the past and of ordering the multitude of discrete facts drawn from that past. The validity and utility of these ideas rest on their ability to provide scholars with a more complete understanding of the processes of change and the dynamics of religious movements in the colonial milieu of pre-independence India.

References

1. *Census, Punjab Report*, 1911, pp. 323 & 326.
2. Anselm L. Strauss, *Mirrors and Masks*, (Glancoe, Illinois: The Free Press, 1959), p. 92.

3. Ruchi Ram Sahni, 'Self-Revelations of an Octogenarian', an unpublished manuscript in the possession of V.C. Joshi, Nehru Memorial Museum and Library, New Delhi.
4. Kenneth W. Jones, *Arya Dharm: Hindu Consciousness in 19th-Century Punjab*, (Berkeley: Univ. of Calif. Press, 1976); Indian edition (Delhi: Manohar Book Service, 1976), pp. 71-2.
5. Kenneth W. Jones, *Arya Dharm: Hindu Consciousness in 19th-Century Punjab* (op. cit.), pp. 22-29. Also see by the same author, 'The Bengali Elite in Post-Annexation Punjab: An Example of Inter-Regional Influence in 19th-Century India', *Indian Economic and Social History Review* (December 1966), pp. 376-395.
6. For standard works on the Arya Samaj, see Lala Lajpat Rai, *The Arya Samaj* (London, Green & Company, 1915); J.N. Farquhar, *Modern Religious Movements in India* (Delhi: Munshiram Manohar Lal 1967); Indra Vidyavachaspati, *Arya Samaj ka Itihas*, 2 vols (Delhi, Sarvadeshik Arya Pratinidhi Sabha, 1957); and Jones, *Arya Dharm* (op. cit.). For bibliographic reference see Kenneth W. Jones, 'Sources for Arya Samaj History' in W. Eric Gustafson and Kenneth W. Jones (eds.), *Sources on Punjab History* (Delhi: Manohar Book Service, 1975), pp. 130-70.
7. The reference on developments within the Sikh community during the second half of the century are not extensive. See N.G. Barrier, *The Sikhs and Their Literature* (Delhi: Manohar Book Service, 1970); Khushwant Singh, *A History of the Sikhs*, 2 vols (Princeton, 1966); Ganda Singh (ed.), *Panjab 1849-1960* (Patiala: Khalsa College, 1962); Kenneth W. Jones, 'Ham Hindu Nahin: Arya-Sikh Relations, 1877-1905', *Journal of Asian Studies* (May 1973); and N.G. Barrier, 'The Sikh Resurgence, 1849-1947: An Assessment of Printed Sources and their Location' in Gustafson and Jones (eds.), *Sources on Punjab History* (Delhi: Manohar Book Service, 1975).
8. For the Ahmadiyah movement, see Spencer Lavan, *The Ahmadiyah Movement: A History and Perspective* (Delhi: Manohar Book Service, 1974); also the author's article in *Sources on Punjab History*; Howard A. Walter, *The Ahmadiya Movement* (Calcutta: Associated Press, 1918); J.N. Farquhar, *Modern Religious Movements in India*; Stephen Fuchs, *Rebellious Prophets* (London: Asia Publishing House, 1965); also see the standard works on Indian Islam.
9. See Jones, 'The Bengali Elite in Post-Annexation Punjab', op. cit., and Jones, *Arya Dharm*, op. cit., pp. 40-3 and 112-15.
10. Jones, *Arya Dharm*, op. cit., pp. 115-19.
11. Ibid., pp. 108-12 & 189-91.
12. Kenneth W. Jones, 'Communalism in the Punjab: The Arya Samaj Contribution', *Journal of Asian Studies* (November 1968); *Arya Dharm*, op. cit., pp. 193-202, and the pages of Lahore *Tribune*.
13. There are many editions of the *Satyarth Prakash*. One of the standard English translations is by Ganga Prasad Upadhyaya, *The Light of Truth* (Allahabad: The Kala Press, 1956). For greater accuracy, the Hindi version is preferred and readily available from any Arya Samaj outlet.
14. Jones, 'Ham Hindu Nahin', op. cit., *passim*.

15. N.G. Barrier, 'Punjab Politics and the Disturbances of 1907', Ph.D. dissertation (Duke University, 1966), pp. 16-17.
16. Jones, *Arya Dharm*, op. cit., pp. 175-76.
17. Ibid., pp. 176-77.
18. Ibid., p. 326.
19. The relation between the government and missionaries is complex and often contradictory. Strain existed, but to those outside of the Christian community the missionaries seemed allied to the government and strongly supported by it. Any disagreements between the two groups were kept within the bounds of the English community. In Punjab, particularly, there were very close ties between many government officials and the Christian missionaries. For references to the missions in Punjab, see John C.B. Webster, 'Mission Sources of Nineteenth-Century Punjab History', in Gustafson and Jones (eds.), *Sources on Punjab History*, op. cit., pp. 171-218; and his recent study, *Christian Community and Change in 19th-Century North India* (Delhi: Macmillan, 1976); and also Stanley E. Brush, 'Protestants in the Punjab: Religion and Social Change in an Indian Province in the Nineteenth Century' (unpublished Ph.D. dissertation, Univ. of Calif., Berkeley, 1971).
20. U.N. Mukherjee wrote a series of articles under the title 'A Dying Race' for the journal *Bengalee* (Calcutta: 1910). These articles received wide attention in Punjab when selections were reprinted in the *Punjabee* during September and October of 1909.
21. *Census, Punjab Report*, 1891, pp. xliv, 93 & 97; *Census, Punjab Report*, 1901, p. 158; and *Census, Punjab Report*, 1911, p. 129.

8

Arun P. Bali

Organization of the Virasaiva Movement: An Analysis in the Sect-Church Framework

THE VIRASAIVA MOVEMENT, which assumed unusual significance and became a social force to be reckoned with in the twelfth century, is intimately linked with the name of Basaveswara. He spearheaded the movement and was mainly instrumental in popularizing it in the Kannada region of South India. Under his leadership, the Virasaiva movement became articulate and assumed a definite shape by AD 1141 and gathered strength and momentum at Kalyana after AD 1162 (Desai, 1968:280). Its adherents are variously called Virasaivas,[1] Lingayats,[2] Lingavants, Lingangis, Sivabhaktas or Sivachars. Lingayat has become a well-known term for members of the Virasaiva community, though they do not use it themselves. The name Sivabhakta or Sivachar is generally used by them. Today, Lingayats or Virasaivas are found throughout the State of Karnatak —where they form the largest single ethnic group, constituting about 15.57 per cent of the State's population'[3]—and also in some districts of neighbouring states like Andhra Pradesh, Kerala, Maharashtra and Tamilnadu. They are concentrated in the Bombay-Karnataka area, Hyderabad-Karnataka area and the border districts of the old princely State of Mysore. A heavy concentration is found in the districts of Dharwar, Bijapur and Belgaum. They constitute 50 per cent of the population of Dharwar district, while in the districts of Bijapur and Belgaum they constitute 40 per cent of the population (Nandi, 1975:32-46).

In this paper, the Virasaiva movement is examined in an historical perspective. However, it is not my intention to provide a complete descriptive account of every aspect of the Virasaiva movement.[4] On the contrary, this paper probes into the Virasaiva movement in terms of one fundamental analytical perspective only: the sect-church framework. The sect-church framework enables us to analyze various aspects of the movement—its belief system, value system, ideology of protest, leadership, modes of recruitment, organizational framework, institutionalization and routinization. Underlying the desire to explore the movement's organizational experience is the realization that the sect-church framework is inadequate to explain the various facets of the movement. In assessing the dynamics and structure of the Virasaiva movement, we will wear two sets of lenses; one to look at the organizational framework and the cementing (or integrating) forces which have sustained the movement, and the other to look at the changing nature of the organizational framework.

The pioneering efforts of Ernst Troeltsch and Max Weber provided a starting-point for the sect-church taxonomy. The church as a type strives to be co-extensive with society in its membership and thus to maximize integration. In an effort to accomplish this, emphasis is laid on sacrament and creed. Troeltsch remarks that the church is that type of organization that is overwhelmingly conservative, which to a certain extent accepts the secular order and dominates the masses; in principle, therefore, it is universal, that is, it aspires to encompass the whole life of humanity. The church-type of religious organization is characterized by the following traits:

1. Claims universality and inclusiveness;
2. exercises religious monopoly and tries to eliminate religious competition;
3. elaborate formal and hierarchical organization; a religious bureaucracy;
4. use of a trained and professional ministry;
5. restricted lay participation;
6. membership is ascribed;
7. closely allied with both temporal and secular powers; and
8. emphasis on religious education.

Further modifications and refinements of the church type have been made. For instance, J. Milton Yinger (1970) has distinguished the 'universal church' from '*ecclesia*' (Greek word for church) and has further dichotomized both into 'institutionalized' and 'diffused norms'.

A sect is a comparatively small group. It aspires for personal inward perfection and aims at a direct personal fellowship between the members of each group. Relationships between members are generally more intimate and all-encompassing than the church. Primary group relations and direct communication predominate. The members of a sect share a strong sense of deprivation[5] and alienation. In an extreme case, it can be purely the religion of laymen, free from both worldly and ecclesiastical authority. A sect repudiates what it views as the compromises of the church, preferring isolation to compromise.

A sect usually exercises more powerful sanctions over its members and tends to control more aspects of their lives. It attempts to maintain distinct spatial or social boundaries between its members and the world through various devices for limiting interaction with outsiders. Taboos are rigidly enforced to prevent contamination by the world and to maintain separation from it. Stripped to its essentials, the presence of one or more of the following traits is necessary for a religious organization to be labelled a sect:[6]

1. Small size and exclusive;
2. at the cultural periphery of society;
3. membership is voluntary;
4. self-perception as a fellowship of an elect or select few;
5. renunciation of—or indifference to—prevailing culture and social organization;
6. rejects organization and strives to maintain maximum democratic participation of members within an explicitly non-bureaucratic character;
7. emphasizes purity of doctrine and usually demands a return to original religious thinking;
8. accepts the ideal of the priesthood of all believers;
9. prefers unspecialized, part-time ministry;
10. emphasizes evangelism and conversion;
11. tends to concentrate on other worldly issues like salvation, deliverance, hell and heaven, to the virtual exclusion of secular interests;

12. high level of lay participation;
13. draws disproportionately from the lower social classes in society;
14. emphasizes direct personal intercourse with God, thereby minimizing sacraments.

Other scholars have enumerated additional salient features of sects than I have done here.[7] Implicit in many of the characteristics outlined above is the protest element. All these traits were present in the Virasaiva movement at the time of its inception. A sect's protest may be either veiled or open. In the case of the Virasaiva movement, protest against the Brahmins was open. It should also be mentioned that many different taxonomies of sect exist. While Clark (1949) distinguishes the following types: pessimistic/adventist sects, perfectionist/subjectivist sects; charismatic/pentecostal sects; legalistic/objectivist sects, and communistic sects; Wilson (1970) distinguishes revolutionist, introversionist, manipulationist, thaumaturgical, reformist and utopian sects.

The sect-church taxonomy has been considered as a singularly useful conceptual tool for the analysis of the organized Christian groups in relation to their environment. This taxonomy has been criticized by many scholars on two main counts. H. Richard Niebuhr is the leading exponent of the first school of criticism. He criticized the Troeltsch-Weber formulation as being static and sought to incorporate it into a propositional scheme based on the assumption that the sect-type is inherently stable and exhibits a tendency to move away from its original 'pure' state towards achieving the status of a church; the basic assumption being, 'sects do not remain as sects' (Niebuhr 1929).

The other strand of thought is represented by Howard Becker, Milton Yinger, Peter Berger and others. Their attempts at a reformulation of the Troeltsch-Weber dichotomization have centred around the definition of the types themselves. The taxonomy of the religious organization as suggested by Troeltsch and Weber in terms of the antithetical concepts of church and sect highlight the fact that these are two terminal points of a social continuum. It leaves unexamined the wide spectrum of organizations within each type. These types are best understood as abstract types, marking the terminal points of a continuum and expressing different ways of negotiating with the secular world and its power. Scholars have pointed out that these are several intermediate points along the continuum. Among them are the 'established sect' or 'institutionalized sect', cult, denomination, and *ecclesia.* It has been necessary to develop these concepts with a view to taking account of sects traversing an alternate path to the predominant sect-to-denomination pattern. There is, of course, yet another path that many sects tread—'the sect-to-oblivion route'.

Niebuhr (1929) and Pope (1942) elaborate the theory that there is an inherent tendency towards deradicalization in the development of sects. They argue that as the process of routinization and institutionalization sets in, the sects tend to compromise with the established religious and secular pattern, to accept their pluralist situation, and increase their organizational complexity and wealth to the point where they become denominationalized. Wilson (1970) has rejected the thesis put forward by Niebuhr and Pope. He challenges the assumption made by them that sects basically have a similar ideology, social composition, organizational framework and developmental pattern.

One of the serious drawbacks of the sect-church typology is that it obscures, to some degree, the nexus between meanings and the functional problems of social organization. The process of sect to church transformation is sometimes regarded as simply a problem of organizational survival through 'compromise' whereas the word 'compromise' may be quite misleading for an interpretation of what is going on from the standpoint of participants in the movement at issue. In the case of the Virasaiva movement, it appears to us that the typology as developed in the context of Christian religion is misleading, because Hinduism has no Church.

We shall now examine the origin and development of the Virasaiva movement in the sect-church framework.

The Formative Period

The Virasaiva movement emerged in opposition to the social ethos of the Brahmin. Prior to its emergence, brahmanic Hinduism came to be hemmed in by the caste and ritual systems. The Brahmin had begun to consider himself as the priestly purveyor of all sacred lore and texts and thwarted all attempts at dislodging him from his niche. Social intercourse among the castes and classes was highly restricted and a network of rules had emerged which inhibited inter-dining and inter-marriage. These were the handiwork of the Brahmins.

All this bespoke of inequality, of differential power, and of the narrowing of effective areas of economic betterment. The outcome of this was the dehumanizing existence which confronted non-Brahmins. For, to be born a non-Brahmin was to be sentenced to a lifetime of bondage to ascriptive or hereditary barriers, insults and humiliations. It was against these blatant evils that Basaveswara and many other Virasaivas reacted vehemently. The Virasaiva movement protested, challenged and waged a relentless crusade against the social evils perpetrated by the Brahmins. In its early years, the movement was involved in militant and aggressive encounters with the Brahmins. It challenged not only the legality of existing norms and values in which all non-Brahmins were encased but also the legitimacy of these was challenged. The preamble of the movement is dominated by the ideology of egalitarianism and democracy. It aimed at establishing a society devoid of caste or class.

In its formative stage, the Virasaiva movement exhibited typical sectarian traits. It was headed by Basaveswara together with a band of loyal followers. Basaveswara's acceptance of a secular position—as Chief Minister and Treasurer to King Bijjala II, the Kalachuri King—accelerated the initial enthusiastic impetus of the Virasaiva movement. Political office was used as a fulcrum to further the movement's cause. The secular position that Basaveswara held furnished material, moral and royal patronage for the movement. He personally initiated newcomers into the movement and converted them to Siva worship. The missionary activities and religious zeal of Basaveswara become a source of suspicion. He exercised a dominating influence on the growth and development of the movement and played a major role in the articulation of its ideology of protest. He proclaimed that all those who submitted to *kudala sanganna* are equal, irrespective of sex, caste and class. They are addressed as *sivasaranas.* To popularize the movement he established the *Anubhava Mantapa*[8] at Kalyana, a colloquium to discuss the various theological, mystical and philosophical aspects of Virasaivism. Members of this colloquium were drawn from diverse social backgrounds. Considerations like sex, age, caste and occupation were inconsequential in gaining membership. The deliberations and discussions at the *Anubhava Mantapa* were conducted under the spiritual guidance of Allama Prabhu and carried on in Kannada—the idiom of the common man. The essence of these deliberations and spiritual encounters are contained in the *Sunyasampadane.*

From these deliberations and discussions emerged the topical contours which undergrid the ideological format of the movement's protest. The Virasaiva movement professed an anti-Brahmanic and anti-ritualistic ethic. It demanded a renunciation of all that formed an integral part of the social ethos associated with Brahmins. The Virasaivas acknowledged only the God Siva as the Supreme Godhead. They granted equality to man and woman both in the secular and ritual spheres and also accorded them the right of worship. They believe that they are immune from pollution (*sutakas*), as they carry the *linga* at all times—from the womb to the tomb—on their person. They do not observe pollution arising from caste (*jati*), birth (*janana*), death (*preta*), spittle (*uchchista*) and menstruation (*rajasa sutaka*). The Virasaivas regarded untouchability as a social evil and made efforts to eradicate it. The hypothesis of rebirth was rejected as they believed in *jivan-mukti*. Work (*kayaka*) was sanctified. The Virasaiva movement prohibited child marriage and encouraged widow remarriage. It envisioned a society devoid of caste and class and sought a fraternal community and universal brotherhood. The credo of the movement is dominated by an egalitarian and democratic ideology, which is at the heart of the movement's continuing reformatory appeal.

The movement seems to have taken birth at Kalyana. It had gathered strength and momentum by about 1162 AD under the leadership of Basaveswara, Allama Prabhu, Cennabasava, Siddharama and others. During this formative phase, the organization of the movement was amorphous and nebulous in character. The leadership was in the hands of charismatic leaders like Basaveswara, Allama Prabhu, and Cennabasava. Most of their energies and resources were spent on articulating the ideology of protest of the movement and teaching the art of personal devotion and attainment of *moksa*. They taught devotion to one God, Siva—personified as *Kudala Sangamma*[9], *Guhesvara*,[10] *Cennamallikarjuna*,[11] and *Kapila Sidda Mallikarjuna*[12] in the *vacanas* composed and sung in praise of Lord Siva. They provided the impetus to intense personal devotion (*bhakti*). The element of *bhakti* was emphasized by the Virasaiva saints, who asked the devotees to follow the *bhakti marga* in their quest for the Ultimate Reality.

Basaveswara and others cherished and nurtured the idea of establishing a society based on egalitarian principles. With this aim in mind they propounded an ethical code enjoining every Virasaiva to adhere to it. The ethical code of conduct to be observed by Virasaivas are the *pancacaras* (five codes of conduct)—*lingacara, sadacara, sivacara, brthyacara* and *ganacara.*[13] Allama Prabhu says that *acara* (good conduct) is essential for all persons, and is the 'source of knowledge'.

The Virasaiva movement brought in its wake the transformation of institutions, changes in the legitimacy of power, and changes in the core values and dominant ideologies which composed the mosaic of the social ethos of the Brahmin. It prophesized the legitimacy of a new social order. The movement waged a fierce crusade against the corpus of beliefs, rites and rituals evolved and nurtured by the Brahmins. It protested against these as they bespoke of inequality, differential power and a narrowing of the access to economic power. The cosmos of brahmanic Hinduism had come to be enmeshed in the ritual cobweb woven by the Brahmins. This alienated the Brahmin from the non-Brahmins, for the latter were denied the right and privilege to perform many of the rituals. Women suffered disabilities as they were not granted access to the performance of many rituals. The Virasaiva movement shunned elaborate ceremonialism and excessive ritualism introduced by the Brahmins. The Brahmin considered himself as the rightful representative of God on earth and regarded himself as the sole mediator or honest broker between God and man. This idea was stiffly opposed by the Virasaivas. Basaveswara and others declared that no one has the power to act as another's spiritual representative before God. They laid emphasis on direct communication with God. They rejected the hierarchical structure of religious authority associated with brahmanic Hinduism. In their opinion, it stood between God and man and alienated them from each other. Since the most notable component of this structure is priesthood, the Virasaiva *sivasaranas* considered themselves as only the first among equals. Basaveswara was impatient with those who argued for the performance of religious rites to realize God. He often exclaimed: 'How can devotion to Siva and adherence to rites agree?' He discarded the sacred thread. He maintained that 'Siva could be won over only by devotion and not either by music or by vedic chants'. He believed in full surrender of oneself to God. Many of the rituals evolved by the Brahmins were either abandoned completely or modified, simplified and refined to meet the exigencies of the times.

The rituals evolved by the Virasaivas[14] and made obligatory on all members of the sect mark a distinct change from those associated with brahmanical Hinduism. The Virasaiva movement professed equality of the sexes and this has been stated unequivocally by Basaveswara and other *sivasaranas*. They stressed that 'all wearers of the *linga* are equal in the eyes of the Lord'. Women were granted the right of worship in the spiritual sphere, and they did not suffer from the social stigma of pollution. Further, the Virasaiva movement granted free access to all Virasaivas, irrespective of their former caste affiliations, to perform the rituals evolved by the *sivasaranas* and enunciated in Virasaiva scriptures. These social values upheld by the *sivasaranas* gave direction to the movement's activities and provided an ideological hub for its entire programme.

The leaders of the Virasaiva movement created an organizational framework parallel to that of the Brahmins in order to sustain, uphold and propagate Virasaiva doctrines. The organizational framework was conceived as a primary medium for fostering, renewing and expressing religious experience. Further, the organizational framework was designed not simply for the purpose of obtaining benefits for the Virasaivas but also to enhance their—as well as the movement's—combat-efficiency in the external world. Basaveswara realized that a formal degree of organization is essential for any social movement. The fact that he established *mathas* in almost all places where Virasaivas resided, and introduced the priestly order of *jangamas* clearly indicate his awareness of the necessity of an organizational machinery to sustain the movement. The *matha-jangama* axis formed the nucleus of the organizational framework of the movement.

During the formative period of the movement, its leaders advocated and allowed open recruitment to its ranks, and considerations like caste, age and sex were deemed irrelevant to the attainment of *moksa* (salvation). This open and voluntary nature of a vocation followed by the members of the movement brought together all strata of society on an equal footing. The unifying theme that came to dominate the movement's ideology in all its ramifications was the concept of egalitarianism. The social groups in which the movement was anchored exhibited a pre-dominantly lower-class social status following (see Table, pages 44-45). The movement enjoyed the support of the class of priests (collectively known as *jangamas*), traders and peasants, and craftsmen.[15] The main recruiting ground for the movement was the lower castes. Many of the early adherents of Virasaivism belonged to lower castes, the bulk of Lingayat saints being outcastes. Basaveswara's death, however, marked a turning point. Later Virasaiva leaders discouraged the lower or impure castes from becoming members of the Virasaiva community. Rules for recruitment were made more stringent for those hailing from these low caste groups and seeking to become members of the movement.

The Virasaiva movement relied heavily on conversion, the major avenue for gaining more members to the community. The movement's leaders directed all their efforts towards converting groups in a bid to mobilize support for the movement's cause. They aimed at group recruitment, or bloc recruitment, through the process of conversion. In group recruitment, members of the group provided each other with social support and negatively sanction those who hesitate to join. The recruitment of isolated individuals was also undertaken, although preference was exercised in favour of groups.

The religious zeal and missionary activities of Basaveswara, coupled with his piety and munificence, played an important role in the spread of the movement to the masses. Within a short span of time it gained the acceptance of the masses, and people from various walks of life began embracing it. Basaveswara personally undertook the work of initiating the newcomers and converting them to Siva worship. Later, the task of recruiting new members was entrusted to the *mathas*. Some of the *mathas* which played a prominent role in converting new members were the Suttur *matha*, Mysore, the Chitradurga Brhan and Taralabalu *mathas*, Sirigere, and the Siddaganga *matha*, Tumkur. However, the Siddaganga *matha* did not evince much interest in conversion. Twelve years have rolled by, observes Sadasivaiah (1967: 205) since the last conversion of about twenty persons took place. Unfortunately, exact figures relating to conversion are not available. Dr. Malledevaru[16] mentioned the conversion of some Tamilians some thirty years ago which had been performed by the head of the Suttur *matha*. He went on to point out that conversions were taking place even today. Conversion was being done by the Suttur and Taralabalu *mathas*, he pointed. In contrast, Dr. Sadasivaiah[17] pointed out that conversion had virtually come to a standstill. During the last twenty years there have not been more than a dozen conversions. Sadasivaiah (1967: 173) points out that 103 persons were initiated in 1956, none were converted in 1957 and 1958, and only four were initiated in

1959 by the Chitradurga Brhan *matha*.

Leaders are the agents of group mobilization and the architects of organization and ideology. The early leaders of the Virasaiva movement were 'either high brahmanas or belonged to the families of traders and hereditary officials. While most of these leaders lived and preached in towns some enjoyed important positions in the government and at the court' (Nandi, 1975: 37-9). The chief religious leaders maintained intimate, personal, *gemeinschaft*-like relationships with the members. The leaders tried to minimize cleavages as much as possible by socializing members to a common set of values and beliefs. Basaveswara was a charismatic leader whose authority stemmed more from real, or supposed, personal virtue, grace or enlightenment than from formalized norms. Like many leaders of sectarian movements, Basaveswara also established an organizational framework to sustain the movement which later became institutionalized as the Virasaiva movement moved towards the church end of the sect-church continuum.

The dominant social religious order was dismayed at the growing popularity of the Virasaiva movement and the increase in its followers. It made a concerted appeal to Bijjala to do something to stem the tide of the Virasaiva-wave. Bijjala tried to nip the Virasaiva mevement in the bud. He and his successors tried to repress the movement by undertaking coercive action designed to protect their very existence. The Virasaivas did not flinch from this challenge. Encounters with the dominant social order and the opposition that the movement faced played an important role in strengthening the group awareness or consciousness and each individual's identity as a participating member of it. Basaveswara came into conflict with Bijiala and they parted company as a result because their ideologies differed in the socio-religious sphere. The break-off point was when Bijjala[18] ordered the beheading of two staunch Virasaivas—namely, Haralayya (an untouchable convert) and Madhuvayya (a Brahmin convert)—following their involvement in an inter-caste marriage. The initial era of goodwill which existed between them disappeared rapidly. Indeed, this episode not only antagonized the Virasaiva community but precipitated a crisis in the leadership of the movement. Factionalism emerged within the movement and there was the inevitable split between the advocates of the 'moderate approach' (which included Basaveswara, Allama Prabhu, Cennabasava, Siddharama and their close associates), and the advocates of the 'militant approach' like Jagadeva, Molleyya, and Bommayya. For the first time in the history of the movement, there was an erosion of faith in the leadership.[19] The advocates of the 'militant approach', who clamoured for retaliation, were frustrated by the conciliatory attitude of the leadership. Internal fighting continued, with rival leaders and groups making active bids for power. The scramble for power and leadership led to a change in the leadership. New protest leaders—Jagadeva, Molleyya, and Bommayya—displaced the earlier leaders. These new protest leaders paid no heed to the earlier leaders' repeated pleas for desisting from adopting a retaliatory attitude. The prospects of an *entente* between the two groups were bleak. The new protest leaders had gone a far way from the road of pacification and directed all their efforts towards avenging the death of Haralayya and Madhuvayya. Their sole aim was to get rid of Bijjala. They felt that Bijjala had to pay the price for his part in the murder of two Virasaiva devotees.

Seeing that their advice was falling on deaf ears, Basaveswara, Allama Prabhu, Cennabasava and their supporters dissociated themselves from the militant elements and departed from Kalyana. As a result, they lost control of the situation. All this seems to have occurred in A D 1167. There was an outburst of violence which engulfed not only the Virasaiva community but also the entire kingdom. Bijjala was promptly assassinated by the new leaders of the movement, leading to chaotic conditions with the Virasaivas unleashing a reign of terror and persecution. This resulted in a direct armed conflict between the Virasaivas and Bijjala's successors. These encounters led to a mass exodus of Virasaivas from Kalyana and Kalyana lost its importance as the centre of the movement as many Virasaivas followed the footsteps of their leaders to places of safety. For instance, many adherents of the faith accompanied Basaveswara to Kudala Sangama, some followed Cennabasava to Ulavi and others to Srisaila. Many others dispersed in various directions in quest of new homes. There was thus a proliferation of centres of Virasaiva activity.

This phase also witnessed the passing away of Basaveswara. This was a major setback to the movement as it was now deprived of its guiding force. Following his death, the reins of leadership were soon in the hands of Cennabasava.[20] Under the leadership of Cennabasava, the movement was able to consolidate its position to a great extent. Cennabasava enriched the philosophy and theology of the movement and is credited with having systematized the metaphysics of Virasaivism. Much credit is due to him for having kept all the elements within the movement intact.

Two events mark the culmination of the formative phase of the movement: (i) the assassination of Bijjala; and (ii) dissociation of the top leaders from the radicals and their retreat from Kalyana to various places. Intense fighting between Somideva, Bijjala's son, and the Virasaivas resulted in the latter's fleeing from Kalyana. The movement met some temporary reverses as a result.

Virasaivism spread throughout Northwest Mysore and 'if tradition is to be believed or accepted, then within sixty years of Basaveswara's death, that is between 1168 to 1228 AD it was embraced from Ulavi (near Goa) to Sholapur, and from Balehalli or Balehonnur (Koppa taluq) to Sivaganga (Nelamangala taluq)[7] (Rice, 1897:476).

To conclude, amorphous and poorly organized at first, the Virasaiva movement ultimately evolved a sustaining ideology, a sense of *espirit de corps* and a high degree of dedication to the movement's aims.

Period of Integration and Consolidation

During this period the movement's early charismatic leadership became institutionalized in the *mathas*, and in the heads of the *mathas*, because, as the movement progressed, it suffered external threats. An official clergy (the *jangamas*) replaced the lay leadership; and easily taught creeds replaced the unwritten, enthusiastically held doctrines of the emergent Virasaiva sect. In the early stages, authority was firmly reposed in a single charismatic figure—Basaveswara, and later Cennabasava—and membership was often defined in terms of a subscription to Virasaiva tenets and doctrines. With the charismatic leaders gone, the question of integration became acute. However, the major crises of integration did not beset the movement until the thirteenth century A D. The response to these integrative crises can be expressed in terms of two related developments: (*i*) formal reorganization of the movement resulting in a sacralization of the bureaucracy; and (*ii*) reconstitution of communications ritual and doctrine to accommodate a widely dispersed membership in such a way as to both reinforce membership as a pattern of behaviour and to protect its members against erosive counter-stimuli from the surrounding environment.

The integrative mechanisms that were reinforced so as to tide over the integrative crises were the weller of *mathas* and the priestly order of the *jangamas*. The Virasaiva movement showed itself proficient in matching continuity and innovation in a blend capable of ensuring integration while preserving the core of Basaveswara's message.

The interregnum between the demise of Basaveswara and the beginning of the reign of Devarayya II (A D 1424-46) was a saga of struggle for Virasaiva movement. However, it managed to overcome the temporary setbacks it suffered following the exit of its early leaders and its persecution at the hands of Jains and Brahmins. During this period, staunch followers of Virasaivism preached the gospel of Basaveswara and other *sivasaranas* wherever they settled. The *mathas* and *jangamas* were actively engaged in fulfilling the tasks assigned to them. They performed admirably the twin functions—of *preservation* and propagation of Virasaiva doctrines, texts, and *vacana* literature; and the formulation of codes of conduct and methods of social control in order to keep alive the precepts and practices of the movement as laid down by the founding fathers. The *mathas* served as storehouses and custodians of the invaluable Virasaiva texts and *vacana sahitya*, protecting them from the ravages of time. Scholars made phenomenal efforts to transcribe the various religious works. They also endeavoured to preserve these invaluable texts from being condemned to the dusty archives of the past. In this period great scholars and authors like Harihara, Raghavanka and Palkurike Somanatha contributed substantially to Virasaiva doctrines by their outstanding works—*Ragales of Sivagana*, *Siddaramacharitra*, and *Basavapuranamu*, respectively. *Somanatha Charitre*, another work of Raghavanka, deals with the life of Adayya who was born in Saurashtra and went to Purigere (modern Laxmeshwar) to carry on his trading activities. It narrates the tale of his confrontation with the Jains there and his triumph in establishing the Virasaiva faith. A volume of literature comprising the *vacanas* of Basaveswara and his compeers has also survived almost intact through this period.

The reign of Devarayya II witnessed a new era of upheaval or renaissance of Virasaiva religion and literature.[21] Chamarasa (*c.* 1430) wrote the famous *Prabhulinga Lile* which deals with the life and teachings of Allama Prabhu, or Prabhudeva, a contemporary of

Basaveswara. Nijaguna Sivayogi (*c.* 1500) employed the '*tripadi*' for explaining the intricacies of Virasaivism as in *Yoganga Trividhi* and *Arvathu Murara Tripadi.* Sarvajna (*c.* 1700), a Virasaiva teacher, was the most famous exponent of rendering *vacanas* in the metrical form of '*tripadis*'. In Devarayya's reign, a hundred and one *viraktas* (ascetics) lived and preached Virasaivism.[22] The paucity of authentic accounts relating to these ascetics is partially compensated for by literary evidence. Available literary evidence clearly supports the viewpoint that they were instrumental in reorganizing Virasaivism and reinterpreting Virasaiva literature, especially the *vacanas* composed by the *sivasaranas* in the twelfth century, and in establishin centres of learning and study not only in the Vijayanagar kingdon but also in other parts of Karnatáka.

Among the *sivasaranas* of this period, Nijaguna Sivayogi is preeminent and the cynosure of all eyes. Tontada Siddhalinga Yati, or Siddeshwara, is another eminent *sivasarana.* Siddeshwara was the first person during this period to render his emotions and sentiments in the form of *vacanas.* He resuscitated the *vacana* form of literary expression, which had fallen into disuse for a long time. The collection of his *vacanas* is called *Satsthalajnana Saramrta.* Siddeshwara epitomized a new mystical upsurge and inspired a fresh band of mystics, who revived the Virasaiva movement and spread the gospel of Virasaivism among the masses. Sarvajna, who lived during the closing years of the Vijayanagar Empire, was another popular *sivasarana* who enriched Virasaiva literature. Muppina Shadakshari (believed to be Nijaguna's contemporary) and Sarpabhushana Sivayogi, or Sappanna, who lived in the first half of the nineteenth century, followed in the footsteps of Nijaguna Sivayogi and preached Virasaivism through their *vacanas* which are full of devotion and mystical ardour.

We now turn to examine the *matha-jangama* axis which was the corporate vehicle of the implementation of a distinctive religious organization. The foundations for the development of the *matha-jangama* axis were laid in the twelfth century by Basaveswara and were charged with the twin objectives of preservation and propagation of the tenets of Virasaivism and its canonical scriptures.

The origins of Virasaiva monasticism are shrouded in mystery. However, scholars have propounded two theories to explain the origins of Virasaiva monasticism. The advocates of one school of thought attribute the founding of the Virasaiva *mathas* to the *panchacharyas* (five prophets)—namely, Revanaradhya, Marularadhya, Ekoramaradhya, Panditaradhya and Visvaradhya. These prophets are believed to have established five *mathas* at Kedarnath in the Himalayas; Ujjini in Bellary district, Srisailam near Nandyal; Rambhapuri, or Balehalli or Balehonnur, in West Mysore; and Benares (Farquhar, 1967:260). These are the five important Virasaiva *pattada mathas* which exist even today. The Virasaiva *mathas* which are located all over Karnataka owe their allegiance to these five *pattada mathas*. The five *pattada mathas* are believed to have been established mainly for propagating the tenets of Virasaivism. They formed the mainspring of the movement's proselytizing activities.

Protagonists of the second school of thought trace the origin of the Virasaiva monastic system to the establishment of the *Sunyasimhasana* or 'Throne of Void' at Kalyana. This *Sunyasimhasana* was established by Basaveswara, and Allama Prabhu was invited to occupy the pontificate. Virasaiva *mathas* are divided into *pattada mathas* and *virakta mathas*. In the early days of the Virasaiva movement, the functions of the *pattada* and *virakta mathas* were clearly demarcated. The *pattada mathas* were entrusted with cases of good conduct (*acara*). This involved liturgical work and also supervision of the spiritual and moral conduct of devotees. The head priests of these *mathas* were empowered to punish all those who violated the social and religious duties enjoined upon them by Virasaiva doctrines. On the other hand, the task of interpreting the tenets of Virasaivism, disseminating the knowledge contained in them to the masses, writing books to elucidate them, and delivering discourses to the people in order to provide a vivid exposition of the intricacies of Virasaivism was entrusted to the *virakta mathas*. However, this division of functions gradually became blurred over the passage of time.

During the phase of integration and consolidation, the Virasaiva monastic system came to be characterized by a hierarchical pyramid, with the chief *matha* (*jagadpitha*) headed by the chief priest (referred to as *swamiji, jagadguru*, or *pattadadevaru*) at the apex. The branch *mathas*, spread over a large number of villages where Virasaivas resided and owing loyalty to the chief *matha*, occupied the lowest position in the hierarchical pyramid. All power—be it spiritual, religious or political power—flowed unidirectionally from the chief *matha* to the branch *mathas*. The entire framework within which the

Figure 1

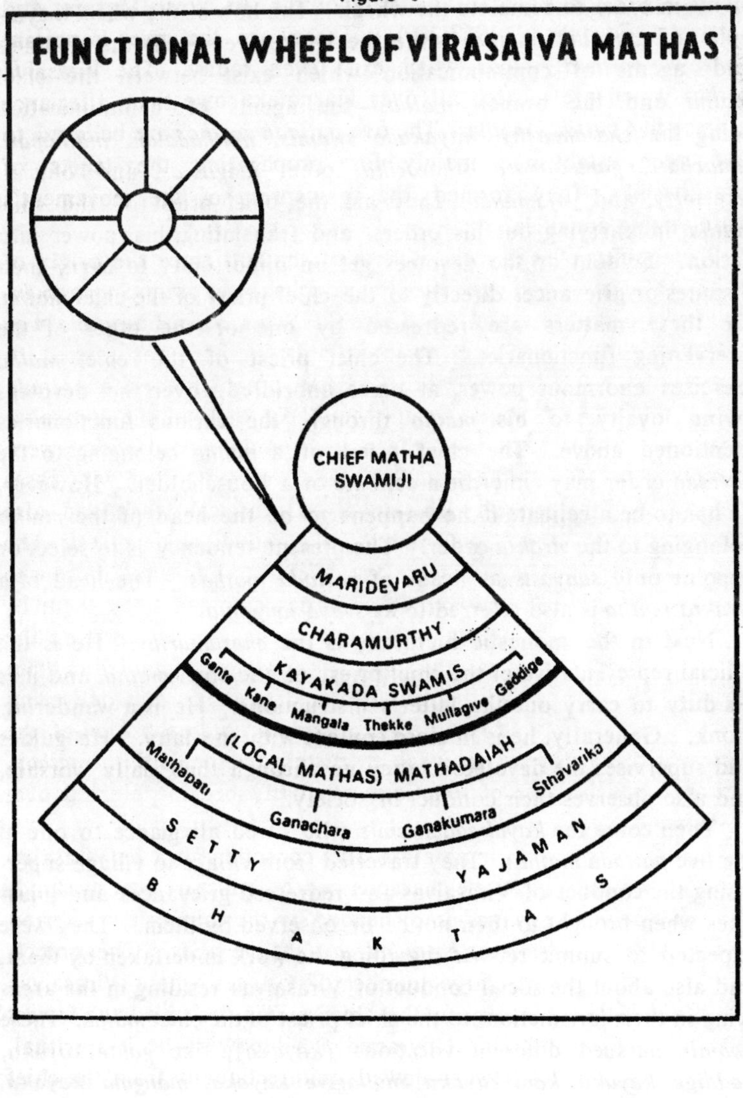
FUNCTIONAL WHEEL OF VIRASAIVA MATHAS
CHIEF MATHA SWAMIJI
MARIDEVARU
CHARAMURTHY
KAYAKADA SWAMIS
Gante
Kane
Mangala
Thekke
Mullagive
Gaddige
(LOCAL MATHAS) MATHADAIAH
Mathapati
Ganachara
Ganakumara
Sthavarika
SETTY YAJAMAN
BHAKTAS

mathas functioned and operated resembles what we shall term 'the wheel'. Figure 1 portrays the 'functional wheel of the Virasaiva *mathas*' (Arun Bali, 1976b:119). What has been portrayed in one segment is just a replica and this can be repeated in the other segments in order to complete the wheel. The hub of the wheel is symbolic of the chief *matha*, while the spokes represent the channels and agents of communication which exist between the chief *matha* and the branch *mathas*—the agents of communication being the *charamurthy*, *kayakada swamis*, *mathadaiah*, *mathapati*, *ganachari*, *ganakumara sthavarika*, other *jangamas*, and officials like *setty*, and *yajamana*. They aid the chief priest of the chief *matha* in carrying out his orders and translating his power into action. Seldom do the devotees get an opportunity to carry their disputes or grievances directly to the chief priest of the chief *matha*, for these matters are redressed by one or the other of the intervening functionaries. The chief priest of the chief *matha* exercises enormous power, at times unbridled, over the devotees owing loyalty to his *matha* through the various functionaries mentioned above. The chief priest of a *matha* belonging to the *pattada* order may either be a celibate or a householder. However, he has to be a celibate if he happens to be the head of the *matha* belonging to the *virakta* order. The present tendency is to select or appoint only *sanyasis* as heads of *pattada mathas*. The head of a *virakta matha* is also referred to as *svaya jangama*.

Next in the monastic hierarchy is the *charamurthy*. He is the official representative of the chief priest of the chief *matha*, and it is his duty to carry out the latter's instructions. He is a wandering monk. Generally, he is in close contact with the laity. He guides and supervises the devotees as they go through their daily worship, and also observes their conduct in society.

Then come the *kayakada swamis* who owed allegiance to one of the five *pattada mathas*. They travelled from village to village supervising the conduct of Virasaivas and redressed grievances and injustices when brought to their notice or observed by them. They were expected to submit reports regarding the work undertaken by them, and also about the social conduct of Virasaivas residing in the areas lying in their jurisdiction, to the chief priest of the chief *matha*. These *swamis* pursued different vocations *(kayaka)*, like *gante kayaka*, *gaddige kayaka*, *kani kayaka*, *mullagive kayaka*, *mangala kayaka*, and *thekke kayaka*. These *swamis* were entrusted with the task of supervising the code of conduct of Virasaivas. A recital of the manner in which the *kayakada swamis* performed their duty of supervising the code of conduct of the Virasaivas and the rules as enjoined in the Virasaiva texts will be found in the section on *jangamas* and social control later in this paper.

In the *mathas* are also found *maris* or *swami*-designates. These *maris* are also referred to as *maridevaru* (or little *swami* or lord) and are trainees in the *mathas* under the aegis of the chief priest himself. They are imparted knowledge of the Vedas, Upanisads, *Saivagamas*, the tenets of Virasaivism, and *Sivayoga* and are given opportunities to acquire proficiency in Sanskrit, Kannada and English. In case facilities for educating *maris* do not exist in a particular *matha* then they are sent to a *matha* where such facilities are available.

The social organization of the branch (*saka*) *matha*, also has a clearly defined social hierarchy. Here the head of the *matha* is addressed as *mathadaiah* (head priest). He is appointed by and is responsible to only one superior officer—the *swamiji* (chief priest of the chief *matha*) and thus his power in relation to his devotees is very strong. He possesses the authority of the church, and is in a position to resist local pressures. He is assisted in his daily routine and in the maintenance and supervision of the conduct of his devotees by a coterie of officials—namely, *mathapati*, *ganacarya*, *gaṅakumara*, and *sthavarika* who belong to the *gurusthala* order and are *jangamas* They are found in every village where Virasaivas reside.

Jangama: The priestly order

The *jangamas* actively involved themselves in the tasks of transmission, propagation, and popularization of Virasaivism and the maintenance of the social cohesion and solidarity within the community (Ghurye, 1964:210). The word *jangama* literally, means a 'moving object'. In Virasaivism, it signifies a person belonging to a religious order and who is an itinerant preacher. Basaveswara considered the *jangamas* to be the living embodiments of Siva, the Lord Himself. He emphasized that every Virasaiva must pay homage to the *jangama*. He forms an important constituent of the trinity of *guru-linga-jangama*. The *jangamas* generally belong to one of the two orders—either *pattada* or *virakta*—depending upon the type of *matha* they owe allegiance to. The *viraktas* (renouncers of wordly pleasures), *pattadadevarus* (head priests), *ayyas* (teachers), *carantis* (wanderers), and *maris* (acolytes) form the five classes into which the *jangamas* are divided.[23] To laymen, all *jangamas* are holy and they worship all without much inquiry as to the school they belong to. Each of the five schools associated with the *Pancacaryas*—Ekoramaradhya, Panditaradhya, Marularadhya, Visvaradhya and Revanaradhya—includes thirteen divisions (*bagis*).[24] *Jangamas* belonging to the same school or divisions (*bagi*) do not intermarry. *Ayyas* may take food from any Lingayat except from members of the barber, washermen and mahar communities and in some cases from oilmen (*teli*) and ferrymen (*ambigara*). *Maris* are generally celibates and wait on *viraktas*. They are potential *pattada devarus* or *swami*-designates. *Carantis* travel from place to place in order to gather contributions, both in cash and kind, from the Lingayat laity for the support of the *mathas*. *Jangamas* preside, participate and conduct almost all Lingayat rites and ceremonies. 'It is a peculiarity among the Lingayats that they esteem the *jangam* or priest as superior even to the deity' (Thurston, 1909 (IV):280). The *jangamas*, who conduct all religious ceremonies connected with the various rites of passage under the suprintendence of the *pattadayyas*, generally belong to the class of Virasaiva clergy known as *gurusthala*. On the other hand, the *viraktas* are expected to spend their time in reading and understanding the intricacies of Virasaiva philosophy, its doctrines and dogmas and transmitting this knowledge to the laity in a lucid and simple manner so that the latter is able to understand and appreciate them.

The major modes of recruitment into the order of *jangamas* were conversion and adoption. *Vanis* and *panchamasalis* can become *jangamas* but it is only when a *jangama* has no child or relation that he adopts a boy from these classes. Certain conditions are prescribed and followed while adopting a boy into the order of *jangamas*. First, the boy must not be married. Second, he must not be the child of a widow by her second husband. Conversion to the priesthood was prevalent in the early days of the Virasaiva movement, but this practice has fallen into disuse in contemporary times.

The *matha-jangama* axis was the major underpinning of the movement's organizational fabric. This axis became the carrier of the movement's ideology of protest; its form remained but the content registered changes over the passage of time.

Social Control: Methods and Agencies

The only sanctions imposed upon erring Virasaivas in their rules of conduct in the early days of the movement, were mainly those of public opinion and social ostracism. Virasaiva saints evoked fear of ridicule, isolation and public censure on those who erred in their observation of the rules of conduct as enunciated in the Virasaiva texts. As a sectarian movement, the Virasaiva movement imposed sanctions over its members and tended to control many aspects of their lives.

It was enjoined on every Virasaiva to report to the leaders of the community any violations of the five codes of conduct (*pancacaras*) that he may notice. This system did not function satisfactorily. Hence the task of ensuring adherence to the five codes of conduct was entrusted to special functionaries like the *mathadaiah*, *mathapati*, *ganacarya ganakumara* and *sthavarika* who belonged to the *guru-sthala* order.

The *mathadaiah* and *mathapati* attended to the task of observing, supervising and guiding the religious practices of the devotees. The *mathapati* was the first person who visited the houses of Virasaivas and his duty was to advise the devotees to wear the *istalinga* along with the sacred beads (*rudraksa*) and smear themselves with holy ash (*bhasma* or *vibhuti*). The former would visit the houses and if he found that wrong practices were being followed or that there were violations in the observance of the codes of conduct, he levied and exorted a fine of five annas.

Those in charge of the maintenance of order in the Virasaiva community and of protecting Virasaivas from harassment by members of other castes and religions, were the *ganacarya* and *ganakumara*. They were to report cases of disputes and quarrels among the Virasaivas as well as any violations of the *acaras* observed by them, excluding religious practices, to the *mathadaiah*. The supervision of temple worship was in the care of the *sthavarika*. Although Virasaiva saints did not approve of worship in the temple, yet their followers did practise temple worship. These five officials were found in every village and were worked under the supervision of a *pattacaradhikari* who travelled extensively.

In addition to these five officials, there were also the *kayakada swamis*, the wandering itinerants, who owed allegiance to one of the five *pattada mathas*. These *kayakada swamis* travelled from village to village supervising the conduct of people and redressing injustice when it was brought to their notice or when observed by them. They adopted the method of self-suffering in order to make the erring Virasaivas realize their folly. There were *swamis* of different *kayaka*, like *gante kayaka* (bell), *mullagive kayaka* (nailed sandals), *kani kayaka* (standing on fours), *gaddige kayaka* (sitting quietly and patiently in a place for days without taking anything), *mangala kayaka* (going around with burning camphor in a plate), *thekke kayka* (to stand embracing the pillar of a house). Upon entering a village a *gante kayakada swami* would ascertain from the *mathadaiah* and *mathapati* about the observance of the codes of conduct on the part of the Virasaivas living in the village. If he found that many Virasaivas were either not observing or were violating the codes of counduct then he would ring his bell up and down the streets until the aldermen of the village came to him and apologized and assured him of proper observance. If convinced of their sincerity he stopped his *kayaka*, i.e. ringing the bell, and having partaken of his food, would proceeds to the next village. The next official to visit the village was the *gaddige kayakada swami*. This official visited the village one month after the *gante kayakada swami's* visit. He obtained a report from the *mathadaiah* and *mathapati* regarding the observance or non-observance of the codes of conduct by the Virasaivas. In the event of no case being reported regarding violations or non-observance, the *gaddige kayakada swami* proceeded to the next village. However, if cases of violations in the codes of conduct were reported, then this *swami* would sit in a prominent place in the street and begin ringing the bells with both his hands. He would stop this only when the people staying in that street promised to abide by the codes of conduct. This was accompanied by the offering of *daksina* to the *swami* by the people.

The visit of the *mullagive swami* followed after an interlude of one month. He resorted to his *kayaka*, which involved standing on a sandal of nails in front of the houses of those Virasaivas who had promised to follow the codes of conduct faithfully but continued to flout them. He stopped his *kayaka* only when the defaulters apologized and paid a fine of rupee one. The *mullagive kayakada swami* then went to the *matha* and took his food before proceeding to the next village.

Another month intervened before the *thekke kayakada swami* visited the village. He ascertained from the *mathadaiah* whether those who had apologized for violating the codes of conduct were now behaving properly. In case there were still a few families who had not given up their bad ways the *swami* went to the house concerned and would embrace a pillar in the house and stand there. He stopped doing so only when the defaulters promised him that they would mend their ways and observe the codes of conduct. He then took his food in the devotee's house and accepted *daksina* before proceeding to the next village.

One month later, the *mangala kayakada swami* visited the village. He also ascertained from the *mathadaiah* whether all the Virasaivas residing in the village were observing the codes of conduct. He ignited camphor in a plate and with this in his hand went from house to house blessing its inmates. He accepted *daksina* from those who offered it.

These *kayakada swamis* visited the villages successively, allowing an interval of one month between each other's visit. The visits of these *swamis* were frequent some fifty years ago. Today, they are rarely seen. The Virasaiva movement attempted to maintain distinct spatial or social boundaries between it and the world through various devices for limiting interaction with outsiders. The order of excommunication (*bahiskara*) was the most severe punishment which the *Swamiji* of the chief *matha* pronounced upon Virasaivas in cases of gross misconduct. The cooperation of the devotees is required to make any punishment effective. Among the laity there are officials known as *setty* and *yajamana*, the former having greater influence than the latter.

This thumb-nail sketch of the various measures adopted by the movement's leaders to ensure proper observation of the five codes of conduct aids us in understanding the solidarity of the community and also the nexus between *mathas* and *jangamas* and the laity. These instruments of social control were effective until the turn of the present century. By preserving and transmitting such values as the Virasaiva movement held dear, the *matha-jangama* axis provided an anchorage for the social order, acting as a primary agency of stability and continuity.

During this phase, the organizational framework enabled the Virasaivas to effectively combat the external social environment and created among them a sense of identity, a feeling that theirs was a religious organization distinct from other groups. This organizational framework came to acquire a high degree of formalism and institutionalization. This phase witnessed increasing tendencies towards the routinization and bureaucratization of the movement's organizational framework.

Many Virasaiva leaders, who strongly influenced the course of development of the movement, emphasized that formal education is central among the social realities of the society they were living in, and urged the *mathas* to embark upon a massive drive to promote education and launch educational programmes in order to accelerate the spread of education within Virasaiva society.

They urged the *mathas* to devote a considerable part of their energies and time to promoting education. In the early days of the movement, the *mathas* provided instruction in Virasaiva philosophy and doctrines. Stress was laid on observance of the codes of conduct and on an understanding the eight aids (*astavaranas*). Imparting sacred lore and familiarizing and acquainting Virasaivas with the tenets of Virasaivism, *vacanas*, and *satsthala* philosophy, and also providing a basic knowledge of both Kannada and Sanskrit in order to enable the Virasaivas to understand the vedas, *Upanisads*, and *Saivagamas*, formed the hard core of the educational activity undertaken by the *mathas*. For the effective implementation of this programme the *mathas* undertook the task of instituting Sanskrit *patshalas* at various places, taking care to ensure that these were located within the area over which the *matha* establishing them could exercise its influence. The Sanskrit *patshalas* were the media through which *Vedic* literature percolated through Virasaiva society. The rationale behind establishing these *patshalas* was that a basic grounding in the fundamentals of Sanskrit was thought necessary; for, many of the texts—like the *Saivagamas*, *Upanisads* and *Vedas*—which the Virasaivas acknowledge as authoritative are in Sanskrit. Sanskrit was also useful to appreciate and understand the Virasaiva tenets, philosophy and texts. There was also the motivation of breaking the monopoly of the Brahmins over Sanskrit learning. Viewed from this perspective, the establishment of Sanskrit *patshalas* appears to be consistent with the movement's aims and objective.

As a sectarian movement, the Virasaivas had attained a high degree of politicization during their confrontation with the Brahmins, and had developed an elaborate organizational network at all levels. All these provided the necessary infrastructure for the development of the non-Brahmin movement at the turn of the present century.

The Virasaivas, backed by their vast organizational network, adopted a militant posture against the Brahmins in an effort to restore parity in the vital areas of social existence.

In the twentieth century, the pre-existing infrastructure enabled the Virasaivas to seek new goals. The Virasaivas agitated for educational benefits and reservation of seats in educational institutions and also sought preferential treatment in education and government employment. Among the goals envisioned by Virasaiva associations were the general advancement of the Virasaiva community, and this included education and a guaranteed share in the modern political process. This theme was wholly in harmony with the forces prevalent in South India in the early years of the twentieth century South India, which were mainly rebelling against the Brahmins.

Over the years, the Virasaiva movement succumbed to the process of institutionalization. It exhibited tendencies of losing its dissenting sectarian status. The process of institutionalization and routinization which beset it can be expressed in two ways: first, there was a regularization and routinization of the movement itself along organized lines. The movement codified its belief and the value systems and provided institutionalized arrangements to enforce the codes of conduct (*pancacaras*) on its members. There was an emphasis upon a formal, hierarchical organization, a religious bureaucracy; for, the very inclusiveness of a large and diverse religious community requires large-scale organization. The *jangamas* developed into a priestly class and isolated themselves from the rest of the community. They thwarted all attempts on the part of non-*jangamas* to encroach upon their privileges, power and prestige. The religious bureaucracy of the movement was characterized by the employment of a professional full-time clergy (*jangamas*) who possess the appropriate credentials of education and formal ordination. The Virasaiva movement has been maintaining relatively good relations with the state and secular powers. Its most extreme stance would, perhaps, be one of a 'loyal opposition'. In a context of religious pluralism, the movement maintains tolerant and friendly relationships with other movements claiming a denominational status. In matters of recruitment there has been a noticeable shift from reliance on conversion to primary reliance on birth for gaining more members, though it has been tolerant of some theological diversity and dispute, something it would not have done in its early days. The movement's membership now shows a bias towards the middle and upper classes of society, in contradistinction to its earlier concentration on low social status following. One witnesses a strong tendency within the movement for higher status persons to assume positions of power and be elected to office. Low-status members within the movement tend to defer to those with more education, a higher status job, and greater prestige.

An important factor leading to the movement losing its sectarian 'sting' and gravitating towards a denominational form, was the upward status mobility of some of its members, following improvements in their social and economic conditions. The movement has a bearing on the upward mobility of Virasaivas in the growth of a differentiated elite and the kinds of ritual, educational and economic gains that they have achieved and the quantum of political power they now enjoy.

The second way in which the process of institutionalization can be visualized is thus: the Virasaiva movement's absorption by the social order following the partial achievement of its goals pursued by its organization and/or its programme. There has been a change in its orientation—from one of opposition to one of accommodation—towards society. 'The more things change, the more they stay the same', runs the French proverb and, generally speaking, it is true. But not this time; the Virasaiva movement, while it bore a resemblance to the past, marked a sharp and surprising departure from the was men had once thought. It contained elements of both visions, but novel ideas predominated. The break with the past, while not total, was loud and enthusiastic and was accompanied by scorn for ideas that everyone had once implicitly believed.

The spirit of sectarianism in Hinduism has a different connotation. It can be traced back to several centuries before our era. The sects which are now most important are relatively recent and emerged only in the twelfth century (e.g., the Virasaiva movement) or later. In the context of Hinduism, sectarianism refers to either worshippers of Siva or Visnu, who were neither in complete sympathy with traditional brahmanism nor excommunicated by it and who had new texts and rites *in lieu* of the old ones or at least to supplement the Vedas and Vedic sacrifices. Most Indian sects are theistic in their origin, that is to say, they take a particular deity (Siva or Visnu or Motner goddess) and identify it as the centre. In the case of the Lingayats or Virasaivas, the supreme Godhead is Siva. In all their *vacanas* 'they speak to Siva and speak of Siva' (Ramanujam, 1973:11).

One of the primary doctrines of sectarian Hinduism is *bhakti* and it is common to both Saivites and Visnavites. The second feature common to all Hindu sects is the extravagant respect paid to *gurus* (or preceptors); the Virasaiva movement is no exception to this rule. In many sects the founder (or other prominent saints) is described as an incarnation (*avatar*) and receives regeneration after death (e.g., Basava, Ramanuja). Membership of a sect can be attained only by initiation (*diksa*) at the hands of a *guru* who teaches a special *mantra* (sacred formula) of which each sect has its own.

Bhandarkar (1965) was among the first to use the term 'sect' to describe the adherents of the Lingayat or Virasaiva philosophy, and his usage was followed by Nandimath (1942). Basham (1954) and Dasgupta (1955). Weber (1958:21) and Hutton (1946:103) consider Lingayats to be an illustration *par excellence* of a religious group becoming a caste. They use the hyphenated term 'caste-sect', despite the fact that the Lingayat ideology rejects the caste system of brahmanic Hinduism. Srinivas (1952:225) considers Lingayats to be primarily a status-honour group. A third usage of the term 'sect' for the Lingayats stems from the approach of Renou and Dumont. Their viewpoint attempts to place Lingayats in relation to the mainstream of 'Hinduism'. According to Renou, there are three salient features which characterize an Indian sect: first, adherence to a particular book and particular divinity; second, a philosophical standpoint of its own, particularly emphasizing *bhakti*; and, third, an ascetic founder who is an historical personality. The Virasaiva movement embodies these three features and judged by these criteria, early Virasaivism exhibited many sectarian traits. McCormack (1963:59-71) says: 'If it is possible to define a single Lingayat tradition and to characterize a sectarian group, Lingayats, as the carriers of that tradition, then the term "sect" may be taken to refer to the "life history" of the carriers of that tradition as a group'.

Lingayat religious specialists are of two types—priests and learned men (*sastris*), both usually belonging to the *jangama* castes, and *Viraktas* (*ascetics*). They use the term '*bhakta*' (devotee) in describing a member of their sect. They do not base their definition on the popular culture's emblems of the Lingayat, namely, the wearing of the *lingam* by members belonging to the group and their practice of vegetarianism. Among the Lingayat priests, the view is common that sect membership follows from the exclusive employment of their services for the celebration of the life-cycle and calendar rites.

Table

Social Composition of Virasaiva Community

Priestly Order	Trading/Commercial	Agricultural	Functional	Miscellaneous
JANGAMA	BANAJIGA			
Aradhya (Lingayat	Adi Banajiga	Ahir Lingayat	Ambis (Ferrymen)	Aidugadayadavaru
Brahmin)	Badagalava	Gauda Lingayat	Ganiga:	Gavinga
Ayya	Bania Lingayat	Gauda Mane	1. Bile Ganiga	Hirẹhasube
Chikkamath	Banna Dava	Gauliga	2. Diksavant Ganiga	Janagonda
Ganacari	Basale	Gurikara	3. Kare Ganiga	Kombe
Ganadhisvara	Bavani	Gurusthala	4. Rasawant Ganiga	Koriavarn
Hiremath	Gada Lingayita	Mallava	5. Silavant Ganiga	Pavaliyoru
Hugar	Gaddigeyava	Nonaba	Jadar:	Sajjana
Mathapati	Joti Banajiga	Panchachara Lingayat	1. Bile Jadar	Sthalavada
Pujar	Kaikola	Panchamasali Totiga	2. Kare Jadar	Tamadi
Sthavara	Kannadiga	Lingayat Reddis:	Koshtis (Hatkars)	Virabhande
Swami	Kanthapavade	1. Narada Lingayats	Lingayat Agasarus	Wara Bande
	Kori Setti	2. Pakanati Lingayats	Lingayat Gaulis	
	Linga Banajiga	3. Pasubumati Lingayats	Lingayat Holeyas	
	Lokavant Banajiga	4. Renati Lingayats	Lingayat Jyandras	
	Melpavade	5. Yellamma Kapus	Lingayat Kapus	
	Nirumelinava	6. Yellamma Reddis	Lingayat Kumbaras	
	Panchamasale Banajiga	Sadarus	Lingayat Kurumas	
	Pattaha Setti	Lingayat-Vokkaligas:	Lingayat Mangalas	
	Pavda Setti	1. Hande-Kurubas	Lingayat Nayandarus:	
	Petemane	2. Kuda-Vokkaligas	1. Non-Silvant	

Silavant Banajiga	3. Pakanaka-Reddis	Nayandaru
Toga Setti		2. Silavant Nayandaru
Turukane Banajiga		Lingayat Panchalas
		Lingayat Parit (Washermen)
		Lingayat Simpis:
		1. Nagalik Simpis
		2. Shiva Simpis
		Malis
		Mochi
		Nhavis
		Neygi
		1. Bilimagga
		2, Devanga
		Sale
		1. Pattusale

Viewed in the light of contemporary sociological observation, it can be said that the widest and most inclusive definition of the Lingayat sect as a political group hinges on the joint (popular) criteria of *linga*-wearing and strict vegetarianism. This group coincides with the group with whom Lingayat priests eat during the celebration of life-cycle or calendar rites, and from among whom the group dining together in the halls of *virakta mathas* is recruited.

By the criteria of religion, as viewed from the perspective of religious specialists, it has been seen that a wider group is cotemplated than is included by the social difinition—'wider' in the sense of greater diversity in caste and status, although religious congregations are localized (McCormack, 1963: 59-71).

From the legalistic perspective, the lawyers stress *linga*-wearing as important in defining the group boundaries of the sect, in addition to the knowledge of the *vacanas* (Sakhare, 1942: 1-10).

Having examined the difinition of sect boundaries of the Virasaiva movement as visualized by their own members, I shall now examine other ways of classifying sectarian movements. Sectarian movements could be distinguished on the basis of the degree of change they seek to bring about. A distinction has to be made between those sectarian movements which aim at making doctrinal changes, from those which have far-reaching social consequences. The Virasaiva movement is an illustration of a sectarian movement of the second category. In the present paper, the focus has been the Virasaiva movement as a sectarian movement and not as a Backward Classes movement—both aspects centring round protest and conflict in different spheres. The main thrust of the argument is the movement's development, with 'sect' and 'church' (dominant religious organization) characteristics intermingled with one another for dominance and power. As the processes of routinization and institutionalization set in, the Virasaiva movement—a militant and aggressive sect to start with—succumbed to the process of deradicalization, and tended to compromise with the established religious and secular patterns, to accept a pluralist situation, and to increase its organizational complexity and wealth to the point where it has become denominationalized. It lacks the fervid zeal of the sect it once was, and is no longer characterized by a rejection of society.

Viewed in the context of a sectarian movement, the Virasaiva movement exhibits tendencies to change and move away from its original programmatic aims towards eventual denominational status, and manifest characteristics of the dominant social order which it had originally repudiated. The Virasaiva movement demonstrates the fact that the sect-church framework is dynamic and when it becomes highly routinized it gives rise to new contradictions, out of which arise splinter movements (sadar *versus* non-sadar). Further, the Virasaiva movement got a new lease of life through new interests. The movement brought about not only reformatory changes in the religious sphere and social ethics but also transformatory changes. The new social ethic led to a diversification of occupation and modernization. It also led to a growth in educational opportunities. With this there was a change in differential access to economic and educational opportunities. There was a change in the tarditional power structure as the Lingayats are one of the major groups in Karnataka.

Sources of Table

SOURCES

H V. Nanjundayya and L.K. Anantakrishna Iyer, *The Mysore Tribes and Castes.* 4 vols. Bangalore: Mysore Government Press, 1928-35.

Edgar Thurston, *Castes and Tribes of Southern India.* 7 vols. Madras: Government Press, 1909.

R.V. Russell and Hira Lal, *The Tribes and Castes of the Central Provinces of India.* 4 vols. Delhi: Rajdhani Book Centre, 1975, (originally published in 1915).

R.E. Enthoven, *The Tribes and Castes of Bombay.* 3 vols. Bombay: Government Central Press, 1920-22.

M.A. Sherring, *Hindu Tribes and Castes.* 3 vols. Delhi: Cosmo Publications (originally published in 1881, reprinted in 1974).

B. Lewis Rice, Mysore: *A Gazetteer Combined for Government.* rev. ed. 2 vols. London: Archibald Constable & Co., 1897.

K. Ishwaran, *Shivapur.* London: Routledge and Kegan Paul, 1968.

C. Parvathamma, *Politics and Religion: A Study of Historical Interaction between Socio-political relationships in a Mysore Village.* New Delhi: Sterling Publishers, 1971.

GAZETTEERS OF INDIA

Bombay State: *Poona District.* rev. ed. Bombay: Government Central Press, 1954.

Bombay State: *Dharwar District.* rev. ed. Bombay: Government Central Press, 1959.

Maharashtra State: *Kolhapur District*. rev. ed. Bombay: Directorate of Government Printing, Stationery and Publications, 1960.
Mysore State: *Coorg District*. Bangalore: Government Press, 1965.
Mysore State: *Bijapur District*. Bangalore: Government Press, 1968.
Mysore State: *Gulbarga District*. Bangalore: Government Press, 1966.
Mysore State: *Chitradurga District*. Bangalore: Government Press, 1967.
Mysore State: *Mandya District*. Bangalore: Government Press, 1967.
Mysore State: *Kolar District*. Bangalore: Government Press, 1968.
Mysore State: *Tumkur District*. Bangalore: Government Press, 1969.
Mysore State: *Raichur District*. Bangalore: Government Press, 1970.
Mysore State: *Hassan District*. Bangalore: Government Press, 1971.
Mysore State *Bellary District*. Bangalore: Government Press, 1972.

CENSUS OF INDIA

1903:1901, vol. I: *India: Ethnographic Appendices*, by H.H. Risley. Calcutta: Superintendent of Government Printing, India.
1903:1901, vol. IX: *Bombay*. Bombay: Government Central Press.
1903:1901, vol. XXIV: *Mysore*. pts. 1-4. Bangalore: Government Press.
1912:1911, vol. VII: *Bombay*. pt. 1: *Report*. Bombay: Government Central Press.
1912:1911, vol. XXI: *Mysore*, pt. 1: *Report*. Bangalore: Government Press.
1912:1911, vol. XXI: *Mysore*, pt. 2: *Tables*. Bangalore: Government Press.
1923:1921, vol. VIII: *Bombay*, pts. 1 & 2. Bombay: Government Central Press.
1923:1921, vol. XXIII: *Mysore*, pt. 1: *Report*. Bangalore: Government Press.
1933:1931, vol. I: *India*, pt. 1: *Report*. Delhi: Manager of Publications.
1933:1931, vol. XXV: *Mysore*, pt. 1: *Report*. Bangalore: Government Press.
1946:1941, vol. I: *India*, pt. 1: *Tables*. Delhi: Manager of Publications.
1953:1951, vol. XIV: *Mysore*, pt. 2: *Tables*. Bangalore: Government Press.

Acknowledgements

Thanks are due to Professor M.S.A. Rao for his thoughtful comments. I thank Dr. (Mrs.) Anjali Arun Bali for her comments on an earlier draft of this paper.

Notes

1. Interpretations of the term 'Virasaiva' are to be found in religious works like *Siddhanta Sikahmani* and *Kriyasara*.
2. The term 'lingayat' is an anglicized form of *lingavant*. The Lingayats derive their name from the Sanskrit word *linga*, (the phallic emblem) with the suffix *ayta*, which means 'the people who bear the *linga*' habitually.
3. See Mysore Backward Classes Committee, *Final Report* 1961, pp. 43-46.

4. For a description of the Virasaiva movement see Arun P. Bali, 'A Sociological Study of Virasaiva Movement'. Unpublished M. Litt. dissertation. Department of Sociology, University of Delhi, Delhi, 1976.
5. Charles Y. Glock distinguishes five types of deprivation: economic, social, organismic, ethical and psychic. For a full treatment of types, see Charles Y. Glock, 'The Role of Deprivation in the origin and Evolution of Religious Groups'. In Robert Lee and Martin E. Lary (eds.) *Religion and Social Conflict*. New York: Oxford University Press, 1964, pp. 24-36.
6. Derived from the studies of N.J. Demerath III and Phillip E. Hammond, *Religion in Social Context: Tradition and Transition*. New York: Random House, 1969, pp 70-1; Liston Pope, *Millhands and Preachers: A Study of Gastonia*. New Haven, Conn.: Yale University Press, 1942, pp. 122-24; Bryan R. Wilson, 'An Analysis of Sect Development'. *American Saciological Review*, 1959, 24:3-15; E.D.C. Brewer, 'Sect and Church in Methodism'. *Social Forces*, 1952, 30(4): 400-8.
7. Pope lists twenty-one characteristics. See Liston Pope, *Millhands and Preachers: A Study of Gastonia*. New Haven, Conn.. Yale University Press, 1942.
8. It is difficult to trace the precise origins and evolution of this institution, which is described in detail in later literary works.
9. Basaveswara addressed his *vacanas* to Lord *Budala Sanganna* or *Kudala Sangamma*.
10. Allama Prabhu composed his *vacanas* in praise of *Guhesvara*.
11. Akka Mahadevi's devotional songs (*vacanas*) were sung in praise of *Cennamallikarjuna*.
12. Siddharama composed his *vacanas* in praise of *Kapila Sidda Malikarjuna*.
13. For a treatment on the *pancacaras* see Arun P. Bali, 'A Sociological Study of Virasaiva Movement'. Unpublished M. Litt, dissertation. Department of Sociology, University of Delhi, 1976, pp. 64-70.
14. For a fuller treatment of Virasaiva rituals and rites of passage, see Arun P. Bali, 'A Sociological Study of Virasaiva Movement.' Unpublished M. Litt. dissertation. Department of Sociology, University of Delhi, 1976, pp. 71-94.
15. See R. N. Nandi, 'Origin of Virasaiva Movement'. *The Indian Historical Review*, 1975, 2(1):32-46.
16. Interview with Dr. H. P. Malledvaru at Mysore on 1 November 1975.
17. Interview with Dr. H. M. Sadasivaiah at Mysore on 28 October 1975.
18. See Bhimakavi, *Busava Purana*: 60-4; *Cannabasava Purana* v.9-20; *Sunya Sampadane* (Gulur) XXI.18; *Raghavanka Caritra* XV.17.
19. Allama Prabhu gives vent to his feelings in many of his *vacanas* regarding the factional fight within the movement's leadership. For a few specimens of these *vacanas* see P.B. Desai, *Basavesvara and his Times*. Dharwar: Kannada Research Institute, Karnatak University, 1968, pp. 214-19.
20. Lingayat traditions represent Basaveswara as having first designated his sister's son, Cennabasava, as his spiritual heir.
21. Refer to P. B. Desai, *Vijayanagara Samrajya* (Kannada), p.69.
22. For a list of the 101 *viraktas*, see G. Shivarudrappa, 'Contributions of

Veerashaiva Mathas to the Development of Education in Karnatak: Historical Survey'. Unpublished Ph. D. thesis. University of Mysore, 1974, appendix.

23. See Maharashtra State Gazetteer, *Kolhapur district*, 1968, p. 171.
24. See Maharashtra State Gazetteer, *Kolhapur district*, 1968, p. 171n.

References

BALI, ARUN P. (1976*a*): 'Some Aspects of Virasaiva Movement: *Matha-Jangama* Axis'. Paper presented to the Workshop on Social Movements at the Department of Sociology, University of Delhi, 24-26 March 1976.

————(1976*b*): 'A Sociological Study of Virasaiva Movement'. Unpublished M. Litt. dissertation. Department of Sociology, University of Delhi.

BASHAM, A.L. (1954): *The Wonder that was India.* London: Sidgwick & Jackson.

BHANDARKAR, R.G. (1965): *Vaisnaivism, Saivism and Minor Religious Systems.* Varanasi: Indological Book House (originally published in 1915).

CLARK, ELMEN T. (1949): *The Small Sects in America* (Revised ed.) New York: Abingdon—Cokesbury Press.

DASGUPTA, S N. (1955): *History of Indian Philosophy.* 5 vols. Cambridge: Cambridge University Press.

DESAI, P.B. (1968): *Basaveswara and His Times.* Dharwar: Kannada Research Institute, Karnatak University.

FARQUHAR, J.N. (1967): *An Outline of the Religious Literature of India.* Delhi: Motilal Banarsidas (first published in 1920).

GHURYE, G.S. (1964): *Indian Sadhus.* Bombay: Popular Prakashan (second edition).

HUTTON, J.H. (1946): *Caste in India.* Oxford: Oxford University Press.

MALLEDEVARU, H.M. (1973): *Essentials of Virasaivism.* Bombay: Bharatiya Vidya Bhavan.

McCORMACK, WILLIAM (1963): "Lingayats as a Sect". *The Journal of the Royal Anthropological Institute of Great Britain and Ireland*, 93 (Part I): 59-71.

NANDI, R.N. (1975): 'Origin of Virasaiva Movement'. *The Indian Historical Review*. 2(1): 32-46.

NANDIMATH, S.C. (1942): *A Handbook of Virasaivism.* Dharwar: The Literary Committee.

NIEBUHR, H.R. (1929): *The Sources of Denominationalism.* New York: Holt, Rinehart & Winston.

POPE, LISTON (1942): *Millhands and Preachers: A Study of Gastonia.* New Haven, Conn.: Yale University Press.

RAMANUJAN, A.K. (translator) (1973): *Speaking of Siva.* Harmondsworth: Penguin Books.

RICE, B. LEWIS (1897): *Mysore: A Gazetteer Compiled for Government.* 2 vols. (rev. ed.). London: Archibald Constable & Co.

SADASIVAIAH, H.M. (1967): *A Comparative Study of two Virasaiva Monasteries.* Mysore: Prasaranga, Manasa Gangotri.

SAKHARE, M.R. (1942): *History and Philosophy of Lingayat Religion.* Belgaum: published by author.

SRINIVAS, M.N. (1952): *Religion and Society among the Coorgs and South India.* Oxford: Clarendon Press.

THURSTON, E. (1909): *Castes and Tribes of Southern India.* 7 vols. Madras: Government Press.

WEBER, MAX (1958): *The Religion of India: The Sociology of Hinduism and Buddhism.* Translated and edited by Hans Gerth and Don Martindale. Glencoe, Ill.: The Free Press.

WILSON, B.R. (1970): *Religious Sects: A Sociological Study.* London: Weidenfeld and Nicolson.

YINGER, J. MILTON (1970): *The Scientific Study of Religion.* New York: Macmillan.

9

Kolleen and Gar Kellom

A Guru-Centered Movement in the Making: Akhand Mahayoga Sangha of Varanasi*

PERHAPS THE MOST dominant figure in the development of modern Indian religion is the guru. Such social movements as the Nirankari movement have had gurus as their leaders, and gurus have achieved recognition throughout the world as teachers and guides for the seekers of all religions. Guru-centered movements in India constitute a phenomenon that has not yet been fully explored by scholars or researchers. Our desire to study the phenomenon of the guru-centered movement comes from a familiarity with gurus in California and a need to understand more clearly what the role of the guru is in Indian religion. At the same time we wanted to learn, under the guidance of a guru, the techniques of meditation that lead towards self-realization as found in the school of Kashmir Shaivism. Although the problems of finding a bona fide guru are complicated by the numerous self-proclaimed gurus who take money and deceive their followers with incomplete knowledge of their traditions, we were fortunate to find rather quickly both a newly declared guru and guide for meditation. When we were initially introduced to Sita Ram Pandey, the adopted son of the famous

*This paper is dedicated to Shri Mahamahopadhyaya Padmavibhushana Pandit Gopinath Kaviraj, Scholar, Philosopher and tantrik of international fame, who died on 12 June 1976.

Pandit Shri Gopinath Kaviraj, we were surprised to learn that he had started to initiate disciples only two years earlier and that only five months had elapsed since he had founded a public organization called Akhand Mahayoga Sangha. After several question and answer sessions at his home in Sigra, Banaras, it became apparent that this was not only an excellent opportunity to study the origin and activities of a guru-led movement with an organization but that the guru was also capable of giving us guidance in the practical techniques of meditation based mostly on the school of Kashmir Shaivism. Both Kolleen and I became initiated disciples of Sita Ram's Sangha and for the duration of our stay in Banaras participated in the activities of the organization while practising meditation under his guidance.

The first section of the paper that follows is an historical account of Sita Ram Pandey's association with Pandit Gopinath Kaviraj and the events that led to Sita Ram's initiation as a guru. The second section is a description of the beginnings and growth of his Sangha.[1]

The Making of a Guru

Dada Sita Ram has emerged only recently as a guru, offering a *Sadhana* (means) leading to self-realization (*atma sakshatkar*) based on his personal experiences and thirty-five years of association with Pandit Gopinath Kaviraj. To describe the events that led to his emergence I shall offer a brief biography of Kaviraj, the events of Sita Ram's life, as well as portraits of the three men who were closest to Sita Ram at the time he was recognized as a guru.

Shri Mahamahopadhyaya Pandit Gopinath Kaviraj is the son of Pandit Vaikunthanath, a brilliant student of English, Sanskrit and Philosophy who died in the first year of his M.A. He was a classmate of the great Swami Vivekananda. Gopinath Kaviraj became a brilliant student in his own right, standing at the head of his class in the Sanskrit wing of Queen's College, Banaras. He first held the post of Director of Research created for him by the Head of the Sanskrit College and later was selected as the Principal of the same school, which has come to be known as the Banaras Sanskrit University. Kaviraj served in that post for 13 years before retiring at the age of 50 to devote himself whole-heartedly to religious and spiritual studies and sadhana'.[2] He received several offers of teaching positions at Lahore College, Mayo College (Ajmer), and Lucknow University, but declined these to remain in Banaras and to devote his life to research in the fields of Sanskrit, literature, history, archaeology, epigraphy and philosophy.

Although he has received no less than five honorary doctorates from Indian universities and the honorary titles of Mahamahopadhyaya (1934) and Padma Vibhushana (1964) from the Government of India, he remained engrossed in a life of spiritual discourse and study at his home at Sigra, Banaras. He also preferred to stay in Banaras because of devotion to his only guru, Sri Swami Visuddhananda Paramahans, a great yogi and master of solar science who gave Kaviraj initiation (diksha) on 21 January 1918 at Hanuman Ghat. Swami Visuddhananda remained at his ashram in Banaras where he was visited by Dr. Paul Brunton who has written one of the only English accounts of Swamiji's power to materialize flower scents and bring a strangled bird back to life by focusing sunlight through a magnifying lens.[3] Gopinath Kaviraj also learned this solar science from his guru, but has never exhibited it to anyone.

SITA RAM PANDEY

The exact relationship of Gopinath Kaviraj with Sita Ram Pandey has been included in most biographies of Kaviraji:[4]

> Sita Ram Pandey came in the shelter of Kaviraji in early 1935, as a helpless child in need of education. Sita Ram was born in Katheli Bazaar, District Basti. After his father's death when he was only two years old, he and his mother resided with the brother-in-law, Pandit Badrinath Tripathi. Pandit Tripathi brought this family to Banaras where he supported them by serving as a pandit. But, unfortunately, only two years after they came to Banaras Pandit Tripathi also died. It was at this time that Sita Ram came under the shelter of Kaviraji, who was then Principal of Queens College. Kaviraji arranged his admittance to Jai Narain High School and Sita Ram took up residence with him as well. In order to support Sita Ram's mother, Kaviraji granted her Rs. 30 per month which she is still getting. After the death of Sita Ram's sister and her husband, the responsibility of their son and daughter also came to Sita Ram. In 1942, after getting the

permission of Kaviraji, he stopped his education and started a very small iron shop. Financial help of Rs. 3,000 for this business was also granted by Kaviraji. In 1952 Kaviraji arranged Sita Ram's marriage and gave him the ground floor of his Sigra house for his home. . . . Sita Ram spends minimal time in economic pursuits, preferring to give himself to spiritual service. In travel and during meals he is always with Kaviraji. Having lived with Babuji he has had the company of great religious personalities like Meher Baba, Shri Ram Thakur, Sita Ram Das, Onkar Nath and Tara Charan Sadhu. Sita Ram has benefited greatly financially and has learned to benefit mankind in the shelter of this great man (Kaviraji).[5]

Sita Ram has told how at the edge of eleven he was influenced by the story of Dhruva, the son of an emperor, who went to the forest to do tapas after being slapped by his step-mother. After reading this story, Sita Ram went to the forest near Chitrakut to search for god. Kaviraji and all who searched for him were unable to find him. Upon his return, Kaviraji recognized his interest in the spiritual line and took him to see Swami Visuddhananda.

Another story that Sita Ram proudly tells is how when travelling with Kaviraji in Poona, he one day passed by a palatial home with a long line of people in front of it. He was curious to know what was happening. Perhaps something was wrong or some rich person was giving alms to the poor. He was told that these people were waiting to get darshan of Meher Baba. Sita Ram then went to Meher Baba's secretary and said, 'Pandit Gopinath Kaviraj is staying in Poona and I have come to arrange an appointment for him with Meher Baba.' The secretary fixed the time for 9.00 a.m. the following day, and offered to send a car. Sita Ram declined the use of the car but said, 'I would like to have darshan of Meher Baba'. Sita Ram returned the next day with Kaviraji to have a second darshan.

While Sita Ram was travelling with Kaviraji and Swami Visuddhananda to Jagannath Puri, it was decided that Sita Ram would receive initiation from Swami Visuddhananda upon their return to Banaras. Sita Ram had already received teaching (*upadesh*) from him but had not been initiated. Before returning to Banaras, however, Swami Visuddhananda died. It was then decided that Siddhi Mata should give him initiation 'because there was no one else who was proper in Kaviraji's view'. Gopinath Kaviraj was not allowed by Visuddhananda to give initiation.

Sita Ram has stated that although Siddhi Mata performed the formality of his initiation, Swami Visuddhananda was his actual guru. At the same time, he considers Gopinath Kaviraj to be the source of all his understanding:

> I have learned many different things from here and there, but the major knowledge comes from Gopinath Kaviraj. My knowledge and methods both come from him.... He has not given more than one method to anyone. Gracefully he has given something to me, and that too as a son, not as a disciple. Only to me. Because if he had given it to me as a disciple then he would have to give to everyone which was not allowed by his guru.[6]

In 1952, when Sita Ram was 26, Gopinath Kaviraj arranged his marriage, although he had previously refused to marry in order to follow a spiritual life. Sita Ram is the father of seven children, five of whom live in the Sigra house with him, along with his wife and his mother. Sita Ram has also had the responsibility of raising the children of his sister and brother-in-law who both died at a very young age.

Sita Ram Pandey earns approximately Rs. 300 per month ($ 34) from his steel wire business in Dal Mandi, Banaras, and earns rent from his house which is located near the center of Banaras. He has virtually nothing to do with the maintenance of his business except for monitoring the records and making periodic trips to Calcutta to buy steel wire.

While sitting by the side of Kaviraji during spiritual discourses, Sita Ram became a fast friend of a Swami from Karnatak, a long-time student of Kaviraji. In about 1965, Sita Ram began to guide the Karnatak Swami in the secret techniques of the *sadhana* of sexual union, *yugala sadhana*. It was through his relationship with this Swami and persons to whom he was introduced by him that Sita Ram gradually began to assume the role of instructor in practical *sadhana* techniques.

Since the age of seven, the Karnatak Swami had been an initiated member of the Virasaiva sect of South India. Upon the death of his uncle, he became the head of the monastery there. He did his M.A. in Philosophy and worked for six years with Kaviraji completing his doctorate. He is still the figurehead of his organization but waits for 'the orders and inspiration' of Kaviraji. He had dedicated his life to Gopinath Kaviraj and considers Sita Ram to be his elder brother.

About the year 1970, this Swami took Sita Ram to see a friend of his—a Professor of vocal music. Sita Ram also began instructing the musician in the techniques of *yugala sadhana* and about three months later he felt as if a millstone had been lifted from his neck. His personal problems were solved. The musician had earlier tried other gurus, but had not found a solution. It is uncertain as to how long he continued *yugala sadhana* with Sita Ram, but in 1974 he came an initiated disciple of Dada Sita Ram in his *sadhana* of self-realization (*atma sakshatkar*).

It is clear that although Sita Ram began his life as a guru by instructing a Swami and a musician in the *sadhana* of sexual union, he has instructed no one else in this line. For reasons unknown to us, Dada Sita Ram gave this instruction to these two men only, neither of whom is practising it at the present time.

However, Sita Ram emerged as a guru when his third disciple gave him wide publicity. The Swami introduced another friend to Sita Ram—a part-time astrologer and a stage actor. He was a joint-owner, along with his younger brother, of a mechanical engineering firm. He had had two other gurus, one of whom now resides in the United States, but could not find a solution to his personal problems. He met the Swami and asked him for guidance in spiritual methods. The latter replied that at present he was in a learning stage himself and could not guide him, but added, 'I will take you to someone who will'. He attended some discussions at Sita Ram's house and began to feel that was drawn to Sita Ram as he had been to his former guru. He then requested initiation but for three months Sita Ram refused saying that he could get initiation only if he discontinued relations with all women except his wife and avoided the company of his old friends. With a view to fulfilling these conditions, the astrologer disciple spent four continuous months in the company of Sita Ram and the Swami in discussions and pilgrimage.

A Display of Power (Shakti Prayog)

The crucial event in the exposure of Dada Sita Ram was an incident that occurred in 1972 at the home of X, a mutual friend of Sita Ram, the Swami and the astrologer. This incident convinced the astrologer that he wanted Sita Ram to be his guru. Further, it marked Sita Ram Pandey's first public step as a guru.

The discussion that evening centered on whether a person could lose the sense of the physical body through meditation. X's wife was eager to know if this could be done in her own *sadhana*, and Sita Ram said that it was possible. The Swami challenged Sita Ram to prove his contention, never having observed Sita Ram's ability in this line. Although Sita Ram was very upset by the challenge, he nevertheless accepted. Arrangements were made to meet the following evening—both Sita Ram and X's wife had empty stomachs to guard against possible nausea and vomitting. X's wife was seated on her meditation seat and Sita Ram placed his hands upon her, administering what the astrologer disciple calls a 'heavy dose' of *shakti*. X's wife presently fainted, and when she returned to consciousness said, with tears in her eyes, 'Why did you make me returned. I have never known such a peace like this before. Please send me back.' For the next three days she was totally engrossed in meditation at her home.

This incident resulted in a disagreement. Sita Ram felt that the Swami should recognize him as his master, having given him instructions for the past seven years. Whereas the Swami felt it an insult that he should be asked to accept any master other than Gopinath Kaviraj.

The astrologer disciple received initiation from Dada Sita Ram and became his first disciple in his present line of *sadhana* for self-realization (*atma sakshatkar*). Since his formal initiation, he has introduced Sita Ram to more than thirty persons who have become disciples (*sishya*) and the first members of the Akhanda Mahayoga Sangha.

Before discussing the organization of the Akhanda Mahayoga Sangha, we shall describe the process of the making of a guru. The guru is a religious teacher, and a moral and spiritual guide, in fact 'spiritual parent', who instructs his disciples in the *Sastars* and conducts the ceremony of initiation. Manu says, 'Of him who gives natural birth and of him who gives knowledge of the Veda, the giver of sacred knowledge is the more venerable father. Since second or divine birth insures life to the twice-born in this world and the next'.[7] The guru is not a mere mortal. He is considered the same as god, who, with his power, carries the responsibility for the sins of his disciples. The relationship between guru and disciple does not terminate until the disciple has attained the state of pure monism.

For Dada Sita Ram, the guru is one who shows the way towards self-realization. A guru shows the way—he carries. He is able to 'make one reach up toward the light of Truth'. He helps his disciples find their inner current. The guru prepares a disciple the way a parent would raise a child or a farmer would till the soil for planting.

The goddess with whom Dada Sita Ram is to be identified is the Divine Mother, Durga: 'First, the goddess upon whom we do *sadhana*, with whom we establish a relationship, is Mother. In all the world the sweetest relation is that of mother'.[8] In the room where Dada Sita Ram receives those who come to see him, there is a picture of Ma Durga beneath the photograph of Gopinath Kaviraj. He says that the guru and the Divine Mother are one, and that to bow at the feet of the guru is to bow at the feet of Ma.

The close rapport that Dada Sita Ram has with his disciples is one of the most distinctive qualities about him as a guru. Nothing is to be kept secret. If any disciple has not been to Sigra for several days he will make a personal call at his home to see what might be wrong. Recently there was a bank executive in Banaras who quit his job, renounced his life and family and began wandering throughout Uttar Pradesh in the manner of a *sadhu*. His wife was terribly upset and came to Sita Ram to seek his help. Sita Ram located her husband in an ashram in Burdwan near Calcutta, and convinced him to return to Banaras where Sita Ram took care of him. He also approached the local mental hospital and the bank and persuaded them to have his absence treated as a result of a mental breakdown and to reinstate him in his job. This man is not an initiated disciple of Sita Ram, but his story again illustrates the kind of activities Sita Ram involves himself with.

Like Kaviraji, Sita Ram accepts no money from those who come to him for initiation. Only sweets and *paan* (betel leaf) may be brought which he then distributes to those who are present. His wife and two older daughters provide tea and food for visitors, and several times a week a disciple may stay at Sigra. He has sometimes been criticized by his family for being too indifferent to them, preferring to sit with his disciples or to travel, than to stay at home. Nevertheless, it is one of the most distinguishing aspects of his guruship that he maintains a personal relationship with each of his disciples.

It must be said at this point that Sita Ram appears to have been greatly influenced by the lives of Swami Visuddhananda and Gopinath Kaviraj. Swamiji's bold attempts to establish a laboratory and locate nine spiritual powers for the welfare of the world, as well as Kaviraji's constant devotion to the needs of those who come to him are mirrored in Sita Ram's actions. The way Sita Ram has formed an organization based upon this concern will be dealt with in next section. We will also discuss the deviations he has made from the traditions of his two spiritual masters, both in his organization and in his *sadhana*.

Another distinctive feature about Sita Ram is his emphasis on the *practical* experience. He believes that the guru is a guide toward self-realization, but not until the disciple's experiences progress toward that realization is he called a proper guru. He emphasizes results. Gopinath Kaviraj was a master of the theories of many schools of Indian philosophy; while Sita Ram places emphasis on commuting theories to practice. Again and again he reminded us that knowledge from books is incomplete. Practical experience is the only source of true knowledge, which books can then broaden. He reminds his disciples of what Swami Visuddhananda said about a yogi: 'Yogi has control over his powers but a bhakt (one taken to devotional path) does not.'[9] Sita Ram considers that no yogi can be a real yogi without a knowledge of *tantra* and how to use that power (*shakti*).

For his knowledge of tantric *sadhana*, Sita Ram consulted three gurus. First was Swami Pranavananda who taught him something of tantric *sadhana* which he shared with Gopinath Kaviraj. Kaviraj then gave him a second tantric *sadhana* which he considered better. Sita Ram consulted a third guru—probably (but not certainly) Janardan Swami of Rishikesh—who gave him more instructions to which Gopinath Kaviraj also added.[10]

One of Sita Ram's constant worries concerns gurus who give no guidance or who, through false guidance, lead people astray. The musician disciple contrasts the twenty-seven years he spent with the previous guru with the two years he has been with Sita Ram by saying that his previous guru was truly a realized soul who had reached the top of the mountain and spoke to all of us below saying: 'Come on up; the way is beautiful'. But the musician found the forest so thick he could not find his way. 'With Sita Ram the way is clear. He takes us step by step.'

As a practical guru Sita Ram knows the tantric techniques of *yugala sadhana* (which he gave to only two of his disciples), the *shakti prayog* and his present line of Raj Yoga with various ways of guidance which he adapts to each individual's needs. He has incorporated this emphasis on experience and the practical application of philosophy into his four stages of *sadhana*

Akhanda Mahayoga Sangha

Beginnings

In this section I will describe the nature, growth and functions of Sita Ram's organization, and how his disciples have been affected since joining the organization and doing *sadhana*. *Akhanda* means cosmic, universal, integral and whole; *Mahayoga* means cosmic communion with the indivisible cosmic consciouness; sangha is a get together of those individuals who wish to share this ineffable experience of that divine infinite radiation.

Sita Ram did not make a conscious decision about initiating disciples, but rather it happened 'automatically' due to the grace of Divine Mother Durga. His nature was like that of Gopinath Kaviraj—not to be attached to mundane affairs but rather to follow the 'inner instructions' of the Mother. After initiating the astrologer in February 1973, Sita Ram initiated four friends of the latter. These five men, along with the musician disciple, constitute the core group of what has come to be known as the Akhanda Mahayoga Sangha in Banaras. The four friends of the astrologer disciple who became Sita Ram's first disciples were two accountants, an inspector and a contractor. While one was from Allahabad the three others were from Banaras. They were all curious about what had changed their astrologer friend's behaviour after being initiated by Sita Ram, and since he refused to take part in their activities they came to Dada Sita Ram with him. Sita Ram was reluctant to give these men initiation, but eventually received 'inner instruction' which was reinforced by the insistence of the astrologer disciple and initiated them. The contractor disciple was the only non-Brahmin in the group.

The contractor led a rather carefree life. In 1973 his brother contracted throat cancer, and died a slow and painful death. His brother's widow committed suicide out of grief. Not long after that, his uncle also died, leaving the contractor in a very disturbed state of mind. He had never had a guru and had read very little of spiritual matters, considering himself 'a worldly man'. He met Sita Ram at the homes of several friends and was impressed with the gift Sita Ram had for explaining spiritual things in a simple way.

The contractor has now dedicated his life to his guru. He has reached the third stage of *sadhana* along with the other four.

After taking his first five disciples Sita Ram refused to initiate anyone else. He said, 'I am not going to have more than five disciples. These five can do all my work'. At this point Sita Ram began to 'feel a kind of fear' of Gopinath Kaviraj. He felt perhaps he had made a mistake by beginning to initiate disciples while Kaviraj had refrained from initiating any one.

In July 1974 these five disciples decided to celebrate Guru Purnima—the traditional day to honour the guru—by doing puja to Dada Sita Ram. The news of this celebration in Sigra spread, and one of the five informed Gopinath Kaviraj that Sita Ram had been initiating disciples. Sita Ram, wanting to have the blessings of Kaviraji, went to see him. He said,

> The day after Guru Purnima I went to see (Kaviraji) and said that by the grace of Divine Mother Durga I have felt four stages within myself and now I want to give this to the rest of the world. He (Kaviraji) replied, 'If you have realized these four stages you mentioned inside yourself, then give them to the world. The world is passing through a very miserable time'.[11]

At this point it is important to explain something of the philosophy of Gopinath Kaviraj and the tradition to which Sita Ram owes so much. It is a tradition that Sita Ram has traced back to 'the guru of the father of Rabindranath Tagore' known as Prabhu Jagat Bandhu. The ideas of Jagat Bandhu have been passed on to Sri Aurobindo and Meher Baba, and then adopted by Gopinath Kaviraj and explained in his book written in 1948. Sita Ram basically accepts this philosophy but has incorporated some of his own ideas, thus providing a distinct ideology to his movement.

The main principle of Akhanda Mahayoga is that in its soul every creature is the same. From the ant to the elephant all of us have the same light (*chaitanya*), the same soul. If one soul is to realize this divine light that is coming from the upper world and be transformed, then all souls will realize it and be similarly transformed.[12] If any one would become a truly realized soul then all will be realized souls provided they are inclined toward or in contact with a person like Sri Aurobindo, Meher Baba or Gopinath Kaviraj. Dada Sita Ram says that contact with him is enough. 'That love will pull you up and when the divine light or god's grace comes you will be transformed'. To this extent Sita Ram concurs with Gopinath Kaviraj, Meher Baba and Sri Aurobindo.

Sita Ram's contribution to this theory is the practical dimension. He says that while great men like Aurobindo and Kaviraj are preparing themselves for the divine light it is not enough for the common person to simply wait until the first soul is realized so that he will also be realized. We should prepare ourselves. Sita Ram explains:

> So I thought, when god's grace comes, when the divine light comes we will get it, but why shouldn't I prepare myself also, so if the divine light comes in my lifetime I will be ready to hold it. In the same way, all those who will be in my contact, I should prepare the same base for them also. . . . That is why I have added the word 'sangha' to Akhanda Mahayoga. Because all of us together under the shadow of the Divine Mother are preparing ourselves for god's grace.[13]

For Sita Ram, therefore, there is an 'immanent spiritual resuscitation' in the world, but it is not something that will fall upon us without our own preparation. The transformation of this mortal world from its pain and suffering depends upon the 'whole-hearted cooperation' of one and all. We are not to be more spectators or merely attached to great souls who will save the human race for good. 'All of us individually will have to be self-awakened in order to usher in the dawn of supreme enlightenment'.[14]

Growth

During the year that followed Guru Purnima in 1974, at least three more friends of the astrologer disciple were initiated: a tailor, a research student and an engineer. With the inclusion of these three men Sita Ram's disciples numbered at least nine by the time of the Guru Purnima in 1975. During this time Sita Ram conceived the plan to start an organization that he felt was inspired through inner instruction from mother Durga. With Kaviraji's permission secured and knowledge of his guruship spreading by word of mouth he agreed to allow his disciples to give his organization publicity. In July of 1975 a Hindi brochure entitled Akhanda Mahayoga Sangha was published with Sita Ram's description of his philosophy, the four stages of *sadhana* and his association with Kaviraji.

After Guru Purnima of 1975, Sita Ram began to initiate with greater frequency. This time he recruited more high-placed individuals—the president of a big company in Kanpur, the manager of a water-works, and the manager of a coal mine. He also initiated two women from Calcutta. The network was growing and the message was spreading. A hotel manager was initiated, who soon thereafter brought Sita Ram his first foreign disciple, a spiritually minded world traveller from Santa Barbara, California. A tourist guide was also initiated, who then began to bring other foreigners to Sita Ram, most of whom were only curious observers. Other members continually brought their friends, relatives and associates to Sigra.

In October 1975, a priest (aged 23 years) of a temple in Banaras became his disciple. In November and December, Sita Ram began to initiate several persons from different walks of life: a sales-tax officer from Calcutta, a lawyer and a businessman. One of the most interesting persons to be initiated during this period and the person who has had an immense impact upon the recent growth of the organization is this businessman. It is relevant to briefly describe here his previous involvement with gurus, his rise through the stages of the Akhanda Mahayoga Sangha to membership of the inner core, and his proselytizing activities for Sita Ram.

The Businessman Disciple

The thirty-two years old businessman is the father of three children. He lives with his wife, father and three children at Banaras. His family is of the Vaisya caste. They migrated from Rajasthan in 1857, penniless after the British seized their land. Starting with the sale of tin pots carried in baskets on their heads, the family today owns a large building complex, as well as a spacious house and several cows. His family has been spiritually oriented since his youth owing to the influence of his mother. He has had over ten gurus. His first guru was a family guru whose lectures on the *Bhagavad Gita* and bhakti he used to attend at the age of 14 years. Three years later, in 1967, Swami (the first disciple of Sita Ram) took him to see Gopinath Kaviraj whom he has visited frequently since then. He always took a burlap *assan* and established a regular place for himself on the balcony outside Kaviraji's room where he could listen to the discussions and take notes.

In 1961 he went to Hardwar to live with a third guru, and learned a *sadhana* called Hansa Yoga in which he practised breathing exercises combined with a diet of one cup of tea, four chapatis and grass vegetable soup each day. After a year-and-a-half in Hardwar his health deteriorated drastically and he began to bleed from his nose. He left Hardwar out of fear that he might die.

His fourth guru was a scholar of Kashmir Shaivism who taught him Sanskrit and with whom he has read many of the works of Abhinava Gupta, Utpal Deva, Kshemaraja and Jai Rath. He has translated six books from Sanskrit into Hindi. He continues to visit his fourth guru frequently.

The businessman also had a guru of Hatha Yoga, a retired major from the Indian Army, and a guru from Gujarat who only gestured and did not speak. He spent time with Anandamayi Ma, with a Muslim near Sarnath who eats only one meal a day, and with a tantrik. He visited many of these gurus simultaneously and by 1975 had begun to talk of starting a yoga center with friends in order to bring many of these gurus to Banaras.

He admits that for most of his life he has had a bad reputation. He has spent much of his time in lawsuits as both defendant and plaintiff, and, by his own admission, was very mean. He was also after women. His life began to take an abrupt turn, however, after meeting Sita Ram Pandey.

He met Sita Ram on 28 November 1975. He told Sita Ram about his idea for a yoga center and Sita Ram invited him to Sigra to visit his own Sangha. At Sigra, he was attracted by the congenial atmosphere, spiritual discourses and Sita Ram's association with Kaviraji. On 18 December 1975, the businessman was initiated into the first stage of Sita Ram's *sadhana*.

He remained very close to Sita Ram during his initial days as a disciple, often telling Sita Ram of his experiences in *sadhana* and discussing philosophy. By 18 January 1976 he had achieved the second stage. He had been doing *sadhana* for eighteen years, had previously learned to locate *susumna* and therefore found the first stage easy. He then vowed to stop all his work and dedicate a full six months to *sadhana* for self-purification. He gave away all the money he had earned by questionable means and stayed in close contact with Sita Ram, receiving instructions for his meditation every few weeks.

According to his family and friends a remarkable change took place in his life after initiation. His family life has once again become happy, and his relations with friends and business associates have improved. This change is so welcome but so unexpected that he wishes to place a garland at the feet of Sita Ram for helping it to take place. He said: 'The thing is that previously I was searching for peace and comfort in the outside world, in worldly affairs, like corruption, court, conspiracy, smuggling. Now I am not able to do those things. . . . I feel one hundred, one thousand times better than I was before.' When we asked him what makes Sita Ram different from his other gurus and if he will still seek other gurus he replied: 'The thing is that Guruji is not different from anyone. He just feels his vibration in everybody and this makes him greater. . . . He will be my last guru. He is my satguru. The journey ends here.'[15]

Ever since his initiation he has been the most active member of the Akhanda Mahayoga Sangha. Besides doing *sadhana* regularly he has devoted himself to building up the organization. Below is a sample of some of his activities on behalf of Sita Ram: (*i*) By means of his brother's printing business he published an English translation of Sita Ram's pamphlet describing the Akhanda Mahayoga Sangha. (*ii*) He has redecorated Sita Ram's visitors' room with a new couch, tapestries, colourful curtains, pillows and a fan for hot weather. (*iii*) He has designed and printed an emblem for the organization which he then presented to most of the members for framing. (*iv*) He has distributed publicity hand-outs of the Akhanda Mahayoga Sangha to radio stations, newspapers, and important and influential persons. (*v*) In Sita Ram's name he plans to publish his translation from Bengali to Hindi of *Akhanda Mahayog* by Gopinath Kaviraj. The book will have an appendix on the origin of the Akhanda Mahayoga Sangha and the proceeds will go toward the organization. (*vi*) He plans to finish his translation into Hindi of *Tantra Lok* and with the proceeds to build a meditation hall behind

Sita Ram's Sigra house with accommodation for out-of-town guests.

To carry out these activities this businessman discontinued his own work and borrowed money from relatives. He has put pressure on Sita Ram to accept money for the organization. When Sita Ram initiated the Duke of Aron from Spain vacationing in Banaras, he lobbied hard to convince Sita Ram to ask the Duke for money. From the point of view of other members he seems to have mounted a single-handed campaign to make Sita Ram and his Akhanda Mahayoga Sangha 'popular'.

There is one more event involving the businessman that is important to mention both from the point of view of the organization and as an example of Sita Ram's influence. This event centers around the former's mother, who for the past eight years has been living in Chitrakut as a *sunya* (non-entity), having left her family because she felt that at their home she was not able to pursue the spiritual line that her father's family had practised. She vowed never to return to Banaras again. When Sita Ram was informed about this and also of the family's desire to have her return to Banaras, he decided to go to Chitrakut and see her. On 23 January 1976, Sita Ram, along with the businessman and the astrologer disciple, left Banaras for Chitrakut. On 27 January they returned with the businessman's mother. Sita Ram completely converted her to his point of view and initiated her.

Following this incident, the businessman's brother-in-law and father-in-law were initiated. His uncle from Delhi, who is a Ph.D. in Philosophy, also made plans for initiation. His uncle claims to be a guru with thousands of followers of his own in the United States. It is certain that the businessman has had a major impact on Sita Ram and the organization of the Akhanda Mahayoga Sangha. He is now considered to be a member of the core group, arousing traces of envy and jealousy from some of the original five.

Ourselves in the Sangha

We came to know of Sita Ram Pandey and the Akhanda Mahayoga Sangha through an Arts Professor from Benaras Hindu University who was known to the businessman disciple. On the evening of Sunday 4 January 1976, accompanied by the Professor and our interpreter, we met Sita Ram.

Sitting across from Sita Ram on cushions were eight disciples, including the American. We were treated hospitably and offered tea and sweets while the astrologer disciple prepared our instant horoscopes. We observed this welcome for several others, and were moved by the genuine good feelings that seemed to prevail.

In the days that followed we learned that Sita Ram's *sadhana* consists of regular meditation in the lotus position with eyes closed for a period of one hour each morning and evening. Each disciple is expected to have a dark, quiet place for this purpose where they place a wool *assan* on top of a grass *assan*, and once seated thereon follow the explicit instructions for locating *susumna* and the *chakras* given in initiation. The only restrictions Sita Ram places on his disciples is that they refrain from eating eggs, onions and garlic because these foods disturb the energy created during *sadhana*. Meat, fish, coffee and all other foods are permitted. He strongly discourages the use of drugs or alcohol but does not prohibit this. No money whatsoever is required at the time of initiation. The initiate is required to bring two kilograms of sweets and a flower garland. Sita Ram also insists that the details of one's initiation are to be kept completely secret.

For Sita Ram to give someone initiation it is not only necessary that he receives 'inner instruction' from the Divine Mother, but that there should be a strong curiosity or thirst on the part of the seeker. Kolleen and I both felt a definite curiosity but were concerned about what an individually oriented *sadhana* would do to our marriage relationship. Would we each become withdrawn, removed and contemplatively silent? Would it pull us apart? We were also suspicious about the lack of women in the Sangha, although we were told that female disciples existed.

As we discussed these concerns, Sita Ram assured us that we both would be given identical lines of *sadhana*. A couple should be considered as 'two wheels of the same cart', we were told—one could not progress without the other. Each individual's advancement would encourage the other. In the end we were basically satisfied with Sita Ram's answers to our first concern. As regards the position of women in the organization, we were aware of the apparent separation in Indian society of the men's world of activity from the domestic responsibilities of women. We were told that women are normally too busy for *sadhana* and that when they do undertake religious practice it is more appropriate for them to do bhakti worship of deities like Ram or Krishna. Although our questions about the women in the Akhanda Mahayoga Sangha remained unsatisfactorily answered, we asked for initiation.

My initiation was scheduled for 9 January and I arrived at Sigra washed and scrubbed, with my two kilograms of sweets, *assans* and flower mala. I was the only person to be initiated that day. Sita Ram and I made our way slowly to the roof and paused a moment to discuss the landmarks of Banaras spread out below us and to enjoy the early morning air. I recall gazing off to the East toward the Ganga where a bird in flight soared just at the horizon line, at first slightly below, then slightly above and then exactly right. I felt strangely like I was out there with him, a feeling I would come to recognize more clearly once I was a disciple of Sita Ram.

Sita Ram then invited me into his rooftop *sadhana* room and instructed me in the techniques of the first stage. This was a most pleasant time and what I experienced there gave me a new feeling of closeness to Sita Ram, if for no other reason than that he took the time to explain what he knew to me so clearly and so sincerely. Even more enjoyable was the time spent meditating together although it was over much before I wanted it to be. We were soon embracing out on the roof again and I felt much like a child as I skipped down the stairs behind my new Guruji to meet the brothers waiting below.

Kolleen's initiation was on 18 January and was similar to mine except for the elimination of part of the practical technique which she would be granted later after a brief examination. There was also a difference in that she was asked, 'To whom do you feel you are closer or with whom do you feel a closer spiritual relationship, your mother or your father?' Kolleen answered that it was her mother with whom she felt a more spiritual bond, which pleased Sita Ram. This seems to indicate that Sita Ram may believe that women tend to feel a closer relationship with their fathers which would cause him to hesitate to initiate women into his Sangha. With that assumption this line of *sadhana* which attempts to bring one toward self-realization through developing a relationship with the Divine Mother would be inappropriate for most women. Apparently Sita Ram felt assured and proceeded with Kolleen's initiation.

In the days that followed we experienced a new closeness with members of the organization that continued to grow during our stay in Banaras. While we had originally been the center of attention whenever we came to Sigra, as time passed we were allowed to fade into the comfortable background of the brotherhood. Sita Ram began to use us as examples of a successful, mediating, foreign couple to those who came to ask about initiation. We became more and more a part of the Sangha and were included in many social activities of the group. We were taken by Sita Ram to visit Gopinath Kaviraj at Anandamayi Ma Ashram and Visuddhananda's ashram. Members of the Sangha frequently visited us at our home. We were invited to attend music concerts. We were also invited for meditation and to the *puja* observed by the Sangh during the Shivaratri celebrations and the solar eclipse of 29 May 1976.

Our position as foreigners in the Akhanda Mahayoga Sangha seemed to have a double significance. Initially we were seen as a curiousity because Sita Ram had only one other American disciple. Soon after initiation we began to hear rumours that Sita Ram might come to visit us in the United States and had hopes that we would be instrumental in establishing an American center for his Sangha.

Throughout our experience with the Akhanda Mahayoga Sangha we saw a continuous flow of people visit Sita Ram. We watched the number of disciples and visitors closely from January to May, and while the attendance on Sunday evenings was higher than on week-days, there was nevertheless a consistent attendance of at least eight people. It appears we came to Sita Ram at a time when he was most active in initiating new disciples. The astrologer disciple informed us that it was only two months before we arrived in Banaras that Sita Ram had begun to initiate frequently. After we became disciples we witnessed the initiations of our interpreter, a surgeon at Banaras Hindu University Hospital, a pharmacist and Hatha Yoga instructor, a salesman from Calcutta and many others.

The salesman from Calcutta was having problems with his marriage and came to Banaras to leave his family for good. He admits that he is an alcoholic but became a member of Alcoholics Anonymous six years ago and proudly showed us his Alcoholics Anonymous coin. He had approached Sita Ram with the idea of starting an Alcoholics Anonymous chapter in Banaras and Sita Ram felt it was a good idea. However, the salesman was attracted by Sita Ram's *sadhana*. He met Sita Ram after a twelve-year search for a guru. One day he saw Sita Ram on a bicycle downtown and he waved and said, 'How are you?' He knew then that was what he wanted, a guru who rides a bicycle and goes about his life like a real person.[16] He received initiation from Sita Ram after coming to Sigra several times with his uncle. He then returned to Calcutta where Sita Ram frequently visits him. In one of his trips to Calcutta he initiated a guru, the head of a Burdwan ashram and many of his disciples.

The exact number of Sita Ram's disciples is not known but he, as well as other core group members, has told us that as of June 1976 there were between fifty and sixty members of the Akhanda Mahayoga Sangha in the Banaras area and about one hundred disciples in the whole of India.

THE FUTURE OF THE AKHANDA MAHAYOGA SANGHA

This rapid increase in initiates since December 1975 and the frequency of Sita Ram's travelling prompted us to ask several members of the Sangha about the future of their organization. The most consistent answer we received was that the organization's future is 'very bright' because Sita Ram has something real to offer to the world. There are so many gurus with phoney messages and Sita Ram's disciples are convinced that he has something to offer which really works. The astrologer disciple says that the future is very bright but warns that the core group must protect Sita Ram from criticism and see to it that no one misleads him.

The businessman disciple, more than anyone, seems to be emerging as the administrative leader of the Akhanda Mahayoga Sangha. Besides his many activities for the Sangha and plans for expansion, he strongly criticizes fellow members for not realizing the necessity of publicity and raising finances.

Sita Ram has active groups of disciples in Banaras and Calcutta—indeed, these groups of disciples compete for his presence. Besides expansion in North India there is frequent reference to establishing foreign centers.

The musician disciple has spoken with friends in Switzerland and London about the possibility of starting a European center. He is also attempting to arrange for an American concert tour for himself and will take Sita Ram with him if he succeeds. None of the members of the Sangha has ever been to the United States but the musician has frequently toured Europe and the USA. Right up to the day we left Banaras it was suggested that we should attempt to organize our friends so that we could invite Sita Ram to California.

We frequently questioned whether Sita Ram should expand his organization and our reservations were often met with agreement. Many disciples feel that Sita Ram is absent from Banaras far too much already. More disciples and more centers would make him less and less available and make it more difficult for him to maintain his personalized style. The musician laments the hierarchy of an organization, yet he is the biggest force behind efforts at international expansion.

It seems to us that Sita Ram likes his organization and believes that he is doing good for the world this way. We noticed an administrative element creeping into his discussions, perhaps due to the influence of the businessman and other growth minded members. When we asked Sita Ram himself about the future of his Sangha, he replied:

> The world is sad and not at peace. The world needs these four stages so I have to give as much as I can and for that we need some publicity and we have to start centers here and there. But right now we are facing a financial problem because, as you know, I do not accept money. But for Akhanda Mahayoga Sangha we need money. I try to contribute as much of my own as I can and to some extent I am satisfied.[17]

Whether Sita Ram will change the basic nature of his guruship away from personal relationships with disciples and continue to refuse financial contributions remains to be seen. It is obvious, however, that there is mounting pressure from some disciples to have a large organization of the style of Swami Muktananda or Maharishi Mahesh Yogi.

Characteristics of the Sangha

As stated earlier, Sita Ram's style of guruship is both personal and practical. The organization he has created reflects these characteristics. The most significant thing about the Sangha is that it appeals almost exclusively to Hindu householders. All of the Indian disciples whom we met were married and most had children. The only unmarried disciple we met was the American. Sita Ram considers the schools of Kashmir Shaivism and Tantrik Philosophy to be important for him because they are best suited to the life of the householder. Sita Ram was convinced by Kaviraji to accept a householder's life-style and to make these philosophies a part of his teaching. Kaviraji took Sita Ram aside when he was ten years old and when he had just returned from wandering in the forest, and told him that 'to live in this world is as necessary as spiritual pursuit'. It was also Kaviraji who convinced Sita Ram to marry and helped him establish a business.

Sita Ram's disciples constantly reiterated that they liked Sita Ram's Sangha and *sadhana* because they were not restrictive. As disciples they were allowed to pursue whatever life they wished. I was told just before my initiation that the path I had chosen was a simple one and it would allow me time and freedom to be myself in every way. Sita Ram has devoted the closing paragraph of his publicity pamphlet to this topic: 'In this yogic *sadhana* one's profession or any occupation will in no way be any hindrance. The two essential requisites are steadfastness of conduct and faith in the intrinsic truth of the path. Apart from this one is free to lead one's life as one wishes.'

There is some evidence, however, that Sita Ram attracts mostly householders who are well established and need not devote much time to their occupations. Sita Ram himself spends very little time on his business affairs and never visits his shop. All core group members are well established financially and have arranged their work and family life to allow ample free time for *sadhana*, spiritual discussion, and socializing with fellow disciples.

We also noticed a definite middle-aged majority in the Sangha. The core group members are all over 40 and in the rest of the Sangha most disciples are over 30. Yet this too is only a temporary tendency because of late there seems to be a greater number of members in their twenties and thirties. It seems to us that because the original members were all middle-aged and financially well established they tended to have friends who were middle-aged and well established. As the Sangha has expanded younger members and their friends have joined.

While certain people—such as the doctor, the musician of international fame, the one who occupied high political offices, and the Duke from Spain—were either given rapid approval for initiation or were actively sought after, certain other members had to wait. It is said: 'we want quality, not quantity'. It is obvious, however, that the more serious and dedicated a disciple the more he pleases Sita Ram.

No low caste members or outcastes were ever seen at Sigra except for Sita Ram's employees. Out of 23 members we surveyed, 8 were Brahmin, 3 were Kshatriya, 3 were Kayasth and 9 were Baniya or Vaisya. We observed no separation of caste within the organization but rather a hierarchy based upon seniority.

The members of the Sangha are also well educated and in most cases seem to be persons with professional degrees or occupations. We met three teachers (with M.As. or Ph.Ds.), two medical doctors, one lawyer, two bank officers, six government workers, eight persons in private business, one reporter and one tour guide. Most members seem to have had college level education and most are well read.

In summary we would say that the membership of the Akhanda Mahayoga Sangha is made up of well-educated, Hindu householders of non-lower castes who tend to be middle-aged, financially well established and professionally occupied. There is, however, another characteristic of the membership that must be dealt with separately; that is that the membership is almost exclusively male.

Sita Ram's first woman disciple was the wife of a banker, who still considers Sita Ram to be her guru, but her husband doesn't allow her to come to Sigra. Sita Ram has also initiated the wives of other disciples. In all there are five female disciples.

Sita Ram was never able to give us a satisfactory explanation of his preference for men in the Sangha. On our last visit to Sigra we asked him again about women and *sadhana*, and he told us again that bhakti was better suited for them. In his scheme of *sadhana*, women tend to fail because of the 'different kinds of mental problems they have to face'.

We recognize that there are certain cultural restrictions operating here—such as on free discourse between men and women in public—yet it is clear to us that aside from the good intentions of many members and aside from the several female disciples Sita Ram has, women are not incorporated into nor do they participate in the Sangha. Perhaps it is too much to expect Sita Ram to deviate further from the traditions of Swami Visuddhananda and Pandit Gopinath Kaviraj by accepting women into what has traditionally been a man's pursuit. Sita Ram has begun to initiate disciples where Kaviraji was forbidden, and he has begun to initiate foreigners and some women which for Visuddhananda was unthinkable.[18] Indeed,

Sita Ram appears to have reached the limits of his innovation on this point, at least for the present. The Akhanda Mahayoga Sangha is, therefore, a brotherhood—clearly a man's organization. This brotherhood plays an important part in what appears to be the chief function of the Sangha.

CHIEF FUNCTIONS OF THE SANGHA

If a common element could be drawn from the stories of all his disciples, it would be that Sita Ram has provided not only personal understanding, but a practical method for solving serious personal problems. The musician had already attempted suicide twice; the astrologer was not only in financial trouble but was living an extremely decadent life-style; the engineer had experienced three rapid deaths of close relatives; another was an opium addict; the businessman was living decadently and illegally; and his mother was in severe mental distress. The salesman from Calcutta, although a reformed alcoholic, was engrossed in financial and marital problems and had come to Banaras to leave his family for good. On our first visit to Sigra, Sita Ram spoke to us on this topic:

> In this *sadhana* the biggest thing is, that bad habits in a man will change from inside, not from outside. For example, my third disciple, he used to need to drink in the evening after 8.00. After coming to our *sadhana* he gave it up. I did not say he should give it up. In this *sadhana* you get so much joy that the joy of drinking becomes inferior by comparison. There is no competition.[19]

In this manner Sita Ram has combined his personal style with a practical method to deal specifically with the problems of the householders who come to him. It is part of the relationship that he establishes with disciples that they surrender themselves to this experience; as a result they will automatically discover activities more fulfilling and a joy that goes beyond solutions they may have sought in alcohol, drugs, women, or illegal business methods. Sita Ram has said that once the awareness of these problems is achieved the transformation of evil tendencies into good takes place simultaneously. It is the association with others trying also to improve their lives that reinforces this process.

Sita Ram not only reforms the personal lives of his disciples but involves a great many of them in new activities as well. For us the Sangha was a source of not only philosophical and spiritual discussions but an instant source for music concerts, festival celebrations, pilgrimage activities, and help for any problems we might have.

Sita Ram has made it clear that he is not capable of dealing with physical pain but the businessman disciple is convinced that Sita Ram will be able to solve this problem as well

It is our conclusion, therefore, that the recent transformation of Sita Ram from the quiet adopted son of Gopinath Kaviraj to Dada Sita Ram, bonande guru with a fast growing organization, is due at least partly to the compassion he has for those who come to him. He has been deeply influenced by two men who have given themselves for the welfare of the world and seems to have interpreted this message in a way that is both personally and practically oriented toward solving serious personal problems. Sita Ram has seemed to assume a role sometimes as brother and other times as counsellor or almost therapist. It is understandable then that the most significant thing to say of his organization and movement is that it too has as its chief function bringing about a change in peoples' lives that is positive and reinforced by the brotherhood instead of enforced ascetic discipline.

Notes

1. For the collection of this information I am greatly indebted to Mr. Virendra Singh, former Assistant Coordinator of the University of Wisconsin Program in Banaras, who began as our interpreter in early sessions with Sita Ram but soon took initiation and became a member of the Sangha. Our information for this portion of the paper comes mostly from over 500 pages of translated interviews with Sita Ram Pandey, members of his Sangha and several outside sources, as well as five months of participant observation.

Understandably, one of our problems during this project was a lack of sufficient knowledge of Hindi. Despite the persistent tutoring of Virendra Singh and the increased skills we gained through hours of conversations in Hindi, it was difficult for us to accurately follow technical discussions. For additional translations we are indebted to several members of Sita Ram's Sangha whose knowledge of English was far superior to our knowledge of Hindi, and particularly to our 'junior guru' Sahaney Sahab.

We are indebted to Pandit Ram Shanker Bhattacharya for his help in understanding the school of Kashmir Shaivism and particularly for his guidance in the reading of *Parmarthasar* by Abhinava Gupta. We are also grateful to Sita Ram for repeatedly taking the time and effort to explain his background to us in Hindi we could understand.

I am most of all grateful to my wife Kolleen who has not only assisted in this project with her skills in language and writing but who has served as my fellow researcher from the inception of this project. This paper stands as a combined effort of our experience with Sita Ram and his organization.

For visas, funding and valuable advice I wish to acknowledge the Berkeley Professional Studies Program of the University of California and particularly to give thanks to Vijayan Puliampet who has labored long and skillfully to organize all the practical matters of our stay in India.

2. *Gopinath Kaviraj Abhinandan Granth*, Akhila Bharatiya Sanskrit Parishad, Lucknow, 7 September 1967.
3. See Paul Brunton's *Search for a Secret India* (1970).
4. What follows is our translation of a paragraph from *Kaviraji: Jeevan Aur Sadhana* by Dr. Bhagwati Prasad Singh (Gorakhpur University) in *Gopinath Kaviraj Abhinandan Granth*, op. cit.
5. See note 1.
6. Session with Sita Ram Pandey, Register Number 7, p. 267.
7. *Sir John Woodruff, Introduction to Tantra Sastra*, Ganesh and Company, Madras (1973), p. 66.
8. Register Number 1, pp. 32-57.
9. Register Number 6, p. 204.
10. Register Number 8, p. 276.
11. Register Number 9, pp. 13-19.
12. See Bibliography under Gopinath Kaviraj.
13. Register Number 7, pp. 258-75.
14. As explained by Sita Ram Pandey in his brochure *Akhand Mahayoga Sangha*.
15. Interview with the businessman disciple, pp. 14-24.
16. Interview with salesman disciple, p. 3.
17. Register Number 9, p. 14.
18. Swami Visuddhananda would not initiate foreigners because he held that this was impure and would dilute the power of his knowledge.
19. Register Number 1, pp. 19-20.

Bibliography

BRUNTON, PAUL (1970): *Search for a Secret India*. New York: Weiser Samuel Inc.

CHATTERJI, JAGDISH CHANDRA (1962): *Kashmir Shaivism*, Research and Publication Department of Government of Jammu and Kashmir.

CHATTERJI, JAGDISH CHANDRA (ED.) (1916): *Parmatha Sara* by Abhinavagupta with the commentary of Yogi Raja. Research and Publication Department of Government of Jammu and Kashmir.

GOPINATH, KAVIRAJ (1967): *Abhinandan Granth*, Akhil Bharatiya Sanskrit Parishad.

————(1948): *Akhand Mahayoga* (Great Integral Yoga). Chakravarti Chatterji and Co. Calcutta.

————(1966): *Aspects of Indian Thought*, published by Burdwan University, Burdwan, West Bengal.

————(n.d.): *A Life Story of the Great Yogi Shri Visuddhananda Parmahansa*, (Basic Principles of Spiritual Life as enunciated by the great Yogi); (Stories of wonderful yogic powers and unbounded love of the great Yogi), Visuddhananda Kanan Ashram, Varanasi.

PANDEY, KANTI CHANDRA (1963): *Abhinavagupta—An Historical and Philosophical Study*. Chowkhamba Sanskrit Series, Gopal Mandir Lane, Varanasi-1.

RAMAKRISHNA MISSION INSTITUTE OF CULTURE (1956): 'Kashmir Shaivism' in *The Cultural Heritage of India*, Vol. IV, pp. 79-97, Gol Park, Calcutta.

RUDRAPPA, J. (1969): *Kashmir Saivism*, Prasaranga, University of Mysore, Mysore.

10

I.S. Marwah

Tabligh Movement Among the Meos of Mewat*

THIS PAPER DEALS with the Tabligh movement which is a religious movement among the Muslims of Mewat who are known as Meos. It aims to discuss the genesis of the movement, its organization, its ideology and its consequences.

Tabligh, in Arabic, literally means to instruct or to educate the people about their religion. Thus, the Tabligh is a religious movement which urges its followers to be regular in the observance of Islamic prescriptions in their daily life (Mines, 1973:68). It can be called a movement in the sociological sense as it has the essential elements of a religious movement; namely, an ideology, an organization through which the message is put across, leadership and a system of recruitment.

From time to time, attempts have been made for the renewal of Islam in the Indian subcontinent. These attempts have taken various forms and have differed in terms of their organization and scope depending on the circumstances and the socio-political content in which they arose. Generally, the aim of these socio-religious movements has been revitalization of Islam in India. Two well-known

*This paper is based on fieldwork conducted in the villages of Gurgaon district of Haryana during the years 1974-76. I wish to thank Professor M.S.A. Rao for his valuable comments and suggestions. I also wish to express gratitude to Dr. J.D. Mehra for his kind help. I am grateful to the Indian Council of Social Science Research for providing me with a contingency grant for fieldwork.

movements arose in the eighteenth and nineteenth centuries—the Shah Wali Ullah movement and the Mujahidin movement.[1] Shah Wali Ullah witnessed the collapse of the Muslim state in India in the eighteenth century. Non-Muslim groups—such as the Mahrathas, the Jats and the Sikhs—had come into power in their respective areas. The British had already established their foothold in Eastern India. Shah Walli Ullah, who had studied theology at Medina in Arabia, attempted to strengthen the Islamic communities of North India by unifying the different Sufi orders under the banner of orthodox Islam. Shah Wali Ullah emphasized *ijtihad* (reasoning) in applying Muslim religious laws, and argued that these laws should be basically based on the *Quran* and the *Hadith*. He emphasized the utility of congregated gatherings such as the Friday prayers and the performance of *haj*. He subscribed to the theory that Islam was the final religious system which supersedes all other religious systems which have become obsolete. He sensed danger to Islam from syncretism or compromise. Islam, he felt, must be made more orthodox and purer. In India, the purity and orthodoxy of Islam was endangered due to the entry of new converts into the fold who continued to practise and believe in non-Islamic elements. So he felt that the non-Islamic elements must be consciously eliminated from the culture of the Muslim communities in India. However, minor deviations could be condoned provided these were not tantamount to being anti-Islamic (Ahmad, 1964:209).

Another Islamic movement which emphasized orthodoxy was the Mujahidin movement started by Sayyid Ahmad Shahid of Baraely (1782-1831). His aim was to purify the Islamic communities in India of all syncretic elements, so that these could be based exclusively on the *Quran* and the *Sunnah*. He wanted to eliminate the following three types of excesses from orthodox Sunni belief: (*i*) Sufism which goes against the tenets of religious law; (*ii*) celebration of Muharram as a public festival, as it is of Shia origin; and (*iii*) non-Muslim elements which have been either borrowed from Hinduism or which have survived among the converts from Hinduism. India was conceived to be an imperfect state (*dar'ul harb*) which was politically controlled by non-Muslims and where, therefore, Muslims could not truly follow the tenets of Islam. To safeguard the Muslims in the imperfect state reformist work must be carried out continuously. The imperfect state could be converted into the ideal theocratic state through a holy war. The Mujahidin movement sought to set up parallel Muslim courts to administer justice in accordance with Islamic principles. It may be noted in this connection that Shaikh Ahmad Sirhindi, the originator of the Mujaddid movement in the seventeenth century, had argued for the superiority of Shariat over Tariqat (Rizvi, 1965:225).

In the later half of the nineteenth century, many movements arose among the Muslims in India. Well-known among these were the Ahmadiyah movement,[2] Sir Sayyid Ahmad's Aligarh movement[3] and the Ahl-i-Hadith movement[4] of Maulvi Muhammad Husayn of Batala. The aim of all these movements was to revitalize Islam in India. There are two different approaches to revitalization: one that emphasized the orthodoxy and purity of religious practices, the other which emphasized modernization through the adoption of Western education. While the former took the position of confrontation against Western culture and education, the latter wished to adopt Western culture and its educational system.

A number of movements arose in the second decade of the twentieth century, which aimed at strengthening the Muslim communities through *tanzim* (organization) and *tabligh* (religious propaganda). These movements arose in the wake of the Shuddhi and Sangathan movements of the Arya Samaj (Mathur, 1972:181-83 and 186-87). More than one organization came into being to carry out *tabligh* among the Muslim communities. But the one which has had the maximum effect and the longest duration was the Tabligh movement among the Meos of Mewat, Started by Moulana Muhammad Ilyas (1885-1944) of Kandhla, district Muzaffarnagar, in Uttar Pradesh. It was started in the Mewat area of district Gurgaon in Haryana (erstwhile Punjab). Later it spread to other parts of the Indian subcontinent. At present it has even assumed an international complexion. Before we discuss the origins of the movement, it will be necessary to describe the social organization of the Meos with special reference to their religious beliefs and rituals, customs and manners which they retained even after they were converted to Islam from Hinduism.

II

Mewat, the land where the Meos live, is a cultural area. It comprises parts of three contiguous districts of Gurgaon, Bharatpur and

Alwar. Gurgaon district forms a part of Haryana and Bharatpur and Alwar districts form part of Rajasthan. Geographically, it lies to the south-west of Delhi, and its Northern boundary comes fairly close to Delhi. The dialect spoken in the area is called Mewati which is closer to the Rajasthani dialects of Hindi. The Meos constitute one of the major communities of the Mewat region. It is claimed that the name of the region is actually derived from the name of this community. The territory of Mewat is divided into different geographical areas by the low Aravalli ranges known as Kala Pahad (black mountain) in Mewat. These ranges have played a very significant role in the history of the Meos in Mewat. Many historical monuments indicative of the past are situated along the ranges. The undulated landscape near the foothills has always provided natural protection to the Meos who claim to have been looters and plunderers. Some historical accounts also refer to the Meos in this role.[5] They always posed a problem of law and order to the rulers in Delhi. Mujeeb (1967:218-19) quotes Barani: 'In the middle of the thirteenth century, the Meos who lived in the hilly areas west and south of Delhi not only plundered people on the highways around Delhi but even stole into the town. They came up to the Haud-i-Shamsi, molested water-carriers and maid servants, who came to draw water, stripping them and walking away with their clothes.'

The Meos are primarily agriculturists. They are mainly dependent on rains except in a small area of Mewat where a canal irrigation system exists. Animal husbandry is the secondary source of livelihood. Those who are close to the hilly ranges also rear sheep and goats. Now milk-selling is catching on in those areas which are located by the side of main roads and where milk chilling plants have been started by the Delhi Milk Scheme.

The Meos claim to be the descendants of Kshatriyas who had embraced Islam.[6] They perceive of themselves as being high caste—*unchi jati* or *unchi qaum*. They practise endogamy rigidly. An element of hierarchy is evident in their relationship with other castes. They treat the Hindu chamars and bhangis as untouchables. They had *jajmani* relationships with both the Hindu and Muslim castes such as kumbhar (potter, Hindu), lohar (black-smith, Muslim), khati (carpenter, Hindu or Muslim), nai (barber, Muslim or Hindu), sakka (water-carrier, Muslim), chamar (leather-worker, Hindu), bhangi (scavenger, Hindu), and mirasi (Muslim). The families of these castes which served the land-owning Meos were known as *tehalavas*. They were paid in kind. Their relationships were enduring and hereditary. Now the traditional pattern of relationships has undergone a great deal of change. Chamars have given up carrying and skinning dead animals. They also refused to accept food and water from the Meos because of the latter were Muslims. The Meos were clients of Brahmins who used to work out auspicious dates for marriages for them. The Muslim mirasi, and *jogi* are still treated as inferior (*chhote log*), and the Meos would not like to accept food from them. However, all Muslims can pray at the same mosque and smoke from the same *huqqa*.

Internally, the Meos are divided into a number of exogamous groups called *pals* and *gots*. The membership of these groups is hereditary and is based on patrilineal descent. Traditionally, Meo society is divided into twelve *pals* and fifty-two *gots*. One often hears the expression '*bara pal aur bavan got*' being used by the Meos whenever they refer to the totality of the Meos. Actually, the number of *pals* is thirteen, although the thirteenth (*pahat*) is referred to as *pallakra*, meaning half *pal*. The number of actual *gots* is more than fifty-two. Each *pal* is traditionally associated with a territory. The region of Mewat can be seen as subdivided into thirteen distinct tracts. Each tract belongs to a *pal*, and is known by the name of that *pal*. The boundaries of *pal* territory are no longer very clear. Earlier, each *pal* had a chief called Chaudhary who played an important role in the political structure.

Each *pal* is further divided into subgroups called *thamas* or *thambas*. A *thama* consists of the putative patrilineal descendants of a common ancestor, generally referred to as *dada*. The *thamas* are named either after the ancestor or after the original village of the ancestor. Each *thama* also has a Chaudhary, whose office is hereditary. The *thamas* have political as well as social functions. These are most relevant in matters relating to marriage and divorce.

A *got* consists of the descendants of a common male ancestor whose genealogical relationship is not exactly traceable. Members of a *got* may be dispersed, but usually a cluster of contiguous villages are inhabited by the *sehgotias* (people of the same *got*). The *gots* are exogamous groups. Many of the Meo *got* names are common with the *gots* of non-Meo communities such as the jats, Gujars, and Minas. The *pals* and *gots* can be further grouped under different *vamsa* or *bans* such as Kachhwas bans, Jadu bans, Tomar bans.

These *vamsa* are common to Meo and Hindu Rajputs.

The Meo household is constituted by the blood relatives and their spouses who reside together and form a *chulah* (hearth) group. It is known as a *ghar* in the Mewati dialect. The households among the Meos can be divided into two main categories: simple household and complex household. Simple households may consist of the elementary family, one-member household, incomplete elementary family or supplemented elementary family. The complex household consists of two or more nuclear families or parts thereof who reside together in one building and possess a common hearth. A complex household may be further subdivided into two basic types: lineal joint family and collateral joint family. The lineal joint family consists of husband, wife, married sons and unmarried sons and daughters. The collateral joint family consists of married brothers living together.

Another set of family type is based upon the polygynous family composed of man and more than one wife. Among the Meos, a polygynous family comes into being due to levirate practice, i.e., when a man marries his brother's (usually elder brother) widow or it may be resorted to when the first wife has failed to bear a child.

The lineal joint family and the collateral joint family are considered to be an ideal social norm in Meo society. Ideally, the residential unity of the patrikin and their wives is cherished. The rule of residence is virilocal. The married sisters and daughters move out to join their husbands' natal families. This allows the parental family to grow into an extended family where the son or sons form the link between the elementary families. Such extended families have the tendency to breakdown after the death of the parents. This may happen even in the lifetime of the parents if the land-holding of the family is insufficient.

The inheritance rules of Meos are strictly patrilineal. Land is equally divided between the sons. Widows have no share in ancestral property. Daughters and sisters have no right of inheritance in property. Daughters may receive a gift of land in the absence of any male heir. The customary laws of inheritance rather than the Shariat prevail among the Meos.

When a separation takes place within the family, a new homestead is built within the common compound called *bakhal*. The households of agnatically related individuals are generally situated within a *bakhal*. The members of the *bakhal* may form a patrilineage which is called *ghariya* or *khas kunba.*

At another level, the lineage group may be called *kunba* and *khandan.* Both the terms are used for patrilineages of varying genealogical depth. The terms are used for the descendants of a common male ancestor and are referred to as *ek dada ki aulad.* Sometimes all families belonging to a *got* in a village may belong to one *khandan.* The terms *khandan* and *kunba* emphasize common descent. The term *kunba* is generally restricted to a definite, closely interacting descent group. It is a descent group which acts as a corporate group at the time of the performance of rituals connected with the life-cycle. Usually the members of this group also form the neighbourhood group. So, the *kunba* is a lineage group where the genealogical relationships are very precisely known, at least to the elders.

There are several views on when and how the Meos embraced Islam.[7] The Meos believe that they were converted during the earlier phase of the spread of Islam in India. They trace their first contact with the Muslims back to Mohammad bin Kasim's attack on Sindh in the eighth century. The Arab invaders worked intently for the spread of Islam in Sindh. The Meos believe that they were spread up to Sindh at that time and must, therefore, have come under the influence of Islam (Shakur, 1974:317).

The second phase of the spread of Islam among the Meos began in the times of Mahmud Ghaznavi in the eleventh century. Sayyid Salar Sahu, Mahmud Ghaznavi's sister's husband, was in command of the royal forces. He established himself at Ajmer and started conquering the areas around Ajmer. His son Sayyid Salar Masud Gazi defeated Tejpal, a Meo chieftain, at Dhandgarh near Rewari. Tejpal is believed to have embraced Islam and thus became the first known Meo Muslim (Shakur, 1974:319-20). Sayyid Salar Masud Gazi is remembered among the Meos. The Meos of Alwar swear by his name. All over Mewat, *pucca* platforms (chabutras) connected with Sayyid Salar Masud Gazi are to be found in the villages. These *chabutras* (square platforms) are believed to be sacred. Lamps are lighted over these *chabutras* on certain occasions. Members of a caste known as Majavars, who claim to be Shaikhs, are responsible for looking after these sacred platforms. The flag of Sayyid Salar Masud Gazi is also considered sacred and used to be worshipped by the Meos in the past.

Although the Meos became Muslims long back, they continued

many Hindu beliefs and cultural practices. Many Meos traced their genealogical relationship with Lord Krishna. Janam-ashtami, the birthday of Shri Krishna, was celebrated. Hindu festivals such as Diwali and Dussehra were also celebrated. They used to participate in the Holi celebrations.

Many Sufi saints, such as Hazrat Khwaja Mohiuddin Chisti and Nizammuddin Aulia, impressed the Meos, and they were held in great esteem. The *mazars* of these saints were treated as holy shrines, and the Meos used to pay homage at these tombs. They also participated in the *urs*. Another mystic, Shah Madar (*c.* 1315-1436), was also a highly revered saint. He was reputed to have possessed miraculous powers and was responsible for the spread of Islam among many non-Muslim communities in India. His tomb exists at Makanpur and the Meos considered it to be sacred. They carried a flag in his honour and went to his tomb in procession, singing songs in praise of Hazrat Madar Shah. Some Sufi saints, who were associated with religious preachings in Mewat, were also remembered. Hazrat Shaikh Musa and Shah Chokha were two such well-known saints. Their tombs were worshipped and annual *urs* were held in their honour. At the local village level, certain deities such as Panchpir, Khera Devta, Chabunda, Bhomiya and Bhairon were also worshipped. These deities were represented either by platforms or by stone slabs. People used to light earthen lamps on them and offer sweets. These offerings were given to the Faqir. Thus, the Meo Muslims retained many Hindu modes of worship.

Indeed, the Meos achieved a cultural synthesis between their original Hindu culture and Islam. The basic structures of family, *pals* and *gots*, and of lineages did not undergo radical transformation after their conversion to Islam. These groups have remained as exogamous units. In the selection of a spouse, one must avoid one's *got*. Members of *gots* and *pals* are looked upon as agnates. Some *gots* are the receivers, others the givers. Some *gots* and *pals* are both receivers and givers. The subdivisions of a *pal*, the *thamas*, are also treated likewise. The rules governing the selection of a spouse are complex and involve various degrees of prohibition such as the avoidance of cross cousins, those from one's own village, or from one's mother's brother's village, etc. These rules of exogamy have shown a great deal of persistence in spite of the Islamic character of the community. By themselves, these rules do not go against the laws of Shariat, but in the case of marriage between prohibited categories of individuals the customary rules are given precedence over the laws of Shariat. The same is the case with laws governing inheritance. The customary inheritance laws of the Meos seem to be closer to traditional Hindu laws than to those based on the Shariat. The Meos also maintained the traditional 'brotherhood' relationships with some of the Jat, Ahir and Thakar clans.

However, changes had taken place over time in many life-cycle rituals due to the impact of Islam. *Khatna* (the circumcision) ceremony was a very important ceremony. It was conducted on a fairly lavish scale, but was treated more as a social occasion than a religious one. The recitation of the holy *Quran* had no place in the ceremony. Marriage was treated as a contract. The Nikah ceremony was conducted through a kazi. Many Hindu elements in the rituals associated with marriage also survived—such as, *manda, ubtan, chak-pujna,* fixing an auspicious date and time through a Brahmin, and the playing of music. The most significant Islamic ritual adopted by the Meos was the practice of burial instead of cremation which was their earlier custom. A funeral feast was given after forty days called *chehallum*. Though these rituals of life-crises were Islamic, many Hindu or traditional elements associated with them remained.

The method of naming children among the Meos was very peculiar. The Hindu practice of using Singh was never given up completely. The essential Hindu name was given a Muslim twist by adding the suffix Khan. Thus these were names like Mangal Khan, Simrath Khan, Sumer Khan, Kapur Khan.

The Meos, especially the males, never gave up their traditional dress, which was no different from their Hindu Jat and Ahir neighbours. Women, however, had taken to Muslim dress much earlier. Women did not observe the Muslim *purda,* although they did practise the *gunghat*.

The traditional folk songs which the Mirasis sang at the time of weddings alluded to the Hindu past of the Meos. The story of the *Mahabharata* was recited on certain occasions. A famous Meo poet, Saadullah, had composed a Mewati version of the *Mahabharata* which was very popular among the Meos. Thus, the Meos retained many aspects of Hindu religion and culture and it is in the context of this lack of a separate and distinct identity that the Tabligh movement arose.

III

The Tabligh movement was started in Mewat after the Arya Samaj had started its reconversion movement (Shuddhi) in Northern India in the earlier part of the third decade of the twentieth century. The Shuddhi movement was basically aimed at such Muslim communities which were considered to have been Hindus in their recent past—the aim being to persuade these communities to return to the fold of Hinduism. This movement caused considerable anxiety among the Muslims, and they started consolidating their position by propagating religious orthodoxy.

The aim of the Tabligh movement was to bring about a re-awakening of faith in Islam among the Muslims in India and elsewhere. It was thought that the Muslims had come to such a sorry state of affairs, particularly in the Indian subcontinent, because they had forgotten the true teachings of Islam. The rich were involved in leading a luxurious life, forgetting their obligations to God. The learned ulemas had not been successful in spreading their knowledge of Islam, or the message of Islam, to the lay Muslims. Many Muslims had started questioning the validity of *Quranic* injunctions. In this context the Tabligh movement aimed at spreading the message of Islam to all Muslims. It aimed at purifying the Muslims and making them orthodox Muslims. The Tabligh movement, however, did not aim at conversion of non-Muslims to Islam but only at making Muslims better and purer Muslims. Its message to the Muslim was '*Ae Musalmano, Musalman bano*' ('call to the Muslims to be devout') (Hasni, n.d.: 15-16).

Ilyas, the founder of the Tabligh movement, felt that a number of Muslim communities living in rural areas had hardly any true knowledge of Islamic practices and laws. Such Muslim communities still, therefore, practised many un-Islamic social customs. They did not either observe the basic tenets of Islamic faith or they were indifferent to these. Hence there was a necessity to teach the basic principles of Islam to such communities.

Ilyas argued that the task of spreading the true faith must be shared by all Muslims. It should not be left only to the learned few—the ulemas. It was the duty of every Muslim to 'teach people to do good deeds and prevent people from bad things'. So people must take up the responsibility of spreading the message of Allah. People should to be made conscious of their obligation to God. *Iman* (belief) had to be created. The aim of Tabligh, in the words of Ilyas, was to spread the message of the Prophet.

Secondly, Ilyas said that the aim of the movement was to inculcate an emotional relationship with God—'to bring the men of Allah, especially the unconcerned, to Allah's path'. Thus, the Tabligh movement essentially professed an ideology of reawakening the faith of Muslims in God and in the message of God, while eschewing un-Islamic beliefs and customs.

Moulana Ilyas

The originator of the movement Moulana Ilyas,[8] was born in 1886. His father Moulana Mohammad Ismail was a tutor to the children of Mirza Ilahi Baksh, an affine of Bahadur Shah, the last of the Mughal emperors. Moulana Mohammad Ismail lived in Hazrat Nizammuddin Aulia's shrine in Delhi. He also acted as Imam of a mosque known as Banglawali masjid in the Nizammuddin complex. Moulana Mohammad Ismail took keen interest in religious education. He had attracted a number of students from Mewat who studied under him in the Nizammuddin mosque. Moulana Muhammad Ismail came from an orthodox family where the *Hadith* and Shariat were greatly emphasized. Moulana Ilyas spent his childhood in Kandhla, where his mother came from, and partly in Nizammuddin. Ilyas' mother was known to be a very pious lady. She spent her time in prayers and in reciting the holy *Quran*. Moulana Ilyas was a very restless child and spent his time in the pursuit of religious training. He had learnt the whole of the *Quran* by heart even as a child. He was very particular in saying his prayers and even talked of organizing a *jihad* (holy war) against those Muslims who did not observe this practice. He spent ten years of his formative period receiving religious instruction from Moulana Rashid Ahmed Gangohi. Moulana Ilyas became seriously ill during his childhood and had to discontinue his studies as 'he suffered the weakness of the brain' (Hasni, n.d.: 48). But he insisted on carrying on with his studies, and later went to Deoband—the center of religious training and learning—at the age of twenty-three and spent about two or three years there. He also spent some time in the Saharanpur madrassa. So, the first twenty-five years of life were spent in receiving religious training in the company of some well-known Moulvis.

Moulana Ilyas took charge of the Nizammuddin mosque after the death of his elder brother, Moulana Mohammed, in 1919. The madrassa was in a very poor financial condition. He worked hard to run the madrassa and even spent from his private coffers to sustain it. He was undaunted by the hard conditions of life in this period and even considered this as necessary to good training and education. One thing which was striking in his life was that the Moulana always considered it his destiny to serve the cause of Islam and Muslims. In 1919, just before he took over as Imam, he barely survived a very serious illness. He attributed this to his mission of serving the people and Allah. During his second visit to Arabia for the performance of *haj* in 1926, Moulana Ilyas dreamt that God would make use of him. He pondered over how he could be of use to God till he realized that the best way was to fulfil his mission of serving Muslims. It was after his return to India that he started the system of *jamats* (organized group) to move about among the peasants teaching them the bare minimum of *Kalma, Toheed* and *Namaj*.

Moulana Ilyas even wanted to start his Tabligh movement in Medina. He had an audience with the governor of Medina and sought permission to start Tabligh. But he returned to India without waiting for the final reply as he thought his mission was to work in India. Later on, he wrote to one of his friends in Medina that he would start Tabligh in Medina if he felt that it was worthwhile to do so (Hasni, n.d.:103).

His hard life and the arduous journeys he undertook in the village had left the Moulana weak and sickness overtook him. In 1943 he had an acute attack of dysentery and never recovered from it. Even during his illness he never gave up saying his prayers. He died in July 1944 in New Delhi.

Moulana Ilyas adopted the six-article (*chhe number*) course of teachings which formed the essence of his movement (Ferozepuri, n.d.:44-105):

(i) *Kalimah:* Every Muslim must be able to recite *Kalimah* which means that there is no God but Allah and Muhammad is his messenger. *Kalimah* stresses the oneness of God. It is believed that the recitation of *Kalimah* can save a man from burning in hell for eternity, provided he fulfils the following conditions: Firstly, one should be familiar with the correct wording of the *Kalimah*. Secondly, the meanings of the *Kalimah* should be known. Thirdly, its implications must be realized, i.e., to submit oneself fully to the Almighty in every action and thought. Fourthly, one must develop complete faith in God. One cannot accomplish anything without the help of God and that Allah is not dependent on anyone else. Success can be achieved only by strictly following the teachings of the Prophet.

(ii) *Namaz:* Every Muslim is enjoined to say prayers at the appointed hours of the day and night. Apart from the ritual of offering prayer, every Muslim must be earnest in his faith. *Namaz* is a pillar of Islam. One who gives up *Namaz* comes close to being a disbeliever. It is enjoined upon Muslims to teach *Namaz* to every child at the age of seven.

(iii) *Illum* (knowledge) *and Dhikr* (remembrance of Allah): Seeking of knowledge has been greatly emphasized in Islam. According to the *Hadith* those who travel out to seek knowledge, will find the path to the heaven easier. Knowledge is what the Prophet Muhammad conveyed to the people. The true knowledge is based on what is mentioned in the *Quran* and the *Hadith*. So every Muslim must acquire the true knowledge of the *Quran* and the *Hadith*. 'Seeking of knowledge is a duty of every Muslim man and woman', says a *Hadith*. There are four dimensions of knowledge: (*a*) Knowledge of the ways of living such as the domestic life and relationships between neighbours and the family. Muhammad has shown the ways of living through his own life which must be treated as a model. (*b*) Knowledge concerning the *Ibadat* such as the prayer, fasting and *haj*. (*c*) Knowledge of the practices which one adopts to earn one's living. (*d*) Knowledge of correct dealings concerning loans, gifts, etc., and between different types of persons.

According to the *Hadith*, knowledge can be acquired either by reading the *Quran*, or by learning the *Quran*, or by listening to the *Quran*. Muslims are also required to learn about the life of the Prophet and his companions. Their lives should form a model. Every Muslim is also required to teach others. Moulana Ilyas laid great stress on learning and teaching. He said: 'It is our duty to teach the ignorant Muslims' (Hasni, n.d.: 305). Moulana Ilyas wanted every Muslim to spare some part of his life for the propagation of knowledge to others. The Moulana thought that the teaching and learning of knowledge should not be confined to the institutions but should reach the common men (*ummat*), who are too busy to go to these institutions. The knowledge of the *din* (faith) can be acquired through association with believers, just as language and culture is learnt through keeping company with cultured and learned persons. This is the most natural way of learning. He said, 'Unless the heart directs, mind will not go in for correct knowledge. The feelings of heart depend on the application and not on bookish knowledge' (Hasni, n.d.: 304). Moulana Ilyas wrote, 'No person can succeed in acquiring knowledge unless he transmits it to the others, especially to those who are less learned' (Hasni, n.d.: 305). According to the Moulana, every Muslim must acquire the knowledge of *din*—establishing a relationship with *din* is an important part of a Muslim's life. So, every Muslim must devote his time for Tabligh and *din*.

The other part of this article is concerned with *Dhikr*. *Dhikr* means remembering the Almighty in praise and glorification. One must always keep God in one's heart as it helps to purify the heart. Some time must be spent every day in remembering Allah and in singing His glory. There are general ways of doing this, such as the recitation of the *Quran* and by offering prayers. Both the *Quran* and the *Hadith* stress the importance of remembering the Almighty. The Tabligh teachings lay stress on the recitation of the third *Kalimah* which means 'Glory be to Allah! Praise be to Allah! There is no god save Allah! Allah is the greatest! There is no power and no strength save in Allah—the sublime—the tremendous' (Waheedazzafer, 1971: 141).

(*iv*) *Ikram-i-Muslim* (Respect for Muslims): Respect for human beings in general, but Muslims in particular, has been stressed. An important element of the *Ikram* is recognition of the rights of others—the rights of seniors, the rights of neighbours, the rights of the poor, etc. In a *Hadith* it is recorded that God helps those who help the men of Allah (Ferozepuri, n.d.:77). 'The idea was to bring back the various factions and different classes in the Muslim society to the fold of the real Islamic brotherhood' (Faruqi, 1971: 65).

(*v*) *Ikhlas-i-Niyat* (Sincerity of Intention): Actions must be performed with the sole intention of pleasing Allah. All matters relating to faith and to worldly affairs must be made subservient to Allah. Anything which is performed with unpious intentions is not acceptable to the Almighty. According to a *Hadith*, 'Allah does not look towards your appearances or your possessions, but he looks into your heart and deeds' (Ferozepuri, n.d.: 86).

(vi) Tabligh: Travelling far and wide in order to spread the message of Allah is the duty of every Muslim. Moulana Ilyas desired that every Muslim should spare some time for the propagation of the faith. This must be done as it was done by the Prophet himself. The above-mentioned five articles must be practised by the *tablighees* (the believrs in Tabligh).

One could learn about the faith by studying in madrassas (religious school) and through books. But a very large majority of people can never hope to go to a madrassa or a maktab (institution of elementary education run by mosques), or they may never be able to devote any time to it because they are too busy with their work. Moulana Ilyas was concerned about the unlettered peasants who formed the majority but knew very little about the faith. Such a large number of people could be made familiar with the true principles of the faith only if it was directly communicated by those who had acquired the knowledge. Moulana Ilyas wanted to restart the practice of groups of people (jamaat) moving about to preach the true faith to the ignorant as was the practice during the lifetime of the prophet.

> We have given up the practice of *jamaats* moving about to preach. This was the basic principle. Prophet Muhammad (peace be upon him) himself moved about to preach. In Mecca, the Muslims were in minority. Every convert to Islam was required to move about to convert the non-believers. When the Prophet reached Medina he started sending *jamaats* to all the four corners. So the movement of preaching to others was basic to Islam. All this had been given up (Hasni, n.d.: 278).

The Mewatis and Moulana Ilyas

It was Moulana Ilyas' father, Moulana Mohammad Ismail, who had first attracted students from Mewat to his madrassa in the Hazrat Nizammuddin complex. The Mewatis used to visit the *dargah* of Nizammuddin Aulia to participate in the annual *urs* and to offer prayers. Moulana Mohammed Ismail started taking an interest in those Mewatis and lured some of them to his Banglawali masjid and persuaded them to join his madrassa. It is said that, in the beginning, he once encountered a group of Mewatis who were on their way to Delhi to work as labourers. He asked them about their. destination and their purpose. He offered to pay them the amount which they hoped to earn as labourers only if they stayed in his madrassa and learnt about Islamic theology. This was the beginning of a long relationship between the Mewatis and the madrassa at Nizammuddin. Moulana Mohammed Ismail had established friendship with some Mewatis of Ferozepur-Namak and Nuh. They had come to regard him as a sacred and pious person and he occasionally paid visits to Mewat (Ferozepuri, n.d.: 9).

When Moulana Ilyas took charge of the madrassa, some Mewatis who had patronized his father and brother as holy men came over to him and invited him to visit Mewat. The Moulana agreed, on the condition that they started a *maktab* in the village to celebrate his visit. That was the only way to honour him, he said. The Mewatis being peasants had never paid sufficient attention to religious schools as they thought these as being useless for their children. The Moulana was very keen to start maktabs and madrassas in Mewat. This he thought was the only way to spread the Islamic faith and the knowledge of Shariat among the ignorant peasant Muslims of Mewat. He was aware of the fact that the Meos were very ignorant of their religion and wanted to create conditions favourable for bringing the Meos closer to Islam. He thought that by opening centers of religious instruction, the younger generation could be reformed. Moulana Ilyas started establishing maktabs and madrassas in Mewat. He even spent his personal income for this. Thanks to his missionary zeal, a large number of maktabs and madrassas were opened in a short span of time.

Disappointment with the Maktabs and Madrassas

Soon the Moulana was disappointed with the progress of the spread of Islam through the regular madrassas and maktabs. First, although a large number of maktabs and madrassas had been opened in Mewat, only a very small number of children were actually studying in them. Secondly, the Moulana feared that those who were trained 'would be lost in the vast expanse of the ignorance' which Mewat represented. Moulana Ilyas was shocked and disappointed to meet a person who was trained in an Islamic school in Mewat but whose beared was shaved off, and whose face, form and dress did not show any trace of Islam (Hasni, n.d.: 81). The Moulana was very keen to spread the basic knowledge of Islam in the whole of Mewat as fast as possible.

Moulana Ilyas was also conscious that many of the customary practices of the Meos went against the Shariat. Some ulemas were trying to stop such practices but had not met with much success. The Moulana came to the conclusion that in order to achieve reform, people must be prepared to accept reform. People must be made conscious of their duty towards God—they must be brought closer to *din* (Faith). This, he said, was like preparing the land fit for cultivation. After the Moulana returned from his second *haj*, in 1927, he called a public meeting at Nuh. At this *ijimah* (religious meeting), the Moulana put forward his idea of the *jamaats* moving from one village to another in order to influence people. This idea met with a very warm response. Within a month, a *jamaat* of eight persons had been formed. The *jamaat* moved out of its village of origin, Ferozepur Nanak, and moved to other villages reaching a town called Sohna next Friday. The Friday congregation prayers were offered at Sohna and again the movement began. The next two Friday prayers were held at Taoru (in Rajasthan) and Nagina (district Gurgaon) towns. This was the first *tablighi jamaat*. It consisted of the Mewatis and toured villages within Mewat. It is claimed that Moulana Ilyas got his idea of the *jamaat* going about persuading people to say their prayers during his stay at Ferozepur Namak in Nuh tehsil in Gurgaon district. A few villagers, who had received training in a religious institution in Delhi, used to exhort their neighbours to attend Friday prayers in the village mosque. When Moulana Ilyas saw this, he was excited by the idea and wanted them to go out to the adjoining villages.

In 1933, the Moulana performed *haj* for the third time, and on his return he plunged himself in the Tablighi work with greater zeal. He went to Mewat with a big group consisting of over one hundred persons. He divided his group into smaller batches and asked them to go to different villages. They were asked to persuade the peasants to say prayers along with them. He then thought of sending the Meos to areas outside Mewat so that they could meet non-Meo Muslims and learn more about Islam from this association. For this he looked towards the adjoining area of Western Uttar Pradesh (Saharanpur and Muzaffarnagar districts) as representative of the Islamic way of life. The first Mewati *jamaat* was sent to Kandhla in Muzaffarnagar district, the birth place of Moulana Ilyas.

Moulana Ilyas was very systematic in his work of Tabligh in Mewat. He had a map of Mewat prepared in which information regarding roads, names of villages, population figures of each village, and names of the prominent Meos was given. A number of *jamaats* were set up, which included non-Meo Muslims, and they started touring the villages in Mewat. In this way the Moulana brought the Muslims of different communities together, hoping to bring them closer culturally. Hasni (n.d.:96) writes, 'After many such tours within and outside Mewat, the Mewatis started hating Hinduistic dress and took to Islamic dress, the bangles of hands and the earrings vanished. Men started sporting beard, anti-Shariat customs of marriage became less. Drinking liquor, to which the Meos were addicted, was given up. Crimes, riots and immoral behaviour began to show decrease in incidence.'

The Moulana exhorted the Meos to go to the well-known centers of Islamic learning such as Deoband, Saharanpur, Raipur (U.P.) and Thana Bhand (U.P.). The *jamaats* were sent to these centers, from where they spread to other villages nearby. Moulana Ilyas was not content with only changing the customs and habits of the Mewatis. He desired that even their language should change into Arabic. At least the students should speak Arabic within the precincts of the madrassa (Hasni, n.d.: 228-29).

The Moulana could not tolerate any infringement of the Shariat laws. In a letter to a friend, the Moulana wrote: 'It should be emphasized that the panchayats and the other activities must be in accordance with the Shariat. If the laws of Shariat are disobeyed or disregarded, then Islam is finished and *kafur* comes up' (Hasni, n.d.: 233).

EFFECTS OF THE TABLIGH

Though the Tabligh movement was initiated in the late twenties of the twentieth century in the Mewat region, its iufluence had been largely imperceptible before Independence. After 1947 its influence increased tremendously, especially in the Haryana region of Mewat. As a result of the Tabligh movement, the degree of Islamic influence on the Meo culture increased considerably. Islamization was conceived of as a transformation of social customs and practices along the lines indicated by the scriptures. The culture of the Meos is undergoing Islamization rapidly. The process of Islamization involves the elimination of non-Islamic or traditional Hindu elements on the one hand, and, on the other, the conscious and deliberate introduction of what are perceived as Islamic practices.

The life-cycle rituals are being Islamized and the Hindu elements are being weeded out. Singing by women when *baraat* party enters the *bakhal* has been declared to be undesirable. Use of turmeric and rice and yellowish cotton thread has been stopped as it is associated with Hindu symbols. The practice of deciding the auspicious day has been given up resulting in the elimination of the role of the Brahmin. *Neq*, the customary gifts for the serving castes which were given by the bridegroom's party at the *bhaddar* ceremony, have been given up. Other customs associated with marriage—such as, *chak pujna, chavand pujna, kuan pujna*, the custom of the newly weds visiting the graves of pirs and bhairon, etc.—have also been stopped. The *tablighi jamaats* and the religious leaders (Mullas and Maulvis) emphasize on reducing the wedding rituals to the barest possible extent. Some new ceremonies, such as *akika* on the birth of a son, have been introduced.

The Tabligh movement also deprecates the holding of *urs* and the custom of visiting the graves of saints (*pirs*) or ancestors, as this amounts to worshipping which goes against the tenets of Islam. So, the worship of *mazars*, of culture heroes and saints (Sayyid) and the local deities has been gradually abandoned.

The celebration of Hindu festivals such as Holi, Diwali and Dussehra, Goverdhan and Teej has also been stopped. In the mixed villages, the Meos are asked to avoid participation in these festivals. Islamic festivals such as Id-ul-Zuha and Id-ul-Fitr, are increasingly given great importance.

Even the celebration of certain Muslim festivals such as Muharram is being discouraged. On Muharram, *tazias* were brought out in big villages. These were taken round the village, followed by a procession of mourners, to be finally dismantled. The decorated *tazias* were considered sacred and women even worshipped them. In some village *chalisa* was also observed. This was meant to mark the fortieth day after the martyrdom of the third Imam Husain and his associates. It was treated as a day of jubilation and a *mela* was held on the day. These festivals are also being discouraged as they are considered to be deviations from orthodox Islamic practices. A non-Meo Imam, who had opposed the observance of Muharram in a village, expressed his indignation to me: 'Those people are ignorant of the true knowledge of Islam. These ten days of the month should be spent in prayer and remembrance only.' The Meos, especially the younger ones, did not like the interference of the Pesh-Imam in their affairs.

The Tabligh movement has resulted in the rapid Islamization of Meo society. Two related processes are involved in this: the gradual elimination of the syncretic elements of the traditional Meo culture which are considered un-Islamic; and the increasing trend towards religious orthodoxy. This has resulted in the weakening of the traditional ties of relationships between the Meos and their Hindu neighbours. At the same time it has created among the Meos a feeling of closeness with other Muslims. The Meos are seeking to establish their Muslim identity througn religious orthodoxy. The Tabligh movement has met with success only in the post-Independence period in Mewat. This happened after the Meos had passed through a traumatic experiences of communal riots and the forced attempt at reconversion at the time of Partition (Aggarwal, 1969: 1677-81). They have started asserting their Islamic identity as a result, and the process of Islamization has helped them in consolidating their position as a minority community. The Tabligh movement can be viewed as an attempt to bring about cultural unity among the diverse Muslim communities in India (Singh, 1973: 76).

A section among the Meos is concerned about this trend towards Islamization. They fear that the Meos might lose their distinct cultural identity. There have been attempts to consciously preserve certain crucial elements of their social structure (Sharma and Srivastava, 1967). In short, the Meos are now facing a cultural crisis—having taken to the path of Islamization they do not wish to lose their ethnic identity altogether in this process.

Notes

1. See Ahmad (1964:201-17) and Mujeeb (1967:277-82).
2. For the Ahmadiyah movement, see Ahmad and Grunebaum (1970:77-84); Farquhar (1919:137-148), and Lavan (1974).
3. See Mujeeb (1967), Ahmad (1967:31-56) and Jain (1965).
4. See Ahmad (1967:113-22) and Titus (1959:195-97).
5. Refer to Elliot and Dawson, Vol. III (1964:103-5); Lal (1963:58) and William Crooke (1907:143-44).

6. See Shakur (1974). The title of the book is itself very suggestive. Also, see Aggarwal (1971).
7. According to the Census Report of 1811, conversion took place about the time of Allauddin-Ghori. See W.W. Hunter (1964), however, who states that conversion took place after the invasion of Mahmud Ghaznavi in the eleventh century.
8. For a detailed account of his life, see Haq (1972). Also see Amir-Ali (1970: 33-45); Aggarwal (1969:1677-81); Ferozepuri (n.d); and Hasni (n.d).

References

AGGARWAL, PRATAP C. (1969): 'Islamic Revival in Modern India—The Case of the Meo'. *Economic and Political Weekly*, 4(42):1677-81.

————(1971): *Caste, Religion and Power: An Indian Case Study*. New Delhi: Shri Ram Centre for Industrial Relations.

AHMAD, AZIZ (1964): *Studies of Islamic Culture in the Indian Environment*. Oxford: Clarendon Press.

————(1967): *Islamic Modernism in India and Pakistan, 1857-1964*. London: Oxford University Press.

AHMAD & GRUNEBAUM (1970): *Muslim Self-Statement in India and Pakistan, 1857-1968*. Wiesbaden: Otto Harrossowitz.

AMIR-ALI, HASHMI (1970): *The Meos of Mewat*. New Delhi: Oxford & IBH Publishing Co.

CROOKE, WILLIAM (1907): *Natives of Northern India*. London: Archibald Constable & Co.

ELLIOT, HENRY M. & JOHN DAWSON (eds.) (1964): *A History of India as told by its own Historians*. Vol. III. Allahabad: Kitab Mahal.

FARQUHAR, J.N. (1919): *Modern Religious Movements in India*. New York: The Macmillan Company.

FARUQI, Z.H. (1971): 'The Tablighi Jamaat'. In *India and Contemporary Islam*. S.T. Lokhandwala (ed.), Simla: Indian Institute of Advanced Study.

FEROZEPURI, MOHAMMAD ISA (n.d.): *Tablighi Tehrik ki Ibtada aur Uske Bunyadi Asul*. Idara Isha' at Dinyat.

HAQ, M. ANWARUL (1972): *The Faith Movement of Moulana Muhammad Ilyas*. London: George Allen & Unwin.

HASNI, S. ABDUL HASAN ALI (n.d.): *Moulana Muhammad Ilyas aur Unki Dini Dawat*. New Delhi: Idara Isha' at Dinyat.

HUNTER, W.W. (1964): *The Indian Mussalmans*. Lahore: Premier Book House. Reprint. (Originally published in 1871).

JAIN, M.S. (1965): *The Aligarh Movement*. Agra: Sri Ram Mehta & Co.

LAL, K.S. (1963): *Twilight of the Sultanate*. New York: Asia Publishing House.

LAVAN, SPENCER (1974): *The Ahmadiyah Movement*. Delhi: Manohar Book Service.

MATHUR, Y.B. (1972): *Muslims and Changing India*. New Delhi: Trimurti Publications.

MINES, MATTISON (1973): 'Social Stratification among the Muslim Tamils in Tamilnadu, South India'. In *Caste and Social Stratification among the Muslims*. Imtiaz Ahmad (ed.), Delhi: Manohar Book Service.

MUJEEB, M. (1967): *Indian Muslims*. London: George Allen & Unwin Ltd.

RIZVI, S.A.A. (1965): *Muslim Revivalist Movements in Northern India in the Sixteenth and Seventeenth Centuries*. Agra: Agra University.

SHAKUR, MOULANA HAKIM ABDUL (1974): *Tarikh Meo Chhatri*, Nuh: Chaudhry Yasin Meo High School, Dist. Gurgaon.

SHARMA, S.L., & R.N. SRIVASTAVA (1967): 'Institutional Resistance to Induced Islamization in a Convert Community'. *Sociological Bulletin*, 16(1): 69-80.

SINGH, YOGENDRA (1973): *Modernization of Indian Tradition*. Delhi: Thomson Press.

TITUS, MURRAY T. (1959): *Islam in India and Pakistan*. Revised edition. Calcutta: Y.M.C.A. Publishing House.

WAHEEDUZZAFER (1971): "Muslim Socio-religious Movements". *In India and Contemporary Islam*. Simla: S.T. Lokhandwala (ed.). Indian Institute of Advanced Study.

11

B.K. Roy Burman

Challenges and Responses in Tribal India

Since the inception of colonial rule most of the tribes of India have exhibited signs of restlessness at one time or the other in varying degrees of intensity. The reasons, of course, vary from one tribe to another and they will be examined in this paper. At the same time, one has to consider whether this restlessness is symptomatic of a deeper challenge posed by tribal India to the contemporary non-tribal social and political systems of the country. One has also to consider whether such a challenge, if it exists, has a global dimension.

To identify the specific features of unrest among different tribes or the general nature of tribal restlessness in perspective, it would be necessary to have a preliminary idea of the structural attributes of the tribes of India. At the level of abstraction, 'tribe' is generally equated with 'primitive' in the academic community and the public at large. However, there are a large number of communities whom most people would recognize as tribes, but who are not primitive.[1] Examples of primitive tribes would be the Sentinelese of the Andaman Islands who seem to have no contact with the rest of the world. Similarly, there are the Jarawas with whom some contact has been established only during the last four or five years. They depend on nature, have a simple technology and do not produce their own food. These are the true primitives. On the mainland, however, there is hardly any community which is primitive in this sense. There are, however, communities like the Malapandarams of Kerala and the

Birhors of Bihar, the bulk of whose population are gatherers and collectors of forest produce. To some extent, they harvest the forest and exchange the crudely processed products with the people of the plains. Again there are tribes like the Sulungs of Arunachal who live in abject poverty and are the serfs of their dominant neighbours like the Tagins. All of them come under the category of primitive or semi-primitive. The Gallongs of Arunachal, and the Kondhs of Orissa and Andhra Pradesh, who practise shifting cultivation, have a distinct social organization and a self-image of being different from their neighbours. They are also considered to be different by their neighbours. They are not primitive in the classical sense; but it would be generally acceptable to treat them as tribals. In India, there are a large number of such people who are post-primitive tribals.[2]

The restlessness of the post-primitive tribals is frequently different in scale and nature from that of the primitive tribals. Before going into this question, it would be necessary to examine the characteristics of the post-primitives in some depth.

There is a point of view which maintains that the communities that are considered to be post-primitives can as well be treated as peasants.[3] But the post-primitives of today are not just peasants. In the ancient world, settled agriculture, particularly when stimulated by urban growth, was the only advanced mode of production available to the primitive tribes. The process of the transformation and sublimation of their culture was also linked up with urban growth. Today, a people coming out of their primitive shell have multiple choices. An Andamanese can survive partly on charity and partly on the sale of curio objects collected from the seaside without being drawn into the orbit of a peasant economy in any manner. Incidentally, what is considered as charity on the part of the settlers in the Andaman Islands, may be looked upon by the Andamanese themselves as a tribute due to them from trespassers on their land. A Kadar or a Chenchu can take to plantation labour directly from his food gathering economy. A middle class can emerge among the Oraons in a welfare state, even without drawing upon the surplus of an agricultural economy. On a different plain, a Gond, dispossessed of his forest wealth, would not commit himself unequivocally to the cultural communication emanating from the town; he will be in search of a mythical kingdom of God or of an autonomous political system. He will want not only to reform the present; but also to restore the past in a manner which is compatible with the present.[4]

The post-primitives are thus multi-nucleated in their social organization and are involved in political and cultural communications at different levels. The simplistic approach of labelling them peasants would be misleading in an understanding of the crucial problems that affect their lives.

Turning to the specific manifestations of restlessness among the primitives and the post-primitives, several parameters can be envisaged:

1. Response to threats to the privacy of habitat.
2. Response to threats to access to and control of resources.
3. Response to disruption of traditional roles in the total interaction set-up.
4. Search for new meanings of the relationship between man and nature.
5. Search for new meanings of the relationship between individuals and society.
6. Search for new frontiers of identity.
7. Search for a more satisfactory system of control of resources.
8. Search for a more satisfactory system of organization of community power at all levels.

It is obvious that while the first three possible origins of restlessness are responses to challenges emanating primarily from outside, the last five are responses to challenges primarily from within. While on a closer examination it would be found that this delineation is rather arbitrary and artificial, it is necessary to have a starting point for analytical purposes.

Response to Threats to the Privacy of Habitat

COUNTER-THREAT

Even now the Sentinelese in the Bay of Bengal do not allow outsiders to land on their island. They threaten the encroachers with bow and arrows. No doubt, their resistance can be easily overcome with the application of force; but the ethos of modern civilization will not allow this. For decades, the Jarawas of middle and south Andaman had also resisted encroachment through counter-threats.

This reticence has recently been overcome by prolonged preventive measures against violence, along with repeated overtures of friendship. It has now been possible to establish contact with the Jarawas. But it is not known what revaluation of values, cognitive shifts and rearrangements in the community power structure took place within Jarawa society, so as to make non-antagonistic contacts with outsiders possible. Counter-threats and violent reactions against colonial expansion in the tribal areas were quite frequent in North-east India during the last century and even during the earlier part of the present century.

WITHDRAWAL

Consequent upon the establishment of industrial centers in primitive settings, the withdrawal of the indigenous people to more outlying areas is a well-known phenomenon. Perhaps in the past, much of this withdrawal was spontaneous, caused by super-natural fear or fear of physical violence. But now market forces operate more relentlessly. With rapid changes in the pattern of land use, land has become a commodity. The tribals feel tempted to sell their land and recede to more outlying areas where the commodity value of land is either non-existent or is very low. The failure of the state in most parts of the country to recognize the corporate nature of ownership of land amongst tribal communities has facilitated such alienation with serious economic and political consequences which will be discussed later.

Response to Threats against Access to and Control of Resources

REVOLTS AGAINST IMPOSITION OF STATE OR STATE SPONSORED CAPITALISM ON PRIMITIVE SOCIAL BASE IN THE FORESTS

During colonial rule, a number of uprisings had taken place among the tribals which centered on the question of forests. Colonial anthropologists and administrators blamed the corrupt practices of the petty forest officials for this. But by doing so they evaded the real issue. Until recently, hill cultivation and collection of forest resources for various domestic purposes were the main sources of livelihood for the tribals. Even where they had taken to settled agriculture, forest produce remained an important subsidiary means of livelihood. In the last century a policy of reservation of forests was introduced by the colonial rulers to enable the extraction of timber and other forest products to serve the needs of the railways and various industries. Forest produce was frequently sold at subsidized rates; hence there were no profits which could be ploughed back to augment productive activities in the forests or to provide reasonable wages for forest labourers. At the same time, nothing was done to introduce advanced modes of production in the other sectors of the economy of the tribals. They soon became pauperized and were forced to work for extremely low wages. It was in this context that malpractices became widespread among petty forest officials. But a sociologist should not overlook that they could not have behaved otherwise. If they enforced the system required by the state too rigidly, either the tribal communities would have ceased to exist physically or they would have been in a state of perpetual revolt. By their corrupt practices the petty forest officials helped the tribals to survive and also to keep the number and the intensity of revolts within limits.

Among the tribal revolts centering around the question of reservation of forests during colonial rule, mention may be made of the revolts of the Garos, Koyas and Kondhs. These revolts rarely attracted the attention of the nationalist leaders carrying on the anti-colonial struggle. As most of them hailed from the plains and did not have any real knowledge of the actual conditions prevailing in the hills, they seem to have been taken in by the propaganda of the apologists of colonial rule that they were fighting the battle of civilization against barbarism; of science against primitivism; of increasing resources as against wasting them. One important exception was the satyagraha launched by the forest dwellers of the Kumaon region. In this movement an important nationalist leader, Gobind Ballabh Pant, played a very important role. One should, however, take note of the fact that the people of Kumaon have had very close social links with the people of the plains for centuries. Hence their struggle could become part of the national liberation struggle more easily.[5]

In some other parts of the country also, the leaders of the forest dwellers tried to link up their uprising with the national movement. For instance, in 1920, Alluru Sitaram Raju, who led the revolt of the Koyas against the oppressive practices of the forest administration, swore by the name of Gandhi.[6] In her fight against the British, Rani Gaidailu of Manipur also referred to Gandhi as her source of inspiration.[7]

It is interesting to note that though the hill peoples' movement failed, in general, to be linked up with the nationalist movement, in several cases the leadership for their movement was provided by non-tribals from the plains. A systematic sociological explanation of this phenomenon is still to be provided. In the meantime, a few tentative observations can be made. First, the tribals were very afraid that in their confrontation with the foreign rulers they might be isolated from the rest of the country. Thus, the outside leaders served as bridges between them and their neighbours. Secondly, they had their own internal contradictions and dilemmas. Sections of the tribals were not free from the cultural influences of their neighbours; while they were those who held on to their ancient traditions. The presence of perceptive individuals from outside, who could restate the relevant aspects of the neighbouring cultures in terms of the tribal idiom and vice-versa, helped to resolve the internal contradictions.

MOVEMENTS AGAINST ALIENATION OF TRIBAL LAND

The colonial administration created conditions in which the large-scale dispossession of the tribals from their agricultural lands became a regular process. In some parts of the country—for instance, Chotanagpur—the tribute paid by the indigenous population to the rulers had been converted into rent shortly before the advent of the British raj. This implied that the rulers, who could dominate over society through their power of causing or preventing physical coercion, started to claim to be the ultimate owners of all the resources under their dispensation. From being coordinators and later rulers of human affairs, they turned into masters of territories.

The ideology of political organization underlying this development was very much different from what had prevailed in the past. This ideology was further reinforced during colonial rule which had the effect of eroding the moral fabric of the old society. The rates at which the rents were charged were enhanced; and the enforcing machinery was made more effective. The distortion, however, took place at the level of the social organization. Even though tribute was converted into rent, during the pre-colonial period it was the community represented by the original settler's lineage which was the recognized unit for paying it. However, during colonial rule the primacy of the state over resources was established on the one hand,

and, on the other, the individual was freed from the moral constraints of community membership, in the utilization and enjoyment of resources. This freedom was really a bondage as the individual was now brought under the direct subjugation of the sate, without the community serving as a cushion. He also lost the security provided by the mutual aid system of the community in crisis situations—like illness, death, etc., or during rites of passage like birth or marriage. At the same time, the reserves at the disposal of the community in the form of forest resources to meet crop failures or other unforeseen events were depleted. The last point is frequently ignored by many analysts of the economic and social history of the tribals. They fail to realize that for the tribals who have taken to agriculture, the adjoining forest is not only a source of a subsidiary means of livelihood but also the last resort for survival which has been preserved through the wisdom of generations.

For instance, in case of drought when cultivation is not likely to yield the expected return, they turn to collection of jungle produce or hunting. It is the destruction of the communal security system and the fact that they are now deprived of their emergency reserves that has made the tribals vulnerable to exploitation by usurious money-lenders and traders. The improvident life-style that is found among many of them is more likely to be the outcome of this situation, rather than the cause of it.

Earlier the tribal individuals could turn to the community to help in times of crisis, but with the penetration of colonial domination the community was no longer in a position to help. Money-lenders and traders now plugged this gap. Many of them were undoubtedly greedy, but it would be wrong to consider this as being only the outcome of perfidious human nature. It was the vagaries of the colonial market economy to which the economy of the tribals was now being linked up, that made the unscrupulous operations of traders and money-lenders almost inevitable. The early expansionist phase of the colonial economy was a concomitant of wars of conquest, punitive expeditions and armed conflicts with potential rivals. The commodity market was very unstable and there were considerable amounts of speculative transactions. The traders in the tribal areas wanted to make hay while the sun shone. If they were sure of a secure market, they would not have diverted part of their capital into money-lending or in taking over land when the tribals failed to repay loans.

As a cummulative effect of these various processes, the tribal communities have been continuously losing their lands. With the expansion of marketing facilities, the extension of the production infrastructure and improvements in agricultural technology in recent years, the rate of dispossession and deprivation has been further accentuated. And, last but not the least, is the contribution of the land survey and settlement operations, where rights are recognized not in terms of the systems prevailing among the tribals, but in terms of those prevailing among the plains people in entirely different ecological and historical contexts.[8]

The response of the tribals to the challenges mentioned above has not been uniform. Tribes like the Bhuiya or Nagesia seem to have submitted to their fate without presenting much organized resistance But tribes such as the Santal, Ho, Oraon, Munda and Bhumij have tried to resist, even resorting to violence. One of the reasons for the differential responses might be that the tribes which offered resistance are the ones who are more stratified internally than the ones which did not offer significant collective opposition. The upper strata of such tribes as the Oraon, Munda, Ho certainly served as the rallying points of their respective tribes.

The case of the Santals was somewhat different. Traditional Santal society was not stratified in the same way as the Oraon, Munda or Ho were. In their case, however, there was a special circumstance which might have been a contributory factor. They had effected an innovation in their social organization by which the primacy of the original settler's lineage was replaced by the supremacy of the tribal council; this in turn facilitated their fanning out, since the later part of the eighteenth century, all over the uplands in the borders of Bengal, Bihar and Orissa which were being rapidly cleared up to serve the various needs of the colonial and mercantile establishments.[9] Their settlement in these areas, in the face of opposition from earlier settlers like the Sauria Paharia and the Malpaharia, was possible largely because of the support that they received from the colonial administration. Thus in the process of their settlement a leadership, with multiple contacts with the outside world, had come into existence. As a consequence, the frustration when they felt themselves betrayed was much more intense; and they were also able to develop a strategy of action so that their revolt in the middle of the last century was not confined to their ethnic group only. Socio-economic interest groups like the oilmen and the weavers, who occupied a position similar to the Santals, were also drawn into it.[10]

Further, it should be noted that social stratification by itself is not enough to mobilize the people to actively resist alienation of their land. The nature of the stratification is an important factor. For instance, though the Gonds were highly stratified, no significant revolt took place amongst them till the forties of the present century. In the middle ages they had established kingdoms, sometimes confronting, sometimes subservient to and sometimes serving as buffers between the Mughal empire, and the kingdoms of the Marathas and Bijapur. The presence of a state structure and the shifting nature of political contacts with the outside world led to both the stratification and segmentation of Gond society.[11] The upper strata emerged as a multi-focal aristocracy. One of their foci of interest was the tribal society itself; the others included the political and cultural elites of the surrounding societies. It was not difficult for the Gond aristocrats to come to terms with the colonial rulers. The old chiefs were converted into new Zamindars and the Gonds oscillated between tribal and peasant forms of social organization. One form tended to neutralize the other and the Gonds could not sustain either a peasant movement or a tribal movement for any length of time.

The histories of such movements as those led by Kangla Majhi of Raipur and Behari Das of Bastar highlight this point. Both of them capitalized on the pauperization and frustration of the tribals. But they were not peasant leaders. They projected themselves as the kings of the tribals. Behari Das claimed to be an incarnation of the late Prabir Chandra Bhanjdeo, who was deposed as the ruler of Bastar, led a tribal confrontation with the government in the sixties.[12] Kangla Majhi surrounded himself with the regalia of a king.[13] These claims to a royal status did not, however, mean that these movements had the capture of state power as a goal. The frontiers of the kingdoms of their fancy are in the minds of men, of their disciples, where the territorial dimension is only incidental. Occasionally they have dabbled in politics, but mostly as junior partners of some of the all-India political parties.

In the early sixties, Kangla Majhi moved for a Gondwana state with rights of management of lands and forests; but even then he did not think of fighting for an independent center of power. He tried to legitimize his actions by claiming that he had received the approval of Jawaharlal Nehru. It is obvious that he could not have received any approval from Nehru for the type of upsurge that he led. But the very fact that he made such a claim and that many of his followers believed it, is extremely important. It shows their faith in the moral ethos of the national liberation struggle, for which Nehru stood. At the same time, it shows their utter confusion about the nature of the organization of state power. It is not proposed to examine the empirical aspects of the movement in greater detail. The movement failed, notwithstanding the fact that a section of Gond aristocracy wanted a separate state for themselves.

The foregoing case studies show that while the presence of internal stratification does not by itself play a decisive role in mobilizing the tribals to take organized action against the loss of their resources, particularly land resources, it still has some relevance in determining the course of events. To see the question in a wider perspective, it would be useful to examine the nature of the mobilization of those tribes where an educated section has emerged which claims leadership roles. One such mobilization is the Jharkhand Mukti Morcha (Jharkhand Liberation Front),[14] which was active in parts of the Santal Parganas and Hazaribag in the early seventies. It is important to note that, according to the 1971 Census, all the fifty-six tribal males and females in the Santal Parganas who declared their primary activity to be political and related works, were at least matriculates. The president of the Morcha was a lawyer, Binod Mahato, and its secretary was an educated Santal, Sibo Soren. They encouraged the tribals to forcibly recover the lands which were deceitfully taken away from them by traders and money-lenders. They also prevented forest contractors from removing trees. It is interesting to observe that notwithstanding alleged Marxist leanings they were not averse to draping themselves with a supernatural aura. Sibo Soren's followers believed that his body could not be pierced by bullets, and that he could ride a motorcycle over a river. It seems that for some time the movement aimed at the capture of state power, but, later on, it limited itself to a set of demands for more comprehensive welfare activities on the part of the state and better execution of existing programmes.

Thus, an agrarian movement that started with a bang ended in a whimper of middle class opportunist politics with a frill of philanthropism. More or less the same is the story of the Jharkhand movement in Chotanagpur proper.[15] the plain tribals movement in the Brahmaputra valley,[16] and the tribal youth movement of Tripura.[17] To some extent, Srikakulam has been an exception.

While there may also be other causes for the dismal history of the tribal agrarian movements, one has first to seek for reasons in the internal structure of the tribal societies themselves. One important clue to the internal structure is provided by the number and types of occupations in which the tribal workers are employed. In this matter, a special tabulation of the 1971 Census data in respect of the Santal Parganas provides interesting information; namely, 72.95 per cent of the total tribal workers of the district were engaged in cultivation. Among the Santals, the numerically most important tribe of the district, 75.13 per cent were engaged in cultivation. But whereas the non-agricultural workers in tribes like the Banjara, Gorait, Ho, Karmali, Kharia, Kisan, Korwa and Paharia can be divided into less than ten occupational groups each, the Santal non-agricultural workers are found in seventy-two occupation groups. If the specific occupations are considered, the number would be much larger. An important problem of ethno-sociology that deserves consideration, and which has a bearing on the fate of tribal agrarian movements, is the ramification that occupational diversities have on the ethnic process. For instance, one would ask whether Santal teachers or clerks or mechanics perceive themselves primarily as teachers or as Santals. Secondly, if they perceive themselves primarily as Santals will they try to reorient Santal culture to meet their occupational needs as teachers, or clerks or mechanics, etc., or will they try to adjust their occupational norms as teachers or whatever to the constraints of the traditional culture centering on cultivation and the subsidiary hunting-gathering economy? Thirdly, if persons belonging to a number of tribes perceive themselves primarily as teachers, clerks, etc., and not as members of their respective tribes, will this lead to ethnic convergence or to ethnic differentiation?

In the politico-historical context of the country in which this process of divergence of occupations is taking place among the tribes, particularly in the context of a welfare state wedded to parliamentary democracy, it seems likely that they would perceive themselves more as members of their respective ethnic groups rather than as workers engaged in particular occupations. But at the same time, they do not find it possible to directly influence the cultural processes of their tribe or, in the reverse, to adjust their occupational norms to the cultural constraints of their tribe. The only course open to them is to try to control the political process of the tribes. The political communication structure of the country as a whole helps them rather than the traditional leaders. The bulk of the tribals who are cultivators have to accommodate them or to completely submit to their leadership. Thus, tribal society assumes the character of a proto-national society where the tribal cultivators do not perceive themselves only as cultivators, but as members of their respective ethno-political entities with a wide spectrum of diversities. And though they may launch struggles on agrarian issues, it becomes possible to divert the struggle to other issues with which their leaders are more concerned.[18]

Response to Disruption of Traditional Roles in the Total Interaction Set-up

While dispossession of traditional resources has been the most important cause of tribal unrest, there are other causes also. But due to shortage of space and also because most of them are ultimately linked up with the question of resources, they will be treated in this paper in a summary manner.

The behaviour of many of the so-called ex-criminal tribes can be understood primarily in terms of the disruption of their traditional roles.[19] For instance, the Banjaras—who used to render commissariat service to the armies in the middle ages and were also engaged in itinerant trade—were pushed out of their occupation with the establishment of the railway line. Many of the immunities and privileges that they enjoyed in the old kingdoms disappeared. They thus suffered not only economically, but also socially. Many of them could not adjust to the new situation and took to crime. The Chenchus of Kurnool district in Andhra Pradesh, who were primarily hunters and gatherers, suffered a terrible economic blow when their forests were taken over by the state. They also served as guides to the traders and pilgrims visiting the famous temple of Srisailam and received payment for this service. With the extension of roads, communication and effective administration, this role also suffered a setback and many of them took to crime. The Bhils of Mewar, who had a similar role in respect of the trade and pilgrim routes passing through their area, also suffered in the same way and responded similarly. The criminal behaviour of some sections of the Savaras who inhabit the border territory between Bengal and Orissa had similar origins. It seems that to many of them crime was not an unmitigated anti-social behaviour; it was a sort of guerrila warfare against encroachment by the technologically more advanced societies on their age-old rights.[20]

It is, however, difficult to say that all these communities uniformly perceived theft, robbery, etc., as a political response to economic challenges or social deprivation. It seems that they have been largely oscillating between looking at the question politically and morally. The moral dilemma finds expression in the views of the Bhagat movements that sweep through the tribal areas from time to time. It is not without significance that while these movements enjoin the tribals to abjure a criminal way of life, they also quite frequently hold out hopes of restoration or establishment of tribal kingdoms. In one way these movements symbolize the urge of the tribal societies concerned to normalize their human relations with those whom they look upon as intruders. In another way, these movements also express their craving for a system of political management in which they do not feel themselves to be aliens.

Search for New Meanings of the Relationship between Man and Nature

Along with the attempts to reorient human relations, a reinterpretation of the relations between man and nature (as described in myths and legends and also as believed otherwise) is also taking place. The Ao Nagas have the myth of origin from six rocks. Some educated persons among them are interpreting it to mean that Ao culture has descended straight from the Stone Age.[21] Among the Jaintias, ecological explanations are being given for the taboos relating to the forests and forest species.[22] Pyschological explanations are advanced by educated Adis for the trials by ordeal—like putting burning amber on the palm of the hand to establish the innocence of a person accused of committing a crime. Among the same people, the belief in Doinyo-Polo (Sun and Moon) as the source of almighty power is replacing the belief in them as the primeval pair.[23] Such reinterpretation is consciously done to promote unity among these who accept the supremacy of the Doinyo-Polo cult over any other cult which has originated from any human being. Such developments are the precursors of the growth of a tribal theology. They also mark an assertion of self-respect and equality with their neighbours. It is significant that, during 1961-71, there was a marked increase in many parts of India in the proportion of tribals returning their religion by the names of their respective tribes, and a corresponding decline in the proportion of those who profess Hinduism or Christianity.

SEARCH FOR NEW MEANINGS OF THE RELATIONSHIP BETWEEN INDIVIDUAL AND SOCIETY

This massive search is highlighted by the cryptic observation of an Andamanese (the population of the Andamanese was about two thousand at the beginning of the century and is now barely two dozen): 'I cannot tell my God how I am. What can I tell you?'[24] Under the spectre of extinction, the communication between his inner self and the world around has broken down. He is lost. Attempts are being made to introduce the Andamanese to community life in an island exclusively of their own; but they hardly stay there for any length of time. Individuals move out, stay at Port Blair, get bored and return. And this goes on in a circuit. An anomie, a meaninglessness, has overtaken them. Many of them are reported to bury themselves in the abyss of time with the aid of opium. Perhaps there are many moments when they look upon themselves primarily as depersonalized beings, rather than individuals sharing a common meaning system or building up a common edifice of life. But again there are moments of resurrection. They try to live in the community, recreate the community. A few years ago, the Andamanese were faced with a crisis. They had only one boy and one girl of marriageable age. Unless they married, the community would die out, but the couple were closely related. The alternative was to exchange bride and bridegroom with another tribe, the Onge, who lived in another island at a distance of about 100 miles. After prolonged deliberation, involving the elders of the community and well-wishers from outside, they decided to make internal adjustments. The boy and the girl had to overcome their inhibition so that the community could live. A child has been born to them.

The Andamanese are, of course, an extreme case. There is hardly any other tribe which faces a real danger of extinction. But many suffer from the agony of tiny numbers, depletion of resources and the encroachments of superior technology. They do not know where to seek shelter. Earlier, those individuals who had the chance to come into closer contact with persons from societies with more sophisticated technologies or who had received modern education, would frequently drift away from their respective communities. They would try to emulate the ways of life of the contact cultures; but they soon discovered that by drifting away from their own culture they did not necessarily get easy entrance into the society they were emulating.

The process of drift and emulation, described as sanskritization in the Indian context, succeeded in creating elite groups in the tribal societies which were internally alienated and externally frustrated. It is not a matter of chance that sanskritization gained momentum during the later phase of colonial rule. The structures that sanskritization tended to create within the tribal societies were in conformity with the structures that colonialism created in Indian society as a whole.[25]

In post-Independence India, in the context of the spread of secular and democratic values (although haltingly) and coupled with the inherent contradictions of sanskritization, a move in the opposite direction is gaining momentum. In North Bengal, the Mech, who in the thirties had changed their clan names to Hindu gotra names and adopted Brahmin priests, have reverted to clan names and given up Brahmin priests.[26] The Rajputization trend among the Mahatos of Bihar is being countered by a conscious trend towards tribalization.[27] It is the story of the prodigal son returning home. This new trend seems to have two contradictory effects on the relations between the individual and society. The tribal individuals feel less overwhelmed by the outside world. The elites of sanskritization turn into the elites of counter-sanskritization. There is only change of postures.

Search for New Frontiers of Identity

The identity dilemma prevails not only at the individual level but at the level of collectivities as well.

As already noted, with the extension of the market economy to every nook and corner of the country, the tribal communities find that their traditional resources are slipping out of their control. There is an instinctive, defensive reaction among the tribes which are similarly placed to join hands. This is a phase of simultaneous reinforcement and reinterpretation of traditions. This phase occurred among the Adi group of tribes of Arunachal Pradesh in the late fifties and early sixties. The Gallong, Padam, Minyong and cognate tribes who have traditions of origin from a common ancestor—Aboteni—moved closer to one another. Earlier, the plains people described them by a common name, Abor, although they themselves remained internally differentiated. There was a bid to give a positive content to their common identity. The old myths and legends started to be looked upon in a different way. The differences were glossed over and common elements were highlighted. This phase of expansion of identity may be described as infra-nationalism. In the phase of infra-nationalism, though there is an awareness of the intrusion of market forces, there is hardly any awareness of the political superstructure at the national level. The dominant traditions that serve as the driving force for the nation state are out of focus, in so far as infra-nationalism is concerned.

A more evolved form of expansion of identity is proto-nationalism. In this phase, an elite, conscious of the political and cultural superstructure at the national level, comes into existence.[28] Besides, there is a widespread awareness of the physical comforts that can be conferred by modern technology and there is a desire to avail of them.

Expansion of identity becomes a matter of conscious choice among several alternatives. This can be illustrated by a case study in the Tengnoupal district of Manipur. Here the numerically dominant tribe is Anal. The other important tribes include the Moyons, Monsangs and Lamkangs. In the early fifties, some educated Moyons and Monsangs realized that in order to be able to take advantage of the various welfare and development activities undertaken by the state, they should be able to function as an effective pressure group in the Territorial Council of Manipur. They initiated a move to unite with the Anals and constitute a single tribe called Pakan. They held several joint meetings and decided that while for common religious services they would use the Anal language, they would use the shawls of the different tribes for different purposes. The move fell through as the Anals were not very enthusiastic about it. But later on, when an Autonomous District Council was introduced in the hill districts of Manipur. the

Anals wanted to revive the move to establish a common identity; this time the Moyons and Monsangs were not interested as they found that they could dominate the scene by forming alliances with other small tribes against the Anals. The Moyons and Monsangs, however, initiated a move among themselves to forge a common identity of the two tribes under the name Mon. As a symbol of their unity, some of them are trying to introduce a common shawl design for ceremonial occasions. While a majority of the more influential leaders of the two tribes have joined this move, small sections of the educated young Monsangs are opposing it as they feel that this will adversely affect their job opportunities at the district level.

Such conscious bids towards identity expansion are found among the tribes of Nagaland, Kerala, Bihar, Orissa, Madhya Pradesh and Gujarat—in fact almost all over India.

In proto-nationalism, there is almost equal emphasis on the self-management of the cultures as well as of the resources associated with the various ethnic groups. The essential difference between proto-nationalism and nationalism is that the former does not consciously strive to capture independent state power, whereas the later does. This does not mean, however, that the elites of proto-nationalism are not interested in the political processes of the state. They are interested, but more as a pressure group than as independent holders of power. One of the reasons for this is that the source of legitimization of power in proto-nationalism is different from the source of legitimization of power in the nation-state. In the case of the former it is the moral bond provided by descent from common ancestors, whereas in case of the state it is the coercive capacity of a territorial unit.

While these differences exist at the level of the ideal, in actual practice there is always a blending of the two. Proto-nationalism, therefore, sometimes takes the form of regionalism,[29] which in fact is the anti-thesis of proto-nationalism.

In regionalism, in the long run, the decisive role is played by the interest group which is inextricably linked up with the production system at the national level. But if such a decisive role continues over a length of time, the leaders of the ethnic groups involved in it feel that they are being used only as instruments to serve interests which are not of immediate relevance to the bulk of their people. An oscillation between proto-nationalism and regionalism takes place. This is what seems to be happening in the Jharkhand Movement in Chotanagpur.[30]

Proto-nationalism is also to be differentiated from sub-nationalism.[31] As noted earlier, proto-nationalism is a phase of expansion of identity; sub-nationalism is a phase of contraction of identity. One results from the expansion of the orbit of development; the other results from the disparities of development. Besides, as in state nationalism, in sub-nationalism the ultimate sanction is the coercive power of the community, whereas, as already stated, in proto-nationalism it is primarily the moral consensus of the community.

SEARCH FOR A MORE SATISFACTORY SYSTEM OF CONTROL OF RESOURCES

Along with the search for new frontiers of identity, a search for a more satisfactory system of control of resources is also taking place.

Among the Mizo group of tribes, the heroes—the leaders of war—seem to have considerably say in the manner of utilization of the productive resources. The institution of hereditary chiefship was a check against the arbitrary functioning of the war leaders. But with the establishment of colonial rule, when the chiefs were recognized as the sole channels of communication with the state, they tended to become autocratic rulers of the Mizo tribes; they not only claimed tributes from those residing in their jurisdiction but even charged rents in kind for the productive activities on the lands. Towards the end of British rule, there were movements against the exactions by the chiefs which were not sanctioned by tribal custom. After Independence and on the recommendation of the Autonomous District Council, chiefship was abolished in Mizoram by law. But no satisfactory system of management of land could be evolved immediately, which led to a number of dislocations.[32]

In Manipur also the egalitarian ideology opposed to the autocratic rights of the chiefs spread among some of the tribes who recognized hereditary chiefs. They tried to follow the elective principle but the elected leaders were not careful to preserve the traditional resources and alienation of land took place to a considerable extent. Besides. as survey and settlement operations are conducted on the assumption that land not belonging to individuals belongs to the state, a problem arose in respect of the community lands in those areas where hereditary chiefs with ownership rights over lands were not recognized by the communities concerned. A trend of reversion to the old system, therefore, is perceptible. But in this matter also opinions are divided.[33] There is an apprehension that it would be easier to take over lands from the chief either by outright purchase or by political corruption, than to nibble away at communal lands through dubious methods.

The dilemmas illustrated by the cases of tribes from Mizoram and Manipur hold good for many other parts of the country in various forms.

Search for a More Satisfactory System of Organisation of Community Power at all Levels

The question of a satisfactory system of control of resources is, in the ultimate analysis, linked up with the question of organization of community power at all levels.

A crucial question in this matter is the unit of organization of community power. In the Kameng district of Arunachal when some of the hamlets of the village Rupa were recognized as separate villages, it created a turmoil. The power elite of Rupa protested as, according to them, the people in the sub-villages had access to common resources in lieu of certain services that they rendered to the main village.[31]

In the Autonomous District Council Areas of North-East India, there is a tussle between the traditional village organization and the District Council in the matter of distribution of power. The conflict has different histories in the different districts. In the Garo Hills, the District Council and the village authorities were able to work out a mutually acceptable system. The village agreed to accept the District Council's authority to manage the community forest on condition that the latter would pay a fixed annuity to the village. In the Khasi and Jaintia Hills, mutual accommodation was not possible because the syiems or tribal chiefs were recognized as feudal rulers by the British and were entitled to certain constitutional safeguards under the Instruments of accession that they signed with the Government of India at the time of Independence. In the post-Independence period, the conflict between the District Council and the chiefs was complicated by the fact that the state government of undivided Assam found it convenient to use the syiems as a counter-force against the District Council. Through this struggle the District Council was able to emerge as a supra-tribal entity rather than a subordinate organ of the state. It became the rallying center for the emerging educated middle class among the tribals.[35] With the formation of the hill state, however, the situation has changed. The District Council is considered by many tribal leaders as a road-block against the effective organization of state power. In this conflict, the erstwhile feudal chiefs seem to have regained some of their lost ground.

There are two angles from which the situation can be considered. From one angle, the conflict between the District Council and the state is a factional conflict between political parties. From another point of view, it symbolizes the conflict between organization of community power in the framework of state structure, versus that of supra-tribal organization. Space will not permit me to elaborate the point in detail. It may, however, be pointed out that under the Sixth Schedule of the Constitution, the rights and responsibilities reposed in the District Council are mostly the formalization of the rights and responsibilities exercised by tribal societies through their traditional structures. On the creation of the hill state if the powers exercised by the District Councils are taken over by the organs of the state, it means not only a difference in the scale of their operation, it also means a qualitative change in the nature of their operation. In other words, it means that traditional tribal institutions are to be replaced by organs of the state. This is a real dilemma for the tribals who have been fighting to establish their identity. They find that their success means the end of what they have stood for all the time. It seems that this dilemma is faced by the Nagas also. A few years ago, they would consider the appellation 'tribal' as a pejorative term. Now Nagas of all political hues would like to describe themselves as a multi-tribal nation.[36]

The search for the viable unit of community power goes on not only at the level of the state within the framework of the Constitution, but also at the level of independent political entities, as has been the case with the Nagas or Mizos for a number of years. Without going into the merits of these cases, it is necessary to appreciate that this search falls into a global pattern. There are similar insurgency movements of tribal or tribe-like communities in different countries of South and South-east Asia. There are also

rumblings in USA, Canada and Australia. One has to give serious thought as to whether all these should be considered as mere ethnic upsurges or whether they have deeper significance for humanity. Though most of these movements have the capture of state power as their formal goal, these may, without the leaders of the movements themselves knowing it, lead to the resurrection of the will of man for communitarian self-management in place of the soulless control by depersonalized organs of the state.[37]

References

1. B.K. Roy Burman (1960): 'Basic Concepts of Tribal Welfare and Tribal Integration'. *Journal of Social Research.* Vol. III, No. 2.
2. B.K. Roy, Burman (1974): 'Perspective for Administration and Development of the Scheduled Tribes'. Workshop on *Perspective on Tribal Development and Administration*, National Institute of Community Development, Hyderabad.
3. Andre Beteille (1974): *Six Essays in Comparative Sociology.* Delhi: Oxford University Press; S.C. Sinha (1965) : Tribe Caste and Tribe Peasant Continua in Central India'. *Man in India.* Vol. 45, No. 1.
4. Personal communication between Dr. B.K. Roy Burman and Shri K.N. Thusu of the Anthropological Survey of India, Calcutta.
5. B.K. Roy Burman (1977): Issue paper for the Seminar on 'The People and the Forest in the Western Himalaya'. Dehra Dun: Himalaya Seva Sangh (Mimeograph).
6. V. Raghavaiah: *Rebellion*. New Delhi: Bharatiya Adimjati Sewak Sangh.
7. Gangumei Kabui (1970) : Jadonang, *Jadonang Volume*, August 1970, Imphal.
8. B.K. Roy Burman (1976): 'Transfer and Alienation of Tribal Land'. *Samatat* Supplement, Calcutta.
9. B.K. Roy Burman (1975): 'Population and Social Process among the Tribes of India'. *Plural Societies*, Winter 1975.
10. K.K. Datta (1940): *Santal Insurrection*, Calcutta.
11. B.K. Roy Burman (1964): 'Gonds'—Synopsis of talk delivered at Tribal Orientation and Training Centre, Udaipur. Mimeographed copies circulated by the office of the Registrar General, India, and also S.C. Sinha, (1962): 'State Formation and Rajput Myth in Tribal Central India'. *Man in India.* Vol. 42, No. 1.
12. Joshi, Sleeping Giant.
13. Field data.
14. H.P. Pradhan: 'Jharkhand Liberation Front'. *Economic and Political Weekly*, 1975. Vol. X, No. 24.
15. Sachchidanand (1972): 'The Tribal Situation in Bihar'. In *Tribal Situation in India*, K. S. Singh (ed.). Simla: Indian Institute of Advanced Study.

16. M.S. Prabhakar (1974): 'The Politics of Script'. *Economic and Political Weekly*, 21 December 1974.
17. Brochure of the Upajati Juba Samity, Tripura, 1975.
18. B.K. Roy Burman (1973): Presidential Address, Annual Conference of Adimjati Sevak Sangh, Srivakulam.
19. B.K. Roy Burman (1973): 'Denotified Tribes—Problem of Integrated Social Planning'. Seminar on Denotified Communities, Moradabad, Uttar Pradesh.
20. Bhargava, *Denotified Tribes*, 1939.
21. B.K. Roy Burman (1973): *Waromung—An Ao Naga Village in Nagaland*. Vol. I, Part VI, *Census of India*, 1961. Delhi: Manager of Publications.
22. B.K. Roy Burman (1976): Proceedings of the Seminar on 'People and Forest in Eastern Himalaya', New Delhi: Himalaya Seva Sangh.
23. Ashang Ering, 'Dayna Polo Cult' (unpublished paper).
24. B.K. Roy Burman (1971): Field note.
25. B.K. Roy Burman (1971): 'National Movements among Tribals'. *Secular Democracy*. Annual Number, Vol. IV, Nos. 3 and 4.
26. B K. Roy Burman (1953): 'Acculturation among the Mech'. Report submitted to the Government of West Bengal.
27. Pasupati Mahato (1974): Proceedings of the Conference of Kudmi. Adivasi Mahasabha.
28. B.K. Roy Burman (1971): 'National Movements among Tribals'. *Secular Democracy*. Annual Number, Vol. IV, Nos. 3 and 4.
29. B.K. Roy Burman (1974): Perspective for Administration and Development of the Scheduled Tribes. Workshop on Perspective on Tribal Development and Administration. Hyderabad: National Institute of Community Development.
30. B.K. Roy Burman (1975): 'Ethnicity in Chotanagpur'. UNESCO Seminar on Inter-ethnic Relations, Kathmandu.
31. B.K. Roy Burman (1971): 'National Movements among Tribals'. *Secular Democracy*. Annual Number, Vol. IV, Nos. 3 and 4.
32. B.K. Roy Burman (1973): 'Demographic and Socio-economic Profiles of the Hill Areas of N.E. India'. *Census of India*, 1961. Vol. I, Delhi: Manager of Publications.
33. B.K. Roy Burman (1977): Note of Customary Laws. Manipur (mimeographed).
34. B.K. Roy Burman (1976): *Rupa—A Sherdullpur Village in Arunachal Pradesh*. *Census of India*, 1971. Delhi: Manager of Publications.
35. B.K. Roy Burman (1973): 'Demographic and Socio-economic Profiles of the Hill Areas of N.E. India'. *Census of India*, 1961. Vol. I. Delhi: Manager of Publications.
36. Saizha (1972): ICSSR Seminar on 'Social Change in Nagaland'. Kohima.
37. B.K. Roy Burman (1972): Issue Paper for the Seminar on 'Social Change in Nagaland'. ICSSR (mimeographed).

12

Joseph Troisi

Social Movements among the Santals*

IN RECENT YEARS sociologists and social anthropologists throughout the world have shown an increasing interest in the study of social movements. In fact, a number of books and articles have been written about these phenomena which represent an important sphere of social activity and social change.[1] This paper is concerned with the significance of three such social movements—namely, the Santal Rebellion of 1855-57, the Kharwar Movement and the Jharkhand Movement—all of which were powerful expressions of the collective protest of the Santals against conditions of economic exploitation and social oppression. As we shall see in this paper, these three movements derived their strength from the idea of the Golden Age so prominent in Santal mythology. This gave meaning and purpose to the religious, economic and political aspirations of the Santals and at the same time legitimized their claim to the land and their attempts to repossess it.

In order to understand better and analyze the nature of these three movements, it will be useful to present a brief overview of the various types of social movements. Rudolf Herberle defines a social movement as a collective effort to transform established

*Earlier versions of this paper were presented at a Workshop on Social Movements organised by the Centre of Advanced Study in Sociology, Delhi University, March 1976, and in *Social Action*, 26(3), July-Sept. 1976, pp. 253-66.

The author wishes to gratefully thank Prof. M.S.A. Rao, Prof. Andre Beteille and Dr. Alfred de Souza for their valued suggestions.

relations within a particular society.[2] Neil Smelser views social movements as directly oriented towards a change in social institutions and social norms.[3] One, however, has to be careful not to identify a social movement merely on the basis of the tactics used to mobilize and involve the masses. Another important factor is the ideological thrust behind every social movement which aims at revamping or restructuring a society. Most writers tend to agree with Paul Wilkinson's view that two basic elements, namely, a minimal degree of organization and a commitment to change, are necessary for the existence of a social movement.[4]

On the basis of the structural changes they seek to bring about in an existing society, social movements may be classified as reformative, transformative or revivalistic.[5] Reformative movements are those that aim only at a partial change or modification in the existing social structure without seeking to replace it.[6] Examples of this are mass insurrections seeking to redress particular grievances. Transformative or revolutionary movements aim at replacing the whole of a particular social structure with a more suitable one. The various rebellions aimed at driving out the British or other colonizers and in restoring earlier rulers and social structures are clear examples of these types of movements. Revivalistic movements are backward looking in the sense that they seek to restore 'the good old days'.[7] Ralph Linton subsumes both revivalistic and perpetuative movements under one typology which he calls nativistic, defining it as 'any conscious organised attempt on the part of a society's members to revive or perpetuate selected aspects of their culture'.[8] This classification, however, is not a rigid one, since a social movement might initially be reformative in nature and become transformative as it gains momentum. In fact, Mclaughlin views revolutionary and reform movements as parts of a continuum.[9]

Social movements can also be classified according to the various typologies based on goals, ideologies and methods of organization. Thus we have religious movements, political movements, agrarian movements, millenarian movements, messianic movements, student movements, etc.[10] A point which must be kept in mind is that the ideology of a movement should not be separated from its social context. As is often the case, it is not the ideology which forms the initial impetus for a movement but it is the situation, say conditions of relative deprivation, which influences the specific characteristics of the ideology.

Social movements among the tribals have been widely prevalent in India during and after the British Raj. Raghaviah reports that there were more than seventy tribal uprisings over a period of nearly two hundred years.[11] This is not astonishing especially when one realizes that, as a result of the socio-political changes which the tribals have been experiencing, a number of administrative, economic, political and religious forces have influenced the tribal communities. Though in some cases the tribal response to these impinging forces has been one of acceptance and adaptation, the reaction of almost all the major tribal communities has been one of resistance giving rise to a number of social movements varying in ideologies and modes of organization and effectiveness.[12] Each of these uprisings expressed the desperation of the tribal groups and invariably they were ruthlessly suppressed.

Following these tribal rebellions and, in certain cases even without such precedence, a number of reformative movements were started with the idea of emulating the Hindu cultural pattern. Thus we have the various Bhagat movements among the Oraons and the Bhils, the Kharwar Movement among the Santals, the Vaishnavite reform movement among the Bhumij, and others.[13] In his book *Rebellious Prophets: A Study of Messianic Movements in India* (1965), Fuchs describes more than fifty social movements among tribals which had certain messianic and millenarian overtones. According to him, these movements were led by prophetic leaders who were believed to possess supernatural powers and who claimed to usher in a terrestrial state of righteousness and justice that would correspond to the widely accepted myth of the Golden Age.

The purpose of the present paper, which is based on data collected mostly from secondary sources such as earlier ethnographic writings, gazetteers, administrative reports and documents, is to understand the interaction of the major historical, cultural, economic, political and religious factors underlying the Santal Rebellion, the Kharwar Movement and the Jharkhand Movement among the Santals. It would appear that the social movements which took place among the Santals tended to serve several interests at the same time. Yet, as will be shown in the course of this paper, the sociological significance of these complex movements can perhaps be best understood if they are viewed mainly as nativistic movements. The three social movements that will be studied here aimed at 'combining traditional cultural elements and values with new themes derived from the oppressing groups, in an utopian vision of a Golden Age'.[14] Though one particular aspect might have predominated over others at a particular stage, they were invariably interrelated so that these movements were in varying degrees economic as well as religious and political.

The Rebellion 1855-1857

The Santals are the largest homogenous tribe in the subcontinent.[15] According to the 1971 Census, they numbered 3,633,459, or 9.55 per cent of the country's Scheduled Tribes' population.[16] They are mostly to be found in Bihar (1,801,304) and West Bengal (1,376,980). They are, in fact, the largest of the Scheduled Tribes of these two states constituting 36.51 and 54.36 per cent respectively of these states' Scheduled Tribes' population.[17] They are also to be found in large numbers in Assam, Meghalaya and Orissa, in Nepal and Bangladesh.

Since the Santals have no written records of their own, various theories have been advanced regarding the origin of these Austro-Asiatic aboriginals, whose own traditions represent them as a race wandering from one country to another. But whatever their origins might have been, authentic records show that by about the middle of the eighteenth century, large numbers of Santals were to be found in Chotanagpur especially in the districts of Hazaribagh, Palamau and Singhbhum, and in the neighbouring districts of Midnapore and Birbhum. Thus as early as 1795, Sir John Shore spoke of the Santals of Ramgarh in Birbhum district.[18] Toward the end of the eighteenth century, the Santals, who were 'very expert in clearing forests and bringing them into cultivation',[19] began to migrate to the Rajmahal Hills situated on the North-eastern side of the Chotanagpur plateau. Two reasons can be given for this migration. Towards the end of the eighteenth century, many of the Chotanagpur jungles had been cleared and there was a considerable influx of population from the infertile uplands which could not support them. Second, the introduction of the Permanent Zamindari Settlement by the East India Company in 1793 'resulted in a general extension of tillage'[20] and in the creation of a new set of landlords based on the English feudal pattern. These landlords began hiring Santal labourers to clear the virgin forests in the Rajmahal Hills' area so as to bring more land under cultivation. They enticed them by promising them high wages and rent-free farms.

This area had been the homeland of the Malers and the Mal Paharias, notorious robbers and cattle lifters who often raided the villages in the plains.[21] Various unsuccessful efforts were made by the British government to win over these tribals and to bring them under control. In 1833 the government demarcated an area surrounding the Rajmahal Hills and comprising 1,366 square miles. It came to be known as the *Damin-i-koh* which literally means 'the skirts of the hills'. The idea behind this move was to declare this hill tract, occupied by tribals, the property of the government. The Santals were now encouraged to settle down in the area. During the next fifteen years, they moved to this region in such great numbers that the population of the area increased by more than twenty-six times. Captain Walter S. Sherwill, who was employed in the government revenue survey of Bihar Province, noted that while in 1838 there were about forty Santal villages in the area with a population of about 3,000, by 1861 the Santal population in the area had increased to 82,795 inhabiting 1,473 villages.[22] The *Damin-i-koh* soon became the centre of Santal life. Little did the government think, however, that these Santals would revolt twenty-two years later.

OPPRESSION

The single most important event in the history of the Santals, the Rebellion of 1855-57, has become part and parcel of their consciousness. This can be seen from the number of dramas and songs celebrating this event and mythologizing its leaders, helping to keep alive in the minds of the present day Santals the memory of this great event. The Santal Rebellion was not 'a mere spasmodic outburst of the crude instincts of the semi-savage Santals',[23] but the outcome of a 'long course of oppression silently and patiently submitted to by these unsophisticated people unaccustomed to fight for their own rights in the legitimate ways of their neighbours'.[24] The Rebellion came at a time when the destitution and sufferings of the Santals had reached an extremely high level because of the oppression and merciless exploitation of the money-lenders, landlords and merchants. In her analysis of peasant uprisings in India, Kathleen Gough points out that 'all of them embodied ideas of freedom from undue economic exploitation or deprivation'[25].

Writing in 1867, twelve years after the outbreak of the rebellion, E.G. Man concluded that four grievances were chiefly responsible for the Santal Rebellion: (i) the grasping and rapacious spirit of the money-lenders in their transactions with the tribals; (*ii*) the increasing misery caused by their iniquitous system of allowing personal and hereditary bondage for debt; (*iii*) unparalleled corruption and extortion of the police in aiding and abetting the *Mahajans* (money-lenders); and (*iv*) the impossibility of the Santals obtaining redress from the courts.[26] There is abundant evidence, as we shall see, that Man's understanding of the Rebellion was substantially correct.

We have already noted how the Santals were induced to migrate to the *Damin-i-koh* with promises which were never honoured. At about the time that they began occupying the *Damin*, Hindu and Muslim traders and moneylenders began to infiltrate the area, and when the Santals took loans, they found themselves trapped in a vicious circle of extortion from which they could not escape in their lifetime. Before long they were reduced to mere tenants while the traders and moneylenders rapidly amassed large fortunes by securing cash and grains from the Santals through various obnoxious means.[27] The immigrant landlords took advantage of the Santals' misfortunes and started exacting heavy taxes which the over-burdened Santals could not pay. As a result they were forcibly ousted out from their property.

Bondage System

One of the devices used to exploit the Santals was the execution of bonds. There were two kinds of bondage systems—the *kamiotee* and the *harwahee*. According to the former, a man borrowed money binding himself to work without pay for the moneylender whenever required till the loan was repaid. Under the *harwahee* system, the borrower had, in addition to personal service, to plough the moneylender's fields whenever required till his loan was repaid. It was thus practically impossible for the borrower to repay the loan because his services were required during harvest time and the other busy seasons of the year, and this did not leave him enough time to plough his own fields or work for wages. As interest was taken in advance, the debtor could never work off his debt. The debtor's children and near relatives were considered liable in the case of his death.[28] As *The Calcutta Review* reported in 1860, the Santal thus 'saw his crops, his cattle, even himself and family appropriated for a debt which ten times paid remained an incubus upon him still'.[29] To make matters worse the Santals were also harassed by some of the Europeans who were then working as railway employees. *The Calcutta Review* of 1856 reports how the Santals quite often saw their houses pillaged, their crops stolen, their women molested and their children murdered by these 'foreign' workers.[30]

The Santals had made many attempts to present their grievances to the government but were repeatedly rebuffed. The courts of law gave more security to the propertied classes and, so far as the Santals were concerned, legalized the rapacity of the money-lenders. Administration in the *Damin-i-koh* area was riddled with abuses. For revenue administration, the area was under the supervision of a superintendent assisted by four *naib suzawalas* who used to visit the area in order to collect rent and settle land disputes. They were notoriously corrupt. For civil and criminal cases, the Santals had to go to the courts at Bhagalpur or Deoghar. It was extremely difficult for the Santals to gain regular access to these courts not only because of the inconvenience of the long journey but also because of the corruption of the *amlahs* (clerks), *mukhtiars* (pleaders) and peons attached to these courts. Since the Santals did not know any other language apart from Santali, they were forced to make use of interpreters and pleaders who were in the pay of their oppressors. As *The Calcutta Review* reported in 1860, while the Santal 'found justice in the shape of the Magistrate so far off and so terribly difficult of access, he found justice nearer home in the shape of Darogahs and thannah police, the authorised agents of the district magistrate, but found it only to find it his bane'.[31] Thus the situation in the *Damin-i-koh* prior to the rebellion was one in which the zamindars, the police, and the revenue and court clerks, managed a combined system of extortion, and subjected the vulnerable and illiterate Santals to forcible dispossession of property, abuse and personal violence and a variety of petty tyrannies.

The Santals were in desperation. The oppression was also felt by those outside the *Damin-i-koh*. Signs of disorder began appearing on the horizon. A Santal *manjhi* (village chief) by the name of Morgo Rajah unsuccessfully attempted to organize the Santals of the southern area into a separate kingdom.[32] In the beginning of 1854, Bir Singh, a Santal *pargana*,[33] proclaimed that in a vision he had of Cando Bonga, the Santals' main spirit, he had received magical charms by means of which the Santals' exploiters would be punished. Soon he had an enthusiastic following and they held a number of meetings at night under the pretence of worship. These meetings often led to various robberies from the houses of traders and money-lenders.

LAND

Though the demands of the Santals preceding the Rebellion were mainly concerned with the improvement of their general economic situation, the question of land had a special significance for them. As Culshaw points out, 'Economic factors alone will not give a solution to the question of why the Santals rebelled. . . . Hunger drove them to despair, but their attachment to the land provided also an emotional basis without which the rebellion might not have taken place.'[31] Here it is worth noting that for the Santals, as also for most of the tribals, land provides not only economic security but a powerful link with one's ancestors. In fact no land is taken possession of unless the spirits first approve of it. This is evident from the number of ominous beliefs associated with the selection of a site for a new village.[35] Thus, for the Santals, land is part of their spiritual as well as their economic heritage. As a result of the extortions of the landlords and money-lenders, the Santals had no security in the possession of the very lands they themselves had made fit for cultivation. In the course of time the *Deku* settlers acquired more and more of the land mortgaged by the Santals.[36]

Another important element in the complex of factors which pushed the Santals into rebellion was the yearning for independence, the dream of the ancient days when they had no overlords. Thus Sidhu and Kanhu, whose home was in Bhognadi near Barhait in the very heart of the *Damin-i-koh*, announced that 'we will kill and make an end of all the *Deku* rule ourselves and whoever does not listen, show him a sword'.[37] This urge for independence reached its climax when Sidhu and Kanhu proclaimed that they had witnessed a divine apparition and had received a divine message from Suba Thakur, the supreme deity of the Santals, urging them to lead the Santals in a rebellion. It is a well-known fact that religion has often acted as an important motivating force in starting various social movements. Thus Sidhu and Kanhu's claim that it was

God's wish that the Santals revolt against their oppressors appeared to be the spark needed to kindle the conflagration. This religious sanction gave the leaders the authority they required to be accepted by the Santals and the news of the apparition was sent by messengers to all the headmen of the *Damin-i-koh*.

MARCH TO CALCUTTA

In spite of all this, however, the Rebellion did not get under way immediately. The leaders first petitioned the local authorities to redress their grievances by regulating the widespread usury and reducing the land tax. They proclaimed that this was necessary since their supreme deity had directed them to collect and pay revenue to the state at the rate of two annas on every buffalo plough and half anna on each cow plough per annum. Besides, the annual rate of interest on loans was to be one paisa in every rupee.[38] The British Superintendent, however, did not pay any heed to these 'godly' directions. The Santal leaders then approached the Commissioner and told him that if he did not redress their grievances they would do so themselves by taking the law into their hands. But again nothing was done. This resulted in a number of dacoities directed once more against the money-lenders who had been the principal agents of their oppression and misery. As was reported by a contemporary, these robberies were 'well merited reprisals for their (money-lenders') unprovoked cruelties'.[39] The authorities, however, thought otherwise and on the complaint of the money-lenders these outrages were treated as ordinary dacoities and the Santal ring-leaders were caught, tried and convicted.

Seeing no way out of their utter misery, Sidhu and Kanhu sent messengers to announce a meeting at Bhognadi. On 30 June 1855 more than thirty thousand Santals armed with bows and arrows began their march towards Calcutta. A police inspector, instigated by some Hindu and Moslem money-lenders, tried to arrest the leaders but this so enraged the mob that they hacked him and nine members of his platoon to pieces. The cry *Hul! Hul!* (Rebel! Rebel!) was now raised everywhere and the Rebellion got under way. After intermittent battles lasting over a year, the rebellion was eventually crushed by the British. The Santal insurgents suffered heavy losses and the ring leaders were rounded up, summarily tried and hanged.[40]

Reforms

Though the Rebellion was manifestly unsuccessful, it served to draw the attention of the British government to the extent of the oppressive conditions under which the Santals were living. It convinced the government of the necessity of adopting ameliorative judicial and administrative reforms. An inquiry was made into the grievances of the Santals by Ashley Aden. The result was the Act XXXVII of 22 December 1855, which formed the territory in and around the *Damin-i-koh* into a separate non-regulation district called Santal Parganas and placed under the control of the Commissioner of Bhagalpur. This new district created from the districts of Bhagalpur and Birbhum, lies between 23°48′-25°18′ North latitude and 86°28′-87°57′ East longitude. It has an area of 14,129 square kilometres.[41] The new district was divided into four subdistricts—Dumka, Deoghar (including Jamtara), Godda and Rajmahal (including Pakaur)—and placed under a Deputy Commissioner and four assistant commissioners.[42]

It was also decided to introduce a special system of administration and an attempt was made to utilize the Santal village organization in administering the area. Thus the Police Rules of 1856 gave police powers to the headman of every Santal village (*manjhi*) and the *pargana* (head of a number of villages). The Deputy Commissioner was given the right to appoint and dismiss a *manjhi* or a *pargana*.[43] A non-regulation system was thus introduced, the main feature of which was a direct communication between the people and their British rulers. This system did away with any intermediary between the Santals and the Assistant Commissioner since complaints were to be made verbally. This innovation was of great importance for, as Culshaw remarks, previously the government was not only geographically remote from the situation but was also completely ignorant of the people's problems. To make things worse, the administration had previously almost been in the hands of the Darogas, who were known to be corrupt.

Another legal measure taken by the government was the abolition of the *kamiotee* system of bondage in 1858. The Santal Rebellion did not, however, only attract the attention of the government to the poignant exploitation and oppression which the Santals were undergoing but also that of a number of Christian missionaries. Thus in 1862 the Church Missionary Society started work in the northern part of the new district.[44]

Kharwar Movement

The period following the Rebellion was not, however, entirely peaceful. Slowly the Santal Parganas district began to slide back into the regulation system and the privileges of the Santals began once more to be taken away from them. To start with, Act XXXVII of 1855 which, as mentioned earlier, set up the district of Santal Parganas, was largely amended by Act X of 2 May 1857 with the result that the size of the district was considerably reduced. This was done on the representations of European indigo planters, zamindars and *raiyats* who pointed out that the designation of their area as a non-regulation district of Santal Parganas was improper since the Santals were not the majority group inhabiting the area.

With the opening of new roads quite a number of Bhojpuris from north Bihar and Bengalis from Calcutta swarmed into the district. They were more than willing to lend money to the spendthrift Santals in exchange for their lands. Though the *kamiotee* system of bondage was abolished, the government neither curtailed the high rates of interest nor made arrangements for cheap agricultural credit to the Santals who had, once again, to resort to the money-lenders.

Since the Santal Parganas was administered as a non-regulation district, a question arose as to whether the Stamp Law should be enforced. The issue was referred to the Advocate-General who decided in 1863 that there was no reason to exempt the district from the operation of any general law passed after 1855. As a result, the Santals were made to pay ever increasing rents, many of their village headmen were dismissed and a lot of rent-free land was seized by the rapacious landlords. A spirit of resentment swept throughout the district bringing the Santals to the point of a mass upsurge once again.

Golden Age

The failure of the Rebellion was, however, still fresh in their minds. They realized that the path to better economic conditions through militant methods was closed and thus could not openly revolt against the British or those whom they supported. This realization was the beginning of a new consciousness which manifested itself in another social movement. Called the Kharwar Movement, it was motivated by the desire to return to an idealized past of tribal independence and glory that is celebrated in Santal myths. According to Skrefsrud, the word Kharwar 'is the ancient name of the Santals and in their minds is inseparably associated with the Golden Era of their history, namely the time when they lived in Campa in absolute independence and had no rent or tribute to pay but only to bring a small offering to pay to their leaders in virtue of their office'.[45]

It is not known exactly when the movement actually started. It, however, achieved prominence when, in 1871, a charismatic leader, Bhagirath Manjhi of Godda sub-division who added the title of babaji to his name, announced that he would restore the Golden Age to the Santals if they returned to the worship of one God and cleansed themselves of their sins. As the 'king' of the 'new Santal Raj',[46] he endeavoured to liberate the Santal country from the oppressors—the sahibs, zamindars and *mahajans*. While exhorting the people to worship the Hindu deity, Ram, whom he identified with the Santal Cando, he assured them that their lands would be recovered. Their present oppression, he explained, was a divine punishment for abandoning the worship of the one God and turning to the veneration of minor and evil spirits. His teaching was in keeping with Santal traditions according to which their ancestors had worshipped only Thakur and had no *bongas* (spirits).[47]

However, since they were unable to recover their land, the number of his followers began dwindling. So Bhagirath changed the style of his preaching, particularly after the severe famine of 1874. He told the people that the Rebellion had failed because they had committed the sin of having sexual relations with non-Santal women.[48] Only if they purified themselves would God, or Ram Cando, restore their lands to them. He instructed the people not to let fowls or pigs pollute the Burma rice (imported by the government because of the famine), and to bathe daily before cooking their food. These new norms of behaviour which Bhagirath sought to impose on the Santals reflected Hindu notions of ritual purity and pollution. The people, however, began to lose faith in Bhagirath and in his teaching when they found out that they had to repay the government for the Burma rice which they had thought was a gift from the gods. Later, when he attempted to politicize the movement by instigating the Santals to refuse payment of taxes on the land they cultivated, Bhagirath was arrested and imprisoned.

After Bhagirath, the movement was kept alive by several babajis who claimed to have received a mandate from Ram Cando to work for the economic upliftment of the Santals. In general they were more preoccupied with religious ideas rather than with political action. In 1880, Dubia Gosain, who came from the vicinity of Deoghra, introduced the worship of the babaji, much as the Hindus revere sanyasis. He smeared his body with ashes and kept long hair and also started taking *ganja*. Using the Census operations of 1881, he instigated the Santals to clamour for a tribal administration. Following his directives, the Santals objected to the numbering of their houses and the recording of their names. Seeing this, the British government took immediate action, arresting Gosain and placing the entire area under the control of the police and the army.

Division

After this, although mention is made of an outbreak during the 1897 famine, the Kharwar Movement went underground and in the next few decades it split into three distinct sects—the Sapha Hor, Samra and Babajiu.[49] Even after this division, these three sects retained the same practices, sharing in common the worship of Ram Cando. Later, however, they became more sanskritized and exclusive. The members of the Sapha Hor observed strict commensal norms which forbade them from eating in the houses of those who did not belong to the sect. These 'outsiders' were not invited to participate in ceremonies and life-cycle events of the Sapha Hor. They abandoned what they considered to be degrading practices, such as the keeping and eating of fowls and pigs and the drinking of *handi* (rice-beer) and other intoxicants. They could eat their morning meal only after taking a purificatory bath. They also recognized Mahadev as their one deity.

In 1930 a new reform movement started by Bangam Manjhi attracted a number of followers. His teachings supported the practices of the Sapha Hor, particularly regarding the daily purificatory bath and abstaining from meat and liquor. To these Bangam added the exclusive use of Khadi clothing and exhorted the Santals not to dance anywhere except in their villages. This movement caught the attention of the local Congress Party leaders. Fuchs reports that 'their meetings were held in full moon nights and some of them were attended by such prominent persons as Sardar Vallabhai Patel and Dr. Rajendra Prasad'.[50] In May 1930, two hundred and ten Santals were invested with the sacred thread, or *janeo*. The *janeo dhari* Santal, that is those who wear the sacred thread, regarded themselves as socially superior to those who did not wear the thread. They were reluctant to intermarry or to have social intercourse with the non-*janeo dhari* Santals. A strong cleavage separated the two groups. Together with various revolutionaries from Bihar and Bengal, the Sapha Hor members played a prominent role in the Indian freedom movement.[51] They took part not only in the various demonstrations organized during the freedom movement but also engaged in acts of violence and sabotage, as a result of which many were arrested and sent to jail.

Thus every now and then the Kharwar Movement was stirred into life again by prophets who claimed divine inspiration and who proclaimed that through their miraculous powers they could deliver the Santals from the oppression and misery they were in. The Movement came to life especially in times of great calamity which were taken by the Santals to be signs of the supreme deity's displeasure.

As a result of the Kharwar Movement, especially the working of its three sects, the Santals began generally moving towards Hinduization with increasing ambivalence. The emulation of Hindu socio-religious practices by the Santals was regarded as a means of raising their status in the eyes of their Hindu neighbours and of putting themselves on an equal footing with them, thus lessening the degree of subordination which was the main cause of their suffering.[52] But in the 1930s, various political events external to Santal society helped to check this drift which to many village elders seemed to be threatening tribal solidarity and autonomy. The path which the Santals were following to free themselves from their misery and oppression was profoundly altered. This change was marked by a shift in emphasis from the socio-religious to the political aspect.

Jharkhand Movement

With the spread of the national freedom movement, a new political consciousness emerged among the tribals of the Chotanagpur plateau, broadly referred to in Indian literature as the Jharkhand,[53] and which, as a result of the high concentration of tribals to be found in the area, constituted what is commonly called Tribal Bihar.[54] Though the Jharkhand Movement, as it later came to be known, did not originate specifically among the Santals, its ideology coincided with the aspirations of the Santals with the result that many soon became members.

Among the various factors which generated this Movement, perhaps the most important factor was the strong antipathy towards the *Deku* who were thought of as being the cause of the ever growing discontent among the tribals of Chotanagpur. The Movement was thus marked by a deep sense of an exclusive *Adibasi* identity and aimed at getting rid of the non-tribal economic exploiters and oppressors. Another important factor in the emergence of this Movement was the advent of Christianity in the area which opened up new vistas to the tribals. The Christian missionaries were the pioneers in spreading education, medical care and social welfare among the tribals, thus giving them new opportunities for economic improvement and freedom. Christianity was also instrumental in rousing the tribals' political consciousness.[55] Many tribal leaders received their education in Christian schools and some were even sent abroad for further training.

A small group of educated tribal Christians, moved by the pathetic state of their brethren, felt the urgent need for a united tribal organization. In 1920 they officially launched the Chotanagpur Unnati Samaj aiming at the uplift of the tribals and at improving their social and economic conditions. Only *Adibasis* were allowed to become members of the Samaj which, especially in the beginning, contributed considerably towards inter-tribal unity in the region. After some time, however, in-fighting began to develop and a few Samaj members left the organization and formed two other organizations—the Kisan Sabha dominated mostly by *Adibasis* from the Anglican and Lutheran Missions and by non-Christians, and the Chotanagpur Catholic Sabha which was chiefly restricted to the Catholic aboriginals of Chotanagpur. This split considerably weakened the mother organization.

The formation in 1936 of Orissa as a Province separate from Bihar had serious repercussions on these three *Adibasi* organizations. Mr. Ignace Beck, the general secretary of the Chotanagpur Catholic Sabha who had great political influence in the area, realized that unless the *Adibasis* presented a common front setting aside all denominational differences, their salvation from economic, political and social exploitation would never be achieved. As a result of his constant efforts, an alliance called the Adibasi Mahasabha was formed. The general conference, which took place in May 1938, officially declared that the Mahasabha would serve as the only organization to represent the interests of the tribals. Asserting its tribal identity it was decided that its leaders were to fight against the *Deku* exploiters, work for improving the economic, social and political status of the *Adibasis* and aim at the formation of a separate *Adibasi* state.

Under the charismatic leadership of Jaipal Singh, an Oxford educated Munda Christian who in 1939 was elected president of the Mahasabha, the movement gathered momentum and spread all over the Chotanagpur plateau. In his bid to universalize the cause of a Jharkhand state, Jaipal Singh sought the co-operation of the non-*Adibasi* residents of the region who were not considered as *deku* having been settled in Chotanagpur for generations. At his insistence, the general session of the Mahasabha, held at Jamshedpur in 1949, decided that though the Mahasabha would remain essentially a tribal organization, its membership would be extended to non-*Adibasi* Jharkhandis.

Following the establishment of a democratic form of government in India based on adult franchise, the Adibasi Mahasabha emerged as a full-fledged political party in 1951. It took the name of Jharkhand Party and the cock as its symbol. In the First General Elections of 1952, the Party won all the thirty-two seats in the Bihar Legislative Assembly which it contested. It emerged as the main opposition party in the state. In Orissa, also, the Party won a considerable victory making it necessary for the ruling party to win over the support of the elected Jharkhandis. Prior to the elections, Jaipal Singh proclaimed that the Jharkhand was the land of the *Adibasis* and that there was little hope of their regeneration unless the non-*Adibasi* exploiters quit the Jharkhand. The mobilizers of the Movement echoed the slogan 'Jharkhand abua, daku *Deku* senoa' which means 'Jharkhand is ours, the dacoit *Deku* will go'.

Three years later, in January 1955, a memorandum was submitted by the executive committee of the Jharkhand Party to the States' Reorganisation Commission emphasizing the economic, political and cultural imperatives for the formation of a separate Jharkhand state.[56] The memorandum stated that ethnically, linguistically and culturally, the *Adibasis* were distinct from the non-tribals. Besides this tribal homogeneity and the fact that the tribals, who formed the biggest community in the area, were losing their identity, there was also a certain geographical contiguity and an administrative separativeness which more than justified the claim for a separate state within the Republic of India. The proposed separate state, to be known as the Jharkhand, was to be made up of six districts of Bihar and nine districts of Bengal, Madhya Pradesh and Orissa.[57] This demand for a separate state was, however, turned down by the States' Reorganisation Commission who pointed out that the Jharkhand tribals did not have a common language.

The protagonists of the All India Jharkhand Party thought that their main objective of a separate Jharkhand state would only materialize if they merged with the ruling Congress Party. Following the merger in September 1963, however, the party was characterized by a number of factions and cleavages. By the time of the General Elections of 1967, three distinct tribal parties had emerged within the Jharkhand—the original All India Jharkhand Party under the leadership of Bagun Sumbrui, a Ho; the Jharkhand Party headed by N.E. Horo, a Munda Christian; and the Hul Jharkhand Party headed by Sibu Murmu, a Santal. While the Jharkhand Party is dominated mainly by Christian legislators of the Chotanagpur division with the support of some Ho Hindu legislators, the Hul Jharkhand Party consists mainly of Santal legislators. As the name *hul*, which means 'rebellion', indicates, the members of this party declared that they were ready to go to any lengths in the cause of their people, even to the point of violence. Though both the Hul Jharkhand and the Jharkhand parties claim affinity with the All India Jharkhand Party and have as their main objective a separate statehood for Jharkhand, a lot of in-fighting prevails among their leaders. After the relative defeat that the Jharkhand parties experienced in the Fourth General Elections, N.E. Horo tried to bring about an alliance between these three parties. His efforts, however, did not meet with any success.

The pattern of leadership among these three parties has been secularized in many ways. With the extension of its membership to non-*Adibasis*, the party started emphasizing the needs of the region as a whole rather than that of the tribals only. This affected the Party's almost exclusively Christian oriented leadership. Till the Third General Elections in 1962, most of the leaders of the

Jharkhand Party, with the exception of a small minority, were educated tribal Christians. Five years later, not only were a considerable number of non-Christian tribals given a Party ticket but non-tribal Jharkhandis were occupying important positions in the three different parties. This factor considerably weakened the influence which the Party initially enjoyed among the *Adibasi* Jharkhandis.

In spite of the intermittent failures which the Party had to face and the fact that the Jharkhandis have not yet attained their goal of a separate statehood, the continuity of the Jharkhand Movement proves that this objective is far from dormant. This is also evident from the several organizations which have emerged in the Chotanagpur plateau aimed at protecting the *Adibasis'* rights, preventing the alienation of their land, improving their socio-economic status and renewing the demand for a Jharkhand state separate from Bihar.[58]

Conclusion

It can now be seen that though the three movements assumed different forms of expression through the process of economic transformation, Sanskritization, and the growing consciousness of a separate ethnic identity leading to a political awareness, their ideological thrust was by and large the same, namely—the restoration of the Golden Age, so much a part of Santal mythology. This rationalized their claim to the land and justified the various attempts to re-possess it from their exploiters. The leaders of the Rebellion and the Kharwar Movement reiterated the slogan that all the land belonged to the Santals, while the Jharkhand Movement claimed that Jharkhand belonged only to the *Adibasi* Jharkhandis. In the three movements the situation of oppression and exploitation made the Santals increasingly conscious of the mythological roots of their ideology.

An analysis of the three movements shows that the leaders foresaw not only economic relief but increased political power and an opportunity to improve the status of the Santals. The Kharwar Movement had two aspects—the political and the socio-religious. Politically it aimed at the restoration of tribal independence and at resisting the paying of land rent. The socio-religious aspect of the movement was characterized by the incorporation of Sanskritic religious symbols and practices such as the giving up of eating meat and drinking rice-beer and other intoxicants, taking to vegetarianism and *ganja* instead, adopting the habit of daily purificatory baths and the use of the sacred thread.

A question arises as to why, as Martin Orans points out, 'while wishing to triumph over the oppressive Hindus, the Santals thought of cashing in on the victory with the traditional Hindu symbols of rank'.[59] Before attempting to answer this question it is worth noting that the tribals of India have been influenced by the traditions of their neighbouring communities, the dominant community often being the Hindus. This is evident from the fact that, by and large, the tribals have borrowed heavily from the ideas and institutions of the Hindus.[60] For at least a thousand years before the advent of Islam in the thirteenth century, the Santals may be said to have been in contact with the Hindus.[61] As a result, various aspects of Santal life—material, social, economic, linguistic and religious—have been affected by Hindu culture.[62] The influence of Hinduism on Santal religious beliefs and practices is manifest in the incorporation of Hindu deities, like Siva, Lakshmi, Parvati, Ram, Kali, Durga, and Krishna, in the Santal pantheon, and in the addition of certain festivals, like the Pata Porob and the Chata Porob, which are believed to be of Hindu origin, to the Santal festival cycle.[63] The institution of *ojhaism* (medicine-man) shows a great deal of Hindu influence. Some of the marriage and funerary ceremonies are closely analogous to certain Hindu practices. Thus the continuous first-hand contact between the Santals and the Hindus did create a condition favourable for acculturation and generally led to reciprocal borrowings. By itself, however, this contact was not a sufficient cause for any radical readjustment. It was mainly with the Kharwar Movement that the acculturation of the Santals towards Hinduism was accelerated. The material conditions of the Santals facilitated the success of the Movement.

As mentioned earlier, the Kharwar Movement arose at a time of acute crisis and desperation among the Santals, when pragmatic methods for the redress of their wrongs by legal and military means had failed. The claim of Sidhu and Kanhu that it was God's wish that the Santals revolt against their non-tribal oppressors gave the leaders the authority they required to be accepted by the Santals and to start the rebellion. The gods could not fail them. The defeat of the Rebellion, however, shook their belief in the efficacy of their *bongas*. As a result of their relative deprivation and constant exploitation, the Santals were anxious to try any means to improve their economic conditions. Pragmatically, they now had three directions in which they could turn—Islam, Hinduism and Christianity. Since even today the Santals have a strong aversion for what they call the *Turuk* (the old Musulman cavalry), the choice of Islam was out of the question. This left only two alternatives—Christianity and Hinduism.

Considering the milieu in which the Santals existed, it is understandable that they adopted the socio-religious practices of the dominant Hindu community who had the advantage of economic power and high prestige. The Hindus thus functioned as the Santals' referents. The Santals believed that by doing so they would raise their status, reduce the degree of subordination in the eyes of the Hiudus, and improve their economic conditions.[64] Martin Orans explains this phenomenon of emulating the practices of the oppressors through what he calls the 'rank concession syndrome', meaning the acceptance of social inferiority.[65] By conceding rank to the dominant Hindus, the Santals placed themselves in an inferior status. Their resentment at their low status produced a tendency towards emulation and what Orans calls 'power incorporative borrowing'.[66] This process is very similar to Srinivas' concept of Sanskritization.

The adoption of Hindu practices, however, did not change the basic characteristics of the Santal religion. As Mukhopadhyay points out, 'the religion of the Austrics is still a distinctive culture and . . . can be seen in its pristine glory even today'.[67] What the Santals aimed at was not conversion to Hinduism but to strike out new directions of their own.

Desirous of maintaining their identity, the Santals found in the Jharkhand Movement an opportunity to emeliorate their social and economic conditions on the one hand, and, on the other, to create a 'great tradition' of their own.[68] Asserting themselves politically, they joined forces with the other tribals of the Chotanagpur region and demanded the formation of a separate Jharkhand state as the homeland of the *Adibasis*. From what has been said earlier, three factors can be pointed out as being crucial in the emergence of the Jharkhand Movement: (*i*) the idea that the Jharkhand was the land of the *Adibasis* and that the non-*Adibasi* exploiters who were ethnically different had brought misery and backwardness to the *Adibasis*; (*ii*) the penetration of Christianity in the area encouraged and supported the emergence of new leadership to improve the socio-economic conditions of the *Adibasis*; and (*iii*) the geographical contiguity and administrative separativeness of the Chotanagpur plateau.

Though the Jharkhand Party, as it emerged in 1952, was a purely political party, the underlying forces behind the Jharkhand Movement were more socio-economic and ethnic rather than political. This latter factor can only be seen as a consequence of the first two factors.[69] In fact, as Surajit Sinha remarks, 'the dramatic initial success of the Jharkhand Party has been due to the fact that the leaders have been able to utilise the intense unfavourable image about the outsiders in the minds of the tribals in this area'.[70]

Our analysis of the three movements shows that the Rebellion was restorative in nature in that it aimed at the expulsion of the British Raj and the Hindu landlords, money-lenders and traders, and sought to usher in the earlier autonomy and social order. It had a religious rationale which was effective in mobilizing the people for the achievement of the primary objective—the restoration of the Santal Raj. The Kharwar Movement primarily aimed at improving the social conditions of the Santals, increasing their ethnic unity, purity and economic prosperity through a reformed religion. After India's Independence, politics became a legitimate sphere which the Santals began to manipulate for the achievement of their aspirations for tribal autonomy and independence.

Notes

1. See for example, Rudolf Herberle, *Social Movements*, New York: Appleton Century Crofts, 1951; A.P.C. Wallace, 'Revitalisation Movements', *American Anthropologist*, 58, 1956, pp. 50-66; W.B. Cameron, *Modern Social Movements*, New York: Random House, 1966; Barry Mclaughlin (ed.), *Studies in Social Movements*, New York: Free Press, 1969; Paul Wilkinson, *Social Movements*, London: Pall Mall, 1971.
2. A similar definition is given by Herbert Blumer in *Symbolic Interactionism: Perspective and Method*, New Jersey: Prentice Hall, 1969.
3. Neil J. Smelser, *Theory of Collective Behaviour*, New York: Free Press, 1962.
4. Paul Wilkinson, op. cit., pp. 26-47.
5. Barry Mclaughlin (op. cit., p. 4), identifies two main types of social movements, namely 'revolutionary' and 'reform' movements.
6. According to Mclaughlin, op. cit., p. 4, 'the reform movement accepts existing norms and values and uses them to criticise the social defects it opposes'.

7. L.K. Mahapatra, 'Social Movements among Tribes of India', in K. Suresh Singh (ed.), *Tribal Situation in India*, Simla: Indian Institute of Advanced Study, 1972, p. 400. To this classification, Mahapatra adds conservative or perpetuative movements which, according to him, aim at perpetuating the status quo and thus are organized to obstruct any current changes.
8. Ralph Linton, 'Nativistic Movements', *American Anthropologist*, 45, 1943, p. 320. He classifies nativistic movements under a four-fold scheme—revivalistic or perpetuative in emphasis and magical or rational in type, (ibid., pp. 231-34). According to Wallace, op. cit., nativistic movements are characterized by a strong urge to do away with whatever is alien to a society's culture, be it persons, customs, norms or values.
9. Mclaughlin, op. cit., p. 4.
10. In Wilkinson's 'typology' social movements are grouped according to a ten-fold classification. See Wilkinson, op. cit., pp. 51-2.
11. V. Raghaviah, *Tribal Revolts*, Nellore: Andhra Rashtra Adimjati Sevak Sangh, 1971. Among the notable tribal revolts in India we find the rebellion of the Maler of the Rajmahal Hills in 1772; the Ganganarain Hangama (1832) among the Bhumij; the Kol uprising of 1831; the Santal rebellion of 1855; the Bhokta rising and the Rai movement of 1857; the rebellion of the Kacha Nagas (1880s); the Sardari or Mulhi Larai (1885); and the Birsa movement (1900) among the Mundas.
12. Kathleen Gough's classification of peasant revolts during the British rule yields five types of action in terms of objectives and methods of organisation: restorative rebellions; religious movements; social banditry; terrorist vengeance; and mass insurrection. See 'Indian Peasant Uprisings', *Economic and Political Weekly*, 9 (32-34), August 1974, pp. 1391-412.
13. In his book *Oraon Religion and Customs* (Calcutta: Editions Indian, 1972, reprint, pp. 227-97), S.C. Roy has enumerated as many as four religious movements among the Oraons. They are the Nemha or Bhuiphut Bhagats; the Bachhi-Dan Bhagats including Vishnu Bhagats; the Kabirpanthi Bhagats and the Tana Bhagats. For a description of how these Bhagat movements have influenced the Bhils, see S.L. Doshi, *Bhils: Between Societal Self Awareness and Cultural Synthesis*, New Delhi: Sterling Publishers (P) Ltd., 1971, pp. 166-75.
14. Kathleen Gough, op. cit., p. 1395.
15. Numerically, according to the *Census of India*, the Gonds and the Bhils are larger. They are, however, very heterogeneous and in fact are considered to be constituents of a group of tribes designated by a common name.
16. This figure, however, must be accepted with some reservations. It does not include fairly large numbers of Santals to be found in certain states like Assam and Meghalaya where they are not listed as Scheduled Tribes.
17. In Bihar, they are mainly concentrated in the districts of Santal Parganas, Singhbhum, Hazaribagh, Dhanbad and Purnea. In West Bengal, they are mostly to be found in the districts of Midnapore, Purulia, Burdwan, Bankura, West Dinajpur, Birbhum and Malda.
18. See Sir John Shore, 'On Some Extraordinary Facts, Customs and Practices of the Hindus', *Asiatic Researches*, Calcutta, No. 4, 1795, pp. 331-50.

Further information about the Santals at this early period has been obtained by H.C. Sutherland, *Report on the Management of the Rajmahal Hills dated 8 June, 1819*, Dumka: Deputy Commissioner's Record Room, 1819; Montgomery Martin, *Eastern India*, London, 1832; Walter S. Sherwill, 'Notes upon a Tour through the Rajmahal Hills' *Journal of the Asiatic Society of Bengal*, Calcutta, 20(7), 1851, pp. 544-606; E.G. Man, *Sonthalia and the Sonthals*, London: Tinsley & Co., 1867.

19. McPherson, H., *Note on the Aboriginal Races of the Sonthal Parganas*, 1908.
20. Hunter, W.W., *The Annals of Rural Bengal*, Delhi: Cosmo Publications, 1975, p. 219.
21. B.B. Bradley-Birt, *The Story of an Indian Upland*, London: Smith, Elder and Co., 1905.
22. Walter S. Sherwill, op. cit., p. 548.
23. Kalikinkar Datta, *The Santal Insurrection of 1855-57*, Calcutta: University of Calcutta, 1940, p. 5.
24. Kalikinkar Datta, ibid., p. 10.
25. Kathleen Gough, op. cit., p. 1395.
26. E.G. Man, op. cit., p. 110.
27. Kalikinkar Datta, op. cit., p. 6.
28. William Le Fleming Robinson who worked for the abolition of this form of slavery in the Santal Parganas, reports the case of a Santal who worked the whole of his life to repay the twenty-five rupees he had borrowed. On his death his son, and later his grandson did the same. See George Yule, 'Report on the Sonthal Pergunnahs for 1858', in E.G. Man, op. cit., pp. 22-27.
29. 'The Sonthal Pergunnahs', *The Calcutta Review*, No. 35, July-December 1860, pp. 510-51.
30. See, 'The Sonthal Rebellion', *The Calcutta Review*, 26(51), 1856, pp. 223-64.
31. "The Sonthal Pergunnahs", *The Calcutta Review*, 35, July-December 1860, p. 525.
32. Ibid.
33. A *Pargana* is in charge of a *Parganait* or *Bungalow*--"a confederacy of village communities".
34. W.J. Culshaw and W.G. Archer, 'The Santal Rebellion', *Man in India*, 25(4), December 1945, p. 219.
35. A. Campbell, 'Superstitions of the Santals', *Journal of the Bihar and Orissa Research Society*, 1(2), May 1915, pp. 213-28.
36. The concept of *deku* has changed from time to time. Originally it referred to the oppressive *zamindars* and Bengali money-lenders. Later it was used to encompass also the North Bihari traders, money-lenders, upper-class people and the Punjabi and Marwari businessmen.
37. W.J. Culshaw and W.G. Archer, op. cit., p. 228.
38. *The Calcutta Review* 1856. According to this report usurious interest rates ranging from 50 to 500 per cent were charged by the money-lenders on loans taken by the Santals.
39. Ibid.

40. For further details about the Santal Rebellion see Kalikinkar Datta, 'Original Records about the Santal Insurrection', *Bengal Past and Present*, Calcutta, 48(1), July-September, 1934, pp. 32-7; R. Carstairs, *Harma's Village —A Novel of Santal Life*, Pokhuria: The Santal Mission Press, 1935; Chotrae Desmanjhi, *Chot. ae Deshmanjhi Reak Katha*, Benageria: The Santal Mission Press, 1938; E. Thompson and G.T. Garratt, *Rise and Fulfilment of British Rule in India*, Allahabad: Central Book Depot, 1958; R.R. Diwakar (ed.), *Bihar Through the Ages*, Bombay: Orient Longmans, 1959.
41. The district is bounded on the north by the districts of Bhagalpur and Purnea; on the south by Burdwan and Dhanbad; on the east by Birbhum, Malda and Murshidabad; and on the west by Bhagalpur, Hazaribagh and Monghyr. The river Ganges separates the district from Purnea and Malda, while the Ajai and Barakar rivers separate it from Burdwan and Dhanbad.
42. In 1872, Deoghar, Godda and Rajmahal became sub-divisions. The Deputy Commissioner went to stay in Dumka, the capital of the district. On 31 January 1881, Jamtara and Pakaur became sub-divisions.
43. Though the final appointment of a *manjhi* lies with the Deputy Commissioner, he, however, takes into consideration the villagers' choice and the traditional custom of appointing the nearest male heir to the office. For a detailed study of the rules of the appointment of Santal headmen see *Scheduled V of the Santal Parganas Tenancy (Supplementary) Rules, 1950.* The same holds good for the post of *pargana*.
44. Their mission was known as The Indian Home Mission to the Santals. Other Protestant societies that have made notable contributions to missionary work in the district are the United Free Church of Scotland, the American Methodist Episcopal Mission, the Plymouth Brethren, the American Seventh Day Adventists, the Wesleyan Mission and the Bengal Baptist Dipti Mission.
45. Letter to the Editor, *The Statesman*, 8 November 1880.
46. Kathleen Gough, op. cit., p. 1396.
47. L.S.S.O'Malley, *Bengal District Gazetteers: Santal Parganas, Vol-22*, Calcutta: Bengal Secretariat Book Depot, 1910, p. 146.

    For the Santal ancestors' belief in one god see P.O. Bodding, *Traditions and Institutions of the Santals*, Oslo: A.W. Broggers Boktrykheri, 1942, p. 132. The belief of the Santals in the power of the *bongas* who are said to constantly manifest themselves to men and to intervene in men's enterprises and affairs, is so strong that it colours their whole life. As N. Datta-Majumdar reports in *The Santal: A Study in Cultural-Change* (Calcutta: Manager of Publications, Govt. of India Press, 1956, p. 101), 'The Santals live not only in their human tribal society but in a greater society consisting of supernatural beings as well.'
48. The Santals are very strict about their marriage traditions, especially those regarding tribal endogamy and clan exogamy. The Santals frequently resorted to a form of social ostracism known as *bitlaha*. Indulging in sexual intercourse with a non-Santal was considered the worst kind of offence. For a detailed analysis of *bitlaha* see Sachchidananda, 'Bitlaha: Analysis of

a Santal Situation', *Man in India*, Ranchi, 49(4), December 1969, pp. 280-8.

49. The name Sapha is derived from the word *sapha* which means 'to clean' and refers to the cleaning out of what were considered to be objectionable or polluting practices. Samra is the name of the village in Godda sub-division where the leader of this sect lived. Babajiu (*jiu* in Santali means 'spirit') represented the original group. See P.O. Bodding, 'The Kharwar Movement among the Santals', *Man in India*, Ranchi, 1(3), September 1921, pp. 222-32, and 'A Santal Sect', *The Modern Review*, Calcutta, 31 March 1922, p. 358.
50. Stephen Fuchs, *Rebellious Prophets*, Bombay: Asia Publishing House, 1965, p. 57.
51. R.R. Diwakar, op.cit.
52. See Edward Jay, 'Revitalisation Movements in Tribal India', in L.P. Vidyarthi (ed.), *Aspects of Religion in Indian Society*, Meerut: Kedar Nath Ram Nath, 1961, p. 303.
53. The word Jharkhand literally means 'a tract of forest'. At various times Jharkhand was also known as 'Khukha' and 'Chotanagpur'.
54. The Chotanagpur plateau lies in the southern portion of the state of Bihar. Being a continuation of the Vindhya range it extends up to Orissa in the south and to Bengal in the east.

    In the Chotanagpur Division there are 3,415,600 Scheduled Tribals or 69.24 per cent of the State's total Scheduled Tribal population and 6.06 per cent of the State's total population. In the district of Santal Parganas which is situated on the Chotanagpur plateau, there are 1,154,281 Scheduled Tribals forming 23.40 per cent of the State's total Scheduled Tribal population and 2.05 per cent of the State's total population.
55. See Sachchidananda, *Culture Change in Tribal Bihar*, Calcutta: Bookland (P) Ltd., 1964, pp. 109-11.
56. It is interesting to note that Jaipal Singh did not sign the memorandum.
57. Similar to the Jharkhand movement among the Jharkhandis we find the Hill States' movement in the Assam Hills; the Adisthan movement among the Bhils, etc. These movements which emerged after India's Independence, aimed at the reorganisation of tribal states within the Indian Union.
58. Among these organizations we find the Birsa Seva Dal which was organized among the *Adibasi* youth at the suggestion of Jaipal Singh in 1968. Other organizations include the Jharkhand Morcha, the Jharkhand Diwas and the Jharkhand Mukti Andolan.

    For further details about the Jharkhand movement see K.I. Sharma 'Jharkhand Movement in Bihar', *Economic and Political Weekly*, 11(1-2), 10 Jan. 1976, pp. 37-43; Jyoti Sen, 'The Jharkhand Movement' in K. Suresh Singh (ed.), *Tribal Situation in India*, Simla: Indian Institute of Advanced Study, 1972, pp. 432-7; L.P. Vidyarthi, 'Aspects of Tribal Leadership in Chotanagpur', in L.P. Vidyarthi (ed.), *Leadership in Tribal India*, Bombay: Asia Publishing House, 1967, pp. 127-44.
59. Martin Orans, *The Santal*, Detroit: Wayne State University Press, 1965, p. 33.
60. See N.K. Bose, 'The Hindu Method of Tribal Absorption', *Science and Culture*, Calcutta, 7(4), October 1941, pp. 188-94; S.L. Kalia 'Sanskritisation

and Tribalisation', in T.B. Naik (ed.), *Changing Tribe*, Chindwara: Tribal Research Institute, 1961.

61. N. Datta-Majumdar, op. cit., p. 53.
62. See Ali Amir, *Then and Now—A Study of Socio-Economic Structure and Change in Some Villages near Vishva-Bharati University, Bengal*, Calcutta: Asia Publishing House, 1960; N. Datta-Majumdar, op. cit.; V.K. Kochar, 'Profile of a Tribal Village', *Vanyajati*, 12(2), April 1964, pp. 80-95; Martin Orans, op. cit.; Charulal Mukherjea, *The Santals*, Calcutta: A Mukherjee and Co. Pvt. Ltd., 1962; Saileshwar Prasad, *Where The Three Tribes Meet*, Allahabad: Indian International Publications, 1974.
63. See P.O. Bodding, *Traditions and Institutions of the Santals*, Oslo: A.W. Broggers Boktrykheri, 1942, p. 158.
64. See also the various Bhagat movements and the Bhumij-Kshatriya movement (Surajit Sinha, 'The Media and Nature of Hindu-Bhumij Interactions', *Journal of Asiatic Society* (*Letters and Science*), No. 23, 1957, pp. 23-37.
65. Martin Orans, op. cit., pp. 123-35.
66. Martin Orans, op. cit., p. 125.
    This implied that the Santals regarded the traits of the dominant Hindus as being endowed with special efficacy.
67. Sankarananda Mukhopadhyay, *The Austrics of India*, Calcutta: K.P. Bagchi and Co., 1975, pp. 14-5.
68. Martin Orans, op. cit., p. 106.
69. K.I. Sharma, op. cit.
70. Surajit Sinha, 'Tribal Solidarity Movement in India: A Review', in K. Suresh Singh (ed.), op. cit., p. 417.

13

Geraldine H. Forbes

The Women's Movement in India: Traditional Symbols and New Roles

THE STATUS OF women was an issue of great concern to nineteenth century reformers in India. Their first efforts were directed against certain customs—*sati*, female infanticide and prohibitions against widow remarriage—seen as detrimental to the status of women. Later they tried to educate women and bring them into public life. By the first decade of the twentieth century, a few Indian women were convinced that they needed an all-India women's organization, run by women, to deal with women's problems. Saraladevi Choudhurani, the founder of the Bharat Stree Mahamandal ('Great Circle of Indian Women') in 1910, wrote the following critique of the male champions of the women's movement:

> They are the so-called social reformers. They advertise themselves as champions of the weaker sex; equal opportunities for women, female education and female emancipation are some of their pet subjects of oratory at the annual show. They even make honest efforts at object lessons in the above subjects by persuading educated ladies to come up on their platform and speak for themselves. But woe to the women if they venture to act for themselves.[1]

Between 1910 and 1920 the number of social organizations for women grew rapidly. Called by various names—Mahila Samitis, Women's Clubs, Ladies' Societies—they emerged in the cities and towns of British India and the native states. In 1917 the women of Madras formed the Women's Indian Association which fostered branches and affiliated many of the small societies already in existence.[2] During the next ten years two additional all-India organizations were founded to represent the interests of women: the National Council of Women in India (1925) and the All-India Women's Conference (1926). By 1932 the national women's organizations could claim a joint membership of over 10,000 women.[3]

It is the activities of these women, in both local and national organizations for women, and the activities of the thousands of women who supported and joined the nationalist movement that together make up what has been termed the 'women's movement'. That no distinction has been drawn between the struggle for Independence and the efforts to improve the status of women partly reflects the similarity in the arguments used to draw women into the two types of activity. According to Mahatma Gandhi, the political movement aimed at social and moral regeneration as germane to the fight for freedom from British domination. And in this regeneration, women had an extremely important part to play: 'The foundation on which society rests in the home and dharma is to be cultivated in the home.'[4] Gandhi urged women to 'come out' and join the struggle, continuously insisting that constructive work—spinning, wearing khadi, teaching and 'serving'—were as important as attending meetings.[5] Similarly, the apolitical social organizations were concerned with 'uplift' which had implications for future generations and the future of India.

While this women's movement has elicited numerous expressions of amazement, delight and wonder[6] and accounts that wax eloquent about the leading women and their activities, many questions remain unanswered. If the activities of women in this period are to be viewed as a 'movement', we need to ask questions about the kind of movement it was, the problems it sought to solve, and who became involved. In the following pages, we will look at two leaders of the 'women's movement': Saroj Nalini Dutt, the founder of the Mahila Samiti movement in Bengal, and Sarojini Naidu, the most famous of the all-India figures associated with the leading social and political organizations of the time. They represent respectively the women who operated in one state, used a regional language and focused exclusively on social uplift; and the women who took all of India as their arena, used English on most occasions, and worked with both social and political associations. Through the efforts of these two women to speak to women about new roles and responsibilities, encourage them to join organizations and mobilize them for activity, it is possible to generalize about the movement itself, in terms of its constituency, the problems it identified and the solutions offered.

Saroj Nalini Dutt (1887-1925), a woman who made her impact primarily in the province of Bengal, was the founder of the women's institute movement in that province. Born near Hooghly, she was the fourth daughter of Brojendra Nath De, a distinguished member of the Indian Civil Service. Her family belonged to the Bengali elite, her father held a much coveted position and her uncle, S.M. Mitra, was a well-known journalist.

The Des and the Mitras were members of the Brahmo Samaj, a theistic society concerned with both religious and social reform. From the time of Rammohun Roy, members of the Samaj had been committed to the improvement of women's status. They encouraged female education and participation of females in social and religious activities, and set up the earliest women's societies for the discussion of self-improvement.[7] Although Saroj Nalini's family held advanced ideas about the role of women, they were not among those who flouted custom and brought upon themselves the wrath of the orthodox community. Saroj Nalini's mother had remained in *purda* to avoid offending her husband's widowed mother, and Saroj Nalini was educated at home, not in one of the new schools for females. Although the surroundings were in conformity with *purda* restrictions, the subjects she studied were not. Saroj Nalini was taught to play tennis, ride horseback, and participate in other outdoor sports. It was in these early years that she learned to observe traditional customs and behave in a manner which would not offend less Westernized Bengalis.

Married to Guru Saday Dutt in 1906, Saroj Nalini became his partner in work and play. At the time of their marriage, Guru Saday was a sub-divisional officer in Kishergunge and future postings took him to other small towns in the mofussil. Saroj Nalini accompanied him to these new places and, whenever possible, joined him on his rounds of the district. She was capable of acting as his secretary, joining in tennis matches and preserving her reputation as an excellent cook and housekeeper. Her husband called her an ideal woman: able to take the best of tradition and combine it with the ideals of the progressive.[8]

Saroj Nalini's village experiences affected her deeply. In her father's home she had experienced a life-style that allowed women considerable freedom. In the villages of Bengal she found that many women were uneducated, secluded and isolated. Distressed by their plight, she decided to take the initiative in forming some kind of society where women could meet with each other and share ideas and problems. The first Mahila Samiti was formed in Pabna in 1913. From Pabna she moved to Birbhum (1916), Sultanpur (1917), Rampurhat (1918) and Bankura (1921), starting a women's institute in each town.

The objectives were to develop friendly cooperation among *purda* women, interest them in the world outside their homes, and arrange lectures on practical subjects. However, these apparently simple objectives had far-reaching implications. This was recognized by some of the men who refused to let their wives attend even one meeting. These meetings, they retorted, would only be the first step, next would come the destruction of the family.[9] In these early years, it was certainly not clear to all concerned what effect these organizations might have on the women who joined. Saroj Nalini Dutt was far more Westernized than most of the women in Bengal, particularly those from the villages, and the controversy still raged about the type of woman produced by education and a free social movement would produce. Even among sophisticated urbanites, moderates fought radicals on the necessity for gradual change, urging an education that would leave the modest behaviour and value system of the Indian female intact.[10] It is not surprising, then, that the country folk were cautious about innovation in this realm.

In addition to providing new social contacts, these early women's societies served two general purposes: they provided a forum for women's demands and a place for adult education. The education offered was related to the role of woman as a nurturer and focused on food and nutrition, child care, hygiene and sewing. In many cases the women were too shy to express demands but there are examples of women using these Mahila Samitis to request the services of a female doctor and to set up schools for girls.[11] Saroj Nalini also attempted to encourage patriotism and a concern for larger issues. The members were given lectures about India and its great patriots, introduced to Tagore's songs and, during World War I, encouraged to manufacture items of clothing and tooth-brushes for the volunteers.[12]

But this was to be patriotism without nationalist overtones. At one time Saroj Nalini had blamed the British for Indian backwardness, but her increased experience in the villages made her change her analysis of the situation. India's condition, she concluded, was not an effect of British rule, but of Indian social customs. There were three areas where major changes were needed: education, social service and unity. Women, as the educators of children, had a vital part to play in the future of the nation. While they had always been taught to care for their families, they now needed to go beyond this and learn to help their fellowmen: 'every man and every woman must also do some work, no matter how little, for the Motherland'. At the same time, people needed to work together. Brotherhood, public spirit and civic spirit would result from striving towards unity.[13] Politics did not claim her interest; Saroj Nalini ignored both the efforts of Indian women to gain the franchise and the involvement of women in the Indian National Congress. Her concern was with strengthening the people first, the fight for freedom could come later.

Who were the people she recruited for the Mahila Samitis? In the beginning, her efforts were directed exclusively towards women who would have been considered 'middle-class'. Their husbands held positions in the government, were professionals or landowners. Labouring women and the wives of craftsmen were not invited. This should not be seen as snobbishness so much caste/class insularity. From the beginning of the nineteenth century, the 'woman problem' had been defined in terms of upper-class and middle-class women. Seclusion, lack of formal education, and restrictions on movement, were seen as the problems to be overcome; lectures, social organizations and literature provided the method of attack. These were neither the problems of the lower class nor were these suitable ways to claim their attention. It was hoped though that the women who took part in these organizations would become aware of the needs of their society and feel confident in the world outside their homes so that they could play a part in social regeneration.[14]

Following trips to England and Japan in the early 1920s, Saroj Nalini became more concerned with the economic position of women and co-incidentally with the problems of lower-middle-class women. She began to orient the Samitis towards economic uplift, claiming that women needed to be taught skills that would allow them to supplement their incomes if married, or support themselves if widowed.[15] However, she continued to see the income women obtained from employment as part-time or supplemental rather than as a necessity for the family. For that reason, women employed full-time, as servants and labourers, were left untouched by her organizations.

After Saroj Nalini's premature death in 1935, her husband and admirers founded the 'Saroj Nalini Dutt Memorial Association for Women's Work in Bengal'. This association continued and expanded her work, establishing additional Samitis and arranging for classes in handicrafts and midwifery, baby clinics and schools to teach domestic science. A number of other organizations were being formed at this time, but they were generally urban-based. However, Saroj Nalini's concern had been with women outside the major towns and cities: 'There can be no real improvements in the country unless we can educate, and widen the ideas of women in the *mofussil* towns and villages.'[16]

Saroj Nalini was convinced that the new role she envisioned for women was not in conflict with a 'traditional' role. In fact, she suggested that the role she encouraged—an enlarged social role which included activities outside the home—was the true 'traditional' role. She appealed to ancient myths, asking her critics if they had not heard to Maitreyi, Gargi and Lilavati. It was not just in ancient times that Indian women had taken a leading part in intellectual life; in modern times she could cite Khana, an authority on agricultural science and economics. Even the customary phrase used to describe the arena of women's work in Bengal, *ghar-sansar* (home-family/world) proved that a woman's legitimate sphere was the world as well as the home. The seclusion of women, a departure from true tradition, had caused the country to fall to a low state. Women, she insisted, needed to be restored to their rightful position.[17]

Thus, this new role for women was not presented as a break with history, but as part of a continuous, though interrupted, development. And the activities suggested were not intended to introduce conflict or tension into family life. Saroj Nalini was deeply concerned that the changes should be gradual; for example, women could remain in *purda* and become more knowledgeable about the world.

From the home it would be possible to learn about nutrition, medicine and world events. In turn, these women would make better mothers and the result would be a stronger, healthier generation of children. Saroj Nalini did encourage some women to cast off the restrictions of *purda*, but only when the husbands favoured it and the change would not offend other members of the family or adversely affect family status.[18]

Saroj Nalini's success in attracting women to these Mahila Samitis must be attributed to her sensitivity and tact in dealing with conservative Hindu society. Whenever possible, she reasoned with her critics, particularly if they were men who were reluctant to have their wives and daughters attend a meeting. But with women she relied more on her actions. While visiting her husband's relatives in Sylhet, she arrived without shoes, properly veiled and attired in a simple sari and jewellery similar to that worn by village women. She was well-received.[19] On another occasion, she arranged a send-off dinner for the volunteers who had joined the British army and was careful to remove her shoes before serving. At a garden party she organized for members of the Mahila Samiti, she paid such close attention to the food restrictions of the various women attending it that even the most orthodox had no cause for complaint.[20] The fact that she was the wife of a senior official was of considerable importance in making the initial contacts, but had she not been sensitive to custom few would have continued to attend the meetings.

The arena of Sarojini Naidu was considerably larger than that of Saroj Nalini—the whole of India instead of just Bengal—and she also envisioned a larger role for women. Nevertheless, these two women were remarkably similar in the arguments they used and the women to whom they appealed. As with Saroj Nalini, Sarojini suggested that women play a larger role in society through social work and politics, without breaking with the past and without neglecting their role as nurturers.

Sarojini Naidu (1879-1949) was born in Hyderabad where her father, Dr. Aghorenath Chattopadhyay, was in the service of the Nizam of Hyderabad. Dr. Chattopadhyay had taken his doctorate in physics from Edinburgh University in 1877 and returned to India to teach. He became the Principal of New Hyderabad College (later Nizam's College) which he founded. He was born and raised in Bengal, became a member of the Brahmo Samaj and a close follower of the great Brahmo reformer, Keshub Chunder Sen.

Deeply committed to female education, he sent Sarojini to Madras High School, Madras Presidency College, and King's College, Cambridge in England.[21] In England she began to write poetry, first with typical English themes and then with Indian themes. Her poetry attracted the attention of Edmund Gosse and other literary figures, and she received considerable praise for her flowing language and effervescence. Upon her return she insisted that she be allowed to marry Dr. Govinda Naidu (from a different caste) and her father finally gave his consent. They took up residence in Hyderabad and had four children.

Sarojini Naidu was a member of an extraordinary family. She herself was an exceptional woman who had had many unusual experiences unusual for an Indian woman at the turn of the century. Nevertheless, she had tremendous influence upon that group which was often labelled as the most traditional in India--the women. She had the sensitivity, tact and skills necessary to relate to more traditional people. From the early part of the century she became a part of the national scene, helping to mould the freedom movement as it developed. The national movement, it would seem, provided this gifted woman with a great opportunity:

> She took with her into politics the graces of the court and city so deeply ingrained in her and the emotional intensity of her personal relationships. Her torrent of impassioned English eloquence gave Indians some of the most stiring oratory of the day. But, above all, she was a person who lived her experience to the hilt, and the national movement provided full scope for marrying the patriot, the poet and the woman in her.[22]

Sarojini had returned to India in 1898 and by 1902 was speaking publicly to women's groups, students and social reform societies about the need for unity, social service and improvement of women's status. She was young and beautiful and her appearances at meetings where Indian women had never spoken publicly thrilled the crowds and captured the imagination of many young women already demanding the right to study and pursue lives different from those of their mothers.[23] Throughout her life she was to continue to inspire people with her oratory and became known as the 'songbird' and the 'nightingale of India'.

Gopal Krishna Gokhale became her first political mentor. He

inspired her with his vision of a free India and by his dedicated service to society through the 'Servants of India Society'. But her early speeches also reflected the theme of Hindu-Muslim unity. Raised in Hyderabad, Sarojini was rare among political leaders in her sensitivity to Muslim problems and appreciation of Muslim culture. Independence, unity and progress for women became entwined themes in her inspiring speeches.[24]

Sarojini had met Gandhi in London in 1914 and the friendship that developed turned into discipleship.[25] But she differed considerably from his other disciples. When she addressed him she used the language of *bhakti* as she adored him, yet she was 'too keen a connoisseur of pleasure to accept the philosophy of renunciation'.[26] She joked and argued with Gandhi, accepted the logic and appeal of his technique, but followed neither his life-style nor directives blindly.

Sarojini had made her first speech to the Indian National Congress in 1906, an organization she joined in 1915. In 1913 she attended and spoke at the Lucknow Conference of the Muslim League and in 1918 she joined the Home Rule League. The following year she was among the first to take the non-cooperation pledge.[27] Her dedication to the political movement was reflected in her election as President of the Congress in 1925, making her the first Indian woman to hold this office. By this time she was clearly established as the most active and influential woman in the Indian political movement.

Her involvement with the woman question dates back to her days in England, or perhaps to her childhood days in her father's home. Interested in the suffragette movement (she had travelled to England with Annie Besant) she was able to meet and talk with some of the leaders of the movement. From the very beginning she had spoken to women and about women, urging social reform to remove the disabilities and urging women to come out of seclusion and perform social service.[28] In 1917, the year the first all-India women's organization (Women's Indian Association) was formed, women's involvement in the political affairs of the day began in earnest. Sarojini, a close friend of Annie Besant, the President, and Margaret Cousins, the Secretary, became a member from the beginning. Shortly after the WIA was formed, an opportunity arose to present a petition to Mr. Edwin Montagu, the Secretary of State for India. The WIA hastily prepared a memorandum asking for women's franchise and

Sarojini Naidu led the delegation to present it.[29]

Sarojini encouraged this type of political activity—i.e., petitioning on issues which affected women's status—but urged women to remain apolitical in terms of party allegiance. She became a member of the All-India Women's Conference which was started in 1926, served as its President in 1930 and was instrumental in keeping this organization out of politics. The AIWC was founded to give women an opportunity to express their views on female education and soon expanded to include social questions. Finally, it was decided that the AIWC was concerned with all questions which affected the welfare of women and children. By 1932 it claimed to be the second most representative body in India.[30] As its President in 1930, Sarojini stated that this was a greater privilege than presiding over the Indian National Congress: 'Yet, this our conference is greater: it is the greatest international gathering in the country where we can demonstrate the individual fellowship of women in the cause of humanity.'[31]

Her tours through India were many, her speeches endless and the people she touched numerous. In some regions—for example, Bengal—she did not speak to women's groups but to men because she did not speak much Bengali and the women of the mofussil were generally unacquainted with English.[32] She spoke English and Urdu fluently but Hindi and Bengali imperfectly, and so delivered the majority of her speeches in English. Because of this, her direct impact, through language, was on that segment of upper-class and middle-class women who had learned English. But she appealed to many other women through the force of her personality, and provided them with a model of fearless activity. This was especially true in 1930 when she took charge of the raid on the Dharsana Salt Works. The sight of this kindly woman, seated on a stool under the hot sun, urging her fellow satyagrahis not to give up, touched many of the village women in the area. They attempted to take water to her and, in spirit, joined the movement against the British.[33]

By 1930 Bombay had become Mrs. Naidu's home and it was this center which was most impressive for the involvement of its women in the civil disobedience movement. Mrs. Naidu cannot take credit for the astounding numbers of women who turned out to meetings and to take part in processions (sometimes numbering as high as 20,000)[34] because Mahatma Gandhi and a number of other luminaries were active in the Bombay-Gujarat area. Nevertheless, Mrs.

Naidu inspired many of the women who joined and many of the leaders (such as Kamaladevi Chattopadhyay) and her presence and impact on the movement was felt in numerous undocumented ways.

While the social organizations drew their membership from the upper- and middle-classes, this was not so of the Independence movement. Its leadership, at least in the cities, came primarily from the elite, but in the countryside many new leaders appeared. Concerning these women, we have difficulty in pinpointing who they were, why they joined and what had inspired them.[35] When the newspapers reported meetings, such as those in Bombay, they listed the names of women such as Sarojini Naidu, Kamaladevi Chattopadhyay and Hansa Mehta, but included little information on the other 10,000 in attendence. The picture was the same for Calcutta, Madras and other major cities. Only the leaders are named, the others become 'four other women', or 'six others'. While the elite women who joined these protests and demonstrations also belonged to social organizations, this was not true of the women who formed the rank and file. Jawaharlal Nehru, among others, had been critical of the women's organizations for not bringing the masses into their movement,[36] but Sarojini insisted that they represented 'modern women' regardless of their social class.[37]

Fundamental to Sarojini's message was the notion that the women who participated in both social and political activities, the 'modern women', were, in fact, traditional. In replying to Nehru's criticism, she defined the modern women: 'We prove that our roots, roots of old days, still feed us, still give us life.'[38] This modern woman did not restrict her life to the home and depend on men to make important decisions about the world, but played a dynamic role: Every women is a creator in the ideals of nationhood. I want the women of India to have consciousness of the great and dynamic nation whose energies have to be mobilized and harmonized for common purposes.'[39] The work to be accomplished was in the political field—working for *swaraj*; and in the social field—working for the uplift of unfortunate people.

When Sarojini elaborated on what she meant by 'roots' she appealed to the *Vedas* and the ancient epics. She was, she claimed, a spiritual decendant of Sita and Savitri. Women would have to learn to act like these Hindu goddesses, not just inside the home (something they had been encouraged to do since childhood) but in their communities and the larger world as well. A woman, she insisted, should be like 'Laksmi, the giver of happiness and prosperity, Saraswati, the embodiment of wisdom and Parvati, the eternal Mother who uplifts the fallen, purifies the sinner, gives hope to the despairing, strength to the weak and courage to the coward and recreates in man the divine energy.'[40]

This theme—that the world could be seen as the extension of the home—was present in many of Sarojini's speeches. The home, she insisted, was the unit of Indian civilization, and within that home 'the mother is the immemorial keeper of that tradition that means purity, honour, love, service and sacrifice for the glory of the nation'.[41] In her speech as the President of the Indian National Congress, she developed an analogy between India as the 'house', the Indian people as 'children' and 'members of the joint family', and the Indian woman as 'Mother'. Women had to work hard to put the national 'house' in order, reconcile the tragic quarrels between joint family members and find a place in the 'house' for all children and foster-children.[42] But she was not willing to let women ignore this larger responsibility and tend only to their own homes. In 1930 she wrote: 'The time has come in my opinion when women can no longer seek immunity beyond the shelter of their sex, but must share equally with their men comrades all the perils and sacrifices for the liberation of the country.'[43] In doing so they would not be breaking with tradition, but following in the footsteps of women who lived in 'the radiant far off yesterdays of our history'. These women had had to 'kindle and sustain the fires of the hearth and altar, to light the beacon lights', and now she was asking women of the twentieth century to do the same thing.[44]

The immediate repercussion of the work of women like Sarojini Naidu and Saroj Nalini Dutt was to bring a number of women into social and political organizations. Gandhi's insistence that constructive work was as important as political work, sanctioned a number of activities which could draw on the leisure-time of middle-class women who were not able to join the political movement directly. There were efforts throughout the country to learn spinning, wear khadi, open khadi shops, work for village uplift and devise programs to help the poor and disadvantaged. While a number of women followed the apolitical lead of women like Saroj Nalini, there were many who joined both political organizations as well as social organizations. However, very few of the rural women, lower-class women, and non-English-speaking women who participated in picket lines and processions connected with the nationalist movement belonged to the national women's organizations or even the local Mahila Samitis and women's circles.

In the first decade following Independence, the legal status of women was transformed. The Constitution recognized sex equality, and various legislations—the Hindu Marriage Act (1955), the Succession Act (1956) and the Adoption Act (1956)—modified the role of women as defined by law and custom. These changes were partly a response to the demands made by women's organizations which had pushed for legislative change since the 1930s. If one looks at the framework which has developed to allow for women's participation in public life, it is apparent that there are few bars to such involvement. However, the number of women in public life—as politicians, professionals or simply labourers—remains small.[45] The liberal framework is undoubtedly a monument to the women's movement; however, the women who have benefitted most from this change belong to the middle-class.

The organizations that emerged as most important in representing 'women's issues' were the national women's organizations. The Women's Indian Association took the lead in asking for the franchise for women, and the pattern of petitioning followed by them was imitated by the other organizations. Their aims called for constructive work as well as petitioning, but uplift proved difficult and unrewarding compared with preparing briefs, meeting with members of parliament and soliciting signatures for petitions. The types of activity they found most rewarding partially determined the kind of issues they championed. Female education, the franchise, legal reform, and the status of women received more attention than the conditions of labouring women, equal pay for equal work, housing for women and equality under the law. The problems of lower-class women did not immediately come to their attention and would not, as long as they remained aloof from the living and working conditions of these women.

But these lower-class women were touched by the nationalist movement. The arguments used to mobilize them were not unlike those used to bring women into Saroj Nalini's Mahila Samitis. They were exhorted to be like the legendary figures of the great epics and praised as embodiments of sacrifice. Connections were made between the poverty of the country and foreign rule, and it was suggested that participation would make possible a better life.[46] While some women were mobilized for the nationalist movement through arguments that stressed the problems of women and encouraged a women's consciousness, it was always done with traditional symbols. The arguments about women's status, the need for education, legal reform and the franchise, generally stayed within the urban areas. Rural women were often appealed to on the same issue as men—i.e., economic exploitation—although in separate groups and in words which emphasized exactly what poverty meant to the woman as nurturer.

Through the involvement of women in picketing and demonstrations, two things happened. Women themselves realized that they were not as weak and helpless as they had come to believe and the men developed a new respect for their strength and ability to suffer. Following 1930-32, when women made a tremendous impression through their involvement in agitational politics, all petitions requesting legislative change or other moves to improve the status of women were prefaced with references to what women had done. The women's organizations co-opted the emotional response to these demonstrations and used it to justify the demands they were presenting. The problem was and has been the lack of a two-way exchange. The social organizations benefitted from the political involvement of the masses of women who neither belonged to these organizations nor had an opportunity to present their grievances as women. These grievances sometimes found a forum in ad-hoc political organizations but they did not find their way into the offices of the national women's organizations where they might have been translated into sophisticated, logical statements and presented to the government and legislative bodies as the demands of India's women.

What, then, was the nature of women's movement during the period 1917-1947? Social reform activities as well as the efforts to serve the nationalist movement were the two main elements of the women's movements. The organizations for women generally tried to remain apolitical but many of their members joined political movements. Their concern for the status of women found release in petitioning, efforts to modify the individual status of women who joined and some efforts at ameliorating the condition of women from the lower classes. The political movement, or the women's part of it, stressed the contribution that women could make in the fight for Swaraj and Swaraj was the answer to all problems. In both cases, the value of women to the nation was stressed. The political leaders put the nation and the struggle for political autonomy first; the women's organizations claimed that the uplift of women was essential to the national cause because women are the mothers of future generations.

Across the board, the arguments put forward to encourage new activities among women were traditional. Women had been publicly aware and active in the past. There were examples in legends and epics, and they could do so again. At the same time, there was no rejection of the traditional role of woman as wife and mother. In fact, women were encouraged to be good wives and mothers and at times it was argued that unless they knew something of the larger world they could not be good wives and mothers. In terms of ideology, this was not a radical movement. Women were seen as having played a major role in ancient times, pushed into a more restricted life at the time of foreign invasions and as being ready to re-emerge in modern times. They were to re-emerge as 'equals' but not equal in the sense demanded by Western feminists, 'not of claiming aggressively an identical place with men in the world but claiming and equalling, though in a different place, not performing identical duties with men but performing duties different because supplementary, fulfilling the duties of man in the life of the country'.[47]

Notes and References

1. Saraladevi Choudhurani, 'A Women's Movement', *The Modern Review*, October 1911, p. 343.
2. By 1930-1, the Women's Indian Association claimed sixty-seven branches, twenty-six centers and 4,000 members. *Women's Indian Association Report for the Year 1930-1*, p. 1.
3. Ibid.; All-India Women's Conference, 6th Session, Madras (Dec. 28 1931—Jan. 1 1932); AIWC Files (136); *Bombay Presidency Women's Council Twelfth Annual Report*, (Dec. 1929-Dec. 1930).
4. M.K. Gandhi, 'Speech at Women's Meeting, Kathal', *Collected Works*, XXVI, Ahmedabad, 1966.
5. Gandhi, 'Speech at Women's Conference, Sojitra (Gujarat)', *Collected Works*, XXVI, Ahmedabad, 1967.
6. For example, see Jawaharlal Nehru, *Toward Freedom*, New York, 1941, pp. 159-61; S. Nayar, 'Our Changing Life in India', in B.E. Ward (ed.),

Women in New India, Paris, 1963, p. 209; Raja Rao, *Kanthapura*, New York, 1963.

7. Prabhat Chandra Gangopadhyay, *Banglar Nari Jagaran*, Kalikata, 1362 B.S., p. 15.
8. Guru Saday Dutt, *A Woman of India: Being the Life of Saroj Nalini*, Mysore, 1941, p. 75.
9. Shudha Mazumdar, *A Pattern of Life: The Memoirs of an Indian Woman*, edited by Geraldine Forbes, Delhi: Manohar Book Service, 1977, ch. 10.
10. David Kopf, 'The Brahmo Idea of Social Reform and the Problem of Female Emancipation in Bengal', in John R. McLane (ed.), *Bengal in the Nineteenth and Twentieth Century*, Michigan State University, South Asia Series Occasional Paper No. 25.
11. See Shudha Mazumdar, op. cit., Ch. 10.
12. Ibid.
13. Guru Saday Dutt, op. cit., pp. 64-5.
14. Shudha Mazumdar, op. cit., ch. 10.
15. Interview with Aroti Dutt, 15 August 1972, Calcutta.
16. Saroj Nalini Dutt 'Women's Welfare Organizations in Bengal', in *Modern Review*, March 1925, reprinted in *Saroj Nalini Dutt Memorial Association for Women's Work in Bengal*, Report for 1925.
17. Guru Saday Dutt, op. cit., pp. 97-8.
18. Ibid., pp. 102-3.
19. Ibid., pp. 81-86.
20. Shudha Mazumdar, op. cit., ch. 10.
21. See Harindranath Chattopadhyaya, *Life and Myself*, v. 1, Bombay: Nalanda Publications, 1947. The two main biographies of Sarojini Naidu were written by women who knew her: Padmini Sengupta, *Sarojini Naidu*, New Delhi, 1974 and Tara Ali Baig. The Films Division of the Ministry of Information and Broadcasting, Government of India, has produced a documentary 'Sarojini Naidu, the Nightingale of India' in 1975. Harindranath Chattopadhyaya, her younger brother, was involved with this project and feels that of all the material available on Sarojini, this best captures her 'spirit'.
22. Nayantara Sahgal, 'Sarojini Naidu', *The Illustrated Weekly of India*, 19 January 1975, p. 21.
23. Interview with Lady Rama Rao, Bombay, 26 April 1976. Lady Rama Rao met and heard Sarojini Speak when she was a student at Madras University in 1908. She was thrilled with Sarojini's voice, beauty and skill as an orator. From this time on, she said, her heart was with the women's movement.
24. Tara Ali Baig, *Sarojini Naidu*, New Delhi, 1974, p 35; Padmini Sengupta, op. cit., pp. 35-6.
25. Quote of Mrs. Naidu's words in Padmini Sengupta, op. cit., p. 40.
26. Nayantara Sahgal, op. cit.
27. Manmohan Kaur, *Role of Women in the Freedom Movement, 1857-1957*, Delhi, 1968; Tara Ali Baig, op. cit., Ch. 2.
28. Tara Ali Baig, op. cit., p. 31.
29. M.E. Cousins, *Indian Womanhood Today*, Allahabad, 1941, p. 33; 'A Ladies' Deputation to Mr. Montagu', *New India*, 25 October 1917, p. 5; 'Women's Deputation to Mr. Montagu', *New India*, 13 December 1917, p. 5.

30. *AIWC on Educational Reform*, January 1927, pp. 1, 13; AIWC Fifth Session, January 1931, p. 38; AIWC Sixth Session, December 1931-January 1932, p. 28.
31. *AIWC Conference, Fourth Annual*, 1930, p. 19.
32. 'Mrs. Naidu's Tour in North Bengal', *Forward*, 27 July 1926, p. 10.
33. See daily articles in the *Bombay Chronicle*, 14-22 May 1930.
34. See *Bombay Chronicle*, May-October 1930.
35. Information on such women can sometimes be found with much digging. For example, the village heroine, Matangini Hazra (Midnapore District, Bengal) has been made the subject of a joint-biography, Indubhusan Das, *Pritilata-Matangini*, Calcutta, 1382 BS. Occasionally histories of the freedom movement include some information and one finds the occasional book which gives thumbnail sketches of the individuals who went to jail, e.g., Suryanath Kamth, *Swatantrya Sangramada Smriti Galu*, Mysore, 1974.
36. *AIWC Conference Fourteenth Annual Report*, pp. 27-29.
37. Ibid., p. 32.
38. *AIWC Conference, Fourteenth Annual Report*, p. 32.
39. 'Sarojini Naidu' *Roshni*, IX, (1957), p. 4.
40. Ibid., p. 4.
41. 'Advice to City Fathers of Karachi', *Forward*, 16 August 1925, p. 15.
42. Manmohan Kaur, op. cit., p. 175.
43. Manmohan Kaur, op. cit., p. 176.
44. Eleanor Morton, *The Women in Gandhi's Life*, New York, 1953, p. 120.
45. Census data indicate a decline in female employment. The percentage of female workers to total females is as follows: 1911—33.73 per cent; 1921—33.73 per cent; 1931—27.63 per cent; 1951—23 per cent; 1961—27.96 per cent; and 1971—11.86 per cent. *The Indian Woman, A Statistical Profile*, Government of India, Ministry of Education and Social Welfare, 1975.
46. For an example from Madras see 'Foreign Cloth Boycott: Ladies Campaign, Alleppey', *The Hindu*, 26 April 1931, p. 3.
47. 'Advice to City Fathers of Karachi', *Forward*, 16 August 1925, p. 15.

Part 2

Select Bibliography on Social Movements in India

Part 2

A Select Bibliography on Social Movements in India

Compiled by Arun P Bali and Anjali Arun Bali

THE SCOPE OF the field of social movements is so vast that it is almost impossible to be exhaustive in preparing a bibliography such as this. Thus, we lay no claims that the listing that follows is comprehensive. Furthermore, we have excluded historical and source materials. Given the diversity of social movements, an attempt has been made to classify them according to major categories. A cautionary note is in order with regard to the procedures followed in this bibliography for classifying social movements.

As we proceed, it will become clear that many social movements have overlapping elements. Thus, for example, the reader may find that a social movement which we have categorized as 'Religious and Sectarian' (Section 7) will contain elements of social reform or caste in its explanatory framework or assumptions. Such elements of a social movement may be separated for purposes of analysis, although in actual practice they are interconnected in many ways.

In all there are twelve sections in the bibliography. Section 1, entitled 'Bibliography of Bibliographies', includes bibliographies compiled by scholars. These provide valuable sources for studying social movements.

Section 2 deals with 'General Works—Ideas and Concepts'. Theory is not only a means of organizing and interpreting our substantive perceptions, it also serves to provide new insights and helps us to discover new patterns and issues. The main reason for including these works is that they provide a frame of reference by which the reader can come to grips with the process of social movements. In this section, some studies of social movements concerning non-Indian situations have also been included. Such studies warrant inclusion because of their theoretical importance.

The locus of change constitutes the signal factor in the taxonomy of social movements for the purpose of this bibliography. The different types of social movements have been broadly classified under the following ten categories, representing sections 3 to 12.

3. Peasant Movements
4. Social Reform Movements
5. Caste Movements
6. The Black Movements
7. Religious and Sectarian Movements
8. Tribal Movements
9. Women's Movements
10. Students' Movements
11. Trade Union Movements
12. National Movements

Although no articles on trade union movements, students' movements and national movements appear in the text, they nevertheless merit inclusion as they constitute major types of social movements. The category of Black Movements is relevant in the bibliography because of the comparative study between Backward Classes movements and Black movements which appears in the main text.

1. Bibliography of Bibliographies

ADAMS, CHARLES J. (ED.) (1965) : *A Reader's Guide to the Great Religions.* New York: The Free Press.

BARRIER, GERALD N. (1974) : *The Sikhs and their Literature: A Guide to Books, Tracts and Periodicals, 1849-1919.* Delhi: Manohar Book Service.

DUBE, S.C. (1977) : 'Bibliography'. In S.C. Dube (ed.), *Tribal Heritage in India: Ethnicity, Identity and Interaction.* Vol. 1. Delhi: Vikas Publishing House.

FARQUHAR, J.N. (1914): *A Primer of Hinduism* (2nd ed.). Oxford: O.U.P.

——— (1967): *An Outline of the Religious Literature of India.* Delhi: Motilal Banarsidass (first published in 1920).

GHOSH, ARUN & RANJIT GHOSH (1976) : *Indian Political Movement in 1919-1971: A Systematic Bibliography.* Calcutta: India Book Exchange.

GUNJAL, S.R. (1967) : *Basava Sahitya Darshana.* Vol. I. Bangalore: Basava Samiti.

GUSTAFSON, W. ERIC & KENNETH W. JONES (EDS.) (1975): *Sources on Punjab History.* Delhi: Manohar Book Service.

INDIA, REGISTRAR-GENERAL (OFFICE OF) (1966) : *Bibliography on Scheduled Castes, Scheduled Tribes and Selected Marginal Communities of India.* Delhi: Manager of Publications.

JAINA, CHOTE LAL (1945) : *Jaina Bibliography.* Calcutta: Bharti Jain Parishad.

MCPHERSON, J.M. *et al.* (1971): *Blacks in America: Bibliographical Essays.* New York: Doubleday & Co.

MAHAR, J. MICHAEL (1964) : *India: A Critical Biography.* Tuscon, Arizona: University of Arizona Press.

RAMDEV, J.S. (1967): *Guru Gobind Singh: A Descriptive Bibliography.* Chandigarh: Punjab University.

ROY, SARAT CHANDRA (COMP.) (1942) : *Bibliography on Tribes*: W.G. Archer (ed.). (In Census of India, 1941, Vol. VII. Appendix, Bihar Caste Tables, 1942).

SHARMA, J.S. (1975): *India's Minorities: A Bibliographical Study.* Delhi: Vikas Publishing House.

SHARMA, J.S. (ED.) (1962) : *India's Struggle for Freedom: Select Documents and Sources.* 3 vols. Delhi: S. Chand & Co.

SHARPE, ERIC J. (1971): *Thinking About Hinduism.* London: Lutberworth Press.

SINGH, GANDA (1965): *A Select Bibliography of the Sikhs and Sikhism.* Amritsar.

TROISI, J. (1976): *The Santhals: A Classified and Annotated Bibliography.* Delhi: Manohor Book Service.

ZELLIOTT, ELEANOR (1972): 'Bibliography'. In J. Michael Mahar (ed.), *The Untouchables in Contemporary India.* Tucson, Arizona: University of Arizona Press, pp. 432-481.

2. General Works—Ideas and Concepts

ABERLE, D.F. (1962): 'A Note on Relative Deprivation Theory as Applied to Millenarian and other Cult Movement'. In S. Thrupp (ed.), *Millennial Dreams in Action: Essays in Comparative Studies*. Comparative Studies in Society and History. The Hague: Mouton, pp. 209-14.

———— (1966): *The Peyote Religion Among the Navaho*. Viking Fund Publications in Anthropology No. 42. New York: Wenner-Gren Foundation.

APTER, DAVID E. (ED.) (1964): *Ideology and Discontent*. New York: The Free Press.

BANKS, J.A. (1972): *The Sociology of Social Movement*. London: Macmillan Press.

BARBER, B. (1941): 'Acculturation and Messianic Movements'. *American Sociological Review*. Vol. 6, pp. 663-8.

BARKUN, MICHAEL (1974): *Disaster and the Millennium*. New Haven and London: Yale University Press.

BELL, DANIEL (1960): *The End of Ideology*. New York: The Free Press.

———— (1964): *The Radical Right*. Garden City, N.Y.: Doubleday.

BELLAH, ROBERT N. (ED.) (1965): *Religion and Progress in Modern Asia*. New York: The Free Press.

BENDIX, R. (1961): 'The Lower Classes and the Democratic Revolution'. *Industrial Relations*. Vol. 1, No. 1 (October), pp. 91-116.

BENSON, J. KENNETH & JAMES DORSETT (1971): 'Church-Sect Replaced'. *Journal for the Scientific Study of Religion*. Vol. 10, No. 2, pp. 138-51.

BERGER, PETER L. (1954): 'The Sociological Study of Sectarianism'. *Social Research*. Vol. 21, pp. 467-85.

———— (1958): 'Sectarianism and Religious Sociation'. *American Journal of Sociology*. Vol. 64, pp. 41-4.

BIENEN, HENRY (1968): *Violence and Social Change*. Chicago: University of Chicago Press.

BITTNER, EGON (1963): 'Radicalism and the Organization of Radical Movements'. *American Sociological Review*. Vol. 28 (December), pp. 928-40.

BLUMER, HERBERT (1939): 'Social Movements'. In Robert E. Park (ed.), *An Outline of the Principles of Sociology*. New York: Barnes & Noble.

———— (1951): 'Social Movements'. In A.M. Lee (ed.), *New Outline of Principles of Sociology*. New York: Barnes & Noble.

———— (1957): 'Collective Behavior'. In J.B. Gittler (ed.), *Review of Sociology*. New York: John Wiley & Sons, pp. 127-58.

BOISSEVAIN, JEREMY (1965): *Saints and Fireworks: Religion and Politics in Rural Malta*. London School of Economics, Monographs on Social Anthropology, No. 30. New York: Humanities Press.

BONDURANT, JOAN V. (1965): *Conquest of Violence: The Gandhian Philosophy of Conflict* (rev. ed.). Berkeley: University of California Press.

BREWER, E.D.C. (1952): 'Sect and Church in Methodism'. *Social Forces*. Vol. 30, No. 4, pp. 400-8.

BRINTON, CRANE (1938): *The Anatomy of Revolution.* New York: W.W. Norton & Co.

BURRIDGE, KENELM (1969): *New Heaven, New Earth: A Study of Millenarian Activities.* Oxford: Basil Blackwell.

CAMERON, W.R. (1966): *Modern Social Movements.* New York: Random House.

CANTRIL, HADLEY (1941): *The Psychology of Social Movements.* New York: John Wiley & Sons.

CHAFFEE, GRACE E. (1930): 'The Isolated Religious Sects as an Object for Social Research'. *American Journal of Sociology.* Vol. 35, pp. 618-30.

CLARK, S.D. (1948): *Church and Sect in Canada.* Toronto: University of Toronto Press.

COCHRANE, D. GLYNN (1970): *Big Men and Cargo Cults.* London: Oxford University Press.

COHN, NORMAN (1970): *The Pursuit of the Millennium: Revolutionary Millenarians and Mystical Anarchists of the Middle Ages* (3rd ed.). New York: Oxford University Press.

CURRIE, ELLIOTT & JEROME SKOLNICK (1970): 'A Critical Note on Conceptions of Collective Behavior'. *Annals of the American Academy of Political and Social Science.* Vol. 391 (Sept.), pp. 34-45.

CURRY, DONALD E. (1970): 'Messianism and Protestantism in Brazil's Sertao'. *Journal of Inter-American Studies and World Affairs.* Vol- 12, pp. 416-38.

DAMLE, Y.B. (1968): 'Reference Group Theory with regard to Mobility in Caste'. In James Silverberg (ed.), *Social Mobility in the Caste System in India.* The Hague: Mouton, pp. 95-102.

D'ANTONIO, WILLIAM V. & FREDERICK B. PIKE (EDS.) (1964): *Religion, Revolution and Reform: New Forces of Change in Latin America.* New York: Frederick A. Praeger.

DAVIES, JAMES C. (1962): 'Toward a Theory of Revolution'. *American Sociological Review.* Vol. 27, No. 1 (Feb.). pp. 5-19.

————(ED.) (1971): *When Men Rebel and Why.* New York: The Free Press.

DAVIS, JEROME (1930): *Contemporary Social Movements.* New York: D. Appleton-Century, Inc.

DEMERATH III, NICHOLAS, *et al.* (1971): 'Criteria and Contingencies of Success in Radical Political Movements'. *Journal of Social Issues.* Vol. 27, No. 1, pp. 63-80.

DESPRES, LEO A. (1969): *Protest aud Change in Plural Societies.* Occasional Paper Series, No. 2. Centre for Developing Area Studies, McGill University, Montreal.

DRUCKER, PETER F. (1969): *The Age of Discontinuity.* New York: Harper and Row.

EDWARDS, LYFORD P. (1927): *The Natural History of Revolution.* Chicago: University of Chicago Press.

EISTER, ALLAN W. (1967): 'Toward a Radical Critique of Church-Sect Typologizing'. *Journal for the Scientific Study of Religion.* Vol. 6, No. 1, pp. 85-90.

EVANS, R.R. (ED.) (1973): *Social Movements.* Chicago: Rand McNally.

FARB, PETER (1969): 'Ghost Dance and Cargo Cult'. *Horizon*. Vol. 11 (Spring), pp. 58-64.

FARIS, E. (1955): 'The Sect and the Sectarian'. *American Journal of Sociology*. Vol. 60, No. 6, pp. 75-89.

FERBER, MICHAEL, & LYND STAUGHTON (1971): *The Resistance*. Boston: Beacon Press.

FINKLE, JASON L., & RICHARD W. GABLE (1966): *Political Development & Social Change*. New York: John Wiley & Sons.

FINN, JAMES (1967): *Protest: Pacifism and Politics*. New York: Vintage Books.

GERLACH, LUTHER & VIRGINIA HINE (1970): *People, Power and Change: Movements of Social Transformation*. New York: Bobbs-Merrill.

GESCHWANDER. JAMES A. (1968*a*): 'Status Inconsistency, Social Isolation, and Individual Unrest'. *Social Forces*. Vol. 46 (June), pp. 477-83.

———— (1968*b*): 'Explorations in the Theory of Social Movements and Revolutions'. *Social Forces*. Vol. 47 (Dec.), pp. 127-35.

GLOCK, CHARLES (1964): 'The Role of Deprivation in the Origin and Evolution of Religious Groups'. In Robert Lee and Martin E. Marty (eds.), *Religion and Social Conflict*. New York: Oxford University Press, pp. 24-36.

GOODE, ERICH (1967*a*): 'Some Critical Observations on the Church-Sect Dimension'. *Journal for the Scientific Study of Religion*. Vol. 6, No. 1, pp. 69-77.

———— (1967*b*): 'Further Reflections on the Church-Sect Dimension'. *Journal for the Scientific Study of Religion*. Vol. 6, No. 2, pp. 270-5.

GRAHAM, ALLAN 1974: 'A Theory of Millennialism: The Irwingite Movement as an Illustration'. *British Journal of Sociology*. Vol. 25. No. 3, pp. 296-311.

GREENE, T.H. (1974): *Comparative Revolutionary Movements*. Englewood-Cliffs, N.J.: Prentice Hall.

GURR, T.R. (1970): *Why Men Rebel*. Princeton, N.J.: Princeton University Press.

GUSFIELD, JOSEPH R. (1957): 'The Problems of Generations in an Organizational Structure'. *Social Forces*. Vol. 35 (May).

———— (1967): 'Functional Areas of Leadership in Social Movements'. In L.P. Vidyarthi (ed.), *Leadership in India*. Bombay: Asia Publishing House.

———— (1968): 'The Study of Social Movements'. In David Sills (ed.), *International Encyclopaedia of the Social Sciences*. Vol. 14. New York: Macmillan Co., & The Free Press, pp. 445-50.

————(ED.) (1971): *Protest, Reform and Revolt: A Reader in Social Movements*. New York: John Wiley & Sons.

HAMPDEN-TURNER, CHARLES (1970): *Radical Man*. Cambridge, Mass.: Schenkam.

HEBERLE, RUDOLF (1949*a*): 'The Sociology of Social Movements'. *American Sociological Review*. Vol. 14. pp. 346-57.

———— (1949*b*): 'Observations on the Sociology of Social Movement'. *American Sociological Review*. Vol. 14, pp. 347-57.

———— (1951): *Social Movements: An Introduction to Political Sociology*. New York: Appleton-Century-Crofts.

———— (1968): 'Types and Functions of Social Movements'. In David

Sills (ed.), *International Encyclopaedia of the Social Sciences.* Vol. 14. New York: Macmillan Co., & The Free Press, pp. 438-44.

HERMASSI, ELBAKI (1976): 'Toward a Comparative Study of Revolutions'. *Comparative Studies in Society and History.* Vol. 18, No. 2 (April), pp. 211-35.

HINE, VIRGINIA H. (1974): 'The Deprivation and Disorganization: Theories of Social Movements'. In Irving I. Zaretsky and Mark P. Leone (eds.), *Religious Movements in Contemporary America.* Princeton, N.J.: Princeton University Press, pp. 646-61.

HOBSBAWM, E.J. (1959): *Primitive Rebels: Studies in Archaic Forms of Social Movements in the Nineteenth and Twentieth Centuries.* New York: W.W. Norton.

HOPPER, REX (1950): 'The Revolutionary Process: A Frame of Reference for the Study of Revolutionary Movements'. *Social Forces.* Vol. 28, pp. 270-9.

HOROWITZ, IRVING LOUIS (1972): 'The Morphology of Modern Revolution'. *The Indian Journal of Sociology.* Vol. 3, Nos. 1 & 2 (Mar.-Sept.), pp. 3-34.

JESSOP, BOB (1972): *Social Order, Reform and Revolution.* London: Macmillan.

JOCANO, F. LANDA (1971): *Ideology and Radical Movements in the Philippines: A Preliminary View.* Singapore: Institute of South-east Asia Studies.

JOHNSON, BENTON 1957: 'A Critical Appraisal of the Church-Sect Typology'. *American Sociological Review.* Vol. 22, No. 1, pp. 84-92.

——— (1967): 'On Church and Sect'. *American Sociological Review.* Vol. 28, No. 1, pp. 64-8.

——— (1971): 'Church-Sect Revisted'. *Journal for the Scientific Study of Religion.* Vol. 10, No. 2, pp. 124-37.

JOHNSON, CHALMERS, (1966): *Revolutionary Change.* Boston: Little, Brown.

JOHNSTONE. RONALD L. (1975): *Religion and Society in Integration: The Sociology of Religion.* Englewood Cliffs. N.J.: Prentice-Hall.

KATZ, HENRYK (1971): 'Social Movements—An Essay in Definition'. *Polish Sociological Bulletin.* Vol. 23, No. 1, pp. 61-75.

KILLIAN, L. (1964): 'Social Movements'. In R.E.L. Faris (ed.), *Handbook of Modern Sociology.* Chicago: Rand-McNally, pp. 426-56.

KOBBEN, A.J.F. (1960): Prophetic Movements as an Expression of Social Protest'. *International Archives of Enthnography.* Vol. 49 (Part I), pp. 117-64.

LAIDLER, HARRY W. (1953): *Socio-Economic Movements.* London: Routledge & Kegan Paul.

LAING, R.D. (1967): *The Politics of Experience.* New York: Ballantine.

LANG, KURT & GLADYS LANG (1961): *Collective Dynamics.* New York: Thomas Y. Crowell.

LANTERNARI, VITTORIO (1955): *The Religions of the Oppressed: A Study of Modern Messianic Cults.* New York: Mentor.

LAUER, ROBERT H. (1972): 'Social Movements: An Interactionist Analysis'. *Sociological Quarterly.* Vol. 13, No. 3, pp. 315-28.

LEIDEN, C. & K.M. SCHMIDT (1968): *The Politics of Violence.* Englewood Cliffs, N.J.: Prentice-Hall.

LENS, SIDNEY (1966): *Radicalism in America.* New York: Thomas Y. Crowell.

LESSA, WILLIAM A., & EVON Z. VOGT (EDS.) (1965): *Reader in Comparative*

Religion: An Anthropological Approach (2nd ed.). New York: Harper & Row.

LINTON, RALPH (1965): 'Nativistic Movements'. In Willian A. Lessa and Evon Z. Vogt (eds.), *Reader in Comparative Religion: An Anthropological Approach* (2nd ed.). New York: Harper & Row, pp. 409-506.

LIPSKY, MICHAEL (1968): 'Protest as a Political Resource'. *American Political Science Review*. Vol. 62, pp. 1144-58.

MAIER, N.R.F. (1942): 'The Role of Frustration in Social Movements'. *Psychological Review*. Vol. 44 (Nov.), pp. 591-2.

MALALGODA, KITSIRI (1976): 'Millennialism in Relation to Buddhism'. *Comparative Studies in Society and History*. Vol. 12, pp. 424-41.

MANNHEIM, KARL (1936): *Ideology and Utopia*. Translated by Louis Wirth and E. Shils. New York: Harcourt, Brace and World.

MARRIOTT, MCKIM (1968): 'Multiple Reference in Indian Caste Systems'. In James Silverberg (ed.), *Social Mobility in the Caste System in India*. The Hague: Mouton, pp. 103-14.

MEADOWS, PAUL (1946) : 'Theses on Social Movements'. *Social Forces*. Vol. 24 (May).

MERTON, R.K. (1968) : *Social Theory and Social Structure* (enl. ed.). New Delhi: Amerind Publishing Co.

MERTON, R K. & ALICE KITT ROSSI (1950) : 'Contributions to the Theory of Reference Group Behaviour'. In R.K. Merton and P.F. Lazarsfeld (eds.), *Continuities in Social Research*. New York: The Free Press, pp. 40-106.

MESSINGER, SHELDON L. (1955): 'Organizational Transformation: A Case Study of a Declining Social Movement'. *American Sociological Review*. Vol. 20, pp. 3-10.

MORRISON, DENTON E. (1971): 'Some Notes Toward Theory on Relative Deprivation, Social Movements, and Social Change'. *American Behavioral Scientist*. Vol. 14, pp. 675-90.

MORRISON, DENTON & ALLAN STEEVES (1967) : 'Deprivation, Discontent, and Social Movement Participation: Evidence in a Contemporary Farmer's Movement'. *Rural Sociology*. Vol. 32, pp. 414-34.

MUKHERJI, P.N. (1976) : 'Social Movement and Social Change: Towards a Conceptual Clarification and Theoretical Framework'. Paper presented to the Thirteenth All India Sociological Conference, Chandigarh, 26-28 December 1976 (mimeographed).

NELSON, HAROLD (1971): 'Leadership and Change in an Evolutionary Movement'. *Social Forces*. Vol. 49, pp. 353-71.

NICHOLAS, RALPH (1973): 'Social and Political Movements'. *Annual Review of Anthropology*. Vol. 2, pp. 63-84.

NIEBUHR, H.R. (1954): *The Social Sources of Denominationalism*. Hamden, Conn.: Shoe String Press.

NIEBURG, H.L. (1969): *Political Violence*. New York: St. Martin's Press.

OBERSCHALL, ANTHONY (1973): *Social Conflict and Social Movements*. Englewood Cliffs, N.J.: Prentice-Hall.

O'DEA, T.F. (1963): 'Sociological Dilemmas: Five Paradoxes of Institutionalization'. In E.A. Tiryakian (ed.), *Sociological Theory, Values and Socio-Cultural Change*. New York: The Free Press, pp. 71-89.

———(1968): 'Sects and Cults'. In David Sills (ed.), *International Encyclopaedia of the Social Sciences.* Vol. 14. New York: Macmillan Co., & The Free Press, pp. 130-5.

OLSEN, MARVIN L. (1968): 'Perceived Legitimacy of Social Protest Actions'. *Social Problems.* Vol. 15, pp. 297-310.

OOMMEN, T.K. (1976): 'Sociological Issues in the Analysis of Social Movements in Independent India'. Paper presented to the Thirteenth All-India Sociological Conference, Chandigarh, 26-28 December 1976 (mimeographed).

———(Forthcoming): 'Methodological Framework and Empirical Reality: Their Interactions in the Study of a Social Movement'. In Yogendra Singh and T.K. Oommen (eds.), *The Craft of Social Sciences in India.*

PINARD, MAURICE (1968): 'Mass Society and Political Movements: A New Formulation'. *American Journal of Sociology.* Vol. 73, No. 6 (May), pp. 682-90.

POPE, LISTON (1942): *Millhands and Preachers: A Study of Gastonia.* New Haven, Conn.: Yale University Press.

PORTES, ALEJANDRO (1971): 'Political Primitivism, Differential Socialization, and Lower Class Leftist Radicalism'. *American Sociological Review.* Vol. 36 (Oct.), pp. 820-35.

PUTNEY, SNELL & MIDDLETON RUSSEL (1961): 'Dimensions and Correlations of Religious Ideologies'. *Social Forces.* Vol. 39 (May).

RAO, M.S.A. (1976): 'Some Conceptual Problems in the Study of Social Movements'. Paper presented to the Thirteenth All India Sociological Conference, Chandigarh, 26-28 December 1976 (Chp. of this Volume).

———(1977): 'Themes in the Ideology of Protest Movements'. In S.C. Malik (ed.), *Dissent, Protest and Reform in Indian Civilization.* Simla: Indian Institute of Advanced Studies, pp. 56-64.

REDEKOP, CALVIN (1974): 'A New Look at Sect Development'. *Journal for the Scientific Study of Religion.* Vol. 13, No. 3 (Sept.), pp. 345-52.

ROCHE, J.P. & S. SACHS (1955): 'The Bureaucrat and the Enthusiast: An Exploration of the Leadership of Social Movements'. *Western Political Quarterly.* Vol. 8, pp. 248-61.

ROY, WALLIS (1974): 'Ideology, Authority and the Development of Cultic Movements'. *Social Research.* Vol. 41, No. 2 (Summer), pp. 299-327.

RUNCIMAN, W.G. (1961): 'Problems of Research on Relative Deprivation'. *The European Journal of Sociology.* Vol. 2, pp. 315-23.

———(1966): *Relative Deprivation and Social Justice.* Berkeley: University of California Press

RUSH, GARY B., & R. SERGE DENISOFF (1971): *Social and Political Movements.* New York: Appleton-Century Crofts.

SCHWARTZ, G. (1970): *Sect Ideologies and Social Status.* Chicago: University of Chicago Press.

SIMMEL, GEORG (1955): *Conflict and the Web of Group-Affiliations.* Translated by K. Wolff and R. Bendix. New York: The Free Press.

SMELSER, NEIL J. (1963): *Theory of Collective Behavior.* New York: The Free Press.

SMITH, D.E. (1965): 'Millenarian Scholarship in America'. *American Quarterly.* Vol. 17, pp. 535-49.

SMITH, M.W. (1959): 'Towards a Classification of Cult Movements'. *Man*. Vol. 59, pp. 8-12.

SNOOK, JOHN B. (1974): 'An Alternative to Church-Sect'. *Journal for the Scientific Study of Religion*. Vol. 13, No. 2 (June). pp. 191-204.

SPIER. LESLIE *et al*. (1959): 'Comments on Aberle's Thesis of Deprivation'. *Southwestern Journal of Anthropology*. Vol. 15, pp. 84-8.

SRINIVAS, M.N. (1952): *Religion and Society Among the Coorgs of South India*. Oxford: Clarendon Press.

————(1966): *Social Change in Modern India*. Berkeley: University of California Press.

STEIN, LORENZO VON (1964): *The History of the Social Movement in France 1789-1850*. Introduced, edited, and translated by Kaethe Mengelberg. Totowa, N.J.: Bedminster Press.

STOUFFER SAMUEL A. *et al*. (*eds*.) (1949): *The American Soldier: Adjustment during Army Life*. Vol. I. Princeton: Princeton University Press.

TALMON, YONINA (1962): 'Pursuit of the Millennium: The Relation between Religious and Social Change'. *Archives Europeenes de Sociologie*. Vol. 3, pp. 125-48.

————(1966): 'Millenarian Movements'. *Archives Europeenes de Sociologie*. Vol. 7, pp. 159-200.

THRUPP, SYLVIA (*ed*.) (1962): *Millennial Dreams in Action: Essays in Comparative Studies*. Comparative Studies in Society and History. The Hague: Mouton.

TILLY, CHARLES (1975): 'Revolutions and Collective Violence'. In Fred I. Greenstein and Nelson W. Polsby (eds.), *Handbook of Political Science*. Vol. 3. Reading, Mass.: Addison-Wesley.

TOCH, HANS (1965): *The Social Psychology of Social Movements*. Indianapolis: Bobbs-Merrill.

TURNER, H.W. (1966): 'A Methodology for Women African Religious Movements'. *Comparative Studies in Society and History*. Vol. 8, pp. 281-94.

TURNER, RALPH (1964a): 'Collective Behavior'. In Robert E. Faris (ed.), *Handbook of Modern Sociology*. Chicago: Rand McNally.

————(1964b): 'Collective Behavior and Conflict: The Theoretical Frameworks'. *Sociological Quarterly*. Vol. 5, pp. 122-32.

————(1969a): 'The Public Perception of Protest'. *American Sociological Review*. Vol. 34, No. 6, pp. 815-31.

————(1969b): 'The Theme of Contemporary Social Movements'. *British Journal of Sociology*. Vol. 20, No. 4 (Dec.), pp. 390-405.

————(1970); 'Determinants of Social Movement Strategies'. In Tamotsu Shibutani (ed.), *Human Nature and Collective Behavior*. Englewood Cliffs, N.J.: Prentice-Hall, pp. 145-64.

TURNER, R., & L. KILLIAN (*eds*.) (1957) : *Collective Behavior*. Englewood Cliffs, N.J.: Prentice-Hall.

TURNER, VICTOR W. (1974): 'Metaphors of Anti-Structure in Religious Culture'. In Allan W. Eister (ed.), *Changing Perspectives in the Scientific Study of Religion*. New York: John Wiley & Sons.

TUVESON, E.L. (1964): *Millennium and Utopia: A Study in the Background of the Idea of Progress*. New York: Harper Torchbooks.

VANDER ZANDEN, JAMES W. (1959): 'Resistance and Social Movements'. *Social Forces*. Vol. 37, pp, 312-5.

WAKEFIELD, DAN (1960): *Revolt in the South*. New York: Grove Press.

WALLACE, A.F.C. (1956): 'Revitalization Movements'. *American Anthropologist* New Series. Vol. 58 (April), pp. 264-81.

WALLACE, A.F.C., *et al*. (1959): 'Toward a Classification of Cult Movements: Some Further Contributions'. *Man*, Vol. 59, pp. 25-8.

WALZER, MICHAEL (1965): *The Revolution of the Saints: A Study in the Origins of Radical Politics*. Cambridge, Mass.: Harvard University Press.

WILKINSON, PAUL (1971): *Social Movement*. London: Macmillan.

WILSON, BRYAN R. (1959): 'An Analysis of Sect Development'. *American Sociological Review*. Vol. 24, pp. 3-15.

————(1961): *Sects and Society*. Berkeley: University of California Press.

————(1963): 'Millennialism in Comparative Perspective'. *Comparative Studies in Society and History*. Vol. 6, pp. 93-114.

————(1970): *Religious Sects: A Sociological Study*. London: Weidenfeld and Nicolson.

WILSON, BRYAN R. (ED.) (1967): *Patterns of Sectarianism: Organization and Ideology in Social and Religious Movements*. London: Heinemann.

WILSON JOHN (1973): *Introduction to Social Movements*. New York: Basic Books.

WORSLEY, PETER (1957): *The Trumpet Shall Sound: A Study of Cargo Cults in Melanesia*. London: MacGibbon and Kee.

YINGER, J. MILTON (1946): *Religion in the Struggle for Power*. Durham, N.C.: Duke University Press.

————(1965): *Sociology Looks at Religion*. New York: Macmillan.

————(1970): *The Scientific Study of Religion*. New York: Macmillan.

ZAKUTA, LEO (1964): *A Protest Movement Becalmed*. Toronto: University of Toronto Press.

ZALD, MAYER N. & ROBERTA ASH (1966): 'Social Movements Organizations: Growth, Decay and Change'. *Social Forces*. Vol. 44, pp. 327-41.

ZEITLIN, MAURICE (1966): 'Alienation and Revolution'. *Social Forces*. Vol. 45 (Dec.), pp. 224-36.

ZYGMUNT, J. F. (1970): 'Prophetic Failure and Chiliastic Identity: The Case of Jehovah's Witnesses'. *American Journal of Sociology*. Vol. 75, pp. 926-48.

3. Peasant Movements

BECK, E.F. BRENDA (1972): *Peasant Society in Konku: A Study of Right and Left Subcastes in South India*. Vancouver: University of British Columbia Press.

BEDFORD, IAN GEORGE (1961): 'Telangana Insurrection: A Study in Cause and Development of a Communist Insurrection in Rural India, 1946-1951'. Unpublished Ph.D. thesis. Australian National University.

BETEILLE, ANDRE (1970*a*) : 'The Causes of Agrarian Unrest'. The *Citizen*. Vol. 1, No. 23 (Feb.).

————(1970*b*) : 'Peasant Associations and the Agrarian Class Structure'. *Contributions to Indian Sociology*. New Series, Vol. 4, pp. 126-39.

————(1971) : 'Class Structure in an Agrarian Society: The Case of the Jotedars'. In *Society and Revolution: Essays in Honour of Engels*. Delhi: People's Publishing House, pp. 208-36.

————(1972*a*) : 'The Study of Agrarian Systems: An Anthropological Approach'. *Man in India*. Vol. 52, No. 2, pp. 150-73.

————(1972*b*) : 'Agrarian Relations in Tanjore District, South India'. *Sociological Bulletin*. Vol. 21, No. 2, (Sept.), pp. 122-51.

————(1974) : *Studies in Agrarian Social Structure*. Delhi: Oxford University Press.

BLAIR, H.W. (1976) : 'Primary and Secondary Characteristics in Peasant Politics at the Micro-level in an Indian Constituency: A Statistical Odyssey'. *Contributions to Indian Sociology*. New Series. Vol. 9, No. 3 (Jan.-June).

CHARLESWORTH, NEIL (1962) : 'Rich Peasants and Poor Peasants in Late Nineteenth Century Maharashtra'. Paper presented at a Seminar in the Institute of Commonwealth Studies, London University, 7 May 1963.

————(1976) : 'Economic and Social Stratification among the Bombay Peasantry: Some More Reflections'. Paper presented at a Seminar in the Institute of Commonwealth Studies, London University, 6 April 1976.

CRANE ROBERT I. (1952) : 'Indian National Congress and the Indian Agrarian Problem, 1919-1939: An Historical Study'. Unpublished Ph.D. thesis. Yale University.

CRAWLEY, W.F. (1971) : 'Kisan Sabhas and Agrarian Revolt in the United Provinces, 1920-1921' *Modern Asian Studies*, Vol. 5, No. 2, pp. 96-108.

DALE, STEPHEN F. (1972) : 'Islam and Social Conflict: The Mappillas of Malabar, 1498-1922'. Unpublished Ph.D. thesis. University of California.

————(1975) : 'The Mappilla Outbreaks: Ideology and Social Conflict in Nineteenth Century Kerala'. *Journal of Asian Studies*. Vol. 35, No. 1 (Nov.), pp. 85-97.

————(1976) : 'The Mappillas During Mysorean Rule: Agrarian Conflict in Eighteenth-Century Malabar'. *South Asia*. No. 6 (Dec.), pp. 1-13.

DHANAGARE, D.N. (1973) : 'Peasant Movements in India, 1920-1950'. Unpublished D.Phil. thesis. University of Sussex.

————(1974) : 'Social Origins of the Peasant Insurrection in Telangana (1964-71)'. *Contributions to Indian Sociology*. New Series. No. 8.

————(1975*a*) : 'The Politics of Survival: Peasant Organizations and the Left-Wing in India, 1925-46'. *Sociological Bulletin*. Vol. 24, No. 1 (Mar.), pp. 29-54.

————(1975*b*) : 'Congress and Agrarian Agitation in Oudh, 1920-22 and 1930-32'. *South Asia*. No. 5.

————(1976) : 'Peasant Protest and Politics—The Tebhaga Movement in Bengal (India), 1946-1947'. *The Journal of Peasant Studies*. Vol. 3, No. 3 (April), pp. 360-78.

DUTT, KRISHAN (1972) : 'Sardar Patel and the Bardoli Movement'. Unpublished Ph.D. thesis. Meerut University.

FUKUZANA, H. (1965) : 'Land and Peasants in the Eighteenth Century Maratha Kingdom'. *Hitotsubashi Journal of Economics*. (June).

GOPALAN, NAYAR C. (1921) : *The Moplah Rebellion*. Calcutta: N.C. Gopalan.

GOUGH, KATHLEEN (1968-69) : 'Peasant Resistance and Revolt in South India'. *Pacific Affairs*. Vol. 16, No. 4 (Winter).

————(1974) : 'Indian Peasant Uprisings'. *Economic and Political Weekly*. Vol. 9, Nos. 32-34 (August).

GOVERNMENT OF INDIA (1969) : 'The Causes and Nature of Current Agrarian Tensions'. Delhi: Ministry of Home Affairs, Research and Policy Division (mimeographed).

GURNANEY, M.U. (1962) : Some Factors Shaping the Indian Labour Movement'. Unpublished Ph.D. thesis. University of Wisconsin.

HARCOURT, M.V. (1977) : 'Kisan Populism and North Indian Politics: The Context of the 1942 Rebellion in Bihar and Eastern U.P.'. In D.A. Low (ed.), *Congress and the Raj*. Delhi: Arnold-Heinemann.

HARDGRAVE, JR. R.L. (1976) : 'Peasant Mobilization in Malabar: the Mappilla Rebellion, 1921'. In R.L. Crane (ed.), *Aspects of Mobilization in South Asia*. Syracuse: Maxwell School, Syracuse University.

————(1977) : 'The Mappilla Rebellion, 1921: Peasant Revolt in Malabar'. *Modern Asian Studies*. Vol. 11, No. 1, pp. 57-99.

HARDIMAN, D. (1975) : 'Peasant Agitations in Kheda District, Gujarat, 1917-1934'. Unpublished D.Phil. dissertation. University of Sussex.

————(1976) : 'Politicisation and Agitation among the Dominant Peasants in Early Twentieth Century India'. *Economic and Political Weekly*. Vol. 9 (28 Feb.).

HAUSER, WALTER (1961) : 'Bihar Provincial Kisan Sabha, 1920-1940: A Study of an Indian Peasant Movement'. Unpublished Ph.D. thesis. University of Chicago.

JOSHI, P.C. (1969) : 'Agrarian Social Structure and Social Change'. *Sankhya*. Series B, Vol. 31, Parts 3 & 4.

————(1970) : 'Factors underlying Agrarian Unrest'. Review Article, *Seminar* (May).

————(1974*a*) : 'Land Reform and Agrarian Change in India and Pakistan since 1947: I'. *The Journal of Peasant Studies*. Vol. 1, No. 2 (Jan.), pp. 164-85.

————(1974*b*) : 'Land Reform and Agrarian Change in India and Pakistan since 1947: II'. *The Journal of Peasant Studies*. Vol. 1, No. 3 (April), pp. 326-62.

KARAT, P. (1976) : 'Peasant Movement in Malabar, 1934-40'. *Social Scientist*. Vol. 5, No. 2 (Sept.), pp. 30-44.

KELKAR, GOVIND S. (1975) : 'Kisan Unrest and the Congress in U.P., 1920-22'. *Economic and Political Weekly*. Vol. 10, No. 52 (Dec.), p. 1987.

MIES, MARIA (1976) : 'Peasant's Movement in Maharashtra: Its Development and its Perspective'. *Journal of Contemporary Asia*. Vol. 6, No. 2, pp. 172-85

MUKHERJI, P.N. (1966): 'Gramdan in Berain: Sociological Analysis'. *Human Organization*. Vol. 25, No. 1.

NEALE, WALTER (1962): 'The Indian Peasant: The State and Economic Development'. *Land Economics*. Vol. 38 (November), pp. 281-91.

NEWELL, RICHARD SMITH (1966): 'Congress Agrarian Reform Policy: A Case Study of Land Redistribution in Northern India". Unpublished Ph.D. thesis. University of Pennsylvania.

OMVEDT, GAIL (1974): 'Revolution and the Rural Proletariat in Contemporary Western India'. *Journal of Contemporary Asia*.

OOMMEN, T.K. (1967): 'Charisma, Social Structure and Social Change'. *The Comparative Study of Society and History*. Vol. 10 (Oct.), pp. 85-9.

————(1971): 'Agrarian Tensions in a Kerala District: An Analysis'. *Indian Journal of Industrial Relations*. Vol. 7.

————(1972) *Charisma, Stability and Change: An Analysis of Bhoodan-Gramdan Movement in India*. New Delhi: Thomson Press.

————(1975): 'Agrarian Legislations and Movements as Sources of Social Change'. *Economic and Political Weekly*. Vol. 10, No. 40.

————(1977): 'From Mobilization to Institutionalization: The Life-Cycle of an Agrarian Movement in Kerala'. In S.C. Malik (ed.), *Dissent, Protest and Reform in Indian Civilization*. Simla: Indian Institute of Advanced Study, pp. 286-301.

POUCHEPADASS, J. (1974): 'Local Leaders and the Intelligentsia in the Champaran Satyagraha (1917): A Study in Peasant Mobilization'. *Contributions to Indian Sociology*. New Series, No. 8.

PRASAD, PRADHAN H. (1975): 'Agrarian Unrest and Economic Changes in Rural Bihar: Three Case Studies'. *Economic and Political Weekly* (14 June).

RANGA, N.G. (1936): 'The All India Kisan Movement'. In H.N. Mitra (ed.), *The Indian Annual Register*. (July-Dec.). Vol. 2, pp. 280-99.

————(1949): *Revolutionary Peasants*. Delhi: Amrit Book Co.

SEN, BHAWANI (1962): *Evolution of Agrarian Relations in India*. Delhi: People's Publishing House.

SEN, SUSHIL (1972): *Agrarian Struggle in Bengal 1946-47*. Delhi: People's Publishing House.

SHAH, S.A. & KATHLEEN, GOUGH (1969): 'Class and Agrarian Change: Some Comments on Peasant-Resistance and Revolt in India'. *Pacific Affairs*. Vol. 42.

SIDDIQI, MAJID HAYAT (1972): 'The Peasant Movement in Pratapgarh, 1920'. *The Indian Economic and Social History Review*. Vol. 9, No. 3.

SINGH, RAJENDRA (1974*a*): 'Agrarian Social Structure and Peasant Unrest: A Study of Land-Grab Movement in District Basti, East U.P.'. *Sociological Bulletin*. Vol. 23, No. 1 (March), pp. 44-70.

————(1974*b*): 'Social Structure and Peasant Revolution—A Case Study of an Abortive Land Grab Movement in Uttar Pradesh'. Paper presented to the XII All-India Sociological Conference, B.H.U., Varanasi, 28-30 October 1974 (mimeographed).

————(1976): 'Peasant Movement in Eastern U.P.'. Paper presented at the Workshop on Social Movements, Department of Sociology, University of Delhi, 24-26 March 1976 (Chapter 3 of this Volume).

SINGH, V.P. (1970) : 'Evolution of a Rural Stratification System in India, 1930-65'. Unpublished Ph D. thesis. University of Wisconsin.

STOKES, ERIC (1970) : 'Traditional Elites in the Great Rebellion of 1857: Some Aspects of Rural Revolts in the Upper and Central Doab'. In Edmund Leach and S.N. Mukherjee (eds.), *Elites in South Asia*. London: Cambridge University Press.

TEWARI, SMITA (1977) : 'Agrarian Relations in Awadh'. Unpublished M.Phil. dissertation. Department of Sociology, University of Delhi.

TOTTENHAM, G.R.F. (1922) : *The Mappilla Rebellion, 1921-22*. Madras: Government Press.

WOOD, CONRAD (1973) : 'An Interpretation of Moplah Violence'. Paper presented at a Seminar in the School of Oriental and African Studies, University of London, 22 May 1973.

————(1974) : 'Historical Background of the Moplah Rebellion'. *Social Scientist*. (Trivandrum), Vol. 3, No. 1 (Aug.), pp. 5-33.

————(1976) : 'Moplah Rebellions between 1800-02 and 1921-22'. *Indian Economic and Social History Review*. Vol. 13, No. 1 (Jan.-Mar.), pp. 97-106.

4. Social Reform Movements

BARRIER, N.G. (1967) : 'The Arya Samaj and Congress Politics in the Punjab, 1894-1908'. *Journal of Asian Studies*. Vol. 26, No. 3 (May).

BHATT, G.S. (1968) : 'Brahmo Samaj, Arya Samaj and the Church-Sect Typology'. *Review of Religious Research*. Vol. 10, No. 1 (Fall).

————(1973) : 'Ideological and Socio-Historical Role of Elites in the Brahmo Samaj and Arya Samaj Movements'. In K.S. Mathur *et al.* (ed.), *Studies in Social Change*. Lucknow: Ethnographic & Folk Culture Society, U.P., pp. 69-98.

BONDURANT, JOAN V. (1965) : *Conquest of Violence: The Gandhian Philosophy of Conflict* (rev. ed). Berkeley, California: University of California.

BONDURANT, JOAN V & MARAGRET, W. FISHER (1966*a*) : 'The Concept of Change in Hindu, Socialist and Neo-Gandhian Thought'. In Donald E. Smith (ed.), *Religion and Politics in South Asia*. Princeton: Princeton University Press.

————(1966*b*) : 'Ethics in Action: Contrasting Approaches to Social and Political Problems in Modern India'. *Australian Journal of Politics and History*. Vol. 12, No. 2, (Aug.).

CHAMUPATI, M.A. (1964) : *Principles of Arya Samaj*. Delhi: New India Press.

CARROLL, LUCY (1976) : 'The Temperance Movement in India: Politics and Social Reform'. *Modern Asian Studies*. Vol. 10 (Part 3), (July), pp. 417-48.

CHAKRAVARTI, S.C. & S.N. RAY (COMPILERS) (1933) : *Brahmo Samaj, The Depressed Classes and Untouchability*. Calcutta: Sadharan Brâhmo Samaj.

CHINTAMANI C.Y. (ED.) (1901) : *Indian Social Reform*. Madras: Thompson & Co.

DUA, VEENA (1969) : 'The Arya Samaj and Politics'. Paper presented at the Ninth All-India Sociological Conference, I.I.T., Delhi, 22-25 November 1969 (mimeographed).

———(1970*a*) : 'Social Organization of the Arya Samaj: A Study of Two Local Arya Centres in Jullundur'. *Sociological Bulletin*. Vol. 19, No. 1 (March), pp. 32-50.

———(1970*b*) : 'Arya Samaj and Punjab Politics'. *Economic and Political Weekly*. Vol. 4, Nos. 43 & 44, (Oct.), pp. 1787-91.

FISHER MARGARET W. & JOAN V. BONDURANT (1956) : *Indian Approaches to a Socialist Society*. Indian Press Digests Monograph Series, No. 2. Berkeley, California: Institute of International Studies of the University of California.

GRAHAM REID (1942) : 'The Arya Samaj as a Reformation in Hinduism with Special Reference to Caste'. Unpublished Ph. D. thesis. Yale University.

GRISWOLD, H.D. (1909) : 'Arya Samaj'. *Encyclopaedia of Religion and Ethics*. Vol. 2, pp. 57-62.

GUPTA, K.P. (1974) : 'Religious Evolution and Social Change in India: A Study of Ramakrishna Mission Movement'. *Contributions to Indian Sociology*. New Series, No. 8.

HEIMSATH, C.H. (1964) : *Indian Nationalism and Hindu Social Reform*. Princeton: Princeton University Press.

ISWAR, SARAN (1966) : *A Handbook of the Arya Samaj*. Benares.

JAVED, RAM CHANDRA (1954) : *Arya Samaj ke Mahapurush*. Jullundur: Yunivarsiti Publishers.

JONES, KENNETH W. (1968) : 'Communalism in the Punjab: The Arya Samaj Contribution'. *Journal of Asian Studies*. Vol. 28, No. 1, pp. 39-54.

———(1973) : 'Ham Hindu Nahin: Arya-Sikh Relations, 1877-1905'. *Journal of Asian Studies*. Vol. 32, No. 3 (May), pp. 457-75.

———(1975) : 'Sources for Arya Samaj History'. In W. Eric Gustafson and Kenneth W. Jones (eds.), *Sources on Punjab History*. Delhi: Manohar Book Service.

———(1976) : *Arya Dharm: Hindu Consciousness in 19th Century Punjab*. Berkeley: University of California Press.

JORDENS, J.T.F. (1977) : 'Reconversion to Hinduism, the Shuddhi of the Arya Samaj'. In G.A. Oddie (ed.), *Religion in South Asia: Religious Conversion and Revival Movements in South Asia in Medieval and Modern Times*. Delhi: Manohar Book Service, pp. 145-61.

KEER, DHANANJAY (1969) : *Mahatma Joti Rao Phooley*. Bombay: Popular Prakashan.

KOPF, DAVID (1970) : 'The Brahmo Samaj Intelligentsia and the Bengal Renaissance'. In R.I. Crane (ed.), *Transition in South Asia: Problems of Modernization*. Program in Comparative Studies on Southern Asia. Durham: Duke University, pp. 7-48.

KUBER, W.N. (1973) : *Dr. Ambedkar: A Critical Study*. New Delhi: People's Publishing House.

LAJPAT RAI, LALA (1915) : *The Arya Samaj*. London: Longmans, Green & Co.

LEONARD, J.G. (1970) : 'Kandukuri Viresalingam: A Biography of an Indian Social Reformer, 1848-1919'. Unpublished Ph. D. thesis. University of Wisconsin.

METCALF, T.R. (1965) : *The Aftermath of Revolt: India—1857-1870*. Princeton; Princeton University Press.

NAG, B.A. (1901): 'The Arya Samaj, its History, Progress and Methods'. *Indian Evangelical Review.* (Oct.).

NAIR, SANKARAN C. (1913): *The Position of Hindu Social Reform Associations.* Madras: India Printing Works.

NATARAJAN, S. (1959): *A Century of Social Reform in India.* Bombay: Asia Publishing House.

NAYAR, BALDEV RAJ (1966): *Minority Politics in the Punjab.* Princeton: Princeton University Press.

OMVEDT, GAIL (1971): 'Jotirao Phule and the Ideology of Social Revolution in India'. *Economic and Political Weekly.* Vol. 6, No. 37, (Sept.), pp. 1969-79.

———(1973): 'The Satyashodhak Samaj and Peasant Agitation'. *Economic and Political Weekly.* (Nov.), pp. 1971-82.

PANDEY, D. (1972): *The Arya Samaj and Indian Nationalism.* New Delhi: Sultan Chand.

PARLEK, R.S. (1973): *Contribution of the Arya Samaj in the Making of Modern India, 1875-1947.* New Delhi: Arya Pratini.

PATHAN, Y.M. (1977): "Mahatama Jotirao Phule and Satyashodhak Samaj". In S.C. Malik (ed.), *Dissent, Protest and Reform in Indian Civilization.* Simla: Indian Institute of Advanced Study.

PULLAPILLY, CYRIAC K. (1976): 'The Izhavas of Kerala and their Historic Struggle for Acceptance in the Hindu Society'. In Bardwell L. Smith (ed.), *Religion and Social Conflict in South Asia.* Leiden: E.J. Brill.

RAM, MUNSHI & RAMA DEVA (1911): *The Arya Samaj and its Detractors.* Kangri, Hardwar: Satya Dharm Pracharak Press.

RAM, PANDIT LEKH (1893): *Arya Samaj Men Shanti Phailane ke Asli Upao* (The Real Means of Spreading Peace throughout the Arya Samaj). Jullundur: Sat Dharam Pracharak Press.

RANADE, M.G. (1901): 'The Saints and Prophets of Maharashtra'. In M.G. Ranade, *Rise of Maratha Power.* Bombay: Bombay University.

RAO, M.S.A (1978): *Social Movements and Social Transformation: A Study of Two Backward Classes Movements.* New Delhi: Macmillan.

SARDA, HAR BILAS (1946): *Life of Dayanand Saraswati, World Teacher.* Ajmer: Vedic Granthalaya.

SASTRI, SIVANATH (1911-12): *History of the Brahmo Samaj.* 2 vols. Calcutta.

SHARMA, PANDIT VISHNU LAL (1912): *Handbook of the Arya Samaj.* Allahabad: The Indian Press.

SHARMA, URSULA (1976): 'Status Striving and Striving to Abolish Status: The Arya Samaj and the Low Castes'. *Social Action.* Vol. 26, No. 3 (July-Sept.), pp. 214-36.

SHASTRI, V.N. (1945): *The Arya Samaj: Its Cult and Creed.* New Delhi: Sarvdeshik Arya Pratinidhi Sabha.

SINGH, BAWA CHHAJJU (1908): *The Teachings of the Arya Samaj.* Lahore: Arya Samaj, Anarkali.

SURI, PUSHPA (1977): 'Some Aspects of the Arya Samaj with Special Reference to the Punjab'. In S.C. Malik (ed.), *Dissent, Protest and Reform in Indian Civilization.* Simla: Indian Institute of Advanced Study.

THURSBY, G. (1972): 'Aspects of Hindu-Muslim Relations in British India: A Study of Arya Samaj Activities, Government of India Policies, and Communal Conflict in the period 1923-1928'. Unpublished Ph.D. thesis. Duke University.

UPADHYAYA, GANGA PRASAD (1954) : *The Origin, Aims and Scope of the Arya Samaj* (2nd edn.). Allahabad: Arya Samaj, Chowk.

————(1956) : *The Light of Truth*. English translation of Swami Dayananda's *Satyarth Prakasha*. Allahabad: The Kala Press.

VIDYAVACHASPATI, INDRA (1957) : *Arya Samaj ka Itihas*. 2 vols. Delhi: Sarvadeshak Arya Pratinidhi Sabha.

VYAS, K.C. (1957) : *The Social Renaissance in India*. Bombay: Vora & Co.

WILLIAM, ROY SMITH (1938) : *Nationalism and Reform in India*. New Haven: Yale University Press.

5. Caste Movements

AGARWAL, L.B. (1934) : *The Harijans in Rebellion*. Bombay: Taraporewala & Sons.

AIYAPPAN, A. (1944) : *Iravas and Culture Change*. Madras: Superintendent, Government Press.

————(1965) : *Social Revolution in a Kerala Village*. New York: Asia Publishing House.

ALEXANDER, K.C. (1968*a*) : *Social Mobility in Kerala*. Poona: Deccan College.

————(1968*b*) : 'Changing Status of Pulaya Harijans of Kerala'. *Economic and Political Weekly*. Special No. (July), pp. 1071-4.

————(1968*c*) : 'Changing Religious Beliefs and Practices of the Pulayas of Kerala'. *Social Action* (Sept.-Oct.), pp. 390-7.

ARNOLD, DAVID & JAMES MANOR (1976) : 'Caste Associations in South India: A Comparative Analysis'. *The Indian Economic and Social History Review*. Vol. 8, No. 3 (July-Sept.).

AURORA, G.S. (1968) : 'Caste and the Backward Classes'. *Man in India*. Vol. 48, pp. 297-306.

AZARIAH, V.S. (1932) : 'The Caste Movement in South India'. *International Review of Missions*. Vol. 21, pp. 457-87.

BABB, L. (1972) : 'The Political Involvement of a Religious Movement: The Satnamis'. In J.M. Mahar (ed.), *The Untouchables in Contemporary India*. Tuscon: The University of Arizona Press, pp. 143-51.

BARNETT, MARGUERITE ROSS (1975) : 'Cultural Nationalist Electoral Politics in Tamil Nadu, South India'. In Myron Weiner and John Osgood Field (eds.), *Electoral Politics in the Indian States*. Delhi: Manohar Book Service.

————(Forthcoming) : *The Politics of Cultural Nationalism in South India*. Princeton: Princeton University Press.

BARNETT, MARGUERITE ROSS & STEPHEN A. BARNETT (1974) : 'A Contemporary Peasant and Post Peasant Alternatives in Tamil Nadu, South India: The Ideas of a Militant South Indian Untouchable'. *Annals of the New York Academy of Science*. Vol. 220 (March), pp. 385-410.

BARNETT, STEPHEN A. (1970) : 'The Structural Position of a South Indian Caste: Kondaikkatti Vellalas of Tamil Nadu'. Unpublished Ph.D. dissertation. University of Chicago.

———(1975): 'Approaches to Changes in Caste Ideology in South India'. In Burton Stein (ed.), *Essays on South Asia.* Honolulu, Hawaii: University Press of Hawaii.

———(1976): 'The Process of Withdrawal in a South Indian Caste'. In Milton Singer (ed.), *Entrepreneurship and the Modernization of Occupations in South Asia.* Durham, D.C.: Duke University Press.

———(Forthcoming): *From Structure to Substance: Change in a South Indian Caste.*

BETEILLE, ANDRE (1965): 'The Future of the Backward Classes: The Competing Demands of Status and Power'. *Perspectives, Supplement to the Indian Journal of Public Administration.* Vol. 11, pp. 1-39.

———(1969): *Castes: Old and New Essays in Social Structure and Social Stratification.* Bombay: Asia Publishing House.

BETEILLE, ANDRE & M.N. SRINIVAS (1965): 'The Untouchables of India'. *Scientific American.* Vol. 213, pp. 13-17.

BHAGAT, M.G. (1935): *The Untouchable Classes of Maharashtra.* Bombay: University of Bombay.

BHAT, CHANDRASHEKHAR (1977): 'Social Mobility among the Waddars of South India with special reference to Mysore'. Ph.D. thesis submitted to Department of Sociology, University of Delhi.

BHATT, ANIL (1971): 'Politics of Social Mobility in India'. *Contributions to Indian Sociology.* New Series, No. 5.

BLAIR, H.W. (1969): 'Caste, Politics and Democracy in Bihar State of India: The Elections of 1967'. Unpublished Ph.D. thesis. Duke University.

BOSE, N.K. (1975): *The Structure of Hindu Society.* Translated by Andre Beteille. New Delhi: Orient Longman.

BRIGGS, G.W. (1920): *The Chamars.* London: Oxford University Press.

COHN, B.S. (1954): 'The Camars of Senapur: A Study of the Changing Status of a Depressed Caste'. Unpublished Ph.D. thesis. Cornell University, Ithaca, New York.

———(1955): 'The Changing Status of a Depressed Caste'. In McKim Marriott (ed.), *Village India.* Chicago: University of Chicago Press, pp. 53-77.

———(1959): 'Changing Traditions of a Low Caste'. In Milton B. Singer (ed.), *Traditional India: Structure and Change.* Philadelphia: American Folklore Society.

CONLON, F.F. (1969): 'The Emergence of the Sarasvat Brahmans, 1830-1930'. Unpublished Ph.D. thesis. University of Minnesota.

———(1970): 'Caste and Urbanism in Historical Perspective: The Saraswat Brahmans'. In R.G. Fox (ed.), *Urban India: Society, Space and Image.* Program in Comparative Studies on Southern Asia. Duke University, Monograph Number 10, pp. 25-38.

———(1974): 'Caste by Association: The Gauda Sarasvata Brahmana Unification Movement'. *Journal of Asian Studies.* Vol. 33, No. 3, pp. 351-65.

———(1977): *A Caste in a Changing World: The Chitrapur Saraswat Brahmans 1700-1935.* New Delhi: Thomson Press (India) Ltd.

COPLAND, IAN (1973): 'The Maharaja of Kolhapur and the Non-Brahmin Movement, 1902-10'. *Modern Asian Studies.* Vol. 7, No. 2, pp. 209-25.

DIEHL, ANITA (1976): 'E. V. Ramaswami Naicker-Periyar: A Study of the Influence of Personality on Social and Political Development, Outlines and Extracts'. Paper presented to 5th European Conference on Modern Asian Studies, Leiden, July 1976 (mimeographed).

DUSHKIN, LELAH (1961*a*): 'The Backward Classes'. *The Economic Weekly*. Vol. 13, No. 43, pp. 1665-83.

————(1961*b*): 'The Backward Classes' *The Economic Weekly*. Vol. 13, No. 45, pp. 1695-1706.

————(1961*c*): 'The Backward Classes'. *The Economic Weekly*. Vol. 13, No. 46, pp. 1729-38.

————(1972): 'The Non-Brahmin Movement in Mysore State'. Association for Asian Studies, New York (mimeographed).

————(1974): 'The Non-Brahmin Movement in Princely Mysore'. Unpublished Ph. D. thesis. University of Pennsylvania, Philadelphia.

FISHMAN, A.T. (1941): *Culture Change and the Underprivileged: A Study of Madigas in South India Under Christian Guidance*. Madras: Christian Literary Society.

FOX, RICHARD G. (1967): 'Resiliency and Change in the Indian Caste System: The Umar of U.P.'. *Journal of Asian Studies*. Vol. 26, pp. 575-87.

GHURYE, G.S. (1932): *Caste and Race in India*. London: Routledge and Kegan Paul.

————(1961): *Caste, Class and Occupation*. Bombay: Popular Book Depot.

GALANTER, MARC (COMPILER & EDITOR) (1965): 'Legal Materials for the Study of Modern India: An Introduction to the Civilization of India'. 4 parts. The University of Chicago, The College, Chicago, Illinois (mimeographed).

GOINDI, S. (1958): 'Backward Classes in U.P.'. Unpublished Ph.D. thesis. Allahabad University.

GOKHALE, B.G. (1976): 'Dr. Bhimrao Ramji Ambedkar: Rebel against Hindu Tradition'. In Bardwell L. Smith (ed.), *Religion and Social Conflict in South Asia*. Leiden: E.J. Brill.

GOUGH, KATHLEEN (1967): 'Kerala Politics and the 1965 Elections'. *International Journal of Comparative Sociology* (Sept.).

————(1970): 'Palakkara: Social and Religious Change in Central Kerala' In K. Ishwaran (ed.), *Change and Continuity in India's Villages*. New York: Columbia University Press.

HARDGRAVE JR., ROBERT L. (1965): *The Dravidian Movement*. Bombay: Popular Prakashan.

————(1966): 'Religion, Politics and the DMK' In D.E. Smith (ed.). *South Asian Politics and Religion*. Princeton, N.J.: Princeton University Press, pp. 213-34.

————(1969): *The Nadars of Tamilnad: The Political Culture of a Community in Change*. Berkeley and Los Angeles: University of California Press.

HARPER, EDWARD B. (1968): 'Social Consequences of an "Unsuccessful" Low Caste Movement'. In James Silverberg (ed.), *Social Mobility in the Caste System in India*. The Hague: Mouton, pp. 36-65.

HAUSER, W. (1967): 'Dynamics of Social Ranking and Political Power Among

Emerging Caste Groups in Bihar'. Unpublished paper prepared for the 19th A A S Meeting, Chicago.

IRSCHICK, EUGENE F. (1969): *Politics and Social Conflict in South India: The Non-Brahmin Movement and Tamil Separatism, 1916-1928*. Bombay: Oxford University Press.

JAYARAMAN, R. (1964): 'The Dravida Movement'. *Economic Weekly*. Vol. 16, pp. 1555-7.

JEFFREY, ROBIN (1974): 'The Social Origins of a Caste Association, 1875-1905: The Founding of the S.N.D.P. Yogam'. *South Asia*. Vol. 4 (October), pp. 39-59.

———(1976*a*): '*The Decline of Nayar Dominance: Society and Politics in Travancore, 1847-1908*'. London: University of Sussex.

———(1976): 'Temple Entry movement in Travancore, 1860-1940'. *Social Scientist*. Vol. 4, No. 8 (Mar.), pp. 3-27.

JOHNSON, M.G. (1975): 'Social Mobility among Untouchables' In G.R. Gupta (ed.), *Main Currents in Indian Sociology*. Vol. 3. Delhi: Vikas Publishing House.

KARVE, D. G. & D.V. AMBEDKAR (EDS.), (1967): *Speeches and Writings of G.K. Gokhale*. Vol. 3. Bombay: Asia Publishing House.

KHARE, R.S. (1960): 'The Kanya-Kubja Brahmans and their Caste Organization'. *Southwestern Journal of Anthropology*. Vol. 16, pp. 348-67.

———(1970): *The Changing Brahmans: Associations and Elites among the Kanya Kubjas of North India*. Chicago: University of Chicago.

———(1971): 'Home and Office: Some Trends of Modernization among the Kanya-Kubja Brahmans'. *Comparative Studies in Society and History*. Vol. 13, No. 2 (April), pp. 196-216.

KHEDKAR, R. V. (1959): *The Divine Heritage of the Yadavas*. Allahabad: Parmanand.

KOTHARI, RAJNI & MARU RUSHIKESH (1965): 'Caste and Secularism in India: Case Study of a Caste Federation'. *Journal of Asian Studies*. Vol. 25, No. 1 (Nov.), pp. 35-50.

KUDVA, V.N. (1972): *History of the Dakshinatya Saraswats*. Madras.

LATTHE, A.B. (1924): *Memoirs of His Highness Shri Shahu Chattrapati, Maharaja of Kolhapur*.

LEONARD, KAREN (1969): The Kayasths of Hyderabad City: Their Internal History, and their Role in Politics and Society from 1850-1900'. Unpublished Ph.D. thesis. University of Wisconsin.

LYNCH, OWEN M. (1969): *The Politics of Untouchability: Social Mobility and Social Change in a City of India*. New York and London: Columbia University Press.

MAHAR, J.M. (ED.) (1972): *The Untouchables in Contemporary India*. Tuscon: University of Arizona Press.

MAHAR, P.M. (1958): 'Changing Caste Ideology in a North Indian Village'. *Journal of Social Issues*. Vol. 14, No. 4, pp. 51-65.

———(1960): 'Changing Religious Practices of an Untouchable Caste'. *Economic Development and Cultural Change*. Vol. 8, No. 3, pp. 279-287.

MANDELBAUM, D.G. (1960): 'A Reformer of his People'. In J.B. Casagrande (ed.), *In the Company of Man*. New York: Harper & Brothers.

McGavran, D.A. (1939): *Indian Oppressed Classes and Religion*. Jubbulpur.

Mayer, Adrian C. (1956): 'Some Hierarchical Aspects of Caste'. *Southwestern Journal of Anthropology*. (Summer), pp. 117-44.

Mines, M. (1966): 'Caste Dominance and Social Mobility in India: A Matrix Theory'. *Cornell Journal of Social Relations*. Vol. 1, No. 2 (Oct.), pp. 51-63.

Moffatt, Michael (1976): 'Untouchables and the Caste System: a Tamil Case Study'. *Contributions to Indian Sociology*. New Series. Vol. 9, No. 3 (Jan.-June).

Molony, J.C. (1932): 'The Depressed Classes'. In John Cumming (ed.), *Political India, 1832-1932: A Cooperative Survey of a Century*. London: Oxford University Press.

Monga, Veena (1967): 'Social Mobility among the Potters: Report of a Caste Conference'. *Economic and Political Weekly*. (June), pp. 1047-55.

Nandi, P.K. (1965): 'A Study of Caste Organization in Kanpur'. *Man in India*. Vol. 45, No. 1 (Jan.-Mar.), pp. 84-99.

Nataraja, Guru (1952): *The Word of the Guru: An Outline of the Life and Teachings of the Guru Narayana*. Ernakulum: Paico Publishing House.

Omvedt, Gail (1973*a*): 'Non-Brahmans and Communists in Bombay: Part I". *Economic and Political Weekly*. (21 April), pp. 749-59.

————(1973*b*): 'Non-Brahmans and Communists in Bombay: Part II'. *Economic and Political Weekly*. (28 April), pp. 800-5.

————(1976): *Cultural Revolt in a Colonial Society: The Non-Brahman Movement in Western India, 1873-1930*. Bombay: Scientific Education Trust.

Oommen, T.K. (1976): 'Scheduled Castes and Scheduled Tribes'. In S.C. Dube (ed.), *India Since Independence*. Delhi: Vikas Publishing House.

Pandey, Rajbali (1968): *Yaduvans ka Itihas* (in Hindi). Varanasi: Krishna Prakasan.

Parathasarathy, T.M. (1964): *D.M.K. History* (in Tamil). Madras: n.p.

Patrao, A.P. (1932): 'The Justice Movement in India'. *Asiatic Review*. Vol. 28.

Periyar, E.V.R. (1965): *Social Reform or Social Revolution* (translated from the Book *Arivin Ellai* in Tamil into English by A.M. Dharmalingam). Madras: Viduthalai Publications.

Popley, H.A. (1918): 'The Awakening among the Middle Classes of South India'. *International Review of Missions*. Vol. 7, No. 27.

Ramaswamy, Uma (1973): 'Backward Classes in Andhra Pradesh: A Study in Social Change'. Unpublished M. Litt. dissertation. Department of Sociology, University of Delhi.

————(1974*a*): 'Scheduled Castes in Andhra: Some Aspects of Social Change'. *Economic and Political Weekly*. Vol. 9, No. 29 (20 July), pp. 1153-8.

————(1974*b*): 'Self Identity among Scheduled Castes: A Study of Andhra'. *Economic and Political Weekly*. Vol. 9, No. 47 (23 Nov.) pp. 1959-64).

Rao, M.S.A. (1958): 'Political Elite and Caste Associations'. *Economic and Political Weekly*. Vol. 3, pp. 779-82.

———(1977): 'Themes in the Ideology of Protest Movements'. In S.C. Malik (ed.), *Dissent, Protest and Reform in Indian Civilization*. Simla: Indian Institute of Advanced Study, pp. 54-64.

———(1978): *'Social Movements and Social Transformation: A Study of Two Backward Classes Movements'*. New Delhi: Macmillan.

REDDY, N.S. (1954): 'Transition in Caste Structure in Andhra Desh with particular reference to Depressed Classes'. Unpublished Ph.D. thesis. Lucknow University.

ROWE, WILLIAM L. (1960). 'Social and Economic Mobility in a Low Caste North Indian Community'. Unpublished Ph.D. thesis. Cornell University, Ithaca, New York.

———(1968): 'The New Chauhans: A Caste Mobility Movement in North India'. In James Silverberg (ed.), *Social Mobility in the Caste System in India*. The Hague: Mouton, pp. 66-77.

———(1973): 'Caste, Kinship, and Association in Urban India'. In Aiden Southall (ed.), *Urban Anthropology: Cross-Cultural Studies of Urbanization*. New York: Oxford University Press, pp. 211-49.

RUDOLPH, LLOYD I. (1960): 'Urban Life and Populist Radicalism: Dravidian Politics in Madras'. *Journal of Asian Studies*. Vol. 20 (May), pp. 5-22.

RUDOLPH, LLOYD I. & SUSANNE HOEBER RUDOLPH (1960): 'The Political Role of India's Caste Associations'. *Pacific Affairs*. Vol. 35, pp. 5-22.

SAMUEL, V. THOMAS (1977): *One Caste, One Religion, One God: A Study of Sree Narayana Guru*. New Delhi: Sterling Publications.

SANGAVE, VILAS A. (1961): 'Changing Pattern of Caste Organization in Kolhapur City'. *Sociological Bulletin*. Vol. 11, Nos. 1 & 2, pp. 36-59.

SANJAL, H. (1971): 'Continuities of Social Mobility in Traditional and Modern Society in India: Two Case Studies of Caste Mobility in Bengal'. *Journal of Asian Studies*. Vol. 30, No. 2, pp. 315-79.

SANJEEVI, N. (1977): 'Literary and Cultural Background of the D.K. and D.M.K.'. In S.C. Malik (ed.), *Dissent, Protest and Reform in Indian Civilization*. Simla: Indian Institute of Advanced Study, pp. 342-53.

SARKAR, R.M. (1966): 'The Bahubir Sammelan—A Case of Social Mobility Movement'. *The Eastern Anthropologist*. Vol. 19, No. 3 (Sept.-Dec.), pp. 225-30.

SEBIRNG, J. (1972): 'The Formation of New Castes: A Probable Case from North India'. *American Anthropologist*. Vol. 174, No. 3.

SHAH, G. (1977): *Caste Association and Political Process*. Bombay: Popular Prakashan.

SHARROCK, REV. JOHN, A. (1919): 'Caste as a Factor in Indian Reform'. *Asiatic Review*. Vol. 15 (July), pp. 402-24.

SILVERBERG, JAMES (ED.) (1968): *Social Mobility in the Caste System in India: An Interdisciplinary Symposium* Comparative Studies in Society and History, Supplement III. The Hauge: Mouton.

SINGER, MILTON B. (ED.) (1959): *Traditional India: Structure and Change*. Philadelphia: American Folklore Society.

SINGH, MOHINDER (1947): *The Depressed Classes—Their Economic and Social Condition*. Bombay: Hind Kitabs.

SINGH, T.R. (1969): *The Madiga: A Study of Social Structure and Change*. Lucknow: Ethnographic and Folk Culture Society.

SMITH, DONALD E. (ED.) (1966): *South Asian Politics and Religion*. Princeton, N.J.: Princeton University Press.

SOMJEE, A.H. (1973): 'Caste and the Decline of Political Homogeneity'. *American Political Science Review*. Vol. 67 (Sept.), pp. 799-816.

SRINIVAS, M.N. (1956): 'A Note on Sanskritization and Westernization'. *Far Eastern Quarterly*. Vol. 15, No. 4.

————(1962): *Caste in Modern India and Other Essays*. Bombay: Asia Publishing House.

————(1963): 'India's Revitalized Caste System'. *The Times* (London), September.

————(1965) : *Religion and Society among the Coorgs of South India* (reprint). Bombay: Asia Publishing House.

————(1966) : *Social Change in Modern India*. Berkeley: University of California Press.

————(1968) : 'Mobility in the Caste System'. In Milton Singer and B.S. Cohn (eds.), *Structure and Change in Indian Society*. Chicago: Aldine.

SRINIVAS, M.N. & ANDRE BETEILLE (1965) : 'The "Untouchables" of India'. *Scientific American*. Vol. 213, pp. 13-17.

STUART-SMITH, T.G. (1938) : 'Movement among the Ezhavas of Travancore'. *Christian Missionary Society Mass Movement Quarterly*. Vol. 21, No. 1 (March).

SURYAVAMSHI, BHAGWANSINGH (1962) : *The Abhiras: Their History and Culture*. M.S. University Archaeology & Ancient History Series, No. 6. Baroda: M.S. University of Baroda.

TANNER, E. SCUDAMORE (1932) : 'The Sudra Movement in the Kistna Church Council Area'. *Christian Missionary Society Mass Movement Quarterly*. Vol. 15, No. 1 (March).

THOMAS, DANIEL (1965) : *Sree Narayana Guru*. Bangalore: CISRS.

TRIVEDI, D.N. (1973): 'Caste, Modernization and Institutionalization of Change'. *The Eastern Anthropologist*. Vol. 26, No. 3 (July-Sept.), pp. 235-45.

VERMA, O.P. (1970) : *The Yadavas and their Times*. Nagpur: Vidarbha Samshodhan Mandal.

WAGLE, N.K. (1970) : 'The History and Social Organization of the Gauda Sarasvata Brahmanas of the West Coast of India'. *Journal of Indian History*. Vol. 48, pp. 7-25 & 295-333.

YADAV, K.C. (1967) : *Ahirwal ka Itihas* (in Hindi). Delhi: Haryana Prakashan.

ZELLIOT, ELEANOR (1969) : 'Dr. Ambedkar and the Mahar Movements'. Unpublished Ph.D. thesis. University of Pennsylvania.

————(1973) : 'Mahar and Non-Brahmin Movements in Maharashtra'. *Indian Economic and Social History Review*. Vol. 7, pp. 397-415.

————(1972) : 'Gandhi and Ambedkar: A Study of Leadership'. In J.M. Mahar (ed.), *The Untouchables in Contemporary India*. Tuscow: University of Arizona Press.

————(1977) : 'The Psychological Dimension of the Buddhist Movement in India'. In G.A. Oddie (ed.), *Religion in South Asia: Religious Conversion and Revival Movements in South Asia in Medieval and Modern Times.* Delhi: Manohar Book Service, pp. 119-44.

6. Black Movements

ALLEN, R.L. (1970) : *Black Awakening in Capitalist America.* New York: Doubleday.

BARBOUR, F.B. (ED.) (1968) : *The Black Power Revolt.* Boston: Sargent.

BENNETT, LERONE (1965) : *The Negro Mood.* New York: Ballantine Books, Inc.

BLALOCK, HUBERT M. (1967) : *Toward a Theory of Minority-Group Relations.* New York: John Wiley & Sons.

BLAUNOR, ROBERT (1969) : 'Internal Colonialism and Ghetto Revolt'. *Social Problems.* Vol. 16 (Spring), pp. 393-408.

BRACEY JR. J.H., A. MEIER & E. RUDWICK (1970) : *Blacks in the Abolitionist Movement.* Belmont: Wadsworth.

BRACEY JR., J.H., A. MEIER & E. RUDWICK (EDS.) (1970) : *Black Nationalism in America.* Bobbs-Merrill Co.

BROOM, LEONARD & NORVAL GLENN (1965) : *Transformation of the Negro American.* New York: Harper & Row Publishers.

BUCK, SOLON J. (1920) : *The Agrarian Crusade.* New Haven, Conn.: Yale University Press.

BULLOCK, CHARLES S., & H.R. RODGERS (EDS.) (1972) : *Black Political Attitudes.* Chicago: Markham.

CAPLAN, NATHAN S. & JEFFREY M. PAIGE (1969) : 'A Study of Ghetto Rioters'. In A.B. Callow (ed.), *American Urban History.* New York: Oxford University Press, pp. 541-8.

CARMICHAEL, STOKELY & CHARLES V. HAMILTON (1967) : *Black Power.* New York: Random House.

CLARK, KENNETH (1965) : *Dark Ghetto.* New York: Harper & Row Publishers.

CRONON, E.D. (1955) : *Black Moses: The Story of Marcus Garvey and the Universal Negro Improvement Association.* Madison: University of Wisconsin Press.

CULVER, D.W. (1953) : *Negro Segregation in the Methodist Church.* New Haven: Yale University Press.

DAVIS, ALLISON *et al.* (1941) : *Deep South.* Chicago: University of Chicago Press.

DOBLER, LAVINIA & EDGAR A. TOPPIN (1965) : *Pioneers and Patriots: The Lives of Six Negroes of the Revolutionary Era.* Garden City, N.Y.: Doubleday & Co.

DOLLARD, JOHN (1949): *Caste and Class in a Southern Town.* New York: Harper & Brothers.

DRAKE ST. CLAIR & HORACE CAYTON (1945) : *Black Metropolis.* New York: Harcourt, Brace & Co.

DUBOIS, W.E.B. (1899) : *The Philadelphia Negro: A Social Study.* Philadelphia.

———(1935) : *Black Reconstruction.* New York: Harcourt, Brace & Co.

ESSIEN-UDOM, E.U. (1962) : *Black Nationalism: A Search for Identity in America.* Chicago: University of Chicago Press.

FRANKLIN, J.H. (1948) : *From Slavery to Freedom.* New York: Knopf.

FRAZIER, E.F. (1926) : 'The Garvey Movement'. *Opportunity.* Vol. 4, pp. 346-8.

———(1966) : *The Negro Family in the United States.* Chicago: University of Chicago Press.

FUCHS, LAWRENCE H. (ED.) (1968) : *American Ethnic Politics.* New York.

GANS, HERBERT J. (1969) : 'The Ghetto Rebellions and Urban Class Conflict'. In Robert Connery (ed.), *Urban Riots.* New York, pp. 76-89.

GESCHWENDER, BARBARA N. & JAMES A GESCHWENDER (1974) : 'Relative Deprivation and Participation in the Civil Rights Movement'. *Social Science Quarterly.* Vol. 54, No. 2 (Sept.), pp. 403-11.

GESCHWENDER, JAMES A. (1964) : 'The Negro Revolt: An Examination of Some Hypotheses'. *Social Forces.* Vol. 43 (Dec.), pp. 248-56.

GINZBERG, ELI, & ALFRED S. EICHNER (1964) : *The Troublesome Presence: American Democracy and the Negro.* New York: The Free Press.

GINZBERG, ELI (ED.) (1964) : *The Negro Challenge to the Business Community.* New York: McGraw-Hill Book Co.

GLENN, NORVAL D. & CHARLES M. BONJEAN (1969) : *Blacks in the United States.* California: Chandler Publishing Co.

GOSNELL, HAROLD F. (1935) : *Negro Politicians: The Rise of Negro Politics in Chicago.* Chicago.

GREFNSTONE, J. DAVID (1969) : *Labor in American Politics.* New York.

HANDAIN, OSCAR (1951) : *The Uprooted.* Boston: Atlantic Monthly Press.

HERSKOVITS, M. (1941) : *The Myth of the Negro Past.* New York: Harper & Brothers.

KILLIAN, LEWIS M. (1953) : 'The Adjustment of Southern White Migrants to Northern Urban Norms'. *Social Forces.* Vol. 32 (Oct.).

———(1968) : *The Impossible Revolution.* New York: Random House.

KILSON, MARTIN (1971*a*) : 'The "Put-on" of Black Panther Rhetoric: On the Function of Polemical Excesses'. *Encounter* (April). pp. 57-8.

———(1971*b*) : 'Politics of Black Ethnicity'. *Dissent* (Aug.), pp. 333-45.

———(1971*c*) : 'Political Change in the Negro Ghetto, 1900-1940'. In Nathan Huggins, Martin Kilson, Daniel Fox (eds.), *Key Issues in the Afro-American Experience.* New York: Harcourt Brace & Co.

KING JR., MARTIN LUTHER (1958) : *Stride toward Freedom.* New York: Harper and Row Publishers.

———(1967) : *Where do we go from Here ?* New York: Harper and Row Publishers.

LECKY, ROBERT S. (ED) (1969) : *Black Manifesto: Religion, Racism and Reparatins.* New York: Sheed and Ward.

LEWIS, MICHAEL (1970) : 'The Negro Protest in Urban America'. In Joseph R. Gusfield (ed.), *Protest, Reform, and Revolt: A Reader in Social Movements.* New York: John Wiley and Sons, pp. 149-90.

LOGAN, RAYFORD W. (1954) : *The Negro in American Life and Thought: The Nadir, 1877-1901.* New York.

McCarthy, Agnes & Lawrence Reddick (1965) : *Worth Fighting For: A History of the Negro in the United States during the Civil War and Reconstruction.* Garden City, N.Y.: Doubleday and Co.

McPherson, J.M. (1964) : *The Struggle for Equality: Abolitionists and the Negro in the Civil War and Reconstruction.* Princeton, N.J.: Princeton University Press.

McPherson, J. M. *et. al.* (1971) : *Blacks in America: Bibliographical Essays.* New York: Doubleday and Co.

McWorter, Gerald A., & Robert L. Crain (1967) : 'Subcommunity Gladiatorial Competition: Civil Rights Leadership as a Competitive Process'. *Social Forces.* Vol. 46 (Sept.), pp. 8-21.

Malcolm X (with Alex Haley) (1966) : *Autobiography of Malcolm X.* New York: Grove Press Inc.

Marshall, Ray (1965) : *The Negro and Organized Labour.* New York: John Wiley and Sons, Inc,

Marx, Gary T. (1969) : *Protest and Prejudice.* New York: Harper and Row.

Marx, Gray T. (ed) (1971) : *Racial Conflict.* Boston: Little, Brown and Co.

Meier, A. & Rudwick, E. (1966) : *From Plantation to Ghetto.* New York: Hill and Wang.

————(1970) : *Black Protest in Sixties.* Chicago: Quadrangle Books.

Myrdal, Gunnar (1944) : *An American Dilemma: The Negro Problem and Modern Democracy.* New York: Harper and Row.

Olsen, Marvin E. (1970) : 'Social and Political Participation of Blacks'. *American Sociological Review.* Vol. 35 (Aug.), pp. 682-97.

Oppenheimer. M. (1963) : 'Current Negro Protest Movements and the Concept of Social Movements'. *Phylon.* Vol. 24, pp. 54-159.

Orum, Anthony M. (1966) : 'A Reappraisal of the Social and Political Participation of Negroes'. *American Journal of Sociology.* Vol. 72 (July), pp. 32-46.

Paige, Jeffrey M. (1971) : 'Political Orientation and Riot Participation'. *American Sociological Review.* Vol. 36 (Oct.), pp. 810-20.

Record, Wilson (1964) : *Race and Radicalism: The NAACP and the Communist Party in Conflict.* Ithaca, N.Y.: Cornell University Press.

Rudwick, E., J.H. Bracey Jr., & A. Meier (eds.), (1970) : *The Rise of the Ghetto.* Belmont: Wadsworth Publishing Co.

Rustin Bayord (1966) : '"Black Power" and Coalition Politics'. *Commentary* (Sept.), pp. 35-40.

Scheniner, Seth M. (1965) : *Negro Mecca: A History of the Negro in New York City, 1865-1920.* New York: New York University Press.

Stampp, K.M. (1956) : *The Peculiar Institution.* New York: Knopf.

Taeuber, Karl E. & Alma Taeuber (1965) : *Negroes in Cities.* Chicago: Aldine Publishing Co.

Verba, Sidney, Bashiruddin Ahmad & Anil Bhatt (1971): *Caste, Race, and Politics.* Beverly Hills: Sage Publications.

Wharton, Vernon Lane (1965) : *The Negro in Mississippi, 1865-1890.* New York: Harper and Row.

WILSON, JAMES Q. (1960): *Negro Politics: The Search for Leadership*. Glencoe, Ill.: The Free Press.

————(1961): The Strategy of Protest: Problem of Negro Civic Action'. *Journal of Conflict Resolution*. Vol. 5, pp. 291-303.

————(1964): 'The Changing Position of the Negro'. In Arnold Rose (ed.), *Assuring Freedom to the Free*. Detroit: Wayne State University Press.

————(1965): *Negro Politics: The Search for Leadership*. New York: The Free Press.

WISH, HARVEY (ED.) (1965): *The Negro Since Emancipation*. Englewood Cliffs, N.J.: Prentice-Hall.

Select Bibliography on Social Movements in India

(B) Religious and Sectarian, Tribal, Women's, Students', Trade Union and National Movements

7. Religious and Sectarian

I. AMONG HINDUS, JAINS AND BUDDHISTS

APTE, S.S. (1965): *Samrath Ramdas: Life and Mission.* Bombay.

ARTAL, R.C. (1909): 'A Short History of the Reformed Shaiva or Veerasaiva Faith'. *Journal of Anthropological Society.* (Bombay), No. 3, pp. 171-262.

BABB, LAWRENCE A. (1972): 'The Satnamis—Political Involvement of a Religious Movement'. In J. Michael Mahar (ed.), *The Untouchables in Contemporary India.* Tucson: University of Arizona Press.

BALI, ARUN P. (1976*a*): 'Some Aspects of Virasaiva Movement: *Matha-Jangama* Axis'. Paper presented to the Workshop on Social Movements at the Department of Sociology, University of Delhi, 24-26 March 1976.

————(1976*b*): 'A Sociological Study of Virasaiva Movement'. Unpublished M.Litt. dissertation. Department of Sociology, University of Delhi.

BANERJEE, A.C. *et. al.* (1956): 'Principal Schools and Sects of Buddhism'. In *2500 years of Buddhism.* New Delhi: Government of India, Publications Division, pp. 97-138.

BARZ, RICHARD (1977): *The Bhakti Sect of Vallabhacharya.* New Delhi: Thomson Press (India) Limited.

BASAVARAJA, K.R. (1973): 'Basavesvara and his Contributions'. In *Sri Kanthika.* Mysore: Geeta Book House.

BEALS, ALAN R. (1974): *Village Life in South India: Cultural Design and Environmental Variations.* Chicago: Aldine.

BHANDARKAR, R.G. (1965): *Vaisnavism, Saivism and Minor Religious Systems.* Varanasi: Indological Book House (originally published in 1915).

BHARIL, C. (1970): 'Social and Political Ideas of Dr. B.R. Ambedkar—A Study of his Life, Services, Social and Political Ideas'. Unpublished Ph.D. thesis. Rajasthan University.

BHATTACHARYA, H. (ED.) (1965): *The Cultural Heritage of India.* Vol. 4: *The Religions.* Calcutta: The Ramakrishna Mission, Institute of Culture.

BHATTACHARYA, JOGENDRA NATH (1866): *Hindu Castes and Sects.* Calcutta. (Reprinted by Editions Indian, Calcutta, 1968, with a foreword by N.K. Bose).

BHATTACHARYA, N.N. (1974): *History of the Sakta Religion.* New Delhi.

BHOOSNURMATH, S.S. (ED.) (1965): *Sunyasampadane.* Rawoor and Advani.

BHOOSNURMATH, S.S. & A. MENEZES (EDS.) (1968): *Sunyasampadane.* Vol. 2 (text and English translation). Dharwar: Karnataka University.

———(1969): *Sunyasampadane.* Vol. 3 (text and English translation). Dharwar: Karnataka University.

———(1970): *Sunyasampadane.* Vol. 4 (text and English translation). Dharwar: Karnataka University.

BRIGGS, G.W. (1938): *Goraknath and the Kanphata Yogis.* Calcutta.

CHAKRAVARTI, CHINTAHARAN (1932): 'The Soma or Sauma Sect of the Saivas'. *Indian Historical Quarterly* (Calcutta). Vol. 8, pp. 221-3.

CHATTOPADHYAYA, S. (1970): *Evolution of Hindu Sects upto the time of Sankaracarya.* New Delhi: Munshiram Manoharlal.

ÇHATURVEDI, PARASURAM (1951): *Uttari Bharat Ki Santparampara* (in Hindi). Prayag.

CHIDANANDAMURTI, (1975): *Lord Basaveshwara.* Delhi: National Book Trust.

CHOPHRA, CHHOGMAL (n.d.): *A Short History of the Terapanthi sect of the Swetamber Jains and its Tenets.* Calcutta: Navayuvak Press.

DAS, SYAMSUNDER (ED.) (1928): *Kabir Granthavali* (in Hindi). Prayag.

DASGUPTA, S.B. (1969): *Obscure Religious Cults.* Calcutta.

DE, S.K. (1961): *Early History of the Vaishnava Faith and Movement in Bengal* (2nd edn.). Calcutta: Firma K.L. Mukhopadhyaya.

DEMING, WILBUR S. (1928): *Ramdas and the Ramdasis.* Calcutta: Association Press, Y.M.C.A.

DESAI, P.B. (1968): *Basavesvara and His Times.* Dharwar: Kannada Research Institute, Karnataka University.

DEVANANDAN, PAUL D. (1959): *Resurgent Hinduism: Review of Modern Movements.* Bangalore: Christian Institute for the Study of Religion and Society.

DUMONT, LOUIS (1970): *Religion/Politics, and History in India.* The Hague: Mouton.

DUTT, N. (1970): *Buddhist Sects in India.* Calcutta: Firma K.L. Mukhopadhyay.

DVIVEDI, HAZARI PRASAD (1950): *Kabir* (in Hindi). Bombay.

ELIOT, CHARLES (1968): *Hinduism and Buddhism: A Historical Sketch.* Vol. 2. New York: Barnes & Noble, pp. 166-290 (originally published in 1921).

FARQUHAR, J.N. (1915): *Modern Religious Movements in India.* New York: Macmillan Co. (reprinted 1967).

FUCHS, STEPHEN (1965): *Rebellious Prophets: A Study of Messianic Movements in Indian Religions.* Bombay: Asia Publishing House.

GHURYE, G S. (1963): *Indian Sadhus.* Bombay: Popular Book Depot.

GOVERNMENT OF MYSORE (1967): *Sri Basavesvara: Eighth Centenary Commemoration Volume.* Bangalore: Government of Mysore.

GRIERSON, GEORGE A. (1921): 'Siva Narayanis'. *Encyclopaedia of Religion and Ethics.* Vol. 11, p. 579.

GUPTA, KRISHNA PRAKASH (1974): 'Religious Evolution and Social Change in India: A Study of the Ramakrishna Mission Movement'. *Contributions to Indian Sociology.* New Series 8, pp. 25-50.

GURUMURTHY, K.G. (1975): 'Veerashaivism and Modernization'. Paper presented at the 62nd Session of the Indian Science Congress Association, Delhi, January 1975 (mimeographed).

HALAKATTI, P.G. (ED.) (1959): *Sivasaraneyava Charitregalu* (in Kannada). Bijapur.

HARPER, EDWARD B. (ED.) (1964): *Religion in South Asia.* Seattle: University of Washington Press.

HUNASHAL, S.M. (1947): *The Lingayat Movement: A Social Revolution in Karnatak.* Dharwar: Karnatak Sahitya Mandira.

———(1957): *The Veerashaiva Social Philosophy.* Raichür: Amaravani Printing Press.

———(1970): *Woman Saints of Karnatak.* Raichur: Taranath Prakashana.

JAIN, J.D. (1966): 'The Changing Pattern of Jain Social Institutions in Uttar Pradesh'. Unpublished Ph.D. thesis. Lucknow University.

JOSHI, T.D. (1970): *Social and Political Thoughts of Ramdas.* Bombay: Vora & Co.

KARVE, IRAWATI & HEMALATA ACHARYA (1962): 'Neo-Buddhism in Maharashtra'. *Journal of the University of Poona, Humanities Section.* Vol. 15, pp. 130-3.

KEAY, E.E. (1931): *Kabir and his Followers.* Oxford: Oxford University Press.

KENNEDY, MELVILLE T. (1925): *The Chaitanya Movement.* Calcutta.

KUMARASWAMIJI, SRI (1949): *The Veerasaiva Philosophy and Mysticism.* Dharwar: Navakalyanamath.

———(1960): *Mirror of Virashaivism.* Dharwar: Navakalyanamath.

———(1969): 'Virasaivism'. In H. Bhattacharya (ed.), *The Cultural Heritage of India.* Vol. 4. Calcutta: Ramakrishna Mission, pp. 98-107.

LORENZEN, DAVID N. (1972): *The Kapalikas and Kalamukhas: Two Lost Saivite Sects.* New Delhi: Thomson Press.

LYNCH, OWEN M. (1969): *The Politics of Untouchables: Social Mobility and Social Change in a City of India.* New York: Columbia University Press.

———(1972): 'Dr. B.R. Ambedkar—Myth and Charisma'. In J. Michael Mahar (ed.), *The Untouchables in Contemporary India.* Tucson: University of Arizona Press, pp. 97-112.

MACNICOL, NICOL (1968): *Indian Theism—From the Vedic to the Muhammadan Period.* Delhi: Munshiram Manoharlal (originally published in 1915).

MAHAR, J. MICHAEL (ED.) (1972): *The Untouchables in Contemporary India.* Tucson: University of Arizona Press.

MALLEDEVARU, H.P. (1973): *Essentials of Virasaivism.* Bombay: Bharatiya Vidya Bhavan.

MALLIK, K. (1950): *Nath Sampradayer Itihas*, (in Bengali). Calcutta.

MANDELBAUM, D.G. (1970): *Society in India*. Vols. 1 & 2. Bombay: Popular Prakashan.

MANOR, JAMES (1977): 'The Evolution of Political Arenas and Units of Social Organization: The Lingayats and Vokkaligas of Princely Mysore'. In M.N. Srinivas, *et al.* (eds.), *Dimensions of Social Change in India*. New Delhi: Allied Publishers.

MCCORMACK, WILLIAM (1959): 'The Forms of Communication in Virasaiva Religion'. In Milton Singer (ed.), *Traditional India: Structure and Change*. Philadelphia: The American Folklore Society, pp. 119-29.

———(1963): 'Lingayats as a Sect'. *The Journal of the Royal Anthropological Institute of Great Britain and Ireland*. Vol. 93 (Part 1), pp. 59-71.

———(1973): 'On Lingayat Culture'. In A.K. Ramanujan (trans.), *Speaking of Siva*. Harmondsworth: Penguin Books, pp. 175 87.

MISHRA, K.K. (1968): 'The Contribution of Religious Movements and Institutions in Indian Nationalism' (in Hindi). Unpublished Ph.D. thesis. Vikram University.

MUDDALINGANNA, V. (1940): 'Bhakti Movement and Caste' Unpublished Ph.D. thesis. University of Mysore.

MUKHERJEE, P. (In Press): *History of the Chaitanya Faith in Orissa*.

NANDI, R.N. (1975): 'Origin of Virasaiva Movement'. *The Indian Historical Review*. Vol. 2, No. 1, pp. 32-46.

NANDIMATH, S.C. (1942): *A Handbook of Virasaivism*. Dharwar: The Literary Committee.

NANDIMATH, S.C. *et. al.* (EDS.) (1965): *Sunyasampadane*. Vol. 1 (text and English translation). Dharwar: Karnataka University.

OREN, STEPHEN A. (1969): 'Religious Groups as Political Organizations: A Comparative Analysis of Three Indian States'. Unpublished Ph.D. thesis. Columbia University.

PANGBORN, CYRUS R. (1976): 'The Ramakrishna Math and Mission: A Case Study of a Revitalization Movement'. In Bardwell L. Smith (ed.), *Hinduism: New Essays in the History of Religions*. Leiden: E.J. Brill.

PARATHASARATHY, V.S. (1970): 'Sociological Study of a Vaishnava Mendicant Sect of Mysore, viz. Dasayya'. Unpublished M. Litt. dissertation. Department of Sociology, University of Delhi.

PARGANIKA, B.L. (1967): 'The Satnami Movement'. *Journal of Social Research*. Vol. 10, No. 1 (Mar), pp. 1-16.

PARVATHAMMA, C. (1967): 'The Social Structure of Lingayats: A Sectarian Caste of Mysore'. *Journal of Sociology and Applied Research* (Jabalpur University). Vol. 1, No. 1.

———(1968): 'The Socio-Economic Drive in Veerasaivism: The Saivite Non-Brahman Caste Group of Mysore'. Paper read at Eighth All India Sociological Conference, Agra, 1 September 1968 (mimeographed).

———(1971): *Politics and Religion: A Study of Historical Interaction between Socio-political Relationships in a Mysore Village*. New Delhi: Sterling Publishers.

———(1972): *Sociological Essays on Veerashaivism*. Bombay: Popular Prakashan.

———(1977): 'Dissent, Protest and Reform Movements in Indian Civilization—Veerasaivism: A Saivite Sectarian Movement in Protest and Reform in Karnataka'. In S.C. Malik (ed.), *Dissent, Protest and Reform in Indian Civilization*. Simla: Indian Institute of Advanced Study.

PATWARDHAN, SUNANDA (1968): 'Social Mobility and Conversion of the Mahars'. *Sociological Bulletin*. Vol. 17, No. 2 (Sept.), pp. 187-202.

———(1973): *Change Among India's Harijans: Maharashtra—A Case Study*. New Delhi: Orient Longman.

PAVATE, S.D. (1927): *Virashaiva Philosophy of the Shaivagamas*. Hubli: W.B. Bile Angadi.

POCOCK, DAVID (1973*a*): 'A Vaishnavite Sect—The Way of Grace'. In David Pocock (ed.), *Mind, Body and Wealth*. Oxford: Basil Blackwell, pp. 94-121.

———(1973*b*): 'A Reformed Sect—the Satsang'. In David Pocock (ed.), *Mind, Body and Wealth*. Oxford: Basil Blackwell, pp. 122-57.

PURI, G.S.P.N. (1966): 'The Origin and Growth of Dashnami Sanyasi Movement in India—Sociology of Religious Organization'. Unpublished Ph.D. thesis. Patna University.

RAGHAVAN, V. (1959): 'Methods of Popular Religious Instruction in South India'. In Milton Singer (ed.), *Traditional India: Structure and Change*. Philadelphia: American Folklore Society, pp. 130-40.

———(1966): *The Great Integrators: The Saint-Singers of India*. Delhi: Publications Division.

RAMANUJAN, A.K. (TRANSLATOR) (1973): *Speaking of Siva*. Harmondsworth: Penguin Books.

RAO, M.S.A. (1974): 'Religious Movements and Social Transformation in India'. In *Religion and Development in Asian Societies*. Sri Lanka: Marga Publications.

RAO, R. RAMA (1924): 'Origin and Development of Siva-Worship with Special Reference to Virsaivism'. *Quarterly Journal of the Mythic Society* (Bangalore) pp. 190-210 & 282-301.

RAO, K. RANGA & K. RADHAKRISHNA MURTY (1972): 'Cultural Matrix and Reference Group Behaviour: A Case of Desanskritization and Islamization of the Telengana Brahmins'. *The Eastern Anthropologist*. Vol. 25, No. 3 (Sept.-Dec.), pp. 241-7.

RECHANNA, G.N. (1960): 'Idea of God in Shaiva Siddhanta and in Veerashaivism'. Unpublished Ph.D. thesis. University of Mysore.

SADASIVAIAH, H.M. (1967): *A Comparative Study of Two Virasaiva Monasteries: A Study in Sociology of Religion*. Mysore: Prasaranga, Manasa Gangotri.

SAKHARE, M.R. (1942): *History and Philosophy of Lingayat Religion*. Belgaum: Published by author.

SAMUEL, V. THOMAS (1977): *One Caste, One Religion, One God: A Study of Sree Narayana Guru*. New Delhi: Sterling Publishers.

SANGAVE, VILAS A. (1959): *Jaina Community: A Social Survey*. Bombay: Popular Book Depot.

———(1962): Changing Patterns of Caste Organization in Kolhapur' *Sociological Bulletin*. Vol. 11, Nos. 1 & 2 (Mar.-Sept.), pp. 36-61.

SEN, D.C. (1922): *Chaitanya and His Age*. Calcutta.

SHIVARUDRAPPA, G. (1974): 'Contributions of Veerashaiva Mathas to the Development of Education in Karnatak: Historical Survey'. Unpublished Ph.D. thesis. University of Mysore.

SIDDHANTASHASTREE, R.K. (1975): *Saivism through the Ages*. Delhi: Munshiram Manoharlal.

SINGER, MILTON (1972): *When a Great Tradition Modernizes*. New York: Praeger.

SINGER, MILTON (ED.) (1966): *Krishna: Myths, Rites, and Attitudes*. Chicago & London: The University of Chicago Press.

SINGH, MOHAN (1937): *Gorakhnath and Medieval Hindu Mysticism*. Lahore.

SINGH, YOGENDRA (1973): *Modernization of Indian Tradition*. Delhi: Thomson Press.

SRINIVASAMURTHY, M.R. (1946): *Bhaktibhandari Basavannanevana* (in Kannada). Bangalore.

STEIN, B. (1968): 'Social Mobility and Medieval South Indian Hindu Sects'. In James Silverberg (ed.), *Social Mobility in Caste System in India*. The Hague: Mouton, pp. 78-94.

STEVENSON, S. (1970): *Heart of Jainism* (reprint). New Delhi. (Originally published in 1915).

SUNKAPUR, M.S. & A. MENEZES (EDS.) (1972): *Sunyasampadane*. Vol. 5 (text and English translation). Dharwar: Karnataka University.

THIPPERUDRASWAMY, H. (1968): *The Virasaiva Saints: A Study*. English trans. by S.M. Angadi. Mysore: Rao & Raghavan.

———(1973): 'Basavesvara: The Revolutionary Saint of Karnataka'. In *Srikanthika*. Mysore: Geeta Book House.

TRIPATHI, B.D. (1967): 'The Religious Mendicants of Uttar Pradesh: A Sociological Study'. Unpublished Ph.D. thesis. Lucknow University.

UBEROI, MOHAN SINGH (1937): *Gorakhnath and Medieval Hindu Mysticism*. Lahore.

VENKANNAIAH, T.A. (1940): *Social Structure of the Virasaiva Saints*. Dharwar: Lingaraj Art Press.

WEBER, MAX (1958): *The Religion of India: The Sociology of Hinduism and Buddhism*. Trans. & edited by Hans Gerth and Don Martindale. Glencoe, Ill.: The Free Press.

WESTCOTT, G.H. (1907): *Kabir and the Kabir Panth*. Cawnpore.

WILSON, H.H. (1958): *Religious Sects of the Hindus*. Edited by Ernst R. Rost (2nd ed.). Calcutta: Susil Gupta (India) Pvt. Ltd.

WURTH, G. (TRANS.) (1864-6a): 'Basava Purana'. *Journal of the Bombay Branch of the Royal Asiatic Society*. Vol. 8, pp. 65-97.

———(1864-6b): 'Canna-Basava Purana'. *Journal of the Bombay Branch of the Royal Asiatic Society*. Vol. 8, pp. 98-221.

YAPANIYA SAMGHA (1933): 'A Jaina Sect'. *Journal of the University of Bombay*. Vol. 1, No. 4, pp. 224-31.

ZELLIOTT, ELEANOR (1976): 'The Medieval Bhakiti Movement in History: An Essay on the Literature in English'. In Bardwell L. Smith (ed.), *Hinduism: New Essays in the History of Religions*. Leiden: E.J. Brill.

II. Among Muslims

Abul Hasan Ali Nadwi, Sayyid (1941): *Ek Ahm Dini Dawat*. Lucknow: Maktaba-i-Islam.

———(1952): *Makatib Hazrat Mawlana Shah Muhammad Ilyas*. Delhi: Kutubkhana Anjuman-i-Traqqi-i-Urdu.

———(1960): *Hazrat Mawlana Ilyas aur Unki Dini Dawat*. Lucknow: Tanvir Press.

Addison, James T. (1929): 'The Ahmadiya Movement and its Western Propaganda'. *Harvard Theological Review*. Vol. 22, pp. 1-32.

Aggarwal, P.C. (1971): *Caste, Religion and Power: An Indian Muslim Case*. New Delhi: Shri Ram Centre for Industrial Relations.

Ahmad, Aziz (1964): *Studies in Islamic Culture in the Indian Environment*. Oxford: Clarendon Press, pp. 55-217.

———(1967*a*): *Islamic Modernism in India and Pakistan, 1857-1964*. London: Oxford University Press, pp. 113-22.

———(1967*b*): 'Problems of Islamic Modernism with Special Reference to the Indo-Pakistan Sub-continent'. *Archives de Sociologie des Religions*. Vol. 23, p. 115.

Ahmad, Aziz & G. Von Grunebaum (1970): *Muslim Self-Statement in India and Pakistan, 1857-1968*. Wiesbaden: Otto Harrossowitz.

Ahmad, Imtiaz (ed.) (1973): *Caste and Social Stratification Among the Muslims*. Delhi: Manohar Book Service.

Ahmad, Q. (1966): *Wahabi Movement*. Calcutta.

Bouvat, L. (1928): 'Chronique et Notes Bibliographique: Les Ahmadiyya de Qadian'. *Journal Asiatique*. Vol. CCXII, pp. 159-81.

Brush, S.E. (1959): 'Ahmadiyyas in Pakistan'. *Muslim World*. Vol. 54 (Oct.), pp. 275-86.

Faridi, Iftikhar (1967): *Tablighi Kam* (Work of Preaching). Delhi: Kutubkhana Anjuman-i-Taraqqi-i-Urdu.

Farquhar, J.N. (1919): *Modern Religious Movements in India*. New York: Macmillan Company, pp. 137-48.

Fisher, H.J. (1963): *Ahmadiyah: A Study in Contemporary Islam on the West African Coast*. Oxford: Oxford University Press.

Gardener, W.R.W. (1920): 'The Ahmadiya Movement'. *Muslim World*. Vol. 10, pp. 59-64.

Garlington, W. (1977): 'The Baha'i Faith in Malwa'. In G.A. Oddie (ed.), *Religion in South Asia: Religious Conversion and Revival Movements in South Asia in Medieval and Modern Times*. New Delhi: Manohar Book Service, pp. 101-17.

Griswold, H.D. (1912): 'The Ahmadiya Movement'. *Muslim World*. Vol. 2 (Oct.), pp. 373-9.

Grunebaum, G. Von (1962): *Modern Islam: The Search for Cultural Identity*. Berkeley & Los Angeles: University of California Press.

Haq, M. Anwarul (1972): *The Faith Movement of Maulana Muhammad Ilyas*. London: George Allen & Unwin.

Hardy, Peter (1964): 'Wahaabis in the Punjab, 1876'. *Journal of the Research Society of Pakistan* (October).

HASAMI, MUHAMMAD THANI (1967): *Sawanih-i-Hazrat Mawlana Muhammad Yusuf Kandhelawi*. Lucknow: Maktab-i-Islam.

HOUTSMA, H.T. (1907): 'Ahmadiya'. *Revue du Monde Musulman*. Vol. 1, pp. 533-76.

HUSAIN, YUSUF (1933): 'The Influence of Islam on the Cult of Bhakti in Medieval India'. *Islamic Culture*. pp. 650-9.

IHTISHAMUL-HASAN, MUHAMMAD (1955): *Musalmanon ki Mawjudah Pasti ka Wahid Itaj* (The Only Remedy for the Present Decline of Muslims). Delhi: Kutubkhana Anjuman-i-Taraqqi-i-Urdu.

JAIN, M.S. (1965): *The Aligarh Movement*. Agra: Sri Ram Mehra & Co.

LAVAN, SPENCER (1974): *The Ahmadiyah Movement: A History and Perspective*. Delhi: Manohar Book Service.

MATHUR, Y.B. (1972): *Muslims and Changing India*. New Delhi: Trimurti Publications Pvt. Ltd., pp. 72-232.

MANZUR NUMAMI, MUHAMMAD (ED.) (1950): *Malfuzat-i-Hazrat Mawlana Muhammad Ilyas* (The Utterances of Mawlana Muhammad Ilyas). Lucknow: Kutubkhana-al-Furgan.

MUJEEB, H. (1967): *Indian Muslims*. London: George Allen & Unwin Ltd.

NIZAMI, K.A. (1961): *Some Aspects of Religion and Politics in Medieval Muslim India in the 13th Century*. Delhi.

——————(1970): Socio-religious Movements in Indian Islam'. *Islamic Culture* (July).

REHATSEK, E. (1880): 'The History of the Wahhabys in Arabia and India', *Journal of the Asiatic Society* (Bombay). pp. 274-401.

RIZVI, S.A.A. (1965): *Muslim Revivalist Movements in Northern India in the Sixteenth and Seventeenth Centuries*. Agra: Agra University.

——————(1977): 'Islamic Proselytisation (Seventh to Sixteenth Centuries)'. In G.A. Oddie (ed.), *Religion in South Asia: Religious Conversion and Revival Movements in South Asia in Medieval and Modern Times*. New Delhi: Manohar Book Service, pp. 13-33.

SABHI AL-HASSAN HASBIMI (n.d.): *Tablighi Tahrik ke Sat Number*. Delhi: Idara-i-Tabligh-i-Islam.

SHARMA, S.L. (1969): 'Structural Continuity in the Face of Cultural Change'. *The Eastern Anthropologist*. Vol. 22, No. 2 (May-Aug.). pp. 177-86.

SHARMA, S.L. & R.N. SRIVASTAVA (1967): 'Institutional Resistance to Induced Islamization in a Convert Community—An Empiric Study in Sociology of Religion'. *Sociological Bulletin*. Vol. 16, No. 1 (Mar.), pp. 69-80.

SMITH, W.C. (1960): 'Ahmadiyya'. *E.I.* 2. Leiden.

——————(1964): *Modern Islam in India*. London: Gollancz.

STANTON, H.V.W. (1925): 'The Ahmadiya Movement'. *Muslim World*. Vol. 15 (Jan.). pp. 10-20.

TITUS, MURRAY T. (1959): *Islam in India and Pakistan* (reprint). Calcutta: Y.M.C.A. Publishing House, pp. 256-69.

WAHIFDUZZAFER (1971): 'Muslim Socio-Religious Movements''. In S.T. Lokhandwalla (ed.), *India and Contemporary Islam*. Simla: Indian Institute of Advanced Study.

WALTER, H.A. (1916): 'The Ahmadiyah Movement Today'. *Muslim World*. Vol. 6, pp. 66-78.

———(1918): *The Ahmadiyah Movement*. Calcutta: Association Press.

III. Among Sikhs

Ahmad, Aziz (1964): 'Sikhism: From Syncretism to Hostility'. In Aziz Ahmad, *Studies in Islamic Culture in the Indian Environment*. Oxford: Clarendon Press, pp. 15(-5.

Banerjee, Indubhushan (1936): *Evolution of the Khalsa*. Vol. 1. Calcutta.

———(1956): *Evolution of the Khalsa*. Vol. 2. Calcutta.

Court, H. (trans.) (1888): *History of the Sikhs*. Lahore.

Cunningham, J.D. (1849): *A History of the Sikhs*. London.

Cust, R.N. (1874): 'The Life of Baba Nanak, the Founder of the Sikh Sect'. *Indian Antiquary*. Vol. 3, pp. 295-300.

Grewal, J.S. (1969): *Guru Nanak in History*. Chandigarh.

———(1972): *From Guru Nanak to Maharaja Ranjit Singh*. Amritsar.

———(1977): 'The Sikh Movement'. In S.C. Malik (ed.), *Dissent, Protest and Reform in Indian Civilization*. Simla: Indian Institute of Advanced Study.

Grewal, J.S. & S.S. Bal (1967): *Guru Gobind Singh*. Chandigarh.

Indian Institute of Advanced Study (1967): *Sikhism and Indian Society*. Transactions, Vol. 4. Simla: Indian Institute of Advanced Study.

Kanwar, Mrigindra Singh (1969): 'Nirmal Panth'. *Proceedings of the Punjab History Congress*. Patiala. pp. 110-19.

Loehlin, C.H. (1967): 'Guru Gobind Singh and Islam'. In *Sikhism and Indian Society*. Transactions, Vol. 4. Simla: Indian Institute of Advanced Study, pp. 127-42.

———(1971): *The Granth of Guru Gobind Singh and the Khalsa Brotherhood*. Lucknow.

Macauliffe, M.A. (1909): *The Sikh Religion*. 6 vols. Oxford: Clarendon Press.

McLeod, W.H. (1968): *Guru Nanak and the Sikh Religion*. Oxford: Clarendon Press.

———(1973): 'The Kukas: A Millenarian Sect of the Punjab'. In G.A. Wood and P.S. O'Connor (eds.), *W.P. Morrell: A Tribute*. Dunedin.

———(1974): 'Ahluwalias and Ramgarhias: Two Sikh Castes'. *South Asia (Journal of South Asian Studies)*, No. 4 (October), pp. 78-90.

Narang, Gokul Chand (1912): *The Transformation of Sikhism*. Lahore.

Ray, Niharranjan (1975): *The Sikh Gurus and the Sikh Society: A Study in Social Analysis* (2nd ed.). New Delhi: Munshiram Manoharlal.

Scott, G.B. (1930): *Religion and Short History of the Sikhs, 1469-1930*. London.

Singh, Bawa Chhajju (1 03): *The Ten Gurus and their Teachings*. Lahore: Punjab Printing Works.

Singh, Bhagat (1969): 'The Role of Sangat in the Development of the Sikh Community'. *Proceedings of Punjab Historical Conference*. pp. 128-36.

Singh, Ganda (ed.) (1969): *Sources of the Life and Teachings of Guru Nanak*. Patiala.

SINGH, GANDA (TRANS.) (1939): *Nanak Panthis, or the Sikhs and Sikhism of the 17th Century* (Eng. trans.). Madras.

SINGH, GURMIT (1966): *Islam and Sikhism: A Comparative Study*. Sirsa, Hissar: Usha Institute of Religious Studies.

SINGH, HARBANS (1964): *The Heritage of the Sikhs*. Bombay.

———(1969): *Guru Nanak and the Origins of the Sikh Faith*. Bombay.

SINGH, KHAZAN (1914): *History and Philosophy of Sikhism*. 2 vols. Lahore.

SINGH, KHUSHWANT (1963): *A History of the Sikhs*. 2 vols. Princeton: Princeton University Press.

SINGH, TEJA (1938): *Sikhism: Its Ideas and Institutions*. Lahore: Lahore Book Shop.

UBEROI, J.P. SINGH (1967): 'On Being Unshorn'. In *Sikhism and Indian Society*. Transactions, Vol. 4. Simla: Indian Institute of Advanced Study, pp. 87-100.

IV. AMONG CHRISTIANS

ALEXANDER, K.C. (1967): 'The Problem of the Neo-Christians of Kerala'. *Man in India*. Vol. 67, No. 6 (Oct.-Dec.), pp. 317-30.

CAMPBELL, ERNEST Y. (1966): 'The Church in the Punjab: Some Aspects of its Life and Growth'. In Victor E.W. Hayward (ed.), *The Church as Christian Community*. London, pp. 137-220.

CAPLAN, LIONEL (1977): 'Social Mobility in Metropolitan Centres—Christians in Madras'. *Contributions to Indian Sociology*. New Series. Vol. 11, No. 1 (Jan.-June)

DIEHL, C.G. (1965): *Church and Shrine: Intermingling Patterns of Culture in the Life of Some Christian Groups in South India*. Uppsala, Sweden: Acta Universitatis, Historia Religionum, No. 2.

FORRESTER, D.B. (1977): 'The Depressed Classes and Conversion to Christianity, 1860-1960'. In G.A. Oddie (ed.), *Religion in South Asia: Religious Conversion and Revival Movements in South Asia in Medievol and Modern Times*. Delhi: Manohar Book Service, pp. 35-66.

GUPTA, R.P. (1969): 'A Sociological Study of Indian Methodist Christian Community (Methodist Church in Southern Asia) in Uttar Pradesh with Particular Reference to Lucknow, Allahabad, Agra and Varanasi'. Unpublished Ph.D. thesis. Lucknow University.

ODDIE, G.A. (1975): 'Christian Conversion in Telugu Country, 1860-1900: A Case Study of One Protestant Movement in the Godavary-Krishna Delta'. *The Indian Economic and Social History Review*. Vol. 12, No. 1 (Jan.-Mar.), pp. 61-80.

———(1977): 'Christian Conversion among non-Brahmans in Andhra Pradesh, with special reference to the Dornakal Diocese, *c*. 1900-1936'. In G.A. Oddie (ed.), *Religion in South Asia: Religious Conversion and Revival Movements in South Asia in Medieval and Modern Times*. Delhi: Manohar Book Service, pp. 67-99.

PICKETT, J. WASKOM (1933): *Christian Mass Movements*. New York: The Abingdon Press.

WIEBE, PAUL D. (1970*a*): 'Christianity and Social Change in South India'. *Practical Anthropology*. Vol. 17 (May-June).

———(1970*b*): 'Protestant Missions in India: A Sociological Review'. *Journal of Asian and African Studies*. Vol. 5 (Oct.).

WIEBE, PAUL D. & S. JOHN-PETER (1972): 'The Catholic Church and Caste in Rural Tamil Nadu'. *The Eastern Anthropologist*. Vol. 25, No. 1 (Jan.-Apr.), pp. 1-11.

WHITEHEAD, HENRY (1913): 'The Mass Movement towards Christianity in the Punjab'. *International Review of Missions*. Vol. 2, pp. 442-53.

8. Tribal Movements

BHADRA, RANAJIT K. (1977): 'Revitalization Movements among the Gond of Madhya Pradesh'. *The Eastern Anthropologist*. Vol. 30, No. 2 (April-June), pp. 131-7.

BHANDARI, J.S. (1973): 'Changing Emphasis in the Religious Beliefs—Study in Ideological Conflict among the Mishing'. In K.S. Mathur *et al.* (eds.), *Studies in Social Change*. Lucknow: Ethnographic and Folk Culture Society, U.P.

BHARDWAJ, GOPAL (1977): 'Socio-Political Movements among the Tribes of India'. In S.C. Dube (ed.), *Tribal Heritage of India: Ethnicity, Identity and Interaction*. Vol. 1. Delhi: Vikas Publishing House, pp. 161-86.

BHATT, VIKAS (1976): 'The Bhagat Movement in Bastar'. Paper presented at the Seminar on Tribal Movements. Anthropological Survey of India, Calcutta (mimeographed).

BODDING, P.O. (1921): 'The Kharwar Movement among the Santals'. *Man in India*. Vol. 3, No. 1 (Sept).

———(1922): 'A Santal Sect'. *The Modern Review*. Vol. 31 (March).

DATTA, KALIKINKAR (1940): *The Santal Insurrection*. Calcutta: Calcutta University.

DATTA MAJUMDAR, NABENDU (1956): *The Santal: A Study in Culture Change*. Department of Anthropology, Memoir No. 2. Delhi: Manager of Publications, Government of India Press.

DE, N. (1964): 'The Tana Bhagats of Chhotanagpur: Studies in Socio-political Movement and Personality Structure'. Unpublished Ph.D. thesis. Patna University.

DESAI, I.P. (1976): 'The Tribal Autonomous Movement in South Gujarat (1970)'. Paper presented at the Seminar on Tribal Movements. Anthropological Survey of India, Calcutta (mimeographed).

———(1977): 'The Vedchbi Movement'. In I.P. Desai and Banwarilal Choudhury, *History of Rural Development in Modern India*. Vol. 2. New Delhi: Impex India, pp. 32-137.

DHAN, R.O. (1967): *These are thy Tribesmen: The Oraon*. Ranchi: Lutheran Church Press.

DUBE, S.C. (ED.) (1977): *Tribal Heritage in India: Ethnicity, Identity and Interaction*. Vol. 1. Delhi: Vikas Publishing House.

GUPTA, B.K.D. (1962): 'Caste-Mobility among the Mahato of South Manbhum'. *Man in India*. Nos. 42-43 (July-Sept.), pp. 228-36.

JAY, EDWARD (1962): 'Revitalization Movements in Tribal India'. In L.P. Vidyarthi (ed.), *Aspects of Religion in Indian Society*. Meerut: Kedar Nath and Ram Nath.

JHA, A.P. (1960): 'Nature of the Santal Unrest of 1871-5 and the Origin of the Sapha Hor Movement'. *Indian Historical Records Commission Proceedings*. Vol. 35, No. 2, pp. 103-13.

KABUI, GANGMUMEI (1976): 'The Zeliangrong Movement: A Historical Study'. Paper presented at the Seminar on Tribal Movements, Anthropological Survey of India, Calcutta (mimeographed).

KALIA, S.L. (1962): 'The Rajmohini Devi Movement in Surguja'. *Bulletin of the Tribal Research Institute*, Chindwara. Vol. 2, No. 1.

KULKARNI, S.D. (1976): 'Adivasis of Maharashtra—A Study of the Bhil Movement in Dhulia District'. Paper presented at the Seminar on Tribal Movements. Anthropological Survey of India, Calcutta (mimeographed).

MAHAPATRA, S.K. (1968): 'Social Movements among Tribes in Eastern India with Special Reference to Orissa'. *Sociologus*. New Series, Vol. 18, No. 1, pp. 46-62.

————(1972): 'Social Movements among the Tribes of India'. In K. Suresh Singh (ed.), *Tribal Situation in India*. Simla: Indian Institute of Advanced Study.

MATHUR, P.R. (1976): 'Political Awakening among the Tribes of Wynad'. Paper presented at the Seminar on Tribal Movements. Anthropological Survey of India, Calcutta (mimeographed).

NAIDU, N.Y. (1972): 'Tribal Revolt in Parvatipuram Agency'. *Economic and Political Weekly*. Vol. 7, No. 18.

NATARAJAN, NALINI (1976): 'Cultural Revivalism among the Christian Khasis of Meghalaya'. Paper presented at the Seminar on Tribal Movements. Anthropological Survey of India, Calcutta (mimeographed).

ORANS, MARTIN (1959): 'A Tribe in Search of a Great Tradition: The Emulation-Solidarity Conflict'. *Man in India*. Vol. 39, No. 2.

————(1965): *The Santals: A Tribe in Search of a Great Tradition*. Detroit: Wayne State University Press.

RAGHAVIAH, V. (1971): *Tribal Revolts*. Nellore: Andhra Rashtra Adimjati Sevak Sangh.

REDDI, N. SUBBA (1972): 'Tribal Unrest and its Aftermath'. Paper presented at the ICSSR-sponsored Conference of Anthropologists, New Delhi. 26-27 May 1972.

ROY-BURMAN, B.K. (1968): 'Some Dimensions of Transformation of Tribal Societies in India'. *Journal of Social Research*. Vol. 11, No. 1.

ROY, S.C. (1921): 'A New Religious Movement among the Oraons'. *Man in India*. Vol. 1, pp. 266-321.

————(1972): 'Revival Movements and Modern Tendencies in Oraon Religion'. In S.C. Roy, *Oraon Religion and Customs*. Calcutta: Editions Indian, pp. 227-97 (first published in 1928).

SACHCHIDANAND (1972): 'Tribal Unrest in India'. Paper presented at the ICSSR-sponsored Conference of Anthropologists, New Delhi. 26-28 May 1972.

SAHA, R.K. (1976): 'Ethnic Movement in Manipur Valley: Politico-Religious upheaval among the Meities'. Paper presented at the Semiñar on Tribal Movements. Anthropological Survey of India, Calcutta (mimeographed).

SAHAY, K.N. (1962): 'Trends of Sanskritization among Oraons'. *Bulletin of the Bihar Tribal Research Institute.*

———(1963): 'Impact of Christianity on the Oraons of the Three Villages in Chota Nagpur'. Unpublished Ph.D. thesis. Ranchi University.

———(1967): 'A Study in the Process of Transformation from Tribe to Caste: Parahiyas of Tolki—A Case Study'. *Journal of Social Research*. Vol. 10, No. 1 (Mar.), pp. 64-89.

SCHNITT, ERIKA (1973): 'Sonat Santal-Samaj—A Sociological Movement among the Santals in Dhanbad District, Bihar, India'. *Sociologus*. Vol. 23, No. 2.

SEN, JYOTI (1972): 'The Jharkhand Movement'. In K. Suresh Singh (ed.), *Tribal Situation in India*. Simla: Indian Institute of Advanced Study.

SHARMA, K.L. (1976): 'Jharkhand Movement in Bihar'. *Economic and Political Weekly*. Vol. 11, Nos. 1-2 (Jan.), pp. 37-43.

SINGH, ROOP (1970): 'The Role of Bhagat Movement in the Inception of Caste Features in the Bhil Tribe'. *The Eastern Anthropologist*. Vol. 23, No. 2 (May-Aug.), pp. 163-70.

SINGH, K. SURESH (1966): *Dust Storm and Hanging Mist: Story of Birsa Munda and his Movement*. Calcutta.

———(1973): 'From Movement to Party: A Study in Tribal Politics in Middle India, 1920-63'. Paper presented at the Nehru Memorial Museum on 29 March 1973.

———(1975): 'Chotanagpur: A Centenary Overview'. *The Bihar Herald Centenary Number*, Patna.

———(1976): 'The Gond Movements'. Paper presented at the Seminar on Tribal Movements. Anthropological Survey of India, Calcutta (mimeographed).

———(1977): 'From Ethnicity to Regionalism: A Study in Tribal Politics and Movements in Chotanagpur from 1900 to 1975'. In S. C. Malik (ed.), *Dissent, Protest and Reform in Indian Civilization*. Simla: Indian Institute of Advanced Study, pp. 317-39.

SINGH, K. SURESH (ED.) (1972): *Tribal Situation in India*. Simla: Indian Institute of Advanced Study.

SINGH, K. SURESH & P.P. MAHATO (1976): 'The Mahato-Kurmi Mahasabha Movement: A Preliminary Appraisal'. Paper presented at the Seminar on Tribal Movements. Anthropological Survey of India, Calcutta (mimeographed).

SINHA, SURAJIT (1959*a*): 'Bhumij-Kshatriya Social Movement in South Manbhum'. *Bulletin of the Department of Anthropology*. Vol. 8, No. 2, pp. 9-32.

———(1959*b*): 'Inter-ethnic Relations and Social Mobility Movement among Some Tribes and Castes of Eastern and Central India'. *Bulletin of Department of Anthropology*. Vol. 8, No. 2.

———(1968*a*): 'Study in Tribal Solidarity Movements—General Propositions.' In Surajit Sinha (ed.), *Research Programmes in Cultural Anthropology and Related Disciplines*. Calcutta: Anthropological Survey of India, pp. 11-17.

————(1968*b*): 'Tribal Solidarity and Messianic Movements'. *Contributions to Indian Sociology*. New Series, No. 11.

————(1972): 'Tribal Solidarity Movements in India'. In K. Suresh Singh (ed.), *Tribal Situation in India*. Simla: Indian Institute of Advanced Study.

SYAMCHAUDHURI, N.K. (1970): 'Tribal Solidarity Movement in Assam: An Appraisal of the Problem'. In Surajit Sinha (ed.), *Research Programmes in Cultural Anthropology and Related Disciplines*. Calcutta: Anthropological Survey of India, pp. 18-24.

TROISI, J. (1976): 'Social Movements among the Santals'. *Social Action*. Vol. 26, No. 3 (July-Sept.), pp. 253-66.

————(1977): 'Religious Beliefs and Practices among the Santals: A Case Study'. Unpublished Ph.D. thesis. Department of Sociology, University of Delhi.

VIDYARTHI, L.P. (1964): 'The Historic March of Jharkhand Party'. *Sociological Bulletin*. Vol. 1, No. 2.

9. Women's Movements

AGGARWAL, R.C. (1974): "Women's Lib in India". *Social Welfare*. Vol. 20, No. 10 (Jan.), pp. 18-22, 28.

ASTHANA, PRATIMA (1974): *Women's Movement in India*. Delhi: Vikas Publishing House.

BAIG, TARA ALI (1976): *India's Woman Power* Delhi: S. Chand & Co.

BAIG, TARA ALI (ED.) (1958): *Women of India*. Delhi: Ministry of Information and Broadcasting.

BASU, APARNA (1976): 'The Role of Women in the Indian Struggle for Freedom'. In B.R. Nanda (ed.), *Indian Women From Purdah to Modernity*. Delhi: Vikas Publishing House.

CHATTOPADHAYA, KAMALADEVI (1975): 'The Women's Movement—Then and Now'. In Devaki Jain (ed.), *Indian Women*. Delhi: Publications Division.

CHATTOPADHYA, KAMALADEVI *et al.* (1939): *The Awakening of Indian Women*. Madras: Everyman's Press.

DASGUPTA, KALPANA (ED) (1976): *Women on the Indian Scene: An Annotated Bibliography*. Delhi: Abhinav Publications.

DESAI, NEERA (1976): 'Struggle for Indian Women's Emancipation: A Movement?' Paper presented to the Thirteenth All India Sociological Conference, Chandiga·h, 26-28 December 1976 (mimeographed).

DEVAKI. JAIN (ED.) (1975): *Indian Women*. Delhi: Publications Division.

KAUR, MANMOHAN (1968): *Role of Women in the Freedom Movement*. Delhi: Sterling Publishers.

MAZUMDAR, VINA (1976): 'The Social Reform Movement in India—From Ranade to Nehru'. In B.R. Nanda (ed.), *Indian Women From Purdah to Modernity*. Delhi: Vikas Publishing House, pp. 41-66.

MEHTA, RAMA (1976): 'From Purdah to Modernity'. In B.R. Nanda (ed.), *Indian Women From Purdah to Modernity*. Delhi: Vikas Publishing House, pp. 113-28.

NANDA, B.R. (ED.) (1976): *Indian Women From Purdah to Modernity.* Delhi: Vikas Publishing House.

SINGH, SITA RAM (1968): *Nationalism and Social Reform in India.* Delhi.

S.N.D.T. WOMEN'S UNIVERSITY (n.d.): *A Select Bibliography on Women in India.* Bombay: Allied Publishers.

10. Students' Movements

ALTBACH, PHILIP G. (1966): 'The Transformation of the Indian Student Movement'. *Asian Survey* (August), pp. 448-60.

———(1968*a*): 'Student Politics and Higher Education in India'. *Daedalus.* Vol. 97 (Winter).

———(1968*b*): *Student Politics in Bombay.* Bombay: Asia Publishing House.

———(1972*a*): *The University in Transition: An Indian Case Study.* Bombay: Sindhu

———(1972*b*): 'Youth and Students in Contemporary Society'. In L.M. Singhvi (ed.), *Youth Unrest: Conflict of Generations.* Delhi: National.

ALTBACH, PHILIP G. (ED.) (1968): *Turmoil and Transition: Education and Student Politics in India.* Bombay: Lalvani.

———(1970): *Student Revolution: A Global Analysis.* Bombay: Lalvani.

ALTBACH, PHILIP G., & R.S. LAUFER (EDS.) (1972): *The New Pilgrims.* New York: David Mckay.

ASTHANA, H.S. & SUMA CHITNIS (1967): 'The Disturbed Campus'. In I.P. Desai, M.S. Gore and Suma Chitnis (eds.), *Papers in the Sociology of Education in India.* New Delhi: NCERT.

BALACHANDRAN, P.K. (1973): 'Anatomy of a Crisis'. *Seminar.* No. 166, pp. 23-8.

———(1977): 'A Sociological Study of Some Dimensions of Student Politics in an Indian University'. Ph.D. thesis submitted to the Department of Sociology, University of Delhi.

CHITRA, M.N. (1966): 'A Student Strike in Mysore—A Sociological Analysis'. *Journal of University Education.* Vol. 4 (March), pp. 149-61.

DASGUPTA, BIPLAB (1974): *The Naxalite Movement.* Delhi: Allied Publishers.

DI BONA, JOSEPH (1966): 'Indiscipline and Student Leadership in an Indian University'. *Comparative Education Review.* Vol. 10 (June).

———(1974): *Change and Conflict in an Indian University.* Bombay: Lalvani.

EAKIN, T.C. (1970): *Students and Politics.* Bombay: Popular Prakashan.

EMMERSON, D.K. (1968): *Students and Politics in Developing Nations.* New York: Praeger.

FISCHER, JOSEPH (1963): 'The University Students in South and South-East Asia'. *Minerva.* Vol. 1, No. 1, (Autumn).

ILCHMAN, W.F. & T.K. DHAR (1970): 'Student Discontent and Educated Unemployment'. *Economic and Political Weekly.* Special No.

INSTITUTE OF CONSTITUTIONAL AND PARLIAMENTARY STUDIES (1966): *Student Unrest—Problems and Perspectives.* Delhi.

KAKAR, S. & K. CHOWDHURY (1969): 'The Student Leaders and Strike'. *Quest*. No. 61 (April-June), pp. 54-62.

KARLEKAR, MALAVIKA (1975): 'Student Politics in West Bengal: The Role of the Chhatra Parishad in the Political Process.' Unpublished Ph.D. thesis. Department of Sociology, University of Delhi.

LIPSET, SEYMOUR MARTIN (1964): 'University Students and Politics in Underdeveloped Countries'. *Minerva*. Vol. 3 (Autumn), pp. 15-56.

LIPSET, SEYMOUR MARTIN & P.G. ALTBACH (1969): *Students in Revolt*. Boston: Houghton Mifflin.

MEHTA, PRAYAG (1971): *The Indian Youth*. Bombay: Somaiya Publications.

OOMMEN, T.K. (1971): *Student Unions in India*. Delhi: Viswa Yuvak Kendra.

————(1974): 'Student Politics in India: The Case of Delhi University'. *Asian Survey*. Vol. 14, No. 9 (Sept.) pp. 777-94.

————(1975*a*): 'Student Power in India: A Political Analysis'. *Political Science Review*. Vol. 14, Nos. 1-2, pp. 10-38.

————(1975*b*): 'Student Power in India: A Political Analysis'. *Political Science Review* (Jaipur). Vol. 14, Nos. 1-2.

REDDY, M. MUNI (1947): *The Student Movement in India*. Lucknow: K.S.R. Acharya.

ROSS, AILEEN D. (1969): *Student Unrest in India: A Comparative Approach*. Montreal: McGill-Queen's University Press.

ROY, RAMASHRAY (1973): 'India—1972. Fissure in the Fortress'. *Asian Survey*. Vol. 12, No. 2, pp. 231-45.

————(1974): 'India—1973. A Year of Discontent'. *Asian Survey*. Vol. 14, No. 2 (Feb.), pp. 115-24.

RUDOLPH, L.I., S.H. RUDOLPH & KARUNA AHMAD (1971): 'Student Politics and National Politics in India'. *Economic and Political Weekly*. Special No. (31 July), pp. 1655-9, 1661-3, 1665-8.

SARKAR, CHANCHAL (1960): 'The Unquiet Campus'. Delhi: The Statesman.

SHAH, B.V. (1968): 'Student—A Sociological Hypothesis'. *Sociological Bulletin*. Vol. 17, No. 1 (Mar.), pp. 55-64.

SHAW, ROBERT C. (1968): 'Student Politics and Student Leadership in an Indian University: The Case of Osmania'. In P.G. Altbach (ed.), *Turmoil and Transition: Higher Education and Student Politics in India*. Bombay: Lalvani.

SINGH, AMAR KUMAR (1968): 'Academic Politics and Student Unrest: The Case of Ranchi University'. In P.G. Altbach (ed.), *Turmoil and Transition: Higher Education and Student Politics in India*. Bombay: Lalvani.

SINGHVI, L.M. (ED.) (1972). *Youth Unrest: Conflict of Generations*. Delhi: National.

VIDYARTHI, L.P. (1976): *Students Unrest in Chotanagpur, 1969-70*. Calcutta: Punthi Pustak.

VISWA YUVAK KENDRA (1973): *The Dynamics of Student Agitation*. Bombay: Somaiya Publications.

11. Trade Union Movements

AGARWAL, R.D. (1972*a*): 'Problems of Unionism'. In R.D. Agarwal (ed.), *Dynamics of Labour Relations in India*. New Delhi: Tata McGraw-Hill Publishing Co.

———(1972*b*): 'Political Dimensions of Trade Unions'. In R.D. Agarwal (ed.), *Dynamics of Labour Relations in India*. New Delhi: Tata McGraw-Hill Publishing Co.

BANAWALIKAR, A.S. (1948): *A Study of Industrial Dissatisfactions* (Being the Report of an Enquiry). Indore: Labour Department.

BAVISKAR, B.S. (1968*a*): 'Union Politics and Management Politics'. *Indian Journal of Industrial Relations*. Vol. 3, No. 3, pp. 300-15.

———(1968*b*): 'Cooperatives and Politics'. *Economic and Political Weekly*. Vol. 3, No. 12, pp. 490-5.

———(1971): 'Factions and Party Politics: General Elections in an Assembly Constituency in Maharashtra'. *Sociological Bulletin*. Vol. 20, No. 1 pp. 54-77.

BOGAERT, M. VAN DEN (1967): 'Trade Unions in Calcutta Docks: Agents of Socio-Cultural Integration'. *Social Action*. Vol. 17, No. 4, pp. 245-62.

CROUCH, H. (1966): *Trade Unions and Politics in India*. Bombay: Manaktalas.

DAS, R.K. (1923) *Labour Movement in India*. Berlin: Walter de Gruyter & Co.

DRAVID, V.V. (1966): *Shramik, Shramik-Andolan Avum Shramik-Vidhan Madhya Pradesh Mein* (in Hindi). Indore: Mazdoor Press, Shram Shivir.

———(1969*a*): 'Indian Trade Union Movement: Retrospect and Prospect' *Indian Worker*. Vol. 17, No. 37, pp. 3-7.

———(1969*b*): 'Trade Union's Role in Economic Development'. *Indian Worker*. Vol. 17, Nos. 45-46, p. 14.

DUFTY, N.F. (1964): *Industrial Relations in India*. Bombay: Allied Publishers.

GHOSH, P.K. (1965): 'Structure of Trade Union Organization'. *Economic Weekly*. Vol. 17, No. 3, pp. 562-5.

GHOSH, S. (1960): *Trade Unionism in the Underdeveloped Countries*. Calcutta: Bookland.

GIRI, V.V. (1959): *Labour Problems in Indian Industry* (2nd edn.). Bombay: Asia Publishing House.

INDIAN NATIONAL TRADE UNION CONGRESS (1950-1972): *INTUC Reports*. New Delhi: INTUC.

JAMES, RALPH (1958*a*): 'Trade Union Democracy: Indian Textiles'. *Western Political Quarterly*. Vol. 11, No. 3, pp. 563-93.

———(1958*b*): 'Politics and Trade Unions in India'. *Far Eastern Survey*. Vol. 27, No. 3, pp. 41-5.

JOHRI, C.K. (1967): *Unionism in a Developing Economy*. Bombay: Asia Publishing House.

JONES, RODNEY W. (1972): 'Linkage Analysis of Indian Urban Politics'. *Economic and Political Weekly*. (17 June), pp. 1195-203.

——————(1974): *Urban Politics in India: Area, Power and Policy in a Penetrated System*. Berkeley & Los Angeles: University of California Press.

KANNAPPAN, S. (1962): 'Gandhian Model of Unionism in a Developing Economy: The TLA in India'. *Indian Journal of Industrial Relations*. Vol. 16, No. 1, pp. 86-110.

KARNIK, V.B. (1966). *Indian Trade Unions: A Survey*. Bombay: Manaktalas.

——————(1974): *Indian Labour Problems and Prospects*. Calcutta: Minerva Associates.

KASSALOW, E.M. (1963): 'Unions in the New and Developing Countries'. In Everett M. Kassalow (ed.), *National Labour Movements in the Postwar World*. Evanston: Northwestern University Press.

KENNEDY, V.D. (1966): *Unions, Employers and Government*. Bombay: Manaktalas.

KOOIMAN, DICK (1976): 'Jobbers and Emergence of Trade Unions in Bombay City'. Paper presented to the 5th European Conference on Modern South Asian Studies, Leiden, July 1976 (mimeographed).

KULKARNI, P.D. (1946): 'Textile Trade Unionism in Bombay'. *Indian Journal of Social Work*. Vol. 7, No. 3, pp. 224-38.

LAMBERT, R.D. (1963): *Workers, Factories and Social Change in India*. Bombay: Asia Publishing House.

MAMKOOTTAM, KURIAKOSE (1977): 'Politics of Trade Unions: A Case Study in Jamshedpur'. Ph.D. thesis submitted to Department of Sociology, University of Delhi.

MAMORIA, C.B. & S.L. DOSHI (1966): *Labour Problems and Social Welfare*. Allahabad: Kitab Mahal.

MRTHUR, A.S. & J.S. MATHUR (1957): *Trade Union Movement in India*. Allahabad: Chaitanya Publishing House.

MATHUR, J.S. (1964): *Indian Working Class Movement*. Allahabad: Central Book Depot.

——————(1965): 'Trade Union Leadership and Industrial Unrest in India'. *Industrial Relations*. Vol. 17, No. 6, pp. 242-8.

MEHTA, ASOKA (1957): 'The Mediating Role of the Trade Union in Underdeveloped Countries'. *Economic Development and Cultural Change*. Vol. 6, pp. 16-23.

MENON, V.K.R. (1960): 'Role of Trade Unions in India's Future Development'. *Productivity*. Vol. 2, No. 2.

MILLEN, BRUCE H. (1963): *The Political Role of Labour in Developing Countries*. Washington, D.C.: The Brookings Institution.

MISHRA, ANJALI (1975) 'Trade Unionism in an Industrial Establishment: A Sociological Study'. Unpublished Ph. D. thesis. Department of Sociology and Anthropology, University of Saugar, Sagar.

MOORE, W.E. & A.S. FELDMAN (EDS.) (1960): *Labour Commitment and Social Change in Developing Areas*. New York: Social Science Research Council.

MORRIS, M.D. (1958): 'Order and Disorder in the Labour Force: The Jamshedpur Crisis of 1958'. *Economic Weekly*. (1 Nov.), pp. 1387-96.

——————(1959): 'Trade Unions and the State'. In Richard L. Park and Irene Tinker (eds.), *Leadership and Political Institutions in India*. Princeton, N.J.: Princeton University Press.

————(1960): 'The Recruitment of an Industrial Labour Force in India with British and American Comparisons.' *Comparative Studies in Society and History*. (April), pp. 305-28.

————(1965): *The Emergence of an Industrial Labour Force in India*. Bombay: Oxford University Press.

MYERS, C.A. & SUBBIAH KANNAPPAN (1970): *Industrial Relations in India*. (2nd rev. & enl. edn.). Bombay: Asia Publishing House.

ORNATI, OSCAR A. (1954): 'Indian Trade Unions Since Independence'. *Far Eastern Survey*. Vol. 23, pp. 113-22.

————(1955): *Jobs and Workers in India*. New York: The Institute of International Industrial and Labour Relations.

————(1957): 'Problems of Indian Trade Unionism'. *Annals of the American Academy of Political and Social Science*. Vol. 310 (March), pp. 151-61.

PANDEY, S.M. (1966): 'Indian Labour Movement: Growth and Character'. *Indian Journal of Labour Economics*. Vol. 9, No. 1, pp. 14-39.

————(1967): 'Rival Unionism in an Industrial Centre: A Study of Kanpur'. *Indian Journal of Industrial Relations*. Vol. 3, No. 2, pp. 138-59.

————(1968): Ideological Conflict in the Kanpur Trade Union Movement, 1934-1945'. *Indian Journal of Industrial Relations*. Vol. 3, No. 3, pp. 243-68.

————(1970): *As Labour Organizes: A Study of Unionism in Kanpur Textile Industry*. New Delhi: Shri Ram Centre.

PANDEY, S.M., & C.M. VIKRAM (1969): 'Trade Unionism in Delhi's Building Industry'. *Indian Journal of Industrial Relations*. Vol. 4, No. 8, pp. 298-321.

PANDHE, M.K. (1958): 'Labour Organization in Sholapur City'. Unpublished Ph.D. thesis. Poona: Gokhale Institute of Politics and Economics.

PATTABHI RAMAN, N. (1967): *Political Involvement of India's Trade Unions*. Bombay: Asia Publishing House.

PUNEKAR, S.D. (1948): *Trade Unionism in India*. Bombay: New Book Co.

————(1958): 'Outside Leadership of Trade Unions: A Bombay Survey'. *Economic Weekly*. Vol. 10, Nos. 26-28, p. 877.

————(1960): 'Trade Union Movement in India'. In V.B. Singh and A.K. Saran (eds.), *Industrial Labour in India*. Bombay: Asia Publishing House.

————(1963): 'Labour in India and the United States'. *Economic Weekly*. Vol. 15, No. 13, pp. 555-8.

————(1967): *Trade Union Leadership in India*. Bombay: Lalvani Publishing House.

RAMANUJAM, G. (1967): *Under the Babul Tree: Study of Indian Labour*. New Delhi: INTUC.

RAMASWAMY, E.A. (1969): 'Trade Unions and Politics'. *Sociological Bulletin*. Vol. 18, No. 2, pp. 137-47.

————(1971): 'Trade Unions and the Electoral Process: General Elections in a Working Class Area'. *Indian Journal of Industrial Relations*. Vol. 7, No. 2, pp. 205-27.

———(1973): 'Politics and Organized Labour in India'. *Asian Survey*. Vol. 13, pp. 914-28.

———(1974): 'The Role of the Trade Union Leader in India'. *Human Organization*. Vol. 33, No. 2, pp. 163-72.

———(1976): 'Trade Unionism and Caste in South India'. *Modern Asian Studies*. Vol. 10 (Part 3) (July), pp. 361-74.

———(1977): *The Worker and His Union*. New Delhi: Allied Publishers.

RAO, A.V. (1967): *Indian Trade Unions*. Honolulu: University of Hawaii Press.

RASTOGI, T.N. (1969): *Indian Industrial Labour*. Bombay: Hind Kitabs.

ROBERTS, B.C. (1964): *Industrial Relations: Contemporary Problems and Perspectives*. London: Methuen & Co.

SHARMA, G.K. (1971): *Labour Movement in India: Its Past and Present*. New Delhi: Sterling Publishers.

SHETH, N.R. (1960): 'Trade Union in an Indian Factory: A Sociological Analysis'. *Economic Weekly*. Vol. 12, Nos. 29-30, p. 1159.

———(1967): 'Society and Industrial Work in India: A Case Study'. *Human Organization*. Vol. 26, Nos. 1-2, pp. 77-9.

———(1968*a*): *The Social Framework of an Indian Factory*. Bombay: Oxford University Press.

———(1968*b*): "Seminar on Trade Unions and Politics in India". *Indian Journal of Industrial Relations*. Vol. 3, No. 3, pp. 316-25.

———(1969*a*): 'Workers' Participation in Trade Union Activities'. *Indian Journal of Industrial Relations*. Vol. 4, No. 3, pp. 279-98.

———(1969*b*): 'Informal Bonds of Factory Workers'. *Economic Weekly*. Vol. 15, No. 8, pp. 359-65.

———(1971): 'Management of Industrial Conflict'. *Indian Management*. Vol. 10, No. 9, pp. 3-9.

SHETH, N.R., & S.P. JAIN (1968*a*): 'Workers, Leaders and Politics: A Case Study'. *Indian Journal of Industrial Relations*. Vol. 3, No. 3, pp. 286-300.

———(1968*b*): 'The Status and Role of Local Union Leaders'. *Indian Journal of Industrial Relations*. Vol. 4, No. 1, pp. 70-89.

SINGH, R.C. (1958): 'Outsiders in the Labour Unions in Bihar'. *Indian Journal of Labour Economics*. Vol. 9, No. 4, pp. 532-44.

SINGH, V.B. (1965): 'Trade Union Movement'. In V.B. Singh (ed.), *Economic History of India: 1857-1956*. Bombay: Allied Publishers, pp. 563-608.

———(1968): *Climate of Industrial Relations: A Study of Kanpur Cotton M*[illegible] Bombay: Allied Publishers.

SIVAYYA, K.V. (1966): *Trade Union Movement in Vishakapatnam*. Waltair: Andhra University Press.

TANIC, ZIVAN (1969): *Workers Participation in Management: Ideal and Reality in India*. New Delhi: Shri Ram Centre for Industrial Relations.

THAKKER, G.K. (1962): *Labour Problems of Textile Industry*. Bombay: Vora & Co.

TRIPATHI, S.D. (1968): 'Politics of a Multi-Union Plant: The Swadesh Experience'. *Indian Journal of Industrial Relations*. Vol. 3, No. 4, pp. 441-58.

VAID, K.N. (1962): *Growth and Practice of Trade Unionism: An Area Study*. Delhi: Delhi School of Social Work.

———(1965): 'Why Workers Join Unions'. *Indian Journal of Industrial Relations*. Vol. 1, No. 2, pp. 208-36.

———(1967): *The New Worker*. Bombay: Asia Publishing House.

———(1968): 'Political Unionism and Industrial Relations in India'. *Indian Journal of Social Work*. Vol. 29, No. 2, pp. 157-67.

VERMA, RAM SINGH BHAI (1952): *Mill Udyog Ke Shoshan Ka Kachha Chitta* (in Hindi). Indore: Mazdoor Press, Shram Shivir.

———(1959): *Textile Wage Board Ke Sammukh Shrâmikon Ka Paksh* (The Case of the Labourers Before the Textile Wage Board) (in Hindi). Indore: Mazdoor Press, Shram Shivir.

———(n.d.): *Indore Ka Mazdoor Andolan, 1932 to 1957* (in Hindi). Indore: Mazdoor Press, Shram Shivir.

WEINER, MYRON (1963): 'Trade Unions'. In Myron Weiner (ed.), *The Politics of Scarcity: Public Pressure and Political Response in India*. Bombay: Asia Publishing House, pp. 79-104.

WILCOX, WAYNE (1965): 'Trade Unions, the Middle Class Intelligentsia, and a Communist M.P.: The Indore Parliamentary Election of 1962'. In Myron Weiner and Rajni Kothari (eds.), *Indian Voting Behaviour*. Calcutta: Firma K.L. Mukhopadhyaya.

12. National Movements in India

ARNOLD, D.J. (1973): 'Nationalism and Regional Politics: Tamilnad, India, 1920-37'. Unpublished Ph.D. dissertation. University of Sussex.

BERNSTORFF, DAGMAR (1976): 'Telangana Regionalism: Structure and Method of a Mass Movement'. Paper presented to the 5th European Conference on Modern South Asian Studies, Leiden, July 1976 (mimeographed).

BESANT ANNIE (1915): *How India Wrought for Freedom: The Story of the National Congress Told from Official Records*. Adyar: The Theosophical Publishing House.

BRODKIN, E.I. (1972): 'The Struggle for Succession: Rebels and Loyalists in the Indian Mutiny of 1857'. *Modern Asian Studies*. No. 6 (July).

BROWN, D. MACKENZIE (1961): *The Nationalist Movement: Indian Political Thought from Ranade to Bhave*. Berkeley: University of California Press.

CASHMAN, RICHARD I. (1974/5): *The Myth of the Lokamanya: Tilak and Mass Politics in Maharashtra*. Berkeley & Los Angeles: University of Chicago Press.

CHIROL, VALENTINE (1910): *Indian Unrest*. London: Macmillan & Co.

DESAI, A.R. (1954): *The Social Background of Indian Nationalism*. Bombay: Popular Prakashan.

DUMONT, LOUIS (1964): 'Nationalism and Communalism' *Contributions to Indian Sociology*. No. 8, pp. 30-70.

FISHFR, FRED B. (1919): *India's Silent Revolution*. New York: The Macmillan Company.

GALLAGHER, J., G. JOHNSON & A. SEAL (EDS.) (1973): *Locality, Province and Nation: Essays in Indian Politics, 1870 to 1940.* Cambridge: Cambridge University Press.

GHOSE, S. (1969): *The Renaissance to Militant Nationalism in India.* Bombay.

GURUNATHAM J. (1913): *The Andhra Movement.* Guntur.

HALAPPA, G.S. (1964): *History of Freedom Movement in Karnataka.* Vol. 2 Bangalore: Government of Mysore.

INGALLS, D.H.H. (1965): 'The Heritage of a Fallible Saint: Annie Besant's Gifts to India'. *Proceedings of the American Philosophical Society.* Vol. 109 (April), pp. 85-8.

IRSCHICK, EUGENE F. (1976): 'Civil Disobedience in Tamil Nadu, 1930-32'. *South Asia (Journal of South Asian Studies).* No. 6 (Dec.), pp. 34-50.

JOHNSON, G. (1973): *Provincial Politics and Indian Nationalism.* Cambridge: Cambridge University Press.

JOSHI, RAM (1970): 'Shiv Sena: A Movement in Search of Legitimacy'. *Asian Survey.* Vol. 10 (Nov.), pp. 967-78.

KATZENSTEIN, MARY F. (1976): 'Origins of Nativism: The Emergence of Siva Sena in Bombay'. In Donald B. Rosenthal (ed.), *City in Indian Politics.* Haryana: Thomson Press, pp. 44-58.

LEONARD, L.G. (1967): 'Politics and Social Change in South India: A Study of the Andhra Movement'. *Journal of Commonwealth Political Studies.* Vol. 5, No. 1 (Mar.), pp. 60-7.

LOVETT, V. (1920): *A History of the Indian Nationalist Movement.* London.

LOW, D.A. (ED.) (1977): *Congress and the Raj: Facets of the Indian Struggle, 1917-47.* New Delhi: Arnold-Heinemann.

MCLANE, JOHN R. (1961): 'The Development of Nationalist Ideas and Tactics and the Policies of the Government of India, 1897-1905'. Unpublished Ph.D. thesis. University of London, School of Oriental and African Studies.

MAJUMDAR, R.C. (1963): *History of the Freedom Movement in India.* 3 Vols. Calcutta: Firma K.L. Mukhopadhyay.

MASSELOS, J. (1974): *Towards Nationalism: Group Affiliations and the Politics of Public Associations in Nineteenth Century Western India.* Bombay.

MATHUR, Y.B. (1972): 'Red Shirt Movement'. In Y.B. Mathur, *Muslims and Changing India.* New Delhi: Trimurti Publications, pp. 233-61.

MENON, P.K.K. (1972): *The History of the Freedom Movement in Kerala.* Vol. 2 (1885-1933). Trivandrum: Government of Kerala Press.

MINAULT, GAIL (1972): 'The Khilafat Movement: A Study of Indian Muslim Leadership, 1919-1924'. Unpublished Ph.D. dissertation. University of Pennsylvania.

MISRA, B.B. (1963): *Select Documents on Mahatma Gandhi's Movement in Champara, 1917-1918.* Patna: Political Science Department, Patna University.

MUKHERJEE, H. & U. MUKHERJEE (1957): *'Bande Matram' and Indian Nationalism, 1906-1908.* Calcutta.

NARAYANA RAO, K.V. (1973): *The Emergence of Andhra Pradesh.* Bombay.

OSTERGAARD, G.N. & M. CURRELL (1971): *The Gentle Anarchists: A Study of the Leaders of the Sarvodaya Movement for Non-Violent Revolution in India.* Oxford: Clarendon Press.

PARK, R.L. (1950): 'The Rise of Militant Nationalism is Bengal: A Regional Study of Indian Nationalism'. Unpublished Ph.D. thesis. University of Cambridge, Massachusetts.

RAO, M.V.K. & HALAPPA, G.S. (EDS.) (1962): *History of Freedom Movement in Karnataka.* Vol. 1, Bangalore: Government of Mysore.

RAY, R.K. (1972): 'Social Conflict and Political Unrest in Bengal, 1875-1925'. Ph.D. dissertation. Cambridge University.

REEVES, P.D. (1966): 'The Politics of Order: Anti-Non-Cooperation in U.P., 1921'. *Journal of Asian Studies.* Vol. 25, No. 2 (Feb.).

SARKAR, SUMIT (1973): *The Swadeshi Movement in Bengal, 1903-1908.* New Delhi.

SAVITA (1970): *Gandhi and Social Policy in India: A Sociological Analysis.* Delhi: National Publishing House.

SEAL, ANIL (1968): *The Emergence of Indian Nationalism: Competition and Collaboration in the Later Nineteenth Century.* Cambridge: Cambridge University Press.

SHAH, GHANSHYAM (1974): 'Traditional Society and Political Mobilization: The Experience of Bardoli Satyagraha (1920-28)'. *Contributions to Indian Sociology.* New Series, No. 8.

SITRAMAYYA, PATTABHI B. (1935): *The History of the National Congress (1885-1935).* Allahabad: Congress Working Committee.

STODDART, BRIAN (1976): 'Agitational Politics in the Tamil-and-Telugu-Speaking Regions of Madras Presidency, 1925-35'. Unpublished Ph.D. dissertation. University of Western Australia.

STOKES, ERIC (1970): Traditional Resistance Movements and Afro-Asian Nationalism: The Context of the 1857 Mutiny Rebellion in India'. *Past and Present.* Vol. 48 (Aug.).

SUNTHRALINGAM, R. (1974): *Politics and Nationalist Awakening in South India, 1852-1891.* Tucson: University of Arizona Press.

TARA CHAND (1964): *History of the Freedom Movement in India.* 2 Vols. Delhi: Publications Division, Government of India.

TUCKER, R. (1976): 'Hindu Traditionalism and Nationalist Ideologies in Nineteenth Century Maharashtra'. *Modern Asian Studies.* Vol. 10 (Part 3) (July), pp. 321-48.

VENKATARANGAIYA, M. (ED.) (1965): *The Freedom Struggle in Andhra Pradesh, 1921-31.* Vol. 3. Hyderabad.

WASHBROOK, D.A. (1976): *The Emergence of Provincial Politics: The Madras Presidency, 1870-1920.* Delhi: Vikas Publishing House.

